The Complete SWIMMING POOL Reference

third edition

Rachel Griffiths
Tom Griffiths

SAGAMORE
PUBLISHING

Publishers: Joseph J. Bannon and Peter L. Bannon
Director of Sales and Marketing: William A. Anderson
Sales Manager: Misty Gilles
Journals Marketing Manager: Emily Wakefield
Director of Development and Production: Susan M. Davis
Technology Manager: Keith Hardyman
Production Coordinator: Amy S. Dagit
Graphic Designer: Julie Schechter

Cover Photo Courtesy of Councilman-Hunsaker

ISBN print edition: 978-1-57167-763-1
ISBN ebook: 978-1-57167-764-8
LCCN: 2014941711

Sagamore Publishing
1807 N. Federal Dr.
Urbana, IL 61801
www.sagamorepub.com

To Coach Bill Campbell (8/9/1923–4/24/2014), whose personal and professional mentoring catapulted me into my career as an aquatics professional at the University of Maryland many, many years ago.

To my daughter Rachel, who by far completed most of the research and writing of this third edition. Her hard work, dedication, and attention to detail are beautifully illustrated in the text.

As she continues to motivate me and energize my efforts, may this book serve as her springboard into a long and rewarding career in aquatics.

— Dr. Tom Griffiths

To my grandmother, Esther Reines (1/28/1926–3/25/2014), who continually reminded us how our valuable work ethic would lead to success and repeatedly praised us for it.

— Rachel Griffiths

CONTENTS

Section IV: Specialty Pools

Section V: Safety, Supervision, and Risk Management

PREFACE

The Complete Swimming Pool Reference, Third Edition combines technical aspects of pool operations manuals with practical information often found in water safety texts. The book is written for all those who own, operate, or otherwise work at swimming pools, including lifeguards, pool operators, pool managers, swimming coaches, diving coaches, swimming instructors, and even residential pool owners.

This book is written clearly and concisely so that even complicated topics are easy to understand. With 33 comprehensive chapters included, there is something for every aquatic professional. New chapters in the third edition include Chapter 1, A Water Safety Primer, Chapter 5, Aquatic Facility Planning and Funding, Chapter 6, Americans With Disabilities Act, Chapter 9, Improving Air Quality in Indoor Pools, Chapter 11, Ultraviolet (UV) Disinfection, Chapter 24, Shallow Water Blackout, Chapter 27, The Virginia Graeme Baker Pool and Spa Safety Act, Chapter 29, Insurance and Aquatic Risk Management, and Chapter 31, Preparing for and Coping With Emergencies.

Reviewing the latest information found in these newly added chapters should certainly place readers on the cutting edge of aquatic facility management and is of vital importance to today's aquatic professionals. This work also includes a variety of references and resources to assist readers who wish to study a topic in greater depth.

INTRODUCTION

Swimming attracts more than 125 million participants annually; this figure represents nearly half of the U.S. population. For years, swimming has been the most popular participant sport in the United States. Only walking has surpassed its popularity in recent years.

According to the CDC, swimming is the most popular recreational activity for children and teens. The Association of Pool & Spa Professionals estimate there are nearly 10 million pools in this country. Six million are privately owned, residential pools. Homeowners maintain an additional three million hot tubs and spas. The number of public and semi-public pools in this country is approaching one million.

People frequent pools for a variety of reasons: fitness, relaxation, instruction, competition, and therapy. Today's swimming facilities do not just accommodate lessons and lap swimmers but are multidimensional fitness and family centers serving all age groups. Many recreational amenities have been added to pools like climbing walls and slides.

During the writing of the first edition of this book in the early 1990s, the drowning rate remained fairly constant, between 7,000 to 8,000 individuals a year. Fortunately, death by drowning was actually reduced to around 5,000 annually during the writing of the second edition of this book. During the writing of this third edition, the drowning rate is now below 4,000. Even though more and more Americans are being exposed to a growing number of aquatic facilities and activities, the fact that the drowning rate is actually decreasing bodes well for our water safety programs. Fortunately, only 10% of these drownings occur in swimming pools, but tragically almost half of these drownings involve small children. Some claim that nearly 500 drownings occur each year in guarded facilities.

Ironically, we build pools in this country to promote health, fitness, and safety, but several risks and hazards are produced with the construction of swimming facilities. This book can help maximize the health and safety benefits of aquatics while reducing hazards and risks. This third edition contains new and improved information on safe aquatic facilities and activities. Aquatic Facility Planning and Funding, ADA, Entrapments, Air Quality/UV, Insurance and Legal Liability, and Shallow Water Blackout are some of the exciting new chapters. Safe, enjoyable, and clean swimming pools should result if the guidelines in this book are followed.

There are many good texts available that can assist the swimming pool owner, operator, or other employees. Some texts are technical and written primarily for swimming pool technicians who need precise information on pool chemistry and filtration. Concerning safety, the American Red Cross along with the YMCA, Ellis & Associates, NASCO, and the StarGuard program are the leaders on lifeguarding and water safety and produce excellent works on these subjects. Residential pool owners are often referred to pamphlets published by swimming pool chemical companies that are easy to follow and understand.

The Complete Swimming Pool Reference, Third Edition, attempts to accomplish the formidable task of combining the most valuable elements of technical, practical, and water safety publications to produce a book that can be used by anyone in aquatics.

It is hoped that anyone associated with a pool, whether it be public or private, will find this book informative and helpful. The needs of homeowners, hotel/motel managers, park directors, pool operators, lifeguards, coaches, and parents are addressed. This book includes many other references and resources that will allow the reader to gain additional information concerning pools and spas. All readers will benefit from this book, from professional pool technicians who service swimming facilities to homeowners who relax in their hot tubs.

How to Use this Book

The information presented in this book progresses from very simple ideas to more complex swimming pool issues. The novice pool owner or operator may wish to concentrate on the earlier sections before moving on to the filtration and chemistry chapters. Conversely, the experienced pool person may wish to skim the initial chapters and spend more time on the later sections in the book. Additionally, some readers will prefer to concentrate on the maintenance and operations sections of the book, while others may want to focus on the safety and human relations portions.

Before addressing each chapter, the reader should carefully read the key terms defined at the outset of each section. Reviewing the key terms will aid the reader in attending to the most critical aspects of each chapter. Appendix B contains a "Personal Pool Profile" that can be completed so the information read can be applied directly to the reader's particular pool.

In addition to this book, there are several other valuable sources of swimming pool and water safety information. The American Red Cross, American Swimming Pool and Spa Association, The Association of Aquatic Professionals, The Centers for Disease Control, Ellis & Associates, StarGuard, The National Aquatic Safety Company, The U.S. Consumer Product Safety Commission, The Association of Pool & Spa Professionals, National Swimming Pool Foundation, The Y, and the National Recreation and Park Association are just a few organizations that can provide the reader with additional information on swimming pools and spas. Websites can be found in Appendix A.

Every pool owner and operator must understand fully the local health codes and ordinances that regulate swimming facilities in their region. This book is not intended to replace or supersede local swimming pool regulations; *The Complete Swimming Pool Reference, Third Edition* only serves as a general guide and helpful reference for those who own or operate swimming pools and spas. The reader must also understand that many state health codes regulating swimming pools are out of date. Much of what is found in these pages is more up to date. Readers must also have a good understanding of the Model Aquatic Health Code (MAHC) and the Americans with Disabilities Act (ADA).

Section I

Pools

We introduce the third edition of the *Complete Swimming Pool Reference* with our latest thoughts and discoveries on water safety. We wanted to lead off with this section because most swimming pool books do not discuss this vitally important topic sufficiently. The use of life jackets in swimming pools—yes, that's right, in swimming pools—as well as the latest advances in drowning detection technologies are discussed here.

Chapter 2 contains a brief, general description of swimming pools, including a classification of different types of pools to provide a basic overview that should be particularly helpful for novices. Topics introduced include circulation, pool configurations, construction materials, finishes, decking, and equipment. Safety, signage, and supervision are also introduced in this section, and chemical balancing is mentioned briefly. These topics are discussed in greater detail later in the book.

Chapter 3 specifically addresses the residential pool. This chapter is a comprehensive treatment of private pools, and the emphasis in this chapter is on safety. Layers of protection and pool barriers are important aspects of this chapter. This chapter is primarily written for homeowners who either have pools or are considering the construction of a pool on their premises. Additionally, residential pool service technicians might find this chapter helpful. Topics such as filtration, circulation, and water chemistry will be presented in Sections II and III.

Chapter 4 discusses public pools in detail. Different types of pools are discussed, as well as construction materials and pool equipment. Ladders, lights, finishes, markers, barriers, programming, and security are covered in this section. Special considerations for outdoor pools are also discussed. Pool areas such as the entrance, locker rooms, first aid room, staff room, and concession areas are also included in this chapter. Chapters 1, 2, and 3 cover swimming pools in general terms.

We wind down this section with two new chapters. Chapter 5 deals with long-range planning and funding for new aquatic facilities, illustrating a rational and detailed approach. Chapter 6 discusses the latest updates with the Americans with Disabilities Act (ADA). This chapter illustrates the many and varied ways of improving the accessibility of your swimming facilities.

1

A Water Safety Primer

As noted in the second edition of *The Complete Swimming Pool Reference* (2003), whenever a hazard is created at the pool, it should be repaired or removed immediately. Accidents at the pool are usually the result of a combination of irresponsible actions on the part of the pool patron, inadequate supervision, and a failure to warn. In this third edition, we provide new approaches to water safety. In this chapter, we focus on strengthening supervision and supplementing supervision.

Supervision

These topics may be mentioned in more depth later in the book. However, this is critically important information for safety in aquatic environments and thus vital to emphasize up front. Safety at the pool is a win for everyone.

Much has changed since the publication of *The Complete Swimming Pool Reference* in 1994 and 2003. For decades, we preached that parental (adult) supervision and vigilant lifeguarding were the cornerstones of drowning prevention programs and the most important Layer of Protection. Although we still believe that close, active, continuous supervision of children by adults and lifeguards is essential, we now believe that in many cases, if not most, technology is more effective than human supervision in regard to drowning prevention. Although this may sound like heresy in some water safety circles, human error is the number one cause of accidents worldwide, and the best of supervision can be spotty. Human beings are unable to remain vigilant for extended periods of time, and distractions are a part of everyday life, particularly in our world of handheld communications and technology. We have spent years researching the role of both technology and supervision in monitoring humans and have made a recent epiphany: Parents and lifeguards will continue to fail to protect lives in the water if they continue to rely *solely* on the human senses to prevent drowning. This is not to assert that we should throw in the towel on supervising, training lifeguards, or improving vigilance. Vigilant supervision is still key. However, the lifeguard toolbox of safety measures must expand to include ALL of the most effective nuts, bolts, and screws for water safety. The water safety culture should shift from *solely supervision* to *strengthening supervision* AND *supplementing supervision*.

Strengthening Supervision

Strengthening supervision is detailed in Chapter 23 and Chapter 24. New cutting-edge research unveils the prevalence of internal noise and other distractions for lifeguards, in addition to the challenges of physical body blindness and cognitive body blindness. This research has led to new strategies to strengthen supervision through methods to help manage internal noise, as well as mix up scanning techniques so scanning does not become too routine and too habitual, which can lead to missing victims in the water. The Complex Quadriplex of Lifeguard Blindness© (CQLB)—the four most significant challenges lifeguards face, along with "the habit of scanning"—illustrates how critical it is to strengthen supervision. However, the CQLB also demonstrates that no matter how strong supervision becomes, it will always have limitations. Thus, supplementing supervision is dire as well.

Supplementing Supervision: Water Safety Technology

Fortunately, many of the technologies we recommend are inexpensive and effective. A major motivation for writing this third edition of *The Complete Swimming Pool Reference* is to change the water safety focus of "solely supervision" to a culture of supervision combined with better pool design and safer technologies for drowning detection and prevention.

Life Jackets

Repeatedly throughout this book, we will encourage readers to promote the use of life jackets in swimming pools, rather than reserving life jackets for open-water use only. We believe that if all nonswimmers would buckle up in life jackets before going into the pool with the same consistency they buckle up in seat belts when they enter automobiles, the drowning rate would drastically decline. Identifying nonswimmers and then floating them in appropriately fitting U.S. Coast Guard-approved life jackets is the cheapest and most effective life insurance policy we can offer those recreating in, on, and around ALL bodies of water. Keep in mind, we still encourage close, active, vigilant supervision by adults whenever nonswimmers are around the water, even when they are wearing life jackets.

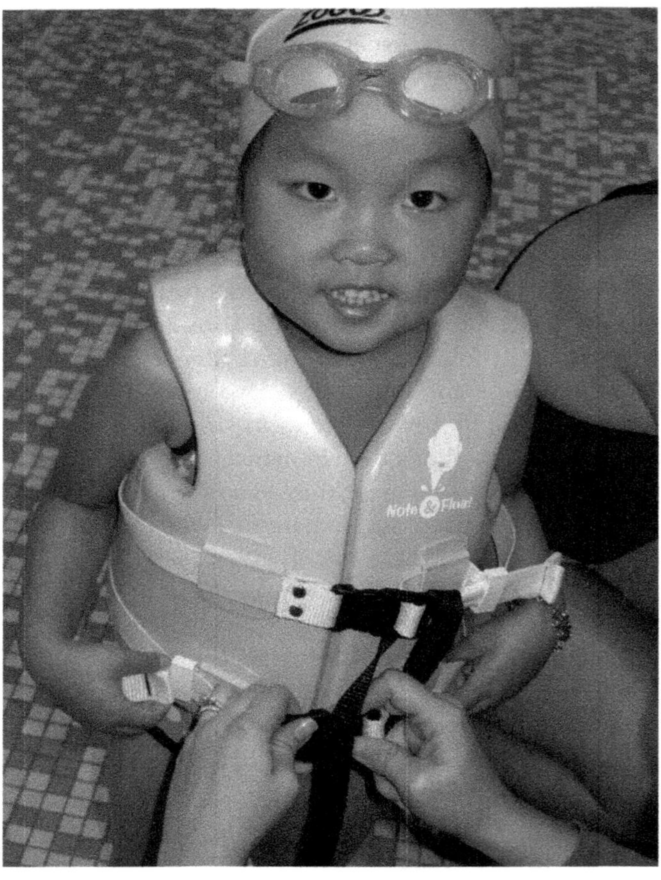

Figure 1.1. Proper fitting of life jackets for young children is important.

Note & Float™

Note & Float™ is a national program designed to reduce the risk of disability and drowning at aquatic facilities. Everyone should buckle up in a life jacket in, on, and around open water, and many state laws require the use of life jackets in watercrafts. Life jackets for nonswim-mers are a must in open water and in swimming pools. Figure 1.1 shows a young nonswimmer excited as she gets buckled in a Note & Float™ life jacket for swim lessons. Life jackets are the cheapest, most effective form of life insurance that can be bought. As new water safety strategies and technologies are developed to keep pools safer, the use of lifesaving tools that already exist is a no-brainer. Life jackets are not new, yet they are not commonplace for pools. Life jackets save lives, so they should be used to save lives at pools as well.

Swimming pool parties are extremely popular throughout the world. Birthday pool parties are especially entertaining. Unfortunately, pool parties are not all fun and games. In fact, more than half of all drownings in guarded swimming pools occur during pool parties. For several reasons, parents, lifeguards, and other supervisors become distracted during pool parties. This is why drowning often occurs at these times. On-duty lifeguards alone cannot prevent pool drowning because in a pool party setting, lifeguards often do not know all the children and do not know who can swim and who cannot. A strong group use policy is needed for pool parties along with the Note & Float™ program.

Note & Float™ is a program that identifies swimmers and nonswimmers and floats nonswimmers in life jackets. The Note & Float™ program instructs patrons (especially children) to wear wristbands that designate swimmers and nonswimmers. Nonswimmers are required to wear a U.S. Coast Guard-approved life jacket, stay within arm's reach of a parent, and stay in shallow water 5 ft and under. See Figure 1.2 for simple safety steps to implement a Note & Float™ program. All nonswimmers should always wear a life jacket at residential pools, at public pools, and in, on, and around open water. Swim lessons are still imperative early and often. In fact, buckling nonswimmers into life jackets helps acclimate children who otherwise would not be able to swim to the water and often is an impetus for swim lesson enrollment. *All children should learn to swim, but before they can, float 'em.*

Child Pool Alarms

Technology can monitor humans better than humans can monitor humans. The original Safety Turtle® is an extra layer of protection for children, which is primarily intended for children who are not supposed to be in the pool. The Safety Turtle® is a colorful turtle-shaped wristband (like a watch), with an alarm, which instantly detects immersion in water and sends a radio signal to the base station (See Figure 1.3.a). The Safety Turtle® is typically used in residential pools, and the base station, often located in the house, alerts the household with a loud, distinctive alarm. The base station also has a rechargeable battery and can be portable for use at a non-residential pool. The Safety Turtle® was designed specifi-

Figure 1.2. Six easy steps for Note & Float on a handy rack card.

cally for young children, locks in place, and can help save lives. This should be used as an extra layer of protection, supplementing (not replacing) supervision, in conjunction with self-closing, self-latching gates, among other necessary layers of protection. We will discuss the Safety Turtle® for improved emergency response in guarded pools in Chapter 4.

The SEAL swim monitoring and drowning detection system is promising new technology that detects a swimmer in distress and alerts lifeguards and parents in time to rescue the swimmer (Figure 1.3.b). The SEAL consists of a central hub that connects with SEALBands that are worn around the neck by swimmers and GUARDBands that are optionally worn by parents, caregivers, and lifeguards. The SEAL triggers visible, audible, and vibrating warnings and alarms on all devices (hub, SEALBand, GuardBands) notifying parents, lifeguards, and other swimmers to initiate a rescue.

Poseidon

For larger municipal pools, Poseidon computer-aided drowning detection systems may be used (see Figure 1.4). As of writing this edition, Poseidon technology systems have detected 22 drowning victims in guarded facilities, resulting in successful rescues. In all cases, the lifeguards initially missed the victims. However, after they were alarmed by the Poseidon system, the lifeguards responded and rescued the individuals. We will discuss the paramount need for water safety technology in-depth in Chapter 23.

Additional Layers of Protection

Swim Lessons

Somewhat surprisingly, our philosophy on swimming lessons has also shifted. After years of suggesting the best years to enroll children in swimming lessons

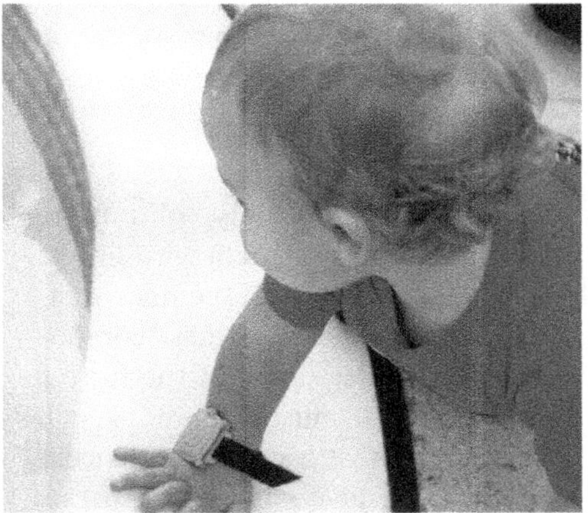

Figure 1.3.a. The Safety Turtle™ wristband sounds an alarm when immersed in water and is an excellent extra layer of protection, especially for residential and unguarded pools. (Photos courtesy of Safety Turtle™)

Figure 1.3.b. The SEAL SwimSafe™ Swim Monitor and Drowning Detection System neckband. (Photo courtesy of SEAL Innovation)

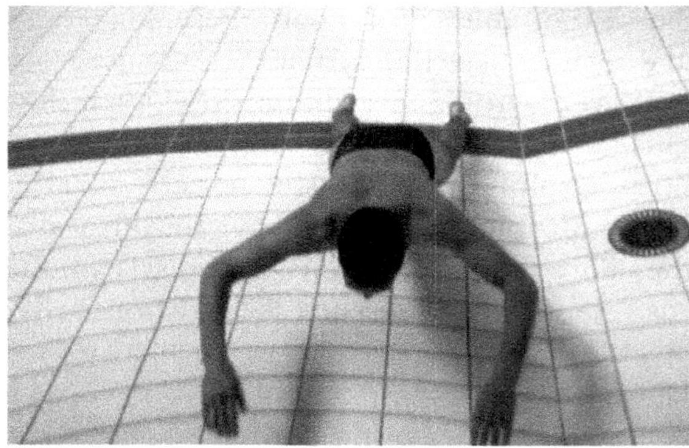

Figure 1.4. Poseidon Technologies, Inc©. computer-aided drowning detection system can alert lifeguards of submerged swimmers in just 10 seconds. (Photo courtesy of Poseidon Technologies, Inc.©).

was between ages 4 and 6 years, we now believe swimming lessons can be beneficial earlier and more often than originally thought. Many quality swim instructors and swim schools are hugely successful at teaching toddlers to swim before ages 1 and 2 years. After reviewing the research, we believe a good guideline for swimming lessons is "early and often," but quality instruction is a must for safety and to get children off to a good start in the swimming pool.

Effective Signage

Although most public pools are plagued with long lists of meaningless rules and regulations that few people take the time to read, many residential pools have no signs at all. As a result, we promote a new strategy of safety signage systems that focuses on four vitally important safety warnings that can result in catastrophic injury and death if not obeyed in public and private pools. Signage should use warning shapes, symbols, and colors, with the most important rules displayed more prominently. The Big Four Rules (see Figure 1.5) include the following:

1. Please Watch Your Children,
2. No Extended Breath-Holding,
3. No Diving in Shallow Water, and
4. Nonswimmers Need Life Jackets.

Figure 1.5. The four most significant warnings and brief explanations are conspicuously displayed at an outdoor swimming pool in California. (Sign design ©Clarion Safety Systems. All rights reserved. Photo courtesy of Aquatic Safety Research Group)

Rules that are not designed to prevent catastrophic injury, drowning, or death (some health codes, no glass on deck, shower before entering, no horseplay, etc.), but need to be posted, can still be displayed, but should be separated from the rules that help prevent fatal events.

Summary

The aquatics industry should not only continue to strengthen supervision, but also supplement with simple technologies such as life jackets. You will see many reasons in this text that illustrate why both of these components are vital to improving water safety in the future. Water safety education is also a must. This book will provide many new and innovative ways to create safer aquatic environments. We will give you plenty to talk about, so be sure to spread the water safety word!

2

A Pool Primer
Basic Characteristics of Pools

On first glance, a swimming pool appears to be a quiet, calm, and still body of water. Pool experts often refer to the perfectly calm pool as a "quiescent pool." But in reality, whether busy or slow in terms of swimmers, a swimming pool is a dynamic system of moving water that continually flows from the pool for treatment and returns cleaned, heated, and sanitized. In fact, a pool is a recycling system whereby the entire volume of water passes through a filtration plant several times each day. As the water travels through the filter, it is cleaned of dirt and other organic debris. Before it returns to the pool, however, it is often heated and must be sanitized using a powerful chemical, most often chlorine. A clean, clear, germ-free pool requires tremendous attention. Large or small, every pool is required to filter and chemically treat its water through this process. When a pool is not filtering or a chemical disinfectant is absent in the water, the pool must be closed immediately. Without filtration and disinfection, the water will turn cloudy and bacteria will grow, thus becoming unsafe for all who enter.

Classifications of Swimming Pools

Some organizations provide many classifications for pools, seemingly from A to Z. Many hybrid and unique pools exist today, and many variations of pool classifications exist across different organizations and states that are often updated and changed. The new Model Aquatic Health Code may also provide further distinctions and classifications of pools. Thus, we prefer to classify pools into three general categories: public pools, semipublic pools, and residential pools. We define these classifications in the following sections.

The Model Aquatic Health Code is "a model and guide for local and state agencies needing to update or implement swimming pool and spa code, rules, regulations, guidance, law, or standards governing the design, construction, operation, and maintenance of swimming pools, spas, hot tubs, and other treated or disinfected aquatic facilities." (www.cdc.gov/healthywater/swimming/pools/mahc/)

Figure 2.1 Fun for everyone at this well planned public pool. (Photo courtesy of Counsilman-Hunsaker)

Public Pools

A public pool is usually a larger pool (more than 1,800 sq ft) that is owned or operated by a legal entity and is made available to anyone who pays a small entry fee. However, some public pools do not charge admission (Figure 2.1). Public pools are also commonly known as municipal or commercial pools.

Semipublic Pools

This pool is similar to the public pool but has specific entry restrictions like that of a fitness center, country club, or hotel or motel pool. Members must qualify and often pay to join before entry into the swimming complex.

Residential Pools

For the purposes of this text, residential pools are private pools that are not regulated by the health department or other regulatory agency. Residential pools are not intended for commercial use and are not owned by more than three families. Again, the number of dwellings considered to be a residential pool may vary across states and may change over time. Specific dimensions are covered in Chapter 3. Public and semipublic pools are usually inspected by a health official, whereas residential pools are not.

Subcategories and Other Aquatic Venues

Further subclassifications of swimming pools exist, which fall under the public, semipublic, or residential categories. These include community and neighborhood pools; agency pools (YMCA/YWCA, Jewish Community Centers, Boy Scouts, Girl Scouts, etc.); school pools; hotel, motel, apartment, or condo pools; water parks; splash pads; spray parks; leisure pools; therapeutic pools; and spas and hot tubs. Because of their popularity, we will discuss residential; community; and hotel, motel, and resort pools in detail later in this text.

Circulation

Although all swimmers see the pool, few have the opportunity to become familiar with the plumbing of the pool. Although this aspect of swimming may not be exciting to all pool owners and operators, an adequate understanding of filtration and chemical disinfection is a must if clean water is to be maintained. For the sake of discussion, a swimming pool plant functions like a closed-loop system. Although swimming pools are not technically "closed loops" (most of the water stays in the system much of the time), we will consider them closed loops in this text for ease of understanding (Figure 2.2).

To understand how a swimming pool functions, consider how the human body works. The heart circulates blood in the body as a centrifugal pump recirculates swimming pool water. The kidneys remove toxic waste from the blood as filters remove debris from the pool water. The veins and arteries carry blood to and from the heart as influent and effluent pipes carry water to and from the pool (Figure 2.3). When we discuss water chemistry later in this book, you will learn that pool water can be either basic and scale-forming or aggressive and corrosive. Scale-forming water blocks the plumbing of the pool as bad cholesterol blocks arteries. On the other hand, corrosive water eats away at the swimming pool plant as cancer deteriorates the human body.

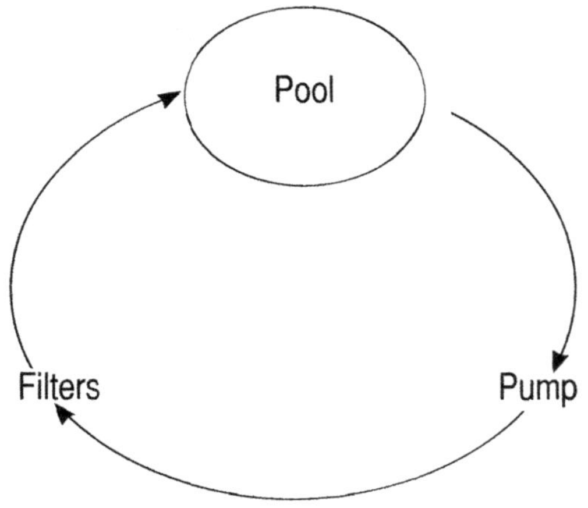

Figure 2.2. Swimming pool circulation simplified: A closed loop.

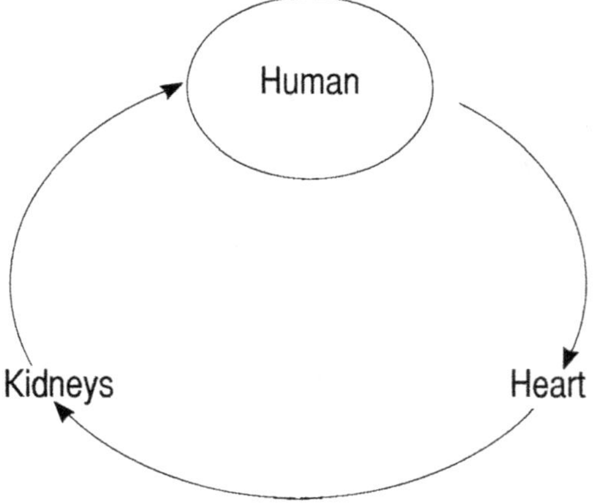

Figure 2.3. Swimming pool circulation is similar to the human body's circulation.

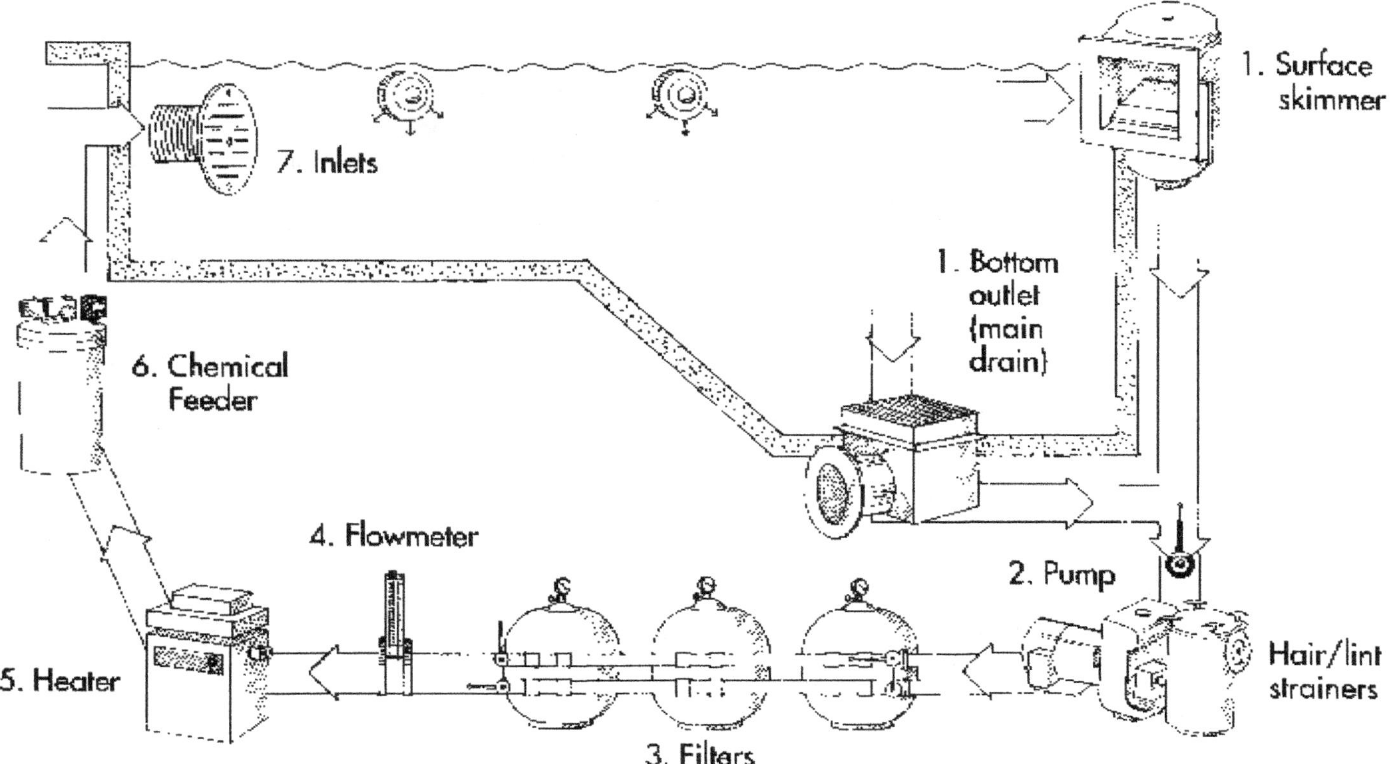

Figure 2.4. Circulation components. (Illustrated by Nancy Bauer)

More specifically, the basic components of a swimming pool and its circulation system include the following:

- vessel or swimming pool basin,
- surge or balancing tank (in larger pools),
- pump,
- hair and lint strainer (except on vacuum filters),
- filter or filters,
- heater (if necessary), and
- chemical disinfectant system.

The water circulates by leaving the pool from outlets around the perimeter found in either surface gutters or skimmers. To a lesser extent, water also leaves through the main drain or bottom outlet. The pool pump then either pushes or pulls the water through the filters. If necessary, the water is heated and then must be chemically treated before returning to the pool by way of inlets located on the pool bottom or pool walls. Typically, hundreds of gallons per minute flow through the filtration plant to be filtered, heated, and chemically treated during this process. Refer to Figure 2.4 for a flow chart illustration of water circulation.

In addition to the pool and the filtration system, knowledgeable pool owners and operators should be familiar with swimming pool construction, pool finishes, decking, accessories, and pool equipment.

Pool Configurations

When the first edition of *The Complete Swimming Pool Reference* was published in 1994, most pools were either rectangular or square in shape. Today, more pools are designed with free-form configurations and include amenities such as waterfalls and walk-in, beach-like entries, commonly known as "zero-depth entry." Pools of tomorrow will be even more creatively constructed and will move even further away from the "boring rectangular" pool design of the past. This is a positive trend that makes the discussion of pool configurations more challenging. When the word *traditional* is used in this text, it refers to older rectangular pools and those with deep ends. Modern swimming pools have mostly shallow water with many having only shallow water.

Many shapes and sizes of pools are available. After years of large pools being built to accommodate many activities, pools are now being constructed of more shallow water for lap swimming, swim lessons, aquacize, safety, and construction costs. Most pools have a shallow end and a deep end, but a growing trend is to construct pools that are all shallow and have no deep water. Shallow water pools are less expensive to build and to operate. Typically, the shallow end of a swimming pool is approximately 3.5 ft deep.

However, many pools are being constructed today with zero-depth or beach-like entries. These types of pools are extremely popular, particularly with younger children and people with disabilities. Whenever possible, competition pools with starting blocks located in shallow water should be moved to the deep end. Headfirst entries must be prohibited from the pool deck in less than 5 ft of water because 95% of all serious diving injuries occur in this depth. Many aquatic professionals now recommend 9 ft of water for headfirst entries from the pool deck. The deep end of the swimming pool ranges from 8 to 13 ft, although "diving" from a board should not be permitted into less than 11 ft. In public pools, the preferred depth is 12.5 ft, or adults may be seriously injured by striking the bottom. The term *springboard diving* in this text does not refer to untrained, unsupervised recreational divers entering the water headfirst. *Headfirst entries* should be used instead of the term *diving* so as not to confuse this with the sport of competitive springboard diving.

Regardless of the type of pool, diving from a board should be permitted into a safe diving envelope only. According to the American Red Cross (2009), a safe diving envelope is an underwater area in front of, below, and to the sides of a diving board that has adequate depth and distance to allow any diver to maneuver safely underwater without striking the bottom or slope of the pool, regardless of the depth of water or the design of the pool. We will discuss this important concept in greater detail later.

In traditional, older swimming pools, the straight, rectangular design is the most common, and other shapes such as T, Z, or L are often used to entertain other activities in the pool without interfering with lap swimming or swim team practice. Creative pool designs are usually built with increased programming in mind (Figure 2.5). As mentioned earlier, free-form pools are becoming more popular today, particularly in the case of leisure pools, water parks, and large resort-type pools, but more municipal pools are following the creative lead of water parks to design family aquatic centers that have many similarities.

Diving Hopper or Spoon-Shaped Pools

Diving hoppers or spoon-shaped pools refer to the deepest section of the pool, which accommodate diving. These are typically found in older, traditional swimming pools. To construct this, a steep slope must be created between the shallow and deep areas of the pool. This is one way of accommodating more than one activity in a rectangular-shaped pool, but it creates problems. The slope itself is problematic. Nonswimmers can slide down the slope into deeper water, and springboard divers can hit the slope with their heads following a dive. The American Red Cross first addressed the dangers of

diving in diving hoppers or spoon-shaped pools and this still holds true today. Black or red lines should be painted across the bottom of the pool to alert swimmers and divers of this slope. A surface line or life line should cross the pool on the surface to prevent novice swimmers from entering the diving area. However, the presence of a life line can neither guarantee the safety of nonswimmers nor replace close supervision. Nonswimmers should always wear properly fitting U.S. Coast Guard-approved life jackets. Although diving hoppers or spoon-shaped pools are a common design for YMCA, high school, and even college pools, a separate diving well often provides more safety and greater programming options. Whenever possible, if a diving board in a particular pool no longer meets the safe diving standards according to the National Collegiate Athletic Association, USA Diving, or the YMCA, either the deep end should be filled in or a climbing wall or other safe similar structure, such as an appropriate slide, should be installed to replace the diving board(s).

Pool Construction

Two basic types of pool construction are available: aboveground and inground swimming pools. We will discuss these types of swimming pools in further detail in Chapter 3. Aboveground pools are usually constructed with aluminum or galvanized panels, although a recent trend is inflatable rubber pools. Aboveground pools are much less expensive than inground pools and can be somewhat portable and temporary. Headfirst entries must be totally banned in aboveground pools.

Inground pools are constructed of a variety of materials including concrete, fiberglass, metal, vinyl, and even wood. Inground pools are more expensive and permanent, and in most cases, diving should be banned in these types of pools as well, unless they are built with competitive diving standards.

Pool Finishes

Regardless of what type of pool finish is selected, the color of the pool basin or finish should be white or at least lightly colored in almost all cases. A white underwater finish provides excellent visibility for safety and aesthetics. White pool basins full of water appear blue, although many naturalistic pools today use dark bottoms. Outdoor pools that use concrete will often have a plaster finish. Many indoor pools are finished with tile. Ceramic tile is the most versatile finish, but not surprisingly, it is also the most expensive. Residential pools are now using vinyl liners, which are both popular and reasonably priced. Vinyl liners can look like tile or plaster, but are much less expensive. On the down side, vinyl liners can be torn or punctured. Stainless steel and fiber-

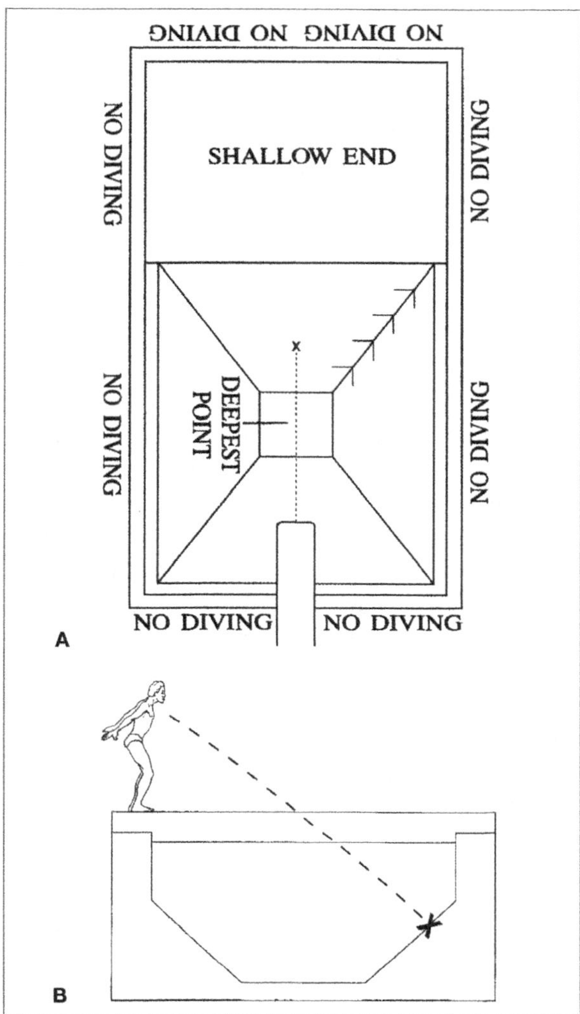

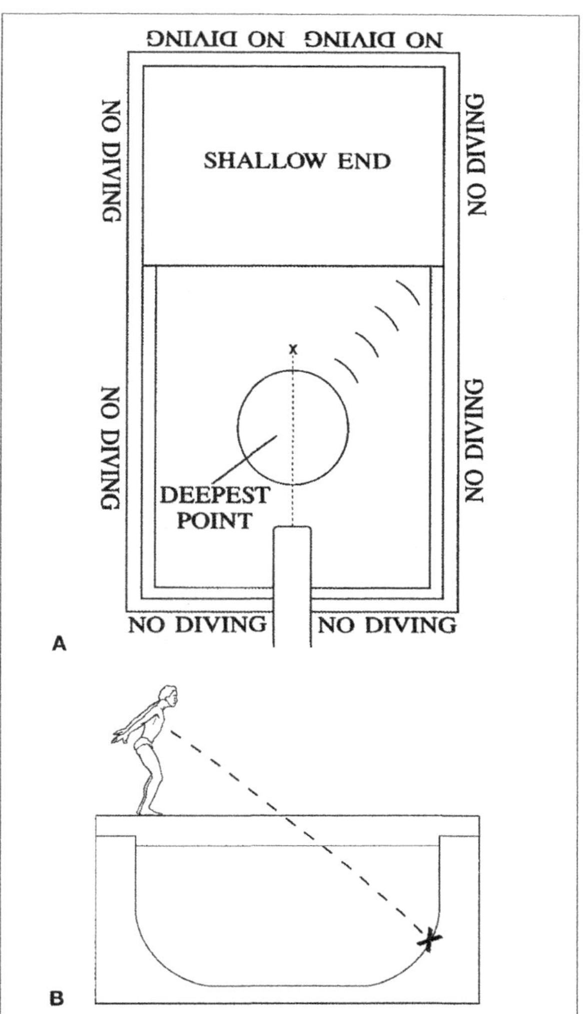

Figure 2.5. Left: A, Top view of hopper-bottom pool. B, Cross-section of hopper-bottom pool. Right: A, Top view of spoon-shaped pool. B, Cross-section of spoon-shaped pool. (From *Swimming and Water Safety,* American Red Cross, 2009)

glass pools are also available. Of course, advantages and disadvantages exist for each pool finish.

Decking

Different materials can be used for deck areas surrounding the pool. Whatever surface is used must be nonslip. Also, the deck must be a flat surface free of depressions or dimples that can collect water and must be sloped away from the pool for proper drainage. Puddles on the pool deck can attract algae, fungi, and worse yet, mosquitoes that can spread the West Nile virus. Decks cluttered with furniture and other pool equipment can obstruct views of the pool and create hazards. Some decking materials that work well include brick, tile, wood, flagstone, terrazzo, concrete, indoor–outdoor carpeting, cocoa mat, flow-through tiles, and exposed aggregate concrete.

Matting or carpeting often remains wet, thus promoting algae and fungi growth. Rubber, interlocking, self-draining deck tiles are becoming popular, but they must also be cleaned regularly, and power washing these is highly recommended. For outdoor pools, artificial grass or astroturf also is becoming more popular. Astroturf for swimming pools should include irrigation openings in the turf that allow for proper water drainage. This surface may become hot in warm weather, which has benefits and drawbacks.

Whatever the deck surface, it must be hosed down regularly to be debris free, and care must also be taken to prevent algae from growing.

Pool Equipment

Ladders, Steps, and Handrails

Ladders should be either recessed into the pool wall or should be removable. Ladders, handrails, and steps should not protrude into lap lanes to prevent accidents. Loose-fitting ladders should be repaired immediately.

Ladders and handrails should be made of stainless steel or another corrosion-resistant material. Plastic or PVC steps should be replaced whenever cracks or signs of wear appear. To prevent trips, slips, and falls, ladders and steps must have nonslip surfaces and the edges should be clearly marked with a contrasting color or colored tile. Ladders should be constructed and be affixed to or found inside pool walls so that children cannot become entrapped between rungs when attempting to swim through them.

Diving Boards and Slides

Before either apparatus is installed, adequate depth must be determined for each piece of equipment. Smaller slides at public and residential pools should probably be reserved for children under age 12 because older, larger individuals might discharge from the slide with too much force. Larger water park slides are designed for all ages. Regardless of the age of the slider or size of the slide, feetfirst sliding is the only way to go. Headfirst sliding must be prohibited for all. Sliders must be certain that no other swimmers or sliders are in the discharge area.

Diving boards should be reserved for deeper flat-bottom pools. Whenever possible, pools should be constructed to allow diving or sliding into a portion of the pool segregated from the general swim area or lap lanes. Rules and regulations concerning their use must be prominently posted. Many colorful playground-type slides are now being adapted for swimming pool use with great success. Playground-type slides and similar simple yet fun features are gaining popularity in swimming pools, adding amenities without as much installation or maintenance as involved with water park waterslides (Figure 2.6). Additionally, playground slides and similar slides often do not require the depth of water necessary for diving boards or other features. When it comes to drop slides, extra care must be taken to ensure that only swimmers use this type of slide because it discharges into water at least 5 ft deep. Nonswimmers must be kept away from these deeper waterslides.

Many diverse options are available for pool slides. Some slides even discharge into a segregated run-out trough with just inches of water. The choices for swimming pool features abound and will continue to grow in the future. New features are exciting, but safety is key for all features.

Figure 2.6. Swimming pool slides and water features.

Water Chemistry

The purpose of the disinfectant (usually chlorine, sometimes bromine) in the water is to keep the water germ free and also clear for aesthetics and safety. Chlorine accomplishes this through sanitation (germ killing) and oxidation ("burning up" organic material). Liquid chlorine works well in this application.

The immediate concern of any pool owner or operator is to keep appropriate disinfectant and pH levels in the pool. Although many pool patrons complain about excessive chlorine levels, most pools in the United States are inadequately chlorinated. Malodorous, burning water comes from the spent form of chlorine called combined chlorine or chloramines, not high levels of the active disinfectant called free chlorine. The pH buffers the disinfectant and also relates to bather comfort.

In addition, the water must be balanced, which requires readings in pH, temperature, total alkalinity, and calcium hardness (see Chapter 16) that many facility owners and operators unfortunately overlook. Balanced water not only keeps swimmers comfortable but also protects the pool shell, plumbing, and related equipment from damage by aggressive or scale-forming water.

The pH and chlorine levels are the primary concern of the aquatic facility operator, who keeps the water healthy and comfortable for pool patrons, that is, user friendly. Temperature, total alkalinity, and calcium hardness levels change more gradually, but must be monitored just the same.

As the pool operator's understanding of basic water chemistry increases, water quality and clarity problems tend to decrease.

Summary

This chapter briefly described and summarized basic characteristics of swimming pools. Other more detailed information regarding pool basics may be found in the references listed. Pool shapes, sizes, construction materials, equipment, circulation, chemistry, and safety were introduced. Regardless of what type of pool is owned or operated, local ordinances and regulations regarding swimming pools, in addition to national regulations (including the Model Aquatic Health Code), must be understood, followed, and wherever possible, surpassed. In addition, The Association of Pool and Spa Professionals is a good resource for swimming pool publications and dealers; APSP can be reached at their website (www.apsp.org) or by phone at 703.838.0083.

*APSP reminds parents that these "layers" are backups to the primary means of accident prevention: **Responsible Adult Supervision**.*

1 Fencing
PURPOSE: To isolate the swimming pool by way of a <u>minimum</u> four-foot-high enclosure.
TYPES: a. Chain link; b. Wooden picket (if non-climbable); c. Ornamental; d. Portable fencing*; e. Natural barrier (thick hedge), if permitted by local code
*Purpose: To temporarily isolate a pool, spa, or hot tub when children are visiting.

2 Automatic, Power Safety Covers
PURPOSE: An impenetrable covering that completely covers the pool, blocking access to water. Cover is operated electronically or by a key independent of all other pool equipment.
TYPES: Meets the latest revision of ASTM F1346 *Standard performance specification for safety covers and labeling requirements for all covers for swimming pools, spas, and hot tubs*

3 Manual Safety Covers
PURPOSE: An impenetrable covering that completely covers the pool, spa, or hot tub, blocking access to water.
TYPES: Meets ASTM F1346 Standard

4 Door Exit Alarms
PURPOSE: Warns parent or guardian when a child opens the door.
TYPES: a. Door announcer/chime; b. Home security system

5 Self-closing/self-latching devices for doors and latching devices for windows
PURPOSE: Keeps all doors and windows leading to the pool, spa, or hot tub area securely closed, limiting access by children.
TYPES: a. Hinge pin replacement; b. Sliding glass door closer; c. Swing arm

6 Fence Gate Closer & Latch
PURPOSE: To close and latch fence gates securely, making a pool, spa, or hot tub inaccessible to a child.
TYPES: Self-latching

7 Fence Gate Alarms
PURPOSE: Sounds when fence gate is open.

8 Infrared Detectors
PURPOSE: Wireless detection alarm that sounds when the area around the pool perimeter is entered.
TYPES: a. Light-beam; b. Body energy

9 Pool Alarms
PURPOSE: An alarm placed in the pool that sounds upon detection of accidental or unauthorized entrance into the water.
TYPES: a. Surface water (wave motion); b. Pressure waves (acoustic); c. Electronic monitoring system

10 Child Alarms
PURPOSE: An alarm clipped on the child that sounds when the child exceeds a certain distance or becomes submerged in water.
TYPES: Clip-on transmitter with in-home receiver

11 Rope & Float Line
A rope & float line should be placed across the pool, alerting swimmers to the separation of the deep end from the shallow end of the pool.

12 Life Ring, Shepherd's Hook
All rescue equipment should be placed near the pool in an easily accessible spot, and should be kept in good condition. These can be used to pull someone in trouble to safety.

13 Posted Emergency Information
Post all CPR, other emergency information, and warning signs, as well as the emergency phone number "911" (or other emergency medical service number), near the pool, spa, or hot tub.

14 Outside Telephone
A cordless or poolside telephone means parents don't have to leave children unattended while they answer the phone. Also, it's a good idea to have one handy to summon help, if needed.

15 Anti-Entrapment Drain Covers and Fittings
Current grates and covers help prevent body or hair entrapment. Make sure that drain covers meet the ANSI/ASME A112.19.2007 standard or latest revision. Safety doors should be installed in all pool cleaner wall suction lines. *Pools, spas, or hot tubs with drain covers that are broken, missing, or not adequately secured should not be used until the proper replacement has been installed. Never allow children to play on or near drains, suction outlets, or jets. <u>There is no backup layer of protection in the marketplace today for a missing or broken drain cover that will protect against all five suction entrapment hazards.</u>*

16 Water Clarity
Clear water aids in identifying soakers and swimmers in distress, helps swimmers avoid collisions and is an indicator that the sanitizer, circulation, and filtration systems are functioning. Poor water clarity suggests the presence of bacteria and/or algae or nutrients for their growth, and that the circulation and filtration systems may not be working efficiently to remove the contaminants from the water.

Figure 2.7. Layers of Protection. (Courtesy of The Association of Pool and Spa Professionals, 2014©)

References

American Red Cross. (2009). *Swimming and water safety* (3rd ed.). Yardley, PA: StayWell.

American Red Cross. (1992). *Swimming and diving.* St Louis, MO: Mosby.

Bibliography

Gabrielson, A. M. (1987). *Swimming pools: A guide to their planning, design, and operation* (4th ed.). Champaign, IL: Human Kinetics.

Human Kinetics. (2008). *Aqua tech: Best practices for pool and aquatic facility operators.* Champaign, IL: Author.

Mitchell, P. (1988). *The proper management of pool and spa water.* Decatur, GA: BioLab.

Recreonics. (1991). *Buyers' guide and operations handbook: Catalog no. 41.* Indianapolis, IN: Author.

Williams, K. G., & Young, R. A. (Eds.). (2011). *Aquatic facility operator manual* (6th ed.). Ashburn, VA: National Recreation and Park Association.

Photo Courtesy of Water Technology, Inc.

3

Residential Pools

Key Concepts

Pool barriers	On-ground pools
Protection layers	Inground pools
Supervision	Chemical safety
Pool covers	Electrical safety
Diving	Insurance
Aboveground pools	APSP

Many homeowners agree that nothing is more satisfying than having a pretty blue pool in the backyard. Whether filled with active people or just sitting there quiet and calm, a pool significantly adds to the quality of life. A swimming pool greatly enhances both exercise and entertaining. Residential pools are definitely a place to rest, relax, party, and work out. Although local health codes and ordinances regulate public pools, they often do not apply to residential pools. In addition, lifeguards do not patrol residential pools, so homeowners should strongly consider additional safety measures that can be installed in and around the pool.

Swimming attracts millions of participants annually. According to The Association of Pool and Spa Professionals (APSP, 2013), there are nearly 8 million residential pools in the United States. This number includes inground and aboveground pools, but it does not include the 6 million hot tubs and spas (APSP, 2013). Of all the newly constructed swimming pools in the United States each year, approximately 60% are privately owned residential pools (APSP, 2013).

Much of the profit in the residential swimming pool industry is obtained through maintenance and repair, and less is derived from new swimming pool installations. In 2005, existing swimming pools accounted for 60% or more of the gross profit for the largest wholesale distributor of swimming pool supplies equipment and related leisure products (POOL 10-Q filed Nov 1, 2006, United States Securities and Exchange Commission Form 10-Q, SCP Pool Corporation.) In an economic downturn, demand for residential swimming pools declines, and in a stable economy, demand seems steady or may increase.

Many pool owners appreciate the recreation and relaxation a swimming pool provides. A trend today to enhance the calming effects of a backyard pool is the addition of a waterfall or other water feature that produces meditative splashing of falling water or lighting. Some people acquire a swimming facility for fitness or therapy. Other people maintain a pool to teach their children to be water safe. Regardless of the reason for having a pool, the type of pool constructed should meet the needs of the homeowner.

Residential pools became more popular in the United States following World War II, when many soldiers were taught water safety skills in the service, thus acquiring a keener appreciation for swimming. Couple that with a booming economy in the United States after the war, and you can easily to see how and why backyard pools took off in America. The fitness movement of the 1970s and development of inexpensive "prefab" pool packages have also contributed greatly to the growth of home pools in this country. The introduction of the vinyl liner pool has also kept the price down on home pools. The pools of today are no longer playthings for the rich. Inground pool costs are similar to new car costs: prices vary. For both pools and automobiles, there are expensive luxurious models and inexpensive, more practical models. Aboveground pools are much less expensive than inground pools. During recessionary periods, inground pool construction tends to decline, whereas aboveground pool purchases tend to remain stable.

Many residential pools run safely and do not experience problems. However, several risks accompany pool ownership.

"Swimming pool time" should be "leisure time" instead of "worry time." Fortunately, the two most feared risks—drowning and spinal cord injury—can be avoided easily. Home pool drownings usually involve small children, and spinal cord injuries most often affect adults.

The leading cause for *not* purchasing a residential pool is that many homeowners perceive pools as a safety hazard for their children. In fact, more than half of the respondents in this survey cited the safety issue for not purchasing a pool. This chapter is dedicated to teaching homeowners how to make residential pools safe for their families. Figure 3.1 shows a well-maintained and aesthetic residential swimming pool, requiring adult supervision.

According to The Association of Pool and Spa Professionals

Residential pools can be classified in many ways, and the definitions vary across states and change over time. For the purposes of this text, *residential pool* shall be defined as any constructed pool, permanent or nonportable, that is intended for noncommercial use as a swimming pool by not more than three owner families and their guests and that is over 24 in. deep and has a surface area exceeding 250 sq ft and/or a volume over 3,250 gal.

Safety

According to the U.S. Consumer Product Safety Commission (CPSC, 2012), nearly 300 children under age 5 years drown in pools, spas, and hot tubs annually. Most swimming pool drownings occur in privately owned residential pools (Laosee, Glichrist, & Rudd, 2012). Tragically, toddlers ages 1 to 3 years account for 75% of home pool submersion or drowning accidents (CPSC, 2012). For every child that dies as a result of drowning, an additional five children are treated in the emergency room for nonfatal submersion injuries (Centers for Disease Control and Prevention, National Center for Injury Prevention and Control, 2012).

Additionally, thousands are sent to the hospital each year as a result of near-drowning incidents, and many of these accidents lead to permanent brain damage. Child drownings occur quickly and quietly, without warning. Children in trouble cannot cry out for help because they spend all their energy attempting to breathe.

In regard to safeguarding children around a swimming pool, no one safety practice or piece of equipment is foolproof. For this reason, pool owners are advised to have a system of safety precautions so that if one fails, another will come into affect. This "layering" of safety techniques and mechanisms is perhaps the best method of protecting children around a pool, but no technique or mechanism should replace close parental supervision.

The most effective and inexpensive form of life insurance a pool owner can purchase is life jackets for all children. Children who cannot swim should wear appropriately fitting U.S. Coast Guard-approved life jackets around or in the water. Children should be in the habit of wearing life jackets whenever they go near or in the pool.

Supervision

It is imperative for children to wear life jackets and for parents or guardians to practice vigilant, in-water, touch supervision to protect their children from drowning in their own backyard.

Parents of most young drowning victims claim they left their child unsupervised for less than 5 minutes. A child can drown in less than 1 minute. Some children

Figure 3.1. A well-designed and maintained residential pool. (Photo courtesy of *Pool & Spa News*)

have drowned while the parent in charge left the pool to answer the phone. Children must never be left alone around a pool for any length of time. More important, parents must not be distracted from watching their children. Just because adults are stationed around the pool does not mean children are safe in the water. Too often, adults talk, read, use their cell phones and other hand-held devices, or even sleep while kids are in the pool. Many people fail to realize that often internal noise, or unrelated thoughts and feelings, such as errands or worry, can be distracting as well. Shields, Pollack-Nelson, and Smith (2011) in their article "Pediatric Submersion Events in Portable Above-Ground Pools in the United States, 2001–2009" reported that in 66% of drowning cases, supervision was present at the time of submersion, and 43% of these children were supervised by an adult. A *lapse* in supervision was recorded in 18% of these cases in which supervision was present (Shields et al., 2011). The lapses in supervision occurred when the supervisor was sleeping, in the house doing chores, asleep in the pool holding the subject, or socializing with neighbors (Shields et al., 2011). Supervision is absolutely vital, but clearly internal noise and external distractions can lead to a *lack* of supervision and *lapses* in supervision. Close, active, touch supervision complemented with technology is critical. A U.S. Coast Guard-approved life jacket is the most effective and least expensive life insurance policy for nonswimmers. Some parents use flotation devices on their children instead of supervising them. Inflatable swimming aids can deflate. Other swimming aids have been known to slip off of children. The only acceptable flotation device is a U.S. Coast Guard-approved life jacket. All floaties and other devices should never be used as a swimming aid for nonswimmers, with the exception of swimming lessons. Whenever more than one adult is present when young children are using the pool, one adult should be specified as the *designated kid watcher* so that no one is distracted from the important task of supervision.

Parents should also refrain from placing too many furnishings and toys around the pool. A pool deck cluttered with swimming accoutrements can obstruct the parents' view of the water, thus impairing supervision and delaying rescue efforts. Children in general are drawn to water. Furthermore, autism is the fastest growing children's disability in America, and autistic children are far more likely to be drawn to the water. When the pool is not in use, all toys and floats should be removed from the pool so that they do not lure a child into the water.

Pool Rules

Many homeowners do not want their aesthetically appealing aquatic landscape ruined with signs, but swimming pool rules and regulations should be clearly marked and observed at poolside. Clearly stated rules will help to eliminate water rescues. Just as there are primary and secondary responsibilities for lifeguards, there is primary and secondary signage. Primary signage lists rules that help prevent catastrophic injury, drowning, and death. Secondary signage is also important to help prevent accidents, injuries, and other unwanted behavior at the pool. However, primary signage should be posted separately from secondary signage. The Big Four Rules that should be emphasized include the following:

> 1. **Please Watch Your Children**
> 2. **No Extended Breath-Holding**
> 3. **No Diving in Shallow Water**
> 4. **Nonswimmers Need Life Jackets.**

"No Running," "No Horseplay," and "No Glass" are rules that are also important and should be included as secondary signage. "Never Swim Alone" is one rule that the family must enforce. If children have had swimming lessons, this does not necessarily mean that they are water safe and do not require supervision. In fact, for some individuals, swimming lessons make them overconfident and careless around the pool.

Barriers

According to the CPSC, nearly half of all children who drowned in residential pools were *last seen inside the house*. Although close supervision is the key to prevent drowning, four-sided barriers also help to keep small children out of the water. The CPSC (2012) posits many of the nearly 300 drownings of children under the age of 5 in backyard pools could be prevented with proper, completely fenced in pools and self-closing, self-latching gates. Several types of manufactured swimming pool barriers are available for homeowners to use, but proper fencing is perhaps the best protection in terms of pool products (Figure 3.2).

Proper fencing for swimming pools is one of the most controversial topics in the swimming pool industry. The CPSC advocates stringent fencing requirements, but many pool builders and owners often find these recommendations too difficult and expensive to achieve.

The CPSC and some states recommend installing a fence on all four sides of the pool, and the house is not allowed to serve as one side of the fence. Pool fences should be a minimum of 4 ft high, but many experts recommend a height of 6 ft. The fence should be composed of vertical slats and be free of footholds or handholds that can aid children in climbing it. Slats must be placed

Figure 3.2. A, B, and C, Effective fencing and gates. D and E, See-through mesh fencing specifically designed for small children can be installed and can be moved in minutes. A, Photo courtesy of Lynn Smith, Clearwater Swimming Pools, Centre Hall, PA; D and E. (Photos courtesy of Protect A Child, Pool Fence Systems)

no greater than 4 in. apart to prevent toddlers from squeezing through. Chairs, benches, and tables should be kept away from the fence. The proper installation of fence gates is important. Gates should be self-closing and self-latching so that after anyone enters or exits the pool, the gate automatically closes and latches. The ability of the gate to close and latch by itself should be checked regularly. The latch should be between 48 and 54 in. high and should be located on the pool side of the fence. This forces a child to reach up and over the fence to manipulate the latch. Gates must never be propped open (Figure 3.3). If this latching arrangement poses a problem for people in wheelchairs, an alternative safe latching mechanism may need to be used.

Whenever possible, the house should not serve as one side of the barrier that protects children from the pool. If the house is a part of the barrier, additional precautions are required. All exit doors and windows leading to the pool should be kept locked whenever small children are in the house. Additionally, windows and doors should be equipped with an audible warning device that will sound whenever an exit from the house to the pool is opened. To use these exits without tripping the alarm, adults can temporarily cancel the alarm for a single opening of a door or a window by using a touchpad or key located out of the reach of children. Pool alarms that emit a loud signal when the pool water is disturbed are becoming popular. Alarms are available in wave motion, electronic detector, and photoelectric sensor varieties. For more information concerning these alarms, contact a local pool supply company.

Swimming Pool Alarms

Alarms that detect swimmers in the water are available for residential pools. These include wristband alarms that children wear in the water such as the Safety Turtle wristband (Chapter 1), surface wave detection alarms, and subsurface wave detection alarms. *An Evaluation of Swimming Pool Alarms* (Whitfield, 2000) found that subsurface pool alarms generally performed better and more reliably than surface wave detection alarms. The CSPC (Whitfield, 2000) recommends that a remote alarm feature that will sound inside the house be used with the pool alarm. Subsurface pool alarms can be used with a cover on the pool, whereas surface alarms cannot. A wristband such as the Safety Turtle alarms when submerged in water. Again, installing as many layers of protection as possible strengthens safety around the water. Pool alarms, along with child wristbands, provide additional layers of protection in a residential pool. Pool covers also should be used.

Pool Covers

Two basic pool covers are available: safety covers and thermal blankets. Safety pool covers come highly recommended for every homeowner with a swimming pool. These covers are usually a nylon mesh material that allows rainwater to pass through but keeps most debris out. Safety covers are often "locked" in place and should support a minimum of 225 lb/sq ft. Some automatic pool covers have a key-operated electric motor switch with a

Figure 3.3. Hotel pool requiring key card access at pool gate. Residential pool owners should consider following the lead of the hotel industry by installing lockable pool gates, in addition to self-closing, self-latching devices. (Photo courtesy of Aquatic Safety Research Group)

power disconnect. A safety cover is the only way to prevent unwanted people and pets from entering the pool water, particularly when the homeowners are away.

Insulating covers or blankets are usually made of a solid material. More than 50% of a pool's heat is lost through evaporation, and a pool cover significantly slows this process and saves both utility and chemical costs. A barrier between the water and the air minimizes the loss of water, heat, and chemicals through evaporation. A thermal blanket is not a safety cover and will not keep people out of the pool.

All pool covers and blankets must be completely removed before anyone enters the pool. Partial removal of pool covers can lead to entrapment and drowning (Figure 3.4) with just a gust of wind. Pool safety covers are extremely valuable when the pool is not in use or the homeowners are away. Sturdy pool covers not only prevent children from entering the water, but also protect against vandalism and even help to keep out debris.

CPR

Although close supervision and effective pool barriers will prevent most child drownings, pool owners must be prepared for emergencies. Anyone owning a pool should have certification in cardiopulmonary resuscitation (CPR). Recovery rates are significantly higher for drowning victims when CPR is applied immediately, as compared with resuscitation efforts that are deferred to the rescue squad. The American Red Cross and the American Heart Association can provide excellent CPR training at minimal cost of time and money. The following lists additional rescue techniques and equipment that will help pool owners to make effective rescues at home.

Telephone

Cell phones are common these days, but when at the pool, a cell phone must be charged, turned on, and readily accessible. Having a specially installed or portable phone at poolside is not a bad idea. 911 (or the local rescue squad number if different) should be clearly marked on the phone, and a highly visible "Phone" sign should be posted so that neighbors and friends can find it easily in an emergency. Emergency procedures should also be prominently displayed by the phone (Figure 3.5). These suggestions may appear to be overly cautious to some people, but when an emergency occurs at the pool and panic sets in, a clearly marked phone with emergency

Figure 3.4. Automatic pool cover and manually attached security covers. (D, Photo courtesy of Vover Pools, Salt Lake City, Utah)

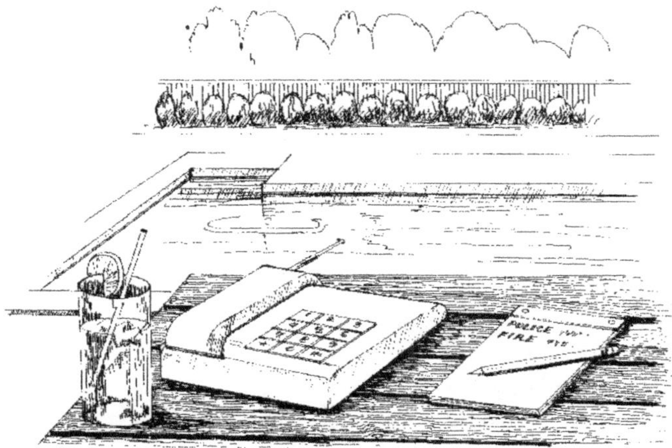

Figure 3.5. Poolside phone for emergencies with important numbers posted.

instructions conspicuously placed at poolside is important. Seconds count in a drowning situation.

Rescue Equipment

To prevent the need for a water rescue, a properly fitting U.S. Coast Guard-approved life jacket is the best insurance policy, particularly for younger nonswimmers. When a rescue must be made, even one involving a small child, entering the water is not recommended because a double drowning may result. Rescue equipment is available, including a long pole (10 to 12 ft long) or shepherd's crook, a large ring buoy with throwing line attached, and a number of extremely buoyant flotation devices. Many rescue devices can be made inexpensively by reusing household items. For instance, an empty plastic milk jug with clothesline rope attached to the handle makes for an excellent "throw-rope." And of course, every pool should have a first aid kit. A written emergency action plan that can be practiced is the best preparation for appropriate efforts to be completed promptly.

Diving and Other Headfirst Entries

Currently, the preferred minimum depth for competitive diving is 11 ft, and the preferred depth is 12.5 ft of water directly below the tip of the board (plummet) and extended in front of the board for 16.5 ft. It will be important to consult the finalized Model Aquatic Health Code when it is released for updated specific diving depth and slope requirements. Headfirst entry from a springboard requires a safe diving envelope that allows a diver to safely maneuver underwater. Considering these dimensions, safe springboard diving in a residential pool would be difficult. Diving from springboards requires supervision regardless of the pool. For the sake of this discussion, diving takes place from a springboard, whereas headfirst entries occur from platforms other than springboards. Chapter 26 discusses diving in depth. The diving that occurs in residential pools is the headfirst entry variety rather than true springboard diving, even though a springboard may be used.

Headfirst entries into swimming pools account for a relatively small percentage of aquatic facility injuries compared to drowning. While most spinal cord injuries result from diving into shallow water, many result from diving into open water. However, due to the significant risk of spinal cord injury present for those who dive headfirst into shallow water and the significant ramifications, it is imperative to try to prevent these injuries at all costs. The greatest risk of neck injuries to adults in residential pools is caused by entering the shallow end of the pool headfirst and hitting the pool bottom or diving into the upslope of the pool bottom (World Health Organization, 2006).

More than 1/3 of spinal cord injuries from diving accidents occur at home swimming pools (University of Alabama at Birmingham, 2011). In 94% of spinal cord injuries, no lifeguard is on duty, and almost half occur during a party (DeVivo & Skear, 1997). Similar to drowning risk factors, males are often victims of spinal injury. This group is at risk more than any other because of their increased height and muscle mass, they have the ability to strike the bottom with tremendous force. Males also tend to engage in more risk-taking behaviors. Additionally, alcohol consumption is a significant contributing factor for spinal injuries resulting from diving into shallow water.

Although many water safety experts teach people how and where to dive safely, entering home pools headfirst from the side, a diving board, or a slide can be extremely dangerous. Adults should always enter the water feetfirst on their first entry into the pool, whether from the side of the deck or the diving board. If entering the water headfirst, adults should use a long, shallow dive and steer up to prevent hitting the bottom. Diving boards in residential pools are best for young children, not adults. However, in most backyard pools, the best advice is to avoid headfirst entries and mandate feetfirst entries only. Warning against head-first entries where prohibited through signage is an important layer of protection, even in residential swimming pools (Figure 3.6.)

Figure 3.6. Effective "No Diving" signage comprehension tested and designed by Clarion Safety Systems©.

Standing front dives should be performed in no less than 9 feet of water (YMCA, 2003, p. 300).

As of this writing, both the National Collegiate Athletic Association (NCAA, 2013) and USA Diving (2013) competitive diving rule books require a minimum of 11'1" to 11'2" for 1 meter diving boards and 12'1" to 12'2" for 3-meter diving boards. NCAA and USA Diving have never experienced a catastrophic diving injury in a supervised facility. Since 1972, the National Federation of State High School Associations (NFSHSA) has allowed high school competitive springboard diving in a minimum of 10 ft of water without ever having a catastrophic neck injury. NFSHSA recommends a depth of 12 ft for newer pools, but continues to sanction events in older 10-ft pools. The Model Aquatic Health Code also is an important reference in this regard. APSP standards do not appear to be adequately stringent to ensure diving safety in residential pools. A lot of deep water is required to make a swimming pool safe for headfirst entries, and most residential pools cannot comply to the depth and distance requirements.

Prohibiting "dumb dives" in residential pools is particularly important. These dives include diving through inner tubes, catching balls while entering headfirst, doing acrobatics, and performing distance dives. When these types of entries are allowed, diving into unsafe depths may result. For instance, a diver out of control could hit the sides or the upslope of the pool where the water is shallow. Another dangerous dive is the "sailor dive," where the diver enters the water headfirst but the hands are kept at the sides.

It must be emphasized that more injuries are caused by swimmers entering shallow water headfirst rather than injuring themselves from diving boards. As did many hotels and motels of the past, some homeowners have attempted to place "big pool" equipment in a small pool. Often, space and water depth is not sufficient to safely accommodate diving boards or slides in a private pool. Today, many diving boards at hotel and motel pools, residential pools, and other small swimming pools have been and continue to be removed for safety. If homeowners are planning to have a diving board, they should consider building a diving-type pool that meets the minimum standards for safe *competitive* diving and *supervision should be constant and vigilant*. Although these accessories are fun to use, they can be dangerous, particularly at parties and especially when alcohol is present. Some pools may have sufficient water depth directly under the tip of the diving board, but unfortunately, showoffs can enter the water near the sides or the upslope where the water is shallow.

Diving boards and slides may not be a good idea for many residential pools. If they exist in a residential pool and sufficient depth and distance are not available, these accessories should be removed. If, however, the owner decides to keep this equipment in the case of marginal depths and distances, ONLY children who are under age 8 years and who are competent and confident swimmers should be allowed to use diving boards or slides, and supervision is a must. Most victims of headfirst entries are males aged 13 years and older without formal training. If individuals older than 8 years cannot be kept from using the equipment in this case, it should be removed. Younger children are usually not large or strong enough to hit the bottom in 9 to 10 ft of water. **Headfirst entries and sliding should always be supervised.**

If headfirst entries are banned at a pool, effective signs prohibiting diving should be posted conspicuously around the swimming facility (Figure 3.6). **Headfirst entries should NEVER be attempted in an ABOVEGROUND POOL.**

Pools and parties are almost synonymous. More than half of all drownings occur at pool parties. Of the few serious neck injuries that occur in pools, many occur during these events. Typically, someone has too much to drink, behavior becomes boisterous, the diver miscalculates a dive while showing off, and a broken neck results. Dangerous headfirst entries come from almost any platform: the pool deck, the diving board, the pool fence, and even the roof of the house. As the height of the dive increases or as the water depth decreases, the chance of serious injury becomes greater.

When planning a pool party, homeowners should separate the alcohol from pool activities. One alternative might be to have swimming first and then to serve drinks after the pool has been cleared and closed.

Hiring a trained lifeguard, whether or not alcohol is served, is always a good practice. Rules should be spelled out in writing beforehand, and the lifeguard should enforce them. Sending a copy of these rules with the invitation is also a good idea. If a residential pool is used at night, adequate lighting is a must. Good illumination is needed so that swimmers can easily read safety signs, see pool walls and bottom clearly, and walk on the pool deck safely. Lighting experts should be consulted before installing backyard lights for the pool. Most important, pool parties need Note & Float™ policies (Figure 3.7) whereby nonswimmers are identified with a wristband and then floated in a U.S. Coast Guard-approved life jacket.

Aboveground, On-Ground, and Inground Pools

When selecting a pool, the homeowner has three basic choices: Should the pool be constructed above, on, or in the ground? According to ANSI/APSP/ICC 4a–2013 American National Standard for Aboveground/Onground Residential Swimming Pools:

1.1.1 Aboveground/onground residential (Type-O) non-diving swimming pools are defined as pools with a shallow area water depth of 36 inches (91 cm) minimum at the wall and a water depth of 48 inches maximum (122 cm) at the wall. This includes portable pools with flexble/non-rigid or rigid side walls which achieve their structural integrity by means of uniform shape, support frame or a combination thereof, and can be disassembled for storage or relocation. 1.2 Aboveground/onground residential swimming pools are for swimming and wading only. No diving boards, slides, or other equipment are to be added to an aboveground/onground pool that in any way indicates that an aboveground/onground pool may be used or intended for diving or sliding purposes.

The aboveground pool tends to be smaller and much less expensive than the inground pool (Figure 3.8). The aboveground pool also has one constant depth; this pool does not have both shallow and deep water.

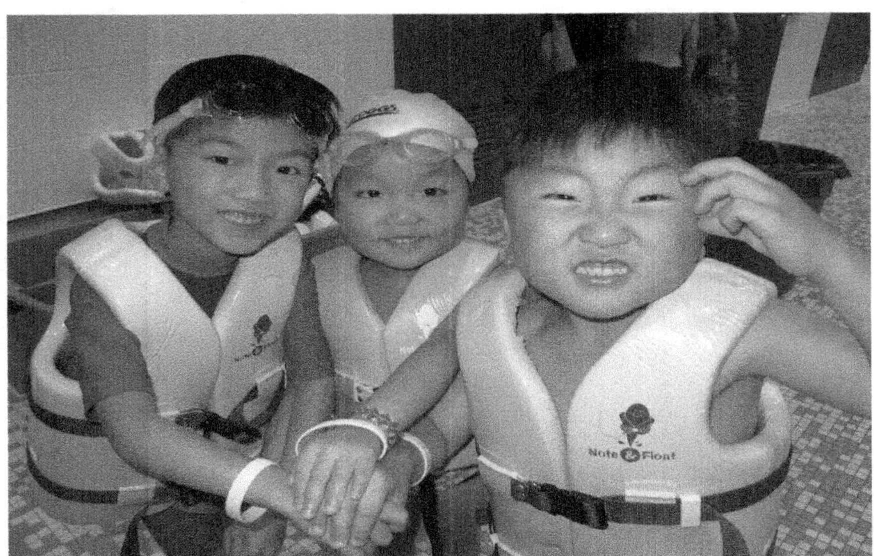

Figure 3.7. A Note & Float™ policy identifying nonswimmers with a wristband and floating them in a properly fitting U.S. Coast Guard-approved life jacket is especially vital for pool parties and other group functions.

Portable pools, including wading pools, inflatable pools, and "soft-sided, self-rising" pools, have gained popularity in recent years. A portable pool is defined as "any movable structure intended for swimming or other water recreation" (Shields et al., 2011, p. 46). Portable pools are relatively inexpensive and available from toy stores, grocery stores, and other locations. However, these pools pose striking safety risks. In the recent study "Pediatric Submersion Events in Portable Above-Ground Pools in the United States, 2001-2009" (Shields et al., 2011), 41% (32 of 78) of submersion cases involving children under the age of 12 occurred in a wading pool. ***Warning:* Portable pools must be effectively covered or drained when not in use. They need to be aggressively supervised when in use.**

Because aboveground and portable pools are small and shallow, activities in the pool must be carefully monitored to prevent accidents. Headfirst entries must **never** be allowed in an aboveground pools. Jumping and cannonballing can be dangerous, too. In fact, only walk-in, feetfirst entries should be permitted in aboveground pools. All other entries should be banned. Jumps, cannonballs, belly flops, and dives can lead to serious accidents. Manufacturers, distributors, and owners should work together toward safe feetfirst entries.

In addition, small children must be kept from swimming through the rungs of A-frame-type ladders. Tragically, some children have been caught between the rungs and have been unable to get to the surface. This pool also appears more temporary than permanent. Construction materials include aluminum, galvanized steel, and even wood.

But perhaps the fastest growing aboveground pool construction material is plastic. Pool plastics are much the same as automobile plastics: raw plastics combined with polymer resins to produce advance composites such as PVC or polypropylenes. These composites enhance strength, flexibility, anticorrosion, and UV resistance and are appealing to the eye. Some aboveground pools are characterized by large, freestanding, and interlocking panels, and others are a continuous roll that is supported by uprights and channels. A vinyl liner is then added to these structures to hold the water. A more recent type of aboveground pool is the large inflatable rubber variety.

The life span for aboveground pools may be less than 10 years, but they are becoming extremely popular, inexpensive to purchase, and quick to install.

The aboveground pool is the least expensive and most affordable pool in the United States. The average household income for pool purchasers is about half of that for inground pool purchasers. Although these figures will change over time, inground pools will likely remain roughly twice as expensive as aboveground pools.

An on-ground residential swimming pool is a removable pool package whose walls rest fully on the surrounding earth and has an excavated area below the ground level where diving and the use of waterslides are prohibited. The slope adjacent to the shallow area shall have a maximum slope of 3:1 and the slope adjacent to the side walls shall have a maximum slope of 1:1.

Aboveground pools tend to be temporary pools, whereas on-ground pools are usually more permanent. On-ground pools are constructed with rigid walls that come in sections. With this rigid wall design comes increased durability and flexibility in size and shape. Sturdy decking is often attached to the wall panels, providing increased strength and permanence. In addition, on-ground pools can be easily identified by fixed piping and electrical equipment for filtration and disinfection, whereas aboveground pools often lack these features.

In-ground pools are more permanent and aesthetically pleasing structures (Figure 3.9). APSP defines an

Figure 3.8. Well-planned above-ground pools. (Courtesy APSP)

Figure 3.9. A very upscale, in-ground residential pool with spa, fire pits, water fall, and a sophisticated, raised coping edge to set it apart from its surroundings. (Photo courtesy of *Pool & Spa News*)

inground swimming pool as any pool whose sides rest in partial or full contact with the earth. A large hole in the ground must be dug, naturally increasing construction costs over the aboveground pool. Although concrete residential pools offer the homeowner strength and durability, they are expensive to build.

More recently, vinyl liner inground pools have become popular (Figure 3.10). A vinyl liner inground pool looks just like a concrete pool but has a sand bottom and paneled sides supporting the vinyl that swimmers do not see. The bottom underneath the liner is usually shaped using sand, cement, or vermiculite to form a solid base. As a result, this type of pool is attractive and lasts longer than an aboveground pool, but costs significantly less than a concrete inground pool. Although the vinyl liner usually lasts a minimum of 10 years, it eventually wears out and needs to be replaced. Vinyl liners are not difficult or expensive to replace. The vinyl liner inground pool has probably made owning a pool a possibility for many homeowners who never thought they could afford one. In general, inground pools can last 30 to 40 years.

Swim Spas (Swim-in-Place Pools)

A still popular and exciting trend in residential pool options is swim spas or swim-in-place pools (see Figure 3.11). These small versatile pools can be quickly and inexpensively installed and provide both aquatic recreation and exercise to homeowners. The current (up to 6.5 mph) in swim spas can be provided by jets, propeller, or paddlewheels. Swim spas are low maintenance; for example, vacuuming is not necessary because the current takes care of the debris through the skimmer. Homeowners interested in this type of pool should try several before purchasing a unit. Like other pools, swim spas come with security covers, and the solid cover appears to be more popular with swim spa owners. Swim spas can also double as hot water spas so when not being used for exercise, they can be used for relaxation.

Swimming Pool Chemicals

Pool chemicals must be kept out of the reach of children. In addition, storing pool chemicals in the garage or an all-purpose shed with gardening supplies is not a good idea. Fertilizers and automotive supplies can cause fire or explosions when mixed with certain pool chemicals.

When transporting chemicals from store to home, pool owners should use a separate cardboard or plastic box to protect the car and passengers from chemical spills. The driver should avoid excessive speeds, turns, and stops. Chemicals should never be left in the car unattended. They should be quickly moved to the proper storage area.

Chemical containers must be stored separately and must not be stacked. Lids must be sealed tightly. Pool chemicals should also be kept off of the floor. If at all

Figure 3.10. Vinyl liner samples. (Photo courtesy of Tom Griffiths)

possible, pool chemicals should be stored in a separate, clean, cool, dry, and well-ventilated building. A small utility shed can be built or purchased for this purpose, but it should be used exclusively for pool supplies. **Before using chemicals, the directions should be read and followed.** Chemicals should never be mixed, and the same scoop should not be used for different chemicals. Chemicals should never be added to the pool when swimmers are present, and eye and face protection should always be used when working with chemicals. To mix pool chemicals with water, the chemicals should ALWAYS be added to the water, NEVER the water to the chemicals. The use of salt to generate chlorine on-site in swimming pools is becoming popular because it eliminates handling and transporting chlorine.

Electrical Safety

All electrical outlets near the pool should be protected by ground fault interrupters (GFI), which are designed to prevent electrical shock. However, electrical appliances should be kept away from the pool. Only battery-operated radios should be allowed near the pool. If outdoor stereo speakers are used, all other stereo components, including amplifiers, should be kept indoors or away from the pool unless they were specifically intended for outdoor use in all types of weather.

All lighting fixtures and electrical appliances must be regularly maintained. Before any electrical repairs are made, the power must be turned off. Better yet, pool owners should call a licensed electrician whenever they have a question about electricity, particularly in a wet environment. Above all, repairing underwater pool lights requires an expert, and all other electrical components must be kept away from the pool.

All electrical appliances should be installed according to the National Electrical Code and any federal, state, or local codes that also apply.

Figure 3.11. Photo courtesy of Endless Pools®.

Pool Maintenance Simplified

Several new developments in the swimming pool industry have helped homeowners maintain clear and clean pools with less stress and strain. Automatic cleaning systems and pool covers are just two new items that have simplified pool maintenance. In addition to security and energy savings, a pool cover, regardless of type, prevents airborne debris such as dust, dirt, and leaves from entering the pool. A pool cover not only keeps heat in the pool and prevents chemicals from evaporating, but also keeps organic debris from entering the water. A solar blanket-type pool cover will pay for itself in a short period of time.

Several automated pool cleaners are also available to homeowners. These devices were developed to save the pool owner time in vacuuming the pool bottom. Most of these devices are designed to operate at night or whenever the pool is free of swimmers. Before purchasing an automatic pool cleaner, the homeowner must be certain that the pool will not have trespassers in the evening. Theft of the machine can occur easily at night. Also, if the machine is tampered with while still in the water, electrocution could result, but this is extremely rare. Simple manual brushing on a daily basis not only keeps the pool cleaner but also offers mild exercise and therapy to the brusher. Hose bibs should be installed near the deck so that deck cleaning can be performed conveniently. However, the hose bib must not create a trip hazard.

Indoor Pools

Some residential pools are constructed inside the home. In this case, excellent ventilation in and around the pool enclosure is important to remove excess heat and humidity; otherwise, damage to the home may result. Both moisture and bad air in the form of chloramines must be effectively vented from the pool.

Creating a good ventilation system for an indoor swimming pool that is energy efficient is nearly impossible. To remove excess humidity and chloramine-laden air, 100% fresh air is often required. Simply stated, in order to have an indoor pool with good air quality, much air must be moved in and out of the pool and unfortunately be wasted. Before attempting to construct an indoor pool, pool owners should consult a ventilation expert specializing in indoor pools. Ultraviolet light may also assist in keeping chloramine smells to a minimum.

Insurance

Experienced and potential pool owners alike should check with their local insurance carrier to ensure they have adequate liability coverage in case an accident occurs in the pool. Most standard homeowner insurance policies automatically extend liability coverage to include swimming pools. This is good news because for the most part, pools are covered by the existing policy, and no additional insurance costs are charged to the homeowner. However, a homeowner policy should have a minimum liability coverage of $300,000. Older policies may have a liability limit of $100,000. If a catastrophic injury occurs, $100,000 may not cover all expenses, and therefore increased liability coverage is warranted. Homeowners may also wish to examine a liability umbrella policy, which covers homeowners for up to $1 million and extends liability coverage to include automobiles.

Summary

For a safe, healthy, and enjoyable home pool atmosphere, the 10 commandments of swimming pool safety should be followed:

- vigilant supervision,
- pool telephone,
- clearly stated pool rules,
- written emergency procedures,
- proper chemical storage and handling,

Review these important steps before beginning pool installation:

- Check property easement requirements.
- Check property setback requirements.
- Check decking requirements.
- Avoid installing a pool within 10 feet/3.05m of a building or structure.
- Avoid overhead power lines.
- Avoid a site where trees and leaves might fall into the pool.
- Avoid raoots and underground piping or cables.
- Avoid slopes within 7 feet/2.13m of the pool.
- Keep sprinklers away from pool walls.
- Avoid the sun's reflection into the residence.
- Situate the pool so that adults are able to watch children near the pool.
- Determine filter and pump location.
- Locate convenient electrical outlets for filter and pump location.
- Check prevailing winds.

(Courtesy of ©2012 The Association of Pool & Spa Professionals)

- effective pool barrier,
- CPR certification,
- lifesaving equipment/life jackets for nonswimmers,
- never swim alone, and
- electrical safety.

The Centers for Disease Control and Prevention has an excellent website that offers swimming safety tips, especially for children (http://www.cdc.gov/healthyswimming/). In addition, the American Red Cross videos *Home Pool Safety: It Only Takes a Minute* and *Water,* *The Deceptive Power* are available at local American Red Cross chapters to assist home pool owners in safeguarding their pools. The American Red Cross also offers a variety of swimming and safety courses that promote water safety. Just because children have had swimming lessons does not mean they can be left unattended at a pool.

For those interested in purchasing a pool, APSP offers pertinent publications and a list of dealers who are members of their organization; APSP can be reached at their website (www.apsp.org) or by phone at 703.838.0083.

Terms and Definitions

Bottom wall rail: The lower portion of the pool frame that guides the pool wall in place. It is usually curved to the arc of the pool wall diameter. It is usually shaped as a modified channel of metal or rigid plastic.

Upright support: The portion of the frame that is adjacent to the aboveground/onground wall in a vertical position that supports the top rail and braces the wall.

Top wall rail: The upper portion of the pool frame that guides the top of the pool wall in place. It is usually curved to the arc of the pool wall diameter. It is usually shaped as a modified channel of metal or rigid plastic.

Joiners, bearing plates, base clips: Metal or plastic connectors that join the bottom or top wall rail and the upright together.

Pool wall: The metallic or reinforced plastic portion of the pool that supports the vinyl liner and contains the hydraulic force of the water.

Liner: Plastic membrane, constructed of vinyl or other compounds, that acts as a one-piece container for the pool water.

Bead receiver: This is used with a beaded or hung liner. Made of metal or plastic with a receptor track to provide a receptor for the vinyl liner bead.

Top rail: The frame part located on top of, or adjacent to, the outer edges of the aboveground/onground pool wall.

Top cap sets: The metal or plastic connectors used to join and cover the exposed gaps between top rails and top joiners.

(Courtesy of ©2012 The Association of Pool & Spa Professionals)

References

American Academy of Pediatrics. Retrieved from www.aap.org

American National Standards Institute & National Spa and Pool Institute. (1991). *Standards for public swimming pools.* Alexandria, VA: The Institute.

American Swimming Pool and Spa Association. (2013). *U.S. Swimming Pool and Hot Tub Market 2013.* Retrieved from http://www.apsp.org.

ANSI/APSP. (2012). *ANSI/APSP/ICC-4 2012 Standard for Aboveground/Onground Swimming Pools.* Association of Pool & Spa Professionals, Alexandria: VA.

Burrow, C. (1992, September 13). All about swimming pools. *The New York Times.*

Centers for Disease Control and Prevention, National Center for Injury Prevention and Control (2012). Web-based Injury Statistics Query and Reporting System (WISQARS) [online]. [cited 2012 May 3]. Available from: URL: http://www.cdc.gov/injury/wisqars.

Centers for Disease Control and Prevention, National Center for Injury Prevention and Control (2012). *Vital signs: unintentional injury deaths among persons aged 0–19 years—United States, 2000-2009.* MMWR 2012; 61:270–6.

Centers for Disease Control and Prevention, National Center for Injury Prevention and Control (2012). *Web-Based Injury Statistics Query and Reporting System (WISQARS)*. Atlanta, GA: US Department of Health and Human Services, CDC. Retrieved from http://www.cdc.gov/injury/wisqars/index.html.

Gabriel, J. (Ed.). (1992). *Diving safety: A position paper.* Indianapolis, IN: USA Diving.

Gabrielson, A. M. (1987). *Swimming pools: A guide to their planning, design, and operation.* Champaign, IL: Human Kinetics.

Griffiths, T. (1995). *The swimming pool.* New York, NY: Simon and Schuster.

Guardex: Hydrotech Chemical Corp, Marietta, GA.

Klein, K. (2007). *Pools.* New York, NY: Rizzoli.

Laosee, OC, Gilchrist, J, Rudd, R. Drowning 2005-2009. MMWR 2012; 61(19):344-347.

National Spa and Pool Institute. (1992). *Pool and spa marketing study for 1991.* Alexandria,VA: Author.

www.fina.org

www.usadiving.org

FINA. (2013). *FINA facilities rules 2013-2017.* www.fina.org.

FINA. (2010). Appendix B - FINA dimensions for diving facilities. Retrieved from www.usadiving.org.

Kowalsky, L. (Ed.). (1991). *Pool/spa operators handbook.* San Antonio, TX: National Swimming Pool Foundation.

Mitchell, K. P. (1988). *The proper management of pool and spa water.* Decatur, GA: BioLab.

National Collegiate Athletic Association. (2013). *Swimming and diving 2012 and 2013 rules.* Indianapolis, IN: The National Collegiate Athletic Association. NCAA.org.

National Spa and Pool Institute. (1983). *The sensible way to enjoy your pool.* Alexandria, VA: Author.

Recreonics. (1991). *Buyers' guide and operations handbook: Catalog no. 41.* Indianapolis, IN: Author.

Shields, B. J., Pollack-Nelson, C., & Smith, G. A. (2011). Pediatric submersion events in portable above-ground pools in the United States, 2001–2009. Pediatrics: American Academy of Pediatrics.

Whitfield, T. W. (2000). *An evaluation of swimming pool alarms.* Retrieved from Consumer Product and Safety Commission website: http://www.cpsc.gov/library/alarm.pdf

Williams, K. G., & Young, R. A. (Eds.). (2011). *Aquatic facility operator manual* (6th ed.). Ashburn, VA: National Recreation and Park Association.

World Health Organization. (2006). *Guidelines for safe recreational water environments, volume 2: Swimming pools and similar environments.*

YMCA. (2003). *Aquatic management: A guide to effective leadership.* Champaign, IL: Human Kinetics.

Bibliography

American Red Cross. (1992). *Swimming and diving.* St Louis, MO: Mosby.

Go Off the Deep End for Pool Safety Tip Sheet. Developed by the University of Alabama at Birmingham, Dept. of P M & R and sponsored by the American Spinal Injury Association (ASIA), the Orthopaedic Research and Education Foundation (OREF) and the UAB Health System. Retrieved from www.spinalcord.org.

Griffiths, T. (1995). *The swimming pool.* New York, NY: Simon and Schuster.

Welch Community Swimming Pool, State College, PA.

4
Traditional Public Pools

Key Concepts

Swimmer loads
Special-use pools
Pool entrance
Pool decks
Apparatus
Underwater lights
Pool finishes
Depth markers
Barriers

Lighting
Food concessions
Programming
Security
Special rooms
ADA
Hotel, motel, and resort pools
Outdoor pools

The primary purpose of the public pool is to provide aquatic opportunities to the public at a minimal cost. For the purposes of this text, the definition of a public pool is any pool other than a residential pool that is intended to be used for swimming or bathing and is operated by an owner, lessee, operator, licensee, or concessionaire, regardless of whether a fee is charged for use.

For the sake of this discussion, public pools may also double as school, YMCA, park and recreational pools, or similar agency pools. The residential pool chapter was written mostly for the residential pool owner, whereas this chapter primarily addresses public pool employees, whether they are the pool manager, coach, instructor, or lifeguard. Standards for public pools are provided by local municipalities, health departments, and the Model Aquatic Health Code. *Local codes should be read, understood, and be on file at all public pools.*

Residential pools most often do not have lifeguards, whereas at public pools, lifeguards are often integral to the safety system. Another important distinction between private and public pools is that public pools are regulated by local ordinances and health codes, making the management of these facilities more complicated. Some professionals make a further distinction by claiming that apartment complex, homeowners' association, and some hotel and motel pools are *semipublic*. However, for the purposes of this discussion, pools will be considered as either public or private.

Because public pools are designed to offer a variety of aquatic opportunities to many individuals, pool sizes and configurations vary. The most popular community pools today usually have creative pool designs that allow for different activities to occur simultaneously. More recently, however, the trend is to build shallow (5 ft or less) rather than deeper (10 ft or more) pools. Many pools today are constructed with a maximum depth of 3.5 ft and are becoming extremely popular. Zero-depth pools with a walk-in or beach-like entry are also becoming popular. Spray playgrounds with water features but no standing water are popular and add a significant margin of safety.

Pool designs should be dictated by programs and priority user groups. A pool cannot be successfully designed or programmed without the target audience in mind. For example, a swimming pool located in a senior citizens' community should have warm, shallow water; deep water is of little value to this group.

ADA

Public Law 101-336, or the Americans With Disabilities Act (ADA), which went into effect on January 26, 1992, extends the Civil Rights Act of 1964 to include citizens with disabilities. The ADA prohibits discrimination against individuals with disabilities in public places including pools. This law entitles all Americans equal opportunity and full enjoyment of public services, facilities, employment, goods, and opportunities. Only private clubs and religious organizations are exempt from this law. Public pools and spas are significantly affected by this law and the requirements for aquatic facilities have evolved over time. John Caden, from SR Smith, has written an excellent chapter for this book specifically on ADA requirements in aquatic settings. The law may require changes in pool policies and procedures, the elimination of architectural barriers, and the addition of services and equipment to aid people with disabilities. Pool modifications might include handrails, ramps, chairlifts, wider doorways,

A

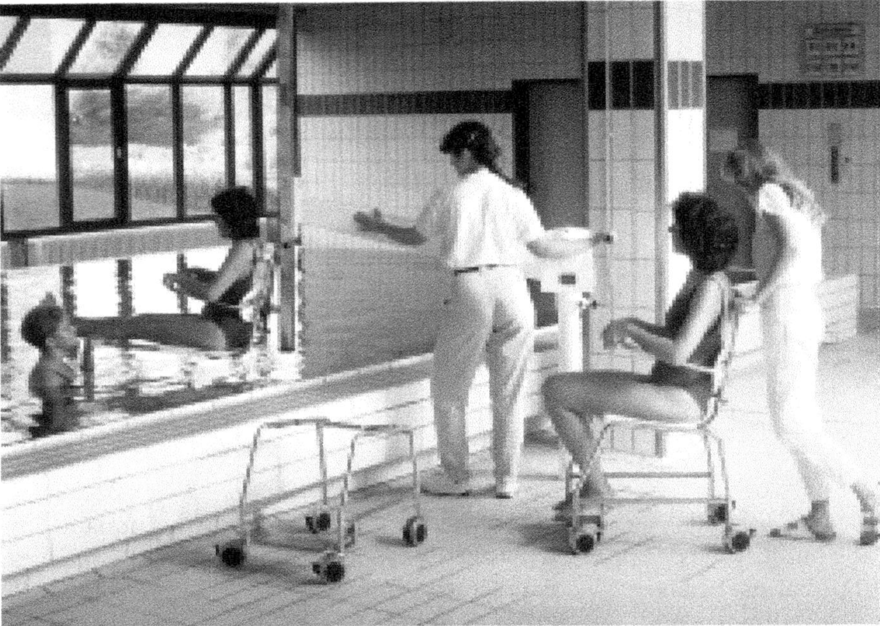

B

Figure 4.1. A: Access ramp may be needed to comply with the ADA (Photo courtesy of Water Technology, Inc.), B: Chairlifts may be used when pool space is at a premium (Photo courtesy of Arjo, Morton Grove, III, C: ADA compliant pool lift. (Photo courtesy of Pentair Aquatic Systems)

C

nonslip surfaces, improved lighting, and assistants who can aid people with disabilities (Figure 4.1). Every public pool operator should be familiar with ADA requirements. A copy of the ADA can be obtained by writing the U.S. Senate Subcommittee on Disability Policy, 113 Senate Hart Office Building, Washington, D.C. 20510. The Department of Justice website (www.ada.gov) provides complete information related to the ADA. The U.S. Access Board also is a helpful resource for ADA information and ways to best implement the guidelines at specific facilities. The U.S. Access Board can be reached via telephone at 800.872.2253 or 800.993.2822 or e-mail at ta@access-board.gov (www.access-board.gov).

Swimmer Loads

Public pools often have a maximum user load that should not be exceeded. State or local pool codes normally establish swimmer loads for public pools and may use any variety of formulas. The criteria used to determine swimmer loads may vary between indoor and outdoor pools, shallow and deep portions of pools, deck surface area, and water surface area. For example, one swimmer load requirement might read "no more than one swimmer per 20 sq ft of surface area." In this case, the entire surface area of the pool would be calculated and then divided by 20 sq ft to determine how many people are allowed to be in the pool at one time. The local regulatory agency that issues the operating permit for the pool is responsible for calculating the maximum swimmer load, but the aquatic facility manager or pool operator must post and enforce the bather load. Swimmer loads are really water quality concepts rather than water safety criteria. Swimmer loads normally are generated during the design stage and are developed so that they do not overburden the water treatment plant. This is why surface area, depth, circulation rate, and filtration area are the most important criteria for establishing swimmer loads. As swimmer loads increase, the hope is that lifeguard coverage will increase, but this is not stated in many swimmer load requirements. Public pool managers must also determine how much of their programming time they will devote to instruction, recreation, therapy, wellness, and competition and which of these activities are priority.

These priorities must be spelled out as specifically as possible.

Special-Use Pools

Whenever possible, separate pools should be constructed for separate programs so that programs do not conflict (Figure 4.2). Additionally, pools can maintain different water temperatures, which is beneficial to different user groups. Next, we will discuss special-use pools that have been used successfully.

The Wading Pool

Traditional wading pools have shallow depth. They typically do not exceed depths of more than 2 ft (24 in.). They are intended for use by children ages 1 to 5 under close supervision. Many refer to this pool as the "kiddie pool" or "familiarization pool." Larger, older children should be kept out of these facilities so that they do not become boisterous and injure younger, smaller children (Figure 4.3). Children who use the wading pool who are not toilet trained should be taken to the restroom

Figure 4.2. Diving, instructional, and racing pools, Stanford University. (Photo courtesy of Counsilman-Hunsaker)

Figure 4.3a. A well-designed water playground for young children. (Photo courtesy of Counsilman-Hunsaker)

Figure 4.3b. This water feature includes fitness skills as well as water play. (Photo courtesy of Counsilman-Hunsaker)

often, and the pool should be drained and cleaned often. Screwed down, tightly secured Virginia Graeme Baker Pool and Spa Safety Act-compliant drain covers are a must, particularly for shallow water pools, to prevent disembowelment and evisceration. Complying with the Act is a requirement to operate a swimming pool. The water depth at the perimeter of this pool should not exceed 18 in. Walls should not extend more than 6 in. above the water surface.

Because wading pools present safety problems for small children, spray pools and water playgrounds with little or no standing water are beginning to replace kiddy pools. With little or no standing water possible in spray pools, they are much safer than wading pools with less chance for drowning, entrapment, and transmission of recreational water illnesses. Interactive features such as splash pads and spray features are also beginning to replace traditional wading pools.

Wading pools with a walk-in entry (zero-depth) are becoming popular because families with children find them easier to use. This pool should be completely separate from the main pool. The greater the distance of the wading pool from the main pool, the less likely a small child will wander into the deeper pool; however, distance from the main pool also creates supervision problems. Whenever possible, a 4-ft barrier or fence with self-closing and self-latching gates should separate the wading pool from other pools.

At some public pools, parents are asked to supervise their children in this pool rather than lifeguards. This is a questionable practice because parents do not realize how quickly a child can drown, are not trained in detecting a drowning child, and often become distracted. If assigning lifeguards to wading pools is not possible, then lifeguards should regularly check on this pool as a part of their normal rotation. Safety lookouts or shallow water lifeguards are also a good idea for this type of pool. Older children should be kept out of this pool because they can injure smaller children. If smaller children are not being properly supervised by their parents or other responsible adults, pool staff should remove the child from the pool and consult with the parents. Younger shallow water lifeguards, as well as senior citizens, may offer quality supervision of these pools.

Suction entrapments are more likely in wading pools than in deep water pools if proper antientrapment layers of protection are not in place. Children are more likely to sit on drains in shallow water. The Virginia Graeme Baker Pool and Spa Safety Act (P&SS Act) was enacted by Congress in 2007 and became effective in 2008 to prevent the hazard of drain entrapments and eviscerations in pools and spas (www.poolsafely.gov/pool-spa-safety-act/). The P&SS Act is consistently updated and open for public comment. In general, "pools and spas are required to have ASME/ANSI A112.19.8-2007 compliant drain covers installed and a second antientrapment system installed, when there is a single main drain other than an unblockable drain" (poolsafely.gov). Pools and spas should be equipped with more than one drain, one or more unblockable drains, or no main drain. In addition, pools and spas with a single main drain other than an unblockable drain are required to have "secondary antientrapment systems," including a minimum of one or more of the following: "safety vacuum release system, suction-limiting vent system, gravity drainage system, automatic pump shutoff system, drain disablement, and/or any other system determined by the Commission to be equally effective as, or better than, these systems at preventing or eliminating the risk of injury or death associated with pool drainage systems" (Consumer Product Safety Commission, 2011, p. 62606).

We will discuss the P&SS Act in further detail in Chapter 27. The Pool Safely website (http://www.poolsafely.gov/pool-spa-safety-act/) provides more information.

As just mentioned, protective covers and antivortex plates on pool outlets and drains are extremely important in the kiddy pool to prevent small children from becoming entrapped. The wading pool should have a separate filtration and disinfection system, but this is not necessarily the case for older public pools. Concerning wading pool circulation, the recommended turnover rate for wading pools is 2 hours or less. Fecal accident policy information should be posted near the wading pool for parents to read.

The Instructional Pool

The instructional pool is typically shallow and filled with warm water and is used primarily for water play and swimming instruction. This pool allows learn-to-swim programs, aquacize, and similar activities to occur while the main pool is being used by the swim team or other large groups. Sizes and shapes of instructional pools vary, but the maximum water depth should be between 3 and a half and 5 ft. Because of the shallow depth of water

in this pool, headfirst entries must be prohibited (Figure 4.4).

The Competition or Main Pool

The competition or main pool has traditionally been the focal point of aquatic programming (Figure 4.5). It contains the most water and has more depth than instructional and wading pools. Most older competition pools have a minimum depth of 3.5 ft, but the recommended minimum depth for competitive pools is now closer to 5 ft to help prevent neck injuries caused by improper racing starts. Currently, organizations have varying minimum water depth requirements between 4.5 ft and 6.7 ft. NCAA and NJSHSA require a minimum of 4 ft, FINA requires a minimum of 4.5 ft, USA Swimming requires a minimum of 4 ft for competition, 6 ft for teaching, and 6.7 ft for championship meets, and the MAHC may require a minimum of 6.7 ft. (S. R. Smith, 2011).

This is where the bulk of aquatic activity occurs and usually contains the racing course for swim team practice and meets. Many lap swimmers gravitate toward this pool. The National Collegiate Athletic Association (NCAA) and USA Swimming organizations can provide dimensions and other recommendations if competitive swimming is to occur in this pool, and the Model Aquatic Health Code should be consulted as well. If starting platforms (blocks) are used in this pool, they should be located at the deep end of the pool. According to Fawcett (2005), "The most common cause of spinal injuries is diving into shallow water less than 5 ft deep." (p. 214). The Aquatic Safety Research Group (2013), along with the majority of current standards, recommends a minimum of 5 ft of water for diving from the side of the pool, although it must be understood that a catastrophic neck

Figure 4.4. Instructional pool used for teaching activities. (Photo courtesy of Mark Hokkanen)

Figure 4.5. Separate racing pool and springboard diving pool.

injury can occur whenever a person enters headfirst into water less than 9 ft deep. For the finalized and most up-to-date starting block water depths, the Model Aquatic Health Code should be consulted.

When not being used by authorized team members, starting blocks should be either covered or removed from the pool deck to prevent injuries. If they cannot be removed, patrons must be prevented from using them. Additionally, signage should be posted indicating that unauthorized use of the starting blocks is not permitted (Figure 4.6).

Figure 4.6. Removable racing start platform can reduce headfirst injuries. (Photo courtesy of Pentair Aquatic Systems)

The Diving Pool

The benefit of a separate diving pool is that deep water activities are removed from the main pool, thus eliminating conflicts between swimmers and divers and other deep water activities. With a separate diving well, a flat bottom profile can be constructed and sufficient water depth provided to prevent neck and back injuries. If competitive diving is permitted in this pool, the preferred depth is 12.5 ft for 1-m diving boards. NCAA, USA Diving, or Fédération Internationale de Natation (FINA) regulations should be followed for construction of a diving board.

The diving well is often used by springboard divers, but when the diving boards are not in use, activities such as scuba diving, synchronized swimming, water jogging, lifeguarding, and water safety courses may be conducted there. Diving wells also tend to keep the water temperature warmer, and this type of deep, warm pool is ideal for water joggers.

Another advantage of the diving pool is that the depth is constant without any slopes. The constant depth should be a minimum of 12.5 ft and can be as much as 17 ft if diving platforms and towers are a part of the facility. Although the diving pool enhances diving safety and improves programming throughout the entire aquatic facility, it is often the most underused pool in the complex because only accomplished swimmers use it and because participants are unable to stand up in it (Figure 4.7). Programming other activities in the pool when the springboard divers are not training is wise. We will discuss specific information about diving boards, stands, rules, and regulations in Chapter 26.

Although separate pools are ideal for both programming and safety, they are much more expensive to construct and maintain than one large pool. Separate pools require separate filtration systems, heaters, surge

Figure 4.7. Separate diving well with competitive springboards and towers at the University of Arizona. (Photo courtesy of Counsilman Hunsaker)

tanks, and disinfection systems. If only one pool can be built, several areas in the pool should be separated from the main pool to allow for activities in addition to lap swimming.

New technology has recently been brought to the United States from Europe that drastically reduces the costs of traditional indoor and outdoor competitive pools. Pre-engineered modular swimming pools combine stainless steel construction with PVC membranes to construct large on-ground competitive pools that do not require extensive excavation. If manufactured and installed for the Olympic Games or another large competitive aquatic event, the pool can be easily removed and installed somewhere else following the competitions. For instance, the water polo pool used in the 1996 Olympic Games was sold and then removed to another location upon completion of the Olympics (Figure 4.8).

This technology shows great promise in the United States in improving the number of world-class

Figure 4.8. A Myrtha® pool at the Greater Richmond Aquatic Partnership. Myrtha Pools® have been used for events including the Olympics for water polo in Atlanta, GA, 1996; the U.S. Olympic Trials in Long Beach, CA, 2004; and the U.S. Olympic Trials, Omaha, NE, 2008. (Photo courtesy of Myrtha Pools®)

swimming venues with a much more affordable, and in many instances portable, pool.

Multiuse Family Pools

As traditional public pools age, they are likely to be converted into multiuse family aquatic centers complete with whirlpools, waterfalls, fountains, slides, lazy rivers, and other activities for families with small children and for seniors (Figure 4.9). Pools designed primarily for competitive and instructional programs are rapidly becoming things of the past. Multiuse family aquatic centers are becoming so popular that their attendance rates far surpass traditional pools. The National Recreation and Park Association, Water Technologies, Counsilman-Hunsaker, and the World Waterpark Association can be contacted regarding this new concept in swimming pools.

Areas outside the pool but within the aquatic facility are important for the functioning of any aquatic facility. They include the entrance, deck area, bathhouses, and snack bar.

Pool Entrance

The entryway to a swimming pool serves many functions, only one of which pertains to admission. This is often "control central" for aquatic facilities and should include ample office and storage space.

The entry area is where the admission policy to the pool is enforced and also the ideal place to disseminate information to pool patrons. Rules and regulations should be posted in this area, along with pool staff pictures and certifications, provided personal and confidential information about employees is not available to the public.

This is also a good location for the first aid kit, telephone, and public address system. For increased accessibility and use, life jackets in a variety of sizes, including sufficient children's sizes should be displayed at the entry area. Automated external defibrillators (AEDs) that are used in case of sudden cardiac arrest may also be placed in this area. This is an ideal place to keep accident report files, health department forms, and other records and documentation. In the case of outdoor pools, this

Figure 4.9. Multiuse family aquatic center or leisure pool. Nonswimmers are buckled up in life jackets even in shallow water. (Photo courtesy of Counsilman-Hunsaker)

area should also provide ample shade and protection from inclement weather. An emergency telephone is desirable in this area. The pool entrance should not be a place where lifeguards are permitted to congregate. Not only does this practice create a poor public image, but it also results in a traffic control problem.

Pool Decking

The deck area must be constructed with a nonslip surface and should surround the entire perimeter of the swimming pool. Pool decks must be designed to remove pool splash-out water, deck cleaning water, and rainwater without leaving standing water. Adequate sloping of decks to drains or perimeter areas is important to protect against puddling and algae growth. Placement of deck drains is imperative for quick and efficient drainage. Continuous perimeter deck drains are favored over intermittent singular deck drains, but if these drains are placed too close to the edge of the pool, hosing of the decks may cause dirty water to pass over the drain and into the pool. Outdoor pools normally have larger decks than indoor pools. The wet areas of a pool deck are located within 10 ft of the edge of the water. Walking and lounging should be provided on deck areas located away from wet areas. "No Diving" warnings should be placed on all pool decks adjacent to water depths of less than 9 ft. These signs should be within 18 in. of the edge of the pool, and the letters must be at least 4 in. tall. Contrasting colors are also recommended for these signs. Hose bibs should be installed around the perimeter of the pool deck to ease cleaning of the entire pool deck area. Floor scrubbers that dispense disinfectant, scrub the deck, and then vacuum up residual soap and dirt are becoming popular for indoor pool decks.

As mentioned in Chapter 3, a variety of construction materials are available. If concrete decks are to be installed, they should conform to the standards recommended by the American Concrete Institute. Attractive, nonslip, flow-through decking materials are becoming a big business within the pool industry. Vinyl and rubber decking tiles, as well as runners, are available to place over existing decks to increase attractiveness and safety (Figure 4.10). However, these types of surfaces tend to trap moisture and should be pressure washed and disinfected so that they do not harbor mold, fungi, and bacteria.

Many facility operators believe that they have inadequate deck space, particularly at indoor pools where space is limited. A spacious deck not only allows for better administration of swimming meets and other events, but also provides an unobstructed view of the water, thus promoting water safety. Naturally, as the deck size increases, and thereby the "footprint" of the building, construction costs increase accordingly. Painted decks, epoxy-coated decks, or carpeted decks are popular, but often require corrective maintenance after several years of use (Figure 4.11).

Ladders and Steps

Pools should have at least two means for patrons to enter and exit at both the shallow end and the deep end of the pool. A good rule of thumb to follow is to have an entry–exit device every 75 ft of pool wall. Ladders must be constructed of corrosion-resistant material such as

Figure 4.10. Nonslip interlocking vinyl tiles. (Photo courtesy of Dri-Dek, Naples, FL)

Figure 4.11. Spacious pool decking that combines a variety of materials including concrete, stamped concrete, and brick. (Photo courtesy of Bomanite, Madera, CA)

stainless steel, although stainless steel requires cleaning and care. All ladders should be recessed completely to eliminate hazards to patrons swimming past them and also to prevent children from swimming between the rungs. Each ladder should have two handrails or handholds. The steps on the ladder must be nonslip. Recessed steps built into the wall must also have two handrails or handholds and nonslip steps, and the recessed treads should drain into the pool to prevent an accumulation of dirt. For specific dimensions of ladders and steps, local and state codes should be consulted. Whenever actual stairways are used in a pool, they should be either recessed from the swimming area or removable. Once again, the steps must be nonslip (Figure 4.13). When stairways are used in a pool, safety devices must be in place to prevent children from attempting to swim through the steps or behind the ladder. Plastic and metal steps should be checked regularly for cracks and other signs of wear. They should also be tightened on a regular basis.

Figure 4.12. Concentric circles carved into the concrete pool deck to make it more nonslip. (Town of Breckinridge Recreation Center, Colorado)

Figure 4.13. Ramps and steps with stainless steel handrails. (Photo courtesy of Pentair Aquatic Systems)

Coping

Pool copings refer to the construction joint or cap that connects the vertical pool wall to the horizontal pool deck. Pool copings must be watertight so that water does not pass to the ground beneath or behind pool walls. Copings must also be constructed with a permanent nonslip surface. Pool copings are often constructed of concrete, stone, or tile. Copings can also serve as handholds for swimmers entering and exiting the pool when a slightly raised lip is provided. Another good idea is to make the coping a different color from the swimming pool deck (Figure 4.14). When this is done, the coping also provides a warning that the edge of the pool is near.

Figure 4.14. Coping divides the deck from the pool. (Photo courtesy of Bomanite, Madera, CA)

Lighting

Lumens and *footcandles* are terms used to measure illumination. In general, lumens describes the magnitude of brightness coming off the light fixture or bulb, whereas footcandles refers to the light that reaches the surface below. Footcandles are easily measured by inexpensive and readily available light meters.

Generally, the Illuminating Engineering Society (IES, 2011) recommends 70–93 footcandles for indoor competition pools and 30 footcandles for public recreational pools.

Many pool professionals recommend 100 footcandles today for competitive swimming pools, and this is important if large championship meets and televised events will occur at the pool. Newly constructed pools are more likely to have 100 footcandles of light, whereas many existing pools have less than 50 footcandles. Indirect lighting is usually used for smaller indoor pools with low ceilings, whereas direct lighting should be used in large indoor complexes with high ceilings. No matter which lighting is used, the light must not glare off the surface of the water. Because most lightbulbs lose their initial brightness quickly, they should be changed often. Additionally, for indoor pools, a practical and inexpensive means of changing the lightbulbs and maintaining the fixtures is imperative. Too many indoor pools have lighting fixtures high in the ceilings over the pools that are almost impossible to reach. Many pool experts appreciate catwalks suspended from the ceiling that contain the light fixtures. Outdoor pools typically require less light than indoor pools. See Figure 4.15 for specific recommendations.

Recommended Lighting Performance Targets

Indoor Pool & Deck Lighting

Function	Recommended Maintained Illuminance Targets[2] (Foot-Candles)				Illuminance Uniformity Targets[3] (Max:Min)			
Competition Level[1]	Level I	Level II	Level III	Level IV	Level I	Level II	Level III	Level IV
Water Surface Luminance	35	25	15	15				
Water Surface Illuminance	70	46	28	28	1.7:1	2.5:1	3:1	4:1
Deck Surface Illuminance	46	19	9	9	2.5:1	4:1	4:1	4:1
Start/Finish & Turning Illuminance	93	70	46		3:1	1.7:1	1.7:1	

The above chart is based on IES standards. Those standards were interpreted and summarized by Keystone Lighting Solutions, LLC. Design professionals & pool operators should reference the source data from IES tables provided in Appendix L1. Additional performance targets and design considerations are included in the IES tables. Keystone Lighting Solutions is not liable for any errors or omissions associated with the above table and it's contents.

Notes

1) Competition Levels are further defined in Appendix L1

2) Illuminance targets are average horizontal (E_h) foot-candles for a reference area that include a depreciation factor from initial installation. Targets assume that at least half of the observers are 25-65 years old. Additional age-based targets can be found in Appendix L1. Foot-candle targets rounded to the nearest unit.

3) Uniformity targets are represented as a ratio of maximum to minimum illuminance (foot-candle) measurements in a reference area. Additional uniformity targets are referenced in the IES tables in Appendix L1.

Recommended Lighting Performance Targets

Outdoor Pool & Deck Lighting

Function	Recommended Maintained Illuminance Targets[2] (Foot-Candles)				Illuminance Uniformity Targets[3] (Max:Min)			
Competition Level[1]	Level I	Level II	Level III	Level IV	Level I	Level II	Level III	Level IV
Water Surface Luminance		15	10	5				
Water Surface Illuminance		28	28	9		2.5:1	3:1	4:1
Deck Surface Illuminance		19	9	9		4:1	4:1	4:1
Start/Finish & Turning Illuminance		46	46			2.5:1	3:1	

The above chart is based on IES standards. Those standards were interpreted and summarized by Keystone Lighting Solutions, LLC. Design professionals & pool operators should reference the source data from IES tables provided in Appendix L1. Additional performance targets and design considerations are included in the IES tables. Keystone Lighting Solutions is not liable for any errors or omissions associated with the above table and it's contents.

Notes

1) Competition Levels are further defined in Appendix L1

2) Illuminance targets are average horizontal (E_h) foot-candles for a reference area that include a depreciation factor from initial installation. Targets assume that at least half of the observers are 25-65 years old. Additional age-based targets can be found in Appendix L1. Foot-candle targets rounded to the nearest unit.

3) Uniformity targets are represented as a ratio of maximum to minimum illuminance (foot-candle) measurements in a reference area. Additional uniformity targets are referenced in the IES tables in Appendix L1.

Figure 4.15. Above-pool lighting recommendations.

Underwater Lights

Underwater lights are not as popular as they once were. Some aquatic facility managers think underwater lights create maintenance problems and are not needed in most swimming situations. Many swimming facilities that have underwater lights rarely, if ever, use them. All underwater lights must be installed according to the National Electrical Code. Ground fault interrupters (GFIs) are also an important requirement. Pool owners should consult an licensed electrician whenever lights need to be installed, repaired, or replaced. Whenever pool owners must handle underwater lights, they must turn off the circuit breaker first. Mishandling of underwater lights may lead to electrocution.

Underwater lights come in two basic types: dry niche and wet niche. The dry niche light unit is placed behind a watertight window in the pool or spa wall. This light can be removed, replaced, or repaired without entering the water. The dry niche light is often handled in the filter room or around the pool shell. A tunnel is created in the pool wall and under the pool deck that houses the light and fixture. A glass lens separates the dry niche light from the pool water. A bulb with too much wattage can damage the lens, which can drain most of the pool and cause flooding. In addition, the lens may break if the light is turned on when the water level in the pool falls below the lens.

A wet niche light is a watertight fixture and a water-cooled fixture placed in a submerged wet niche in the pool or spa wall and is accessible only from the pool or spa (Figure 4.16). This light must be removed from the pool and placed on the pool deck for repairs. With the wet niche light, both the light and the person repairing it get wet. As a result, many individuals prefer working with dry niche lights. Wet niche lights are cooled by the surrounding pool water and may explode if lighted out of the water.

Lighting fixtures should be 2 to 3 ft below the surface of the water with an additional level of lights at 8 and 10 ft depths for deeper pools.

Pool Finishes

Although many pool finishes are available, some are not appropriate for public pools. Most public pool finishes should be light or white in color for good visibility and to allow lifeguards to see objects on the bottom easily. Of all the pool finishes, perhaps plaster is the most popular, particularly with concrete pools. Plastered pools are often referred to as marbledust, "Marcite," and "Marblelite." This pool finish may have to be replastered every 8 to 10 years. Tile as a pool finish is durable and attractive but also extremely expensive. Once a pool basin is tiled, it rarely, if ever, needs to be repaired or replaced. Often, because of the great expense of tile, pools will combine plaster and tile applications. The tile in this case would be reserved for the water line on the pool wall or racing lines on the pool bottom. Rubber-based paints can also serve as a pool finish. Paints used in this fashion should be chlorinated rubber-based paints that are resistant to pool chemicals and unbalanced water. These paints are popular when used for renovation projects. Epoxy paints are expensive, but they form a hard, impervious surface that many public pools require. Painted pool finishes will have to be repainted frequently, about every 5 years. Perhaps the biggest problem pool owners experience with painting a swimming pool is not providing for sufficient curing time before they refill the pool. Regardless of the type of pool finish used, it must provide good visibility, ease

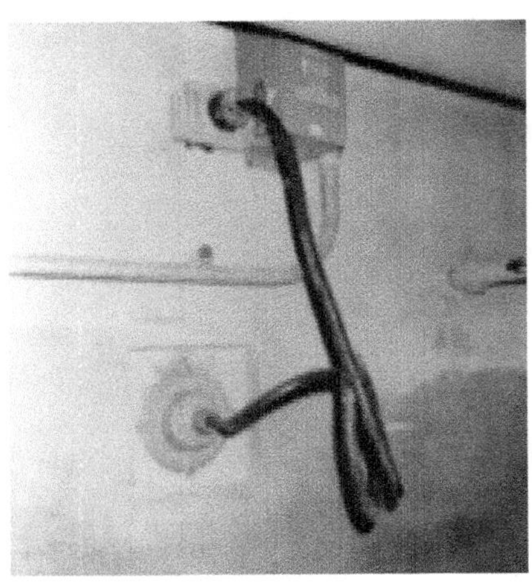

Figure 4.16. A, Dry niche underwater lighting fixture. B, Wet niche underwater lighting fixture. (Photo courtesy of Pentair Aquatic Systems)

of cleaning, and a nonslip surface. Although vinyl-lined pools are popular in private residences, they are usually not compatible with public pool use because the finish can be somewhat slippery, and vinyl may not be able to withstand heavy swimmer loads or the vandalism that is more likely to occur in a public pool.

Depth Markers

Depth markers are integral to every pool, but they are particularly important for public pools (see Figure 4.17). These markings may be painted or tiled, and they must plainly and conspicuously identify the water depth. These signs must appear both on the vertical pool wall just above the water line and horizontally on the pool deck or coping close to the edge of the water (no more than 18 in. from the water). Depth markings must be clearly visible to both the swimmer in the water and the patron on the pool deck. Depth markings on the pool deck must be slip resistant and appear at the minimum and maximum water depths and wherever the slope of the bottom changes. Depth markers should appear periodically on the pool deck when a 2 ft change in water depth occurs, but local codes and pool ordinances must be checked before installation of these markers. Contrasting "warning" colors such as red, black, and yellow should be used whenever possible.

Depth markers must be a minimum of 4 in. high (6- to 8-in. numbers are strongly recommended) with the numbers being a contrasting color from the background.

The depth markings should be permanently installed, and whenever possible, meters and feet should be indicated.

Safety Markings

A Penn State study (Popke, 2012) determined that catastrophic shallow water dives create permanent paralysis in less than a second. Because these dives are difficult to predict and supervise, warnings are necessary. Depth markings are an important public pool requirement in many states, but additional signs and markings should be used at public pools. Headfirst entries from the side of the pool must be prohibited in less than 9 ft of water. If headfirst entry is permitted in water depths between 6 and 9 ft, it should be for supervised, shallow water racing starts only. Diving warnings must be given to pool patrons at regular intervals wherever the water is shallow. "No Diving" signs should be placed on the deck near depth markings. Making these warnings larger than the depth markers may be wise. Some pools incorporate a no diving zone by painting a red or orange line around the edge of the deck and conspicuous "No Diving" text and symbols. (Figures 4.18 and 4.19).

Because headfirst accidents can result in catastrophy, additional precautions against headfirst entries into shallow water should be taken. The international "No Diving" symbol is now readily available in pool tiles that can easily be added to existing pool decks. We will further discuss signage in Chapter 25.

Figure 4.17. Tiled depth markings and no diving warnings around pool perimeter. (Photo courtesy of Counsilman-Hunsaker)

Figure 4.18. "No diving" markers. (Photo courtesy of Aquatic Safety Research Group)

Figure 4.19. Tile symbolic "no diving" warning and horizontal depth marking. (Photo courtesy of Aquatic Safety Research Group)

Warning lines should be painted or tiled on steps or the pool bottom whenever a significant change in depth occurs. These warning lines should be approximately 4 in. wide and colored black, dark blue, or red (Figure 4.20). A boundary line should be placed on pool bottoms to divide deep water from shallow water. A buoyed line (life line) should also be installed across the surface of the pool above the break point and about 2 ft closer to the shallow end of the pool. Warning lines on pool steps, edges, ledges, and other possible obstructions can caution swimmers of abrupt changes in depth or surface structures. The use of these warnings and equipment are highly recommended to keep nonswimmers out of deep water, but they are not foolproof. Parents must watch their children, and adults must exercise common sense.

Pool rules and regulations should be posted at the entrance of the pool, in the locker rooms, and at locations where these rules are particularly pertinent (Figure 4.22).

Pool rules and regulations should follow a three-strikes-and-you're-out guideline. The concept is that patrons can easily view (at a minimum) the four most important pool safety rules in three conspicuous locations. The rules should be posted at the entrance of the pool, in locker rooms, and at locations where these rules are particularly pertinent. States, regions, departments, health codes, specific aquatic venues, and other regulatory bodies often have specific rules that are required or advised. These rules and regulations should be posted, but not all on one sign or in one location. Pools can suffer from "sign pollution"—too many rules posted together so that the most important messages are lost among less meaningful rules.

Figure 4.20. Warning lines on pool bottom. (Photo courtesy of Tim Gervinski)

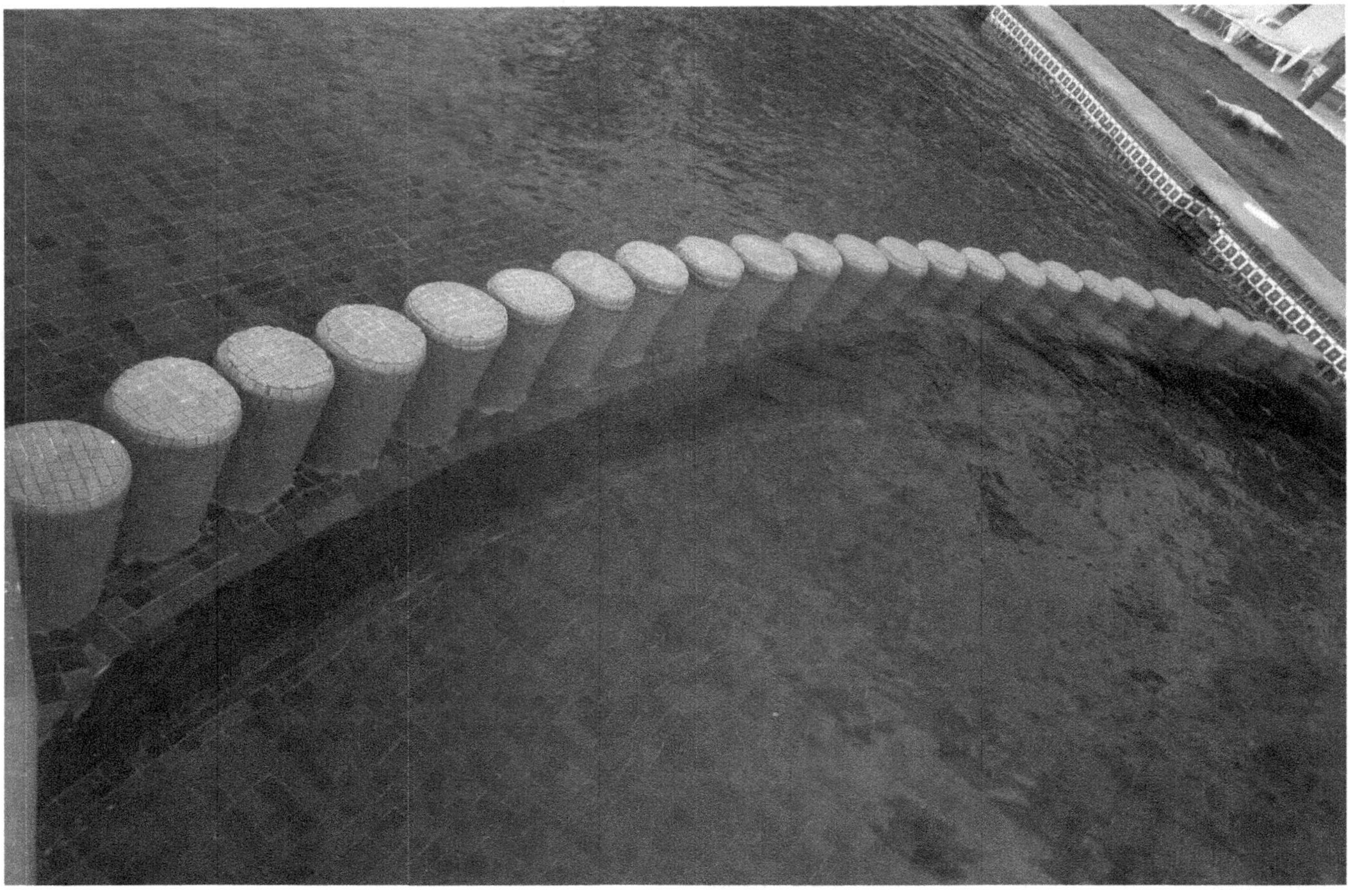

Figure 4.21. Very effective "lifeline" made of concrete pillars, which prevents small non-swimmers from slipping into deep water over their heads. (Photo courtesy of Aquatic Safety Research Group)

Figure 4.22. Too many posted pool rules.

The Big Four Rules must be emphasized: "Please Watch Your Children," "No Extended Breath-Holding," "No Diving in Shallow Water," and "Nonswimmers Need Life Jackets." These safety rules prevent potentially catastrophic injury and drowning and should be placed separately and more prominently than housekeeping rules. Think of the popular saying in music and performance when addressing signage: "If everything is big, nothing is big." When it comes to signage, important signage should be large and prominent. On the contrary, if every housekeeping and other rule, regulation, and request is posted as though it is just as important as the vital safety rules, few to none of the rules will be noticed or read. Just as there are primary and secondary responsibilities for lifeguards, there is primary and secondary signage.

General signage at any pool is extremely important. Rules and regulations not only help to prevent lawsuits, but more important, also help to prevent accidents. Particularly in geographic locations with a multicultural character, universal graphic signs with warnings shapes, colors, and symbols can be more effective.

As mentioned in the previous chapter, the use of contrasting colors similar to highway warning signs also helps to convey the appropriate message.

Lifeguarding Equipment

Many states require that elevated lifeguard chairs be maintained at public pools. Though elevated chairs give lifeguards an improved vantage point from which to supervise swimmers, lifeguards have been known to injure themselves climbing in and out of the chairs. The vertical ladders on the back of the traditional chairs also present challenges and hazards to lifeguards. Lifeguard chairs may either be permanently installed in the pool deck or be portable. Portable lifeguard chairs provide many advantages, but they require slightly more deck space. Perhaps one of the most promising advances in lifeguard stations is elevated stations with steps on the front as opposed to ladders on the back. The steps allow lifeguards to enter and exit more easily and safely than the ladders on traditional lifeguard chairs.

In addition, these lifeguard stations provide standing positions in addition to seats. All in all, the latest technologies in lifeguard stations provide additional safety for patrons and lifeguards.

Lifeguard chairs must be strategically placed to avoid blind spots and glare from the sun. Chairs should also be positioned closer to sections of the pool that have greater risks. Whenever possible, shade and water should be provided at each chair. First aid kits, gloves, and face shields to protect lifeguards from bloodborne pathogens should be located at every chair. If a water rescue must be initiated from the elevated chair, guards must be trained and reminded not to dive into the water from the chair. Many good lifeguards have been seriously injured by diving from lifeguard chairs. A good rule of thumb to determine the number of lifeguard chairs is one elevated chair per 2,000 sq ft of pool surface area. This should not be interpreted to mean that one lifeguard is required every 2,000 sq ft. Local swimming pool codes should be checked before elevated lifeguard stands are purchased or installed (Figure 4.23).

Figure 4.23. Portable elevated lifeguard chair. (Photo courtesy of Pentair Aquatic Systems)

Because lifeguards are human beings and cannot be perfect, boredom, fatigue, and distractions may lead to a lack of vigilance. A new industry has been developed in underwater surveillance. Underwater video cameras and computers can now alert lifeguards and managers when a body is on the bottom in less than 10 seconds.

In addition to elevated chairs, lifeguards and pool patrons must have rescue equipment conveniently and conspicuously available to them. Lifesaving equipment should include the following:

- A strong, light pole at least 12 ft long with a large, blunt hook located at one end, often called a shepherd's crook.
- A ring buoy or other throwing device with a line attached. Although many codes state that a line must be attached, larger more buoyant ring buoys may be more effective without a line attached.
- An emergency telephone with important numbers listed. This phone should be restricted to emergency use only. A 911 call box with audio alarm comes highly recommended.
- A backboard for trained individuals to use in case of a neck or back injury (Figure 4.24).
- U.S. Coast Guard-approved life jackets to "float" nonswimmers.

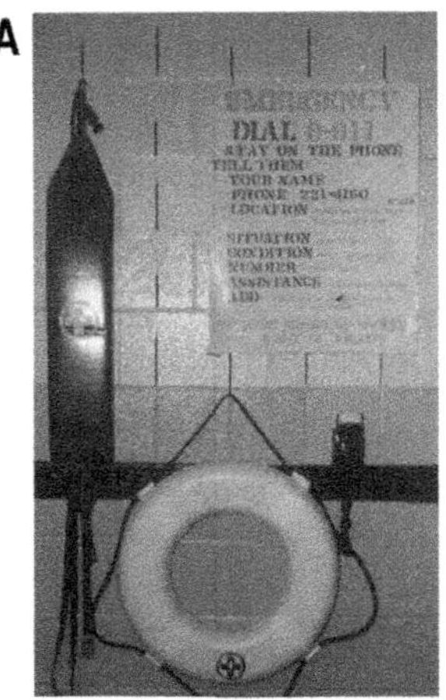

Figure 4.24. A, Rescue tube, ring buoy, and emergency procedure posted. B, Ring buoy. C, Backboard for care of spinal injuries. (A, Photo courtesy of Tim Gervinski)

Outdoor Pools: Special Considerations

Outdoor pools face problems that are often not concerns for indoor pools. First and foremost, lifeguards and patrons should be educated about the harmful effects of ultraviolet (UV) rays produced by the sun. Whenever possible, ample shade should be added to outdoor pools and sunblock should be available free to employees and on sale for patrons (see Figure 4.26). With all the information available on skin cancer today, not providing protection from the harmful rays of the sun would be irresponsible. Although large beach umbrellas are often the simplest remedy in this regard, they can often become airborne during windy conditions and have caused serious accidents. When umbrellas are used for shade, they must be fastened securely and taken down when a storm is approaching. It is also highly recommended that lifeguards wear polarized sunglasses to reduce glare in order to see below the surface, to prevent eye fatigue, and to protect their eyes from harmful UV rays. Fortunately, a variety of new shade products are available.

Indoor pools are protected from the UV rays of the sun. Unfortunately, outdoor pools are bombarded with these damaging rays, which also dissipate chlorine levels and promote algae growth. When pools are located in sunny, hot regions, keeping sufficient levels of chlorine in the pool is extremely difficult. For this reason, many outdoor pool operators now use stabilized chlorines that are not affected by UV rays. Stabilized chlorines are able to withstand sunlight and remain in the water longer, thus saving money and avoiding low chlorine levels.

The use of stabilized chlorines saves significant sums of money. We will discuss the disadvantages to stabilized chlorines in detail in Chapter 12. As a general rule of thumb, states *below* the Mason-Dixon Line are more likely to use stabilized chlorines than states *above* the Mason-Dixon Line.

Outdoor pools often have trouble with algae growth. This is caused not only by the sun but also by wind, rain, and other organic materials being blown into outdoor pools. Sunlight significantly affects algae growth. As the weather warms up and as the weather changes, aquatic facility managers must be prepared to deal with increased algae growth. Daily brushing of the pool bottom and walls goes a long way in preventing algae growth.

Lounge chairs are often provided at outdoor pools. Pool furniture is moved and abused greatly during the course of a season. Sturdiness and stacking ability are requirements for selecting pool furniture. Cleaning pool decks and lounging areas becomes extremely difficult if chairs cannot be stacked. Also, lounging areas should be kept away from the wet deck areas and as far away from the pool deck as possible so that they do not obstruct the lifeguards' view of the the pool or impede rescue efforts. Whenever possible, lounging areas should be kept separate from pool and deck areas (Figure 4.27).

Some outdoor pools lock their lounge chairs to fences to keep vandals from spreading them out over the lawn and from throwing them into the pool at night. Lounge chairs can be easily and permanently stained during the summer months. Wiping them down with warm, soapy water may keep them clean longer. Some companies also completely refurbish these chairs during the winter months.

Sidebar 4.1

Layers of Protection

Installing as many layers of protection as possible is important at traditional public pools, just like in residential pools (Chapter 3). Technology is always progressing and at faster rates throughout the years. Utilizing drowning prevention technology tools can aid lifeguards in saving lives as an additional layer of protection. Poseidon Technologies, Inc. sells the Poseidon Drowning Detection System, using underwater surveillance to detect if a swimmer is motionless in the pool and alert the lifeguards (Figure 4.25). This system has saved many lives in cases where lifeguards initially missed the victims. Emergency buttons help facilitate rescue efforts. When an emergency occurs, the closest person presses the button, alerting the facility at large when a lifeguard/lifeguard(s) initiate a rescue. A new automatic facility alarm system for emergencies has been developed by Safe-Turtle™. The Safety Turtle™ for Lifeguards is a water sensor attached the lifeguard's rescue tube or wrist and automatically signals when a rescue is underway, alarming the pool and front desk simultaneously. Keeping afloat on new technologies available can help facilities become safer with extra layers of protection.

A Summary of Outdoor Pool Concerns

- Airborne debris
- Algae grows more readily
- Damage to the skin caused by UV rays from the sun
- Lighting
- UV rays dissipate chlorine
- Vandals at night

Pool Cleanliness

Outdoor pools are typically more difficult to keep clean because undesirable materials may enter the pool. Leaves, grass clippings, and other foreign objects are of particular concern. Leaves not only clutter the pool bottom but also can easily clog skimmers and gutters, thus reducing proper filtration. Pollen, dirt, dust, rodents, and other small animals often find their way into outdoor pools. Once again, these are unsightly and reduce the flow of water to filters.

Experienced pool operators increase the surface skimming of their pools as more objects find their way into the pool. With increased skimming action, less debris will sink to the bottom. If a large amount of debris sinks to the bottom of the pool, pool operators will then take more water from the bottom outlet (main drain) to pull the undesirable material out of the pool.

A good pool cover, as well as windscreens on perimeter fences, can reduce the amount of undesirable matter that goes into the pool. Whenever possible, trees and shrubs and even lawns should be kept away from the edges of the pool to prevent leaves and clippings from entering the pool.

Barriers

The entire aquatic facility must be bordered with a strong, durable fence or wall, preferably 8 ft in height. Fencing requirements vary in different states and for different types of pools. The minimum fencing requirements must be met. All barriers must be designed to deter unauthorized entry and should not have external handholds or footholds. Chain-link fences, which is popular, durable, and relatively inexpensive, provide easy climbing access for trespassers (Figure

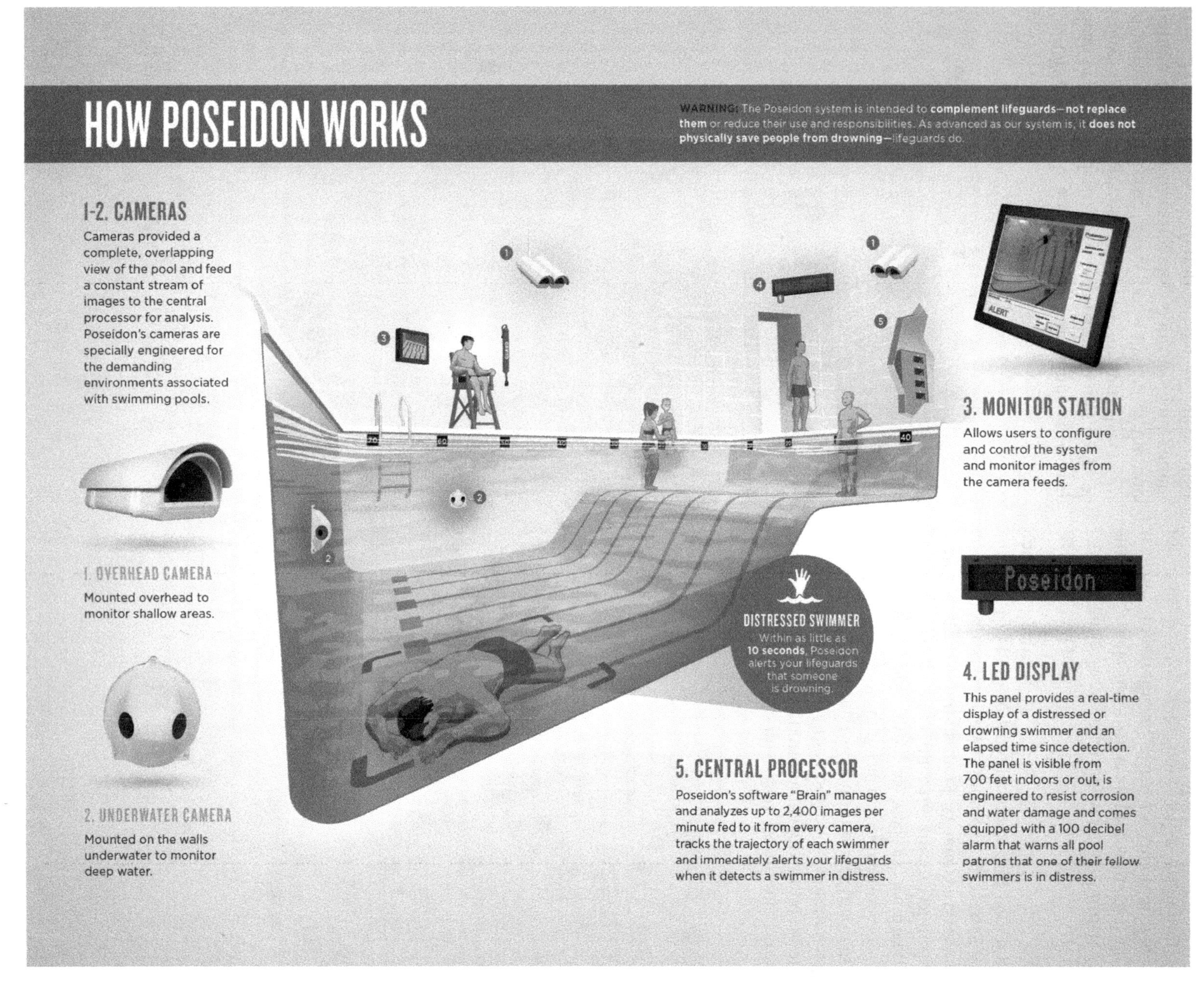

Figure 4.25. Drowning technology that works and saves lives that lifeguards are unable to see. (Photo courtesy of Poseidon Technologies, Inc.)

4.28). A better but more expensive alternative to chain-link fences are fences with vertical slats. Fences must be checked on a regular basis for holes and other openings. Signage located periodically on the fence should warn trespassers about unlawful entry. A large double-doored gate must be available for the entry of emergency vehicles and chemical deliveries.

Lighting

Outdoor pools should have adequate lighting for security reasons, even if nighttime swimming is not planned. A night watchman is also a good idea if trespassers and vandalism are a possibility. This night watchman can also provide other pool services, such as vacuuming and bathhouse cleanup. When lighting is planned for evening swimming and programs, care must be taken so that excessive glare is not produced on the surface of the water. Glare at night will inhibit the lifeguards' ability to watch and protect patrons.

Food Concessions

Anytime food is served at a swimming facility, whether it is sold on the premises or brought in by patrons, it must be consumed in special areas reserved for eating and drinking only (see Figure 4.29). Smoking should also be banned at most swimming facilities. USA Swimming bans smoking anywhere in an aquatic facility during a swimming competition. Keeping an aquatic facility clean can be a nightmare if eating and drinking are allowed anywhere in the facility. Snack bars should provide tables, recycling, and refuse cans clearly marked

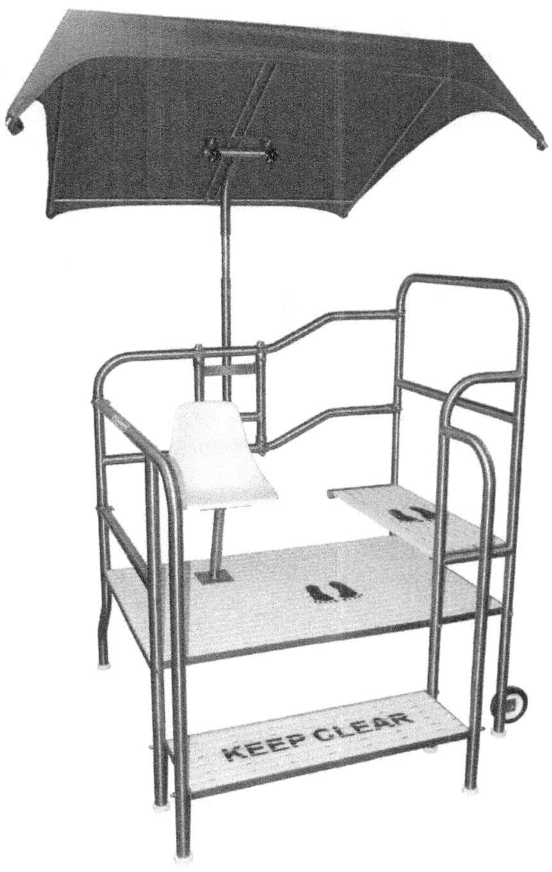

Figure 4.26. Elevated lifeguard stand protected by umbrella from both sun and rain. (Photo courtesy of Pentair Aquatic Systems)

Figure 4.27. Swimming pool furniture on pool deck. (Photo courtesy of Counsilman-Hunsaker)

Figure 4.28. An 8-ft chain-link fence securing a semipublic pool.

Figure 4.29. A concessions area for eating and drinking at an outdoor facility. (Photo courtesy of Water Technology, Inc.)

and kept away from pool decks. Fencing and signage also help to keep food and drink away from pool and deck areas. Above all, glass must be kept out of the facility. Particularly with outdoor pools, as food and drink consumption increases, so will bees and flies.

Food can be dispensed at pools in two basic ways: self-service vending machines or full-service snack bars. Many public pools enjoy the profits of a full-service snack bar, but several disadvantages exist, including personnel and hygiene concerns. A popular trend today is to contract out food concessions to an outside group or organization. Recycling programs and zero-waste biodegradable products are strongly urged for any aquatic facility with a concession stand on the premises.

Public pools must have a minimum of one drinking fountain, but preferably one per 2,000 sq ft of pool surface area, whether or not food and beverages are served. Because burns, bee stings, and cuts are a possibility at outdoor pools, the staff may be required to have additional training and additional first aid equipment may be needed.

Programming

Programming is an important aspect of the public pool that is not normally a part of a private pool. Once again, to program correctly, pool management needs clear priorities. Activities that must be programmed are

- vacuuming (early in the morning to allow dirt to settle);
- lessons (mid-mornings and late afternoons);
- team practice (early morning after vacuuming and early evenings);
- recreational swimming (all other times);
- lap swimming (before and after people go to work, at lunch time, and whenever possible during the day); and
- special groups, shows, and events.

Each of these activities should be prioritized with the individuals in charge. Also, if outside groups rent the facility for special practices or programs, a comprehensive group use policy should be in place and should be signed off on by all parties involved. Extra lifeguards and a Note & Float™ program are important for groups using the aquatic facility.

Security

Securing the pool from trespassers and vandals after the pool closes is a difficult but important task. Not only can someone be seriously injured after hours, but also a great potential for vandalism exists. The outdoor pool can be safeguarded at night in several ways. Motion-activated security lights often work best for swimming pools.

Security Light

Every outdoor pool should have a bright light that illuminates the surface of the pool and surrounding areas. With such a light, police officers and security guards can drive by and look at the surface of the water. Surface water that shows sign of activity may indicate that someone has been in the pool. Most pools turn totally quiescent within 10 to 15 minutes of the last swimmer exiting the pool.

Electronic Devices

Several electronic devices defend against unauthorized entry into the pool. Water sensors can detect almost any water disturbance and can activate an alarm at the local police station. Closed-circuit television cameras, electronic eyes, and other electronic burglar alarm-type devices can protect the pool but can be expensive. Security cameras are for the safety of the building/facility, but they are security cameras, not safety cameras. They do not prevent drowning.

A Night Watchman

Hiring a person to watch the pool in the evening appears to be a boring and expensive proposition. However, if the person assigned to security in the evening can also perform duties such as pool vacuuming and bathhouse cleaning, this situation may save the pool money. A night watchman is a good idea for many outdoor pools. This employee does not need to make arrests or physically deal with intruders, but rather should call police upon unlawful entry. Older, mature lifeguards and desk attendants often fill this capacity.

Locker Rooms

Locker rooms, showers, and toilet facilities are integral to every aquatic facility. A wonderful experience at a swimming facility can be easily ruined by a bad impression of the locker room facility.

In addition, with the advent of *recreational water illnesses*, swimming patrons want and need to know how to prevent themselves from getting sick in swimming facilities. The locker room is perhaps the best place to post this information. The facility fecal accident policy should be posted conspicuously and should

1. require soapy showers before swimming,
2. require children and adults to wash their hands after using the toilets,
3. require children's diapers to be checked often, and
4. ban all individuals who have had diarrhea within the past 2 weeks, among other practical protocols.

Separate dressing and sanitary facilities should be provided for each gender. All new aquatic facilities should consider adding family or unisex changing facilities for parents with younger children of the opposite sex and individuals that do not use gender-defined bathrooms. These rooms must be well lighted, drained, and ventilated. Mold, fungi, and algae are prone to grow if special precautions are not taken. Locker rooms and sanitary facilities must also be planned to allow for daily housekeeping and regular maintenance.

Partitions separating dressing rooms, showers, and toilets in aquatic facilities are often troublesome areas. Partitions must be constructed of durable materials, yet because of the high humidity content and general wetness in this area, they must not be prone to water damage and mold. In addition, partitions should be installed so that cleaning walls and floors with hoses, mops, and brooms is not only possible but also convenient.

All locker room and shower floors must have a nonslip surface, yet be smooth enough to ensure ease of cleaning. Carpet, runners, and the like have nonslip surfaces, but often create slip hazards and are difficult to clean, and they may harbor fungi, mold, and bacteria. Ample floor drains must be installed for proper drainage. Floors must be sloped toward drains not less than one fourth of an inch per foot, with an adequate number of floor drains for proper and complete drainage.

Tiled floors are excellent for locker rooms, but of course, they are expensive. The grout between individual tiles helps to make tile floors nonslip; therefore, the smaller the tile, the more nonslip the surface will be. Although larger tiles are more aesthetically appealing to many, they are often more slippery than floors composed of smaller tiles. Tiles that are 1 in. x 1 in. and 2 in. x 2 in. work best for a nonslip surface. The larger the tiles, the more slippery they become. If individual tiles are larger than the foot size of swimmers, the floor becomes more slippery. This is because larger tiles allow swimmers' feet to hydroplane on water before hitting the grout between tiles. Smaller tiles provide recessed grout that allows water to drain from individual tiles and also provides a roughened surface for swimmers.

Concerning lavatories and urinals for male swimmers, one lavatory (sink) and one toilet for the first 100 users and one additional for every 200 users is a good rule of thumb. These fixtures should be roughly doubled for female swimmers. Pool operators should consult local and state codes to be certain their facility is in compliance.

A minimum of two showerheads should be available for each gender, and for every additional 50 swimmers, a showerhead should be added. The water temperature at discharge should not exceed 90°F, and the flow rate of each showerhead should not exceed 2 gal/min. Thermostats and water heaters for showers should not be accessible to users. Fortunately, low-volume showerheads are now available that save significant amounts of water but maintain strong water pressure.

Soap dispensers should be available at each lavatory but must be made of an unbreakable material. Likewise, only unbreakable mirrors should be located above each lavatory. Sanitary napkin dispensers should be available in all female facilities. All plumbing fixtures must be in accordance with local plumbing codes. Fixtures should be easy to clean and resistant to corrosion.

Electrical outlets in locker room areas deserve special attention. All outlets must be installed with GFIs and located away from wet areas and lavatories. Wall-mounted hair and hand dryers are preferred over personal handheld dryers.

Spectator Areas

Whenever possible, spectator and visitor areas should be isolated from decks and swimming pool areas (see Figure 4.30). Shoes and street clothes are not compatible with wet deck areas and can cause problems in traffic control and deck sanitation. If spectators must be allowed within the pool perimeter and deck area, they should be separated from areas that bathers use. If possible, spectators should have separate toilet facilities.

At least one drinking fountain should be available for spectators and guests.

Operation and Management

As mentioned earlier in this chapter, all facets of aquatic administration are affected by the ADA.

Hiring and supervising personnel, programming, facility management, and other areas of pool management must follow ADA guidelines. All pool owners, operators, and staff must become familiar with this law to mainstream people with disabilities into aquatic facilities and programs.

Every public aquatic facility should be maintained under the direct supervision of a properly trained aquatic facility operator or manager. The pool operator must be trained in sanitation, safety, pool maintenance, record keeping, legal liability, and other important areas. Many states require the pool operator to be certified, and some municipalities train and certify pool operators who work in their region. The American Pool and Spa Association, the National Recreation and Park Association, the National Swimming Pool Foundation, and the Aquatic Safety Research Group offer excellent 2-day training and certification programs in pool operations.

In most cases, lifeguards should be required at a public swimming facility. They should wear the proper attire and be easy to recognize. Lifeguards should be certified in lifeguarding techniques, first aid, and CPR, but more important, the pool manager or operator should specifically train lifeguards for the facility at which they will be working. This key link between pool operator and lifeguard must not be overlooked. It is important to qualify lifeguards in addition to certifying

Figure 4.30. Bleachers above the pool deck providing good spectator viewing area for competitions. (Photo courtesy of Counsilman-Hunsaker)

them. Certified lifeguards are not necessarily qualified. A certification card is not enough alone. Lifeguards should become qualified through preseason and in-service trainings.

Above all, lifeguards must be supervised constantly. More information will be presented on lifeguards in Section V.

Job descriptions must be given to all employees, including lifeguards. Written and oral instruction are needed for all procedures, including water rescues and other emergencies. These instructions are also needed to maintain pool water, including chemical disinfection and adjustments, filtration, backwashing, vacuuming, and water testing, to name a few.

Pool rules, regulations, policies, and priorities must be written and posted in a conspicuous place. Pool patrons should also receive a written copy. Lifeguards and pool personnel must also understand and enforce all rules, as well as OSHA (Occupational Safety and Health Administration) and right-to-know laws.

Swimmer loads are determined by criteria established by the local health department or other regulatory agency.

The maximum allowable number of swimmers in a pool at one time can be determined by pool surface, depth, water volume in gallons, and other factors. Indoor and outdoor swimming facilities usually have different swimmer loads. Pool management must know and observe swimmer limits prescribed for their pools. Swimmer limits are sometimes written on the pool permit. Lifeguard-to-swimmer ratios, such as one lifeguard for every 25 swimmers, appear to be well intended but are extremely difficult to enforce. Depending on the type and skill level of pool patrons, this lifeguard-to-swimmer ratio may be increased or decreased, but perhaps emergency response time and square footage of water surface may be better indicators of the number of lifeguards required.

All required pool applications and permits should be submitted with the state or local authority. Pool permits must be renewed annually and should be posted for all to see at the aquatic facility.

Public pools must be maintained in accordance with local and state codes and must pass all inspections by the regulatory agency to remain open. Health departments and other regulatory agencies provide minimum standards, and most aquatic facilities may want to exceed these printed standards. Permits are often revoked or suspended when the pool constitutes a health or safety hazard to users. The facility operator should close the pool or park immediately upon discovering any unsafe condition. While the facility is closed, the hazard must be removed, repaired, or replaced before the pool is reopened to the public. For example, if a rung on a

ladder is loose, it must be tightened immediately, or a pool patron might slip and fall while exiting the pool. If an antivortex plate is missing, the spa or pool must be closed until it is replaced. When poor water clarity obscures the bottom of the pool at its deepest point, or if the bottom drain is not visible in any part of the pool, the entire pool must be closed and not reopened until the water is cleared. These and other safety violations can cause a facility to be closed until the deficiency is corrected.

Pool management would also be wise to meet regularly with fire, police, ambulance, and EMT officials to ensure that the emergency action plan at the aquatic facility is consistent with emergency care procedures by the professionals responding in the local municipality. Lifeguards and the emergency response team should be trained to work well together. All pool records should be kept for a minimum of 5 years.

First Aid Room

Every public pool should have a first aid room that is reserved for emergencies only and is fully stocked with emergency equipment and supplies. The larger the facility, the larger the first aid room should be. The first aid room should have a cot, several blankets, a sink, and if possible, a shower and a toilet. Lifeguards and other employees should not use this as a staff room.

Some large water parks even station a registered nurse in the first aid room during operating hours. Spine boards and other emergency equipment required by local codes should also be stored here. The first aid room may be an ideal place to post staff first aid and CPR certifications. When questions concerning the requirements of the first aid room arise, pool operators should contact the local health department or another regulatory agency. Blood-borne pathogen information and personal protective equipment should be located in the first aid room.

The location of this room is important. Not only should it be visible to all patrons, but it also must be readily accessible to emergency vehicles. It should have immediate access to outside streets. A phone dedicated for emergency use only should be located in the first aid room. Emergency numbers and procedures should be posted clearly and conspicuously near the phone (Figure 4.31).

Staff Room

Whenever possible, a separate staff room should be available for lifeguards and other employees to rest and relax, away from swimming pool patrons. At an outdoor facility, this is important because it allows lifeguards to be out of the sun. If a separate building or room is not

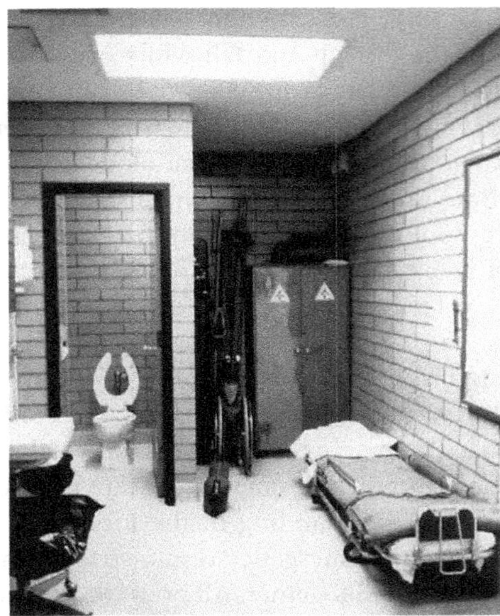

Figure 4.31. First aid room. (Photo courtesy Mark Hokkanen)

possible, perhaps a tent would be helpful. A refrigerator, sofa, and reading materials, particularly related to water safety and emergency care, would be beneficial. Employees only should be allowed in this area.

Hotel, Motel, and Resort Pools

Although hotel, motel, and resort pools are public pools, technically, they are semipublic. Although the public is admitted, the usual entrance restriction is that the swimmer be a guest of the hotel, motel, or resort. Swimming pools at hotels, motels, and resorts are a high selling point for the hotel/motel/resort and valued by guests. Guests are more attracted to hotel, motel, and resorts that have a pool or multiple pools. Aesthetic, well-maintained, and specialty pools are especially enticing for travelers.

Hotel, motel, and resort pools are mentioned separately in this chapter not only because of their popularity, but also because they have special problems associated with them. Apartment and condominium pools have similar concerns as hotel or motel pools except for the transient clientele.

A common problem with many of these facilities is a design problem. Many hotel, motel, and resort pools are smaller pools with many "big pool" amenities placed in them. Although most of these types of pools have removed their diving boards, many still have slides even when they do not have sufficient surface area or depth to allow for these activities. Another safety concern with these pools is the clientele that uses the pool. The following generalities often exist at many hotel, motel, and resort pools:

- transient clientele,
- patrons may not understand rules,
- alcohol consumption,
- very old,
- partying,
- very young,
- patrons unfamiliar with pool, and
- no lifeguard on duty.

It is wise to discuss these variables further to better understand the risks associated with hotel, motel, and resort pools. Many individuals who use these pools are either on vacation or attending professional meetings. Because they are away from home, they are unfamiliar with the pool dimensions and safety practices in the locality of the hotel. Alcohol is often consumed. In addition to traveling professionals, these pools attract retired individuals and young families with small children who are on vacation. As a result, a heterogeneous or mixed-ability group is found in a relatively small body of water. To make matters worse, lifeguards are generally not on duty (Figure 4.32). Because the pool is designed to be aesthetically pleasing to guests, child barriers are often missing; therefore children can easily wander into the pool. In addition, hotels, motels, and resorts may not have knowledgeable staff to run the pool.

For the reasons mentioned above, this special category of pool probably needs extra attention and may require the services of a professional pool company that can manage the pool properly. Another alternative would be to have staff members trained as licensed aquatic facility technicians through the American Swimming Pool and Spa Association or certified as pool operators by the National Swimming Pool Foundation, the National Recreation and Park Association, the YMCA, or a similar organization. In addition, guests must be warned that

Figure 4.32. Hotel/motel pool with "No Lifeguard on Duty" sign. (Photo courtesy of Aquatic Safety Research Group)

the pool is unguarded and not monitored by the staff. Signs such as "Parents: Please watch your children—It only takes seconds for a child to drown" and "Enjoy our pool, but please be careful and exercise common sense" should be created and added to the semipublic pool landscape. More than any other type of pool, hotel and resort pools without lifeguards on duty need a Note & Float™ policy. Accessible U.S. Coast Guard-approved life jackets in a variety of sizes should be a staple at every swimming pool.

Summary

Public aquatic facilities require diligent planning, management, and supervision. People working in and around the water should be trained in several areas including first aid, CPR, lifeguarding, water safety instruction; be licensed aquatic facility technicians; or be certified pool operators. For specific certification requirements, pool operators should contact local authorities responsible for swimming pools. Lifeguards alone cannot ensure the safety of the patrons attending these facilities; the entire management and support staff must be committed. A Note & Float™ policy, providing life jackets for nonswimmers to wear at all pools, guarded and unguarded, is essential for patron safety.

References

American Concrete Institute. Retrieved from http://www.concrete.org/general/home.asp

American National Standards Institute & National Spa and Pool Institute. (1991). *Standards for public swimming pools.* Alexandria, VA: The Institute.

Aquatics Safety Research Group. Retrieved from www.aquaticsafetygroup.com

Illuminating Engineering Society. (1989). *Current recommended practice for sports lighting* (IES RP-6). New York, NY: Author.

Pool and Spa News.

Popke, M. (2012). *Extra Vigilance Necessary with 3-Meter Diving Boards.* Athletic Business Newswire.

S. R. Smith. (2011). Starting block height and depth requirements. Retrieved from www.srsmith.com.

Bibliography

American Red Cross. (1992). *Swimming and diving.* St. Louis, MO: Mosby.

Clayton, R. D., & Thomas, D. G. (1989). *Professional aquatic management* (2nd ed.). Champaign, IL: Human Kinetics.

Consumer Product Safety Commission. (2011, October 11). Virginia Graeme Baker Pool and Spa Safety Act: Interpretation of unblockable drain. *Federal Register, 76*(196), 62605–62607.

DiLaura, D., Houser, K., Mistrick, R., & Steffy, G. (2011). *The lighting handbook: IES HB-10-11.* New York: NY: Illuminating Engineering Society (IES).

Fawcett, P. (2005). *Aquatic facility management.* Champaign, IL: Human Kinetics.

Gabriel, J. (1992). *Diving safety: A position paper.* Indianapolis, IN: USA Diving.

Gabrielson, A. M. (1987). *Swimming pools: A guide to their planning, design, and operation* (4th ed.). Champaign, IL: Human Kinetics.

Kowalsky, L. (Ed.). *Pool/spa operators handbook.* San Antonio, TX: National Swimming Pool Foundation.

National Spa and Pool Institute. (1992). *Pool and spa market study for 1991.* Alexandria, VA: Author.

National Spa and Pool Institute. (1983). *The sensible way to enjoy your pool.* Alexandria, VA: Author.

Pope, J. R., Jr. (1991). *Public swimming pool management.* Alexandria, VA: National Recreation and Park Association.

Williams, K. G., & Young, R. A. (Eds.). (2011). *Aquatic facility operator manual* (6th ed.). Ashburn, VA: National Recreation and Park Association.

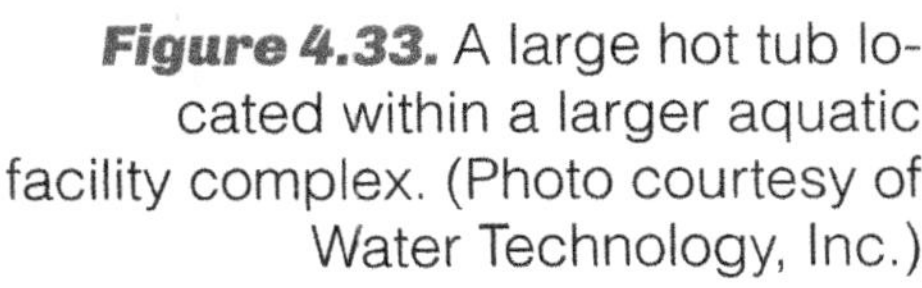

Figure 4.33. A large hot tub located within a larger aquatic facility complex. (Photo courtesy of Water Technology, Inc.)

Photo courtesy of Water Technology, Inc.

5
Aquatic Facility Planning and Funding

by Kevin Post

Key Concepts

Obsolete pools
Repair/restore/replace
Needs assessment
Recreation amenities
Therapy pools
Operations planning
Funding
Partnerships
Certificates of obligation and participations
Design and construction

The numerous small neighborhood pools of small towns and cities across the United States have faced significant challenges. The standard rectangular pool has over time become less intriguing in comparison to other attractions available for children and families. In the 1980s, the popularity of water parks boomed, drawing crowds to exciting attractions involving water, which might have further made the rectangular neighborhood pool seem less enticing. Many pools fell into disrepair, some shut down, and others began to add features, hoping the whole family would come back more often and stay longer.

Today, municipal swimming involves fewer but larger innovative aquatic centers and water parks that entice all the senses: the sights and sounds of families interacting in refreshing free-form pools and wave pools, splashing down waterslides, romping in zero-depth pools, lap swimming in designated lanes, and laughing in inner tubes floating down lazy rivers underneath waterfalls. The intriguing ambience includes sparkling water, coconut sunscreen, soft towels, and sunshine. Taste buds are tantalized with juicy drinks and healthy sandwiches for robust appetites resulting from plausible, entertaining exercise. These are memory-making places where families are eager to frequent, sometimes in lieu of vacations.

Residents are proud of these places and are willing to "pay to play" if the proper experience is provided. The public is continually updated regarding environmental stewardship and knows that increasing the community profile generates revenue and property values. The public sector aquatic center remains successful by sustaining a clean, friendly, environmentally responsible, and fun reputation (see Figure 5.1).

Physically and/or Functionally Obsolete Pools

The pools from the 1950s and 1960s are becoming physically obsolete, thus experiencing high maintenance costs due to outdated filtration and/or leaking pool shells. The physically obsolete pool not only compromises the environment and swimmers by wasting and improperly filtering water, but also depletes the budget.

Older pools can become functionally obsolete when they experience a lack of swimmers due to a shortage of newer recreation amenities. Functionally obsolete pools often sit empty, yet families drive an hour or more to a

Figure 5.1. Space Bowl Water Slide at Liberty Lagoon Water Park is just one of many exhilarating rides offered at larger facilities. (Photo courtesy of Counsilman-Hunsaker)

new water park to find recreational value; and they do not mind paying for it when they find it.

Repair/Restore/Replace

Repairing the pool is when the owner patches the leak, cleans up rust and mildew on finishes, and applies other "Band-Aid" fixes. Restoring the pool is when the owner saves the existing pool and replaces parts and equipment systems, adhering to code and safety upgrades. Replacing the pool is when the owner removes the entire pool and builds a brand new pool.

Although repairing and renovation seem less expensive, in the long term, the same components may not stir the community into more pool usage, and repairs can go on indefinitely. Moreover, renovation may need to be changed again in 10 years because remodel work provides an improved systems environment, but will not fundamentally change the physical aspects to accommodate contemporary programs that swimmers seek today.

When the choice is to repair and/or renovate an obsolete pool, a common mistake is timing decisions, either rushing into building a new pool without the due diligence of gaining community consensus or waiting too long due to indecisive feelings regarding the targeted (or mistargeted) features. The longer the waiting period, the more it will cost due to delays and changing expectations. Lack of timely decisions may result in getting off track with city council changes and other key staff changes, delaying site selection(s) and resulting in more design dilemmas. The best idea is to have a committee representing the community make careful decisions using research backed by clear and accurate information.

Step 1: Needs Assessment

When looking at the opportunity for replacing, expanding, or adding/changing features, an internal aquatic project team or steering committee typically acquires a feasibility study and works with the public. The feasibility study provides projected first dollar costs and yearly operational expenses for the first five years, giving the committee a clearer understanding of pro forma and design solutions.

Building a municipal aquatic center at a new or existing site requires a due diligence process. The key difference in the public sector versus the private sector is consensus building through community outreach. If the project is not properly completed, people may withdraw support because the program is not relevant to their desires and affordability. The community must be included in the showcase of potential new facilities, the proposed program mix, and the desired activity menus

as they develop. Private aquatic development is often controlled by a few people with financial performance being the primary driver, whereas the public sector aquatic development must not only be sustainable but also stand up to public scrutiny. Features and amenities are analyzed via community meetings and stakeholder and staff interviews.

The best place to start is to appoint an internal aquatic project team. The team, sometimes referred to as the steering committee, is relied on for decision-making protocol. The committee is usually made up of local political leadership, the park director or staff members, other recreational professionals, community residents, aquatic staff or swim coaches, school representatives, and other interested parties.

A professional consulting team may work with the steering committee to prepare a feasibility study. The time period from commencement of the study process to the decision to go to referendum (or council vote) can take 120 to 160 days. The teams work together to develop a clear mission statement using a common vocabulary that keeps everyone on track. The mission may include aquatic training, lessons, therapy, and/or recreational benefits as goals. The committee may have to try several times to precisely state the varied mission to its diverse audience.

Identifying relevant needs through community outreach includes focus groups, stakeholder interviews, and sometimes resident surveys. Surveys gauge potential customers' inclinations, gauge how much of the market the project could or should attract, and shows the community that the committee cares about what they think. Focus groups, conducted in real time, reveal residents' tastes, even prompting unanticipated paths, which can be a smorgasbord of invaluable knowledge. Community outreach certainly takes time, but community buy-in is crucial, although often the community already desires trends they see in peer communities.

Community Feedback

Community feedback uncovers valuable information within the community and finds opportunities. This internal inventory assesses how the community and staff view and ultimately use the recreational offerings in the area. Community input is important to understand, as civic spaces are extensions of the people who use them. Use of public programs and activities tends to come when residents feel they are being listened to and reacted to, and thus they are improving their community assets. Mining the information reveals every facet of value, identifies which customers and prospects represent the best opportunities, and creates an understanding of market potential.

For the recreation professional, leading and facilitating a feasibility study is worth the time and effort. Design decisions made today will likely last 50 years. Consequently, the best idea is to build realistic expectations by testing the appetite of the community. Municipal facilities must look at community consensus and public funding, making sure the facility will be sustainable with inclusive programming.

Adding Recreation Amenities

When an obsolete pool is replaced, the community may see a chance to segregate creative water play areas for various age groups (see Figure 5.2). For example, toddlers (aged approximately 0 to 3) enjoy shallow pools with gentle water features and play areas out of the way of the more active areas. Once children grow out of the toddler stage (aged 1 to 3), they enjoy romping in zero-depth free-form pools and make their adventurous way across water walks and participatory play features with "just-their-size" waterslides. Older children (older than 7) speed down large waterslides and enjoy towering water play structures. Teens (aged 13 to 18) appreciate gathering spots such as action islands with access to deep water pools and extreme features (i.e., swirl slides and surfing mechanisms). Lazy rivers and current channels accommodate just about everyone, and spas and lap lanes are geared more toward adults.

Staff may suggest that the aquatic center needs a cohesive theme to stand out. With the continued advances in water features in both safety and realism, fantasy retreats can provide water jungles, pirate coves, and rainforest temples, to name a few. Geographical features specific to a region can include culture, wildlife, or geological formations at the entrance or throughout the park. Color theming and music can lend a resort impression of the French Riviera, the Mediterranean, ancient Mexico, or the Caribbean. With slides, waterfalls, and water play products available in look-alike bamboo, thatch, wood, tile, and brick, and with features such as palm trees, castles, forts, ships, and animals, any theme can be achieved (Figure 5.3).

The Improved Competition Pool

Perhaps the community desires a natatorium that allows for year-round competitive swimming. Competitive swimmers can be a loyal group if opportunities for practice, training, and meets are offered. In many areas, competitive swimmers, water polo players, master swimmers, and even synchronized swimmers and divers are the voice identifying the need

Figure 5.2. A multifaceted family aquatic center...something for everyone! (Photo courtesy of Counsilman-Hunsaker)

Figure 5.3. Themed aquatic facility. (Photo courtesy of Counsilman-Hunsaker)

for more and/or improved pools. Championship venues have seen a rise in building "fast" pools that feature wide gutter construction, carefully calibrated water depth, gutter hung touchpads, and well-designed and properly tensioned floating lane lines. Climate-controlled venue natatoriums offer a year-round light-filled swimming experience with a 50-m x 25-yd pool or a 25-m x 25-yd pool (see Figure 5.4).

Other amenities include 1-m and 3-m springboards with wide safe steps, a timing system, full-color video scoreboard, high-quality sound system, and ample spectator seating. A swimmer's ability to see pool wall targets, floor markings, and other swimmers is critically related to good visibility, which depends on water clarity, state-of-the-art filtration and chemical treatment systems, and 100 footcandles of light, more if televised. All surfaces touched by the swimmer, such as walls and starting blocks, need to be slip resistant. A movable bulkhead offers versatility to accommodate other aquatic lessons, fitness, and activities outside the swim team.

Figure 5.4. A well-designed competition pool with ample deck space. (Photo courtesy of Counsilman-Hunsaker)

Considering a Therapy Pool

A therapy pool can provide warm water to assist people with strained muscles, arthritis, and other aquatic therapy needs and a place for aerobics and gentle water exercise. Due to the associated health benefits of the warm water wellness experience, therapy pools have grown in medical-based popularity. Aquatic therapists provide rehabilitation movements to clients in warm water pools that involve exercise and motion to increase the dynamics of blood pressure and blood and lymph circulation, as well as to decrease swelling in skin and other tissues. Users include athletes who are injured, patients after an operation, people with disabilities (permanent and temporary), people who suffer from arthritis, people with diabetes, women who are pregnant, aging baby boomers, people who are enthusiastic about meditation, and people who are obese.

Ergonomically well-designed aquatic therapy environments offer easy access ramps, perimeter railings, aerobic steppers, treadmills, underwater benches, flexible pool depths for multiple programmatic needs, high-quality water chemical treatment systems, and an appropriately designed heating, ventilating, and air-conditioning and dehumidification (HVAC/DH)

system. Pleasing environments—tranquil waterfalls, natural daylight, aromatherapy, and ambient music from a built-in sound system—cradle the mind and body in a relaxing, soothing, and peaceful way.

Concepts

Diversity and entertainment of the selected attractions are weighed as to how the additional features will fit into the overall user comfort of the established facility (see Figure 5.5). The design team must understand triangulation between elements to avoid jeopardizing segregated age group areas. For example, placing a teen action island inside the configuration of the lazy river near the large waterslides will not disrupt the senior water walking environment on the other side of the park or placing spray features inside the entrance for a plaza effect that immediately invite children to zip around the playful, interactive fountains will not disrupt the toddler area safely out of harm's way in a more private area.

Figure 5.5. Lazy river and children's play area. (Photo courtesy of Counsilman-Hunsaker)

Step 2: Operations Planning

Once a concept and capital budget are established, the ongoing (second dollar) costs must be determined and budgeted. Operations models include three basic scenarios: subsidy, break even, and positive cash flow. Subsidy uses tax dollars to pay operating expenses, and the break-even model is able to pay its own operating expenses. Positive cash flow is the facility that is able to pay its own operating expenses and build revenue. Although older facilities are typically subsidized due to higher costs of maintenance and fewer swimmers, a sustainable model is the norm for new facilities, with fiscal operations driven by programming revenue.

To operate an aquatic center, a thorough marketing plan that includes the mission is vital. Relevant programs with details stating exactly what the program does must be conveyed so that participants are satisfied and become loyal users of the facility.

Developing the unique recipe of success for each community is the key to a great project. How the public perceives the facility will also be how the facility is used. Facility expectations are judged from the moment the public enters the gate. Professional presentation in the friendly, fun, clean, and controlled atmosphere must constantly be examined and carried out by management in its policy.

Creating an economic engine to support the vision will provide a fiscally sustainable enterprise including water, features, and programs in concert with the community for many years to come. Although the taste buds of the investor may focus success around financial performance, the municipal developer has a more complex palette that blends the flavors of cost, recreation amenities, programs, and community needs.

Step 3: Funding Your New Aquatic Facility

Once the city confirms the concepts, the study matches need with political and financial realities by defining funding options. With an opinion of revenue potential and an estimate of operating expenses that subsequently determine cash flow and debt, funding opportunities are across the board, similar to differences in construction costs throughout the nation. Funding might be a school district, YMCA, or a hospital partnership. It might be the sale of bonds, operating leases, or other creative means such as private contributions.

As a practical matter, the likelihood of building and opening a new aquatic center without extensive and direct financial support is fairly remote. Many funding methods are available for building municipal pools. Financing generally occurs in one of the forms or methods outlined below.

Direct Funding

Direct appropriations. A city is permitted by law to directly appropriate money to the development, construction, and operation of an aquatic center. This includes money either spent directly on the project or contributed to another entity established for this purpose.

Private contributions. For different reasons, various private individuals and corporations may support an aquatic project. The center could build civic pride, promote economic development, and enhance community facilities. Properly structured, any of the financing and ownership options selected will permit tax deductible giving from most private contributors. Historically, contributions from outside sources have not exceeded matching funds.

Sample commemorative gift opportunities include the following:

- Pool structure $1,000,000
- Entrance/offices $ 500,000
- Balcony $ 500,000
- Campaign name itself $ 250,000
- Locker rooms $ 250,000
- Large brick and 1-year membership $ 10,000
- bricks/tiles (contributors) $ 500

Partnerships/joint use agreements. Joint use agreements and collaborations with other municipalities, educational institutions, businesses, health care providers, and other organizations and institutions can be significant sources of revenue and programming opportunities. A joint use agreement has the potential to increase programming opportunities and financial support. Although this process is difficult to manage in terms of organizing the different priorities and agendas of the different organizations, it has proven worthwhile in many communities.

A partnership can be a positive experience for the desired aquatic facility. Recent years have provided many examples of existing partnership relationships to establish major facilities. Partnerships have allowed organizations to create useful recreational facilities that otherwise would not have been possible.

The following are reasons an organization may wish to engage in a partnership relationship:

- cost to provide government service is high,
- creates budget and creative programming opportunities,
- spreads the risk among partners,
- merging resources creates a higher level of service delivery,
- offers entrepreneurial opportunities not always affordable to public agencies,
- planning can be an impetus for new perspectives and creative thinking, and
- encourages a market-driven approach rather than a product-driven approach.

The desire to partner with others is popular when mutual interest exists in building a capital asset. What potentially exists in partnership relationships frequently occurs between one or more sectors such as two or more public sector organizations, the public sector and not-for-profit organizations, and the private sector and the public sector.

Partnership relationships usually exist in one of two forms: investment partnerships and program partnerships.

- *Investment partnerships:* public sector organizations such as schools or park organizations, and/or the private sector, and/or the not-for-profit engage in equity construction of a capital asset. In recent years, these facilities have included gymnasiums and fitness facilities.
- *Program partnerships:* public sector organizations such as schools or park organizations, and/or the private sector, and/or not-for-profit organizations engage in the provision of programs to benefit the community or facility. These programs are typically outsourced by the public sector or not-for-profit sector organization to the private sector. In these instances, the public sector is better off managing the activity rather than producing it. In recent years, these programs have included facility management, specialized training programs, and specific skill activities.

Establishing an investment partnership relationship can be tricky, especially for a partnership involving several entities. The structure of such a relationship must allow for consistent operations, policy making, and operational management of the facility after it is open. The relationship has the potential to be complex and challenging given the financial structure, the differences in the makeup of the policy-making boards, and the administrative structures of each entity.

Program partnerships would come after the investment partnership relationship is created and executed. Program partnerships could be as complex as determining financial access to the facility and the allocation of time or identifying how the facility will incorporate programs. The partners will need to discuss each of these issues so a clear idea of financial and operational issues are understood and agreed upon among the partners before the facility is ready to open.

Typically, before any successful partnership is undertaken, three critical considerations must be addressed.

1. *A common vision:* All partners must share a compelling picture of the possibilities. This does not mean that everyone necessarily needs to have the same goals, but all partners must be able to achieve their goals within the "big picture" of the project.
2. *Impact of the new relationship:* The agencies involved must see value. If the involved agencies see the partnership creating the ability to improve productivity, efficiency, and profitability and achieving the desired goals, then the desired impact is mutual and the partnership is closer to achieving the desired goals.
3. *Knowing through intimacy:* Intimacy (closeness, sharing, and trust) is never achieved easily or quickly. To achieve intimacy, agendas must be clear; the ideas of all potential partners regarding the goals of the project must be out in the open. The partners must have similar interests but separate expertise regarding the project, that is, each partner should "bring something to the table."

Capital Markets Financing

These methods of financing involve capital markets. The options are not mutually exclusive in every case. In fact, the final financing for the new facility is likely to be a package of various financing sources that collectively reach the needed total. Options include the following:

- local discretionary sales surtax,
- sale of general obligation bonds,
- sale of certificate of obligation,
- sale of revenue bonds,
- sale of certificates of participation, and
- sale of lease revenue bonds.

General obligation bonds and revenue bonds are issued directly by the city. A third-party owner, set up expressly for this purpose, uses the tax-exempt issuing authority of the city to issue certificates of participation and lease revenue bonds. The city would lease the aquatic center from this entity.

The suitability, structure, requirements, costs, advantages, and disadvantages of each form of financing are different. The remainder of this section summarizes some of these features.

Financing, in most cases, requires the sale of bonds. For any bond to be sold, an independent bond rating institution must evaluate the entity that the bond will represent. This rating determines the bond price and interest rate and, as a result, the overall worth of the bond.

General Obligation Bonds

In selling general obligation bonds (also known as council manic bonds), a municipality obligates itself to levy and collect sufficient property taxes without limit as to the rate or the amount in order to pay principal and interest as it comes due. General obligation bonds with low interests rates are one way to finance capital improvement projects (e.g., parks, facilities, and streetscapes).

Tax status to investors. Income from general obligation bonds generally is exempt (to the investor) from federal income taxes.

Issuance requirements. Should general obligation bonds become a part of the financing package, the issuer must accomplish the following:

- ***Internal approvals:*** The city has an internal approval process before any bond issue can proceed. The city council must endorse the proposed bond. General obligation bonds could be used if approved by the voters.
- ***Voter approval:*** A general obligation issue must go before the voters and must secure the approval of a majority of the voters.
- ***Compliance with indebtedness limits:*** The city faces indebtedness limits based on the aggregate property value in the tax bases.

Certificate of Obligation

With certificate of obligation bonds, the debt instrument is secured by the revenue from the proposed facility, and the municipality obligates itself to levy and collect sufficient property taxes, without limit as to the rate or the amount, to pay principal and interest as it comes due.

Tax status to investors. Income from certificate of obligation bonds is generally exempt (to the investor) from federal income taxes.

Issuance requirements. Should certificate of obligation bonds become a part of the financing package, the issuer must accomplish the following:

- ***Internal approvals.*** The city has an internal approval process before any bond issue can proceed. The city council must endorse the proposed bond.
- ***Compliance with indebtedness limits.*** The city faces indebtedness limits based on the aggregate property value in the tax bases.

Revenue Bonds

Revenue bonds are to be repaid out of the revenues generated by the operation of the aquatic center. The investor bears the risk that the center's revenues will prove insufficient to cover interest and principal payments on the bonds. The city retains the facility's revenue in excess of debt service requirements.

The facility may not generate sufficient revenue to cover all debt service obligations. A revenue bond may be appropriate if an entity were to underwrite the operating cost of operating the community aquatic center and thereby release the revenue stream to secure revenue bonds.

Tax status to investors. Like general obligation bond interest, income from revenue bonds generally is exempt (to the investor) from federal income taxes.

Issuance requirements. The requirements to issue revenue bonds are slightly less restrictive than general obligations. In this case, the city must accomplish the following:

- ***Internal approvals.*** The city has an internal approval process before a bond issue can proceed. The city council must endorse the proposed bond.
- ***Compliance with indebtedness limits.*** The city faces indebtedness limits based upon the aggregate property value in the tax bases.

Certificates of Participation (Municipal Lease)

A certificate of participation (COP) is not a debt issue per se. Instead, the investor purchases a proportional share of lease income that the issuer expects to receive over the life of the COP. It also differs from the bond financing options we previously discussed in that the issuer is not the city, but rather an independent entity created specifically for this purpose. This entity sells the COPs, uses the proceeds to develop the community aquatic center, and then leases the completed center to the city. It secures the means to pay the holder of the COP from the rental income it receives from the city.

In general, a COP must have sufficient revenue generated by the facility to pay for debt service. The aquatic recommendations developed will unlikely generate enough positive cash flow after operations to meet this requirement. By dedicating gross revenues of the facility to support the COP, this structure might be worth considering. Under this scenario, operating expenses would be paid by another source, possibly a corporate sponsor.

Third-party lessor. A third-party entity, who would function as the lessor, would construct and own the aquatic center (initially, at least). In general, three possible entities exist for this purpose:

- private sector entity (e.g., a leasing company or a private investment group),
- constituted authority (e.g., a Joint Powers Authority established by the city for this purpose), or
- a not-for-profit corporation.

City as lessee. The city would be the lessee of the aquatic center, making periodic lease payments to the owner of the facility. The respective share of the lease payments each would make would be a negotiated amount that is based on upcoming contributions, ongoing usage, and other factors.

Kinds of municipal leases. Two leases may be structured:

- ***Operating lease.*** The city makes payments exclusively to use the center.
- ***Financing lease.*** The city makes payments to both use the center and accrue ownership in the facility. Thus, a financing lease functions as a purchase-over-time arrangement for the city.

Impact on indebtedness. Ordinarily, the lease obligations incurred by the municipality are not treated as debt. Consequently, entering into a municipal lease ordinarily is not subject to voter approval or debt limitation provisions.

Financing cost. Ordinarily, the cost of municipal lease financing may range from 20 to 50 basis points above comparable financing through general obligation bonds. The reason for the higher rate is that the lessor is at risk throughout the life of the lease that the city will decline, for any reason, to appropriate the funds to make their periodic lease payments. No other risk compares in a general obligation bond.

Lease Revenue Bonds (Municipal Lease)

In most respects, lease revenue bonds function like certificates of participation (the option we previously discussed). The essential difference between these two is the legal nature of the financing instruments that the independent entity (the lessor) is selling. A lease revenue bond is an obligation of the issuing authority, whereas the certificate of participation provides merely for the flow-through of that authority's rental income from the city to the holder of the COP.

Impact on indebtedness. Ordinarily, the lease obligations the municipality incurs are not treated as debt. Consequently, entering into a municipal lease ordinarily is not subject to voter approval or debt limitation provisions.

Financing cost. The cost of lease revenue bonds may be slightly less than the cost of certificates of participation because the only security behind the certificates of participation is the pass-through of the rental income from the city.

Step 4: Design and Construction

Once the voters approve the referendum, a professional design team with project experience can be hired. The design process includes schematic design, design development, construction documents, bid, and construction. Construction can take from 6 to 12 months where the climate is temperate, 9 to 15 months where the weather is seasonal, and 1 to 2 years for a large indoor aquatic complex.

Success also relies on the skills and craftsmanship of licensed construction professionals. Municipalities understand the difference between qualifications-based selection and low bid. They prequalify the experienced swimming pool contractor and understand that a design–bid–build process includes specifications that clearly identify the requirement for contractor qualifications. Specifications must indicate work that others will complete; a specification that is not proprietary increases competition among bidders. Outlining the scope of work to be included within the pool package creates a tighter bidding environment. Multiple vendors and manufacturers typically assist in maintaining a fair and competitive bidding environment.

If the construction manager (CM) model is chosen, the CM coordinates with the design professionals on issues related to design. The CM coordinates bidding and selection of contractors and negotiates final pricing and assists in the preparation of contractor contracts. The CM establishes lines of communication with inspection agencies and coordinates construction site meetings with contractors and the architect and other related professionals. The CM coordinates punch list preparation, requests warranty information, and closes out the project. Figure 5.6 shows a sample project timeline from determining that existing facilities are obsolete through opening day.

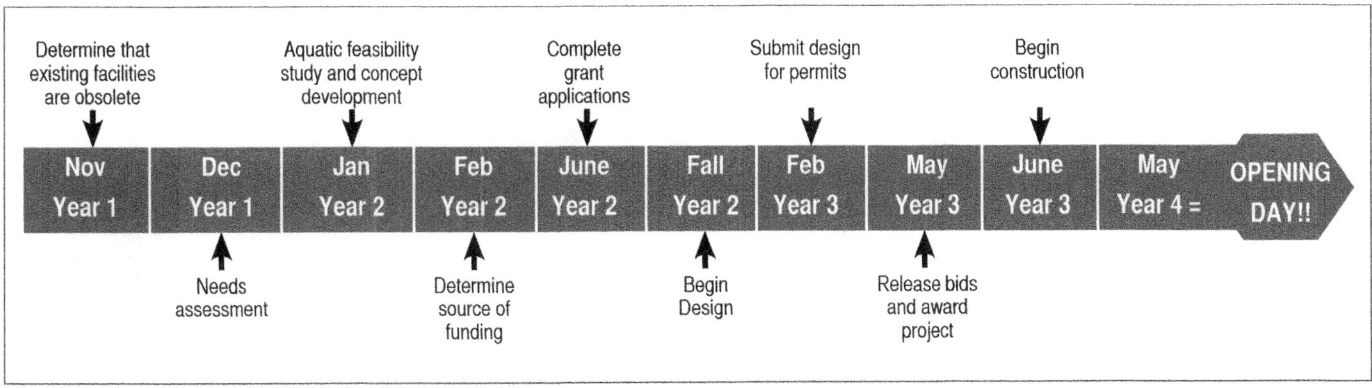

Figure 5.6. Example of a project timeline. (Courtesy of Counsilman-Hunsaker)

Opening Day!

Once the new aquatic facility is in place, the facility operator should ensure that staff, which is typically more than 50% of the annual expense budget, understand and convey all new processes and procedures in a positive environment. In order to win and maintain participants, lifeguards, front desk attendants, instructors, maintenance crews, concession operators, and managers must work to provide services, programs, and amenities that have been thoroughly analyzed and well planned. The staff at modern aquatic centers combine excellent customer service with community outreach to achieve customer loyalty and maintain a place where proud families can make great memories year after year.

Summary

The most daunting task, building a new aquatic facility, can be easier and more simplified with appropriate planning, although it does take time. First, the decision must be made whether to repair, restore, or replace a facility. If the facility will be replaced, following the four steps of needs assessment, operations planning, funding your aquatic facility, and design and construction, can create a smoother path to opening day. Organization and planning are critical in constructing a new facility and can result in significant benefits financially, in the community, and for recreation down the road.

Figure 5.7. A popular lazy river in a busy water park. (Photo courtesy of Counsilman-Hunsaker)

6

Americans With Disabilities Act (ADA)

by John Caden

Key Concepts

ADA background
ADA structure
ADA enforcement
  and compliance
Means of access
Pool lifts
Stationary vs. mobile
  hoists

Landings
Sloping
Safe harbor
Handrails
Ramps
Aquatic wheelchairs
Transfer systems

Introduction

Of all the people who can benefit from the wonderful effects of being in the water, seniors and people with disabilities can benefit the most.

Water can be safe. It compensates for and protects a person with poor balance, reducing the fear of falling. Being in the water reduces stress and pressure on joints or weak limbs. Water also provides exercise opportunities that benefit anyone from a Paralympic swimmer to a senior seeking a low-impact cardio workout by walking across the pool.

In the past, people with physical challenges may have had difficulty using a public pool, as most pools were not accessible. In 2010, the Americans With Disabilities Act (ADA) was expanded and now requires pool operators to provide a means of access into pools in their facilities.

This chapter will provide an overview of the subject of accessible swimming.

ADA Background

Evolution

The ADA is a wide ranging antidiscrimination legislation that grew out of the civil rights movement of the mid-1960s that resulted in laws prohibiting discrimination on the basis of race or gender.

The challenge with eliminating discrimination against people with disabilities is that much of this discrimination is in the form of physical barriers that prevent a person from gaining access to a place. If you cannot enter an office, you cannot be denied a job. If you cannot enter a commercial building, you cannot be denied services. The primary challenge of the ADA is how to effectively remove these physical barriers.

This monumental task was given to a government department commonly referred to as the U.S. Access Board. This group defines accessibility. The U.S. Access Board determines the correct width of a doorway, the

Figure 6.1. ADA-compliant swimming pool lift. (Photo courtesy of S. R. Smith)

number of accessible parking spaces in a parking lot, and the number of accessible rooms in a hotel.

The U.S. Access Board was established as part of the Rehabilitation Act of 1973, which addresses nondiscrimination in federal facilities. Federal facilities are not regulated by the ADA but rather the Architectural Barriers Act of 1968 and the Uniform Federal Accessibility Standards (UFAS) that were published in 1982. The content of UFAS was the precursor to the ADA.

Once Congress passes a law, it authorizes a department of the government to regulate that law. This includes both developing and enforcing regulations associated with that law. The responsibility for regulating and enforcing the ADA has been given to the Disability Rights section of the Department of Justice (DOJ).

Figure 6.2. Access ramp for accessibility into swimming pool. (Photo courtesy of Counsilman-Hunsaker).

The rulemaking process for government departments is well defined. In the case of the ADA, the process begins with the U.S. Access Board developing accessibility guidelines. These guidelines are then passed to the DOJ to be codified into regulatory language. Prior to issuing regulations, the DOJ must first publish proposed regulations in order to provide the public with the opportunity to comment on them. This is called a notice of proposed rulemaking. After public comments, and prior to the final rules being published, the Office of Management and Budget reviews the new regulations to assess their impact on the economy. At the end of this process, the regulations and an implementation timetable are published in the *Federal Register*.

The ADA was signed into law by President George H. W. Bush on July 26, 1990. In 1991, the first set of ADA regulations went into effect. Elements affected by these regulations are now part of the fabric of everyday life in the United States. These regulations resulted in curb cuts, accessible parking places, accessible bath and hotel rooms, ramps, braille signage, and wayfinding signage.

Almost immediately after the release of the 1991 regulations, the U.S. Access Board began to revise these regulations to include areas not covered or addressed in the 1991 version.

Around 1995, the U.S. Access Board began work on accessibility requirements for swimming pools. After several revisions, much discussion, and public comment, in September 2003, the U.S. Access Board released the *Americans With Disabilities Act Accessibility Guidelines for Swimming Pools*. This document is commonly referred to as ADAAG 2004.

Because the U.S. Access Board has no enforcement authority, these guidelines were just that—guidelines. That eventually these guidelines would become law was a foregone conclusion. They were released early to serve as a guidance document for new construction and for pools undergoing modifications. The objective of this early release was to enable new construction projects to build to these standards so that they would not have to renovate when these guidelines became law.

The final version of the ADAAG was passed from the U.S. Access Board to the DOJ in 2006. In 2008, the DOJ issued a notice of proposed rulemaking (NPRM) that was the precursor to the revision of the 1991 regulations. In this NPRM, the DOJ, bowing to lobbying pressure, proposed changes to the ADAAG developed by the U.S. Access Board. Of interest to the swimming pool community, the DOJ proposed that large pools would only be required to provide one means of access and smaller existing pools would not need to be accessible at all.

During the public comment period that followed the release of this NPRM, the backlash against these proposed changes was overwhelming and resulted in DOJ abandoning their proposed revisions to ADAAG and reverting to the U.S. Access Board's original recommendations.

On July 26, 2010, the revision of the ADA was signed into law. Coincidentally, this date was the 20th anniversary of the signing of the original ADA. The new regulations were published in the *Federal Register* on September 15, 2010, and went into effect on March 15, 2011. Full compliance with these regulations was supposed to be required by March 15, 2011. As written, the ADAAG had gray areas that were subject to interpretation. Basically, the rules stated that all swimming pools should be accessible, but specific details on how to accomplish this requirement were not provided.

The entity being subjected to the rules could then decide how to follow them. With respect to swimming pools, the ADA (§ 242.2) stated that an accessible entry should be provided for swimming pools and listed the access means permitted. The rule did not specify whether pool lifts needed to be fixed, whether lifts could be shared between pools, or whether a pool lift should remain in place at all times. The decision on these issues would revert to the facility operator to interpret and implement a program that provides the required access in a manner that works best for his or her facility. This decision would expose the facility to possible ramifications if the access program was deficient. In such a case, the facility could be sued or fined. However, lobbying groups pushed the DOJ to provide specific detail on these gray areas.

On January 31, 2012, the DOJ published the technical assistance document *Accessible Pools: Means of Entry and Exit*. In this document, the DOJ, for the first time, introduced the requirement that pool lifts are required to be fixed elements. Additionally, the DOJ stated that each pool requires its own pool lift and that pool lifts must be in place whenever a pool is open.

Rather than clarifying the situation, this interpretation resulted in more confusion. This interpretation lacked detail on issues such as attachment requirements. Congress discussed whether the DOJ exceeded their authority and failed to follow prescribed rulemaking procedures.

Because of this confusion, the DOJ initially extended the compliance date for swimming pools until May 21, 2012. At the same time, they issued an NPRM seeking public comment on whether this date should be extended further. On May 24, 2012, the DOJ issued another update to their January 31 document, extending the compliance deadline until January 31, 2013.

Enforcement

Even though the new regulations are now in effect, accessibility police are not combing the country looking for instances of noncompliance. The ADA is essentially a complaint-driven statute. This means that a person must file a complaint with the DOJ to initiate action by that department. If the department becomes involved in such a complaint, they have the ability to levy fines upwards of $50,000 against offending parties.

In most cases, the ADA is enforced by complaints lodged directly against an offending facility by a private plaintiff. Many of these cases usually are resolved through mediation, but they may also end up in court.

In this case, a losing defendant may be required to pay the plaintiff's legal fees.

Local governmental agencies, such as health or building departments, have no authority to enforce the ADA. They do, however, have the ability to enforce local building codes, many of which contain accessibility provisions. Enforcement of this type generally only occurs with new construction or modifications or in cases where either a building permit or a certificate of occupancy is issued. Local agencies can withhold these permits if compliance with local building codes is not met. In most cases, local authorities will not become involved with existing facilities, unless a situation arises that requires a permit.

Structure

The ADA is divided into sections, or Titles. Title I, for example, deals with discrimination in the workplace. The two areas of interest to the aquatics industry are Title II and Title III. Title II lists the regulations for local and state government-owned facilities. This includes parks and recreation departments, public schools, and universities. Title III facilities are any privately owned, public accommodation. This includes facilities such as hotels, health clubs, private schools, and community centers.

Facilities not governed by the ADA include private homes, apartments, condos, homeowners' associations, and private clubs. The rule of thumb is that if these facilities restrict the use of their pools to residents/members and their guests, they are not under ADA jurisdiction. However, if any of these facilities were to provide a public accommodation, they would relinquish that exemption. The following are examples of how that can happen:

- if an apartment complex sold memberships to their pool,
- if a condominium operated as a hotel,
- if a homeowners' association hosted swim meets that included swimmers from outside their community, and
- if a private club rented out its facilities to outside organizations for outings.

These would all be considered public accommodations that require the facility to meet ADA barrier removal requirements.

Means of Access

The ADA permits five means of access for pools:

- swimming pool lifts,
- sloped entries,
- transfer walls,
- transfer systems, and
- accessible pool stairs.

Swimming pool lifts. Swimming pool lifts are the most popular means of access, as virtually anyone can use them and as they are the least expensive to install.

Swimming pool lifts or hoists transfer individuals from the pool deck into a pool and from the pool back to the deck. Patient lifts are regulated in the United States by the Food and Drug Administration (FDA).

Any company in the United States that manufactures a product that is regulated by the FDA is required to register their manufacturing facility with the FDA and to ensure that the facility employs current good manufacturing processes in their operation. A requirement of a good manufacturing process is the use of a prevailing standard in the design and manufacture of such products.

The only existing standard that defines requirements for patient lifts is ISO10535:2006. This standard not only provides design and manufacturing criteria, but also defines the various categories for patient lifts. Two types of patient lifts or hoists are available: stationary hoists and mobile hoists. (Internationally, the term *hoist* is used to define these types of products, as the term *lift* refers to an elevator. Because ISO standards are written in Europe, the term *hoist* is used in their publication.)

Stationary hoist. A stationary hoist lifts, transfers, or moves a person within a predefined area and is fixed to a wall, ceiling, or floor; or is mounted or placed in or on other allied devices; or is freestanding (Figure 6.3).

Fixed stationary hoist. A fixed stationary hoist is permanently attached to a surface, such as a pool deck.

Figure 6.3. Stationary hoist. (Photo courtesy of Aquatic Access)

Mounted stationary hoist. A mounted stationary hoist uses a device, such as a sleeve, to secure it to a surface, such as a pool deck.

Freestanding stationary hoist. A freestanding stationary hoist stands on the floor and lifts and moves people with disabilities in an area limited by the reach of the system. The device uses either counterweights or noncantilevered design to maintain its stability during use. In the United States, freestanding stationary hoists used for swimming pools are often called portable pool lifts.

Mobile hoist. A mobile hoist is fitted with a device or devices (e.g., wheels) that are freely movable and propellable along the floor and lifts, transfers, or moves people with disabilities independent of a fixed installation or other allied device.

The basic difference between a mobile hoist and a stationary hoist is that mobile hoists are used to transport the user from place to place, such as from a bed to a bath or toilet facility. Stationary hoists require the user to actually be brought to the device to be transferred to the intended destination, which is adjacent to the stationary hoist.

A good example of a mobile hoist is a Hoyer lift. This type of hoist is common both in health care facilities and in private residences.

Mobile hoists are usually not used for pool lifts. Because they involve moving a person from place to place, such as the locker room to the pool, they require an attendant. This alone will disqualify this type of lift from ADA-regulated facilities.

Stationary hoists, especially ceiling-mounted versions, can be found in many health care applications. Swimming pool lifts are a good example of a stationary hoist. Current designs for swimming pool lifts feature all three types of stationary hoists (i.e., those fixed in place, those placed in an allied device such as a deck anchor, and those that are freestanding).

Swimming pool lifts can be further broken down as discussed below.

Noncantilevered lifts. Noncantilevered lifts have the seat attached to and rotate around the anchor point. Noncantilevered lifts are limited to simple pool designs that feature either no gutter or recessed gutters. Water-powered lifts are good examples of noncantilevered lifts.

Cantilevered lifts. Cantilevered lifts are designed to allow the seat to extend out from the anchor point. Cantilevered lifts provide access to a greater number of pool designs, including rim-flow gutters, roll-out gutters, or any design where a substantial horizontal distance from the loading point to the water exists. Two types of cantilevered lifts are available: nonrotating and rotating.

Nonrotating cantilevered lifts. Nonrotating cantilevered lifts extend the seat directly out from the loading point. These lifts have similar range of motion restrictions as those found with noncantilevered lifts and are most effective with simple pool edge designs with no gutter.

Rotating cantilevered lifts. Rotating cantilevered lifts have the ability to raise and rotate the seat position over the deck and extend the seat out and over obstacles in the path to the water. They can work effectively with almost any pool design.

Noncantilevered lifts are usually fixed in place. They can also be mounted in a deck anchor. The primary limitation for these lifts is that, in most cases, they have to be connected to a water supply. On the other hand, cantilevered lifts can be fixed, anchored, or freestanding.

Design criteria and appropriate testing protocols for patient lifts are contained in ISO10535:2006. Adherence to this standard will ensure a safe product with respect to structural integrity, stability, electrical or electronic safety, and operation. Although the FDA requires documentation that supports standard compliance to be available, it does not have a scheduled audit process for Class III devices, which include patient lifts. However, products sold internationally, especially into the European community, generally must prove compliance with a prevailing standard. If a company is ISO9001 certified, they can self-certify their products as all of their processes are audited annually. Other companies can employ independent certification agencies to document their compliance to a standard.

Currently, the Underwriters Laboratory (UL) does not have a process for swimming pool lifts. The UL is an independent safety science consulting and certification company.

To ensure operational consistency among the different products on the market, the ADA (§ 1009.2) provides requirements for swimming pool lifts. The U.S. Access Board developed these requirements based on existing standards, such as ISO10535, public comment, and industry knowledge and experience. The ADA (§ 1009.2) lists nine elements required for swimming pool lifts. Some of the elements are design specific, that is, they are required to be incorporated into the design of the lift. The balance is site specific and relates to the installation of the lift. A summary of the requirements follows.

Pool lift location (site specific). The lift should be located where the water is no deeper than 48 in. If the entire pool is deeper than 48 in., the lift can be located anywhere along the deck.

Seat location (site specific). In the raised, or loading, position, the center line of the seat must be located a minimum of 16 in. from the edge of the pool. This allows for a safe transfer on and off of the lift seat.

Clear deck space (site specific). On the side of the seat opposite the water, a clear deck space should be provided parallel with the seat. The space should be a minimum of 36 in. wide and should extend forward a minimum of 48 in. from a line located 12 in. behind the rear edge of the seat. This requirement ensures adequate space adjacent to the lift to allow for a wheelchair approach. This requirement can also be design specific if a portion of the lift extends into the clear deck area.

Seat height (design specific). The height of the lift seat should be designed to allow a stop at 16 in. minimum to 19 in. maximum measured from the deck to the top of the seat surface when in the raised (loading) position. This is essentially wheelchair height and a stopping point within this range will ensure the lift seat aligns with the wheelchair. Many lifts, especially cantilevered lifts, have a larger range that accommodates users who do not use a wheelchair.

Seat width (design specific). The seat should be a minimum of 16 in. wide. This requirement provides a wide enough surface to facilitate transfers.

Footrests and armrests (design specific). Footrests are required, and they must move with the seat. Footrests prevent a user's feet from dragging on the deck surface. Armrests are optional, but if used, the armrest on the side opposite the water must be able to be moved clear for transferring.

Operation (design specific). The user must be able to use the lift unassisted from both the deck and the water.

Submerged depth (both design and site specific). The lift should be designed to submerge the top of the sitting surface of the seat a minimum of 18 in. below the level of the water. This depth provides buoyancy that facilitates movement on and off of the lift seat.

Lifting capacity (design specific). Lifts should have a minimum 300-lb lifting capacity and be capable of sustaining a static load of 1.5 times the rated load. These are the only published requirements for swimming pool lifts the DOJ provides. The term *ADA compliant* is used extensively in marketing and advertising for pool lifts, but what does it mean? Because the requirements for pool lifts include elements that are either design specific or site specific, compliance with the regulations is having a compliant product installed in such a fashion that the installation itself is compliant. Not every lift is compliant in every application.

For example, suppose that a facility purchases a pool lift that has the ability to lower the seat 25 in. below the deck. The ADA requires that the seat of a pool lift should be submerged a minimum of 18 in. below the water line. The pool in question has a deck to water distance of 6 in. If 6 in. is added to the required 18-in. submerged depth, the seat will need to be lowered 24 in. below the deck to have a compliant installation.

In this case, this is the correct purchase, as the 25-in. range of the lift will meet the requirement. However, if the deck to water distance for the pool were 10 in. and not 6 in., this lift would not work, as the seat would need to be lowered 28 in. below the deck to get the required 18 in. of submerged depth. A lift with a larger range of motion would need to be ordered to get enough seat deep in the water.

Most manufacturers will work with facilities to ensure that the lift that is ordered will work for the intended pool. In fact, many manufacturers will not ship a lift unless the facility has completed a deck profile worksheet that allows the manufacturer to verify that the lift will work in that installation.

At the end of the day, the final responsibility for ensuring that a facility complies with the ADA falls on the facility owner. This being said, most manufacturers and pool professionals will provide guidance to meet this requirement.

A number of ways exist to ensure that a lift meets ADA requirements. Many manufacturers have had their products verified by a third party to demonstrate their compliance with the ADA. This information will help, but in most cases, this is only half of the battle. Compliance is a combination of a compliant product and a compliant installation. Third-party testing labs generally have no way to review individual installations.

Sloped entries. Sloped entries, or ramps, are similar to ramps installed on dry land. These features require a significant investment to install, but are basically maintenance free once in place.

Ramps are effective in pools where there are a large number of swimmers who are ambulatory who may have difficulty with steps or ladders, such as a pool used by seniors (Figure 6.4).

As with swimming pool lifts, the ADA prescribes specific criteria for sloped entries.

Sloping. Ramp runs should have a running slope not steeper than 1:12. For ramps located on dry land, a few exceptions exist. For existing facilities, if the entire rise of the ramp is no greater than 6 in., a ramp may have a running slope between 1:12 and 1:10. Also, if a ramp has a rise that is no greater than 3 in., the running slope may be between 1:10 and 1:8. A ramp may never be steeper than 1:8 in any situation.

Because entry into a swimming pool will result in a rise that is greater than 6 in., these exceptions will rarely affect the slope requirement for a ramp entry. For pools that have been constructed with a beach-like or zero-depth entry, the slope of the ramp must be no greater than 1:12. Many such pools have been designed with ramps having a running slope of 1:10, which would disqualify them as approved means of access.

The only exception to the sloping requirement is a wading pool, where the sloped entry would extend from the edge of the deck to the deepest part of the pool.

Figure 6.4. Ramp into leisure pool and pool stairs. (Photo courtesy of Counsilman-Hunsaker)

The cross slope of ramp runs should not be steeper than 1:48. Where sloped entries are provided, the surfaces should not be slip-resistant.

Landings. Ramps should have landings at the top and the bottom of each ramp run. The landing clear width should be at least as wide as the widest ramp run leading to the landing. The landing clear length should be at least 60 in. (1,525 mm) long. Ramps that change direction between runs at landings should have a clear landing at least 60 in. (1,525 mm) x 60 in. (1,525 mm).

Sloped entries should extend to a depth of no less than 24 in. (610 mm) and no greater than 30 in. (760 mm) below the stationary water level. This facilitates transfer on and off of a wheelchair. Where landings are required, at least one landing should be located between 24 in. (610 mm) and 30 in. (760 mm) below the stationary water level. In wading pools, the sloped entry and landings, if provided, should extend to the deepest part of the wading pool.

Handrails. At least two handrails should be provided on the sloped entry (Figure 6.5). The clear width between required handrails should be between 33 in. (840 mm) and 38 in. (965 mm). Handrail extensions are not required at the bottom landing serving a sloped entry. Additionally, where a sloped entry is provided for wave action pools, leisure rivers, sand bottom pools, and other pools where user access is limited to one area, the handrails should not be required to comply with the clear width requirements. Sloped entries in wading pools should not be required to provide handrails.

The top of the gripping surfaces of handrails should be between 34 in. (865 mm) and 38 in. (965 mm) vertically above the ramp surface and be at a consistent height above the surface. These requirements for stair and ramp

Figure 6.5. This good design wisely separates the ramp from activity in the main pool.

Figure 6.6. An aquatic wheelchair made of noncorrosive materials.(Photo courtesy of Water Technology)

Figure 6.7. Aquatic wheelchair made of noncorrosive materials designed for access into the water.

handrails are for adults. When children are the principal users in a building or facility (e.g., elementary schools), a second set of handrails at an appropriate height can assist them and aid in preventing accidents. A maximum height of 28 in. (710 mm) measured to the top of the gripping surface from the ramp surface is recommended for handrails designed for children. Sufficient vertical clearance between upper and lower handrails of at least 9 in. (230 mm) should be provided to help prevent entrapment.

Aquatic wheelchairs. Personal wheelchairs and mobility devices may not be appropriate for submerging in water. Some may have batteries, motors, and electrical systems that when submerged in water may cause damage to the personal mobility device or wheelchair or may contaminate the pool water. Although not a requirement, providing an aquatic wheelchair made of noncorrosive materials and designed for access into the water will protect the water from contamination and avoid damage to personal wheelchairs or other mobility aids (Figures 6.6, 6.7).

Transfer walls. Transfer walls are low walls that allow a user to sit on the top of the wall and pivot into the water. They are convenient for both users of wheelchairs and swimmers who are ambulatory. The requirements for transfer walls are listed below.

Clear deck space. A clear deck space of at least 60 in. (1,525 mm) x 60 in. (1,525 mm) with a slope not steeper than 1:48 should be provided at the base of the transfer wall. Where one grab bar is provided, the clear deck space should be centered on the grab bar. Where two grab bars are provided, the clear deck space should be centered on the clearance between the grab bars.

Height. The height of the transfer wall should be between 16 in. (405 mm) and 19 in. (485 mm) measured from the deck.

Wall depth and length. The depth of the transfer wall should be between 12 in. (305 mm) and 16 in. (405 mm). The length of the transfer wall should be at least 60 in. (1525 mm) and should be centered on the area of clear deck space.

Surface. Surfaces of transfer walls should not be sharp and should have rounded edges.

Grab bars. At least one grab bar should be provided on the transfer wall. Grab bars should be perpendicular to the pool wall and should extend the full depth of the transfer wall. The top of the gripping surface should be between 4 in. (100 mm) and 6 in. (150 mm) above the transfer wall. Where one grab bar is provided, at least 24 in. (610 mm) of clearance should be provided on both sides of the grab bar. Where two grab bars are provided, clearance between grab bars should be at least 24 in. (610 mm).

Pool stairs. As the name implies, pool stairs lead into a swimming pool (Figure 6.8). Since stairs can only be used by swimmers who are ambulatory, their utility for most people with disabilities is limited. The requirements for pool stairs are listed below.

Treads and risers. All steps on a flight of stairs should have uniform riser heights and uniform tread depths. The height of a riser on pool stairs has no limit, provided the heights are uniform. Treads should be at least 11 in. (280 mm) deep. Open risers are not permitted.

Handrails. The width between handrails should be between 20 in. (510 mm) and 24 in. (610 mm). Handrail extensions are not required on pool stairs. As with handrails used on ramps, the top of the gripping surfaces of handrails should be between 34 in. (865 mm) and 38 in. (965 mm) vertically above the ramp surface and be at a consistent height above the surface.

Transfer systems. Transfer systems are a means of entry that are a cross between transfer walls and pool stairs. The user transfers onto the top platform of the system and proceeds to transfer, step by step, into the water and back up after a swim. To use a transfer system, a person would require strong transferring skills. The requirements for transfer systems are listed below.

Transfer platform. A transfer platform is provided at the head of each transfer system. Transfer platforms should be at least 19 in. (485 mm) deep and 24 in. (610 mm) wide.

Transfer space. A clear deck space of at least 60 in. (1525 mm) x 60 in. (1525 mm) with a slope not steeper than 1:48 should be located and be centered along the 24-in. (610 mm) side of the transfer platform. The side of the transfer platform serving the transfer space should be unobstructed.

Figure 6.8. Ramps, steps, and handrails. (Photo courtesy of Water Technology, Inc.)

Height. The height of the transfer platform should be between 16 in. (405 mm) and 19 in. (485 mm) measured from the deck.

Transfer steps. Transfer step height should be a maximum of 8 in. (205 mm). The surface of the bottom tread should extend to a water depth of at least 18 in. (455 mm) below the stationary water level. Where possible, the height of the transfer step should be minimized to decrease the distance an individual is required to lift up or move down to reach the next step to gain access.

Surface. The surface of the transfer system should not be sharp and should have rounded edges.

Size. Each transfer step should have a tread clear depth of between 14 in. (355 mm) and 17 in. (430 mm) and should have a tread clear width of at least 24 in. (610 mm).

Grab bars. At least one grab bar on each transfer step and the transfer platform or a continuous grab bar serving each transfer step and the transfer platform should be provided. Where a grab bar is provided on each step, the tops of gripping surfaces should be between 4 in. (100 mm) and 6 in. (150 mm) above each step and transfer platform. Where a continuous grab bar is provided, the top of the gripping surface should be between 4 in. (100 mm) and 6 in. (150 mm) above the step nosing and transfer platform. Grab bars should be located on at least one side of the transfer system. The grab bar located at the transfer platform should not obstruct transfer.

Requirements. The type and size of a pool will determine which means of access are appropriate.

For swimming pools, the five means of access are split into two categories: primary and secondary. Swimming pool lifts and sloped entries are the primary means of access for swimming pools. Transfer walls, transfer systems, and accessible pool stairs are secondary means of access.

Primary means of access are the only types that users can use by themselves. Secondary means of access can only be used in conjunction with a primary means. Primary means of access are so classified because they can be used by more users than the secondary choices. The size of the swimming pool determines the number of access means required.

Large pools with an outside perimeter of 300 ft or more are required to have two means of access. At least one of these must be a primary means of access, (i.e., either a swimming pool lift or a sloped entry). The other means of access can be any of the five types.

Smaller pools under 300 ft in size are required to have one means of access and it must be a primary, meaning either a swimming pool lift or a sloped entry.

Special pools. Other aquatic facilities, such as spas, wading pools, leisure rivers, and wave action pools, have different requirements.

Spas. Spas are required to have one means of access and it can be a pool lift, transfer wall, or transfer system. In this case, all of these means of access are regarded as primary means. If a swimming pool lift is used in a spa, the footrest requirement is waived.

Wave action pools and leisure rivers. Wave action pools and leisure rivers are also required to have one means of access, regardless of the size of the pool. Many of these types of pools are over 300 ft in size, but still require only one means of access. The allowable means of access for these types of pools are pool lifts, sloped entries, or transfer systems. Again, in this application, all of these are considered primary means of access.

Wading pools. Wading pools are required to have one means of access, and it must be a sloped entry extending into the deepest part of the pool. Sloped entries in wading pools are not required to have handrails.

Catch pools. Catch pools are pools located at the bottom of a slide or flume ride. These types of pools are not required to be accessible.

Compliance

The degree to which a facility must comply with the ADA depends upon its status. A new facility being designed to incorporate changes would have an easier time complying with these accessibility provisions than an existing facility with existing walls and pool decks. Incorporating these accessibility provisions is generally referred to as barrier removal.

Barrier Removal

New facilities or facilities undergoing major modifications must FULLY comply with the ADA. Existing facilities must comply with the regulations to the extent that compliance is *readily achievable*, that is, able to be carried out without much difficulty or expense (Figure 6.9).

What is and is not readily achievable is subjective and is considered on a case-by-case basis. The decision on whether a modification is readily achievable is the responsibility of the facility owner. If a barrier removal modification is not considered to be readily achievable, the facility would not be required to make the modification.

Although this determination is subjective, the DOJ provides consultation to assist in determining whether a barrier removal modification is readily achievable. Factors to consider in making this determination include the nature and cost of the modification, along with legitimate safety concerns that may arise.

For example, as mentioned, the 2010 regulations require wading pools to have a sloped entry extending into the deepest part of the pool (Figure 6.10). A sloped entry can be provided in two ways: using a portable ramp or regrading the pool to provide the required slope.

Using a portable ramp for this purpose would not be practical, as it would likely create a legitimate safety hazard for children playing in the pool. The cost to regrade the pool to provide the required slope would likely cost more than the original cost to build the pool. Barrier re-

Figure 6.9. Chair for accessibility installed in an existing facility as a result of the 2010 ADA requirements. (Photo courtesy of Aquatic Safety Research Group)

moval for this pool would not be considered to be readily achievable, and modification would not be required. However, barrier removal is an ongoing responsibility. What is not readily achievable today may change in the future.

For example, if a facility decided to relocate the wading pool to make way for a gymnasium expansion in the future, at that time, the wading pool would need to be brought up to 2010 specifications.

Other Issues

Safe Harbor. A frequent question is, are existing pools "grandfathered" and are they required to provide accessibility? *Safe Harbor* is the ADA term for grandfathering.

If accessibility requirements for an element that was originally defined within the 1991 regulations were changed in the 2010 revision, that element would not need to meet the 2010 standard until a major renovation occurs. This is called a Safe Harbor.

For example, under the 1991 regulations, parking lots were required to provide one van space for every eight accessible parking spaces. The 2010 revision changed this to one van space for every six accessible spaces. A facility that complied with the 1991 regulations does not have to change their parking lot until their regularly scheduled repaving and striping.

On the other hand, if an element was not addressed in the 1991 regulations and is now included in the 2010 revision, Safe Harbor does not apply. There is no original rule to "grandfather."

This is the case for swimming pools. Regulations for pools were not in the 1991 regulations, but these facilities are now included under the 2010 revision. Therefore, there is NO Safe Harbor for swimming pools. All existing pools, regardless of their age, are required to comply with the accessibility requirements to an extent that is readily achievable.

Scoping. Another frequently asked question regarding compliance is, does every pool within a facility needs to be accessible? *Scoping* is the term the ADA uses to define the percentage of an element that needs to be accessible. This process helps to determine the number of accessible rooms in a hotel or the number of accessible parking places in a parking lot.

The U.S. Access Board purposely did not include a scoping provision for swimming pools. This means that every swimming pool needs to be accessible. There is, however, a scoping provision for spas that are arranged in a cluster. In this situation, 5%, or at least one of the spas, need to be accessible.

Providing Accessible Pools

Now that we have reviewed the requirements for accessible swimming pools, we will discuss the process for bringing an aquatic facility into compliance in the next section. We will start with the barrier removal analysis.

A barrier removal analysis is an audit of a facility to determine (a) whether the facility falls under ADA jurisdiction and (b) what elements within the facility would need to be modified to provide access for people with disabilities. This process is required for all Title II facilities and strongly recommended for Title III facilities.

In the case of a swimming pool, once a facility has been determined to be subject to the ADA, the pools

Figure 6.10. Lazy rivers with means of accessibility. (Photo courtesy of Counsilman-Hunsaker)

should be identified as to the type and size to determine what type of access will be required for each. If the facility has existing means of access, these components should be reviewed to ensure that they comply with the ADA.

For example, in the past, facilities may have purchased a swimming pool lift that requires an attendant to operate. Such lifts do not meet the independent operation requirement and would need to be replaced. Additionally, many facilities have installed pool stairs where the width between the handrails does not meet the requirements. Also, as mentioned previously, facilities with beach-like or zero-depth entries may either have too steep a slope or lack handrails to meet the requirement for sloped entries.

Implementation Plan

The barrier removal analysis forms the basis for an implementation plan. The implementation plan is the most important component of preparing to create an accessible environment for an aquatic facility. It outlines all responsibilities under the ADA and puts these responsibilities in a "big picture" overview. This exercise not only will help the facility owner to plan the required barrier removal modifications according to the facility's terms, but also will shield the facility against punitive remedies in the event a needed change was inadvertently overlooked.

The implementation plan begins with a list of all barrier removal issues and a determination of whether the modifications are readily achievable. If the modification is not readily achievable, the reason for this determination should be clearly presented as part of the plan.

The selected means of access should be identified. If the means of access already exists, the plan should note that it conforms to the ADA. If the means of access needs to be ordered, this also should be noted, along with a timetable for issuing the order and expected installation date.

Any new policies or procedures that are a result of accessibility accommodations should also be listed. This could be a new check-in procedure for guests that lets them know the pool is accessible, along with procedures for using the access equipment.

Finally, any equipment used to provide accessibility within a facility must be maintained in proper working order. Setting up and implementing an effective maintenance program is important.

Reviewing all barrier removal modifications with the staff makes sense. They should know the steps the facility has taken to create an accessible environment and the reasons for doing so. Revised policies and procedures should be reviewed to ensure that the staff understand them and follow them. Once the access equipment is or-

dered and installed, staff should be trained to operate it.

Sensitivity training is important so that staff are comfortable working with people with disabilities. This type of training can be coordinated with a local disability advocacy group. It could include a roundtable discussion with people with various disabilities to provide staff members with a firsthand understanding of the challenges these potential swimmers face.

These activities need to be thoroughly documented in a written format and kept on file within the facility. This is NOT a requirement, but shows that a facility owner or manager has proactively addressed barrier removal responsibilities under the ADA. Having this activity documented will greatly reduce possible exposure to punitive action in the event a complaint is filed in regard to facility accessibility.

Financial Assistance

Barrier removal, regardless of its scope, is a financial burden to any facility. Fortunately, this type of expense can be eased in number of ways.

Tax credits. First and foremost, a tax credit is available for smaller companies with annual revenues under $1 million or that employ 30 or fewer full-time employees. This credit can be used to offset roughly half of the expense of barrier removal up to a maximum of $10,000. Any company who thinks they qualify for this credit should consult a tax advisor. In addition, the IRS allows a deduction of up to $15,000 per year for barrier removal modifications.

Leasing programs. A facility owner seeking equipment to be used for barrier removal should consider a leasing program. A leasing program will spread out the cost of this purchase over several years and is also a tax deductible business expense.

Grants. Finally, grants are an additional option. Many local civic and charitable organizations have funds set aside for projects that improve the community. An accessible swimming pool would be in that category.

Figure 6.11. Warm water therapy pool with a transfer wall. (Photo courtesy of Water Technology Inc.)

Programming

Most pools have programming for specific groups, such as activities for children, swimming teams, and aquatic exercise. These activities drive people to the facility. Once a pool becomes accessible, the challenge becomes developing new programming to attract swimmers with disabilities to the facility.

A pool operator can reach out to different groups for ideas and assistance in developing programming opportunities. Local aquatic therapists, physical therapists, and rehab specialists are great resources for advice on the programs that could be implemented for people with disabilities. The Special Olympics and Paralympics can assist in expanding competitive swimming programs to include this group of athletes. "Accessibility programming" should not be limited to people in wheelchairs.

Seniors can greatly benefit from the effects of aquatic activity, but many seniors are not comfortable with traditional water entry methods, such as ladders and stairs. An accessible pool could turn into the fountain of youth for many older citizens (Figure 6.11). Whether they are lap swimmers or walk back and forth across the pool, water exercise provides buoyancy to relieve joint pressure, light resistance for improved cardio workouts, and safety. Many seniors avoid exercise for fear of falling down and breaking a hip. Water exercise prevents this from happening. Pool managers could also schedule off-hours as senior-only swim time, where these swimmers would not be intimidated by a crowded pool.

Many wounded veterans can participate in more robust programs, such as scuba classes, or use water features such as FlowRiders.

New programming opportunities are limited only by the imagination. All of these activities will increase the number of people who use a pool and can only be offered if the pool is accessible.

Marketing

Many facilities have questioned the need for removing barriers in a swimming facility. Their complaint is that they have never had people with disabilities attempt to use their pool. Of course, if the pool had previously been inaccessible, people with disabilities would have had no reason to go to the pool. However, once the pool becomes accessible and the proper programming is in place, these accessible programs should be marketed. The pool manager should let the public know that the facility is user friendly for swimmers with disabilities.

Many avenues are available for spreading the word regarding the accessibility of the facility:

- Directly contact local physical therapists and rehabilitation centers and tell them about new aquatic accessible programming.
- Contact centers for independent living, senior centers, and veterans' organizations and invite them to visit the facility.
- Publicize the facility's accessibility programs. This will attract more participants. Local newspapers and other media outlets are always on the lookout for human interest stories. Take advantage of this free advertising.
- Use the Internet. People with disabilities use the Web as their link to the world. Use this technology to list accessible activities for swimmers with disabilities.

Summary

This chapter is a comprehensive discussion of the Americans with Disabilities Act as it relates specifically to aquatic facilities. Reading and understanding the material within this chapter will give you a complete understanding of the ADA as it applies to your facility. When in doubt, check out the references and resources provided. Complying with the ADA in aquatic facilities is morally, ethically, and legally the right thing to do.

Resources

Numerous resources on the Internet can help pool operators to stay ahead of the curve with respect to pool lift accessibility. The following websites can be excellent starting points to learn more on this subject:

- The DOJ website, www.ada.gov, provides complete information relating to the ADA.
- The Association of Pool and Spa Professionals, www.apsp.org, is the trade association website that also has ADA information, including three webinars and a handy question and answer sheet that summarizes the regulations.
- United States Access Board, http://www.access-board.gov/

Section II
Mechanical

Section II addresses the mechanical aspects of swimming pools, specifically circulation and filtration. Chapter 7 discusses the principals of swimming pool circulation. Particular attention should be paid to the concepts of swimming pool "turnovers." Components of the circulation system are also discussed and include pool outlets, surge tank, hair and lint strainer, pump, filters, heater, chemical feeders, and other pool gauges, valves, and meters. Although good descriptions are given in this chapter for each of the circulation components, trained electricians, plumbers, and pool engineers can offer invaluable experience to novice pool owners and operators.

Chapter 8 deals specifically with swimming pool filtration. The three basic types discussed are sand, diatomaceous earth, and cartridge filters, although a variety of types within each category are evaluated. The reader should visit a swimming pool dealer to closely examine the various types of filters firsthand. The filter photographs and illustrations provided in Chapter 8 can certainly aid the reader in better understanding filtration, but seeing filters in person is a valuable experience. Filtering rates and backwashing techniques are an important part of the chapter.

Chapter 9 deals with improving air quality in indoor swimming facilities particularly with those having high bather loads and high chloramine levels. The latest technologies and instrumentation for improved air quality will be discussed here.

Figure 7.1. Regenerative Media (RM) filter. (Photo courtesy of Water Technology, Inc.)

7 Circulation

Swimming pool water must be circulated continuously through filters whenever the pool is open for swimming, and for most pools, circulation should be maintained 24 hours a day. The circulation system must be capable of drawing water from the pool and then distributing cleaned, heated, and treated water evenly throughout the pool. The circulation process is expanded here. Several pieces of equipment and apparatus are responsible for pool circulation:

- pool outlets;
- purge or balancing tank;
- hair and lint strainer;
- pump;
- filters;
- heater;
- chemical feeders;
- pool inlets; and
- gauges, valves, and meters.

Turnovers

Collectively, the equipment listed is responsible for swimming pool circulation. More important, however, pool circulation equipment must maintain certain "turnover" requirements. Many states require that public pools "turnover" every 8 hours, but the trend has moved toward a 6-hour turnover for large and deep competition pools and even faster for shallow leisure-type pools. Figure 7.1 shows percentages of pool water filtered each turnover. This means that in a pool that contains 120,000 gal, an equivalent amount of water must pass through the filtration plant and return to the pool at least every 6 hours, or four times a day. However, this does not mean that every drop of water in the pool must be filtered every 6 hours, but rather that 120,000 gal must be recirculated. In fact, during one turnover, less than half of the water in the pool goes through the filter, according to Gage and Bidwell's Law of Dilution. As depicted in the following illustration, turnover rate is crucial to water clarity in a swimming pool (Figure 7.2).

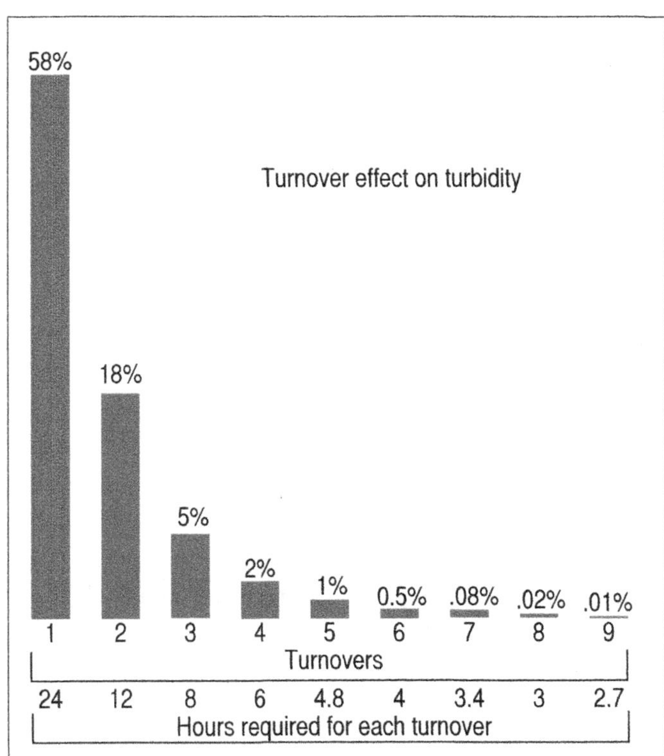

Figure 7.2. Ninety-five percent of the pool water is filtered in three turnovers according to Gage and Bidwell's Law of Dilution. The percentages represent the percent of unfiltered water in the swimming pool.

The turnover rate of a pool can be determined with only the pool volume and the flow rate, as indicated by the flow meter in gallons per minute (GPM). In most pools, the turnover rate is expressed in hours, whereas in hot tubs and spas, the turnover is expressed in minutes.

To determine the turnover rate (TR) for swimming pools, the following formula should be used:

$$\text{TR in hours} = \frac{\text{gallons of pool water}}{60 \times \text{flow rate in GPM}}$$

To determine the turnover rate for hot tubs and spas, the following equation should be used:

$$\text{TR in minutes} = \frac{\text{gallons of spa water}}{\text{flow rate in GPM}}$$

Water clarity depends on good turnover rates. Proper turnover rates are particularly important to public pools with high swimmer loads. Without adequate turnovers, swimming pool water will not stay clear.

Conversely, if a pool vessel meets the turnover requirement and the water is cloudy, the culprit is probably a lack of chemical oxidation, not filtration. Table 7.1 lists general turnover rates. The Model Aquatic Health Code includes specific and up-to-date suggested turnover rates.

Table 7.1
Ideal Turnover Rate

	Light–Moderate Swimmer Loads	Heavy Swimmer Loads
Public pools	6–8 hr	4–6 hr
Public spas	< 30 min	10–20 min
Residential pools	8 hr	6 hr
Residential spas	< 30 min	< 30 min
Wading pools	2 hr	

By studying these graphs, pool operators can easily determine flow rates needed to achieve desired turnover rates for pools and spas without performing the math. By matching the water volume of a given pool in the column on the left with the desired turnover rate on the right, they can find the required flow rate, which is below this intersection on the bottom of the graph. For example, an 80,000-gal pool that needs a 6-hour turnover would require a flow rate of 222 GPM.

Dilution With Freshwater

"Dilution is the solution to pollution." Although this theory has tragically caused the pollution of our oceans, it can be used in aquatic facilities to improve water quality and clarity. Particularly in Europe, many pool operators add freshwater as a regular water treatment regime. This is done for swimmer comfort, and some pool pollutants can only be reduced through dilution.

Emptying the Pool

For some reason, many facility operators in the United States believe that swimming pool water should be replaced every year by emptying the vessel completely and then refilling with freshwater. Pools should only be emptied when absolutely necessary (repairs or cleaning) because more structural harm and safety concerns can be raised when the pool is completely emptied. Most aquatic facilities, including outdoor pools in the wintertime, should be kept full for as long as possible or until repairs must be made to the shell or plumbing.

Pool Outlets

We will now discuss the sequence of how the water flows during circulation starting with pool outlets. Pool outlets are the exit points through which water leaves the swimming pool. The water is filtered and heated when necessary and is then chemically treated before returning to the pool. The pool outlets are where the circulation process begins. Most of the water leaving the pool goes through a perimeter gutter or skimmer system. The swimming pool vessel is designed to collect slightly more water than it can actually hold. Therefore, water continually flows out of the vessel, predominantly from the surface instead of the bottom. Some states require 10% of all water leaving the pool exit through the main drain or bottom outlet.

The system of surface overflow should be designed to handle the bulk of water returning to the filtration system because the surface is where the majority of contaminants are located. Surface overflow of water is often referred to as the perimeter overflow system or surface collection.

Some states recommend 75% of the water leaving the pool vessel come from the surface and only 25% come from the bottom outlet (main drain). Some jurisdictions state that *no less* than 50% of the water leaving the pool must come from the surface and *no more* than 50% must come from the bottom outlet. The term *main drain* is a misnomer because draining the pool occurs rarely and is not the only function of this outlet. As already mentioned, the main drain also serves as an important outlet for pool water circulation.

The main drain serves as the bottom outlet for swimming pool circulation, but is less significant when compared with the surface-skimming action. The bottom outlet should not be placed directly under a diving board because divers will be tempted to play with the drain grate, and divers may get their fingers caught in these drains. In previous editions, we recommended that the surface area of the grates covering the drain be much greater (about 10 times) than the orifice of returning water to the filters to dissipate suction and prevent bathers from becoming stuck to the outlet. Today, measures to prevent body suction entrapments are strongly urged and highly recommended, and design requirements for submerged pool outlets are now federally mandated by the Virginia Graeme Baker Pool and Spa Safety Act (P&SS Act). The P&SS Act, commonly referred to as the VGB Act, requires that all submerged pool outlets, as well as a second antientrapment system, be certified or engineered to meet the requirements within ANSI/APSP-16-2011 when there is a single main drain other than an unblockable drain. The P&SS Act is open for public comment as new requirements and successor requirements are created and adjusted. Thus, during the writing of this edition, the requirements are still subject to change. *Pool Safely* is a great resource for up-to-date requirements and standards for the P&SS Act (http://www.poolsafely.gov/pool-spa-safety-act/). Because a missing or broken outlet cover can be catastrophic, at the least, for practical purposes, all grates covering drains and outlets must be secured, should be unable to be removed without the use of tools, and should be checked often to avoid dangerous entrapments.

In shallow pools, some states allow a reverse flow pool. A reverse flow pool uses floor inlets with no floor outlets on the bottom of the pool, unless the outlet is used for draining purposes only. This design eliminates the hazards associated with suction entrapment on submerged outlets. If submerged outlets are used, they should be located in the deepest part of the pool. At least two bottom outlets are usually preferred for all VGB-certified manufactured outlets. A single outlet is only acceptable if it meets the requirements of ANSI/APSP-16 and if a registered professional designs it. In all cases, these grates will exceed a dimension of 18 in. x 23 in. Consult ANSI/APSP-16 and ANSI/APSP-7 for all drain requirements.

Gutters vs. Skimmers

Although they both remove water from the surface of the pool, gutters and skimmers are significantly different in design. Gutters are troughs that are installed continuously around the perimeter of the pool. In general, larger public pools tend to have gutters, whereas smaller pools (residential, hotel, motel, etc.) tend to use skimmers. Usually, the larger the gutter is, the better the skimming action. Gutters are available in many designs.

Figure 7.3. Virginia Graeme Baker Pool & Spa Safety Act-compliant drain cover installed. (Photo courtesy of Water Technology, Inc.).

Two basic design differences in gutters are below-deck and deck-level gutters.

Deck-level gutter systems are popular because they produce great skimming action and a flat pool surface that is ideal for competitive swimming. Waves will probably not splash back into the pool once the water reaches the deck-level gutter. A popular deck-level design is the rim-flow gutter, which is characterized by a large surge trench that surrounds the pool and collects surface water through slotted coping stones or grates on the deck level (Figure 7.4). The water level and deck level are the same in this design. Because the skimming action is superior in these designs, rim-flow gutters may be loud as a result of the water pouring into the perimeter trench located just below the deck.

Another deck-level overflow system, the roll-out gutter, is similar to the rim-flow gutter but does not have a large surge trench. Because swimmers step into the roll-out gutter to enter the swimming pool, the surface should be nonslip. Additionally, because a large surge trench is not available at the perimeter of the pool, a more turbulent, choppy pool may result.

Recessed gutters are found below the deck level (Figure 7.5). They are found more often in indoor pools and work in the same manner as a deck-level return, but they are located around the perimeter of the pool, just inside the pool walls, just below deck level. Typically, in a pool with recessed gutters, the water surface lies 12 to 18 in.

below the deck. Older pools have small gutter troughs, whereas newer pools, particularly those built for competitive swimming, have wide, deep troughs, resulting in faster times for competitive swimmers.

Skimmers are individual exit ports or boxes located intermittently around the pool. Although the lids covering skimmer baskets are located on deck level, the skimmer baskets are located below deck level, just below the water surface of the pool. The lids or cover plates of skimmers can often be displaced, creating a safety hazard.

Bathers walking on the pool deck will step on these lids, so they must be secure and have nonslip surfaces. The removable baskets found in each skimmer box collect leaves, grass, and other large debris that can hamper circulation and filtration. Skimmer baskets that are neglected (not cleaned regularly) often hinder good skimming action. Clogged skimmer baskets with leaves, grass, and other debris can render a pool cloudy quickly because they will stop the flow of water to the filters. Skimmers are usually placed every 500 to 800 square ft of water surface area or about 20 ft apart. Pool operators should check local codes before installing skimmers to at least meet but hopefully exceed minimum requirements. Skimmers are inexpensive to install, but cannot skim surface water as well as the gutter system, and are not recommended for competitive swimming venues. Although a skimmer system is fine for smaller pools, a gutter system is recommended for large public pools and

Figure 7.4. A, Wide, competitive perimeter overflow gutters under racing platforms. B, Perimeter overflow gutter at large outdoor pool. C, Perimeter overflow gutter in indoor pool with 6-in. freeboard. (A, Photo courtesy of Pentair Aquatic Systems C, Photo courtesy of Water Technology, Inc.)

Figure 7.5. Recessed gutter with good skimming action on indoor pool. (Photo courtesy of Steve Manual)

competition pools. Some states do not allow skimmers in swimming pools with surface areas greater than 1,600 square ft.

Weirs are doors or flaps that maintain a one-way skimming action by regulating the flow of water into the skimmer basket and are an integral part of the skimmer system (Figure 7.6). Once debris enters a skimmer basket, the weir prevents it from returning to the pool if the skimmer is flooded. When the weir is in place, the flow of water is controlled fairly well. Too often, however, weirs are pulled out by children or float out from the throat of the skimmer. Without the weir in place, skimmers do not work as effectively as they should. Weirs must also be equipped with a Styrofoam flotation device and will

not function properly without it. Warn children about playing with weirs because being one-way gates, weirs can trap arms and hands in the skimmer.

Unfortunately, children like to play with floating weirs in the pool and may remove them from the skimmer box for their entertainment.

Whether a gutter or skimmer system is used, the water level in the pool is of paramount importance if these surface overflow systems are to work effectively. The water level must be maintained at the top of the gutter line. In the case of skimmers, the water level should be maintained at least 3 in. up the weir, but no more than halfway above the opening. Water allowed to rise above these recommended levels will flood either the gutter or the skimmer.

Conversely, when the water level is too low, water will not go into the gutter or the skimmer. Dry skimmers and gutters result in the water returning to the filters through the bottom outlet, which is not desirable and is even illegal in some states.

An ideal water level is one that allows for optimum skimming action by maintaining a "thirsty" gutter. A thirsty gutter aggressively pulls water out of the pool, over the lip, and into the gutter drains. It should look and sound like a miniature waterfall. In fact, a thirsty gutter with good skimming action is often a noisy gutter; water cascading out of the pool through the surface collection system can be heard clearly from the pool deck. To produce this effect, the water level in the gutter must be below the water level in the pool.

Conversely, thirsty skimmers can suck air if not enough water flows out of the pool into the bucket, which may in turn damage the pump. An ample amount

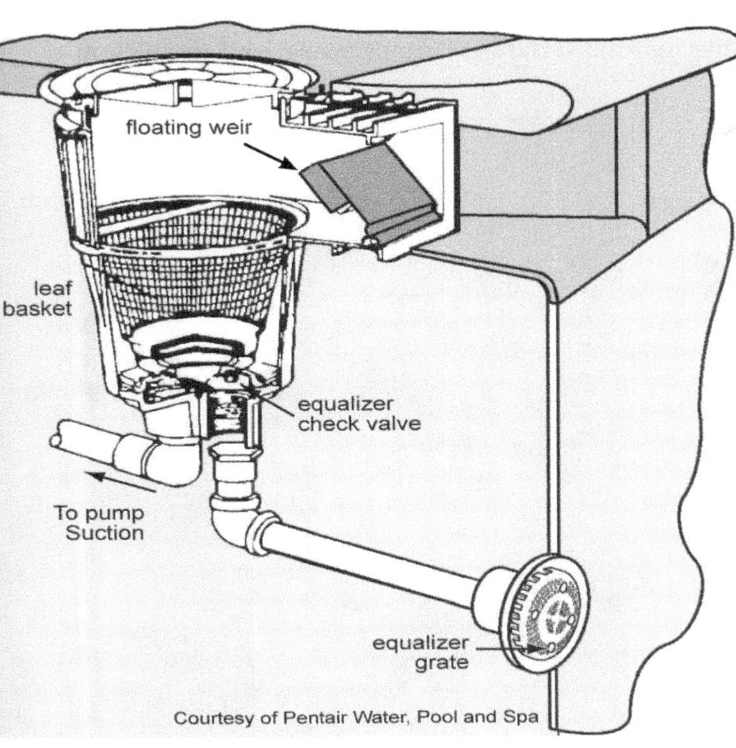

Figure 7.6. Typical skimmer cross section. (Photo courtesy of Pentair Water, Pool, and Spa)

of water should always be in skimmer baskets. Many skimmers also contain throttle plugs to regulate the flow of water. To ensure consistent skimming action, some skimmers must be throttled. Skimmers closest to the pump tend to have the strongest suction. These skimmers need to be throttled back. Skimmers located farthest from the pump have much less draw, so they need to be opened fully.

When gutters or skimmers are flooded by a water level in a swimming pool that is too high, water must be removed from the pool by opening the appropriate valves and sending water to the waste or sewage treatment plant. If the water level in the pool is too low, water must be added to the pool from the local water source. This addition of new water is called "make-up" water. The addition of make-up water can be performed manually or even automatically with the use of solenoid valves. Automatic fill valves now are strongly recommended in most pools.

Many other surface overflow systems are available, including recessed gutters and prefabricated gutters, but the functions are the same. Some work better than others, usually because of the size of the gutter trench.

The Surge (Balancing) Tank

Pools with gutters should have surge or balancing tanks, which are designed to reserve large volumes of displaced swimming pool water (Figure 7.7). Surge tanks must be large enough to hold a large capacity of water so that when the pool load is suddenly increased, water will not be lost. Without a sufficiently sized surge tank, water in the pool displaced by swimmers would overflow the surge tank and enter the waste stream. Balancing tanks with float valves prevents overflow. Pools with skimmers do not have these tanks.

The purpose of surge tanks is twofold: to hold a reserve capacity of water when a large number of bathers enter the water and to protect the pump by maintaining a water level in the tank that is above the suction port of the pool pump. This second benefit protects the pump from surges of water flowing into the pump and also prevents the pump from sucking air. Skimmer pools do not normally have surge tanks, and consequently an auxiliary pipe can be added to the bottom of the skimmer and connected to the pool wall to prevent the skimmer from sucking air. If the water level in the skimmer becomes too low, water is then pulled through this pipe to prevent the pump from sucking air. In older pools, however, this auxiliary pipe, or equalizer, may be painted over or plastered shut and therefore is no longer functional. All skimmer equalizers must terminate in a VGB-compliant fitting, as these are submerged outlets that must meet ANSI/APSP-16 requirements.

The surge tank is an important component of the circulation system because pool pumps require a constant source of water that has little resistance to suction and that is free of air. The water in the surge tank is lower than the water level in the pool when the pump is running. The float valve in the surge tank helps to balance the water coming into the tank, regulating flows between the gutters and the bottom outlet. An open or closed and vented concrete tank in the filter room or near the pool may also serve as the surge tank.

The surge tank works in the following fashion. Outgoing pool water flows by gravity from the pool vessel through the surface collection system and the bottom

Figure 7.7. A, Large surge/balancing tank for public pool. B, Outdoor view of a below grade surge tank.(Photo courtesy of Water Technology, Inc.).

outlets and into the surge tank. When the gutters are flooded, more water is taken from the surface. When the pool is quiet and the gutters are almost dry, more water is taken from the bottom outlet. Although the amount of water in the surge tank varies, the main function of this component is to keep suction into the pump constant.

Hair and Lint Strainer

Perhaps one of the most important yet most neglected components of the circulation system is the hair and lint strainer (Figure 7.8). This device is a mesh basket located in the circulation system just in front of the pool pump to protect the pump from large visible debris. The only filtration systems that do not require hair and lint strainers are vacuum filters because the pump follows the filter. Therefore, in a vacuum system, the pool pump is protected by the filter bed, thus eliminating the need for the protective hair and lint strainer. We will discuss pressure and vacuum filter systems in detail later in this chapter.

The hair and lint strainer is often neglected because cleaning it can be messy. Although the hair and lint strainer is easy to clean, the pool operator often gets wet, and what is found in the basket is often unpleasant (hair, lint, mice, Band-Aids, goggles, bathing caps, etc.). Some health codes require extra hair and lint baskets on hand so that a clean basket can replace the dirty one immediately without stopping filtration. When checking the hair and lint strainer, the pump must be turned off and valves on either side of the basket need to be closed on flooded suction systems. These baskets should be checked at least whenever the filters are backwashed and whenever the pumps are turned off. Experienced pool operators prefer to check the hair and lint strainer every day for good water flow and circulation. A dirty hair and lint strainer can almost stop a filter flow rate, thus leaving the pool with no filtration. Also, if the lid on the hair and lint strainer is not replaced securely, air might be sucked into the system. The number one source of air leaking into the pool is through the lid on the hair and lint strainer. Finally, because many hair and lint strainers are located next to the pump, they can be filled with water to prime the pump when the system is restarted. Today, many hair and lint strainers come with clear acrylic lids to make inspection of the basket easier.

The Pool Pump

The *placement* of the pool pump is important. If the pump is located before the filters, the filtration system is a pressure system. If the pump is located after the filters, the filtration system is a *vacuum system*. In the pressure system, the pump pulls the water from the pool or surge tank and pushes water through the filters. In the vacuum system, the pump draws water from the filters and then pushes the water back to the pool. Vacuum and gravity filter systems do not require a hair and lint strainer because the filters screen foreign objects that could harm the pump.

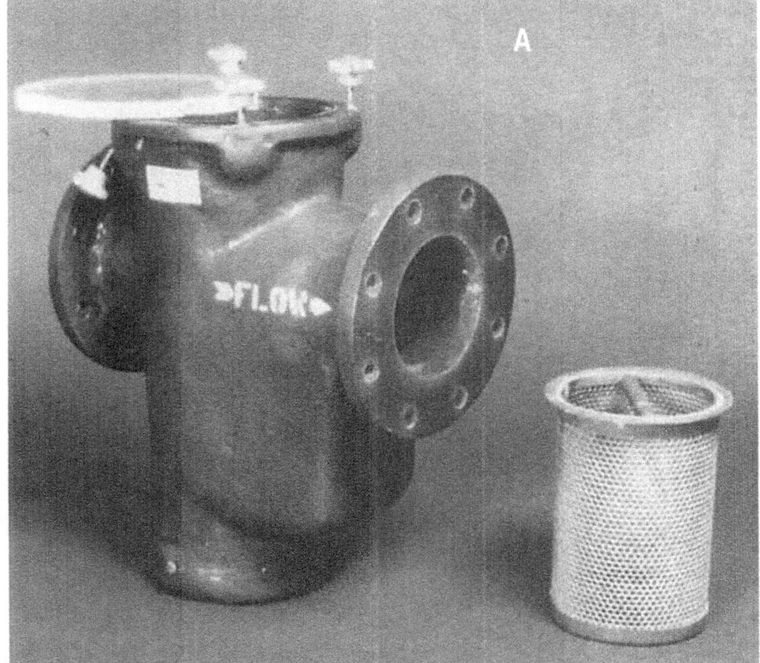

Figure 7.8. A, Fiberglass cover on hair and lint strainer allows pool operator to check basket without stopping filtration. B, Stainless Steel Strainer. (Photo A courtesy of Brock Enterprises, Hamden, CT. Photo B courtesy of Neptune Benson)

Pump placement is also important for maintenance and repairs. If indoors, the pump should be positioned as close to the pool as possible. It should be placed in a cool, dry place and secured on a rigid platform. Care must be taken to keep water, dust, and chemicals away from the pump. If the pump is kept outdoors, the pump should be shielded from the elements, particularly the sun and rain, and should be kept in a well-ventilated area.

The pump is the heart of the circulation system of the pool, but many pool owners and operators do not understand how a swimming pool pump works. To maintain clean, clear swimming pool water, a pump must move the water through the pipes and filters. As the water travels through pipes, valves, and fittings, friction or resistance to flow is created. Additionally, some portions of a circulation system are higher than others, thus requiring additional force to move the water. Pool pumps must overcome gravity and the resistance to flow to circulate water effectively.

Swimming pools use a *centrifugal* pump exclusively (Figure 7.9). The centrifugal pump is simple with only one moving part, the impeller. Centrifugal pumps take water from the suction side into the center, or eye, where the impeller spins and imparts velocity to the water inside the pump (Figure 7.10). The impeller then throws water off its edges at a high velocity. The pump casing converts this water velocity energy to water pressure, which is required to move the pool water through the filters and back to the pool.

Because the pump impeller fits snugly in its casings, hair and lint strainers become important in protecting the pump from damage caused by foreign objects in the water (Figures 7.11.a and 7.11.b). The impeller is also subject to premature corrosion if the pool water remains unbalanced on the acidic side of the pH scale.

An important benefit of using a centrifugal pump is that if a valve is closed on the pressure side of the pump, no damaging pressures develop. As pressure increases in a centrifugal pump, the power required by the pump decreases significantly. As a result, the water spins and churns within the pump and is not supposed to cause damage to the piping, but much depends on the location of the valves. The pump may eventually overheat if the discharge valve remains closed, but pipes and filters should not be damaged by excessively high water pressures. However, circulation pipes have cracked, filter lids have popped, and when pump temperatures have become too hot, PVC piping has actually melted.

Pump Sizing and Pipe Sizing

Pool pumps and pipe sizing go hand in hand because both are dependent upon each other for performance. Selecting the best pump and piping for any pool is best left to the manufacturer's recommendations and certified engineers. Feet of head (a measurement of resistance to flow) and the recommended flow rate in gallons per minute are the criteria needed to select the correct pump for any pool. Pipe diameters, lengths, elbows, and fittings should be considered when determining feet of head. A typical swimming pool may have from 40 to 70 feet of head.

A common problem with pool pumps is the piping in relation to the horsepower of the pump. In general, the suction pipe should be at least as large, if not larger,

Figure 7.9. Numerous centrifugal pumps for a large water park operation. (Photo Courtesy of Water Technology, Inc.)

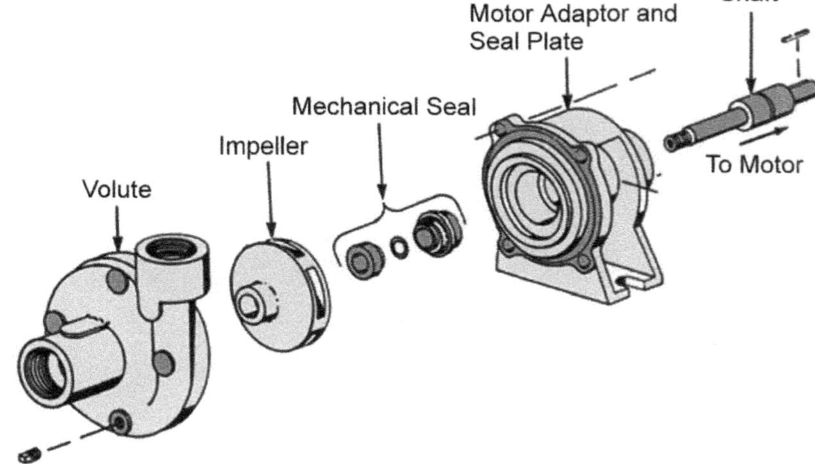

Figure 7.10. Centrifugal pump, exploded view. (Courtesy of the ©The Association of Pool & Spa Professionals, 2014)

Figure 7.11.a. High performance residential pool pump. (Photo courtesy of Hayward Pool Products, Elizabeth, NJ)

Figure 7.11.b. Commercial pool pumps. (Photo courtesy of Water Technology, Inc.)

than the pump pipe connection. The smaller the pipe is, the greater the resistance. Suction side piping must be kept as straight as possible with as few elbows and obstructions as possible. The efficiency of the pump is compromised and resistance is increased with too many additions to the suction side piping. Contact the manufacturer or dealer for complete pipe sizing information.

Undersized pool pumps "burn up" early, whereas oversized pool pumps can cause channeling of filter beds, the breakage of filter laterals, and increased capital and operating costs.

The important factors needed to size pool pumps properly are *gallons per minute* and *total dynamic head*. Feet of head must be measured on both sides of the pump, the vacuumside and the pressure side.

The following exercise can be used to evaluate an existing pump's size. The pressure side of the system is downstream from the pump. A pressure gauge can be used to measure the pressure in pounds per square inch (psi), and this number should be multiplied by a constant of 2.31 to find the feet of head for the pressure side.

The suction side of the system is located upstream of the pump. A vacuum gauge or manometer on the suction side can be used to measure the vacuum in inches of mercury (Hg). The vacuum gauge reading should be multiplied by a constant of 1.13 to find suction feet of head. In cases where the pump is close to the pool or surge tank and located below operating water level, the suction side may actually be under positive pressure. In this case, a compound (psi/Hg) is recommended. But these calculations are often best left to pump specialists rather than pool operators.

The total feet of head for this system can be determined by adding the pressure feet of head to the vacuum feet of head or by subtracting the suction side from the discharge side if positive pressure exists on the suction

side. The required flow rate in gallons per minute and the total feet of head requirements can be used to determine a pump curve. The point at which both gallons per minute and total feet of head intersect on a pump curve determines the pump size needed.

For pools that require the pump to be located below the pool level, a *flooded suction pump* is used because it has more "pushing" power and achieves 1,750 rpm. Pumps located above the pool must have more "pulling" power, so *self-priming pumps* that achieve 3,400 rpm are used in this instance.

Although the process of pump and pipe sizing is simple, a registered engineer, licensed electrician, or local swimming pool supplier can be helpful. Before constructing or renovating a pool, these professionals should be consulted to determine the appropriate pump size for the pool in question. Whenever in the pump room, pool operators should use their senses of sight, hearing, and touch (look, listen, and feel) to check on the pump. If the pump looks and smells hot and is louder than normal, the pump should be turned off and a pump specialist should be summoned.

The Filter

If the pool pump is the heart of swimming pool circulation, then the filters are the kidneys Figures 7.12-7.14 show filter tanks with different mountings. The filters remove suspended particles from the water, which is essential in reducing turbidity and increasing water clarity. Suspended particles that the filters remove include dirt, dust, hair, and oil. Filters DO NOT remove dissolved particles or bacteria. Basically, pool filters strain unwanted solids from the water before they are returned to the pool. We will discuss the basics of filtration here, and we will discuss the specifics of each filter in detail in Chapter 8.

Figure 7.12. Several vertical filter tanks. (Photo courtesy of Neptune-Benson)

Figure 7.13. Horizontally mounted filter tanks. (Photo courtesy of Neptune-Benson)

Figure 7.14. Horizontally mounted filter tanks. (Photo courtesy of Neptune-Benson)

As mentioned previously, placement of the pool pump determines whether the filter system is a pressure system or a vacuum system. In a pressure system, the pump is located before or upstream of the filters, whereas in a vacuum system, the pump follows the filter. The pressure filter system not only contains the pump upstream of the filter, but also the filter medium, which is enclosed in a tank, under pressure. The vacuum system can be detected easily because the pump is downstream of the filter, and often the vats or tanks are open, allowing the medium to be viewed. The vacuum system in not under pressure.

Regardless of the type of filter system, or medium, used, the process of filtration remains the same. The filter surface area, or bed, creates small pores through which dirt lodges and is unable to pass. Dirt can also trap additional dirt; therefore, a dirty filter is often an effective filter. When water no longer flows efficiently through the system because of accumulated dirt, the filter media must be cleaned or replaced.

Filters will produce clear, clean water when properly sized, installed, and operated. The effectiveness of any filtration system, as evidenced by water clarity, depends on several interrelated factors: the filter medium, the amount of filter area, the flow rate, and the turnover rate. Water clarity depends on the oxidizing chemical, such as chlorine, to do most of the work. The following saying in the pool industry holds true: "The chlorine burns the trash and the filter removes the ash."

The filter media can be divided further into two types: permanent and temporary. Permanent media can be reused and does not have to be replaced regularly. Sand is the most common permanent filter medium. Temporary media must be replaced after each filter cleaning or backwashing. Diatomaceous earth, or DE, a temporary medium that was once popular, is now being replaced by regenerative DE, which is known as regenerative media (RM). For the purposes of this text, we will discuss filter media in the following order: sand, DE, RM, and cartridge.

Sand Filters

Many types of sand filters are available for swimming pool use. Sand is a low-maintenance medium that lasts for years. It is easy to clean and relatively inexpensive to purchase. Sand filters use a specially graded sand, shaped like triangles, that when poured into a filter creates tiny caves, crevices, or pores that trap dirt as pool water flows through the sand bed. Advantages of sand filters include the permanent medium, low cost, and ease of operation. Three basic sand filters are available: sand and gravel, high rate pressure sand, and vacuum sand. We will discuss sand filters in detail in Chapter 8.

Recycled glass is now being used in sand filters with success. The glass is lighter and apparently traps more dirt. Another new alternative to sand is zeolite, a naturally formed porous mineral that holds significantly more dirt than sand does. Sodium activation of the zeolite enhances ion exchange to absorb ammonia ions. This tends to keep chloramine production in the filter tank and reduces chloramine production in the pool. Zeolite shows great promise, particularly in pools troubled by chronic chloramine problems.

DE Filters

DE filters use the fossilized remains of aquatic marine life called *diatoms*. These skeletal remains look like microscopic snowflakes and perform a superior job of filtering because they have the ability to trap more dirt and screen finer particles than sand does. The advantage of DE is the high water clarity it produces because of its ability to screen out even the smallest of particles. The disadvantage of this system is that the medium is temporary, needing to be replaced after each filter cleaning. The cleaning of DE filters also tends to be more labor intensive. Some suggest that DE may become more difficult to dispose of in the future. Biodegradable cellulose alternatives are available for DE.

Regenerative Media Filters

Regenerative media filters (RMF) function similarly to conventional DE filters in terms of turbidity removal and high water quality (see Figure 7.15). The advantage over conventional DE filters is the the medium can be reused many times. This is accomplished by mechanical movement of the septa up and down within the water in the filter housing. The medium and dirt particles are expelled from the septa and into suspension. The filter then goes into the precoat cycle, where the medium and dirt particles realign, opening void space in the medium for additional filtering cycles. RMF also can use a DE medium; however, the most popular choice is perlite. Perlite is a volcanic byproduct with none of the disposal or health concerns of DE. We will discuss detailed information regarding RMF in Chapter 8.

Cartridge Filters

Cartridge filters are now mostly used for smaller applications in swimming pool filtration. Sand and DE filters use natural media, whereas cartridge filters use artificial media. The filter medium in a cartridge system is a synthetic fabric. The cartridge filter system is small and does a fine job of removing particulate matter. Perhaps the greatest advantage of this system is that water is not wasted during backwashing; cartridge filters are hand-cleaned. The disadvantage of this system is that the filters are difficult to keep clean and wear out quickly.

The Heater

Particularly in a multiuse pool, water temperature is perhaps the most critical variable of all swimming pool factors because different populations require different water temperatures for comfort. A change of only a few degrees in water temperature is significant for patrons, whereas this is not the case for air temperature. When a swimmer is immersed in water, body heat is lost approximately 200 times faster than when surrounded by air of the same temperature. This helps to explain why swimmers become chilled so quickly in water. A pool that is too cold will not attract patrons. A pool that is too warm will not only drive the more competitive swimmers away but will also cost additional money to heat.

The following are temperature ranges for a variety of aquatic activities:

Competitive swimming:	79°F to 81°F
Youth instruction:	83°F to 86°F
Senior citizens and special populations:	84°F to 86°F
Therapeutic swims:	86°F to 90°F

Figure 7.15. Defender® regenerative media filter. (Photo courtesy of Neptune-Benson)

The best compromise temperature for all user groups in a multiuse pool is 82°F to 83°F.

These temperature ranges may not please all patrons, particularly when only one body of water is available. When these activities are conducted indoors, the air temperature should be maintained about 4° to 6° warmer than the water temperature.

Pool heaters are sized to raise water temperature for a given volume between 20°F and 40°F. The rise in temperature should be gradual, approximately 1°/hr. When undersized, a pool heater will heat the water too slowly; when oversized, the cost of installation and operation will increase. Also, an oversized heater requires a lot of space.

The fuel source will vary in geographic regions. Smaller pools often use propane heaters that are designed to heat the water quickly. In some areas, solar heaters are a good heat source.

The following information contains basic information that pool operators may need when dealing with the pool heater.

Thermostat

The thermostat regulates the heater, which in turn heats the pool, and is a temperature control device that shuts off the heater when the water temperature reaches the desired temperature. Turning the dial to the highest setting will not speed up the heating process. The best idea is for the pool operator to set the thermostat for where the water temperature should be and be patient while waiting for results. Only the person in charge of the pool should be allowed to touch the thermostat.

Bypass Valve

Swimming pool heaters are not designed to heat all the water being circulated. The bypass valve maintains a constant flow of water through the heat exchanger, thus preventing damage to the heater components. If the bypass valve is fully open, no pool water is being heated; when the bypass valve is completely closed, all the swimming pool water is targeted for the heater, overloading and perhaps damaging it.

British Thermal Unit

The British thermal unit (BTU) is a measurement used to define the capabilities of heaters. One BTU is capable of raising the temperature of 1 lb of water by 1°.

Heat Exchanger

The heat exchanger is a device with coils, tubes, or plates that absorbs heat from any fluid, liquid, or air and transfers that heat to another fluid (pool water) without intermixing.

Proper water balance (see Chapter 15) is of paramount importance to the operation and longevity of pool heaters. Aggressive water will destroy heater components, whereas scaling water will clog heating elements.

When a pool heater malfunctions, sometimes the solutions are simple:

1. **No water flow to the heater.** The filter, hair and lint-strainer, skimmer, or main drain may be blocked.
2. **No fuel.** The heater's fuel line may be clogged or the fuel tank may be empty. In the case of an electric heater, check the circuit breaker. The gas line pressure may not be within the required operating range.
3. **Thermostat.** This control device may either be turned down or broken.
4. **Timer switch.** Many pool heaters are on a timer. Be certain the toggle switch is turned "on."

Whether sizing a new heater or repairing an existing heater, pool operators should contact a swimming pool supply company or a heating specialist. If electrical work is required, contract a licensed electrician.

Chemical Feeders

Swimming pools are equipped with chemical feeders that add chemicals to the circulation system of the pool to maintain proper chemical levels (Figure 7.16). Faulty feeders can lead to unacceptable chemical levels, leading to pool closure. Erosion feeders, diaphragm pumps, and peristaltic pumps are common pool feeders. Centrifugal pumps are not typically used as chemical feeders.

Erosion feeders operate simply. Solid, slow-dissolving chemicals such as bromine sticks and calcium hypochlorite or trichlor tablets are placed into a special canister in the circulation line through which pool water circulates through the container and slowly dissolves the solid chemical. Chemicals such as dichlor are not placed in an erosion feeder because they dissolve quickly.

> **NOTE: Never add chemicals other than those the manufacturer specifies. The improper use of chemicals in an erosion feeder may lead to a fire or dangerous explosion.**

Although erosion feeders are simple devices, finding the proper placement and plumbing for the feeder is not easy. The high chemical concentration coming from the erosion feeder can damage circulation equipment located downstream. However, placing the erosion feeder away from the pump may cause poor flow through the feeder. Before installing an erosion feeder, pool operators should consult more than one pool specialist.

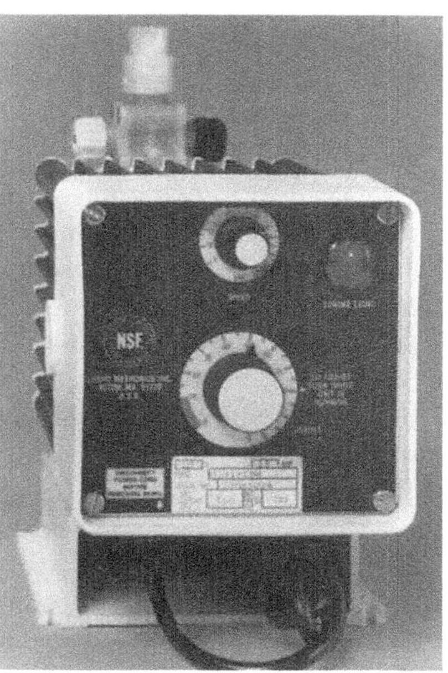

Figure 7.16. A, Peristaltic chemical feed pump is virtually nonclogging because chemicals do not contact pump parts. B, Positive displacement diaphragm chemical feed pump used for liquid chlorine, corrosive acids, and thick polymers. (Photo courtesy of Brock Enterprises, Hamden, CT)

Diaphragm and *peristaltic pumps* have been used to feed chemicals to pools for many years (Figure 7.17). The chemicals that these pumps add to the circulation system should be covered or their gases might corrode the pump. The pump should also be kept away from the chemical vat. Peristaltic pumps seem to be easier to operate because they have no ball and check valves that are notorious for clogging and needing service.

The following description does not discuss the specific mechanics of each pump but is useful. The chemical feeder head is located between two lines of plastic tubing. One line is suction tubing, and the other line is

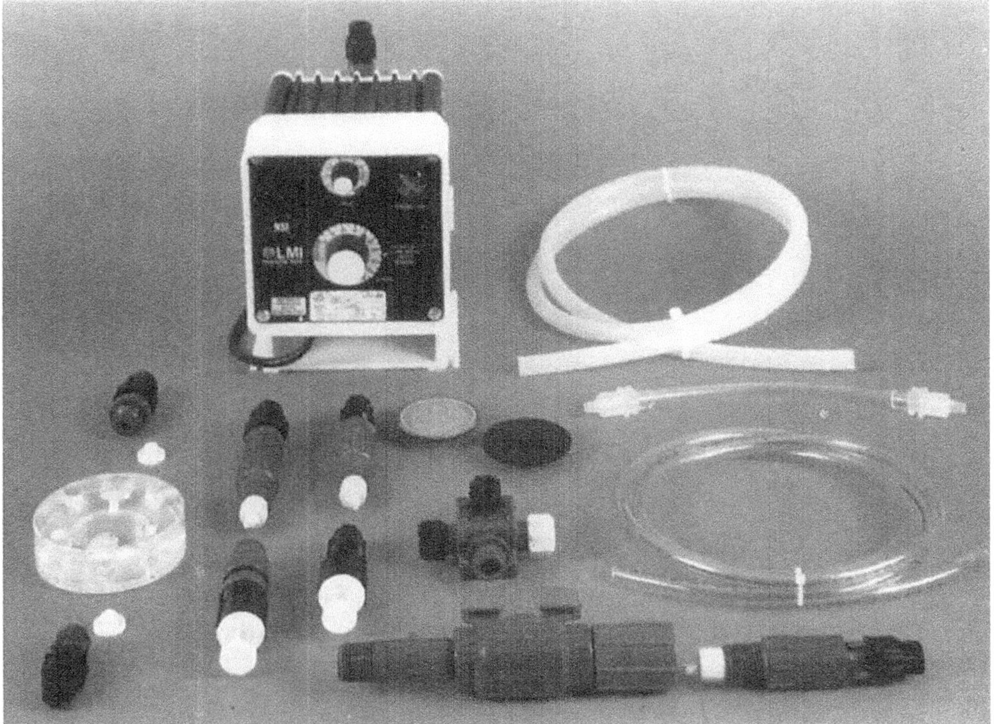

Figure 7.17. Chemical feed pump parts and accessories. (Photo courtesy of Brock Enterprises, Hamden, CT).

pressure or discharge tubing. The chemical feeder head is designed to first create a vacuum in suction tubing, which pulls liquid chemical from a vat into the head and then pushes the chemical through pressure tubing that is connected to the circulation system. Many problems associated with chemical feeders can be attributed to the plastic feeder lines. Each line has a one-way check valve that becomes dirty and must be cleaned or replaced regularly. The end of the suction line that is immersed in liquid is called the foot strainer. The foot strainer is easily clogged, needs to be cleaned often, and may need to be replaced periodically. At the end of the discharge tube is the injector, which also must be cleaned or replaced often.

Both diaphragm and peristaltic pumps, as they are positive feed pumps, need to be cleaned regularly because the feed lines could become pressurized and cause chemical spills if the valves and injectors were to become clogged.

Additionally, the plastic lines themselves often become clogged. The best preventive maintenance for the tubing, valves, and injectors is running a muriatic acid solution (10%) through the chemical feeder and its lines. This must be done with extreme care because muriatic acid and chlorine must not be mixed together. If periodic acid cleaning does not help, the lines and valves should be replaced. Chemical feeders that pump soda ash slurry, DE slurry, and liquid chlorine are particularly susceptible to clogging. Newer pumps have built-in, freshwater flushing devices that prevent clogging.

Inlets

Swimming pool inlets are the last items in the circulation loop through which heated and chemically treated water is finally reintroduced to the pool (Figure 7.18). The best distribution is accomplished through pool bottom or floor inlets. Wall inlets are also used, particularly in smaller pools. Inlets must have covers that are designed to better distribute water and that can be adjusted to direct flow. Inlets can be tested by placing a hand over each inlet to feel for water pressure coming into the pool. A more sophisticated way is to add brightly colored dye in the skimmers or gutters; inlets that are clogged will not show dye coming through them. Blocked inlets can mean pool closures in some states. Inlets are usually made of chrome-plated bronze, plastic, or other corrosion-resistant material.

Valves, Meters, and Gauges

Numerous valves, meters, and gauges are found in the circulation system of the pool. All are important in

A
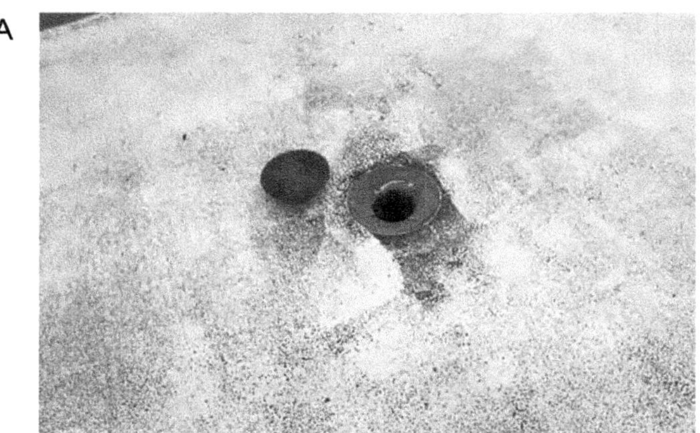

B

C
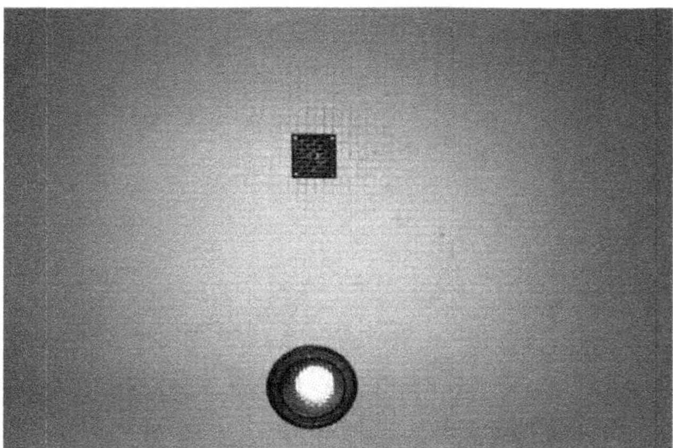

Figure 7.18. A, Bottom inlet for outdoor pool. B and C, Side wall inlet for indoor pool. (Photo courtesy of Steve Manual)

maintaining and adjusting the water circulation of the swimming pool. Valves control the flow of the circulating water and may be ball, gate, butterfly, or float valves. Regardless of the type, valves should be "exercised," that is, opened and closed periodically. This keeps the valves from sticking and prevents scaling and should be done especially for valves that are seldom used.

Gauges usually measure pressure in pounds per square inch. Pressure gauges monitor filtering efficiency by measuring pressure going into (influent) pressure filters and coming out of (effluent) filters. Vacuum filters use vacuum gauges.

Perhaps the most important reading in a filter room regarding circulation comes from the flow meter (Figure 7.19). The location of the flow meter is extremely important. For accurate readings, the flow meter should be placed on a long, straight, uninterrupted length of pipe, free of elbows, gauges, and other instruments. Flow meters should be selected on their ability to be read, removed, cleaned, and replaced. Flow meters are required in most municipalities and read in gallons per minute.

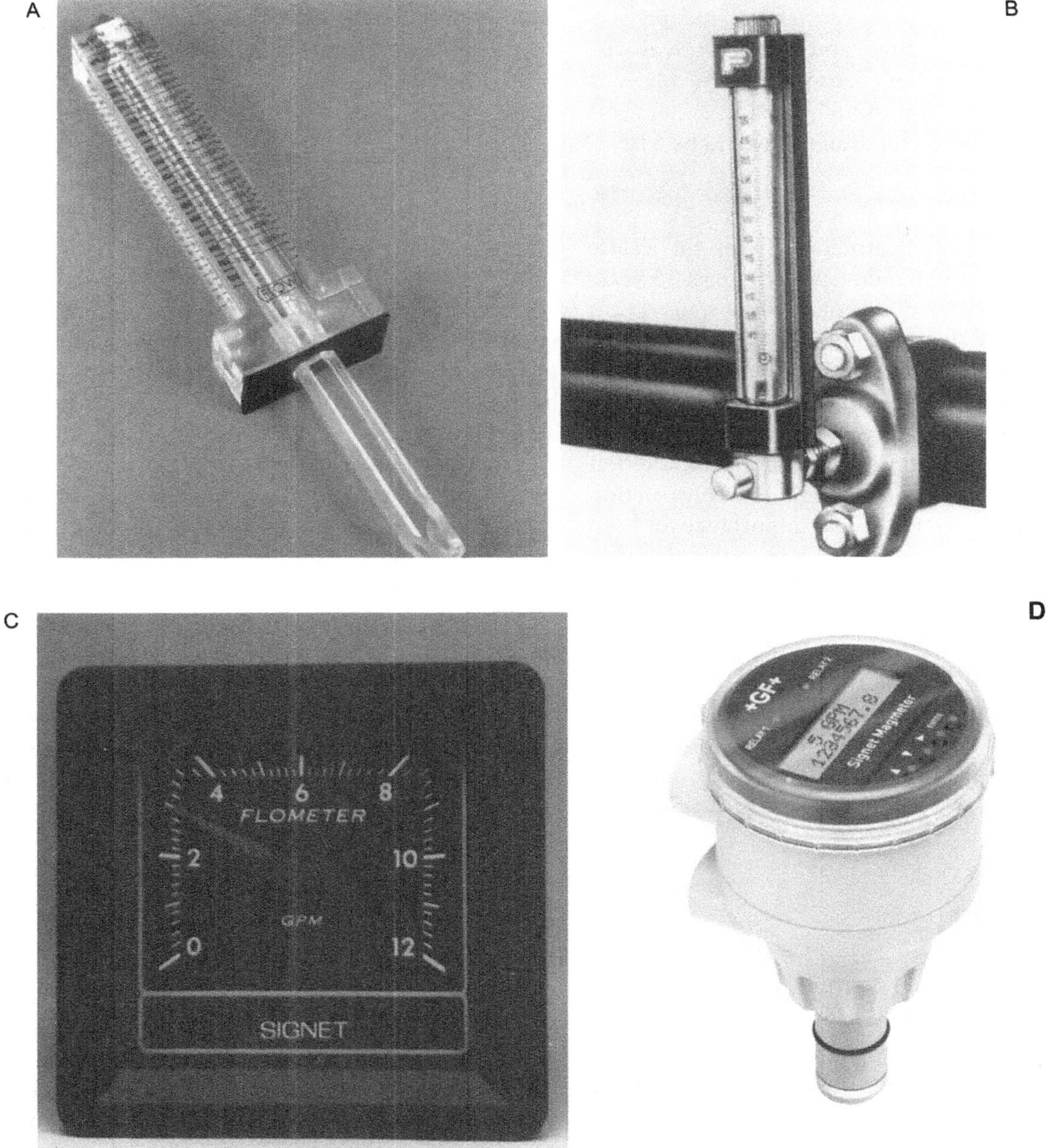

Figure 7.19. A, Economy flow meter is inexpensive. B, Direct impact flow meter is accurate and reliable. C, This flow meter is easy to read, accurate, and reliable. D, Insertion style magnetic flow meter with digital display. (Photos A, B, and C courtesy of Brock Enterprises, Hamden, CT. Photo D courtesy of Water Technology, Inc.)

Flow meters should be removed and cleaned with an acid solution periodically. Most flow meters require a rubber or Teflon gasket to prevent leakage. Once a flow meter is installed, it remains reliable as long as it is kept clean. Additionally, if a flow meter is installed backwards, that is, the impact tube is not facing into the flow of water, no water will enter the tube; thus, the meter will not indicate flow. If the flow meter is clean and installed properly and the reading is low, then the pump, filters, hair and lint strainers, and other components of the circulation system should be checked immediately. As with many other circulation components, a nonfunctioning flow meter may lead to closure of the pool. Inexpensive flow meters are not as accurate and do not work as well as the more expensive types. Because the flow meter is vital to the daily operation of a circulation system, investing in the best flow meter available would be wise.

Design of Leisure Pool Filtration Systems

The design of water-treatment systems for leisure pools has progressed tremendously in the past 15 years (Figure 7.20). Widespread use of shallow-water pools for leisure use and activities, combined with high swimmer loads, has resulted in treatment systems much larger than those installed in conventional pools.

Many components comprise the successful design of a leisure pool, whether indoor or outdoor. In addition to special features, the proper design and construction of the filtration system is of utmost importance for both owner and operator. The real lesson here is that there are no inexpensive routes or shortcuts to safe, clean, sparkling water for your facility guests.

It is important to keep in mind that filtration and disinfection are two separate issues; they do, however, become dependent upon each other during this complex process.

Figure 7.20. A family aquatic leisure center with a competitive pool. (Photo courtesy of Counsilman-Hunsaker)

The distinction between indoor and outdoor leisure pools is a valuable point of discussion that needs to occur for a proper design. Indoor and outdoor pools alike need to filter out particulate matter and, at the same time, disinfect the water. This certainly seems straightforward enough, especially if one is still thinking in terms of the traditional pool with its high water volume and a relatively light bather load.

But the products of high body loads need to be removed more quickly and efficiently than ever. This high load is common to both indoor and outdoor pools. Although there are some similarities, each type of pool is faced with different challenges that must be considered for the proper design of the filtration system.

Turnover

The discussion of turnover (the amount of time required to pump the nominal pool-water volume once through the filtration system) is one that will generate different opinions from designers, contractors and clients.

At a high (or fast) turnover, the treatment system is capable of dealing with large amounts of particulate matter and contaminants. There is a price to be paid to handle the higher flow, however, in terms of the filter area and the number of filter vessels required. The result may very well be an increase in the required mechanical space. An example: For a 100,000-gallon pool with a six-hour turnover, the flow is 278 gallons per minute (gpm), while the flow for the same pool with a two-hour turnover is 833 gpm.

The increased flow requires larger pipes, more supply inlets to distribute the treated water and a properly sized return system to feed the used water back to the filtration plant. The higher flows (with the correspondingly larger piping), the increased space requirement in the mechanical room, and the increased size and/or number of filters have become common in today's successful leisure-pool facilities.

Some of the more progressive state health departments have begun developing guidelines for leisure facilities that aim to lower the number of design variances required. As part of those guidelines, they recognize the importance of lower turnovers and are attempting to develop rules to govern that issue. The ANSI/APSP-9 guidelines will also address turnovers. The design industry has developed some unwritten turnover-time guidelines that have been used on many past and proposed indoor and outdoor facilities. See Table 7.2.

Table 7.2

Turnover Time Guidelines

Type of Pool	Outdoor	Indoor
Spray areas	15 to 30 min.	15 to 30 min.
Children's activities	15 to 30 min.	15 to 30 min.
Slide pool	1 hr.	30 min. to 1 hr.
Tube ride	1 to 2 hrs.	30 min. to 1 hr.
Zero-depth pool	1 to 2 hrs.	30 min. to 1 hr.
Activity pool	1 to 2 hrs.	1 hr.
Wave pool	1 to 2 hrs.	1 hr.
Slow/action river	2 to 3 hrs.	1 to 2 hrs.

One can see that these times are dramatically lower faster than the traditional six to eight hours used in the past. They are, however, required to maintain clean water with high bather loads.

Filtration

For all filtration systems, regardless of the type of filter(s) used, the filter size is based on turnover and the associated flow per square foot of filter area.

At the previously calculated flow of 833 gpm (for a 100,000-gallon pool with a two-hour turnover) and a filtration rate of 8.5 gpm/sf, one requires 98 square feet of filter area, equivalent to two 96-inch-diameter single cell vertical filters or three 48-by-96 inch horizontal filters.

At a flow of 15 gpm/sf, one needs 56 square feet of filter area, meaning one 102-inch single cell vertical filter or two 48-by-72 inch horizontal filters.

If a full ozone system is used for additional disinfection, taller vertical tanks with special ozone linings are recommended.

All filters are based upon a specified flow in gallons per minute (gpm) and square foot (sf) of filter area. Pressure sand filters, depending on their design, will handle from 3 to 20 gpm/sf, as do vacuum sand filters (open tank filters). Diatomaceous earth (DE) filters, with a much thinner active filter depth through the coated leaves (or septums), typically are rated at 1 to 2.5 gpm/sf.

Flow rates for all filters are set by an independent testing agency; the most prominent in the United States is the National Sanitation Foundation. Approved filters are listed in an NSF publication that provides sizes, models and flows that have been tested. Today, most local health departments recognize the NSF as the accepted standard.

The most common type of filtration in the United States is pressure sand filtration. It is primarily used for ease of operation, space efficiency and durability.

Some of the most successful applications use the midrange filtration rates of 7.5 to 12 gpm/sf, which result in excellent efficiencies for the removal of particulate matter, allowing the sand bed to hold larger amounts of dirt, and extending the backwash cycle.

Backwashing can be a frequent occurrence for these leisure facilities, depending upon the bather load, although that is not necessarily a nuisance, it may actually be a benefit because some dilution with fresh makeup water is effective in handling the heavy bather loads, both with respect to particulates and bacteriological contaminants.

Indoor and Outdoor

Bather Load
Estimate the projected daily attendance. Is the facility properly sized, or will it be overloaded from Day One?

Backwash Discharge
Today, many cities and public agencies require that chlorinated backwash water go to sanitary sewer lines with limited capacity, which may require a holding tank for an adequate discharge rate. If such a proper discharge rate capability is not provided, it may result in a "short cycling backwash" by the operator that can reduce the efficiency of the filter in a very short time.

Composition of Makeup Water
High iron and/or manganese concentrations, high chloramines levels from the water treatment facility—these are among the contaminants that can make operations a challenge if not accounted for in the design phase. It's also important to understand the water parameters to select the proper disinfectant and method of pH control.

Outdoor

Pool Location
Rural or urban? This is important for estimating the potential amount of external contaminants, such as blowing soil or other products that may settle on the water's surface.

Suntan Oils
What are the amounts of oils and other skin-care products that will need to be dealt with? It is hoped that some can be removed prior to filtration because they will certainly affect the efficiency of the operation.

Indoor

The indoor pool area becomes an environment of its own. While there are none (or fewer) of the airborne particulate contaminants with which outdoor pools must contend, some interesting challenges arise.

HVAC System

The design of the heating, ventilating, and air conditioning system becomes an essential element toward the success of the facility (Figure 7.21).

The most powerful filtration and disinfection systems available will not perform adequately if the basic chemistry byproducts and airborne contaminants are not removed from the enclosure. That is less important in lightly used, high water volume facilities with low water temperatures (in the range of 79 to 82 degrees Fahrenheit) than in highly frequented, low water volume facilities with higher water temperatures (between 85 and 90 degrees).

Higher temperatures generally mean higher evaporation rates, higher bacteriological activity, higher heat loss and, if not properly exhausted, stale, uncomfortable air that may lead to health concerns for patrons and staff. As if that were not enough, research has indicated that some chemical off-gases can actually be reabsorbed into the water, resulting in very interesting operations problems.

It is essential in the design of indoor pool facilities that the number of air changes per hour is carefully considered along with the proportions of fresh air entering the facility. The special operating condition of the indoor aquatic facilities require the marriage of proper water treatment, oxidation, and disinfection along with air quality to achieve a successful facility.

Summary

Although the pump and the filter receive the most attention in the circulation system of a pool, at least a dozen other components require daily attention. All circulation components must be continually monitored to ensure good water clarity and quality, particularly hair and lint strainers, the chemical feed pumps, and the flow meter.

References

Mitchel, K. (1988). *The proper management of pool and spa water*. Decatur, GA: BioLab.

Pool Water Treatment Advisory Group. (1995). *Swimming pool water: Treatment and quality standards*. Norfolk, United Kingdom: Author.

Bibliography

Gabrielson, A. M. (1987). *Swimming pools: A guide to their planning, design, and operation* (4th ed.). Champaign, IL: Human Kinetics.

Mitchel, K. (1988). *The proper management of pool and spa water*. Decatur, GA: BioLab.

Pope, J. R., Jr. (1991). *Public swimming pool management, I and II*. Alexandria, VA: National Recreation and Park Association.

Recreonics. (1991). *Buyers' guide and operations handbook: Catalog no. 41*. Indianapolis, IN: Author.

Williams, K. G., & Young, R. A. (Eds.). (2011). *Aquatic facility operator manual* (6th ed.). Ashburn, VA: National Recreation and Park Association.

Figure 7.21. Indoor HVAC System (Photo courtesy of Water Technology, Inc.)

8 Filtration

Key Concepts

- Sand filtration
- High rate sand
- Sand and gravel
- Pressure filters
- Vacuum filters
- Filter rates
- Channeling
- Mud balls
- Freeboard
- Backwashing
- Flocculants
- Multiport valves
- Diatomaceous earth
- Regenerative media
- Precoat
- Slurry feeding
- Filter septa
- Cartridge filters

A key to good filtration is the ability of the filter media to screen and trap dirt. Different filter media have different entrapment capabilities. Before we discuss each filter type specifically, we will more closely examine filter media. The following chart illustrates how effectively different media filter swimming pool water.

Grain of table salt	90 to 100 microns
Human hair	70 microns
Visible to the naked eye	35 microns
Sand filtering capability	20 to 25 microns
Talcum powder	5 to 10 microns
Cartridge filtering capability	5 to 10 microns
Red blood cells	8 microns
Average bacteria	2 microns
DE filtering capability	1 to 3 microns

Note. 1 micron is equal to .0000394 in. or 1 millionth of a meter.

Filters that do not allow particles of 15 microns or larger to pass through produce outstanding water clarity. Water clarity results from a lack of turbidity, which is colloidal or particulate matter in suspension. A nephelometer measures water clarity by assigning turbidity units. Good water clarity does not exceed 0.5 nephelometer turbidity units. Remember, when the view of the pool bottom becomes obstructed because of poor water clarity, the pool should be closed.

We will discuss different filtration systems including sand, diatomaceous earth, regenerative media, and cartridge (Figure 8.1).

Sand Filtration

Although sand filters are perhaps the most widely used filters in the swimming pool industry because they are the easiest to use, they are probably the least efficient for trapping dirt. The permanence of sand as a medium and the ease of backwashing are reasons for their popularity. When maintained properly, sand filters produce high water clarity. The faster the water travels through the filter, the lower the filtration efficiency. Slower filtering rates and deeper filtering beds of sand naturally keep more dirt in the filter and out of the pool.

Sand filters use a sand medium that seldom needs to be replaced, and they come in many designs. Sand filters include pressure sand and gravel, pressure high rate sand, vacuum sand, and in rare instances, gravity sand. We will also discuss alternatives to sand in this section.

Pressure Sand and Gravel

Between the 1920s and 1950s, large sand and gravel filters were used to filter the water in many swimming pools throughout the United States. In this filter system, sand is layered on top of gravel and stone of different sizes. The filters are extremely large and require large quantities of sand and gravel in the filters and a great deal of space in the filter room to store them.

Pressure sand and gravel filters are often called "rapid" sand filters, but compared with today's filtering rates, old sand and gravel filters are slow. The old rapid sand filters have filtering rates that vary from 1.5 to 5 GPM/sq ft of filter surface area, whereas popular high rate sand filter systems of today filter at a rate of 12 to 20 GPM/sq ft of filter surface area. In discussions of conventional sand and gravel filters, the term *rapid* should probably be avoided. Too many pool operators confuse rapid filters with high rate filters, thinking they are the same, when they are significantly different.

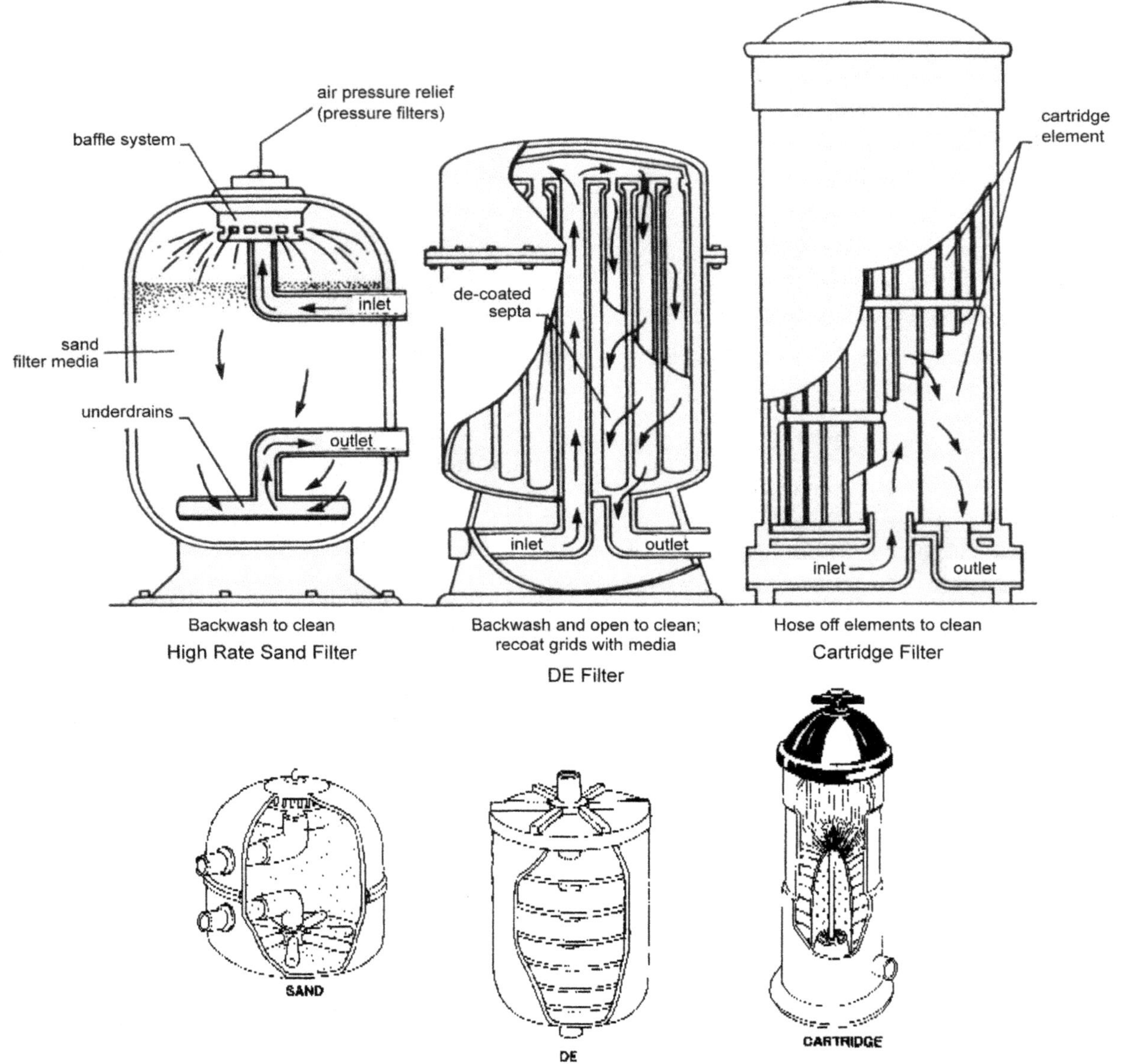

Figure 8.1. Types of pool and spa filters. (Courtesy of ©The Association of Pool & Spa Professionals, 2014)

Sand and gravel filters are rarely installed in today's pools because they are too large, too costly, and require extensive amounts of time and water to backwash. Only older, larger pools still use pressure sand and gravel filters. In many cases, sand and gravel filters in older pools have filter tanks that are taller and wider than the pool operator. For instance, a 180,000-gal pool would require two sand and gravel filters, 11 ft in diameter.

We will discuss the dynamics of the pressure sand and gravel filters in the following paragraphs. Sand and gravel systems are usually found in banks of between two and four filters, with most pools having three filters. The filters may be positioned either vertically or horizontally (Figure 8.2).

By definition, water enters a closed pressure tank containing sand and gravel. The water enters the top of the tank through a distributor or baffle. At this point, the water is spread out evenly with a showerhead plumbing arrangement so that the incoming water does not disrupt or "channel" through the filter bed. The water then travels downward through the top layer of sand and then through the gravel and stone. When the water finally arrives at the bottom of the tank, it is pushed out of the filter through perforated underdrains, or "laterals," which collect the filtered water and return it to the pool. Before the filtered water is returned to the pool, it is heated and then treated. The top layer of sand is 12 to 20 in. deep, but the majority of filtering is accomplished in the first three inches. The particle size of the sand should be between 0.4 and 0.6 mm, which is approximately a #20 sand.

Filtering rates for pressure sand and gravel filters vary, but on average, sand and gravel filters water at a

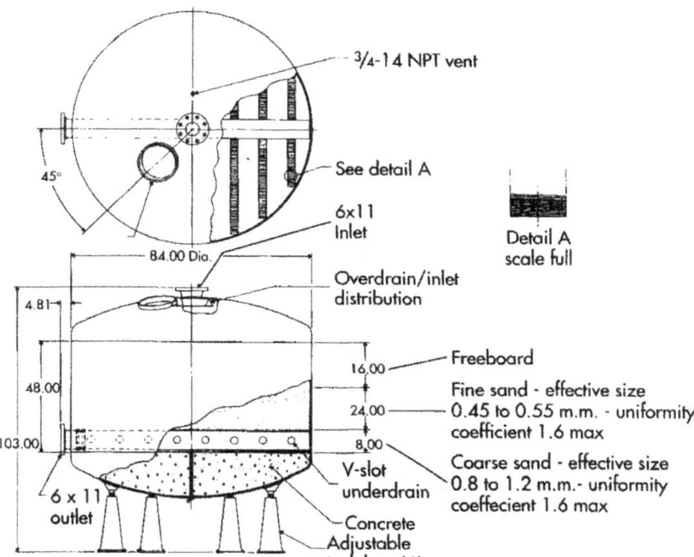

Figure 8.2. Conventional sand and gravel (rapid rate) filter. (Courtesy of Filtrex, Wayne,NJ)

rate of approximately 3 GPM/sq ft of surface area. This is a relatively slow filtering rate.

Freeboard refers to the amount of air space between the top of the sand and the ceiling of the tank. This freeboard is necessary because during the backwash cycle, sand and water are forcefully displaced upward. For backwashing, this extra room allows the filter media to "expand."

Backwashing refers to cleaning pressure filter systems by reversing the flow of water in the filter tank and pushing the accumulated dirt to waste. Backwashing should be performed before filtering effectiveness becomes impaired. An extremely dirty filter will be accompanied by a significant pressure increase inside the tank and a drop in the filter flow rate. The manufacturer's recommendation should be followed for backwashing. When the pressure difference between the water pressure going into the filter (influent) and the water pressure leaving the filter (effluent) reaches a predetermined point, the filters should be backwashed. Many filters are not backwashed until a pressure differential of at least 5 psi occurs. Backwashing every Saturday, for instance, is not a recommended practice unless the swimmer load is consistent during the week. A dirty filter can often be an effective filter because dirt helps to filter dirt.

One problem associated with backwashing a pressure sand and gravel system is that the backwashing flow rate must be about 4 times greater than the filtering flow rate. Backwashing flow rates must be maintained between 12 and 15 GPM to remove all the dirt from the filters. This is in contrast to the normal filtering flow rate of 3 GPM. Such high backwashing rates can be attained by backwashing each filter in this system individually and successively. This is accomplished by isolating each tank so that backwash water only travels through one tank at a time. Backwashing all the filters in a sand and gravel system may last from 15 to 30 minutes.

Many pool operators keep the flow of water reversed until the backwash water, as viewed through a sight glass tube, becomes clear. Not surprisingly, backwashing sand and gravel filters is costly in terms of time and water. Conversely, lengthening the backwash cycle introduces much more water to the pool for healthy dilution.

Flocculants are sometimes added to the top of the sand and gravel filters to assist in the filtering process. Flocculants such as aluminum sulfate create a gelatinous mass that floats on top of the filter and collects additional dirt. Flocculants are used only in conjunction with pressure sand and gravel filter systems, and this is somewhat difficult to do well; good flocs are dependent on the right pH.

The top layer of sand in a pressure sand and gravel system may encounter problems. Most of these problems are caused by ineffective backwashing flow rates. *Mud balls* may form by a combination of hair, lint, and other organic materials. *Channeling* is caused by holes in the sand bed that can result in and lead to poor filtration. *Calcification* of the sand layer may also occur when the pool water is not balanced, particularly regarding high levels of calcium hardness and total alkalinity. To prevent these problems, the sand should be raked clean and inspected once a year. Maintaining balanced water and proper backwashing rates is sufficient to avoid these problems.

In summary, sand and gravel filters produce finely filtered water. They typically have long filter cycles, which means backwashing less frequently, and sand media last at least 10 years, if not longer. But as sand and gravel systems age, they are often replaced by newer, more advanced filtering systems that take up less room and are far less costly to purchase and install.

Dr. Tom's Tip

If you still have older sand and gravel filters, do not get rid of them until absolutely necessary. Chances are the new filtration system will not produce water clarity equivalent to the older, larger sand system. When you finally have to replace the sand and gravel system with high rate sand, get bigger and larger tanks with more sand.

High Rate Sand

High rate sand filters became popular in the late 1950s and early 1960s primarily because of the reduction in both size and cost of the equipment (Figure 8.3). High rate sand systems filter and backwash at approximately the same rate, which is between 15 and 20 gal/sq ft of surface area. Because of these high filtering rates, less sand in smaller tanks is required, thus significant space is saved. Backwashing can also be accomplished in 5 to 7 minutes because all tanks are backwashed simultaneously.

High rate sand filters use *depth filtration*; that is, they use the entire sand bed to trap dirt. Cartridge and diatomaceous earth (DE) filters use only the surface of the media. Sand and gravel filters use the top 3 to 4 in. of sand.

Freeboard in a high rate sand filter can vary, but too much sand in the filter tank will find its way back to the pool through inlets during the backwash cycle. An insufficient amount of sand will result in a filtering bed that is too small to trap sufficient amounts of dirt.

Mud balls, channeling, and calcification of the filter bed can also occur in high rate sand filters, but generally these problems are easier to correct because of the smaller size of the tank and the increased accessibility to the filter bed. High rate sand filters require the sand replaced more often than other filters. This is because the individual sand granules in this system become smooth and lose their ability to trap dirt at high filtering rates. The sand life in a high rate sand filter will vary from pool to pool but should last 3 to 7 years.

Some high rate sand filter systems have oversized pumps. When this occurs, channeling results and the

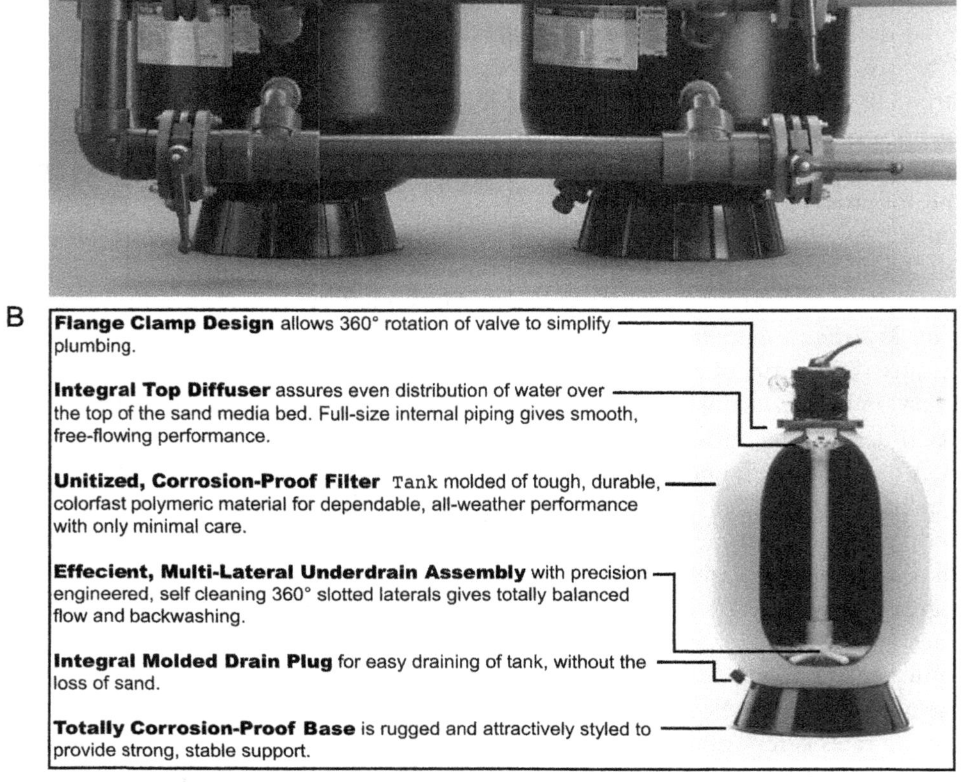

Figure 8.3. A, Commercial high rate sand filters. B, Residential pool high rate sand filters. A, Photo courtesy of Pac-Fab, Sanford, NC. (B, Photo courtesy of Hayward Pool Products, Elizabeth, NJ)

powerful pool pump pushes the dirt through the filter and back into the pool. If the pump size is in question, the pool operator should contact a local pool company or pump dealer.

Backwashing should be performed whenever the flow of water becomes restricted through the filter because of an accumulation of dirt. This usually occurs when the pressure differential between the influent pressure gauge and the effluent pressure gauge on the filters reaches between 15 and 20 psi. However, the manufacturer's recommendations should always be followed.

As mentioned previously, dirt in the filter helps to trap dirt that comes from the pool. Backwashing too often will keep the sand too clean and allow dirt to pass through the filter bed. Not backwashing enough will cause the flow rate to drop and will result in cloudy water.

Some swimming pools, especially smaller pools such as pools found in private residences, have only one high rate sand filter tank. Many companies now manufacture a multiport valve that requires owners and operators to turn a handle to control all circulation functions (Figure 8.4).

Figure 8.4. Multiport valve.

The various functions controlled by the multiport valve are clearly marked on the top of the tank and include the following items.

Filter

The circulation system is in the filter mode most of the time. The filtering cycle is used for normal filtration and is also used for vacuuming in some pools.

Backwash

Backwash is used for cleaning dirty filter media. Some high rate sand filters are backwashed when the pressure in the tank increases by 6 to 8 psi beyond the starting pressure. To backwash a multiport filter tank, the pump must be turned off first. The dial is then turned from "filter" to "backwash," and the pump is restarted. When the backwash water leaving the filter turns clear, as evidenced through the sight glass, the pump is turned off before the dial is reset.

Rinse

The rinse cycle is used following each backwash. Once the dial is positioned to "rinse," the pump is restarted and filter media are rinsed clean for 30 to 60 seconds.

Waste

The waste mode is used to bypass the filter when draining or lowering the pool level and for vacuuming unusually heavy debris. During this cycle, the water leaves the pool and goes directly to waste.

Recirculate

The recirculate cycle moves the water through the swimming pool system by bypassing the filter. This cycle is often used when adding chemicals.

Closed

When the filter is below the deck level, pool water may be lost if the filter is not closed when the pump is not running. This mode is used only when the pump is turned off.

Vacuuming

The vacuuming cycle is used for vacuuming directly back into the filter. Water is returned to the pool during vacuuming in this cycle. Vacuuming directly to waste, particularly with heavy debris, may be wise.

In some regions, backwash can be recycled for gardening, washing cars, or other uses. Chlorine levels in backwashed water dissipates rapidly, particularly if it is sprayed out of the system. However, health codes must be checked before treated swimming pool water is reused.

Vacuum Sand

The original vacuum sand filters used in the swimming pool industry, also known as gravity sand filters, filtered water slowly and required a lot of room. Today's vacuum sand systems are open high rate filter systems that allow the pool operator to view the filter media and water flowing through the filter (Figure 8.5). As mentioned previously, this arrangement does not have a hair and lint strainer because the pump follows the filter.

Many vacuum sand filter systems come in two configurations: "wet well–dry well" or "wet well only." The filter tank is a large open rectangular tank, usually made of stainless steel to resist corrosion. The wet well houses the filtering sand, and the adjacent dry well contains the required piping, gauges, valves, and controls. A collection manifold, or lateral, is located at the bottom of the sand. The sand in the vacuum filter tank is as much as 8 ft below the water level of the pool. To protect the surface of the filter bed, a water flow diversion screen is placed just above the sand bed. The filter tank provides ample space between the sand bed and the top of the filter tank. This extra space serves as a surge tank to store water when excessive bather loads are experienced. Water flows by gravity from the pool outlets to the wet well with sand media, and then the pump draws the water through the sand and pushes it back to the pool. The pump is located in the dry well adjacent to the sand in the wet well. Vacuum sand filters can filter up to 20 gal/min/sq ft of surface area. This filter also uses most of the filter bed for filtering. Backwashing can be accomplished in as little as 2 minutes.

The vacuum sand is a rugged, efficient, and low maintenance system. It allows for easy inspection, access, and maintenance of the filter bed. One disadvantage of the vacuum system is the dry well, which houses the recirculation equipment. To access this equipment, the pool operator must use a ladder to climb down into the dry well. Once in the dry well, the operator has little room in which to work. However, newer vacuum sand systems do not have the dry well, and the recirculation equipment can be set up in an open and accessible mechanical room.

New Alternatives to Sand Filtration

Alternatives have been introduced to sand filter technology: zeolite and recycled glass. Zeolite has been used since the time of Julius Caesar, but only recently in swimming pool filtration. Zeolite uses a combination of natural minerals and volcanic material rather than sand to fill the filter tank. According to manufacturers, zeolite collects more dirt and traps ammonia in the media. Lacking ammonia in the pool means significantly less chloramine production in the pool. Zeolite filtration produces improved water clarity and significantly reduces chloramines. Some suggest *recycled glass* as a replacement for sand because it is lighter and supposedly the sharper edges of the glass catch more dirt.

DE Filtration

DE filters use the fossilized skeletal remains of marine life, sometimes referred to as diatoms. DE is a white powder composed of billions of microscopic skeletons that are millions of years old. Under a microscope, DE resembles small sponges or snowflakes. Each diatom is actually 90% air space and only 10% fossil. DE filtration produces superior water clarity because of the ability of this irregular-shaped filter medium to screen out the smallest of particles. Unlike sand, DE filters dirt by trapping dirt within DE pores and holes, as well as between particles.

DE is a light, porous white powder that clings to the fiber filter septa and allows water, but not dirt, to pass through the media before returning to the pool. The filter elements come in many shapes and sizes. Tubes or cylinders are often used in pressure systems, whereas rectangular and circular leafs are common in vacuum systems. Most DE filters are designed to filter at 1 to 3 GPM/sq ft of surface area.

Although DE produces great water clarity, as a medium, it is temporary, meaning it must be replaced often. Many DE filters require new DE after every backwashing. In addition, the filter septa to which the DE filter cake clings must be cleaned periodically. Disposing of old DE is becoming more of a problem in many municipalities throughout the United States. Finally, when handling DE, pool operators must wear protective masks so that they do not inhale the diatoms.

We will discuss the following DE filters: the pressure system, which uses a closed, pressurized tank; the regenerative DE filter, which is also a pressure system and readjusts the DE in the tank to extend filter cycles; and the vacuum system, which uses an open tank. The filter septa to which the DE clings are composed of porous fabrics that come in many shapes and sizes. DE leafs and discs filter on two sides instead of one. The DE filter septa hold the DE but allow filtered water to pass through. Manifolds are attached between filter elements (septa) that allow the filtered water to return to the pool.

Pressure DE

DE is a temporary filtering medium, whereas sand is a permanent medium. This difference is highlighted during the backwashing cycle. Although the filtering process for pressure and regenerative DE filters is similar to pressure sand systems, the backwashing cycle is significantly different. Pressure DE filters reverse the flow of water for backwashing, but when this is done, the DE in the tank is flushed out to waste and must be replaced (Figure 8.5). Thus, new DE must be placed on the filter septa after each cleaning, requiring additional work. This new coating of DE is called the "precoat" and must be

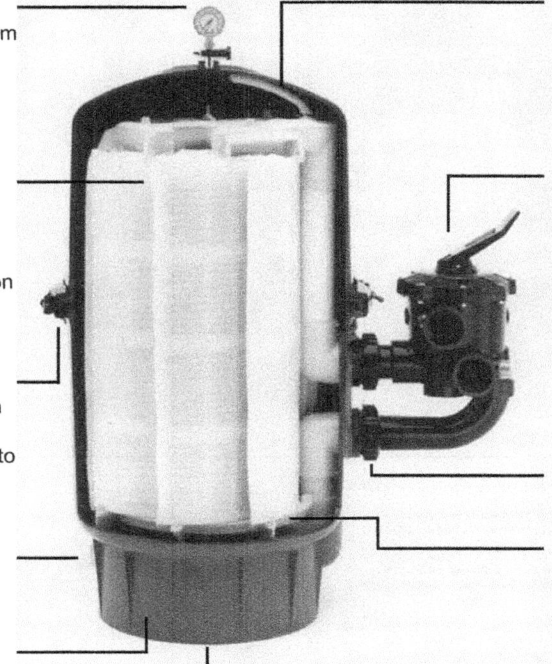

Figure 8.5. Vertical grid pressure DE filter. (Photo courtesy of Hayward Pool Products, Elizabeth, NJ)

accomplished slowly and evenly. The plumbing layout of pressure DE systems is almost identical to the plumbing layout of pressure sand systems because the hair and lint strainer and pump precede the filter. Both the sand and DE pressure filters are enclosed in tanks, so the difference is somewhat subtle to the untrained eye. Additionally, the filter septa are difficult to inspect and to clean in pressure DE systems.

Before purchasing or installing a pressure DE system, the pool operator must ensure the filter septa are easily accessible.

Regenerative Media Filters

Regenerative media filters (RMF) add a feature that extends the life of precoat media in pressure RMF filters (Figure 8.6). Precoat media filters operate on the premise of surface filtration. Because of this, only approximately 10% of the filtering capability is attained. Removing the media from the septa with the surface dirt and particles within the filter tank allows the media to be reused, significantly extending filter cycles.

Under normal operating procedures as the precoat media accumulate dirt, an increased resistance (pressure differential) to flow is experienced. "Bumping" forces water through the inside of the tubes, causing media and dirt into suspension within the tank. During the regeneration cycle, the individual media particles and trapped surface dirt realign on the filter septa, creating new void spaces facing the influent water. Bumping the filter in this fashion recycles media to extend filter cycles before recharging (backwashing) is required. This regeneration process returns filtration to near the original resistance. An RMF should be bumped at least once daily, regardless of pressure. This daily bump slows the buildup of oils and dirt on media surfaces, extending filtration cycles.

RMF may be bumped multiple times before recharging is necessary. Therefore, recharging does not occur nearly as often with an RMF system as with a typical precoat media system, thereby saving significant water, chemicals, time, and money.

Filters without the mechanical bump feature can be regenerated by shutting off the pump, closing influent and effluent valves for several minutes, and allowing media to fall off by gravity. This may work with fresh media, but once oils and dirt accumulate on the surface, this method is ineffective as media will cling to the septa.

Figure 8.7 illustrates the four cycles of regenerative DE filtration.

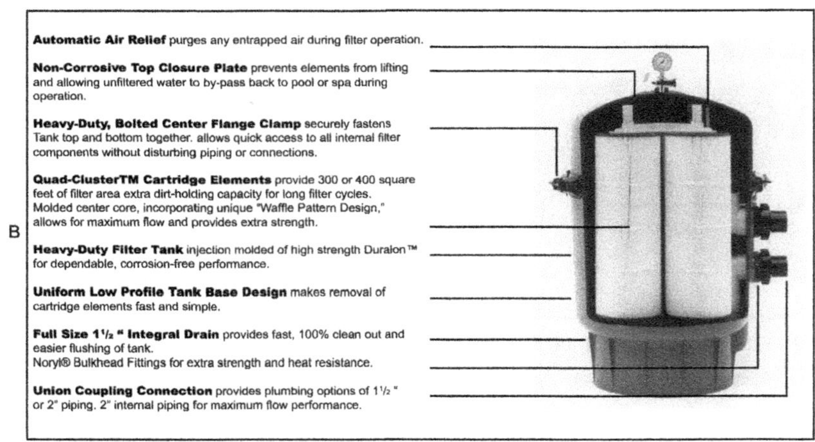

Figure 8.6. A, Pleated, cylindrical cartridge filters of various sizes. B, Cartridge filters. (A, Photo courtesy of Brock Enterprises, Hamden, CT. B, Photo courtesy of Hayward Pool Products, Elizabeth, NJ)

Precoat mode

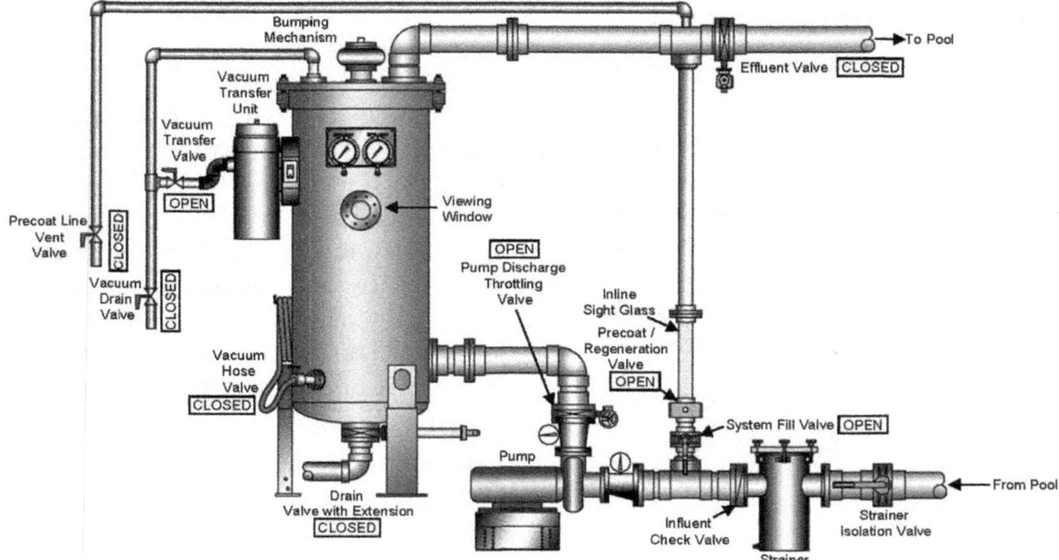

Figure 8.7. Four cycles of regenerative DE filtration. *(cont.)* (Courtesy of Neptune-Benson)

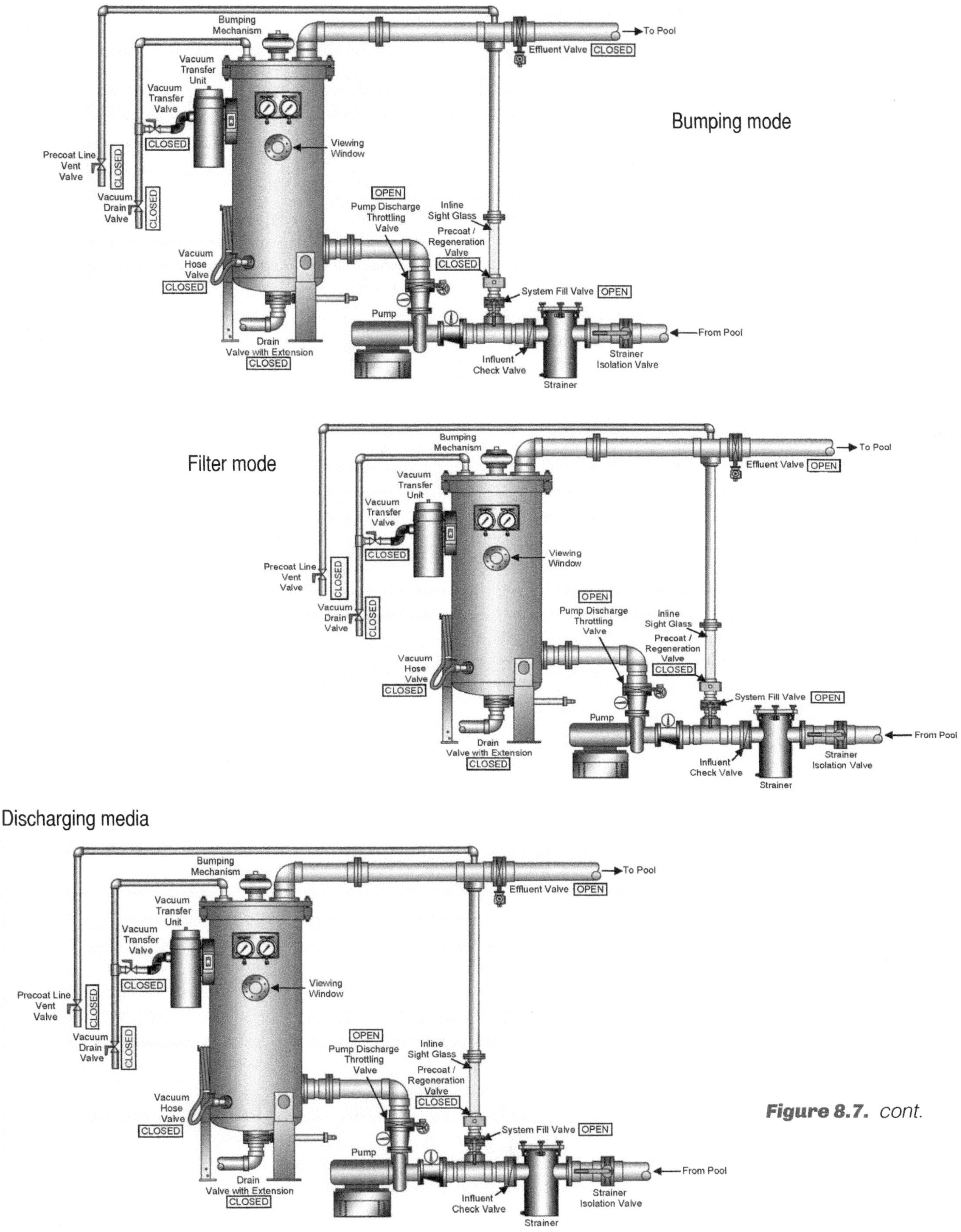

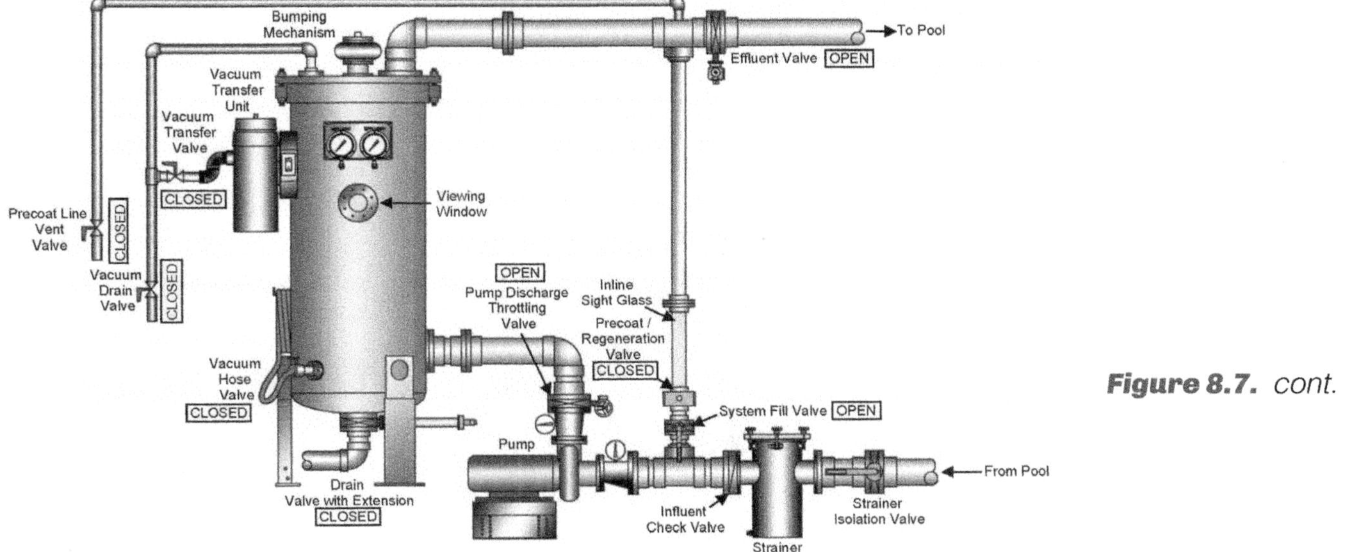

Figure 8.7. *cont.*

Vacuum DE Systems

DE vacuum filters use open tanks with the pool pump following the filter tank (Figure 8.8). No hair and lint strainer is required because the filter protects the pump. The major difference between the DE and sand vacuum systems is how the filter elements are cleaned. Concerning vacuum DE systems, when the filter media become dirty, they are manually hosed off the filter elements. *Backwashing* is not an accurate term to describe cleaning vacuum DE filters because the flow of swimming pool water is not reversed to clean the filter media.

An advantage of this system is that the filter elements, as well as the DE filter cake, can be easily inspected. As the white DE becomes dark brown, pool operators can get a better feel concerning when to backwash. Additionally, if the filter elements have holes that allow DE to pass back into the pool, this problem can be easily detected and repaired. Cleaning the filter septa also becomes easier because the filter elements are easier to remove.

Because DE is the only temporary filter medium we discuss in this text, we will discuss several unique features associated with DE.

Filter Cake

Filter cake is the DE layer that clings to the filter septa or leaves and strains the dust, algae, oil, and other swimming pool debris. The filter cake catches almost everything that passes through it, including large bacteria, and produces outstanding water clarity as a result.

Precoat

Precoat refers to the layer of filtering DE placed on the filter septa to initiate the filtering process or after each backwashing or filter cleaning. Precoating filter cake should be between $\frac{1}{16}$ and $\frac{1}{8}$ in. thick. The amount of DE needed in a DE filter is measured by volume instead of weight. Although many formulas are available, a good rule of thumb is a 1-lb coffee can of DE for every 5 sq ft of filter area. If a 40-sq ft DE filter needs to be recharged, it would require approximately eight cans of DE. Many methods of precoating can be used, but most include recirculating the water within the tank without sending it back to the pool.

Slurry Feeding

Slurry feeding is a procedure used to extend the filter cycle on DE systems. During normal filtration, the porous DE becomes saturated with dirt quickly and eventually becomes impervious. This occurs more quickly during heavy swimmer loads. Small amounts of diluted DE added to the system help the older DE to catch dirt. Slurry feeding systems must be designed so that the mixing equipment does not damage the fragile DE. High-speed agitators used to mix DE in water can pulverize the diatoms, rendering them less effective in filtering

Figure 8.8. A, Vacuum DE discs. B, Large, rectangular DE leafs. (Photo courtesy of Brock Enterprises, Hamden, CT)

dirt. Slurry mixers must be designed to dilute the DE in water slowly and gently.

A rough method of slurry feeding is to throw a coffee can or two of DE into the filtering tank periodically. When too much DE is added to the original precoat through slurry feeding, the filtering of water can be impeded. When excessive amounts of DE have been added so that the DE on one filter element touches the DE clinging to the adjacent filter septa, "bridging" has occurred, and all DE must be removed. Regenerative DE filters accomplish what slurry feeds accomplish without additional DE.

Cleaning Filter Septa

Cleaning filter septa is required periodically because scale, oils, and other organic materials eventually build up on the elements and must be removed with special cleaners. A strong cleaning agent called trisodium phosphate (TSP) is often used to lift oil and grease from the fabric of the septa. After TSP is applied, muriatic acid is then used to remove scale buildup. If muriatic acid is used prior to TSP, oils and grease will be almost impossible to remove. Because of environmental concerns (TSP is not biodegradable and is banned in some states), alternatives to TSP are now highly recommended to avoid the use of phosphates.

Additionally, whenever muriatic acid is used, strong vapors are released. Care must be taken not to breathe these fumes.

Handling DE

Because DE is a light powder, if not handled carefully, it can wind up all over the filter room. Caution must be exercised so that the fine powder is not inhaled. Protective masks covering the nose and mouth will help prevent breathing in the DE. Some believe that breathing microscopic DE particles may cause silicosis of the lungs. The filter room floor should also have floor drains to permit the washing of DE from the floor. When wet and/or used, old DE does not have the same concerns.

In summary, although several disadvantages are associated with DE filters, DE still represents one of the most efficient filter media that produces highly polished water. Although it requires additional work and special handling, DE produces sparkling, clear water.

If water clarity is the most important consideration when designing a swimming pool, then DE filters should be considered. Some swimming pool experts (and I am one of them) claim they can tell when a DE filter is being used by the polished appearance of the water.

Cartridge Filters

The latest technology in swimming pool filtration involves the use of cartridge filters. Cartridge filters have been used for many years in science and industry. Although the original cartridge filters were developed for residential pools during the 1950s, cartridge filters are now used in many pools. The first generation of cartridge filtration used depth filtration, and the second generation (since 1970) moved to surface filtration. Cartridge filters use artificial media. The filter element is made up of a pleated polyester cloth or other synthetic fabric that traps dirt. As spaces and pores become clogged with dirt, the cartridge filter needs to be cleaned or replaced. This usually occurs when the pressure rises to about 10 psi above the starting pressure. Cartridge filters for pools resemble air filters that protect automobile carburetors (Figure 8.8).

The advantages of cartridge filter systems include the following:

1. Cartridges are cleaned by hand and do not require much water to clean; therefore, they conserve water.
2. Cartridge filter systems are simple to disassemble, analyze, repair, and replace. Most cartridge filter maintenance does not require tools.
3. Cartridge filtration systems require little space and eliminate much of the valving and piping required by more traditional pool filters.

The disadvantages of cartridge filter systems include the following:

1. The filters are difficult to clean and some technicians claim that only 65% to 75% of the cartridge filtering capacity is recovered after each cleaning. New filters are required often.
2. Plastic lid covers that hold cartridge filters in the pressure tank can crack. The plastic lids should be checked often and replaced when necessary. When O-rings and gaskets are used to secure the cover, they should be lubricated regularly.

Pool owners and operators who use cartridge filters recommend having extra filters to replace the dirty cartridge being cleaned. Many dirty filters require soaking in TSP or a TSP substitute. Muriatic acid might also be needed after the oils are removed. Because a number of filters must be purchased during the swimming season, cartridge filtration becomes expensive in most applications. Cartridge filtration appears to be more popular with hot tubs. Cartridge filters are designed to filter at a rate of .375 to 1 GPM/sq ft of surface area.

For example, a swimming pool with a flow rate of 475 GPM would require a high rate sand filter bed with 31 to 32 sq ft of surface area—475 GPM divided by 15 GPM/sq ft equals 31.66 sq ft of filter surface area. When the surface area for DE filters is calculated, the answer should be divided by 2 because two sides of every DE filter element do the filtering.

Summary

Before a filtration system is selected for a swimming pool, needs must be prioritized. Operations cost versus capital cost must be considered. RMF can be more expensive but will save money in the long run. Ease of operation and backwashing must be weighed against how clear the water must be. Although filter media must be cleaned regularly, filters can be cleaned or backwashed too often.

In summary, three filtering factors determine water clarity in a swimming pool: the filtering rate, the amount of filtering media, and the effectiveness of media. Table 8.1 includes typical characteristics of common filters.

Dr. Tom's Tip

When backwashing, extend the length of the backwash to purge the pool of extra water. This will require more freshwater to refill your pool after the backwash, but freshwater is your best chemical. Also, when sizing tanks for your aquatic facility, whenever possible, select tanks with larger, wider sand beds. Finally, inspect the sand in the filter tank at least once a year to prevent maintenance problems.

Table 8.1

Filter Type	Filter Media	Filter Rate
Conventional sand and gravel	Permanent sand and gravel	3 GPM/sq ft
High rate sand	Permanent sand	12–20 GPM/sq ft (15 GPM/sq ft average)
RM	Perlite	1–2 GPM/sq ft
DE	Temporary DE	2 GPM/sq ft
Cartridge	Semipermanent fibrous material	.375 GPM/sq ft

Note. To determine how much surface area of a particular filter media is required, use the following simple formula:

$$\frac{\text{flow rate in GPM}}{\text{GPM/sq ft}} = \text{Sq ft of filter surface area}$$

Bibliography

Gabrielson, A. M. (1987). *Swimming pools: A guide to their planning, design, and operation.* Champaign, IL: Human Kinetics.

Mitchel, K. (1988). *The proper management of pool and spa water.* Decatur, GA: BioLab.

Pool & Spa News. Los Angeles, CA. www.poolspanews.com/

Pope, J. R., Jr. (1991). *Public swimming pool management, I and II.* Alexandria, VA: National Recreation and Park Association.

Recreonics. (1991). *Buyers' guide and operations handbook: Catalog no. 41.* Indianapolis, IN: Author.

Service Industry News. Torrance, CA.

Taylor, C. (1989). *Everything you always wanted to know about pool care.* Chino, CA: Service Industry Publications.

Torney, J. A., & Clayton, R. D. (1970). *Aquatic instruction, coaching and management.* Minneapolis, MN: Burgess Publishing.

Washington State Public Health Association. (1988). *Swimming pool operations.* Seattle, WA: Author.

Williams, K. G., & Young, R. A. (Eds.). (2011). *Aquatic facility operator manual* (6th ed.). Ashburn, VA: National Recreation and Park Association.

Improving Air Quality in Indoor Pools

Richard C. Scott, Erik Knight, Ryan Smedema, contributors

Key Concepts

- Chloramines
- Monochloramines
- Dichloramines
- Trichloramines
- Pneumonitis
- Superchlorination

The most important problem to solve in the design of indoor swimming pool facilities is the control of air quality. Air quality is an important issue that can be a struggle for indoor pools. Code-mandated minimum turnover rates are not always appropriate turnover rates. Quality filters, water treatment systems, and a chemical controller are capable of providing good water quality if the operator frequently manually tests the water, adjusts the equipment carefully, and is technically competent in pool operations.

The Problem: Chloramines

Air quality in indoor pools also can be corrosive and damaging to facilities and can lead to health concerns (often lung related) for patrons and lifeguards. Even the best managed pools can develop chloramines. These are by-products of the chlorination process, which tend to form when the free available chlorine interacts with the organic load brought into the water by bathers.

The three chloramines are monochloramine, dichloramine, and trichloramine. Monochloramines and dichloramines stay in the water, but trichloramines become airborne in a gaseous state when agitated (splashing). Leisure pools have much higher levels of chloramines due to their higher bather loads and pattern of usage. These pools also produce more humidity in the air due to water sprays, waterslides, and other features that agitate the water. This contributes to the off-gassing of volatile organic compounds.

Damage to Facilities

As a gas, trichloramines have an the atomic weight that is heavier than oxygen, so trichloramines like to stay low in the building. They form a thick (yet invisible) cloud. This cloud hovers above the surface of the pool and wet deck and slowly swirls around with the existing airflow. It continues to build as more chloramines are released from the water. Eventually the chloramine cloud will build so high that it emits an odor that people on the deck can smell.

Depending on the location of the return vent in the natatorium, eventually the chloramines can build high enough to be pulled into the air-handling system. At that point, the corrosive chloramine cloud begins doing the most damage to the facility because it is being circulated around the entire room, corroding metal in its path.

Health

Medical research shows correlations between indoor pool air and illness. The most prominent of these conditions is granulomatous pneumonitis. Pneumonitis is characterized by inflammation and sometimes permanent scarring of lung tissue. In this case, it is caused by inhaling airborne chloramines, a condition known as "lifeguard lung."

Lung scarring usually occurs only after extended amounts of exposure to chloramines. Lifeguards, swimmers, and coaches have the most exposure and therefore the most risk. However, swimmers, unlike lifeguards, are breathing almost exclusively chloramine-laden air during practice because they breathe only from the surface level of the water. Not only do chloramines release from the surface of the water, but they also hang there because the gas is heavier than the air. The most common medical condition in swimming is asthma.

The more concentrated the chloramine gas, the more noxious it will be. Dilution of the pool air with outside air is often exercised. However, chloramines can still be harmful when diluted.

Solutions

Improved Water Quality

In the previous edition of this book (2009), ultraviolet light lamps were introduced as a "very promising technology," with "new lamps available to destroy some chloramines as well as viruses and bacteria" (p. 102) As foreseeable during the writing of the 3rd edition of *The Complete Swimming Pool Reference* (2014), ultraviolet light is now rather common on new aquatic facility designs and retrofits.

This technology has basically replaced the ozone technology due to its lower costs and easier operations and maintenance requirements.

The situation of chloramines is minimized when the level of chlorine is not overwhelmed by a sudden demand. Fine-tuning the chlorine level to anticipate demand is part of the operational plan for which the operator has control.

> *Note:* Superchlorination is a traditional treatment for chloramines. It may not be as effective as newer methods and technologies, which will be explained in Chapter 13.

When superchlorination is done to remove chloramines from the pool, a large amount of oxygen is required for the process to work. Also, the air in the natatorium must be exhausted. A manual override for 100% outside air is absolutely essential. (Special protection may be required to prevent coils from freezing with temperatures below 35°F.) This should be designed into the system. Some manufacturers refer to the required equipment as a "purge cycle."

At most facilities, lap pool water temperature will be 80°F to 84°F. The natatorium air should be 85°F with 50% to 60% relative humidity. Air temperature that is 1° to 2° above water temperature will slow evaporation. When a therapy pool or whirlpool is included in the natatorium, the air temperature cannot be kept above the water temperature of 86°F to 92°F because bathers and staff will become too hot.

Improved Air Quality

The priorities for the mechanical system design are

- first—indoor air quality,
- second—control of humidity and condensation, and
- third—energy conservation or economy.

For ventilation, 2 cfm/sq ft of the total natatorium floor area is usually acceptable. This can mean about three and a half to six air changes per hour, depending on the height of the natatorium, but may need to be as many as 10 for leisure pools with low ceilings. The new Model Aquatic Health Code (MAHC) includes total outside air requirements. The MAHC has not been adopted by any governing body during the writing of this third edition, but it provides outside air requirements for natatoriums

and pool rooms. In any case, the natatorium should be kept at a negative pressure by exhausting slightly more air than is supplied. This will help in avoiding moisture and odor migration to other portions of the building.

The lowest initial cost systems are designed with 100% outside air using rooftop units or units mounted on a concrete slab on grade. This type of design typically does not have good energy performance because the units must operate on 100% outside air all the time. No air can be returned through the units because they have little or no protection against the natatorium environment. This system provides high indoor air quality at low initial cost with higher operating costs. For projects in some climates, this type of design may be a reasonable design response.

Higher cost units with stainless steel construction, high grades of aluminum, or coated steel have been used successfully on some projects. In this case, a portion of the air is exhausted and a portion is returned through the unit, about 50% up to 100%. See Figures 9.1 and 9.2 for examples of large tubular air ducts. Many times, these types of units will use a method of heat recovery, such as plate heat exchangers, run-around coils, heat pipes, or heat wheels. The heat recovery will extract heat from the return/exhaust air and transfer the energy into the outside/supply airstream. The outside air is used to reduce humidity, so large volumes for ventilation and outside air are required. In most climates, mechanical cooling or dehumidification is required to maintain temperature and humidity. These units must also have the capability to provide 100% outside air when superchlorination is done. These units provide excellent air quality, low initial cost, and moderate operating cost.

The most expensive heating, ventilating, and air-conditioning (HVAC) units are mechanical dehumidification units. These units are built to withstand the natatorium air, but are costly, are complex, and have more maintenance problems than simpler units. Manufacturers usually recommend four or five air changes per hour and current code minimum for outside air (.48 cfm/sq ft of pool and deck area). We know from experience that they have taken care of the humidity and condensation problems well, especially in lap or competition pool installations. However, their record is imperfect in leisure pool projects.

Usually the first priority, indoor air quality, is neglected. Based on the criteria of six air changes per hour and MAHC minimum for outside air, these units will work in the natatorium but are expensive. If this is the design approach the mechanical engineer takes, a minimum of two units is recommended. When one unit is disabled, the natatorium may operate with partial HVAC capability. Many operators who have had units down for replacement of circuit boards or compressors were

Figure 9.1. Large tubular air ducts. (Photo courtesy of Water Technology, Inc.)

Figure 9.2. Tubular air ducts at the juncture of the ceiling and wall, running the length of the 50 meter pool. (Photo courtesy of Counsilman-Hunsaker)

thankful they could operate because they had two units.

The two main approaches to supply and return air ducts are (a) supply low and return high and (b) supply high and return low. Both systems have advantages and will work. Most projects use a design that supplies high and returns or exhausts low because the chlorinated air just above the surface of the water has the worst air quality of anywhere in the natatorium. Taking a large portion of the exhaust or return air from this level ensures that the poor air quality at this level will be diluted. Other approaches will work. It is critical that the circulation of air through the space is complete and not short-circuited as happens when the supply and return are both high.

PVC-coated spiral ducts are recommended. Aluminum or galvanized ducts will work, but run the risk of rust stains at screw holes where the galvanizing is compromised. Stainless steel and fiberglass ducts cost a premium and are poorer choices than aluminum. All metallic ducts should be coated with Tnemec high build epoxy.

In the design of the air supply ducts, caution needs to be exercised to avoid blowing air at a velocity that would chill bathers on the pool deck. Usually the velocity of the air across the deck should be below 25 ft/min. Directing air flow on the water is generally avoided because it causes quicker evaporation, but it improves air quality by moving the poorer quality air on the surface into the return airstream.

In the past, many natatoriums were designed with inadequate heating and ventilating systems. If the designs for these systems are based on code minimums or other industry guidelines, indoor pools are almost guaranteed to have air quality problems. Traditionally, the solution to these problems was to provide supplemental water treatment and to increase the amount of outside air.

As outside air levels are increased, energy conservation should be considered as well. A method of heat exchange should be designed into the project. Variable frequency drives on all fan motors and a controls system with night setbacks and unoccupied modes are recommended to provide an energy-efficient environment that also prioritizes air quality. Every project is unique and a variety of equipment can work successfully at different levels of project budgets.

Since the second edition of this book, new technology has been developed. The newest development in elimination of chloramines is a source-capture method. Some experts suggest that ultraviolet light could kill all chloramines if they were exposed to ultraviolet light for a long enough period of time. However, an average turnover is 4 to 6 hours, which means trichloramines would have to stay waterborne for at least 4 to 6 hours before they could release into the air. But trichloramines can become airborne in seconds. UV will be discussed in Chapters 10 and 11. Sphagnum moss, a relatively new method for public pools which can also help improve air quality will be discussed in chapter 10. Source-capture is an effective method to catch chloramines as they become airborne. Traditionally, water quality was used as a primary solution to chloramines.

The Paddock Evacuator™ is currently the only product that uses this method (Figure 9.3). Source-capture works by "vacuuming" the chloramines off the surface of the water as they are produced.

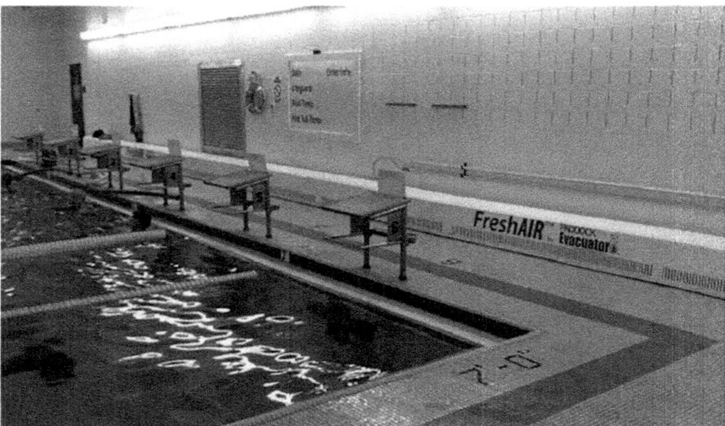

Figure 9.3. Paddock Evacuator™ Wall Mount Evacuator™ exhausts chloramines off the pool surface out of the building. This add-on system can be installed in a variety of locations including the pool gutter. (Photo courtesy of Paddock Evacuator™)

Because chloramines are a heavy gas, source-capture pulls air from the surface of the water and/or wet deck to capture only the lowest chloramine-laden air in the building. It is specifically engineered for each facility so it exhausts only the correct amount of air and nothing more. It also eliminates the need to open doors or to introduce more outside air through the air system. This controls chloramines before they become a problem, which can save maintenance and replacement costs, as well as prevent chloramine-related health concerns for swimmers.

The Paddock Evacuator™ appears to be a more practical, affordable, and effective solution than what has been offered to date. It has significant potential to combat chloramines as they develop. We believe one of the most promising aspects about the evacuator is that it can be added to existing facilities with chloramine problems without replacing the HVAC system. As chloramines remain a challenge for many aquatic facilities, new technology offers hope.

Summary

The number one problem for indoor pools, particularly during competitive swim team season, is heightened chloramine levels. This chapter provided insights that can reduce your chloramine levels during your busiest times in order to maintain good air quality to protect your facility and safeguard your swimmers. This chapter offered you the latest advances in air handling and water chemistry to provide a safe environment to all swimmers.

Photo courtesy of Taylor Technologies, Inc.

Section III
Water Chemistry

Section III is a pool operator's paradise! The next several chapters focus on the many different concepts concerning swimming pool water chemistry. Swimming pool water undergoes a variety of important chemical changes that take place continually. To promote safety and enjoyment in swimming pools, these chemical changes must be constantly monitored. Sparkling clear, clean water depends on good filtration, water balance, disinfection, but most importantly, chemical oxidation. The focus now is on water balance, disinfection, and oxidation. While other textbooks may illustrate the chemical reactions taking place in swimming pool water by way of chemical equations, this text simply describes how the chemicals are functioning and performing without complicated and intimidating formulas and equations. Keeping it simple in this regard has been more successful in teaching water chemistry concepts to pool professionals.

In general, pH and chlorine levels receive much attention in the swimming world. pH and chlorine levels are important because they determine whether the pool water will be "people friendly," that is, safe, comfortable, and enjoyable for swimmers. These levels are monitored on an hourly basis in most heavily used aquatic facilities and every other hour in less used pools.

The Saturation Index, usually referred to as water balance, is also extremely important to maintenance. Water balancing, which is often overlooked by pool personnel, is important in predicting if the swimming pool water is "plumbing friendly." Unbalanced water is either aggressive (corrosive) or basic (scale forming). Aggressive pool water will corrode pipes, filters, heaters, valves, walls, floors, and whatever else it comes in contact with. Conversely, basic water clogs pipes, filters, and heaters with deposits of scale. Using the human body as an analogy for swimming pool chemistry, aggressive water is like cancer, while basic water is similar to bad cholesterol. Water balance, as measured by the Saturation Index, should be monitored weekly or monthly, depending on the pool characteristics. If the chemicals remain within the published ideal ranges, the water is pretty much balanced and there might not be the need to calculate the Saturation Index.

Water chemistry as it applies to aquatic facilities not only helps to maintain crystal clear water but also keeps the water microbe free. Unfortunately, when it comes to swimming pool water, it is possible to have clear water that is not clean water. Understanding the concepts in this section aids the aquatic facility owner/operator in maintaining clear and clean swimming pool water.

10

Disinfection and Supplemental Sanitizers

Key Concepts

- Iodine
- Ozone
- Ionization
- Enzymes
- Chlorine generation
- UV

Swimming pool disinfection is the process of destroying living microorganisms, such as bacteria, to prevent the transmission of disease. To provide efficient and continuous bacteria control, the disinfectant must have residual properties, that is, a minimal level of active, available chemical disinfectant in the swimming pool at all times.

The role of disinfection is extremely important, and it is easily achieved. Oxidation of organic debris (hair, lint, body oil, sweat, urine, etc.), however, might require higher levels of chemical disinfectant in pool water. Chemical compounds that do not have residual properties may not be used as primary swimming pool disinfectants (sanitizers).

The best way to ensure a germ-free pool is to have a weekly bacteria analysis conducted on the pool water. Some states require this test for public pools. The analysis must be conducted under the direct supervision of a public health officer or a certified laboratory. The absence of coliform indicates germ-free water. The coliform count should not exceed 2 bacteria colonies/mm of pool water. The bacteria count should not be greater than 200 bacteria colonies/mm of pool water. Local health department swimming pool codes and the MAHC should be consulted for harmful coliform levels. In the United States, *E. coli* testing is becoming highly recommended for pools and beaches instead of fecal coliform. Apparently, *E. coli* is a better predictor of water quality.

Many swimming pools use chlorine as a disinfectant. Chlorine is a member of Group VIIA of the periodic chart, along with fluorine, bromine, iodine, and astatine, all of which are referred to as halogens. Of the halogens, only chlorine, bromine, and iodine are suitable for swimming pool disinfection. Chapter 12 is devoted to chlorination and bromination. In this chapter, we will discuss supplemental disinfectants, some of which are old and others which are more recent, including iodine, ozone, ionization, chlorine generation, ultraviolet light, sphagnum moss, and enzymes. Most of the alternative disinfectants are referred to as "chlorine-free" sanitizers.

Iodine

Iodine is a halogen-like chlorine and bromine that also can be used for swimming pool disinfection. Iodine was first investigated in the 1950s for use in swimming pools, but its use did not become popular even though it showed potential. Municipalities that allow the use of iodine usually require a higher residual than chlorine or bromine, but again, the application of iodine is rare. For that reason, we do not discuss iodine in length in this edition.

Ozone

Ozone has been a popular means of water disinfection in Europe since the early 1900s. Today, many swimming pools and spas in Europe are treated with ozone. Although ozone disinfection has not been used much in the United States, it has gained respectability as a sanitizing alternative to chlorine and bromine. The increased popularity of ozone in the United States can probably be linked to environmentally conscious consumers who are concerned about the perceived dangers of using chemicals, particularly chlorine, in swimming pools.

Ozone kills virtually all bacteria, algae, mold, and viruses on contact. Ozone also produces an odorless, tasteless pool because chloramines are not produced during ozonation. Ozone has the unique ability to completely destroy urea that swimmers introduce into the pool, thereby eliminating the formation of obnoxious chloramines.

Proponents of ozone claim that when it is used for swimming pool disinfection, there is no bleaching of hair and suits, no smell or eyeburn, and no buildup of total dissolved solids.

Basically, ozone is a form of oxygen that is produced when ultraviolet (UV) rays react with oxygen in the earth's atmosphere. During electrical storms, ozone is often produced when lightning moves through oxygen molecules. Ozone is also known as "energetic oxygen." Ozone is a powerful disinfectant and oxidizer and is even more powerful than chlorine in some respects. Ozone effectively kills many types of bacteria and viruses. For instance, ozone kills *E. coli* 25 times faster than hypochlorous acid, which is produced by chlorine.

Ozone is unstable and does not last long in pool water as a result. Therefore, ozone must be produced onsite and then added to the swimming pool circulation system. Ozone has a half-life of 22 minutes. This means that half of the ozone produced will decompose and be rendered useless every 22 minutes. As a result, ozone must be constantly produced and reintroduced to the pool.

Ozone can be produced with two methods: corona discharge and UV generation.

Corona discharge ozone generation is the more traditional and larger of the two methods of producing ozone. It requires a continual supply of high-voltage electricity that produces large quantities of ozone at high concentrations. A special chamber is needed to house the corona discharge equipment, which reacts with specially dehumidified air. What results in the chamber is similar to an electric storm in the atmosphere, and ozone is produced. Once the ozone is manufactured, it is introduced into the pool with either a venturi-suction system or an air compressor. The trend in ozone delivery appears to be away from compressors and toward venturi injectors. In both cases, ozone bubbles are mixed with swimming pool water that is returning to the pool. The corona discharge equipment can be expensive, and professional installation is a must because of the required combination of water and electricity. For large aquatic facilities, the corona discharge method is preferred.

UV ozone generation uses UV lamps, which produce low levels of ozone, which in turn attack oxygen molecules as air is passed in front of the lamps. Air dryers and compressors are sometimes added to the UV system to increase ozone production. UV lamps require little power, but they generate far less ozone than the older corona discharge method. As a result, UV ozone applications are better suited for smaller aquatic facilities.

European ozonation for pools is characterized by large corona discharge chambers, followed by deozonation chambers using activated charcoal filters. Water purified by ozone must be "deozonated" before returning to the pool so that dangerously high levels of ozone are not reached. Ozonation followed by activated charcoal rids the pool water of obnoxious tastes and odors.

Most states mandate that ozone be used as a supplementary sanitizer only. Health codes require a minimum level of halogen residual to ensure water sanitation. Chlorine or bromine must also be added to ozonated pools because algae growth is actually encouraged in the presence of ozone. Only small residuals need to be maintained for the halogens in this case, but two forms of disinfectants are required when ozone is used as the primary disinfectant. Also, although ozone is safer on pool walls and floors than traditional disinfectants, it corrodes copper and other metals. Because ozone is measured in parts per billion, a special test kit is required.

Ozonation systems are extremely expensive to install. As technology improves and the cost of installation decreases, ozone as a primary pool disinfectant in the United States should gain popularity. The 1984 Olympics held in Los Angeles and the 1996 Olympic games in Atlanta both used ozone in their pools, and NASA plans to use ozonated drinking water in its proposed space station. For commercial pools, ozone is not as popular now as it was when the second edition of this book was printed. The supplemental sanitizer of choice currently seems to be UV systems.

Ionization

Although ionization in commercial pools in the 1980s and 1990s was pushed, the use of ionization in commercial pools has seen a drastic reduction since 2000. Ionization is an electrochemical process of converting electrically neutral (noncharged) atoms, molecules, or compounds into electrically charged ions. These ions, which are either positively (+) or negatively (-) charged, have disinfecting properties in pool water. In the swimming pool industry, ionization is usually accomplished by the use of copper and silver electrodes to produce copper and silver ions. The production of these ions is also referred to as electrolysis. Both copper and silver serve as algaecides and bactericides.

The advantages of using an ionization disinfection system for swimming pools include reduced chemical usage, no effect on pH, and little maintenance or monitoring of disinfecting chemicals.

Ionization with copper and silver does not provide oxidation, however. As a result, an oxidizer is needed to deal with organic debris, and many health departments require a halogen residual regardless of the disinfection system. Both copper electrodes and silver electrodes must be cleaned and changed often. Another drawback of ionization is green and black staining that may result from using copper and silver. Some states may also be concerned about dealing with discharge water that contains these metals. Some pool experts claim that ionization is more appropriate for smaller low-usage pools rather than high-load public aquatic facilities. Perhaps the biggest drawback to ionization systems is that the electrodes must be cleaned and replaced often. Ionization systems were used to purify drinking water during NASA's Apollo missions.

Chlorine Generation

Salt chlorine generators first became popular in Australia during the 1960s, and to this day, many residential pools down under still use this technology. Chlorine generation requires electrical devices to produce chlorine from salts that have been predissolved in the pool water. Ordinary food grade salt or sodium chloride (NaCl) can be converted to sodium hypochlorite (NaClO) through electrolysis made possible by electrodes in a separate salt solution chamber. This is not a water softening technique, however.

This on-site production of sodium hypochlorite reacts with water to produce hypochlorous acid or active chlorine (or hyprobromous acid) that provides effective sanitation. Chlorine generation commonly uses an electrolytic cell containing anode and cathode plates. The major advantage of this system is that disinfecting and sanitizing chemicals do not have to be purchased, stored, and handled. In this regard, salt chlorine generation might produce a safer chlorine-free environment without the safety equipment and procedures required by traditional chlorine forms. Most recently, this system has become popular in Alaska because shipping hazardous pool chemicals there can be cost prohibitive. Chlorine generation is also becoming more popular in private residential pools because it eliminates potentially hazardous chemicals in garages and backyard toolsheds where they are more likely to be mishandled.

Another distinct advantage of chlorine generation is regeneration. In this system, combined chlorine is converted back to free available chlorine after it is used for disinfection. Although the future looks promising for chlorine generation, disadvantages exist with its use. The system as it is used today is expensive to install, but as this system continues to grow in popularity, the cost should come down. Chlorine generation requires a swimming pool salt level to be approximately 3,000 ppm, or 3 g/l, and as a result, the perception is these swimming pools taste salty. In reality, the salt generated by pool water is one twelfth of the salinity of ocean/sea water or of saline solution. Salt water can be corrosive on the plumbing of a pool, but only when the saline level becomes excessive, over 6,000 ppm, or 6 g/l.

Ultraviolet Light

UV light is a popular sanitizer. In the second edition of this book, UV light was explicated as a supplemental sanitizer used in conjunction with hydrogen peroxide. This combination has become less favorable. However, today UV systems are becoming a fixture in heavily used swimming pools and are recommended by regulatory bodies. UV light is a natural component of the electromagnetic radiation emitted by the sun and addresses the parasite *Cryptosporidium*. Swimming pool professionals also appreciate UV systems for their ability to decrease chloramines. Often, pool operators who add UV find that they rarely need to shock their pool as a result of the system. Many components are involved in choosing an appropriate UV system for the facility. Installation, maintenance, and features of a UV system must also be carefully considered. We will discuss UV in more depth in Chapter 11.

Sphagnum Moss

Sphagnum moss, which was originally used in residential pools and spas, is making headway in larger public and private commercial pools. The moss operates similarly to a tea bag (Creative Water Solutions, 2014). The moss is placed into a contact chamber that is designed to optimize interaction of the moss with the pool water. There are two types of contact chambers used in commercial pools and spas; one resides in the surge/balance tank of pools, and the other can be placed offline from the water circulation system in both pools and spas (NSF50 certified). The moss is placed into the contact chamber, where it interacts with the pool/spa water and acts as an absorptive filter, binding cations like calcium and iron, and inhibiting and reducing organic contamination. The moss greatly improves water quality, water clarity, and maintains balanced water using less chemicals and effort. The moss improves air quality by reducing the formation of disinfection byproducts, reduces and removes scale through the binding of calcium

Figure 10.1. Sphagnum moss as it is harvested. (Photo courtesy of Creative Water Solutions, 2014)

ions, and reduces corrosion and overall chemical usage by reducing organic contamination. This results in reduced water consumption, increased heat exchanger efficiency, reduced energy use, and reduced chemical use, among other benefits (Creative Water Solutions, 2014). Although the sphagnum moss reduces the need for supplemental chemicals, sphagnum moss is compatible with most common pool and spa chemicals. State-required chemical residuals, such as chlorine, are still a necessity in the pool or spa. The use of sphagnum moss in swimming pools and spas has proven to be an effective way to save costs, chemicals, energy, and water.[1,2]

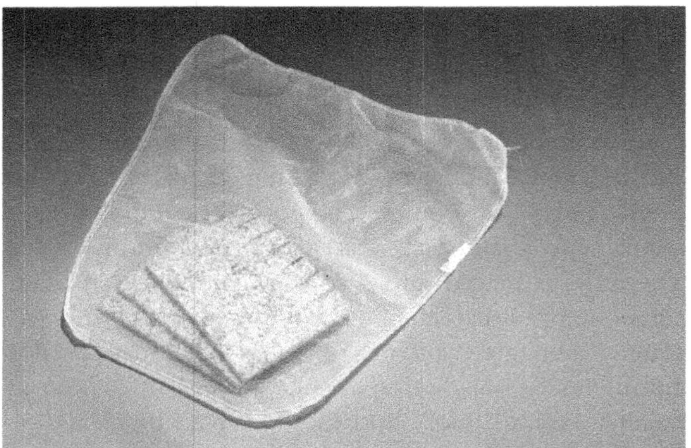

Figure 10.2. Sphagnum moss before it is added to the contact chamber. (Photo courtesy of Creative Water Solutions, 2014)

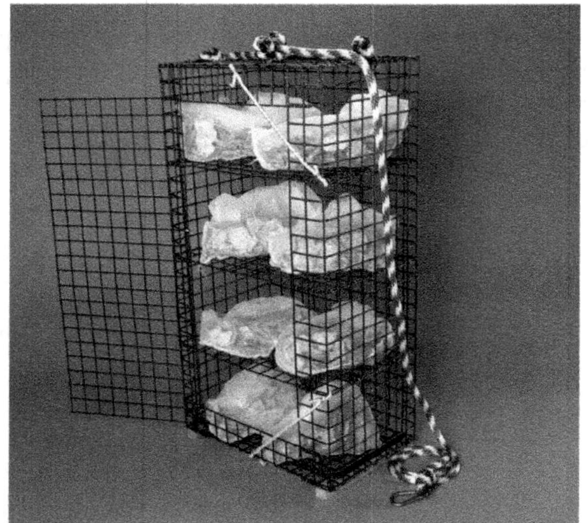

Figure 10.3. Contact chamber for Sphagnum Moss that is used in the surge/balance tank. (Photo courtesy of Creative Water Solutions, 2014)

---

[1]University of Maryland, University Sustainability Fund, Grant Recipient: Sphagnum Moss Swimming Pool Water Treatment System - Campus Recreation Services 2010–2011 (http://www.sustainability.umd.edu/content/about/fund_recipients_moss.php)

[2]Creative Water Solutions, 2014

Enzymes

Enzymes are now being sold in the pool industry as the "natural" way of ridding the water of impurities. Enzymes digest organic wastes such as body oils, dead skin, mucus, soap, deodorants, and other contaminants that bathers add to the water. Enzymes alone cannot disinfect pools, but they should significantly reduce the need for chemical sanitizers. Apparently, pool and spa enzymes are helpful in removing scum lines off sides. Enzyme use has become particularly popular in spas and hot tubs.

Summary

Some nonchlorine disinfectants are gaining popularity in the United States; others have come and gone. Although chlorine remains the primary swimming pool disinfectant in the United States, its competitors are gaining ground. Primary concerns for selecting a pool disinfectant are cost, effectiveness, availability, and ease of handling. Selecting a pool disinfectant without a local supplier can be frustrating. Before selecting a supplemental sanitizer, the pool operator should consult with individuals who already use the particular sanitizers for pros and cons because most pool chemical salespersons do not manage pools. Just about every pool chemical has advantages and disadvantages, and educating oneself before switching chemicals is imperative. Once the switch is made, safe storage and handling procedures must be followed. Finally, not many chemicals offer strong oxidation, strong disinfection, and residual properties the way chlorine does.

> **Dr. Tom's Tip**
>
> A performance contract may be your best bet before you switch to a new chemical system (or filter for that matter). Before the switch is made, objectively measure the water clarity in terms of NTUs (Nephelometric Turbidity Units) through a certified lab. After installation, if the NTUs are not at least as good as before, you know you are not getting what you paid for.

Bibliography

American Water Works Association. (1971). *Water quality and treatment* (3rd ed.). Denver, CO: Author.

ATG UV Technology. (2012). MAHC regulations for UV and swimming pools. Retrieved from http://www.atguv.com/news/61/mach_regulations_for_uv_swimming_pools

Centers for Disease Control and Prevention. (2013). Triple As of healthy swimming: Awareness, action, advocacy. Retrieved from http://www.cdc.

gov/healthywater/swimming/protection/triple-a-healthy-swimming.html

Creative Water Solutions. (2014). http://www.cwsnaturally.com/

Ewoldt, J. (2012). Moss making itself useful in city pools. *StarTribune*. Retrieved from http://www.startribune.com/lifestyle/158363865.html

Gabrielson, A. M. (1987). *Swimming pools: A guide to their planning, design, and operation* (4th ed.). Champaign, IL: Human Kinetics.

Kowalsy, L. (Ed.). (1991). *Pool/spa operators handbook*. San Antonio, TX: National Swimming Pool Foundation.

Mitchel, K. (1988). *The proper management of pool and spa water*. Decatur, GA: BioLab.

Pool & Spa News, Los Angeles. http://www.poolspanews.com/

Pope, J. R., Jr. (1991). *Public swimming pool management I and II*. Alexandria, VA: National Recreation and Park Association.

Recreonics. (1991). *Buyers' guide and operations handbook: Catalog no. 41*. Indianapolis, IN: Author.

Service Industry News, Torrance, Calif.

Shorewood Hills Pool. (2012). Moss filter system. Retrieved from http://www.shorewoodpool.com/moss-filter-system

Taylor, C. (1989). *Everything you always wanted to know about pool care*. Chino, CA: Service Industry Publications.

Torney, J. A., & Clayton, R. D. (1970). *Aquatic instruction, coaching and management*. Minneapolis, MN: Burgess Publishing.

University of Maryland. (n.d.). University sustainability fund: 2010–11 grant recipient: Sphagnum moss swimming pool water treatment system – Campus Recreation Services. Retrieved from http://www.sustainability.umd.edu/content/about/fund_recipients_moss.php

Washington State Public Health Association. (1998). *Swimming pool operations*. Seattle, WA: Author.

Williams, K. G., & Young, R. A. (Eds.). (2011). *Aquatic facility operator manual* (6th ed.). Ashburn, VA: National Recreation and Park Association.

UV System. (Photo courtesy of Tom Schaefer, Engineered Treatment Systems)

11

Ultraviolet Light (UV) Disinfection

Tom Schaefer, Engineered Treatment Systems LLC
Emperor Aquatics
Contributors

Key Concepts

- Ultraviolet light (UV)
- Dose pacing
- Lamps
- System features
- Installation
- Advance controls

Ultraviolet disinfection is a reliable control for recreational water illnesses and harmful chloramines. Ultraviolet-C (UV-C) light has the ability to cause permanent damage to many nuisance microorganisms in water. Certain protozoan parasites are considered "chlorine resistant"; *Cryptosporidium parvum* is one such pathogen that chlorine has difficulty disinfecting. An outbreak of *Cryptosporidium*, or Crypto, in Milwaukee in 1993 made 400,000 people ill and hospitalized 4,400 people (Corso et. al., 2003).

The Centers for Disease Control and Prevention (CDC, 2013) recommends the use of ultraviolet (UV) light disinfection. UV light is a method of secondary disinfection to address Crypto and to destroy inorganic and some organic chloramines. UV light is designed to achieve a 3-log, or 99.9%, inactivation of Crypto. The consideration of UV light as a method to both reduce combined chlorine levels and achieve disinfection goals is recommended, and the majority of aquatic consultants are specifying UV light for new construction and renovations of indoor pools.

What Is UV Light?

UV light is a natural component of the electromagnetic radiation emitted by the sun. The majority of radiation produced during this process is absorbed by ozone in the earth's upper atmosphere. UV light, specifically UV-C light (240 to 280 nm), acts as a natural disinfectant by inactivating almost all exposed microorganisms found in water and on surface matter. Human exposure to UV-C results in retinal and skin burns; however, humans are not exposed to appreciable amounts of UV-C due to filtering in the atmosphere.

Situated in the electromagnetic spectrum between X-rays and visible light, UV light has many beneficial properties. UV light is split into four main categories: UV-A, UV-B, UV-C, and Vacuum UV. The area between 240 and 280 nm is UV-C, commonly known as the *germicidal region*.

UV lights are used in a chamber through which swimming pool water passes (Figure 11.1). The lights radiate sufficient energy to highly disinfect the water that passes through the chamber. UV light treats 100% of the filtered water (sterilize, by definition, is 100%).

Figure 11.1. Treatment chamber. (Photo courtesy of Engineered Treatment Systems)

However, UV radiation does not provide oxidation. Water that contains too much organic debris and body wastes will hinder the UV disinfecting process.

State and federal agencies, through their swim regulatory arms, require minimum chlorine levels (residual) be maintained in pools for public safety. Additionally, these same agencies regulate the use of UV systems when applied to pool applications. Used together, chlorine and UV disinfection have improved both water safety and air quality. USA Swimming discussed the impact of UV technology on indoor air quality: "The Facilities Department of USA Swimming strongly recommends that all indoor pools, both new and existing, have UV systems installed…When compared to chlorine feeder systems, UV systems involve a higher initial capital cost. However, over the life of the pool, UV technologies reduce the on-going operating and maintenance costs. This can be significant" (www.USAswimming.org).

For the purpose of comparison, characteristics associated with germicidal disinfection (UV, ozone, and free chlorine) are listed below.

Cryptosporidium UV Disinfection

A minimum Fluence (UV Dose) of U.S. EPA 3 log calculated 40 mj/cm² is recommended and provides high log instant treatment inside the UV system vessel, but does not leave a residual.

Cryptosporidium Ozone Disinfection

This requires contact time of 8 minutes held at an ozone concentration of 2.3 mg/l (Peeters, Mazás, Masschelein, Villacorta Martiez de Maturana, & Debacker, 1989).

Cryptosporidium Chlorine Disinfection

This requires 10 days at a chlorine level of 1 mg/l to provide a 99.9% kill (CDC, 2013a).

As the information above suggests, UV disinfection is the only "instant treatment," but it is also the only treatment without residual capabilities. State and federal agencies require a residual disinfectant, typically chlorine, be maintained at a specific level in pool water for health reasons. Although 100% of the filtered water is highly treated, the faster the turnover rate, the better UV works.

Today, many pool facility managers and operators witness the substantial benefits UV systems provide on a daily basis, yet others remain skeptical. UV systems, once thought of as a luxury, have become a necessity for achieving a healthy and safe pool environment in the eyes of many. This is due in part to the increasing efficiency of UV systems and the long-term results operators have witnessed.

Log Reduction Disinfection

UV treatment is logarithmic. When the UV energy used is doubled, the log reduction also doubles.
- 90% = 1 log reduction
- 99% = 2 log reduction
- Tripling the 1 log dose increases the kill rate hundredfold (99.9%)

Low-pressure (monochromatic) UV lamps have the majority of their output energy (35% to 40%) within the Germicidal Action Spectrum (240 to 280 nm), specifically 254 nm. (The sun is not monochromatic, a low-pressure lamp is.)

Medium-pressure lamps are polychromatic, and unlike low pressure lamps, which have a peak output of 254 nm, medium-pressure lamps have a broader output between 185 and 400 nm (see Figure 11.2).

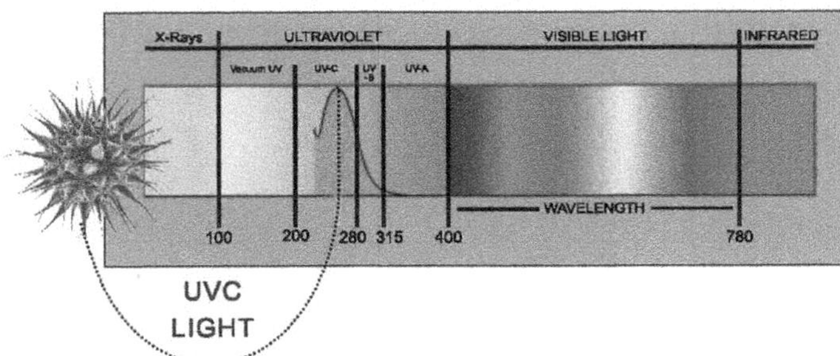

Figure 11.2. The UV-C area of UV light between 240 and 280 nanometres, commonly known as the germicidal region. (Courtesy of Engineered Treatment Systems)

Although medium-pressure UV systems are generally more common throughout the industry, low-pressure UV systems have evolved. Fifteen years ago, medium-pressure UV lamps offered a smaller footprint with higher spectral output (specifically UV-C) than low-pressure lamps. For example, a 5 kW (5,000 W) medium-pressure UV lamp converts 13% (11% to 15%) of its input power (5,000 W) into UV-C light (650 W). Fifteen years ago, to produce the same 650 UV-C W with original low-pressure standard output UV lamps, 27 lamps (65 W/lamp) were required. Today, low-pressure UV lamps that are more powerful exist. Over the past 15 years, low-pressure UV lamp technology has evolved to achieve 4 times the power of their original low-pressure standard output predecessors. This translates to fewer low-pressure lamps required per system, significantly narrowing the gap between low-pressure and medium-pressure UV systems. Today's most powerful low-pressure UV lamp is the amalgam style. Instead of 27 low-pressure standard output UV lamps that together yield 650 UV-C W, only seven low-pressure amalgam UV lamps are required to equal the same amount of UV-C watts. Low pressure lamp technology continues to evolve and improve. Low-pressure UV systems may be a reasonable option in smaller pools.

In general, medium-pressure UV appears to be favorable in larger pools. When the costs involved have been calculated, medium-pressure systems have lower operating costs for all but the smallest flow rates. Both low-pressure and medium-pressure UV systems can help eliminate Crypto, but for chloramine control, a medium-pressure system seems to be advantageous. In the system selection process, accurately sized validated UV systems to protect the investment against potential future health codes and matching flow rate on the validation certificate are important.

Two UV systems are available: traditional axial UV and inline UV. With an axial UV system, the inlets and outlets are located at either end of the chamber. This allows for replacements or retrofits of existing UV units, resulting in increased flexibility. Inline systems are often preferred for modern facilities and facilities with restricted plant room space, as they are installed directly into the pipework and offer a smaller footprint and increased performance and efficiency. A UV system typically includes the following parts: 316-l stainless steel chambers, UV monitoring, automatic internal wiper systems, strainer baskets, and the option for power control to conserve energy when chloramines are low (ATG UV Technology, 2012).

Dose Pacing

Dose pacing maintains the specified level of energy (joules) in the water that is needed for either disinfection or chloramine reduction by providing the exact amount of intensity (lamp power) required. Dose pacing has several advantages, such as reducing power usage, extending the life of the lamps, and extending the quartz life.

Lamps

UV disinfection is beneficial, yet the type of UV lamp, medium pressure or low pressure, along with the system as a whole, should be carefully considered for the specific facility (Figure 11.3 shows a UV lamp). Similar to standard fluorescent lamps, UV lamps are made of quartz, which allows UV energy to pass through. The life of UV lamps is typically 12 to 18 months, affected by over-temperature/nonflow events, starting and stopping of the UV system, and lamp power. The starting and stopping of the system can shorten the life of the lamps, whereas keeping them on low power overnight can extend the life of the lamps.

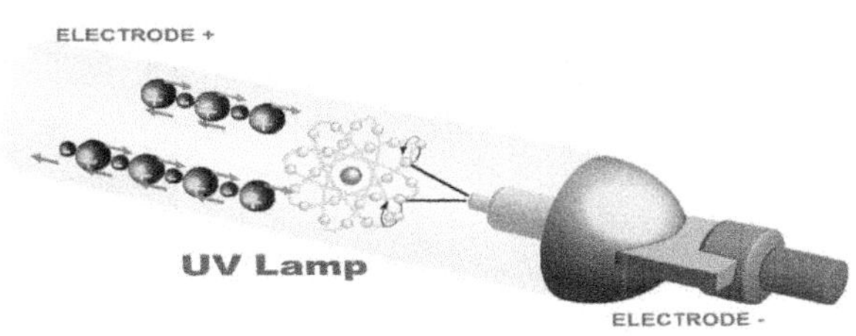

Figure 11.3. Electricity excites liquid mercury to a gas, resulting in the emission of UV energy. (Courtesy of Tom Schaefer, Engineered Treatment Systems)

All UV systems use UV lamps. These lamps play a critical role in establishing the operating performance of a system, capital cost, cost of ownership, and serviceability. Select the UV system that will be the best fit for your facility. When choosing a UV system, pool operators should consult the Model Aquatic Health Code (MAHC) regulations to ensure the system is not only the best fit for their facility, but also compliant with current MAHC guidelines. The MAHC recommends a recognized and capable third party validate the system, among additional specifications. Validation is important. It provides owners and operators with proof that the system will perform as it should. Validation gives a clear route for states considering UV for *Cryptosporidium* reduction to mandate a validation standard for pools. Validation will also be included in the finalized MAHC. Currently, the National Science Foundation advises some states on UV treatment and validation.

Features—Automatic Wipers

UV is used, primarily to disinfect, in almost every industry that uses water, including semiconductor, pharmaceutical, petrochemical, food, beverage, aquaculture. In these industries, when there are organics in the water that can accumulate on the quartz sleeve, internal wipers are used to remove deposits that block the emission of beneficial energy into the water from the quartz sleeve. In commercial aquatics, the quartz sleeve develops deposits from body oils, lotions, and cosmetics. Hard water, iron, or manganese also contribute to scale buildup on the quartz.

The wipers can be automatic or manual. If pool operators were to ask a UV supplier about the effectiveness of manual wipers, they would be told to buy automatic. Manual wipers rely upon humans to actuate them every time; if even a few cleanings are missed, deposits accelerate and the systems will have to be drained, disassembled, manually cleaned, and reassembled. Regardless of industry, automatic wipers are preferred over manual wipers. For optimal performance and accountability, a UV monitor and automatic internal wiper should be considered standard for commercial aquatics. Both low- and medium-pressure UV systems offer automatic internal wipers. Some companies use chemical injection ports to qualify for an NSF-50 requirement of being able to clean without manual disassembly. In this case, the UV chamber is mounted in a bypass. The bypass is engaged, cleaning solvents are injected into the bypass, and then they are drained and rinsed so that no chemical solvents will be added to the pool water when the UV bypass is opened. Accumulation of deposits is a continual process; the frequency of chemical cleaning will directly affect UV performance.

Installation

Installation of the UV system should be located after filtration, but before chemical injection (see Figure 11.4). The UV systems should be installed in a bypass, allowing for servicing while the pool is open. NSF-50-listed systems must be installed in a bypass (see Figure 11.5) if they do not have internal automatic wipers. The UV should be installed after the heaters. A factory-trained technician should install and start the system.

Ultraviolet Installation Detail

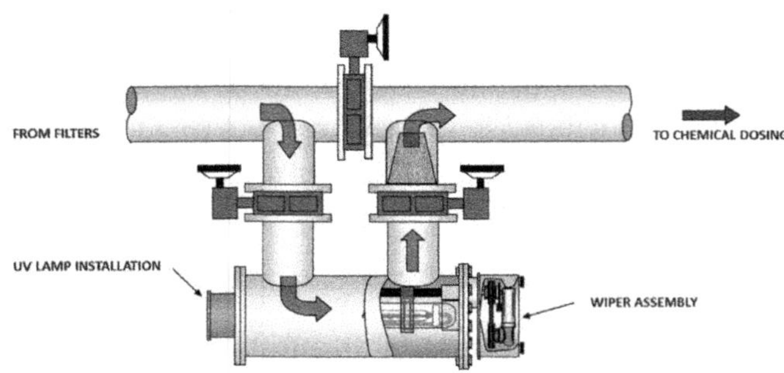

Figure 11.4. Standard bypass design allowing for service to the UV while the pool is open. (Photo courtesy of Tom Schaefer, Engineered Treatment Systems)

A properly specified UV system

- is simple and easy to maintain,
- has validated system performance,
- has monitors that measure UVC energy to ensure the correct dose of UV,
- has control panels that easily interface with existing building management systems,
- has a compact design that requires minimal space, and
- meets UL, MET, and/or ANSI/NSF-50 standards and validated to the U.S. EPA's *Disinfection Guidance Manual.*

The main cost benefits from installing a properly specified UV system include

- a custom unit design that is available for restricted space applications;
- simple maintenance and installation;
- improved health and safety;
- improved water quality, reducing the need for excessive backwashing; and
- improved air quality, reducing building maintenance.

UV systems have several requirements:

- They must be interlocked with feature pumps.
- They must have calibrated UV monitors.
- The output of every lamp must be monitored.
- Data logging of system performance must be automatically recorded.
- Systems with internal wipers must be properly maintained with 2–3 hours of labor every 6 months or twice seasonally.
- Low-pressure UV systems must have wipers and monitors in compliance with existing health codes.
- The validation report certificate must match the design flow rate (NSF-50 Annex H is not proper validation).
- The validation certificate must be submitted to the health department.

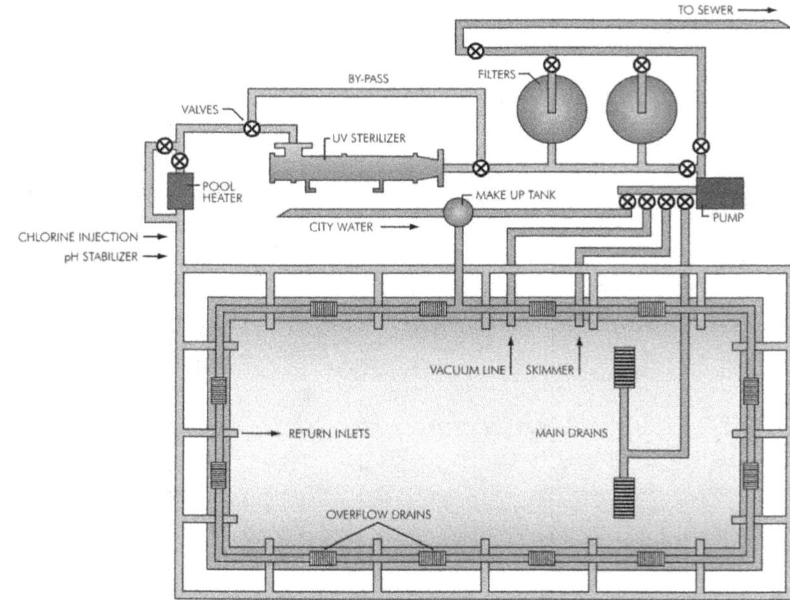

Figure 11.5. Placement of a UV sterilizer in a swimming pool circulation system. (Photo courtesy of Emperor Aquatics)

Table 11.1

Medium Pressure and Low Pressure Selection Criteria

Selection Criterion	Medium Pressure	Low Pressure
Installation/footprint	Small–medium	Medium–large
Service/required area	Small–medium	Large
Water/temperature	Unaffected	Affected
Operation/Electrical	Less efficient	More efficient
Spares/# required	Small	Medium–large
Monitoring/accuracy	Direct line of sight	Limited to none
Power control/lamp	Yes	No
Chloramine/control	200–300nm	254 nm only

(Table courtesy of Tom Schaefer, Engineered Treatment Systems)

Advanced Controls

The newest generation of chemical controllers can determine chloramine levels in the water. A signal to the UV system can adjust lamp power based on the chloramine level. This option will reduce energy consumption and, in theory, extend lamp life.

Summary

UV disinfection in swimming pools is quickly gaining popularity in the aquatic industry as a secondary disinfection system. Many agencies and regulatory bodies recommend UV systems for swimming pools. UV systems kill microorganisms (including *Cryptosporidium parvum*) and chloramines and reduce the need for shocking. As UV systems have many parts, from different lamp outputs to varying controls, the pool operator should carefully consider the type of UV system to install. The pool operator should consult and understand health agency and other regulatory body standards, such as the MAHC.

References

ATG UV Technology. (2012). MAHC regulations for UV and swimming pools. Retrieved from www.atguv.com/news/61/mach_regulations_for_uv_swimming_pools

Centers for Disease Control and Prevention. (2012). Cryptosporidiosis surveillance: United States, 2009–2010. *Morbidity and Mortality Weekly Report, 61*(SS05), 1–12.

Centers for Disease Control and Prevention. (2013a). Healthy swimming/recreational water. Retrieved from http://www.cdc.gov/healthywater/swimming/

Centers for Disease Control and Prevention. (2013b). Triple A's of healthy swimming: Awareness, action, advocacy. Retrieved from http://www.cdc.gov/healthywater/swimming/protection/triple-a-healthy-swimming.html

Corso, P. S., Kramer, M. H., Blair, K. A., Addiss, D. G., Davis, J. P., & Haddix, A. C. (2003). Cost of illness in the 1993 Waterborne Cryptosporidium outbreak, Milwaukee, Wisconsin. Retrieved from http://wwwnc.cdc.gov/eid/article/9/4/02-0417.htm

Peeters, J. E., Mazás, E. A., Masschelein, W. J., Villacorta Martinez de Maturana, I., & Debacker, E. (1989). Effect of disinfection of drinking water with ozone or chlorine dioxide on survival of Cryptosporidium parvum oocysts. *Applied and Environmental Microbiology, 55*, 1519–1522.

USA Swimming. (n.d.) The Air Quality Issue. Retrieved from www.USASwimming.org

(Photo courtesy of Water Technology, Inc.)

12

Chlorination and Bromination

This chapter looks in-depth at chlorination, the most popular means of disinfecting and oxidizing swimming pool water in the United States (Sidebar 12.1). More than 90% of all pools in the United States use chlorine. Although pool owners and operators have experimented with alternative sanitizers, chlorine still offers them an effective and economical way of keeping pool water clean and safe. Chlorine provides three important functions simultaneously:

1. **Disinfection** (sanitation) of bacteria, viruses, algae, and other pathogens and oxidation of organic debris and swimmer waste.

2. **Oxidation** assists the filtering process by burning up solid waste particles in the water. Many alternative sanitizers offer disinfection without oxidation, necessitating the purchase of additional chemicals.

3. **Residual properties,** meaning that chlorine remains in the water for extended periods in order to be available to disinfect and oxidize as the need arises with increased swimmer loads.

We will discuss numerous forms of chlorine, including the advantages and disadvantages of each. We will address bromine, another halogen similar to chlorine in many aspects, later in this chapter.

Disinfection and Oxidation

As mentioned previously, chlorination provides both disinfection and oxidation. Disinfection kills germs and algae to prevent the transmission of disease and other swimmer discomforts. Oxidation supplements the filtering process by burning up or bleaching out many organic impurities that swimmers introduce to the pool. Pool practitioners rightly say, "Chlorine burns the trash, and the filters remove the ash." Chlorine has the ability to burn up many smaller impurities that pass through filters. Killing bacteria is a relatively easy task for chlorine; small amounts of free chlorine (0.4 ppm) will destroy many pathogens. On the other hand, a more difficult responsibility of chlorine is to destroy particulate organic matter. This often calls for higher chlorine levels because heavy swimmer loads create a larger amount of organic debris. For oxidation purposes, free chlorine levels can vary greatly, but often fall somewhere between 2.0 and 10.0 ppm. Dull-looking pool water is often blamed on poor filtration, when in reality, insufficient oxidation is the real culprit.

Hypochlorous Acid

Regardless of the type of chlorine used, hypochlorous acid (HOCl) is the primary chemical used for swimming pool disinfection. Chlorine reacts with water to produce hypochlorous acid, which in turn disinfects through a electrochemical process. Hypochlorous acid penetrates the cell walls of bacteria, killing them. Hypochlorous acid is effective as a disinfectant, an algaecide, and an oxidizer. Used at proper levels, hypochlorous acid does not taste, smell, or burn.

$$Cl_2 + H_2O = HOCl + HCl$$

HOCl is a mild acid that disinfects and oxidizes swimming pool water and is the active killing agent produced by the reaction of chlorine in water. Many pool experts refer to HOCl as free chlorine (FC). HCl is hydrochloric acid, which is a powerful acid. As pH rises, HOCl breaks apart, or disassociates (also referred to as ionization), in the following manner:

$$HOCl = H+ + OCl-$$

H+ refers to the hydrogen ion and OCl- represents the hypochlorite ion. The hypochlorite ion (OCl-) is not very active, and its killing power is insignificant. The higher the pH is, the less HOCl is available to disinfect and oxidize. At higher pH levels, more HOCl is required, and bacteria and algae will take longer to kill. The likelihood of swimmer infections such as swimmer's ear and sore throats may also increase. As pH levels decrease, the effectiveness of HOCl increases (Table 12.1). To prevent HOCl from losing its killing power, pH levels should be maintained between 7.2 and 7.8. Below a pH of 7.2, HOCl becomes corrosive. We will discuss pH in detail in Chapter 15.

In Figure 12.1, at a pH of 7.5, about 50% of the free chlorine is active HOCl. At the elevated pH 8.0, a mere 21% of the free chlorine is active HOCl.

Forms of Chlorine

Chlorine is available in three basic forms: gas, liquid, and solid. Within these three forms, many are commercially available, each of which we discuss below.

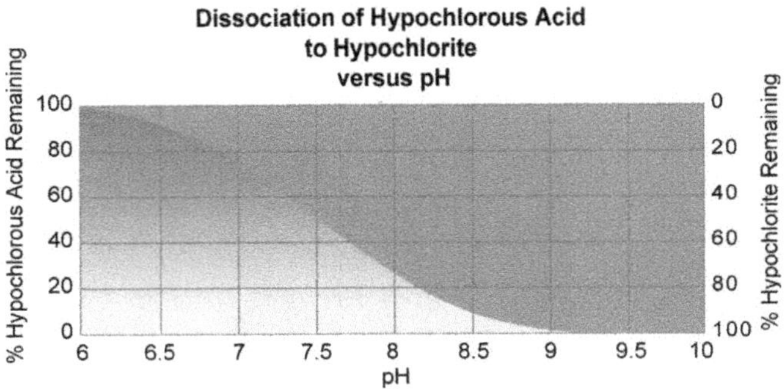

Figure 12.1. Dissociation of hypochlorous acid to hypochlorite with increased pH. (Courtesy of The Association of Pool & Spa Professionals © 2012)

Gas Chlorine (Cl_2)

Of all the chlorines available for swimming pool use, gas chlorine is the most cost effective because it consists of 100% available chemical. Pound for pound, gas chlorine is the cheapest and strongest of all chlorines, but perhaps not surprisingly, it is also the most potentially dangerous.

Since the 9/11 attacks on the World Trade Center in New York City in 2001, there has been a heightened awareness of terroristic threats to the United States. Although an effective form of chlorine, gas chlorine is now examined more carefully because of its potential for use by terrorists. Fewer pools use it today because of these concerns.

Gas chlorine is extremely toxic and can be lethal. Those who use gas chlorine seldom want to part with it, and those who use other disinfectants often fear gas chlorine.

Table 12.1

Chlorine-Based Sanitizing Agents

The most common forms of chlorine sanitizers used in pools and spas are:

Chemical Name	Common Name	% Available Chlorine	pH	Physical Form	Stabilized
Calcium hypochlorite	Cal Hypo	47%, 65%, and 78%	~11	granular and tablets	no
Sodium hypochlorite	Liquid chlorine or bleach	10%–15%	~13	liquid	no
Lithium hypochlorite		35%	10.7	powder	no
Chlorine generators	Variable; commonly	~1% for brine typesalt —produces sodium hypochlorite solution			no
Sodium dichloro-s-triazinetrione	Dichlor	56% and 63%	6	granular	yes
Trichoro-s-triazinetrione	Trichlor	85% and 90%	3.0	granular and tablets	yes
Elemental chlorine	chlorine gas	100%	0–1	gas in cylinder	no

(Courtesy of The Association of Pool and Spa Professionals © 2012)

Gas chlorine is compressed into large metal cylinders, where it liquefies under pressure. As a liquid, it is amber colored and is 1.5 times heavier than water. When released from the tank, the chlorine returns to the gaseous state. Chlorine gas cylinders used for public aquatic facilities normally weigh 150 lb and must conform to Chlorine Institute standards. For every pound of chlorine used, about a half pound of hydrochloric acid is produced, which in turn lowers the pH. As a result, for every pound of chlorine gas added to pool water, an additional pound of soda ash must be added to maintain the pH in the ideal range.

In addition to lowering the pH, the HOCl that chlorine gas produces dissipates quickly in sunlight. To combat this loss of chlorine outdoors, some pool operators stabilize their chlorine in sunlight by adding cyanuric acid (CYA). As one would expect, the use of CYA has pros and cons, which we will discuss later. Generally, aquatic facilities in the south tend to need stabilized chlorine more than aquatic facilities in the north.

Perhaps the greatest shortcoming of gas chlorine is the specialized equipment needed to prevent and escape a gas leak. The following gas chlorine equipment is required in most states:

1. A separate fireproof room reserved for gas chlorine apparatus exclusively. The chlorine room should be detached from the filter room (Figure 12.2).
2. Stored tanks, whether empty or full, must be chained to a wall and capped.
3. A fan and vent located near the floor (remember, chlorine gas is heavier than air) that can exchange the air in the room between 1 and 4 minutes. This fan should run continually.
4. A self-contained breathing apparatus located outside the room. Canister gas masks are ineffective in high gas chlorine contents (Figure 12.3).
5. A high chlorine detection system.

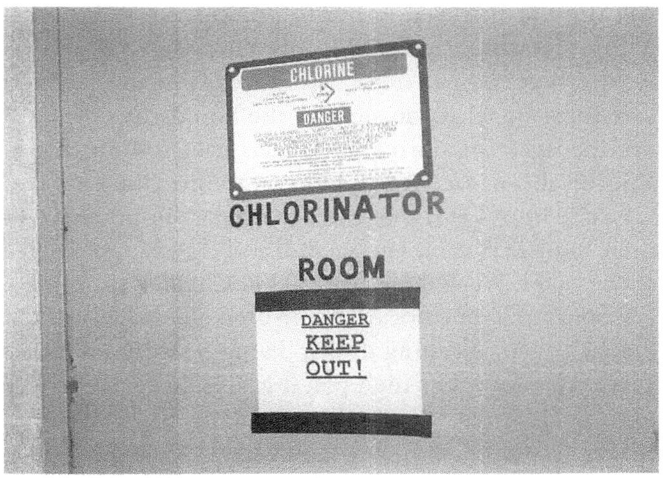

Figure 12.2. Separate, secure gas chlorine room.

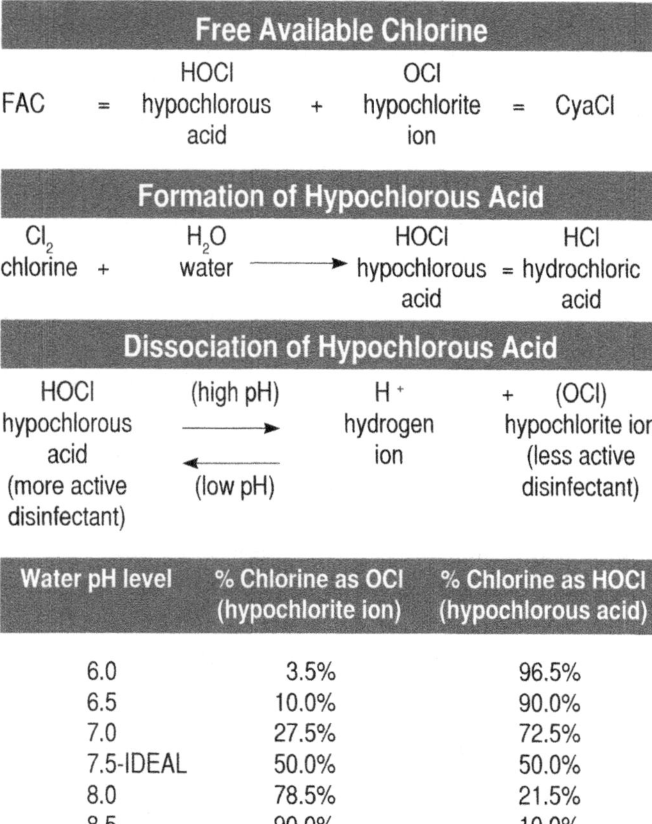

Free Available Chlorine					
FAC	=	HOCl hypochlorous acid	+	OCl hypochlorite ion	= CyaCl

Formation of Hypochlorous Acid

Cl_2 chlorine + H_2O water $\longrightarrow$ HOCl hypochlorous acid = HCl hydrochloric acid

Dissociation of Hypochlorous Acid

HOCl hypochlorous acid (more active disinfectant) $\xrightarrow{\text{(high pH)}}$ $\xleftarrow{\text{(low pH)}}$ H⁺ hydrogen ion + (OCl) hypochlorite ion (less active disinfectant)

Water pH level	% Chlorine as OCl (hypochlorite ion)	% Chlorine as HOCl (hypochlorous acid)
6.0	3.5%	96.5%
6.5	10.0%	90.0%
7.0	27.5%	72.5%
7.5-IDEAL	50.0%	50.0%
8.0	78.5%	21.5%
8.5	90.0%	10.0%

Figure 12.3. The effect of pH on the killing power of chlorine. (Courtesy of The Association of Pool and Spa Professionals © 2012)

6. An emergency action plan to handle a gas leak. One important question must be answered before using gas chlorine: What is the role of the pool operator in the event of a gas leak? Is the primary responsibility of the pool operator to stop the leak or to evacuate the facility and call for help? Where hazmat (hazardous materials) teams exist, pool operators should work with them to establish emergency procedures. Pool operators should probably be trained to handle gas leaks only when hazmat personnel are not available.
7. Pool operators should check gas leaks daily by using ammonia hydroxide (household ammonia) in either a cloth or a misting spray bottle. If a leak exists when the ammonia is applied, a noticeable white cloud will be produced.

Because the mandated safety requirements for the safe handling and transportation of chlorine gas have become stringent, the expense of constructing a gas chlorine storage room and injection system today is much greater than it was a few years ago. Many installations today call for high chlorine shutdown and evacuation systems.

The greatest chance for a gas chlorine leak is when tanks are being changed. For this reason, self-contained breathing apparatus should be worn whenever changing tanks. Perhaps the most common error during this process is using a bad lead washer between the regulator and tank. A new lead washer should be used for every tank change. A worn lead washers must be removed from the tank valve before placing a new washer in the valve. Old washers should be discarded so that they cannot be re-used. Also, a good rule to follow is to never enter a gas chlorine room alone; the buddy system should be used. Gas tanks should never be changed when patrons are present in the facility.

Finally, only mature, well-trained staff should handle gas chlorine. If younger, less experienced workers are responsible for chlorination, gas chlorine should probably not be used. During a chlorine emergency, the Chlorine Emergency Plan Team (CHLOREP) can be contacted at (800)-424-9300.

Residential pools should not use gas chlorine. When handled and managed properly, gas chlorine can provide the cheapest and best disinfection and oxidation to swimming pool water.

Sodium Hypochlorite (NaOCl)

The most popular liquid form of chlorine is sodium hypochlorite (NaOCl). Perhaps its greatest advantage is found in its convenient and safe handling. Sodium hypochlorite (12% to 15% active chlorine) is only slightly more powerful than liquid bleach (5% to 6%). Sodium hypochlorite is most often referred to as either liquid chlorine, sodium hypo, or bleach. Sodium hypochlorite is available in a clear yellow liquid that is normally stored in large plastic drums. This type of liquid chlorine is introduced to the pool by a chemical feeder located in the filter room. Although sodium hypochlorite is more expensive than gas chlorine, it is usually much less expensive than other chlorines and could be the most popular form of chlorine used in the United States.

The chemical reaction taking place for liquid chlorine in swimming pool water is similar to that of gas chlorine:

$$NaOCl + H_2O = HOCl + NaOH$$

NaOCl (sodium hypochlorite) when mixed with water produces hypochlorous acid that disinfects and oxidizes. Another by-product is NaOH, which is sodium hydroxide, a strong basic (alkaline) that raises pH. As a result, whenever sodium hypochlorite is used for disinfection, an acid or CO_2 gas must be added to the pool water to decrease the pH. Muriatic acid (hydrochloric acid) is inexpensive and effective in lowering the pH for public pools. Residential pools and smaller swimming facilities

seem to prefer sodium bisulfate, a safe, convenient, dry acid that is more expensive. A basic rule of thumb is to add 1 gal of muriatic acid for every 4 to 5 gal of sodium hypochlorite. Acids used for lowering pH should be diluted before adding them to the pool water. Acids should be added to cool water in a clean clear plastic container.

Although sodium hypochlorite is readily available and easy to handle, it does not come without pitfalls. Sodium hypochlorite's biggest downfall is its short shelf life. As storage temperatures increase, the percentage of available chlorine decreases cause by autodecomposition. It must be stored in a cool, dark room, which is often difficult to find at swimming pools. Because liquid chlorine decomposes so quickly, large quantities should not be stored for long periods of time. In addition, liquid chlorine may be delivered to the facility in a weakened state, that is, with less than 12% effective chlorine. Depending on the environment in which it is stored, sodium hypochlorite usually does not maintain much strength beyond 30 days, but perhaps fewer. For facility managers to ensure they are getting what they paid for, they can test the chlorine effectiveness with a special test kit to ensure a 12% level of chlorine.

Like gas chlorine, HOCl produced by sodium hypochlorite is unstable, meaning that it loses its strength in sunlight. Again, it may be stabilized if the pool operator wishes to deal with CYA.

Another disadvantage includes the elevating effect sodium hypochlorite has on the pH of pool water. When sodium hypochlorite is used, a strong acid must also be added to maintain the pH within the ideal range. Another problem associated with the use of sodium hypochlorite is that it tends to clog chemical feeders pumping it into the pool. This occurs because of the scale produced by the high pH that sodium hypochlorite contains. When chemical feeders are used to inject sodium hypochlorite, they should be broken down and acid washed on a monthly basis to prevent clogging. Some pool operators will use the chemical feeder to pump fresh water, then pump muriatic acid for cleaning purposes. The manufacturer's guidelines must be followed in this case, and care must be taken not to mix the liquid chlorine with acid because this forms dangerous gas. Sodium hypochlorite also has a strong tendency to raise the total dissolved solids (TDS) that can accumulate in pools. Over time, high TDS values give a dull and cloudy appearance of the water. We will discuss TDS in Chapter 15.

Sodium hypochlorite can be used effectively around the facility for cleaning decks, diving boards, and other areas. Because of its high pH, it is also an excellent way to superchlorinate the pool, particularly when gas chlorine is used as the primary sanitizer.

Household bleach should be substituted for sodium hypochlorite only as a last resort because it can clog a filter medium. One gal of sodium hypochlorite equals the strength of 1 lb of gas chlorine, and 2 gal of household bleach equals 1 gal of industrial liquid chlorine. Gloves and a face shield should be worn when working with sodium hypochlorite and also when working with the acids required to lower pH when liquid chlorine is used (Figure 12.4).

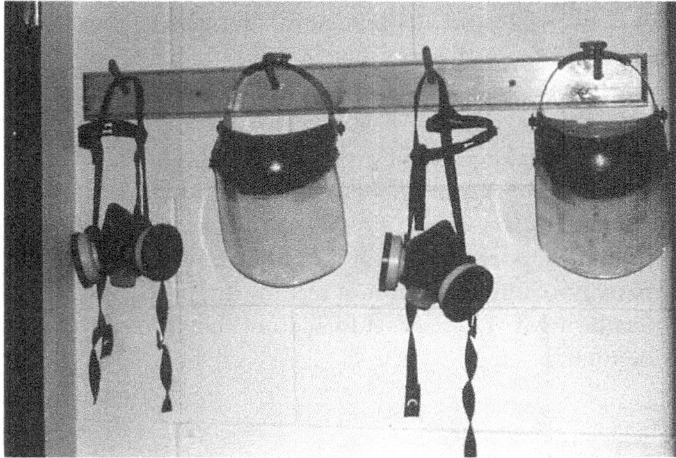

Figure 12.4. Protective equipment for safely handling sodium hypochlorite.

In summary, sodium hypochlorite is an effective disinfectant and oxidizer that is safe and easy to handle. Provided it is stored properly and pH levels are adjusted downward, pool operators can be satisfied with sodium hypochlorite.

Calcium Hypochlorite (Ca(OCl)$_2$)

Calcium hypochlorite has been the leading solid form of chlorine in recent years. "Cal hypo," as it is sometimes referred to, is a white solid and is available in granular and tablet form. It contains 65% available chlorine, has a long shelf life, and is easy to store. Still, a cool, dark place and a tightly secured lid will extend the life of calcium hypochlorite.

In larger pools, the solid briquettes are placed in a feeder that must be cleaned regularly to prevent calcium buildup. In smaller operations, tablets are placed in erosion feeders or surface skimmers. Like liquid chlorine, granular calcium hypochlorite can be used for cleaning and disinfecting around the pool, provided the resulting white powder is not allowed to remain in the facility when people are in attendance. It can also be broadcast over the pool for superchlorination, although when used in this fashion, it may cause cloudiness and leaves a slight residue on the pool bottom. Brushing the pool bottom after shocking and before the pool opens is important. Although this method of superchlorination is popular, some pool experts do not recommend it. Calci-

um hypochlorite should not be broadcast in a vinyl liner pool because undissolved granules may burn or bleach the liner. If cal hypo is used in this fashion, it should be predissolved for a vinyl-lined pool. The chemical reaction that occurs when calcium hypochlorite enters the pool water is as follows:

$$Ca(OCl)_2 + H_2O = 2HOCl + Ca(OH)_2$$

Two molecules of HOCl are produced in this case that disinfect and oxidate. Ca(OH)$_2$ represents calcium hydroxide, a moderate alkaline by-product that slightly increases pH and calcium hardness.

Critics of calcium hypochlorite often claim it clouds the water and elevates the calcium hardness, but when cloudiness does occur, the water clears quickly. In most pools, a higher calcium hardness is usually desirable, so the second criticism is not always valid. Calcium hypochlorite has only a minimal effect on pH and may cause it to rise slightly. Many aquatic facility owners and operators keep some calcium hypochlorite for several pool-related purposes, most of which are related to cleaning. Because many pools have calcium hypochlorite readily accessible, a risk of fire or explosion is present. Any organic material added to calcium hypochlorite can cause combustion. Soda, oil, sweat, paper, soap, other chemicals, and just about anything will cause a fire in this case. For this reason, calcium hypochlorite should be stored separately to prevent other chemicals from being accidentally mixed with it. Chlorine drums must be also kept dry and off the floor. Separate chemical scoops and buckets should be used for application of calcium hypochlorite. Trichlor, a stabilized chlorine, should never be mixed with calcium hypochlorite. Unfortunately, some pool operators have mistakenly placed both chlorines in the same chemical feeder, causing a violent explosion. The problem with the incompatible solid forms of chlorine is that they all look alike, making it easy to improperly mix them.

Calcium hypochlorite is also unstable and will dissipate in sunlight quickly. A little more than 1.5 lb of calcium hypochlorite equals 1 lb of gas chlorine. Calcium hypochlorite is more often seen in residential pool applications rather than in public or commercial settings. Granular calcium hypochlorite also serves as an excellent algaecide on pool decks and pool bottoms, particularly sloped areas.

Chlorine gas, sodium hypochlorite (liquid), and calcium hypochlorite (solid) have been referred to by some water chemists as the Big Three because they are the most commonly used forms of chlorine to date. Each form of chlorine has pros and cons associated with its use. Other forms of chlorine are also valuable in swimming pool sanitation.

Lithium Hypochlorite

Lithium hypochlorite is a powdered chlorine that is extremely soluble in water. Lithium hypochlorite is approximately 35% effective. It dissolves quickly, making it ideal for superchlorination, particularly for vinyl-lined and painted pools, as well as hot tubs. Although lithium hypochlorite is intended to be used as a primary disinfectant, it is often used just for superchlorination because it is expensive.

In particular, it is used in dichlor and trichlor pools because these stabilized chlorines should not be used for shocking because they elevate the CYA levels to unacceptable levels.

Lithium hypochlorite stores and handles well; it is not flammable. Some pool operators prefer lithium because it contains no calcium, which may produce scale-forming water. Lithium hypochlorite is usually dissolved in water first and then pumped into the recirculation system. Lithium hypochlorite will raise the pH slightly, and it is also an unstable chlorine that is lost rapidly in sunlight.

Stabilized Chlorines

All chlorine forms mentioned thus far have been of the unstabilized variety. This means these chemicals last longer in indoor pools than outdoor pools because the deteriorating UV rays of the sun dissipate chlorine. In an attempt to stretch chlorine in outdoor pools, CYA has been added to some chlorine compounds. Stabilized chlorine products represent a somewhat controversial type of chlorination.

Chlorine can be stabilized in two ways: CYA can be added to a chlorinated pool or prestabilized chlorine can be purchased from pool suppliers in the form of chlorinated isocyanurates. Whether CYA is added to chlorinated pool water or stabilized chlorinated isocyanurates are used, the process of protecting chlorine from the UV rays of the sun is the same. CYA is a ringlike molecule that latches onto HOCl molecules to form a more stable atomic structure. This combination of CYA and free chlorine delays chlorine loss, but cannot stop it altogether. Pool operators say that chlorine stabilized with CYA works as if it had sunscreen or as if it was time released. So stabilized chlorine lasts longer than unstabilized chlorine in outdoor pools, but some experts question whether stabilized chlorine is as effective as its counterpart. Too much stabilizer can possibly "bind up" free chlorine, rendering it ineffective and turning the pool water dull and hazy.

The main problem associated with the use of stabilized chlorine is that CYA levels in the water will increase as the stabilizer continues to be used. Most states prohibit CYA levels greater than 100 ppm. The greater the CYA level is, the less effective HOCl will be. Pool operators say as you raise the CYA level, you subtract the free chlorine level. Once the CYA level reaches 100 ppm, the only way of lowering CYA in the pool is by draining water from it. This is particularly a problem for trichlor users because this stabilized chlorine is 50% CYA, and the 100 ppm limit is attained quickly in this case.

Many technicians recommend keeping the CYA levels between 30 and 40 ppm. At that range, HOCl is being protected from the sun, but it still remains an effective killer. Some supporters of stabilized chlorine, however, think the 100 ppm CYA limit is an arbitrary figure. Some pool technicians would prefer to see a higher CYA limit and suggest CYA limits between 150 and 200 ppm. Unfortunately, too many pool operators use stabilized CYA indoors, and whether CYA is applied indoors or outside, many pool operators do not test for it. These two misapplications of stabilized chlorine are dangerous and unfortunate.

> **Dr. Tom's Tip**
>
> For the first time in my career, I added a mere 5 ppm of CYA to my million-gallon outdoor pool with amazing results. Not only was my chlorine use reduced significantly, but my pool water also increased in clarity and polish. If experimenting with straight CYA, use as little as possible the first time.

Apparently, "locking up" free chlorine with CYA and reducing its effectiveness is not the only problem associated with stabilized chlorine. Some health officials believe that high CYA levels in the water may be hazardous to humans. Because swimming pool water can be swallowed and absorbed by the skin, this could be a real concern. High levels of CYA in the body may lead to liver and kidney damage, and that is why health officials recommend low levels of CYA. Conversely, some manufacturers state that CYA levels of 10,000 ppm are not harmful, so it appears this debate will not be short lived.

The two most popular commercially available stabilized chlorines are dichlor and trichlor. Dichlor (sodium dichloro-s-triazinetrione) is a stabilized chlorine commercially produced by combining soda ash, CYA, and chlorine. This stabilized chlorine is sometimes referred to as sodium dichlor. Dichlor is 56% or 62% effective and is presently available in a granular form only. One advantage of dichlor is that it has a neutral pH, so it has little effect on pH levels in pool water. If dichlor is used as a primary sanitizer, an unstabilized chlorine should be used for superchlorination because high levels of CYA will be reached quickly in this case. It is easily stored and handled, and it dissolves quickly. Dichlor is usually predissolved and introduced to the pool through a liquid chlorinator.

Trichlor (trichloro-s-triazinetrione) is another stabilized chlorine that is produced commercially and is available in tablets, sticks, and granules. Unlike dichlor, trichlor dissolves slowly and as a result can be introduced into pools through erosion feeders, floaters, and skimmers. The popularity of trichlor can probably be linked to this fact; homeowners can drop trichlor tablets or sticks into a floater or feeder, and chlorine will be found in the pool regardless of the amount of sunlight. Erosion feeders and floaters are inexpensive and easy to use. If introduced through a skimmer, however, it may damage the skimmer and the plumbing near the skimmer. When trichlor is administered through a floater, children may be tempted to play with it, which is not desirable. Trichlor is powerful, having an available chlorine content of almost 90%. Trichlor is highly acid and lowers the pH of swimming pool water.

The stabilized chlorines dichlor and trichlor are often called organic chlorines. Inorganic chlorines are unstabilized and lost easily in sunlight. Stabilized chlorines should be used only in outdoor pools. Stabilized chlorines were developed to increase the longevity of chlorine in sunlight. Because indoor pools have no deteriorating UV rays, stabilized chlorines are inappropriate indoors. Why worry about and test for CYA levels when UV rays are not present? As mentioned previously, although CYA protects chlorine from the sunlight, it also reduces the ability of chlorine to disinfect.

Perhaps the greatest benefactors of stabilized chlorine are smaller pool owners, hotel and motel pools, and pool service companies who have difficulty keeping chlorine levels up in a number of pools. These individuals would rather use stabilized chlorine than risk closure of their pools by health officials for inadequate chlorine levels. In addition, the savings on chlorine are great. Although stabilizer is an additional cost, it saves significant money by saving chlorine and reducing service calls.

But like other disinfectants, stabilized chlorine has drawbacks. Constantly monitoring and controlling CYA levels is a major concern that requires additional testing procedures. Although easy to use and cost effective, dichlor and trichlor are not good algaecides. Again, stabilized chlorines should be used only outdoors. As stabilized chlorines are used, the levels of CYA climb higher.

Draining the pool somewhat and refilling with freshwater is the only way to reduce CYA levels.

A preferred way of stabilizing pool water is to add CYA to the water to a predetermined CYA level of between 30 and 50 ppm, and then the pool can be chlorinated with a traditional form of chlorine without increasing CYA levels. In summary, stabilized chlorines are both popular and controversial. All pros and cons should be studied before stabilized chlorine are used. A local chemical suppliers can be contacted for details.

Bromination

Bromine, like chlorine, is a member of the halogen family, with excellent disinfection and oxidation properties. Bromine was isolated in 1826 by French scientist Atoine-Jérôme Balard. It is one of five halogens, which are nonmetallic chemical elements. Fluorine, chlorine, iodine, and astatine are the other halogens. Bromine and mercury are the only elements that ordinarily are in a liquid state. Reddish-brown bromine is highly corrosive and easily volatilizes into a gas that irritates the eyes and mucous membranes (Herman, 1991). Elemental bromine is a difficult and dangerous liquid to handle. Elemental bromine reacts with water in the following fashion:

$$Br_2 + H_2O = HOBr + HBr$$

Rather than producing HOCl such as chlorine, bromine produces two disinfecting agents. HOBr, or hypobromous acid, is the primary disinfectant, and HBr, or hydrobromic acid, reduces pH levels.

Elemental bromine is not available for swimming pool use in the United States. The primary source for bromine is seawater and potash mines, and bromine has also been used in photographic processing, dyes, gasoline, and disinfectants and as a poison gas in World War I.

In most applications, bromine became less common. However, in the 1950s, bromine was first combined with chlorine in tablet form and began to see use in swimming pools (Herman, 1991). Today, the industry has moved away from bromine in large public pools. It rarely works as well as chlorine in these venues. Bromine is still common in spas and therapy pools, as it is more stable and lasts longer in hot water.

Although elemental bromine has been used successfully in Europe, the United States has switched to sodium bromide salts in combination with other compounds such as chlorine to increase its effectiveness and ability to be handled. This two-part system includes an oxidizer that activates the bromine. Bromine in this form is available in sticks or tablets. The oxidizer is often chlorine or potassium monopersulfate, a nonhalogen oxidizing agent, and in some cases, ozone. The bromine–potassium monopersulfate combination is usually reserved for small pools that can be hand fed. The more popular combination is bromine–chlorine. The combination of bromine and chlorine produces hypobromous acid (HOBr) as the primary disinfectant and hypochlorous acid (HOCl), which serves as a regenerative catalyst and also assists with disinfection and oxidation.

Bromine has several advantages. Perhaps the greatest advantage is that combined bromine, or bromamines, does not irritate, burn, or smell the way combined chlorines or chloramines do.

Along those lines, chloramines must be "shocked" out of the water, whereas bromamines break down on their own.

Bromine is more stable at elevated temperatures than chlorine, so its use in hot water is preferable to chlorine. This explains why bromine is the preferred disinfectant in hot tubs and spas. Combined chlorines and bromines are produced quickly in hot water environments due to the relatively high swimmer load and the increased amounts of perspiration in the water due to the heat.

Bromamines are effective as disinfectants, whereas chloramines are not, giving bromine the advantage in hot water.

Because it is a fairly strong oxidizer (but not as strong as chlorine), bromine is combustible like chlorine and must be stored carefully. Bromine may also smell, turn the water green, and cause staining and sudsing if not maintained at appropriate levels. Generally, it is more expensive than chlorine. Another disadvantage of bromine is that it is unstable and will be lost rapidly in sunlight. Unfortunately, CYA cannot be used to stabilize bromine. Perhaps the best application for bromine is in hot tubs and spas, whereas chlorine should be reserved for larger pools.

Although pool operators can use a DPD chlorine test to determine the bromine level as long as the appropriate conversion factor is applied to the reading, better test kits test for both chlorine and bromine (look for two sets of standards on the sanitizer side of the color comparator). Some test strips measure chlorine or bromine.

Summary

Chlorine is the most commonly used swimming pool disinfectant in the United States, but many different forms of chlorine are used in aquatic facilities. Once again, pool operators must consider cost, effectiveness, availability, and ease of handling when selecting chlorine. Chlorine must be handled with extreme care. Bromine is also a popular swimming pool disinfectant, but it is more commonly used in hot tubs and spas.

Dr. Tom's Tip

The problem with most aquatic facilities in the United States is that we keep our free chlorine levels too low, particularly in heavily used pools, which promotes chloramine production. Try keeping your chlorine levels .5 ppm higher than you normally do for clearer, sweeter smelling water.

Bibliography

American Water Works Association. (1971). *Water quality and treatment* (3rd ed.). Denver, CO: Author.

Gabrielson, A. M. (1987). *Swimming pools: A guide to their planning, design, and operation* (4th ed.). Champaign, IL: Human Kinetics.

Herman, E. (1991, April 22). Sniffing out a sanitizing specialist. *Pool Spa News.* www.poolspanews.com/

Kowalsky, L. (Ed.). (1991). *Pool/spa operators handbook.* San Antonio, TX: National Swimming Pool Foundation.

Mitchel, K. (1988). *The proper management of pool and spa water.* Decatur, GA: BioLab.

Pope, J. R., Jr. (1991). *Public swimming pool management, I and II.* Alexandria, VA: National Recreation and Park Association.

Recreonics. (1991). *Buyers' guide and operations handbook: Catalog no. 41.* Indianapolis, IN: Author.

Taylor, C. (1989). *Everything you always wanted to know about pool care.* Chino, CA: Service Industry Publications.

Taylor Technologies. (2012). *Test kit selection guide.* Sparks, MD: Taylor Technologies, Inc. www.taylortechnologies.com

Torney, J. A., & Clayton, R. D. (1970). *Aquatic instruction, coaching, and management.* Minneapolis, MN: Burgess Publishing.

Washington State Public Health Association. (1988). *Swimming pool operations.* Seattle, WA: Author.

Williams, K. G., & Young, R. A. (Eds.). (2011). *Aquatic facility operator manual* (6th ed.). Ashburn, VA: National Recreation and Park Association.

13 Superchlorination

With today's advances in water chemistry, superchlorination may not be as vitally important as it once was. For older, traditional pools that might not have the latest chemical and filtration technologies, superchlorination may still be needed. The addition of high-quality UV systems are now used to drastically reduce chloramines levels, rather than using traditional superchlorination methods. See Chapter 11 for more information.

Before discussing the role superchlorination plays in the swimming pool industry, we must first discuss combined chlorine or chloramines. As mentioned in Chapter 12, hypochlorous acid (HOCl) is a by-product produced by the addition of chlorine to pool water. HOCl is an excellent disinfectant and oxidizer. HOCl is referred to as free chlorine (FC).

Editor's note: The first edition of this book called this free available chlorine, or FAC, but the term *available* has since been dropped. *Available* is an ambiguous term that has only led to confusion in the past. So instead of having FAC, CAC, and TAC, we have dropped the *A*s and now use FC, CC, and TC.

Pool operations would be simplified if the free HOCl produced remained free and active in the water, but unfortunately it does not. Free chlorine combines with contaminants such as algae, dust, pollen, urine, perspiration, and other ammonia–nitrogen compounds (most important, urine and sweat) to form combined chlorine (CC). *Chloramine* is another term used to describe CC. Technically, the three types of chloramines are mono-chloramines, dichloramines, and trichloramines, but in this text, we will call them chloramines. The obnoxious "chlorine odor" found at many pools is not FC, but rather CC, or chloramines. Chloramines not only smell but also irritate eyes and mucous membranes and cause cloudy water. Ironically, the swimmers who complain about chlorine irritation and odor are the cause of it because of the ammonia compounds they naturally carry with them into the pool. The chlorine smell is caused by too little, not too much, chlorine. For instance, an aquatic facility that has been effectively superchlorinated will have no detectable chlorine odor, even with high FC levels (Figure 13.1).

Chloramines are perhaps the number one problem facing heavily used indoor chlorinated pools. As swimmer loads increase, so does the likelihood of chloramine formation. Chloramines are not effective disinfectants. The more traditional way to rid a pool of its chloramines is by adding an amount of new chlorine that is 10 times greater than the existing CC count. Table 13.1 illustrates this concept. More recently, however, products have been developed to remove ammonia from the water so that chloramine production is reduced. We will discuss this following the section on shocking. In outdoor pools, chloramines are still a problem, but often go unnoticed because the outside air and breezes whisk the chloramines away before they are noticed—no harm, no foul.

A traditional DPD color matching test is typically used to determine the FC and total chlorine levels (TC). With these levels, FC can be subtracted from TC, resulting in a CC count in parts per million. With a DPD test kit, the FC can be found by adding five drops of the Reagent No. 1 and five drops of Reagent No. 2 (or a No. 1 DPD tablet) to the water sample. With this FC sample, another five drops of DPD No. 3 (or a No. 3 DPD tablet) can be added to determine TC. FC can be subtracted from TC to find CC.

A much improved way of testing for chloramines is Taylor Technologies' FAS-DPD titration method for FC and CC. The white powder in this test kit should be applied to the pool sample in a test vial; the water will turn pink in the presence of FC.

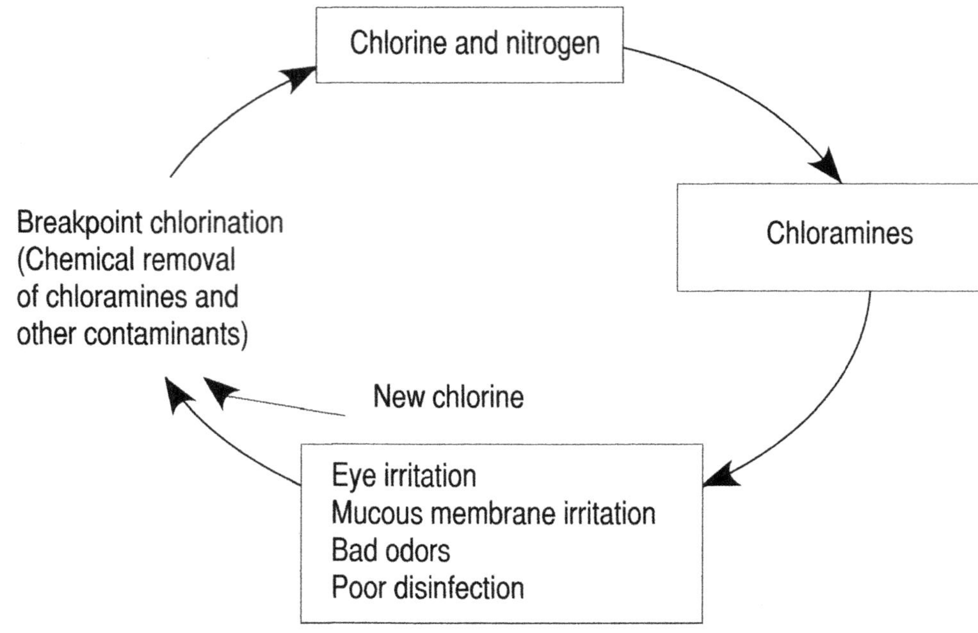

Figure 13.1. Chloramine cycle. (From *Basic Pool and Spa Technology*, 2nd ed., by the National Spa and Pool Institute, 1992, Alexandria, VA: Author)

Table 13.1
Determining Breakpoint Dosage

Chlorine	Amount
TC	1.8 ppm
FC	-1.1 ppm
CC	0.7 ppm
	x 10
Breakpoint dosage	7.0 ppm

Then a titrating reagent should be added drop by drop until the pink sample water turns clear. The total number of drops required to turn the pink water clear should be multiplied by 0.2 ppm or 0.5 ppm (depending on the volume of the sample used) to get the FC reading. The same process can be used to determine the CC reading. The advantages of the FAS-DPD method are it can read FC at levels that would bleach out the result of a traditional DPD test (it reads as high as 20 ppm accurately); it can read CC as low as 0.2, the point at which it is recommended to shock the water (DPD tests can only go as low as 0.5); and no color matching is required—great, if the tester is red color-blind. Aquatic facility managers will find the FAS-DPD method shocks more effectively.

Superchlorination, Breakpoint, and "Shocking"

Subtle differences exist among superchlorination, breakpoint chlorination, and shocking, although many aquatic facility managers consider them synonymous. Although clarifying these concepts may be helpful, understanding how to prevent and destroy chloramines is more important than knowing the exact terminology.

Superchlorination usually refers to the periodic, intentional elevation of FC by pool operators to prevent algae, odors, irritation, and cloudiness. In this case, FC is often raised to between 3 and 10 ppm. Pool operators normally estimate a level they think will work for them.

Breakpoint chlorination, on the other hand, refers to a specific and measurable point at which all organic impurities, including CC, are oxidized. The point at which this will occur (FC approximately 10 times greater than the CC count) can be found with a test kit. The problem with superchlorinating but not reaching the breakpoint is that even more troublesome chloramines are created. Even if the word *superchlorination* is used to mean what is done to restore sparkling, clear water to a pool, the calculation Breakpoint Dosage = 10 x CC level should be used (see Table 13.1).

Shocking is an even more ambiguous term than superchlorinating because not all products sold as shocks have chlorine in them. Some have potassium monopersulfate instead. Many aquatic professionals who have a

UV system installed in their swimming pools claim they rarely need to shock their pools.

Chlorine-based shocks can sanitize the water by killing harmful invaders such bacteria, viruses, yeast, and algae, and they can also oxidize (chemically "burn up") the CC; CC's predecessors, ammonia compounds such as sweat and urine; and organic contaminants such as dirt, pollen, lotions, and perfumes.

Shocks made from potassium monopersulfate cannot sanitize water. They oxidize well, though. Therefore, potassium monopersulfate must be used in conjunction with a registered sanitizer, most commonly chlorine. By cleansing the water of organic contaminants, these non-chlorine shocks leave the sanitizer available for its highest purpose: keeping swimmers safe from disease and infection. Because potassium monopersulfate shocks have no breakpoint phenomenon, they will not create more CC if not enough is added to remove all the chloramines in the water. We will discuss this subject more later.

The point of this discussion is to highlight the importance of eliminating CC in swimming pools, regardless of how that is accomplished, but preferably before the chloramines become obnoxious. Knowing the difference between superchlorination, breakpoint chlorination, and shocking is icing on the cake.

When should a pool be treated? When a test kit reveals a CC level of between 0.2 and 0.4 ppm, the pool should be superchlorinated to 10 times the CC count. Usually at 0.4 ppm CC, eye irritation and chlorine odors become offensive. If the CC levels are at 0.4 ppm, then enough chlorine should be added to raise the FC level to 4.0. Again, if the amount of new chlorine is less than 10 times the CC level, even more chloramines will be created, compounding the existing problem. When treating a pool, overchlorinating is always better than underchlorinating. Underdosing is a common but costly mistake that many aquatic facility operators make.

As the new chlorine attacks chloramines, it converts the chloramines to nitrogen, which leaves the pool as a harmless gas. Potassium monopersulfate shocks and oxidizes ammonia groups to nitrogen gas. For this reason, outdoor pool operators have greater success than indoor pool operators because indoors pools may not allow the gas to escape. To be honest, outdoor pools rarely need to be superchlorinated because sunlight and wind take the malodorous chloramines away. Likewise, shocking should not be performed on a pool that is covered. When shocking an indoor pool, doors and windows should be opened to allow sufficient ventilation for the nitrogen gas to escape. Large box fans are also recommended to blow air across the pool when shocking. This helps to blow the chloramines higher into the air so they can be exhausted out of the building. Reaching break-

point is extremely difficult in an indoor pool with an energy-efficient dehumidification and air recirculation system. These cost-effective and energy-efficient systems often promote poor air quality by recirculating the chloramine-laden air into the pool area and not allowing it to escape. As a result, newer pools are experiencing an increase in exercise-induced asthma cases, particularly in competitive swimmers because of chronic chloramine problems.

Once breakpoint is accomplished, the pool should remain closed until the FC level drops to an acceptable range (3.0 to 5.0 ppm) on its own. The addition of sodium thiosulfate will neutralize excessively high amounts of FC when the pool needs to be reopened to the public shortly after superchlorinating.

In general, superchlorination should be performed more frequently in many indoor pools around the country. Many aquatic facility managers and operators irrationally fear high levels of chlorine in the water and are therefore reluctant to raise the existing levels significantly, even if only for a short time. These individuals must realize that it is CC that causes problems, not FC. Some European pools that still use chlorine often maintain FC levels from 8 to 10 ppm. The "burning out" of organic contaminants and chloramines is a routine practice that is highly recommended and should probably be performed much more than it is currently.

Calculating Dosages

To rid the chloramines from a pool, 10 times the amount of CC in new FC must be added to the pool. Since a 120,000-gal pool weighs approximately 1 million lb, then it follows that 1 lb of gas chlorine will raise the FC 1 ppm in a 120,000-gal pool. One gallon of sodium hypochlorite and 1.6 lb of calcium hypochlorite are equivalent to 1 lb of gas.

EXAMPLE 1

For example, if a CC of 0.4 ppm is found in an 80,000-gal pool, how much chlorine must be added to successfully cleanse this pool?

1. The total amount of chlorine needed to burn out the chloramines needs to be found: 10 x 0.4 ppm CC = 4.0 ppm FC must be added to 80,000 gal.
2. The "pool factor" needs to be found: 80,000 gal ÷ 120,000 gal = a pool factor of 0.66.
3. FC of 4.0 x a pool factor of 0.66 x 1 lb of gas, OR 1 gal of liquid, OR 1.6 lb of calcium hypochlorite.

ANSWER

4.0 x .66 x 1 lb = 2.64 lb of gas chlorine
4.0 x .66 x 1 gal = 2.68 gal of sodium hypochlorite
4.0 x .66 x 1.6 lb = 4.21 lb of calcium hypochlorite

Note: These answers are using percentage of available chlorine. For practical purposes and to ensure that breakpoint chlorination is achieved, the above figures should be rounded up to 3 lb of gas, 3 gal of liquid, and 5 lb of calcium hypochlorite.

EXAMPLE 2

CC levels in a 240,000-gal pool are found to be 0.5 ppm. How much chlorine is needed to clean this pool successfully?

1. 10 x 0.5 ppm = 5.0 ppm FC must be added
2. 240,000 ÷ 120,000 = pool factor of 2
3. 5.0 ppm x 2 x 1 lb of gas, OR 1 gal of liquid, OR 1.6 lb of calcium hypochlorite

ANSWER

10 lb of gas
10 gal of sodium hypochlorite (liquid)
15.75 lb of calcium hypochlorite

Perhaps an even easier way to determine how much chlorine to add to a pool is to figure how much the FC level must be raised and then refer to a chart furnished by many pool chemical companies. Adjustments might be required for pools containing a larger volume of water than is found on the chart. One example found below is furnished by test kit maker Taylor Technologies (Table 13.2).

Gas chlorine is not a practical form of chlorine with which to shock because it takes too much time to inject the chlorine into the pool, and most gas chlorine regulators are not capable of delivering sufficiently high dosages.

Chlorine gas levels may climb slowly and even dissipate while being added. The advantage of shocking with sodium and calcium hypochlorite is that they can be broadcast directly quickly into the pool when the facility is closed in large amounts and therefore reach breakpoint more rapidly. Calcium hypochlorite used for shocking may cause temporary cloudiness. Another advantage of using sodium hypochlorite to shock, particularly when gas is the primary disinfectant, is that it elevates the pH while shocking, so pH adjustments are usually not needed. Because of its fast solubility in water, lithium hypochlorite is also becoming popular for superchlorination.

Table 13.2

Amount of Chlorine Compound to Introduce 1 ppm Chlorine

Volume of Water - U.S. Gallons							
% Available	400 gallons	1,000 gallons	5,000 gallons	10,000 gallons	20,000 gallons	50,000 gallons	100,000 gallons
10 %	0.51 fl oz	1.28 fl oz	6.40 fl oz	12.8 fl oz	1.60 pt	2.00 qt	1.00 gal
12 %	0.43 fl oz	1.07 fl oz	5.33 fl oz	10.7 fl oz	1.33 pt	1.67 qt	3.33 qt
35 %	0.15 oz	0.38 oz	1.91 oz	3.82 oz	7.63 oz	1.19 lb	2.38 lb
45 %	0.12 oz	0.30 oz	1.48 oz	2.97 oz	5.94 oz	14.8 oz	1.85 lb
60 %	0.09 oz	0.22 oz	1.11 oz	2.23 oz	4.45 oz	11.1 oz	1.39 lb
65 %	0.08 oz	0.21 oz	1.03 oz	2.05 oz	4.11 oz	10.3 oz	1.28 lb
75 %	0.07 oz	0.20 oz	0.95 oz	1.77 oz	3.77 oz	9.50 oz	1.17 lb
90 %	0.06 oz	0.15 oz	0.74 oz	1.48 oz	2.97 oz	7.42 oz	14.8 oz
100 %	0.05 oz	0.13 oz	0.67 oz	1.34 oz	2.67 oz	6.68 oz	13.4 oz

(rev. 10/05)

Volume of Water - Liters							
% Available	2,000 L	4,000 L	20,000 L	40,000 L	80,000 L	100,000 L	400,000 L
10 %	20.0 mL	40.0 mL	200 mL	400 mL	800 mL	1.00 L	4.00 L
12 %	16.7 mL	33.3 mL	167 mL	333 mL	667 mL	833 mL	3.33 L
35 %	5.71 g	11.4 g	57.1 g	114 g	229 g	286 g	1.14 kg
45 %	4.44 g	8.89 g	44.4 g	88.9 g	178 g	222 g	889 g
60 %	3.33 g	6.67 g	33.3 g	66.7 g	133 g	167 g	667 g
65 %	3.08 g	6.15 g	30.8 g	61.5 g	123 g	154 g	615 g
75 %	2.83 g	5.63 g	28.3 g	56.3 g	113 g	141 g	563 g
90 %	2.22 g	4.44 g	22.2 g	44.4 g	88.9 g	111 g	444 g
100 %	2.00 g	4.00 g	20.0 g	40.0 g	80.0 g	100 g	400 g

(rev. 10/05)

(© Taylor Technologies, Inc. Reprinted with permission.)

Alternatives to Shocking

Traditional superchlorination may work well in some facilities, but not at all in others, particularly those with high swimmer-to-volume ratios and heavy organic loads entering the water. In addition, pool closure following superchlorination is often required. When chloramine problems persist after proper superchlorination techniques have been applied, the following alternatives should be considered.

Monopersulfate-Based Oxidation

An alternative to traditional superchlorination is a nonchlorine shocking agent called potassium monopersulfate. Monopersulfate is also known as potassium peroxymonosulfate or monopotassium persulfate. Potassium monopersulfate is an oxygen-based chemical that oxidizes like chlorine but without the disadvantages associated with superchlorination. Drawbacks of shocking with chlorine include closing the pools for 8 to 10 hours, bleaching of vinyl liners and similar equipment, and misjudging breakpoint, thereby adding too much chlorine, or worse yet, too little chlorine.

Potassium monopersulfate destroys organic wastes without having to climb to a predetermined breakpoint. One pound per 10,000 gal is the recommended dosage based on compounds with 42% active ingredient. The dosage will vary using products with 32% active ingredient. Perhaps the greatest advantage of these nonchlorine products is that swimmers can return to the water within 1 hour of treatment. This advantage becomes even more important during large competitive swimming events, when shocking may be required, but closing the pool is not possible. Nonchlorine shocking agents do not sanitize and are somewhat expensive.

Additionally, water containing monopersulfate requires a special "deox reagent" for testing FC and CC levels. Otherwise, the monopersulfate will skew the test results. Taylor Technologies can be contacted for more information at 1-800-TEST KIT (837-8548).

> **Dr. Tom's Tip**
>
> Although monopersulfate works extremely well, do not depend on these products exclusively for oxidation. Whenever possible, I suggest alternating between nonchlorine and traditional chlorine shocking for best results.

Granulated Activated Carbon (GAC) Filters

When regular shocking has failed repeatedly in a facility, some aquatic facility operators have been able to remove ammonia by adding a secondary granulated activated carbon (GAC) filter. This system is not used to filter all the pool water, but rather a smaller slipstream of water drawn off the main circulation line or only the source water being added to the pool. The GAC filter helps to remove the ammonia in the pool and chloramines that are produced. Municipal water authorities are increasingly using ammonia and/or chloramines for drinking water disinfection to prevent trihalomethane formation, which worsens the chloramine problem in pools that use this source water.

Zeolites

Zeolites can also be used to curb chloramines. Zeolites are a family of granular, extremely porous volcanic materials capable of removing ammonia from the water and trapping particles down to five microns in size. Zeolites with a high (80%) percentage of clinoptilolite can be used as alternative filter media instead of #20 silica sand in typical sand filter systems. The organic zeolite material has an affinity for ammonia; therefore, any ammonia deposited in the water by swimmers stays in the filter media and is unable to form chloramines in the pool. The product works well and when it does become saturated with ammonia in the filter tank, the filter bed is treated with a saltwater solution to reduce the ammonia instead of shocking the pool. This regeneration process that includes backwashing and the saltwater bath must be performed at least every 6 months, but perhaps more in a heavily used facility. The pool water is tested for ammonia levels rather than chloramine levels in this case, so an ammonia test kit is required.

> **Dr. Tom's Tip**
>
> I once replaced the sand in 12 sand filter tanks for three indoor pools with zeolite on the Penn State campus. This immediately rid the entire facility of all chloramines. Zeolites work amazingly well in eliminating chloramines but this is only a short-term (1-2 year) solution. Eventually, new HVAC systems and UV must be permanently installed.

Other Alternatives

Hydrogen peroxide, UV light, and ozone reduce the use of chlorine and chloramines as a by-product. Good ventilation makes chloramines bearable, particularly for competitive swimmers who are most adversely affected by them. Once chloramines are present, increasing the ventilation across the surface of the water does wonders in lessening their effects. This can be accomplished expensively and more efficiently by improving the heating, ventilating, and air-conditioning (HVAC) systems that handle the air in the facility and/or inexpensively by adding a variety of large fans on the pool deck. This is the primary reason why outdoor pools are not plagued with chloramine problems—no harm, no foul.

Summary

Good pool chemistry requires constant monitoring of TC and FC to determine the presence of CC, also known as chloramines. As chloramines develop, the pool should be treated to remove them, otherwise eye irritation, foul odors, and cloudy water will result. Preventing chloramine buildup through periodic superchlorination to breakpoint is important. Chloramines can also be destroyed with potassium monopersulfate, a nonchlorine shock. All facility users should shower before swimming. Less chloramine would be produced if everyone showered to remove contaminants that have an affinity for chlorine. Zeolites can keep ammonia products in the filter media so that chloramine production is reduced in the pool.

To best review superchlorination, the chlorine cycle that takes place in swimming pools should be examined (Figure 13.3).

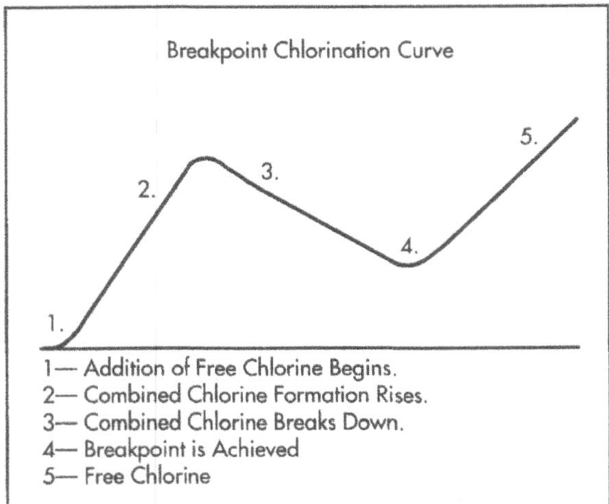

Figure 13.3. Breakpoint chlorination curve. (From *Service Industry News*, Torrance, CA, 1993)

Bibliography

Gabrielson, A. M. (1987). *Swimming pools: A guide to their planning, design, and operation* (4th ed.). Champaign, IL: Human Kinetics.

Knoop, D. F., & Redd, R. (1991, March/April). Shocking news: Analyzing the options. *Aquatics*.

Kowalsky, L. (Ed.). *Pool/spa operators handbook*. San Antonio, TX: National Swimming Pool Foundation.

Mitchel, K. (1988). *The proper management of pool and spa water*. Decatur, GA: BioLab.

Osinski, A. (2002, March). *Eliminating chronic natatorium chloramine problems*. Paper presented at NRPA Aquatics Conference, Palm Springs, CA.

Pool and Spa News, Los Angeles. www.poolspanews.com/

Service Industry News, Torrance, CA.

Taylor, C. (1989). *Everything you always wanted to know about pool care*. Chino, CA: Service Industry Publications.

Taylor Technologies. *Pool and spa water chemistry: A testing and treatment guide with tables*. Sparks, MD: Author.

Taylor Technologies. (2012). Test kit selection guide. Sparks, MD: Taylor Technologies, Inc. www.taylortechnologies.com

Williams, K. G., & Young, R. A. (Ed.). (2011). *Aquatic facility operator manual* (6th ed.). Ashburn, VA: National Recreation and Park Association.

14

Pool Calculations

Key Concepts

- Rectangular pool volume
- Circular pool volume
- Oval pool volume
- Hybrid pool volume

Pool Volume Calculations

Much of the preceding discussion dealing with chemical adjustments assumes that pool owners and operators know the volume or gallons contained in their pools. This is not always the case, however. If the pool volume (pool capacity) is not known, the total gallonage is simple to compute. For the purposes of this text, pool volume and pool capacity are synonymous and are expressed in gallons.

Knowing the pool capacity is a must if chemical adjustments are to be made correctly. The following formulas can be used to calculate pool capacity in gallons:

Rectangular Pool Volume
Length x Width x Average depth x 7.5 gal = Pool gallons

Circular Pool Volume
Diameter x Diameter x Average depth x 5.9 gal = Pool gallons

or

$$\pi \times r^2 \times h$$
$$\pi = 3.14$$

Oval Pool Volume
Maximum length x Maximum width x Average depth x 5.9 gal = Pool gallons

Note: Average depth is calculated by taking the depth of the deep end, adding it to the depth of the shallow end, and dividing by 2 in a pool with a constant slope. There are 7.5 gal in 1 cubic foot of water.

Pool/Spa Equivalent Measures

1 sq. ft. (1 sq. ft. or 1ft.²)	=	a square 12 in. wide x 12 in. long = 144 sq. in.
1 cubic ft. (1 cu. ft. or 1ft.³)	=	a cube 12 in wide x 12 in. long x 12 in. high
1 cubic yard (1 cu. yd. or 1 yd³)	=	27 cubic ft, or a cube 3 ft. on each side
1 cubic ft. of water	contains	7.48 gallons
1 cubic ft. of water	weighs	62.4 lbs.
1 gallon of water	=	.134 cubic ft.
1 gallon of water	weighs	8.33 lbs.
1 part per million (ppm)	example:	1.33 oz. of chemical per 10,000 gallons, or 8.3 lbs. per million gallons of water

Metric Equivalents

1 meter (1 m)	=	39.37 in. 3.2808 ft. 1.0936 yards
1 foot (1 ft. or 1')	=	.3048 meter (m)
1 yard (1 yd.)	=	.9144 meter (m)
1 square foot (1 ft.²)	=	.0929 square meter (m²)
1 square yard	=	.836 square meter
1 cubic meter (m³)	=	35.314 cubic feet; 1.308 cubic yards
1 cubic meter	=	264.2 gallons
1 gallon	=	3.786 liters (L)
1 liter (L)	=	.2642 gallons

Figure 14.1. Equivalent measurements. (Courtesy of 2012 The Association of Pool & Spa Professionals)

Area of a Rectangle or Square

Area = L × W

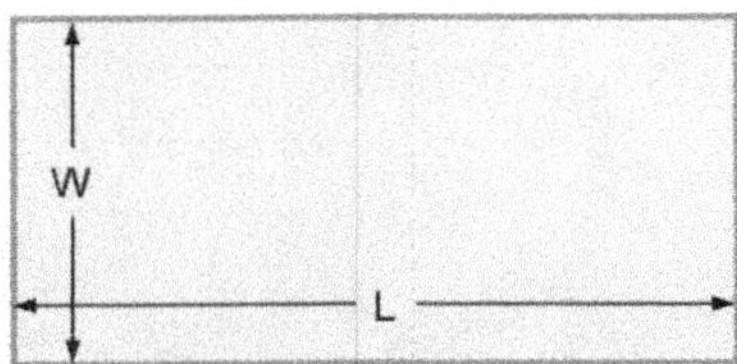

Example:
L = 30 ft. / 9 m   W = 15 ft. / 4.5 m
Area = 30 × 15 = 450 ft.²
Area = 9 m × 4.5 m = 40.5 m²

Area of a Right Triangle

Area = (L × W) ÷ 2

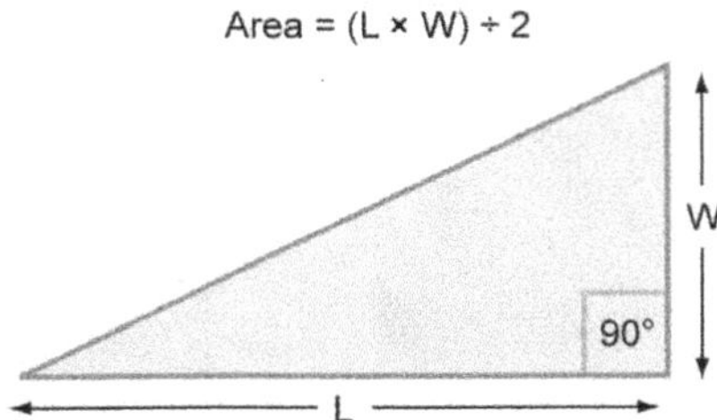

Example:
L = 10 ft. / 3 m   W = 5 ft. / 1.5 m
Area = (10 × 5) ÷ 2 = 25 ft.²
Area = (3 × 1.5) ÷ 2 = 2.25 m²

Area of a Circle

Area = π × r² (or 3.14 × r × r)
r = d ÷ 2

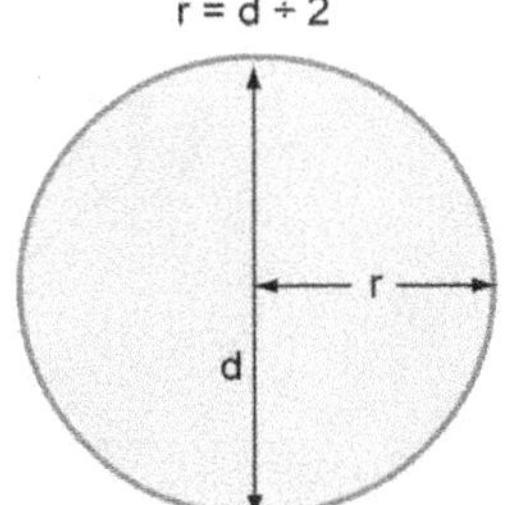

Example:
d (diameter) = 10 ft. / 3 m
r (radius) = 10 ÷ 2 = 5 ft. / 1.5 m
Area = 3.14 × 5 × 5 = 78.5 ft.²
Area = 3.14 × 1.5 × 1.5 = 7 m²

Kidney-shaped Area

Area = (W₁ + W₂) × L × 0.45

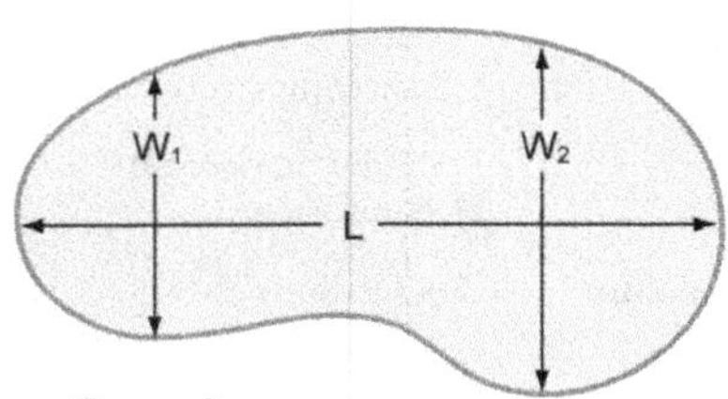

Example:
W₁ = 4 ft. / 1.2 m   W₂ = 6 ft. / 1.8 m
L = 10 ft. / 3 m
Area = 10 × 10 × 0.45 = 45 ft.²
Area = 3 × 3 × 0.45 = 4.05 m²

Area of an Oblong-shaped Oval

Area = (L × W) + π r²
or
(L × W) + (3.14 × r × r)

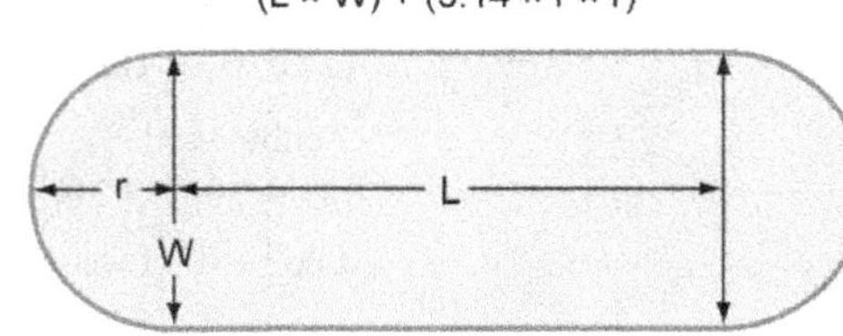

Example:
L = 10 ft. / 3m   W = 5 ft. / 1.5 m
r (radius) = 2.5 ft. / 0.76 m

Area = (10 × 5) + (3.14 × 2.5 × 2.5)
50 + 19.63 = 69.63 ft²

Area = (3 × 1.5) + (3.14 × .76 × .76)
4.5 + 1.81 = 6.31 m²

Area of an Ellipse (Oval)

Area = r₁ × r₂ × π
or
r₁ × r₂ × 3.14

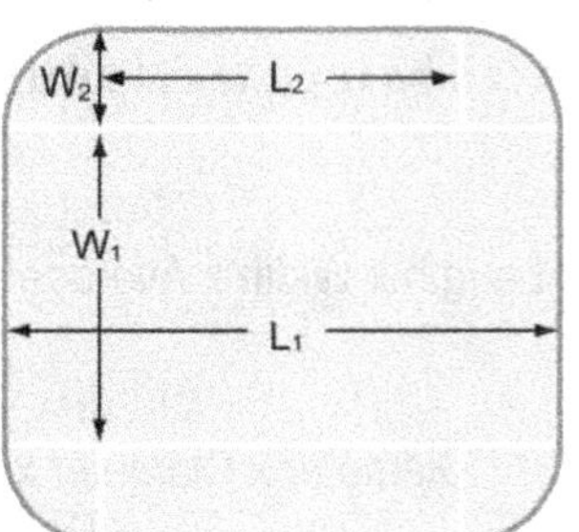

Example:
r₁ (short radius) = 8 ft. / 2.4 m
r₂ (long radius) = 12 ft. / 3.6 m
Area = 8 × 12 × 3.14 = 301.44 ft.²
Area = 2.4 × 3.6 × 3.14 = 27.13 m²

Area of a Trapezoid

Area = ((W₁ + W₂) ÷ 2) × L

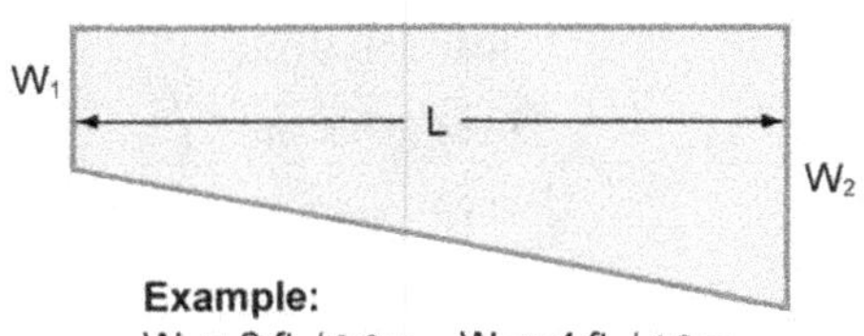

Example:
W₁ = 2 ft. / 0.6 m   W₂ = 4 ft. / 1.2 m
L = 10 ft. / 3 m
Area = ((2 + 4) ÷ 2) × 10 = 30 ft.²
Area = ((.6 + 1.2) ÷ 2) × 3 = 2.7 m²

Area of an Octagon

Area = (L × W) − (4 × (A × B ÷ 2))
= (L × W) − (2 × (A × B))

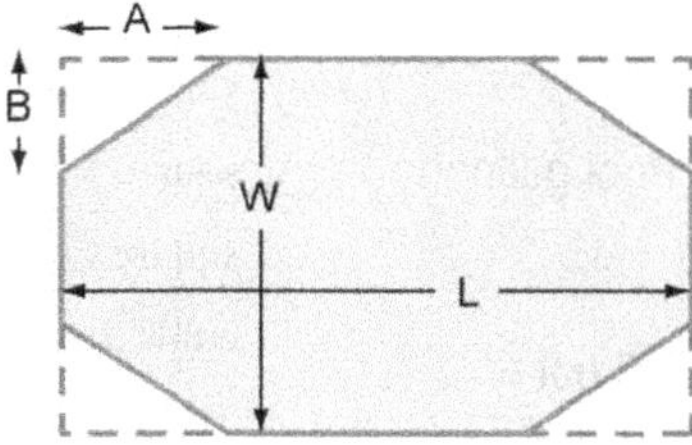

Example:
L = 12 ft. / 3.6 m   W = 9 ft. / 2.7 m
A = 3 ft. / 0.9 m   B = 2 ft. / 0.6 m
Area = (9 × 12) − (2 × (3 × 2)) = 96 ft.²
Area = (3.6 × 2.7) − (2 × (0.9 × 0.6)) = 8.64 m²

Area of a Rounded Rectangle

Area = (L₁ × W₁) + (2 × (L₂ × W₂))
+ (W₂ × W₂ × 3.14)

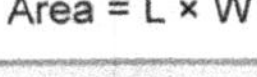

Example:
L₁ = 10 ft. / 3 m   W₁ = 6 ft. / 1.8 m
L₂ = 6 ft. / 1.8 m   W₂ = 2 ft. / 0.6 m
Area = (10 × 6) + (2 × (6 × 2))
+ (2 × 2 × 3.14) = 96.56 ft.²
Area = (3 × 1.8) + (2 × (1.8 × 0.6)
+ (0.6 × 0.6 × 3.14) = 8.69 m²

Figure 14.2.a. Calculating area of shapes. *Note:* Measurements are given for illustrative purposes only. Metric measurements are not equivalent. They have been rounded for simplification. (Courtesy of 2012 The Association of Pool & Spa Professionals)

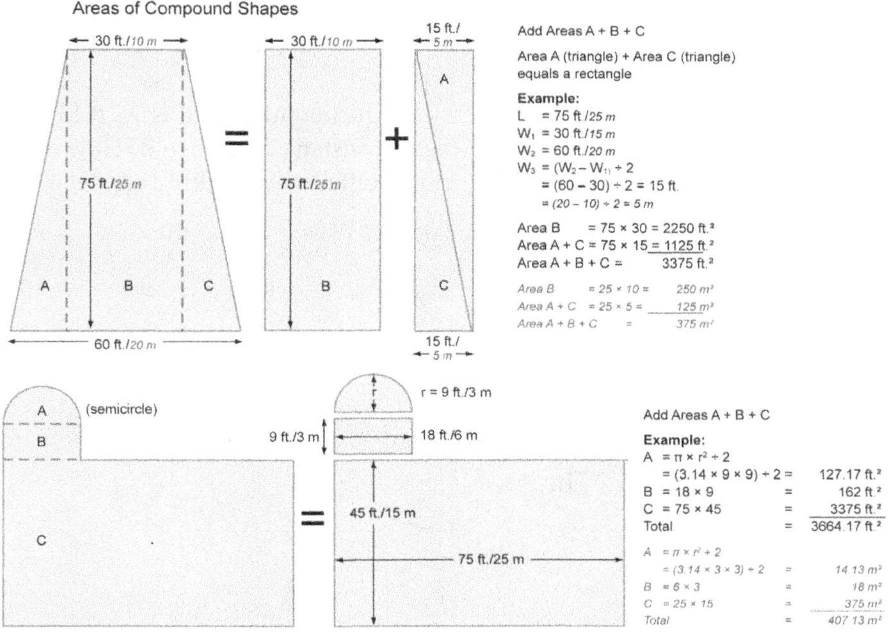

To estimate the area, count the number of grids that fall completely inside the pool perimeter: these grids equal 4 square feet each. Count the grids that fall ¾ within the perimeter: these equal 3 square feet each. Count the grids that fall ½ within the perimeter: these equal 2 square feet each. Finally, count the grids that fall ¼ within the perimeter: these equal 1 square foot each.

As you count, mark each grid with a symbol, such as a dot or an X, or a color, to show that it has been counted. Be careful not to count any grids twice. Then, total the number of square feet to estimate the surface area.

For irregularly-shaped pools and spas, measure the longest dimension in one direction (d_1), then the longest direction crosswise, or perpendicular, to it (d_2):

Surface area = $d_1 \times d_2$

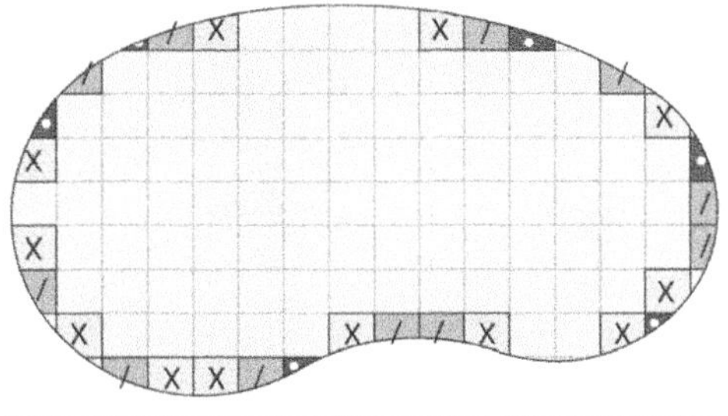

Grid type	Number of grids		Area per grid ft.²/m2		Total Area ft.²/m2
☐	91	×	4 ft.² / .36 m²	=	364 ft.² / 32.76 m²
X	12	×	3 ft.² / .27 m²	=	36 ft.² / 3.24 m²
◪	11	×	2 ft.² / .18 m²	=	22 ft.² / 1.98 m²
▣	6	×	1 ft.² / .09 m²	=	6 ft.² / 0.54 m²
			Total estimated area		428 ft.² / 38.52 m²

Figure 14.2.b. Estimating the area of free-form shapes.(Courtesy of 2012 The Association of Pool & Spa Professionals)

**Finding Area:
Useful Abbreviations and Formulas**

L = Length   W = Width

d = diameter   r = radius (= diameter ÷ 2)

π (pi) = 3.14   D = Depth

Area of a rectangle = lenth x width

Area of a triangle = (base x height) ÷ 2

Circumference of a circle = 3.14 x diameter

Area of a circle = 3.14 x radius^2

Kidney-shaped area = $(W_1 + W_2)$ x L x 0.45

Area of an ellipse (oval) = $(r_1 \times r_2)$ x 3.14

Area of a trapezoid = ([W1 + W2] ÷ 2) x L

Figure 14.3. The basic terms and mathematical formulas used to determine area. Whenever a mathematical function appears in parentheses ( ), it must be completed before continuing with the rest of the formula. (Courtesy of 2012 The Association of Pool & Spa Professionals)

To calculate the pool volume for irregular-shaped pools with a variety of depths, the pool should be divided into separate geometric sections and calculated individually, and then the results should be totaled.

The first three examples that follow are for constant depth pools, and the last three examples pertain to pools with variable depths.

EXAMPLE 1

A rectangular pool is 75 ft long and 45 ft wide and has a constant depth of 4 ft. How many gallons does this pool contain (see Figure 14.4)?

Length x Width x Avg. Depth x 7.5   = Pool capacity in gallons

75 ft x 45 ft x 4 ft x 7.5 gal   = 101,250 gal

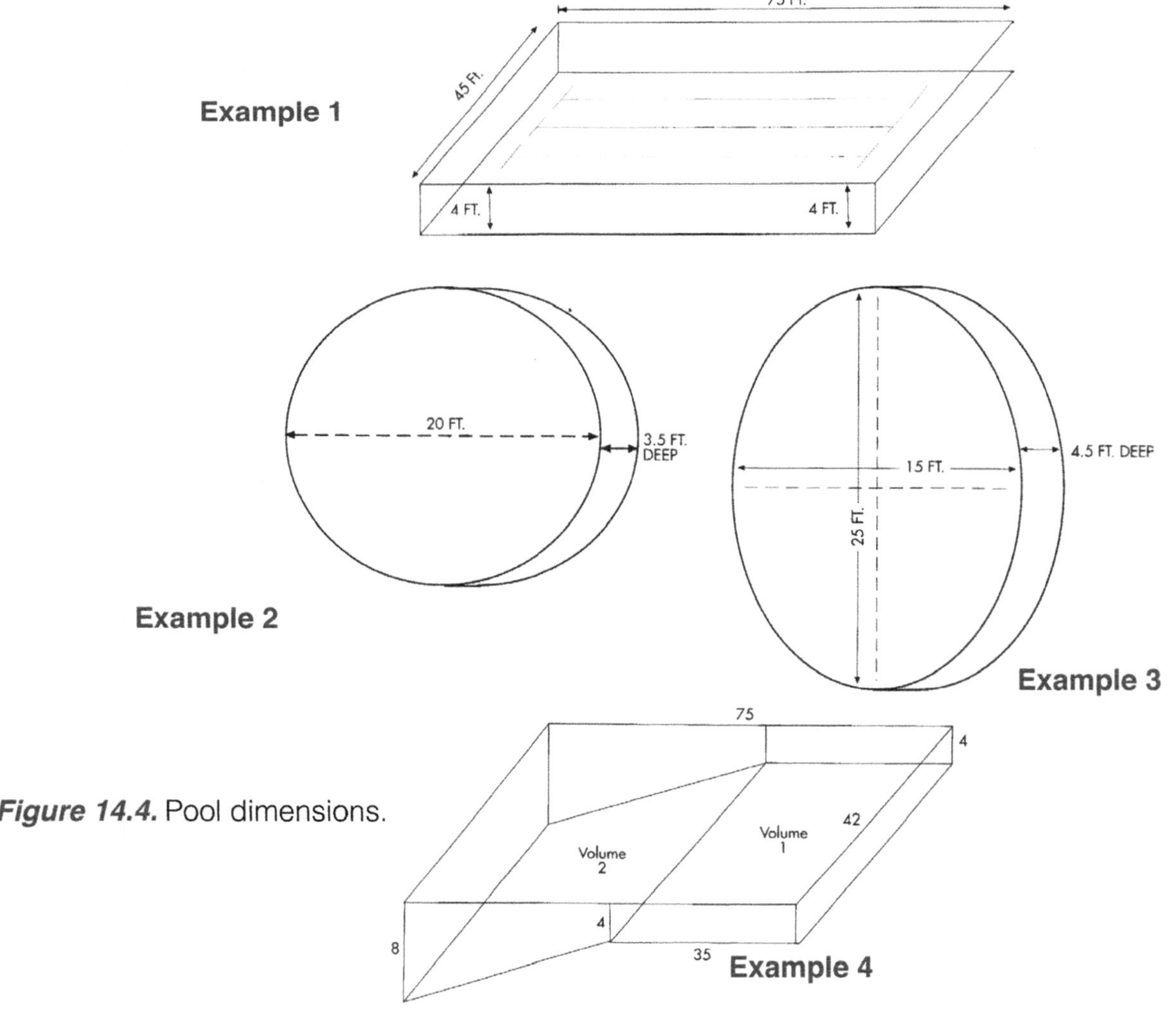

Figure 14.4. Pool dimensions.

EXAMPLE 2

A circular swimming pool is 20 ft across (diameter) and has a constant depth of 3.5 ft. How many gallons does this pool hold (see Figure 14.3)?

Diameter x Diameter x Depth x 5.9 gal = Pool capacity
                                                    in gallons
20 ft x 20 ft x 3.5 ft x 5.9 gal = 8,260 gal

EXAMPLE 3

An oval pool is 25 ft at its maximum length and 15 ft at its maximum width. The pool has a constant depth of 4.5 ft. What is the pool capacity of this pool (see Figure 14.3)?

Maximum length x Maximum = Pool volume
width x Average depth x 5.9 gal

25 ft x 15 ft x 4.5 ft x 5.9 gal = 9,956 gal

EXAMPLE 4

A rectangular pool has a shallow section and a deep section. The pool is 75 ft long (25 yd) and 42 ft wide. The shallow section is 35 ft long and extends from the shallow end of the swimming pool to the beginning of the deep section. The deep section begins where the shallow section ends at a depth of 4 ft and ends at a depth of 8 ft. To calculate the pool's capacity, it should be divided into two sections. For the purposes of this problem, the shallow section will be Volume 1 and the deep section will be Volume 2. After both volumes are computed, they are added together for the entire pool capacity. The diagram in Figure 14.3 will aid in the calculations.

Volume 1 = shallow section
Length x Width x Depth x 7.5 gal = Volume

35 ft x 42 ft x 4 ft x 7.5 gal = 44,100 gal

Volume 2 = deep section
Length x Width x Average depth x 7.5 gal = Volume
$$40 \text{ ft} \times 42 \text{ ft} \times \left[\frac{4 \text{ ft} + 8 \text{ ft}}{2}\right] \times 7.5 \text{ gal} = \text{Volume 2}$$
40 ft x 42 ft x 6 ft x 7.5 gal = 75,600 gal

Volume 1 (shallow section)   44,100 gal
Volume 2 (deep section)   + 75,600 gal

Answer = 119,700-gal pool volume

EXAMPLE 5

A pool is 75 ft long and 45 ft wide with three sections within the one pool. The shallow section is 45 ft long and 45 ft wide and runs from 3.5 ft deep to 5 ft deep. The middle or sloped section of the pool runs from 5 ft deep to 14 ft deep where the diving section begins. This section is 15 ft long and 45 ft wide. The diving section of the pool is 14 ft deep and 15 ft long and 45 ft wide. What is the volume of this pool in gallons? For ease of calculations, this pool will be divided into three sections: diving section (Volume 1), middle section (Volume 2), and shallow section (Volume 3; see Figure 14.5).

Volume 1 = diving section
Length x Width x Depth x 7.5 gal = Volume 1
                                     (diving section)
15 ft x 45 ft x 14 ft x 7.5 gal = 70,875 gal

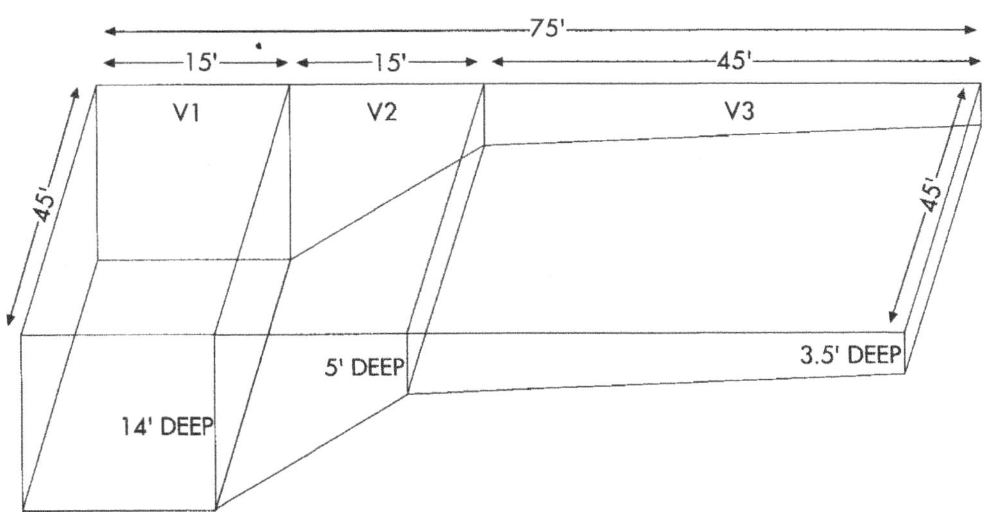

Figure 14.5. Example 5

Volume 2 = middle section

Length x Width x Avg. = Volume 2 (middle)
depth x 7.5 gal

$$15\text{ ft} \times 45\text{ ft} \times \left[\frac{14\text{ ft} + 5\text{ ft}}{2}\right] \times 7.5\text{ gal} = \text{Volume 2 (middle)}$$

15 ft x 45 ft x 9.5 ft x 7.5 ft = 48,093 gal

Volume 2 = shallow section

Length x Width x Avg. = Volume 2 (shallow)
depth x 7.5 gal

$$45\text{ ft} \times 5\text{ ft} \times \left[\frac{5\text{ ft} + 3.5\text{ ft}}{2}\right] \times 7.5\text{ gal} = \text{Volume 2 (shallow)}$$

Volume 2 = shallow section

45 ft x 45 ft x 4.25 ft x 7.5 gal   = 64,546 gal

Volume 1	70,875 gal
Volume 2	+ 48,093 gal
Volume 3	+ 64,546 gal

Answer = 183,584 gal

EXAMPLE 6

An irregular-shaped pool has a main racing pool section and a deeper diving section attached but off to one side. The main pool is 75 ft long and 42 ft wide and ranges in depth from 3 ft at the shallow end to 5 ft at the deep end. This section can be called Volume 1. The diving section is 30 ft long and 35 ft wide. The water depth in this section runs from 5 ft to 12 ft. This section can be called Volume 2. What is the capacity of this pool in gallons (Figure 14.6)?

Volume 1

Length x Width x Average depth x 7.5 gal = Pool volume

$$75\text{ ft} \times 42\text{ ft} \times \left[\frac{3\text{ ft} + 5\text{ ft}}{2}\right] \times 7.5\text{ gal} =$$

75 ft x 42 ft x 4 ft x 7.5 gal = 94,500 gal

Volume 2

Length x Width x Average depth x 7.5 gal =

$$30\text{ ft} \times 35\text{ ft} \times \left[\frac{5\text{ ft} + 12\text{ ft}}{2}\right] \times 7.5\text{ gal} =$$

30 ft x 35 ft x 8.5 ft x 7.5 gal   = 66,937 gal

Volume 1	94,500 gal
Volume 2	+ 66,937 gal

Answer = 161,437 gal

Summary

Swimming pool chemical manufacturers often provide chemical dosage charts with their products. Pool

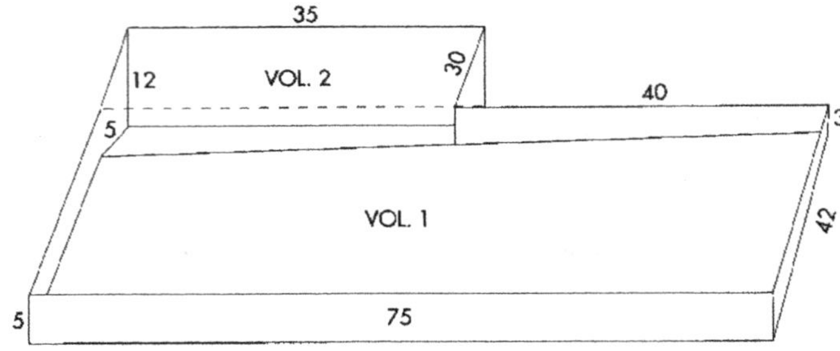

Figure 14.6. Example 6

owners and operators should ask for these charts. When in doubt about how to adjust water chemistry, the chemical distributor should be contacted. Chemical dosage charts make chemical adjustments easy. Calculating the pool volume is the only chore left for the pool operator, and if this chapter has not been fully understood, a local pool store or dealer should be consulted.

References

Kowalsky, L. (Ed.). (1991). *Pool/spa operators handbook.* San Antonio, TX: National Swimming Pool Foundation.

Williams, K. G., & Young, R. A. (Ed.). (2011). *Aquatic facility operator manual* (6th ed.). Ashburn, VA: National Recreation and Park Association.

Bibliography

The American Water Works Association. (1971). *Water quality and treatment* (3rd ed.). Denver, CO: Author.

BioGuard Lab. (1981). *The pool book.* Decatur, GA: Author.

Kowalsky, L. (Ed.). (1991). *Pool/spa operators handbook.* San Antonio, TX: Swimming Pool Foundation.

Mitchel, K. (1988). *The proper management of pool and spa water.* Decatur, GA: BioLab.

Pool and Spa News, Los Angeles. http://www.poolspanews.com/

Service Industry News, Torrance, CA

Taylor, C. (1989). *Everything you always wanted to know about pool care.* Chino, CA: Service Industry Publications.

Taylor Technologies. (2003). *Pool and spa water chemistry: A testing and treatment guide.* Sparks, MD: Author.

The Association of Pool & Spa Professionals. (2012). Service tech manual (4th ed.). Alexandria, VA: Author.

Washington State Public Health Association. (1988). *Swimming pool operations.* Seattle, WA: Author.

Williams, K. G., & Young, R. A. (Ed.). (2011). *Aquatic facility operator manual* (6th ed.). Ashburn, VA: National Recreation and Park Association.

15

pH, Water Balance, and Chemical Adjustments

Swimming pool water may come from one of several sources including municipal water companies, private wells, and surface runoff. Sources such as lakes and reservoirs are the most common suppliers. This source water used to fill swimming pools is usually called "make-up" water. Make-up water may not provide perfectly balanced water and may have components that are not compatible with aquatic facilities. In addition, the environment may introduce substances into the pool water to affect its balance.

Water balance refers to water that is neither corrosive nor scale-forming. The factors that determine the balance of water are pH, total alkalinity (TA), calcium hardness (CH), total dissolved solids (TDS), and temperature, but by far, the three most important factors are pH, TA, and CH. For swimming pool equipment to function effectively and have a long useful life, balanced water is a must. Unbalanced water can destroy a pool shell and its plumbing in only a few years.

Most health departments regulating public pools are only concerned with pH and chlorine readings. Many health department officials concentrate on pH and chlorine values rather than other chemical components of water balance such as TA and CH because they do not directly affect the health and well-being of pool patrons. However, the importance of all elements of water balance cannot be overlooked by pool owners and operators. In the New York City area, for example, water generally has a pH of approximately 6.5 and a TA of about 10 ppm.

This extremely aggressive water would destroy a swimming pool and its components quickly if left unbalanced. On the other hand, aquatic facilities supplied with water from Lake Michigan often have perfectly balanced water. For this reason, it is a good idea to test all water balance factors of an aquatic facility's make-up water.

Because the chemical condition of pool water is in a constant state of flux, the addition of chemicals must be done periodically. Safety is important for both the pool patron and the person performing the chemical adjustments. Second, adding the right amount of chemical to the pool is also important because miscalculations can cost valuable time and money to rebalance the pool water within appropriate chemical parameters.

Because safety is of the utmost concern, and because most chemical adjustments are done manually, we will now discuss chemical safety.

Safe Chemical Handling

Follow these tips to make chemical adjustments safely.

- Chemicals should be stored properly. This includes keeping all chemicals locked in a separate storage facility that is dry, dark, and cool and has adequate ventilation. All chemicals should be stored in sealed containers and kept away from heat sources.
- Gloves and goggles should always be worn when chemicals are to be handled. Separate clean, dry scoops and buckets should be used for each chemical. Scoops and buckets should be marked for the chemical for which they are intended.
- All chemical instructions should be read, understood, and followed.
- A water hose should be kept nearby to assist in the cleanup of chemical spills.
- Chemicals should be kept away from pool patrons. Swimmers should not be present when major chemical adjustments are being made.

- When mixing chemicals, CHEMICALS SHOULD BE ADDED TO WATER, NEVER WATER TO CHEMICALS.

Suggested Chemical Ranges

Before discussing how to make specific chemical adjustments, we will review once again the suggested chemical ranges for swimming pools and spas. At the end of the chapter, Table 15.11 is a listing available through the Association of Pool & Spa Professionals). The figures from APSP are suggested standards only. Local and state health codes may differ and should be consulted on an annual basis.

Specific Chemical Adjustments

Increasing Chlorine

Except when UV is used to supplement chlorination, superchlorination is recommended for most pools on a regular basis. Not only does superchlorination destroy chloramines, a persistent pool problem, but it also kills algae and oxidizes organic debris, which in turn "polishes" the water. Chloramines (combined chlorine [CC]) can be destroyed completely only when 10 times the CC level is added in new free chlorine (FC). Because many forms of chlorine are used in swimming pools today, superchlorination can become confusing. The following information should clarify how to superchlorinate any swimming pool, regardless of type or size. This information will also be helpful to pool owners and operators attempting to raise chlorine without superchlorinating.

Before chemical adjustments are made, the first question that needs to be answered is, how many parts per million must be added to the pool for the desired change? In the case of superchlorination, the question is, how many parts per million of chlorine must be added to achieve breakpoint? In Chapter 16, we discussed the important relationship of CC = TC - FC. A test kit can be used to find both TC and FC. FC can be subtracted from TC to find CC. Once the chloramine level has been computed, this number can be multiplied by 10 to find how much FC should be added to the pool. For example, a pool with 0.4 ppm of CC would require 4.0 ppm FC to burn off all CC. A pool with 0.8 ppm CC would need an FC level of 8.0 ppm to destroy all chloramines.

Since a 120,000-gal pool (which is a fairly standard-sized public pool) weighs approximately 1 million lb, 1 lb of gas chlorine added to this 1 million-lb pool would add 1 ppm. With the example in the preceding paragraph, 4 lb and 8 lb of gas, respectively, would oxidize 0.4 ppm and 0.8 ppm CC levels.

One gal of sodium hypochlorite (liquid) is equal to 1 lb of gas, and 1.6 lb of calcium hypochlorite (dry) is also equivalent to 1 lb of gas. Although gas chlorine is an excellent primary sanitizer, sodium and calcium hypochlorite are often preferred as superchlorinators.

To introduce high chlorine concentrations into a particular pool, the size of that pool also becomes important because not every pool is 120,000 gal. A "pool factor" must be created by dividing a particular pool's gallonage by 120,000 gal before multiplying by the amount of chemical. For instance, if a 60,000-gal pool had a CC level of 0.5 ppm, how much chlorine would have to be added to burn out all chloramines? To kill all chloramines, 10 times 0.5 ppm CC or 5.0 ppm FC is needed.

EXAMPLE 1

$$\begin{matrix} \text{5 lb gas} \\ \text{or} \\ \text{5 gal liquid} \\ \text{or} \\ \text{8 lb cal hypo} \end{matrix} \quad X \quad \frac{60{,}000}{120{,}000} \quad = \quad ?$$

$$\begin{matrix} \text{5 lb gas} \\ \text{or} \\ \text{5 gal sod hypo} \\ \text{or} \\ \text{8 lb cal hypo} \end{matrix} \quad X \quad \frac{.5 \text{ pool}}{\text{factor (pf)}} \quad \begin{matrix} = \text{2.5 lb gas} \\ = \text{2.5 gal liquid} \\ = \text{4 lb cal hypo} \end{matrix}$$

EXAMPLE 2

In a 190,000-gal pool, a CC level of 0.6 ppm is found. How many parts per million of FC must be added, and how much chlorine must be added to achieve this?

To rid a pool of 0.6 ppm CC, 6.0 ppm must be added to the pool. In a 190,000-gal pool, the following calculations are necessary.

$$\begin{matrix} \text{6 lb gas} \\ \text{or} \\ \text{6 gal sod hypo} \\ \text{or} \\ \text{9.6 lb cal hypo} \end{matrix} \quad X \quad \frac{190{,}000}{120{,}000} \quad = ?$$

$$\begin{matrix} \text{6 lb gas} \\ \text{or} \\ \text{6 gal sod hypo} \\ \text{or} \\ \text{9.6 lb cal hypo} \end{matrix} \quad X \quad 1.58 \text{ (pf)} \quad \begin{matrix} = \text{9.48 lb gas} \\ = \text{9.48 gal sodium hypo} \\ = \text{15.16 lb cal hypo} \end{matrix}$$

EXAMPLE 3

In a 250,000-gal pool, a CC level of 0.8 is found. How many parts per million of FC is needed to burn out all chloramines? How much chlorine will be needed to accomplish this?

An FC level of 10 times greater than the CC level is needed to rid the pool of all chloramines. In this case, 8.0 ppm FC must be added to the pool.

8 lb gas
or
8 gal sod hypo
or   X $\dfrac{250,000}{120,000}$ =   **?**
12.8 lb cal hypo
or
8 lb gas

8 gal sod hypo   16.64 lb gas
or   X   2.08 (pf) =
12.8 lb cal hypo   16.64 gal sod hypo

                                                  26.62 lb cal hypo

In order to reach breakpoint chlorination, the FC needs increased by at least 10 times the CC levels. For that reason, all values found in the answers to the problems above should be rounded up. Falling short of breakpoint will waste chlorine and add to chloramine development.

For individuals who do not wish to make calculations, numerous charts and tables are available that have a variety of chlorine levels and pool sizes (Tables 15.1-15.3).

Table 15.1

Amount of chlorinating agent per gallons in pool to introduce 1 ppm FC

Volume of Water - U.S. Gallons							
%Available Chlorine*	400 gallons	1,000 gallons	5,000 gallons	10,000 gallons	20,000 gallons	50,000 gallons	100,000 gallons
10 %	0.51 fl oz	1.28 fl oz	6.40 fl oz	12.8 fl oz	1.60 pt	2.00 qt	1.00 gal
12 %	0.43 fl oz	1.07 fl oz	5.33 fl oz	10.7 fl oz	1.33 pt	1.67 qt	3.33 qt
35 %	0.15 oz	0.38 oz	1.91 oz	3.82 oz	7.63 oz	1.19 lb	2.38 lb
45 %	0.12 oz	0.30 oz	1.48 oz	2.97 oz	5.94 oz	14.8 oz	1.85 lb
60 %	0.09 oz	0.22 oz	1.11 oz	2.23 oz	4.45 oz	11.1 oz	1.39 lb
65 %	0.08 oz	0.21 oz	1.03 oz	2.05 oz	4.11 oz	10.3 oz	1.28 lb
75 %	0.07 oz	0.20 oz	0.95 oz	1.77 oz	3.77 oz	9.50 oz	1.17 lb
90 %	0.06 oz	0.15 oz	0.74 oz	1.48 oz	2.97 oz	7.42 oz	14.8 oz
100 %	0.05 oz	0.13 oz	0.67 oz	1.34 oz	2.67 oz	6.68 oz	13.4 oz

(rev. 10/05)

When breakpoint is the goal, the chemical should be added as quickly as possible. Broadcasting calcium hypochlorite around the pool or "walking" sodium hypochlorite along the perimeter are two common procedures. Pool patrons should not be present when this is occuring. Also, pH levels should be paid attention to while superchlorination is occuring.

Although "shock" products containing potassium monopersulfate will not remove CC, using one of these products proactively to cleanse water of organic contaminants can help prevent the formation of CC. Consult the chemical packaging for the dosage requirements.

Lowering Chlorine

If chlorine levels need to be lowered, the addition of sodium thiosulfate is recommended. A good rule of thumb when adding sodium thiosulfate is 1 lb/100,000 gal of water to reduce the chlorine level by 1 ppm. If the size of a particular pool to be treated is different than 100,000 gal, it should be divided by 100,000 gal to find the pool factor. For instance, if a pool is 150,000 gal and has an FC of 10.0 ppm that must be lowered to 2.1 ppm, how much sodium thiosulfate must be added to this pool to reduce the chlorine level by 8.0 ppm?

8 lb sodium thiosulfate   X $\dfrac{150,000}{100,000}$ = ?

8 lb X 1.5 (pf) = 12 lb sodium thiosulfate

When using sodium thiosulfate, caution should be exercised. If too much sodium thiosulfate is added to the pool, it will be extremely difficult to get chlorine readings, resulting in a waste of time, chlorine, and money. Unlike chlorine, sodium thiosulfate should be added a little at a time. Sodium thiosulfate is normally used after superchlorination only when chlorine readings are exceedingly high. In some regions, sodium sulfite or sodium bisulfite is used instead of sodium thiosulfate. Some pool owners and operators prefer sodium sulfite because its chemistry is more predictable and less is required to lower chlorine or bromine.

pH

Many aquatic experts agree that pH is the most important element in swimming pool water chemistry. Every chemical produced or introduced into the pool is either affected by or has an effect on pH. pH not only promotes or inhibits the work of disinfectants but also determines the water balance in the pool.

Simplified, pH is a numerical value that indicates whether water is acidic or basic. Swimmers are comfortable in water that is slightly basic, usually between 7.2 and 7.8 (Figure 15.1). Water dissociates much like hypochlorous acid to form hydroxide (OH-) ions and hydrogen (H+) ions. The concentration of hydrogen ions determines the pH of water. *pH* actually means potential of hydrogen. The greater the hydrogen concentration is, the lower the pH. The lower the pH is, the more acidic and the less basic the pool water. When the hydrogen ion concentration is equal to the hydroxide ion concentration, the water is neutral. Neutral water such as distilled water has a pH of 7, but a pH of 7.0 is considered too acidic for pool water. The pH scale extends from 0 to 14 with values below 7 being *acidic* and values above 7 being *basic*. The smaller the pH value is, the more acidic the water. The larger the pH value is, the more basic the water.

Acidic water is aggressive, and basic water is scale-forming. Acidic water can deteriorate metal surfaces including filter tanks, valves, pipes, heaters, and other pool plumbing. Corrosive water can also burn skin and eyes and even erode tooth enamel. Scale has the opposite effect. Scale is a white precipitate that builds up on pipes, pumps, and other pool equipment, making them either less effective or nonfunctional. Basic water can also cause cloudiness and skin irritation. The higher the pH is, the less effective the disinfectant is and the more hazy the water becomes.

The pH scale is a logarithmic concept that is important to understand, yet is somewhat complicated. On the pH scale, each unit division represents a tenfold increase or decrease in acidity. Each division on the scale is a multiple of 10. For instance, beginning at the neutral value of 7, a pH of 6 is 10 times more acidic than a pH of 7, a pH of 5 is 100 times more acidic than a pH of 7, and a pH of 4 is a 1,000 times more acidic than a pH of 7. In the other direction, a pH of 8 is 10 times more basic than a pH of 7, a pH of 9 is 100 times more basic, and a pH of 10 is a 1,000 times more basic than a pH of 7. A movement of just 0.5 on the pH scale will result in a 280% increase or decrease in acidity depending on which direction the pH changes. Hopefully, this discussion illustrates how significant relatively small pH changes affect water balance. The pH values of most swimming pools should be maintained between 7.2 and 7.8. As the pH climbs closer to 7.8, bather comfort may increase, but more chlorine will be required at this elevated pH. As the pH lowers toward 7.2, less chlorine is needed, but bather comfort is reduced. Many pool owners and operators consider a pH of 7.4 to 7.5 ideal.

Raising pH

To raise pH, basic or alkaline compounds are used. Soda ash (sodium carbonate) is the most common substance used to increase pH. Soda ash is a fine white powder that is usually mixed with water first and then injected by a chemical feeder pump into the pool water.

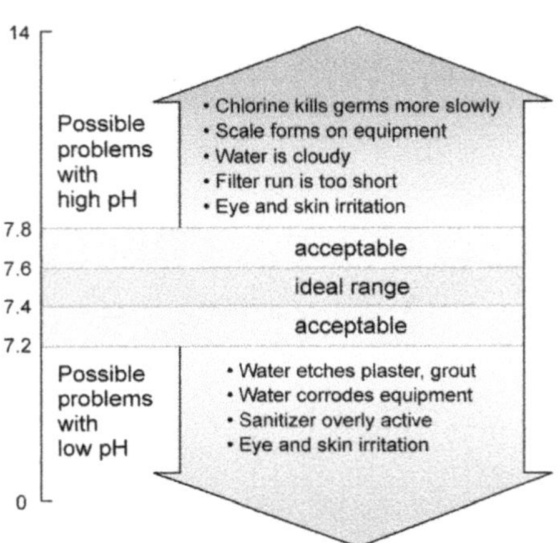

Figure 15.1. Problems with high and low pH. (Courtesy of The Association of Pool & Spa Professionals)

Soda ash feeders are notorious for becoming clogged, particularly around the ball check valves and the injector. Soda ash feeders must be cleaned regularly. Running a solution of muriatic acid periodically through the feeder often prevents clogging, but this must be performed regularly. Soda ash can also be added directly into the pool, but it should be mixed with water first, and it will cloud the water, so it is best to use this technique at night, after the pool closes.

In some pools, sodium hydroxide (caustic soda) is used instead of soda ash. Sodium hydroxide is a liquid that is extremely effective in raising pH and less expensive than soda ash, but it is somewhat difficult to handle and freezes between 50°F and 60°F. Although sodium bicarbonate raises the pH, it is not intended for that purpose. Sodium bicarbonate should only be used to raise TA.

Gas chlorine significantly lowers the pH, so when gas chlorine is used, soda ash is also added to raise the pH, but some pool operators and owners prefer caustic soda because it has a higher pH value.

Gas chlorine causes the pH of the pool water to drop dramatically. As a result, for every 1 lb of gas chlorine added to the pool, a corresponding 1.5 lb of soda ash should be added.

If the pH must be raised for any reason, particularly when gas chlorine is not in use, Table 15.2 may be used. A base demand reagent from a test kit is needed in this case to determine how much soda ash or caustic soda must be added to raise the pH to the desired level.

Lowering pH

When the pH needs to be lowered, an acid must be introduced into the water. Either muriatic acid or sodium bisulfate may be used reduce pH (Tables 15.3 and 15.4). Likewise, an acid demand reagent is required to determine the amount of acid needed to lower the pH to the desired level. In addition, it is important to pre-

Table 15.2

To Raise pH Employing the Taylor Base Demand Procedure Using Soda Ash (Sodium Carbonate, 100%)

Drops of Taylor Base Demand Reagent*	Volume of Water - U.S. Gallons						
	400 gallons	1,000 gallons	5,000 gallons	10,000 gallons	20,000 gallons	50,000 gallons	100,000 gallons
1 drop	0.21 oz	0.51 oz	2.56 oz	5.13 oz	10.3 oz	1.60 lb	3.20 lb
2 drops	0.41 oz	1.03 oz	5.13 oz	10.3 oz	1.28 lb	3.20 lb	6.41 lb
3 drops	0.62 oz	1.54 oz	7.69 oz	15.4 oz	1.92 lb	4.81 lb	9.61 lb
4 drops	0.82 oz	2.05 oz	10.3 oz	1.28 lb	2.50 lb	6.41 lb	12.8 lb
5 drops	1.03 oz	2.56 oz	12.8 oz	1.60 lb	3.20 lb	8.01 lb	16.0 lb
6 drops	1.23 oz	3.08 oz	15.4 oz	1.92 lb	3.85 lb	9.61 lb	19.2 lb
7 drops	1.44 oz	3.59 oz	1.12 lb	2.24 lb	4.49 lb	11.2 lb	22.4 lb
8 drops	1.64 oz	4.10 oz	1.28 lb	2.56 lb	5.13 lb	12.8 lb	25.6 lb
9 drops	1.85 oz	4.61 oz	1.44 lb	2.88 lb	5.77 lb	14.4 lb	28.8 lb
10 drops	2.05 oz	5.13 oz	1.60 lb	3.20 lb	6.40 lb	16.0 lb	32.0 lb

(rev. 4/04)

(© Taylor Technologies, Inc. Reprinted with permission.)

Table 15.3

To Lower pH Employing the Taylor Acid Demand procedure Using Muriatic Acid (20° Baumé/31.45% HCl)

Drops of Taylor Acid Demand Reagent*	Volume of Water - U.S. Gallons						
	400 gallons	1,000 gallons	5,000 gallons	10,000 gallons	20,000 gallons	50,000 gallons	100,000 gallons
1 drop	0.37 fl oz	0.92 fl oz	4.58 fl oz	9.16 fl oz	1.15 pt	1.43 qt	2.86 qt
2 drops	0.73 fl oz	1.83 fl oz	9.16 fl oz	1.15 pt	1.15 qt	2.86 qt	1.43 gal
3 drops	1.10 fl oz	2.75 fl oz	13.7 fl oz	1.72 pt	1.72 qt	1.07 gal	2.15 gal
4 drops	1.47 fl oz	3.67 fl oz	1.15 pt	1.15 qt	2.29 qt	1.43 gal	2.86 gal
5 drops	1.83 fl oz	4.58 fl oz	1.43 pt	1.43 qt	2.86 qt	1.79 gal	3.58 gal
6 drops	2.20 fl oz	5.50 fl oz	1.72 pt	1.72 qt	3.44 qt	2.15 gal	4.30 gal
7 drops	2.57 fl oz	6.41 fl oz	1.00 qt	2.00 qt	1.00 gal	2.51 gal	5.01 gal
8 drops	2.93 fl oz	7.33 fl oz	1.15 qt	2.29 qt	1.15 gal	2.86 gal	5.73 gal
9 drops	3.30 fl oz	8.25 fl oz	1.29 qt	2.58 qt	1.29 gal	3.22 gal	6.44 gal
10 drops	3.67 fl oz	9.16 fl oz	1.43 qt	2.86 qt	1.43 gal	3.58 gal	7.16 gal

(rev. 9/94)

(© Taylor Technologies, Inc. Reprinted with permission.)

Table 15.4

To Lower pH Employing the Taylor Acid Demand Procedure Using Dry Acid (Sodium Bisulfate, 93.2%)

Drops of Taylor Acid Demand Reagent*	Volume of Water - U.S. Gallons						
	400 gallons	1,000 gallons	5,000 gallons	10,000 gallons	20,000 gallons	50,000 gallons	100,000 gallons
1 drop	0.49 oz	1.23 oz	6.16 oz	12.3 oz	1.54 lb	3.85 lb	7.70 lb
2 drops	0.99 oz	2.46 oz	12.3 oz	1.54 lb	3.08 lb	7.70 lb	15.4 lb
3 drops	1.48 oz	3.70 oz	1.16 lb	2.31 lb	4.62 lb	11.6 lb	23.1 lb
4 drops	1.97 oz	4.93 oz	1.54 lb	3.08 lb	6.16 lb	15.4 lb	30.5 lb
5 drops	2.46 oz	6.16 oz	1.93 lb	3.85 lb	7.70 lb	19.3 lb	38.5 lb
6 drops	2.96 oz	7.39 oz	2.31 lb	4.62 lb	9.24 lb	23.1 lb	46.2 lb
7 drops	3.45 oz	8.63 oz	2.70 lb	5.39 lb	10.8 lb	27.0 lb	53.9 lb
8 drops	3.94 oz	9.86 oz	3.08 lb	6.16 lb	12.3 lb	30.8 lb	61.6 lb
9 drops	4.44 oz	11.1 oz	3.47 lb	6.93 lb	13.9 lb	34.7 lb	69.3 lb
10 drops	4.93 oz	12.3 oz	3.85 lb	7.70 lb	15.4 lb	38.5 lb	77.0 lb

(rev. 9/94)

(© Taylor Technologies, Inc. Reprinted with permission.)

dissolve or dilute these acids before they are added to the pool water. If added directly to the pool without dilution, muriatic acid or sodium bisulfate may reduce the TA without any appreciable effect on pH. The most common acid used for this purpose, particularly in large public pools, is muriatic acid (hydrochloric acid). Muriatic acid is corrosive and relatively inexpensive, but it must be handled carefully. If muriatic acid container lids do not fit snugly, muriatic fumes escaping from the container can cause severe damage to electrical equipment such as telephones and automatic chemical controllers. Rubber gloves and safety goggles should always be worn when working with muriatic acid. Muriatic acid is often used to lower the pH when sodium hypochlorite is used to chlorinate the pool. Unfortunately, both liquid chemicals look alike and are often improperly and mistakenly mixed together. This dangerous mixture produces chlorine gas and can cause serious accidents and too often does.

A safer alternative to muriatic acid is sodium bisulfate, which is often referred to as *dry acid* because it comes in a white granule. Sodium bisulfate is much easier to handle, but it is expensive. Many residential and smaller pools use sodium bisulfate or dry acid.

Total Alkalinity (TA)

TA is a measure of the resistance of water to changes in pH and is measured in parts per million. The higher the TA is, the more difficult it is to change pH with either acid or soda ash.

Carbon dioxide (CO_2) is a relatively new method of lowering pH in swimming pools. This gas is inherently safe to use, as evidenced by its use in restaurants to produce the carbonation in soft drinks. CO_2 also raises the TA as it lowers the pH, which is another advantage for pools with low TA. This gas is also kind to metals and does not emit corrosive gases. CO_2 can be used in the equipment room safely and conveniently. CO_2 mixed with water forms carbonic acid, which in turn liberates hydrogen ions, which lowers pH. To use CO_2 successfully at a pool, an expert must install the system, a local supplier must be available, and it should be delivered in bulk. Some claim when they used CO_2, they noticed an increase in algae growth. But CO_2 is becoming more popular in the United States because it is less likely to improperly mix with other chemicals, and therefore it offers increased safety. Before CO_2 is chosen for an aquatic facility to lower pH, an important caveat must be explored. Unlike many other pH-reducing chemicals, CO_2 increases TA. *If TA already tends to be high (130 to 150 ppm), CO_2 should probably be avoided because TA will rise to excessively high levels and then require the addition of muriatic acid, which would defeat the purpose of changing to CO_2.* A pool with sodium hypochlorite will experience a continual and significant rise in pH, and muriatic acid, sodium bisulfate, or CO_2 must be added in this case.

pH levels are determined with a test kit. Although many pH reagents are available, phenol red is the most common pH test reagent for swimming pool water. pH reagents should be replaced annually. pH levels should be checked with chlorine levels on an hourly basis in most pools.

The lower the TA is, the more likely pH is to change; even slight changes in chemicals, swimmer loads, and weather can significantly affect pH or cause "pH bounce." Pool operators experiencing difficulties either adjusting pH levels or maintaining a target pH should analyze the TA.

More specifically, TA is a measurement of alkaline components in the water. These components include carbonate (CO_3^{-2}), bicarbonate (HCO_3^{-1}), and hydroxide (OH^{-1}), with other alkaline materials making minor contributions. In the ideal pH range for pools (7.2 to 7.6), bicarbonates contribute the most.

pH and TA in swimming pools are closely related. When pool water has a low pH, all carbonate ions are converted to bicarbonates and no calcium carbonates are formed. As a result, without calcium carbonate available, the water becomes corrosive to the shell, equipment, and plumbing. Conversely, when pool water has a high pH, calcium precipitates out of the water and causes cloudiness.

Most pools should maintain TA levels from 100 to 150 ppm. Many health departments do not dictate ideal ranges for TA because they only affect pool plumbing and not people's health. Vinyl liner and fiberglass pools may need a slightly higher TA (125 to 175 ppm). TA should not drop below 100 ppm, except in regions that have high CH levels or when calcium hypochlorite is the primary sanitizer. In this case, when the CH in a pool is greater than 500 ppm, the TA may be allowed to drop to no less than 80 ppm.

When in doubt about the recommended TA level for a particular pool, a pool builder or local pool supply company should be consulted. When cyanuric acid (CYA) is added to pool water to stabilize chlorine, it artificially elevates the TA level. When the TA is low (less than 80 ppm) and the CYA level is high (more than 60 ppm), one third of the CYA reading can be subtracted from the TA level for a true TA level.

Raising Total Alkalinity

A low TA not only makes it difficult to maintain the ideal pH, but may also eventually lead to highly aggressive water that could damage filters, the pool shell, heaters, and other equipment. Low alkalinity is also associated with green water and the etching of plaster. Low TA (below 50 ppm) can also be linked to eyeburn.

Sodium bicarbonate ($NaHCO_3$) should be added to raise TA. Sodium bicarbonate is also known as baking soda, bicarb, and bicarbonate of soda. Sodium bicarbonate only slightly affects the pH. Although soda ash also tends to raise the TA, sodium bicarbonate is the recommended chemical for this purpose.

TA must be maintained between 100 and 150 ppm to keep pool water balanced. When total alkalinity must be increased, sodium bicarbonate (baking soda) is added to the pool. A good rule for this chemical adjustment is 15 lb of sodium bicarbonate for each 10 ppm increase in TA in 100,000 gal of water. To determine the pool factor with this formula, the size of the pool being used can be divided by 100,000 gal. In addition, Table 15.5 can be used to make these calculations.

Table 15.5

To Raise Total Alkalinity Using Baking Soda (Sodium Bicarbonate, 100%)

Desired increase in ppm	Volume of Water - U.S. Gallons						
	400 gallons	1,000 gallons	5,000 gallons	10,000 gallons	20,000 gallons	50,000 gallons	100,000 gallons
10 ppm	0.90 oz	2.24 oz	11.2 oz	1.40 lb	2.80 lb	7.00 lb	14.0 lb
20 ppm	1.79 oz	4.48 oz	1.40 lb	2.80 lb	5.60 lb	14.0 lb	28.0 lb
30 ppm	2.69 oz	6.72 oz	2.10 lb	4.20 lb	8.41 lb	21.0 lb	42.0 lb
40 ppm	3.59 oz	8.97 oz	2.80 lb	5.60 lb	11.2 lb	28.0 lb	56.0 lb
50 ppm	4.48 oz	11.2 oz	3.50 lb	7.00 lb	14.0 lb	35.0 lb	70.0 lb
60 ppm	5.38 oz	13.4 oz	4.20 lb	8.41 lb	16.8 lb	42.0 lb	84.1 lb
70 ppm	6.28 oz	15.7 oz	4.90 lb	9.81 lb	19.6 lb	49.0 lb	98.1 lb
80 ppm	7.17 oz	1.12 lb	5.60 lb	11.2 lb	22.4 lb	56.0 lb	112 lb
90 ppm	8.07 oz	1.26 lb	6.30 lb	12.6 lb	25.2 lb	63.0 lb	126 lb
100 ppm	8.97 oz	1.40 lb	7.00 lb	14.0 lb	28.0 lb	70.0 lb	140 lb

(rev. 9/94)

(© Taylor Technologies, Inc. Reprinted with permission.)

The ideal range of 100 to 150 ppm for TA is approximate. In geographical areas with hard source water, the TA may be lowered to 80 ppm. Conversely, in the case of fiberglass or vinyl-lined pools, the TA may need to be elevated to 125 to 175 ppm.

Lowering Total Alkalinity

High TA causes the pH to stick at a certain level, making it difficult to change. Much time and money can be spent on moving the pH even slightly. Additionally, high TA leads to scale buildup and may cause cloudy water.

To lower TA, an acid must be used. Muriatic acid (liquid) and sodium bisulfate (powder) are two acids commonly used for this purpose. Muriatic acid is more commonly used in public pools. TA should be adjusted prior to adjusting other chemicals, particularly pH and CH (Figure 15.2).

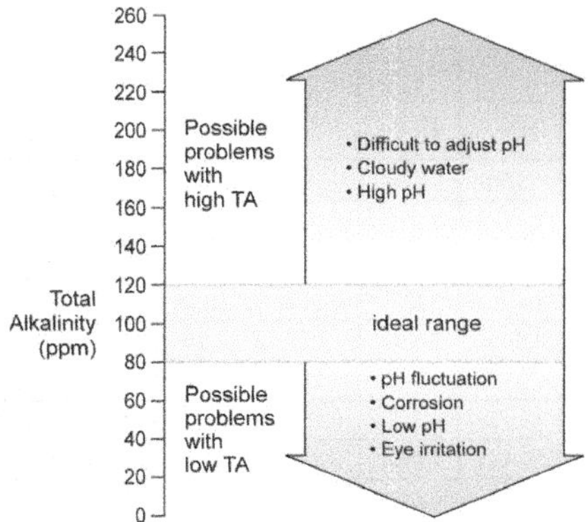

Figure 15.2. Problems with high and low total alkalinity (TA). (Courtesy of The Association of Pool & Spa Professionals)

When TA becomes excessively high, a strong acid such as muriatic acid or sodium bisulfate must be added to the pool water (Table 15.6). Muriatic acid used to reduce TA should be added to the pool full strength, undiluted. This should be done in the deep end of the pool. The pool operator should pour the acid into one spot. When done in this fashion, a low pH is achieved, resulting in the conversion of carbonate alkalinity to carbon dioxide that is released from the water. This procedure may be repeated in several areas over several days until the desired level of TA is achieved.

Table 15.6
To Lower Total Alkalinity Using Muriatic Acid
(20° Baumé/31.45% HCl)

Desired decrease in ppm	Volume of Water - U.S. Gallons						
	400 gallons	1,000 gallons	5,000 gallons	10,000 gallons	20,000 gallons	50,000 gallons	100,000 gallons
10 ppm	1.02 fl oz	2.56 fl oz	12.8 fl oz	1.60 pt	1.60 qt	3.99 qt	2.00 gal
20 ppm	2.04 fl oz	5.11 fl oz	1.60 pt	1.60 qt	3.20 qt	2.00 gal	3.99 gal
30 ppm	3.07 fl oz	7.67 fl oz	1.20 qt	2.40 qt	1.20 gal	3.00 gal	5.99 gal
40 ppm	4.09 fl oz	10.2 fl oz	1.60 qt	3.20 qt	1.60 gal	3.99 gal	7.99 gal
50 ppm	5.11 fl oz	12.8 fl oz	2.00 qt	3.99 qt	2.00 gal	4.99 gal	9.98 gal
60 ppm	6.13 fl oz	15.3 fl oz	2.40 qt	1.20 gal	2.40 gal	5.99 gal	12.0 gal
70 ppm	7.16 fl oz	1.12 pt	2.80 qt	1.40 gal	2.80 gal	6.99 gal	14.0 gal
80 ppm	8.18 fl oz	1.28 pt	3.20 qt	1.60 gal	3.20 gal	7.99 gal	16.0 gal
90 ppm	9.20 fl oz	1.44 pt	3.59 qt	1.80 gal	3.59 gal	8.99 gal	18.0 gal
100 ppm	10.2 fl oz	1.60 pt	3.99 qt	2.00 gal	3.99 gal	9.98 gal	20.0 gal

(rev. 9/94)

(© Taylor Technologies, Inc. Reprinted with permission.)

Sodium bisulfate (dry acid) should be mixed in cool water then introduced to the pool in the same manner as muriatic acid. Broadcasting either acid diluted over the pool is not recommended. The TA is not effectively reduced by broadcasting, particularly when diluted acids are used (Table 15.7).

Table 15.7
To Lower Total Alkalinity Using Dry Acid (Sodium Bisulfate, 93.2%)

Desired decrease in ppm	Volume of Water - U.S. Gallons						
	400 gallons	1,000 gallons	5,000 gallons	10,000 gallons	20,000 gallons	50,000 gallons	100,000 gallons
10 ppm	1.37 oz	3.44 oz	1.07 lb	2.15 lb	4.30 lb	10.7 lb	21.5 lb
20 ppm	2.75 oz	6.87 oz	2.15 lb	4.30 lb	8.59 lb	21.5 lb	43.0 lb
30 ppm	4.12 oz	10.3 oz	3.22 lb	6.45 lb	12.9 lb	32.2 lb	64.5 lb
40 ppm	5.50 oz	13.7 oz	4.30 lb	8.59 lb	17.2 lb	43.0 lb	85.9 lb
50 ppm	6.87 oz	1.07 lb	5.37 lb	10.7 lb	21.5 lb	53.7 lb	107 lb
60 ppm	8.25 oz	1.29 lb	6.45 lb	12.9 lb	25.8 lb	64.5 lb	129 lb
70 ppm	9.62 oz	1.50 lb	7.52 lb	15.0 lb	30.1 lb	75.2 lb	150 lb
80 ppm	11.0 oz	1.72 lb	8.59 lb	17.2 lb	34.4 lb	85.9 lb	172 lb
90 ppm	12.4 oz	1.93 lb	9.67 lb	19.3 lb	38.7 lb	96.7 lb	193 lb
100 ppm	13.7 oz	2.15 lb	10.7 lb	21.5 lb	43.0 lb	107 lb	215 lb

(rev. 9/94)

(© Taylor Technologies, Inc. Reprinted with permission.)

Calcium Hardness (CH)

Hardness is a term often used to refer to the mineral content of water. All water supplies have varying amounts of calcium and magnesium that make water "hard." In swimming pools, calcium accounts for nearly 95% of the hardness. The hardness of water is created by water moving over soil, rocks, and other solids. Although calcium and magnesium are the major contributors to hardness, other elements such as carbonates, chlorides, nitrates, sulfates, and other mineral salts help to make water hard.

Although many households prefer "soft" water, this type of water can be disastrous in swimming pools. Pool water must have a high degree of hardness, or the pool itself and its equipment will deteriorate. Although the U.S. Geological Survey considers water having more than 180 ppm of CH "very hard," this level is actually too "soft" for most swimming pools.

Soft water foams, whereas very hard water does not. Hot tubs that foam may need the CH adjusted. Swimming pools with less than 200 ppm of CH are considered "hungry" for calcium and as a result will dissolve any source of hardness, but particularly plaster and grout. Pool tiles fall off frequently in many pools low in calcium. Low hardness will also adversely affect the water balance in the pool.

As measured in swimming pools in parts per million, CH indicates calcium (Ca) content of the water. The recommended range for CH is between 200 and 400 ppm (Figure 15.3). This text does not examine total hardness, which is the sum of two types of hardness: carbonate and noncarbonate. These types of hardness are also referred to as temporary and permanent.

Typically, low CH is more of a problem to swimming pools than high CH. Low CH combined with low pH

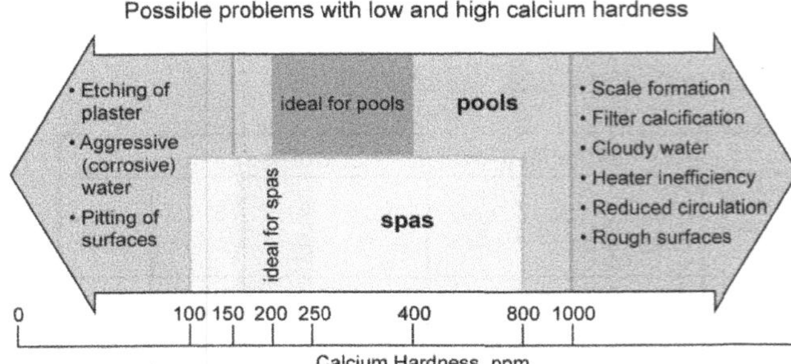

Figure 15.3. Problems with low and high calcium hardness (CH). (Courtesy of The Association of Pool & Spa Professionals)

Table 15.8

To Increase Calcium Hardness Using Calcium Chloride (77%)

Desired increase in ppm	Volume of Water - U.S. Gallons						
	400 gallons	1,000 gallons	5,000 gallons	10,000 gallons	20,000 gallons	50,000 gallons	100,000 gallons
10 ppm	0.77 oz	1.92 oz	9.61 oz	1.20 lb	2.40 lb	6.01 lb	12.0 lb
20 ppm	1.54 oz	3.85 oz	1.20 lb	2.40 lb	4.81 lb	12.0 lb	24.0 lb
30 ppm	2.31 oz	5.77 oz	1.80 lb	3.61 lb	7.21 lb	18.0 lb	36.1 lb
40 ppm	3.08 oz	7.69 oz	2.40 lb	4.81 lb	9.61 lb	24.0 lb	48.1 lb
50 ppm	3.85 oz	9.61 oz	3.00 lb	6.01 lb	12.0 lb	30.0 lb	60.1 lb
60 ppm	4.62 oz	11.5 oz	3.61 lb	7.21 lb	14.4 lb	36.1 lb	72.1 lb
70 ppm	5.38 oz	13.5 oz	4.21 lb	8.41 lb	16.8 lb	42.1 lb	84.1 lb
80 ppm	6.15 oz	15.4 oz	4.81 lb	9.61 lb	19.2 lb	48.1 lb	96.2 lb
90 ppm	6.92 oz	1.08 lb	5.41 lb	10.8 lb	21.6 lb	54.1 lb	108 lb
100 ppm	7.69 oz	1.20 lb	6.01 lb	12.0 lb	24.0 lb	60.1 lb	120 lb

(rev. 9/94)

(© Taylor Technologies, Inc. Reprinted with permission.)

and low TA will significantly increase corrosivity. As the aggressiveness of the water increases, the solubility of calcium carbonate also increases. This means that plaster and marcite pool finishes will deteriorate quickly because calcium carbonate is a major component of both plaster and marcite. The dissolving or breakdown of these pool finishes is called etching.

Low CH also leads to corrosion of metal components in the pool plant, particularly in heat exchangers. Calcium carbonate usually provides a protective film on the surface of copper heat exchangers and heat sinks. This thin layer prevents much water-to-metal interaction, but does not adversely affect the heating process. Without this protective layer caused by low CH, heat exchangers and associated parts can be destroyed prematurely. Strangely enough, as water temperature increases, solubility of calcium carbonate decreases. The recommended range for most pools is between 200 and 400 ppm, but there is nothing wrong with having 500 to 600 ppm in swimming pool water. CH should be tested monthly in most pools and has the least significant effect on the water balance when compared to pH and TA.

Raising Calcium Hardness

If CH needs to be raised, calcium chloride dihydrate should be added to the pool. Calcium chloride should be predissolved before it is added to the pool. Calcium chloride is the chemical that must be added when CH needs to be raised. When added to water, calcium chloride produces a significant amount of heat. As a result, after the total amount of calcium chloride that is needed is determined, this amount can be halved and then applied to the pool in two equal doses. To dissolve chemicals, chemicals should be added to water, NEVER WATER TO CHEMICALS (Tables 15.6 and 15.8).

Lowering Calcium Hardness

In rare instances, the CH may be too high in a swimming pool. The resulting scaling can cause a host of pool problems, including

1. reduced circulation,
2. filter calcification,
3. heater inefficiency,
4. rough pool surfaces, and
5. eye irritation.

The only practical way of removing CH from the water is to drain varying amounts of water from the pool, depending on how high the calcium level is, and then to replace it with water of lower hardness. This may also be accomplished by prolonging the backwash cycle. If source (make-up) water has exceedingly high CH, pH and TA levels may have to be lowered. However, the pH should never be allowed to drop below 7.2, and the TA should never be allowed to fall below 80 ppm.

If high CH is still a problem after draining water and adjusting pH and TA levels, a water softener may be required to reduce the CH level. Sodium phosphate water softeners are not recommended for pool use, but sodium zeolite softeners are. Some sequestering agents may also be used to prevent calcium carbonate scale formation in water with high CH.

As temperature climbs and evaporation rates increase, water leaves the pool, but the minerals remain; thus CH increases. Water heaters naturally have a difficult time with calcium buildup. Also, if calcium hypochlorite is used as the primary disinfectant, CH levels will rise (Table 15.9). As mentioned previously, lowering CH is both rare and difficult to do. Pool heaters are noto-

Table 15.9

To Increase Calcium Hardness Using Calcium Chloride Dihydrate (CaCl$_2$ -2H$_2$O)

Desired calcium increase	Gallons of water			
	1,000	5,000	10,000	50,000
10 ppm	2 oz	10 oz	1.25 lbs	6.25 lbs
25 ppm	5 oz	1.6 lbs	3.12 lbs	15.6 lbs
50 ppm	10 oz	3.2 lbs	6.24 lbs	31.2 lbs

Note: 16 oz equals 1 lb; 1 oz equals 28.35 g

rious for calcium buildup, so they should be drained and cleaned whenever possible. Also, if calcium hypochlorite is used as the primary disinfectant, CH levels will tend to rise. Draining water from the pool and adding new water with a lower CH level is one way to lower CH. Another technique is to add water softener, but this is expensive. Before a water softener is added, pool experts should be consulted because some water softeners are not recommended for pool use.

Increasing Stabilizer (CYA)

The addition of CYA will protect unstabilized chlorine such as gas, sodium hypochlorite, and calcium hypochlorite from the UV rays of the sun. The combination of CYA and FC is a dynamic process that allows additional chlorine to be released while some FC is being consumed. CYA only protects chlorine in sunlight and has no disinfecting properties. The optimal CYA level is between 30 and 50 ppm. For the first application of CYA to a pool, the target level should be about 50 ppm. Table 15.10 describes how much CYA should be added for the level desired. Again, CYA should be added to outdoor pools ONLY.

Decreasing Stabilizer (CYA)

Although a controversial limit, below 100 ppm is the CYA level most states require pools to maintain. When the stabilized chlorines (dichlor and trichlor) are used, the CYA levels can increase rapidly. Some pool operators also complain of increased algae growth and cloudiness when CYA levels rise above 100 ppm. As CYA levels approach 70 ppm, the effectiveness of chlorine is greatly reduced. The only way to reduce CYA levels is to drain some of the pool water.

Table 15.10

NSPI Suggested Chemical Standards for Spa

	Minimum	Ideal	Maximum
Free chlorine (ppm)	2.0	3.0-5.0	10.0 (For NSPI Pools 2,3,6,10)
Combined chlorine (ppm)	None	None	0.2
Bromine (ppm)	2.0	4.0-6.0	10.0 (For all NSPI Pools)
pH	7.2	7.4-7.6	7.8
Total alkalinity (ppm)	60	80-100* 100-120†	180
TDS (ppm)	300	1000-2000	3000
Calcium hardness (ppm)	150	200-400	500-1000+
Cyanuric acid (ppm)	10	30-50	150‡

From ANSI/NSPI-1: Standard for public swimming pools, Alexandria, Va, 1991, The Institute.

* For liquid chlorine, calcium hypochlorite, and lithium hypochlorite.

† For gas chlorine, dichlor, trichlor, and bromine compounds.

‡ Except where limited by health departments requirement, often to 100 PPM.

(Courtesy of Taylor Technologies, Inc.)

Key

NSPI-1 Public Inground Pools
NSPI-2 Public Spas
NSPI-3 Residential Permanent Spas
NSPI-4 Residential Aboveground/Onground Pools
NSPI-5 Residential Inground Swimming Pools

NSPI-6 Residential Portable Spas
NSPI-9 Aquatic Recreation Facilities
NSPI-10 Public Swim Spas
NSPI-11 Residential Swim Spas

Total Dissolved Solids

TDS can be best described as the total of all solids dissolved in water. If all the water in a swimming pool were allowed to evaporate, TDS would be accumulated on the bottom of the pool much in the same way white deposits are left in a boiling pot after the water has evaporated. Some of this dissolved material includes hardness, alkalinity, CYA, chlorides, bromides, and algaecides. TDS also include bather wastes, such as perspiration, urine, body oil, and suntan lotion.

TDS levels are a general indicator of pool or spa water quality. Pools with less than 1,000 ppm TDS usually have good water clarity, whereas pools with more than 3,000 ppm may have poor water clarity, but this is not true in every case. One of the first signs of high TDS is a dull or cloudy appearance of the water.

TDS accumulate over time. The more chemicals and people that are added to pool water, the faster the TDS levels will increase. In general, "new" water in recently filled pools will have a low TDS level, whereas "old" water that has been in a pool or spa for a long period of time will have a high TDS level. A rough rule of thumb is that the TDS level will double during the first year after a pool is filled. Most make-up water has less than 400 ppm TDS. By comparison, saltwater in the ocean has a TDS level of approximately 35,000 ppm. Not surprisingly, when pool water has excessively high TDS levels, the water will actually taste salty.

High TDS values can lead to pools problems (Figure 5.4), including a reduced chlorine efficiency, algae growth, aggressive water, and worst of all, cloudiness.

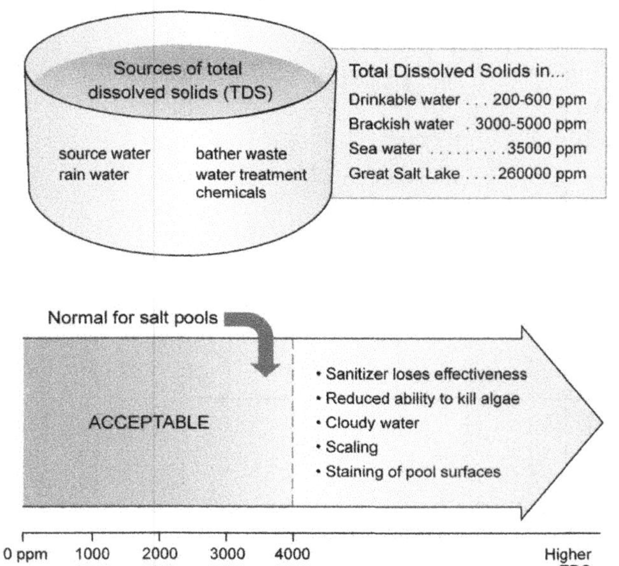

Figure 15.4. Problems with high total dissolved solids (TDS). (©2012 The Association of Pool and Spa Professionals)

Hot tubs and spas have a more significant problem with TDS levels than pools because the swimmer load is relatively higher; more chemicals are added for superchlorination and sudsing; and as water temperature increases, calcium carbonate becomes less soluble. Increased corrosion is due to the increased electrical conductance that a high-TDS pool promotes, resulting in electrolysis or "galvanic" corrosion.

To reduce the TDS level in a pool requires replacing some or all of the water with freshwater that has normal TDS levels. For several reasons, hot tubs should be "dumped" regularly according to a formula (found in Chapter 19). Pool operators, however, can control TDS levels by adding freshwater on a daily basis. Emptying a pool should not be a seasonal or annual occurrence unless the TDS elevate so high that the water becomes cloudy.

TDS have only a minimal effect on the Langelier Saturation Index, which we will discuss next. Because corrosiveness increases as TDS increase, it is a good practice to subtract a tenth (.1) from the Langelier Saturation Index for every 1,000 ppm TDS above 1,000.1.

Measuring TDS requires a portable electronic analyzer. Every owner and operator of a hot water pool should consider this TDS analyzer as a standard piece of equipment, but it may not be required for most public pools. If a high TDS level is suspected at larger public pools, a local pool supplier may be called to analyze the water.

Temperature

As temperature increases, calcium carbonate becomes less soluble, causing it to precipitate out of solution at higher temperatures. Additionally, temperature is one of five factors considered in the Langelier Saturation Index (SI), but it is the least significant of the five factors. The SI determines whether water is corrosive or scale-forming. The SI compares different values of pH, CH, and TA for water of varying temperatures. As temperature increases, the water balance tends to become more basic and scale-producing. However, as temperature drops, water becomes more corrosive.

In addition to helping determine water balance, temperature will also affect algae growth (as temperature increases so does algae growth), chlorination, and evaporation.

Water Balance and the Langelier Saturation Index

In 1936, Professor Wilfred Langelier, a sanitary chemist at the University of California, Berkeley, developed a formula to predict the scaling tendency of municipal water supplies. Professor Langelier was interested in protecting distribution piping in water supply systems from corrosion and excessive scaling by permitting a thin layer of calcium carbonate scale to form on the inside walls of the pipes. The SI originally had nothing to do with swimming pool maintenance and was adapted for this purpose much later.

The original index has been simplified for swimming pool use. Pool owners and operators should note that chlorine and other disinfecting chemicals are not a part of water balance. Before examining the specifics of this index, we will review results of unbalanced water: corrosiveness and scaling.

Aggressive Water

Aggressive (corrosive) water is "hungry" water that attempts to "eat" everything with which it comes in contact. Aggressive water dissolves metals, particularly copper and iron, which leads to stains. Aggressive water also dissolves and etches plaster. A swimming pool plant with corrosive water in it is being "eaten away" and destroyed by the water. An SI with a minus (-) value indicates corrosive water.

Scaling Water

Scaling water is the opposite of aggressive water and does not corrode, but rather "clogs" and "clouds." Unlike hungry aggressive water, scaling water may be considered overfed or overstuffed, containing too many components and inert materials. The excess will precipitate, leaving coarse deposits on surfaces, clogging pipes and valves, and calcifying filter media. Basic water that is only slightly scaling may produce a beneficial protective coating on all pool parts. An SI with a plus (+) value indicates basic or scale-forming water.

Equilibrium

Perfectly balanced water is said to be in equilibrium with calcium carbonate. Zero (0) on the SI indicates water in the state of equilibrium that will neither precipitate calcium carbonate in the form of scale nor dissolve the pool shell and equipment in an attempt to increase calcium carbonate.

Although the SI calculation has been criticized over the years, it still has value in swimming pool applications. It is simple to use and should be conducted on a bimonthly basis for most aquatic facilities. The following factors are needed to determine water balance:

1. pH,
2. TA,
3. CH,
4. temperature, and
5. TDS.

Only pH, TA, and CH are normally adjusted to achieve water balance and are the Big Three contributors to water balance. Pool water will often be balanced if pH, TA, and CH are kept within the recommended ranges.

The Saturation Index

To use the SI, pH is measured with phenol red. Readings for TA, CH, and temperature are taken with a standard pool test kit and a thermometer. Once true values are found, they are converted to the factors found in the SI table listed below. Once TA, CH, and temperature are converted to alkalinity factory, calcium factor, and temperature factor, they are totaled and a constant of -12.1 is added to the sum (Table 15.11).

Table 15.11
The Langelier SI Table

Table 1 (TF) temperature		Table 2 (CF) calcium hardness		Table 3 (AF) total alkalinity	
Degrees F	TF	CH(ppm)	CF	TA(ppm)	AF
32	0.1	5	.3	5	.7
37	0.1	25	1.0	25	1.4
46	0.2	50	1.3	50	1.7
53	0.3	75	1.5	75	1.9
60	0.4	100	1.6	100	2.0
66	0.5	150	1.8	150	2.2
76	0.6	200	1.9	200	2.3
84	0.7	300	2.1	300	2.5
94	0.8	400	2.2	400	2.6
105	0.9	800	2.5	800	2.9
128	1.0	1000	2.6	1000	3.0

$$SI = pH + TF + CF + AF + -12.1$$

The Formula

$$SI = pH + TF + CF + AF + -12.1$$

The first and second editions of this text (1994, 2003) assert an SI index of -0.5 and +0.5 is acceptable. An index of more than +0.5 is scale-forming. An index below -0.5 is corrosive. The current trend in water chemistry is to maintain -0.3 and +0.3.

EXAMPLE 1

A pool has a pH of 8.0, a TA of 150 ppm, a CH of 400 ppm, and a temperature of 86°F. Is the pool water corrosive, scaling, or neutral?

$$SI = pH + TF + AF + CF + -12.1$$
$$SI = 8.0 + 0.7 + 2.2 + 2.2 + -12.1 = +1.0$$

The SI indicates that the pool contains water that is too basic, and as a result, it is scale-forming. This water would precipitate calcium carbonate. The easiest adjustment to make for water balance would be to reduce the pH by adding an acid such as muriatic acid. By reducing the pH to 7.3, which is within the ideal range, the SI would be changed to +0.3, which is acceptable.

However, if a more balanced pool is desired, the TA could be reduced to 80 ppm, which would result in an SI of +0.1 when combined with a 7.3 pH.

$$SI = pH + TF + AF + CF + -12.1$$
$$SI = 7.4 + 0.7 + 1.9 + 2.2 + -12.1 = +0.1$$

The example above demonstrates an important point concerning the SI and water balance. There is a one-to-one relationship between pH and the SI, so pH has the greatest effect on changing water balance. Also, the acid used to lower pH will also lower TA.

EXAMPLE 2

If a pool has a pH of 6.8, a TA of 50 ppm, CH of 30 ppm, and a temperature of 78°F, is the pool corrosive, scaling, or balanced?

$$SI = pH + TF + AF + CF + -12.1$$
$$SI = 6.8 + 0.6 + 1.7 + 1.0 + -12.1 = -2.0$$

The pool in this example is extremely corrosive. Several changes must be made to the water chemistry to protect the pool. Using the SI once again, we find a pH of 7.5, CH of 400 ppm, and a TA of 80 ppm would result in an SI of +0.1.

$$SI = pH + TF + AF + CF + -12.1$$
$$SI = 7.5 + 0.6 + 1.9 + 2.2 + -12.1 = +0.1$$

By reviewing the ideal ranges recommended for swimming pools, we quickly determined that in both examples the water would be out of balance without running an SI because most parameters were well above or below what they should be. In Example 1, high pH, TA, and CH levels indicated that this pool was basic. On the other hand, low pH, TA, and CH levels in Example 2 predict the aggressiveness of the pool water.

Some water test kits contain a calculator or slide rule that computes the SI for the user without having the user do the math. The pool owner or operator uses the actual values for pH, TA, CH, and temperature found with the standard tests and manipulates the calculator for the SI. These devices are accurate, are easy to use, are inexpensive, and are becoming popular (Figure 15.5).

Most pools cannot remain balanced for long periods of time because they are in a state of "dynamic equilibrium." Significant changes in the water occur daily. Also, make-up water in general tends to be either aggressive or scaling. When adding chemicals to balance a pool, pool owners and operators should compensate for the tendencies of a particular pool to "drift" toward the minus or plus side of the SI. As a result, many experienced pool owners and operators will move their "target" SI to the other side of 0 from the SI usually found.

As mentioned previously, pH most significantly affects water balance. Conversely, the temperature of pool water has about one tenth as much effect on water balance as pH. Furthermore, TDS have even less effect on water balance than either pH or temperature. A change of 1,000 ppm TDS has the same effect as changing the pH by 0.1.

To sum up the effects that different components have on the SI, we offer the following comparison by Williams (2011):

To change the SI by .1,

1. change the pH by .1,
2. change the water temperature by 8°F,
3. change the TA by 30 ppm,
4. change the CH by 50 ppm, and
5. change the TDS by 1,000 ppm.

The SI provides a basic starting point from which owners and operators may begin to balance their pool water. The SI examines water balance through a wide-angle lens, but many pool operators need a telephoto lens to perfectly balance their water. The SI was developed for closed-loop water systems, not dynamic, open water systems such as swimming pools.

Jock Hamilton, president of the United Chemical Corporation, developed a water balancing scale that is similar to the SI but uses only three factors instead of the five factors needed to calculate Langelier's scale. He also recommends maintaining a higher pH range to 8.2. The Hamilton Index uses total hardness, TA, and pH. Whether this method of water balance is more accurate

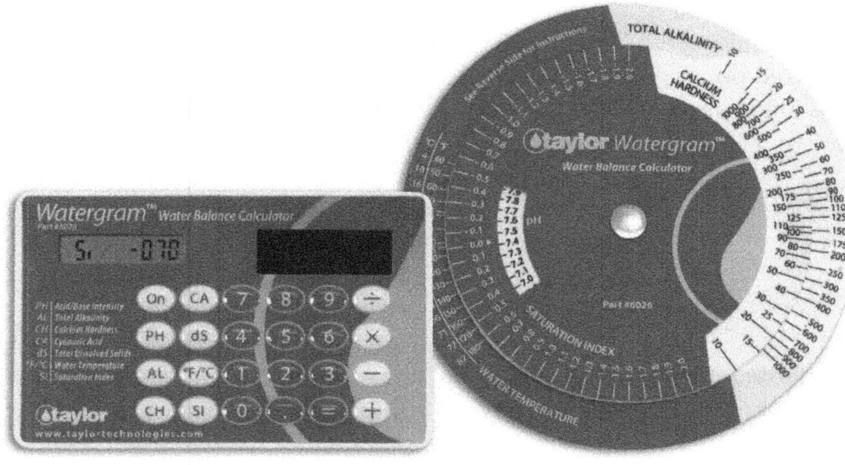

Figure 15.5. Pool calculators can solve many problems. (Photo courtesy of Taylor Technologies, Sparks, MD)

than the Langelier Index has yet to be determined. The Hamilton Index is even easier to use than the Langelier Index.

Summary

pH is one of the most important pool factors and should be checked hourly in most commercial pools. pH is the most important factor in balanced water that is neither aggressive nor scaling. The pool and all its associated parts will last longer and work more efficiently if the water is balanced. The recommended ranges for pH, TA, CH, and TDS are found in Table 15.12.

It cannot be overstated that water balance is by far one of the most neglected areas of aquatic facility management.

Table 15.12
Chemical Operational Parameters

These guidelines set forth the suggested operational parameters for the proper chemical treatment and maintenance of pools and spas. Applicable health department guidelines and label directions supersede these parameters. Chemical treatment alone will not produce sanitary pool and spa water. A filtration system in proper operational condition is also required to attain clear and sanitary water.

KEY

APSP-1 Public Inground Pools
APSP-2 Public Spas
APSP-3 Residential Permanent Spas
APSP-4 Residential Aboveground/Onground Pools

APSP-5 Residential Inground Swimming Pools
APSP-6 Residential Portable Spas
APSP-9 Aquatic Recreation Facilities
APSP-11 Water Quality for Public Pools and Spas

A. Sanitizer Levels

1. Sanitizer Residual
A residual of an EPA-registered sanitizer shall be present at all times and in all areas of the pool or spa.
One of the following EPA-registered sanitizer systems shall be used: Chlorine; or Bromine; or PHMB; or Metal-based systems.

1. Free Chlorine, ppm

Standard	Minimum	Ideal	Maximum	Comments
APSP-1 APSP-4 APSP-5 APSP-9 APSP-11	1.0	2.0–4.0	The U.S. EPA has established a maximum chlorine level of 4.0 ppm for re-entry of swimmers into the water. However, state or local health codes may allow or require the use of chlorine levels above 4.0 ppm.	Hot water/heavy use may require operation at or near maximum levels. • Test kits are available for a variety of free chlorine ranges. • Free chlorine test color (DPD) may be completely or partially bleached by chlorine levels greater than 5 ppm to give a false low reading. For appropriate test kit, consult pool professional or test kit manufacturer. Regular oxidation is recommended and remedial practices may be necessary.
APSP-2 APSP-3 APSP-6 APSP-11	2.0	2.0–4.0	The U.S. EPA has established a maximum chlorine level of 5.0 ppm for re-entry of swimmers into spas. However, state or local health codes may allow or require the use of chlorine levels above 5.0 ppm.	Public Spas and Swim spas: During hours of operation, test the water hourly, record the results, maintain the ideal range continually and shock treat at the end of the daily use period. Residential Spas and Swim spas: Maintain these levels continually during hours of operation. Test water before use. During extended use test water hourly. Shock treat water after use

2. Combined Chlorine, ppm
(High combined chlorine results in reduced sanitizer efficacy. Take remedial action to reduce combined chlorine.)

Standard	Minimum	Ideal	Maximum	Comments
APSP-1 APSP-3 APSP-4 APSP-5 APSP-6 APSP-9 APSP-11	0	0	0.2	Signs of combined chlorine: Sharp chlorine-like odor and eye irritation (e.g., mucous membrane).
APSP-2 APSP-11	0	0	0.5	

(continued)

Table 15.12 (cont.)

3. Total Bromine, ppm
NOTE: Refer to manufacturer's product label for specific use concentrations. Use concentrations vary between different types of brominating compounds.

Standard	Minimum	Ideal	Maximum	Comments
APSP-1 APSP-4 APSP-5 APSP-9 APSP-11	1.0	2.0–3.0 Residential Pools 3.0–4.0 Public Pools	The U.S. EPA allows maximum bromine levels of up to 8.0 ppm for re-entry of swimmers into the water. However, state or local health codes may allow or require the use of bromine levels above 8.0 ppm.	• Hot water/heavy use may require operation at or near maximum levels. • Public swimming pools require maintenance of higher Total Bromine residuals than residential pools. • Regular oxidation is recommended. Residential: During hours of operation, maintain these levels continually. Test water before use. During extended use test water hourly. Shock treat water after use. Public: During hours of operation, maintain the ideal range continually. Test the water hourly and record results. Shock treat water after use.
APSP-2 APSP-3 APSP-6 APSP-11	2.0	2.0–4.0 Residential spas and swim spas 4.0–6.0 Public spas and swim spas		

5. Metal-Based System
Any metal-based system used must incorporate an EPA-registered sanitizer; follow product manufacturer's EPA-accepted label for use and/or operation requirements.

B. Chemical Values
NOTE: When operating outside the ideal ranges, an LSI calculation should be performed to ensure the water is balanced.

1. pH

Standard	Minimum	Ideal	Maximum	Comments
All facilities	7.2	7.4–7.6	7.8	If pH is too low: • rapid dissipation of sanitizer • plaster and concrete etching • eye discomfort • corrosion of metals • vinyl liner wrinkling If pH is too high: • low chlorine efficacy • scale formation • cloudy water • eye discomfort

2. Total Alkalinity (Buffering) ppm as $CaCO_3$*

Standard	Minimum	Ideal	Maximum	Comments
All facilities	60	80–100 for calcium hypochlorite, lithium hypochlorite, and sodium hypochlorite	180	If total alkalinity is too low: • pH bounce • Corrosion tendency If total alkalinity is too high: • Cloudy water
	60	100–120 for sodium dichlor, trichlor, chlorine gas and bromine comlb.	180	• Increased scaling potential • pH tends to be too high or to drift upward more rapidly. * These target values are based on the alkalinity from bicarbonate and carbonate only. Alkalinity should be corrected to account for cyanuric acid (see APSP-11, Section A 7.5).

Table 15.12 (cont.)

3. Total Dissolved Solids (TDS) ppm				
All facilities	NA	NA	1500 ppm greater than TDS at pool or spa start-up. (Start-up TDS includes source water TDS and any other inorganic salt added at start-up or later.)	An increase in TDS may indicate an accumulation of impurities during the course of operation. Excessively high TDS (excluding the amount of sodium chloride added) may lead to hazy water and scale formation, corrosion of fixtures, and may inhibit sanitation. TDS can be reduced by partial draining and addition of fresh water. For Spas: TDS should be periodically reduced by draining. (See Section K, Water Replacement Procedure)

4. Calcium Hardness, ppm, as CaCO₃				
APSP-1 APSP-4 APSP-5 APSP-9 APSP-11	150	200–400	1000	Total alkalinity and pH may need to be adjusted to the lower end of their respective ranges if hardness is over 500 ppm.
APSP-2 APSP-3 APSP-6 APSP-11	100	150–250	800	

5. Heavy Metals				
All facilities	NA	NA		If excessive heavy metals (such as copper, iron and manganese) are present: • Staining may occur • Water may discolor • Filter cycle may decrease and require more frequent back-washing • May indicate pH too low, corrosion, metallic source water, excessive metal ions from treatment chemicals, etc.

6. Langelier Saturation Index (LSI)				
All facilities	−0.3	0.0– ±0.5	±0.5	

C. Biological Values

(Maintaining adequate sanitizer levels is critical to prevent growth of algae and bacteria)

1. Visible Algae

Standard	Minimum	Ideal	Maximum	Comments
All facilities	None visible	None visible	None visible	If algae growth is observed, recommendations may include but are not limited to: • Superchlorinate the pool or spa. Superchlorination should not be performed when PHMB is used. • Use an EPA-registered algicide according to label directions. • Supplement with brushing and vacuuming. Some algicides may cause foaming.

2. Bacteria

All facilities	(See APSP-11)	(See APSP-11)	(See APSP-11)	Public Facilities: If bacteria count exceeds local health department requirements, superchlorinate and follow proper maintenance procedures. Superchlorination should not be performed when PHMB is used. Residential Facilities: Maintain proper sanitizer level and pH to control bacteria.

Table 15.12 (cont.)

D. Stabilizer (when used)				
1. Cyanuric Acid, ppm				
All facilities	10	30–50	100	If stabilizer is too low: Chlorine residual is rapidly destroyed by sunlight. If stabilizer is too high: May reduce chlorine efficacy against algae and pathogens. The effect of cyanuric acid on slowing the oxidation of organics, kill rates of bacteria, viruses, and algae has been demonstrated, primarily in controlled laboratory studies. However, no disease outbreaks linked to cyanuric levels in properly sanitized pools have been reported. NOTE: Cyanuric acid is not recommended for indoor pools or spas where protection from sunlight is not necessary. Cyanuric acid does not stabilize bromine sanitizers.
E. Oxidation				
Regular oxidation is recommended for pools and spas with normal bather load as a preventive treatment				
1. Chlorine Products				
APSP-1 APSP-4 APSP-5 APSP-9 APSP-11	As needed	Weekly	Determined by bather load, weather conditions	Some high-use pools may require oxidation several times per week. Regular oxidation is recommended to prevent the build-up of contaminants, maximize sanitizer efficiency, minimize combined chlorine, and improve water clarity. Chlorine should not be used to oxidize a pool or spa sanitized by PHMB.
APSP-2 APSP-3 APSP-6 APSP-11		At the end of each day facility is used.		

2. Potassium Monopersulfate				
Standard	**Minimum**	**Ideal**	**Maximum**	**Comments**
APSP-1 APSP-4 APSP-5 APSP-9 APSP-11	As needed	Weekly	Determined by bather load, weather conditions, etc.	Some high-use pools may require oxidation several times per week. Regular oxidation is recommended to prevent the build-up of contaminants, maximize sanitizer efficiency, minimize combined chlorine and improve water clarity. Potassium monopersulfate will measure as combined available chlorine in DPD test system. Refer to test kit manufacturer's directions. Potassium monopersulfate should not be used to oxidize a pool or spa sanitized by PHMB.
APSP-2 APSP-3 APSP-6 APSP-11		At the end of each day facility is used		
F. Remedial Practices				
1. Superchlorination				
All facilities				Follow label directions. Use a registered chlorine sanitizer. Do not re-enter pool or spa until water meets the prescribed values in Section A. Do not superchlorinate a pool or spa treated by PHMB. Some symptoms that may indicate a need for superchlorination are: • Cloudy water • Slime formation • Musty odors • Difficulty in maintaining a sanitizer residual • Algae and/or high bacteria counts • Eye irritation from chloramines For fecal response guidelines, refer to http://www.cdc.gov/healthywater/swimming/index.html

Table 15.12 (cont.)

2. Superchlorination to establish breakpoint, dosage in ppm				
APSP-1 APSP-2 APSP-4 APSP-5 APSP-9 APSP-11	At least 10 times combined chlorine			High dosage may be required to satisfy chlorine demand. If combined chlorine persists, water replacement should be considered. Superchlorination should not be performed when PHMB is used.

3. Shock Treatment and Shock Oxidizers				
All facilities				Some conditions that may indicate a need for a shock or a shock oxidizer are: • Cloudy water • Difficulty in maintaining a sanitizer residual • Periods after heavy bather use • Adverse weather. Shock oxidizers are not sanitizers. They are effective in oxidizing organic contaminants. If the purpose is to treat bacteria or visible algae, an EPA-registered shock product should be used; follow label directions. Spas should be shocked or shock-oxidized on a daily basis when used.

4. Chlorine Dioxide

Standard	Minimum	Ideal	Maximum	Comments
		As needed	Determined by occurrence of biofilms in skimmer or plumbing, or by abrupt disappearance of hydrogen peroxide.	White or pink-colored biofilms can infest the plumbing of PHMB pools and eventually spread onto pool surfaces. On other occasions, the biofilms will be hidden from view, but will cause a rapid decrease in hydrogen peroxide. Chlorine dioxide kills the peroxide-degrading organisms, but should be used only to treat the plumbing and not the pool itself. Follow label directions.

5. Clarification/Flocculation				
All facilities		As needed		Follow manufacturer's directions.

6. Algicides				
All facilities		As needed		Use U.S. EPA-registered products. Follow manufacturer's directions. Use of some algicides may cause foaming.

7. Foam Control				
All facilities		As needed	There shall be no persistent foam (foam remaining in a spa after the jets are turned off).	Foam may harbor persistent microorganisms. If foaming is not adequately controlled, consider a daily shock or oxidation treatment, water replacement, or an appropriate anti-foam agent. Follow manufacturer's directions.

8. Nitrates				
All facilities				Nitrate ion is a nutrient for algae and a number of bacteria. Elevated algae and bacteria populations associated with elevated nitrate ion concentrations create a significant chlorine demand. Nitrate ion is at the highest oxidation state of nitrogen, and does not have a chlorine demand.

9. Phosphate				
All facilities		No requirements		Phosphate is an oxidized form of phosphorous. Phosphorous is a non-metallic element and an essential nutrient for all living organisms, including bacteria and algae. Phosphate does not create a chlorine demand since the phosphate ion does not react with free chlorine. However, inadequate maintenance and sanitization can allow algae and bacteria to reproduce rapidly by using phosphorous as a nutrient. Under these circumstances, the multiplying algae or bacterial populations will cause chlorine demand.

Table 15.12 (cont.)

G. Temperature

| All facilities | Personal preference | 78–94 °F *(26–34°C)* depending on pool type and use
Up to 104 °F *(40 °C)* depending on spa type and use | 104 °F *(40 °C)* | If temperature is too low:
• Bather discomfort
If temperature is too high:
• Excessive fuel requirement
• Increased evaporation
• Bather discomfort
• Increased scaling potential
• Increased use of sanitizers
Overexposure to hot water may cause nausea, dizziness, and fainting.
The Consumer Product Safety Commission states: "Hot tub water temperatures should never exceed 104 degrees Fahrenheit." Temperatures well below 104 °F *(40 °C)* are recommended for extended use (exceeding 10–15 minutes) or for pregnant women, people with certain medical conditions or medications, and for young children. |

H. Water Clarity

Standard	Minimum	Comments
All facilities	The deepest part of the pool or spa and/or main drain shall be visible and sharply defined. Pools: Pool water shall be of a clarity to permit an 8 in. *(203 mm)* diameter black and white Secchi disc or main suction outlet (main drain) located on the bottom of the pool at its deepest point to be clearly visible and sharply defined from any point on the deck up to 30 feet *(9.14 m)* away in a direct line of sight from the disc or main drain. Spas: The bottom of the spa at its deepest point shall be clearly visible.** ** This test shall be performed when the water is in a non-turbulent state and bubbles have been allowed to dissipate.	If water is turbid: • Sanitizer level may be low • Filtration/circulation system may require maintenance or increased run (filtering) time • Improper chemical balance (Section B) • Consult remedial practices (Section F)

I. Supplemental Sanitizers

1. Ozone
Concentration in air above pool or spa water, ppm

Standard	Minimum	Ideal	Maximum	Comments
All facilities			0.1 ppm over 8 hour time-weighted average and 0.3 ppm for any 15 minute period	• Serves as oxidizer of water contaminants. • Ozone shall be used only in conjunction with an EPA-registered sanitizer. • Indoor installations should have adequate ventilation. • When ozone is used for indoor installations, air monitoring is required. See OSHA Standard 29 CFR 1910.1000 Table Z-1.

Table 15.12 (cont.)

2. UV				
All facilities				UV lamps shall be used only in conjunction with an EPA-registered sanitizer.
J. Oxidation Reduction Potential (ORP)				
APSP-1 APSP-2 APSP-9 APSP-11				When an ORP controller is used, it shall not be relied upon as a method for measuring the concentration of sanitizer in the water. The sanitizer level shall be measured with traditional wet chemical methods capable of detecting specific sanitizer residuals (e.g. DPD, N, N-diethyl-p-phenylene diamine for free available chlorine), to ensure that the minimum sanitizer residual is maintained. For PHMB-treated pools, levels for ORP values are not applicable. ORP reading may be affected by a number of factors including, but not limited to, pH, probe condition, cyanuric acid, sanitizer type, and supplemental oxidizers. Follow manufacturer's recommendations.

(c) APSP 2014

References

Olin Corporation. (1992). *The complete pool care book.* Stamford, CT: Author.

Williams, K. G., & Young, R. A. (Eds.). (2011). *Aquatic facility operator manual* (6th ed.). Ashburn, VA: National Recreation and Park Association.

Bibliography

The American Water Works Association. (1971). *Water quality and treatment* (3rd ed.). Denver, CO: Author.

The Association of Pool and Spa Professionals. (2012). *Certified maintenance specialist workbook.* Alexandria, VA: The Association of Pool & Spa Professionals.

Gabrielson, A. M. (1987). *Swimming pools: A guide to their planning, design, and operation* (4th ed.). Champaign, IL: Human Kinetics.

Kowalsky, L. (Ed.). (1991). *Pool/spa operators handbook.* San Antonio, TX: National Swimming Pool Foundation.

Mitchel, K. (1988). *The proper management of pool and spa water.* Decatur, GA: BioLab.

Pool & Spa News, Los Angeles.

Pope, J. R., Jr. (1991). *Public swimming pool management, I and II.* Alexandria, VA: National Recreation and Park Association.

Service Industry News. Torrance, CA. http://www.poolspanews.com/

Taylor, C. (1989). *Everything you always wanted to know about pool care.* Chino, CA: Service Industry Publications.

Taylor Technologies. (2011). *Pool and spa water chemistry: A testing and treatment guide with tables.* Sparks, MD: Author.

Tepas, J. J. (1989, June 19). Putting Langelier in perspective. *Pool and Spa News.* http://www.poolspanews.com/

Washington State Public Health Association. (1988). *Swimming pool operations.* Seattle, WA: Author.

Williams, K. G., & Young, R. A. (Eds.). (2011). *Aquatic facility operator manual* (6th ed.). Ashburn, VA: National Recreation and Park Association.

Courtesy of Counsilman-Hunsaker

16
Water Testing

Sanitary water is free from infection and disease-causing organisms such as bacteria, viruses, and yeasts; from slippery algae that can cause falls and spoil the appearance of the water; and from bather wastes, dirt, dust, leaves, grass, and the like. Water cannot stay sanitary by itself. Sanitation is achieved with the addition of a disinfectant, most commonly chlorine.

Balanced water will neither corrode nor scale the surfaces or equipment of the pool.

Corrosion is an eating-away of a material, such as a metal pool fixture. Scaling refers to deposits on surfaces that are unsightly and rough to the touch, as on plaster, and that can also block water flow when they build up on pool piping. Both conditions can lead to big repair bills, so keeping water chemically balanced is important. This is achieved by managing four interrelated factors: pH, total alkalinity, calcium hardness, and water temperature. A change in one can affect all others, and that is why proper and vigilant water testing is important.

Just because swimming pool water looks good does not necessarily mean that it is free from harmful microscopic organisms or chemically balanced. A vigilant water-testing program will permit pool operators to detect emerging pool problems before most patrons notice them. Proper use of a swimming pool test kit is a must for all pool owners and operators. Even though many aquatic facilities are wisely moving to automated systems for monitoring and adjusting water chemistry, manual testing must still be performed to calibrate the equipment, to ensure the system is performing properly, and to meet the requirements of public health authorities. Perhaps the two greatest problems in water quality management are testing that is too infrequent and use of reagents that have spoiled or are too old to produce accurate results.

Types of Tests

Several methods are employed to analyze water conditions (see Figure 16.1).

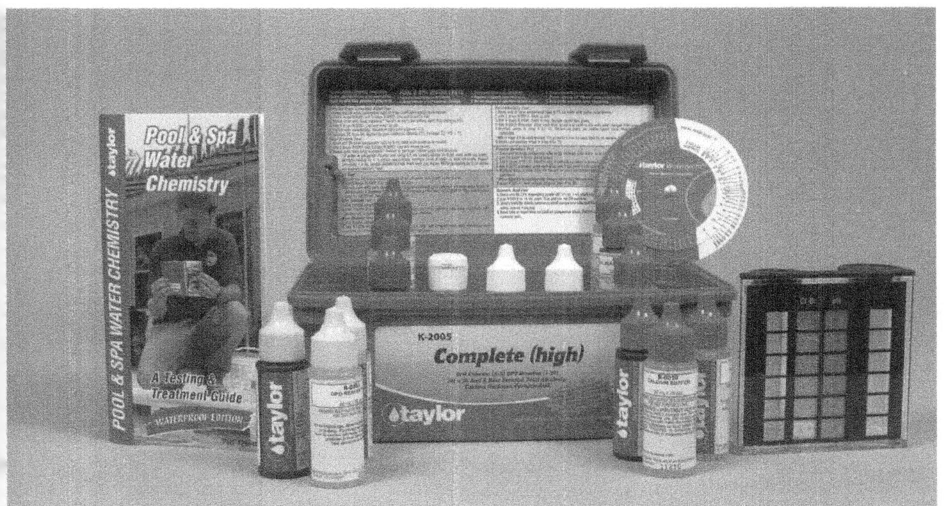

Figure 16.1. A comprehensive water testing kit for use on pools or spas sanitized with chlorine or bromine, complete with color-coded instructions and water balance calculator. (Photo courtesy of Taylor Technologies, Sparks, MD)

Colorimetric

Colorimetric tests operate on the theory that the more you have of a chemical substance in the water, the darker the treated sample's color will become. A chemical indicator added to a sample of pool water will produce a certain color. Testing for chlorine with DPD is a good example. Comparing the pink of the treated sample with reddish color standards provided with the test kit will determine the level of chemical in the water. pH also is commonly measured with a colorimetric test. These color standards range from yellow-orange to deep pink. Proper lighting is important when a color-matching test is conducted, and the manufacturer's guidelines should be followed closely in this regard. Because artificial light alters perception, testing in daylight is recommended. Test kit companies actually sell lights that simulate daylight for indoor water testing. Some people afflicted by color blindness might have problems differentiating between shades of red. This condition makes reading a DPD test result for chlorine (or bromine) difficult for a small number of people. FAS-DPD chemistry, which we discuss later in this chapter, is a good alternative for these individuals.

Titrimetric

During a titrimetric test, one reagent is added to the sample to turn it a certain color and then a second reagent is added gradually, drop by drop (titrated), until the water changes color dramatically. The number of drops needed for this color change should be counted to determine the concentration of the analyte. Both total alkalinity and calcium hardness are usually measured in this manner. The FAS-DPD test mentioned above is also a titration. It goes from deep pink to colorless, a change even a person who is red color-blind can see.

Turbidimetric

This test produces a precipitate that will eventually obscure a black dot on the bottom of the test vial. The amount of the cloudy solution it takes to hide the dot determines the parts per million. This test is usually reserved for measuring cyanuric acid. Melamine is the reagent added to the water sample in this case.

Sampling Techniques

To achieve accurate results, the pool operator or owner needs to properly collect and handle the water sample so that the test is not contaminated. These guidelines should be followed:

- Hands should be washed with soap and water and rinsed well before a sample is collected.
- Vials used to collect the sample should be rinsed several times in the water that is to be tested. Also, vials

used as test cells should be washed with a detergent periodically and rinsed well with distilled water.
- The water collected must be a "representative" sample, that is, it should not be collected from the surface where contaminants collect or in front of an inlet where water with high chemical concentrations is found. Every attempt should be made to collect water samples from 12 to 18 in. (elbow deep) below the surface and from several different locations around the pool.
- Proper sample volume is extremely important. The bottom of the meniscus should touch the fill line indicated on the test cell when viewed at eye level. The meniscus is the curved surface that forms when water fills the chamber (Figure 16.2).

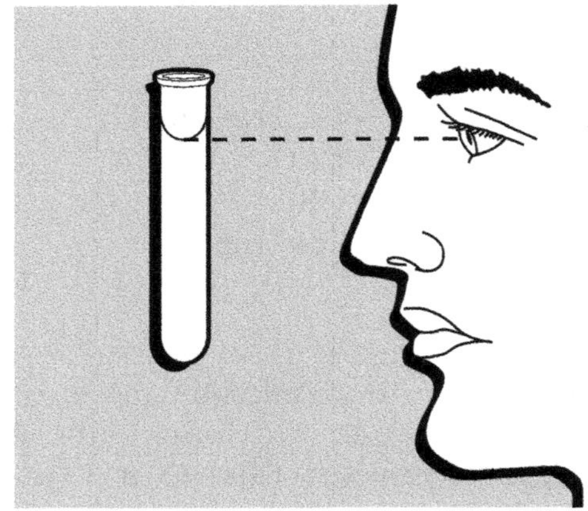

Figure 16.2. Water samples display a curvature at the surface called a meniscus. (Illustration courtesy of Taylor Technologies, Sparks, MD)

Test Kit Procedures

Many test kits are available to pool owners and operators (Figure 16.3). Although prices vary, test kits are inexpensive compared to the cost of the vessels they protect. A commercial-grade test kit with all the tests needed to ensure sanitary, balanced water is recommended for aquatic facilities. When a test kit is used, the following rules should be applied:

- Directions should be read and followed carefully. They are simple to follow and often color coded for user friendliness.
- The tester should mix reagents thoroughly by swirling the test vial using wrist action. Magnetic stirrers are available for purchase to aid stirring.
- Only reagents that the test kit manufacturer specifies should be used. Test kits and reagents should not be interchanged. Even different test kit models from the same manufacturer often require different reagents. This is particularly true for phenol red used to test pH.

- Reagents have a shelf life and should be replaced at least annually or at the beginning of each swim season.
- All reagents should be marked with the date of purchase. Whenever possible, reagents should be purchased directly from the manufacturer to ensure freshness.
- When reagents are mixed with the water sample in the test cell, the cover or caps provided should be used. If fingers are used to cover the sample, it could become contaminated. When reagents are mixed into a sample, the sample should not be shaken vigorously because this may cause a false reading. The capped sample should be swirled carefully or gently inverted to mix it with the reagent.
- Environmental influences impact the effectiveness of reagents even more than age. Extreme heat or cold and prolonged exposure to air, sunlight, humidity, or even treatment chemicals will quickly degrade them. For this reason, the test kit should be stored at room temperature (between 36°F and 85°F) in a dark, dry area away from other chemicals. Reagents should not be stored outside in the sun or a hot shed. THEY SHOULD BE KEPT OUT OF REACH OF CHILDREN.
- Reagents are easily contaminated. Chemical droppers or reagent bottles should not come in contact with foreign substances. The caps should be replaced tightly after each use. Bottle caps should not be inadvertently switched. Reagents should be kept in the carrying case when not in use. AGAIN, THEY SHOULD BE STORED OUT OF REACH OF CHILDREN.

Dr. Tom's Tip

When you notice a change in drop size, eliminate static buildup on the dropper bottle tip by wiping with a clean, damp paper towel.

- When reagents are added to the water sample, the reagent dropper should be held vertically to get the correct drop size. The reagent should not dribble down the inside walls of the vial; it should be dropped directly into the sample.
- Separate test vials should be used for different tests if instructed.
- The reading should be taken promptly; the sample should not sit.
- The tester should read the sample by holding it at eye level. A white card should be used as a background when the manufacturer recommends it. The test should be read in the daylight, but not directly into the sun. Better yet, a special lamp that simulates daylight indoors should be used.
- After a water test is complete, the sample should not be thrown back into the pool. The chemicals should be disposed of in a deck drain or other waste receptacle.

Dr. Tom's Tip

Perhaps the most popular yet worst place to keep a test kit is on a lifeguard chair or a poolside table. In this case, it is too exposed to the elements and too accessible to other people. To prevent tampering, reagent degradation, and accidental poisoning, keep the test kit in an office if possible or in a mechanical room if you must, but keep it away from people and the elements. Also, minimize the number of people taking the water readings. This will produce more reliable results.

pH Testing

pH is measured on a scale of 0 to 14. A pH of less than 7 is on the acidic side; as the number gets lower and closer to 0, the solution becomes more acidic. A pH more than 7 is on the basic side; as the number gets higher and closer to 14, the solution becomes more basic. Although a neutral pH is 7.0, that is too low for most swimming pools. As a rule, swimming pool water should be maintained between 7.2 and 7.8 on the pH scale, and more ideally between 7.4 and 7.6. Do not be fooled by the differences being only decimals. The pH scale is logarithmic, and a pH of 6 is 10 times more acidic than a pH of 7 and 100 times more acidic than a pH of 8.

Testing for pH is one of the simplest and most standardized of all pool tests. This is a colorimetric test that uses phenolsulfonephthalein, more commonly known as phenol red. Phenol red is usually a liquid reagent, although tablets are available. Phenol red is an effective indicator of pH between the values of 6.8 and 8.4. To test for pH, generally either five drops of phenol liquid or one tablet is added to a water sample. The sample color will become progressively darker as pH levels increase. The color of the treated water sample must be compared to the color comparator provided with the test kit. Phenol red will turn yellow at lower levels of pH and then orange at slightly higher levels. The lighter shades of red indicate proper pH levels; dark red indicates an excessively high level of pH (at or above the end of the test's range).

With a chlorine reading over 10 ppm, the phenol red indicator may turn dark purple. If this occurs, the tester should wait until the sanitizer level returns to normal range and then retest the pH. The temperature of the test sample should be between 60°F and 90°F. *Note:* Not all phenol red formulations are alike. The tester must use the preparation designed for use with the test kit. The reagent number should be checked carefully before a refill is bought.

Other pH reagents that can be used are bromothymol blue (pH 6.0 to 7.6) or cresol red (pH 7.2 to 8.8).

Digital "pocket" pH meters can also be used to determine pH levels in a pool. These meters include a submersible electrode and electrical circuitry to quickly monitor and display pH readings. Even more sophisticated meters, called colorimeters or photometers, eliminate the need for color matching with the human eye when pH and other important chemical parameters are being tested. Digital readouts from meters take the subjectivity out of water testing. Although meters can be extremely accurate, they are also fragile, they may need to be calibrated frequently, and the good ones require a bigger upfront investment (see Figures 16.4 and 16.5).

If pH is found to be low, a base demand test should be conducted with a base demand reagent to determine how much soda ash (caustic) to add to raise the pH to the desired level. Likewise, when pH is high, an acid demand test should be conducted with an acid demand reagent to determine how much muriatic acid or sodium bisulfate to add to return the pH to the recommended range. Both reagents are found in a quality test kit. In both cases, the number of drops required to change the color of the existing pH test sample to a color within the appropriate range determines the amount of chemical to be added.

Chlorine and Bromine Testing

The DPD Method

The most common method of testing for chlorine is a color comparison test with DPD reagents, which turn the water sample pink. DPD is short for N,N-diethyl-p-phenylenediamine. DPD chemistry can determine two types of chlorine residuals: free chlorine (FC) and total chlorine (TC). Once these levels are found, combined chlorine (CC) can be calculated by subtracting FC from TC. Although required FC levels vary from state to state, most pools should probably maintain their FC level between 2.0 and 4.0 ppm. Higher FC residuals are becoming more widely seen in water quality guidelines. Whenever possible, CC levels should not exceed 0.2 ppm, which is easier said than accomplished, particularly in busy indoor facilities.

Orthotolidine (OTO), once the standard test for chlorine, is no longer recommended. The OTO method cannot distinguish between the active sanitizer and CC, is prone to errors, and is a suspected carcinogen. Because OTO turns a water sample yellow, the old-fashioned test kits can be picked out easily because they have yellow color standards on the sanitizer side of the comparator rather than the pink color standards used in DPD test kits. To sum up, a DPD test should be used because it distinguishes between FC and CC.

DPD tests are available in both liquid and tablet form. Although DPD tablets have a longer shelf life, some individuals have a problem with managing and disposing of the foil and cellophane packets containing the tablets, which tend to make a mess. Users must also

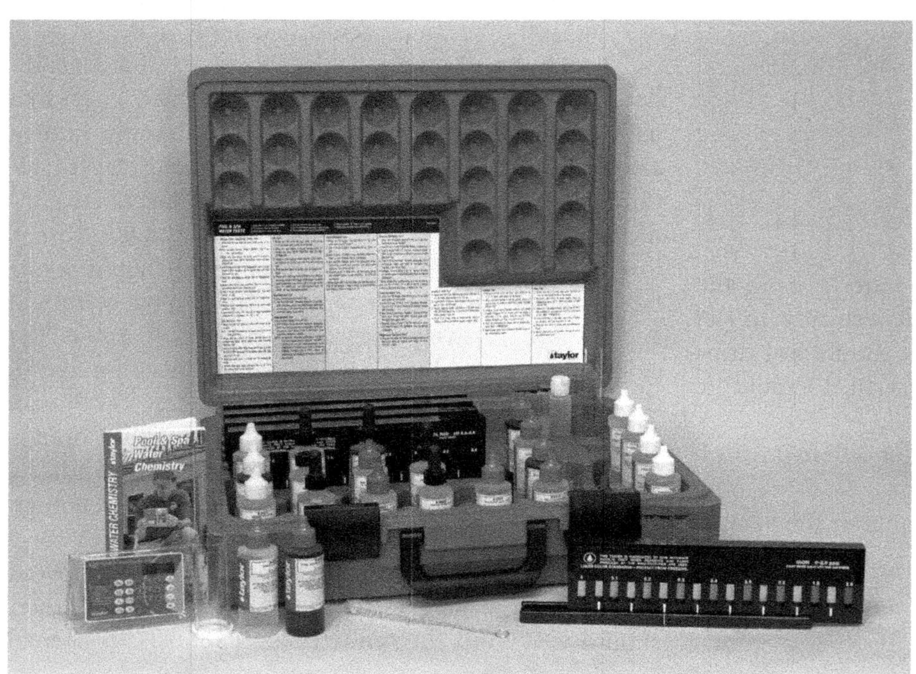

Figure 16.3. A commercial-grade test kit with liquid color standards, rather than color comparator printed on paper. (Photo courtesy of Taylor Technologies, Sparks, MD)

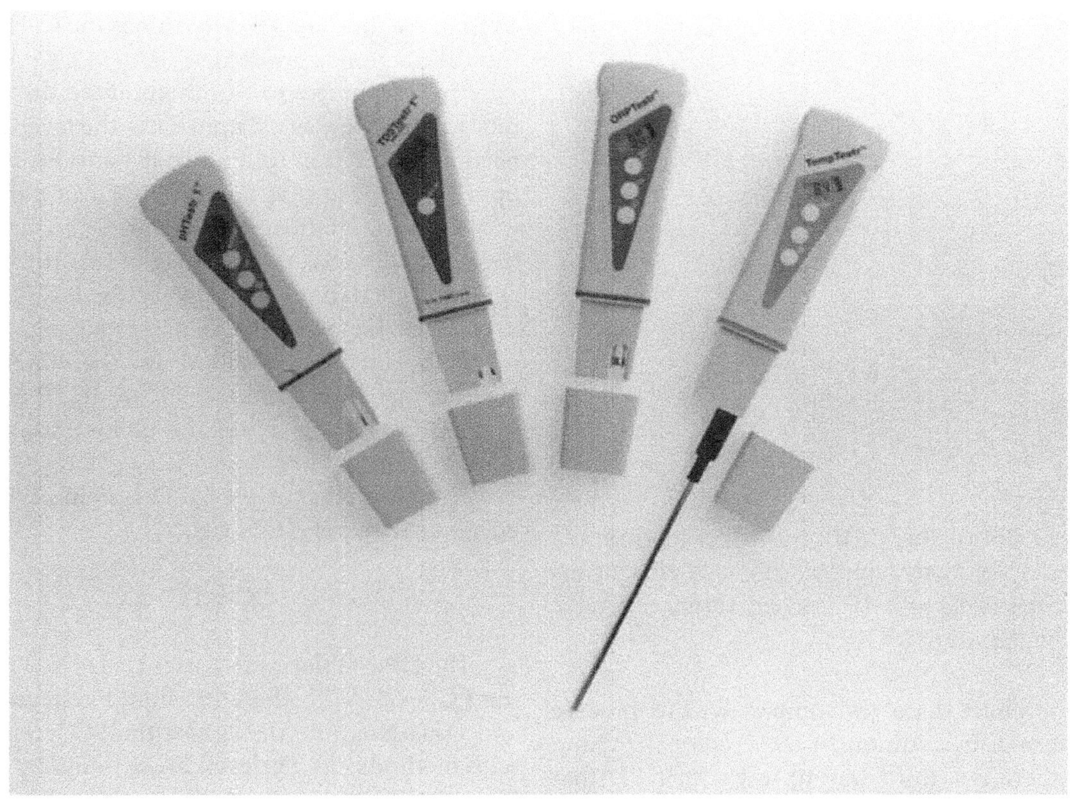

Figure 16.4. A pocket-sized pH meter (far left) alongside of TDS, ORP, and temperature meters.

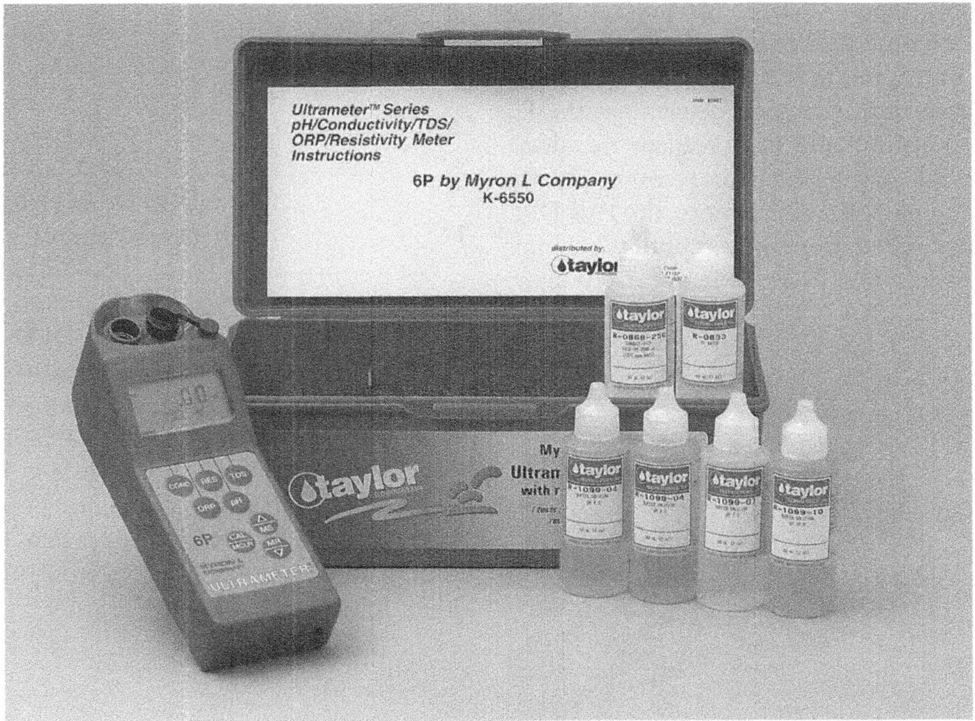

Figure 16.5. Some meters test multiple parameters. (Photo courtesy of Taylor Technologies, Sparks, MD)

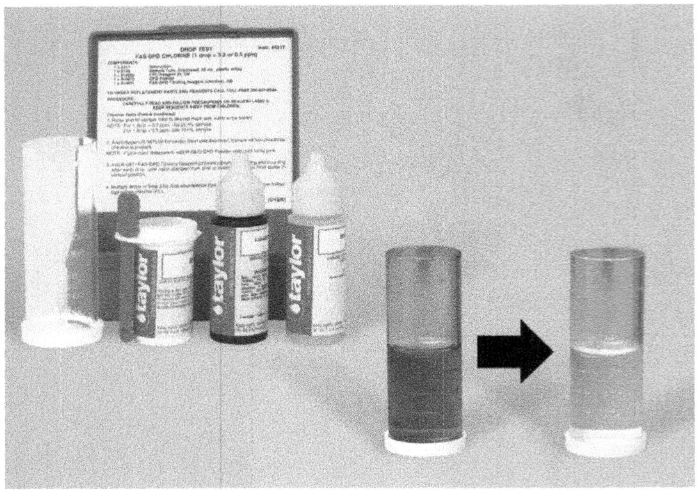

Figure 16.6. Count the drops needed to change the sample's color from pink to colorless when performing an FAS-DPD test. (Photo courtesy of Taylor Technologies, Sparks, MD)

make sure the tablet dissolves completely; this process cannot be rushed. In addition to these color-matching procedures, there is a third way to test with DPD that does not require comparing different shades of pink. The ferrous ammonium sulfate (FAS) variation of the DPD test involves use of one powder and two liquid reagents. A tiny amount of DPD powder is added to the sample, which turns it pink. Then FAS-DPD titrating solution is added one drop at a time until the solution makes a permanent change from pink to colorless. The number of drops needed to make this happen determines the FC level. Next, five drops of liquid DPD reagent are added, and if there is any CC in the pool at or over 0.2 ppm, the solution will turn pink again. Once more, the FAS-DPD titrating solution is added drop by drop until the sample goes from pink to colorless. The number of drops need-

ed to make this happen determines the CC level directly (no subtraction is needed).

The advantages to this method are that it can accurately read as low as 0.2 ppm CC—the level at which you need to take action to remove it—and FC as high as 20 ppm (something that might be seen in a pool shocked with chlorine). Other tests cannot determine values between 0 and 1 and do not read over 5 or 10 ppm. Another advantage is that anyone can see the change from color to colorless happen, even a small group of people, mainly men, who are red color-blind, and therefore have a terrible time matching pinks (see Figure 16.7). The FAS-DPD method is available as a stand-alone test or as part of a combination test kit.

The advantage of the DPD system is that it distinguishes between FC and CC.

$$CC = TC - FC$$

The DPD tablet system uses DPD No. 1 to determine the FC level. With the DPD liquid system, DPD No. 1 and DPD No. 2 do this. Once the FC level is found, in both methods, the TC level can be found by adding DPD No. 3 to the treated sample. The first reading (FC) should be subtracted from the second reading (TC) to find the CC level. If the color does not change from the first test (FC) and the second test (TC), then no CC exists in the pool. A summary is found below:

Test	DPD Reagents Required
FC	DPD No. 1 tablet or DPD liquids No. 1 & No. 2
TC	treated sample + DPD No. 3

Bromine is also tested with DPD, but because all forms of bromine are efficient sanitizers, only the total bromine level is measured. Certain test kit manufacturers offer color comparators with values for both chlorine and bromine; however, if they do not, bromine may be measured with the standard chlorine test. The comparator reading can be multiplied by 2.25 to find the bromine reading because bromine is 2.25 times heavier than chlorine.

Figure 16.7. Some meters test multiple parameters. (Photo courtesy of Taylor Technologies, Sparks, MD)

A word of caution is in order when a high level of sanitizer is suspected. When chlorine and bromine levels are exceedingly high (beginning at about 10 ppm and 22 ppm, respectively), the sanitizer will bleach the DPD reagent immediately as it enters the test tube, falsely indicating that no chlorine or bromine is in the pool water or the level is low. Not realizing this will likely cause the pool operator to add even more sanitizer! Therefore, when a high level of sanitizer is expected and no color develops with the specified addition of DPD No. 2, one more drop of DPD No. 2 can be added. If there is still no color, or if pink appears but only for a brief moment, the water is superchlorinated. This test sample should be discarded and another test should be performed with a new 50/50 water sample (half pool water and half tap or distilled water). Then the result should be multiplied by 2. In the case of extremely high chlorine levels, the dilution may need to be one-third pool water and two-thirds unchlorinated water, in which case the results should be tripled.

Be aware that ozone, iodine, or oxidized manganese in the sample can cause false DPD readings for chlorine and bromine because they are chemically similar. Also, if the sample contains residual from a potassium monopersulfate nonchlorine "shock" added to the water within the past 24 hours, it will cause false readings in tests that employ DPD No. 3. For a Taylor test kit, this interference can be removed from the sample with a special "deox reagent" that must be purchased separately.

Test Strips

The technology for test strips came from the medical diagnostics industry. Strip performance has steadily improved since these "dry chemistry" tests were introduced to pool and spa owners in the mid-1990s. Although regulated public pools cannot use them for testing because their accuracy is still seen as inferior to "wet chemistry," they are popular with consumers as quick checks of water quality (see Figure 16.8).

The best-selling strips read chlorine and/or bromine, pH, and total alkalinity simultaneously. Other models are available for as many as six factors per test strip, as well as for specialty tests such as salt or nitrate.

Directions for this use are straightforward—really there is no learning curve—but every manufacturer's directions differ slightly. Some say dip in and out of the water quickly, some say swirl in a circle gently, some say swish back and forth for a certain amount of time. But all manufacturers tell how long to wait before comparing the color that develops to the color chart that is provided and how much time is available before the "window" for a correct reading closes (see Figure 16.9). Most important, the specific instructions for each test strip product should be followed.

Figure 16.8. Quick, easy handheld test strips for residential pool owners. (Photo courtesy of Taylor Technologies, Sparks, MD)

Unfortunately, there is no way to look at a test strip to determine whether it is contaminated or has outlived its useful life. Whenever the pads of a test strip come in contact with wet or oily fingers, they are contaminated. Also, the cap on the bottle containing the test strips should be tightly closed so that air and humidity do not spoil them.

Strips should not be used past the expiration date printed on the container, and the chemically impregnated pads should not be touched.

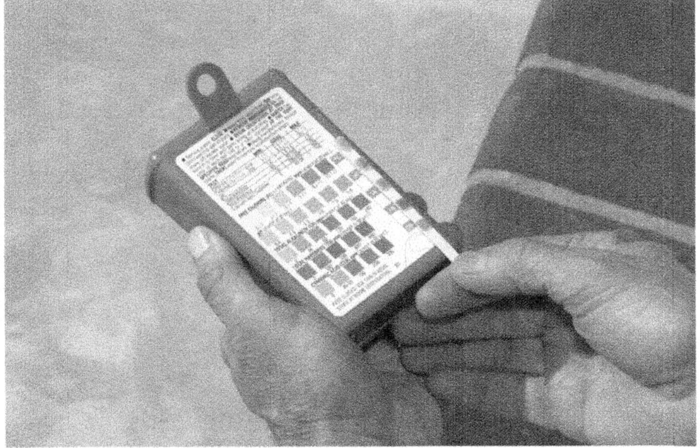

Figure 16.9. Comparing test strip results with ideal ranges. (Photo courtesy of Taylor Technologies, Sparks, MD)

Oxygen-Reduction Potential Testing (ORP)

Perhaps the most sophisticated instrument available to pool personnel for measuring the amount of disinfectant in the water is the oxygen-reduction potential (ORP) analyzer (see Figures 16.10 and 16.11). This ORP method of chemical analysis is also known as the redox method. ORP is a measure of the oxidizing capability or "work value" of any sanitizer used in water. ORP is a qualitative measure, whereas standard test kit procedures offer a quantitative measure of a sanitizer in the water. Rather than measuring sanitizers in parts per million, the ORP analyzer measures in millivolts (mV). This electrochemical measurement uses silver and silver chloride electrodes to determine the electrical potential of sanitizers in the water. Apparently, ORP levels predict the killing rate of *E. coli* organisms much more accurately than traditional chlorine readings. Pathogens cannot survive in water measuring more than 650 mV. As a result, the World Health Organization recognizes 650 mV as the minimum ORP level for drinking water, and Germany and other European countries have adopted 750 mV as the minimum ORP level for public pools and spas. When used with chlorine, ORP measures the level of hypochlorous acid as it disassociates according to pH levels.

Perhaps the greatest advantage of the ORP system is that the pool water is monitored continually (Figure 16.12). In addition to continual monitoring, many ORP systems have been expanded to include the ability to adjust chemicals automatically. Some ORP systems come with a digital readout for chlorine and pH levels, whereas others have a printout. ORP controllers even report verbally in English, through a speech synthesizer, the chemical balance of the pool water. To receive a chemical report of pool conditions, users dial the controller's

Table I	
pH ELECTRODE READINGS	
pH SCALE	mV
0 (HIGHLY ACIDIC)	+420
7.0 (NEUTRAL)	0
7.5 (IDEAL)	-30
8.0 (BASIC)	-60
14 (HIGHLY BASIC)	-420

TABLE II	
ORP ELECTRODE READINGS	
mV	CONDITIONS
BELOW 650	UNSANITARY WATER (Germs, Bacteria)
654	MINIMUM LEVEL
700 to 750	IDEAL LEVEL

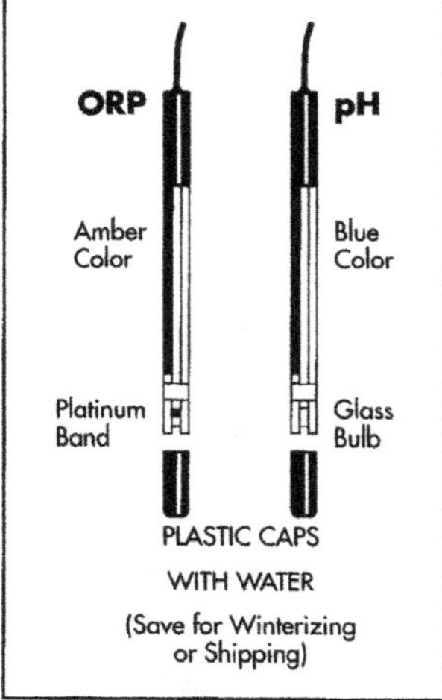

Figure 16.11. Examples of chemical sensors—pH and ORP sensors. (From *Basic pool and spa technology* (2nd ed.), by the National Spa and Pool Institute, 1992, Alexandria, VA: Author)

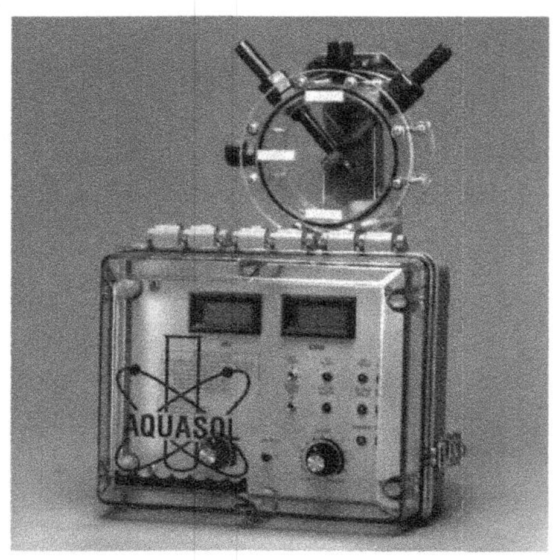

Figure 16.10. Oxygen-reduction potential (ORP) automatic control system. (Photo courtesy of Aquasol)

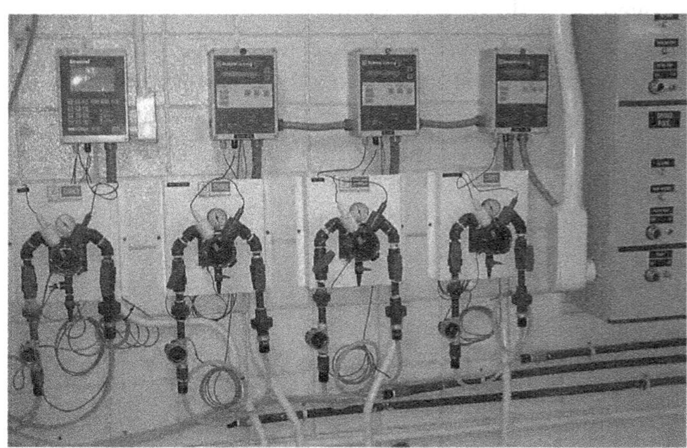

Figure 16.12. ORP automatic controllers located above pool disinfectant pumps. (Photo courtesy of Counsilman-Hunsaker)

phone number or access the information through a computer. Handheld models are also becoming popular.

One slight disadvantage of the ORP system is that the sensors need to be cleaned and replaced periodically. This is not a major drawback. Also, all ORP analyzers must be calibrated and checked against results from the manual means of testing sanitizers. Despite these concerns, ORP testing appears to be the most accurate, reliable, and sophisticated method of analyzing water sanitation, but it should still be backed up with manual testing of the water on a daily basis.

Total Alkalinity Testing

Total alkalinity should be tested weekly (best) or bimonthly with a low swimmer load. Total alkalinity is a key aspect of water balance. A total alkalinity reading is required to determine the saturation index and also aids in controlling wide swings in the pH of pool water. Total alkalinity readings should be between 60 and 180 ppm with 80 to 120 ppm being preferred in most aquatic facilities. Total alkalinity is measured by means of a titration ("drop") test. A specified volume of water is taken from the pool, the chlorine residual is neutralized with thiosulfate, a chemical indicator is added, and then the sample is titrated with an acid until the sample color changes dramatically. The indicator commonly used for total alkalinity tests is bromcresol green or methyl red. As one of two common titrants (sulfuric acid or hydrochloric acid) is added to the sample, it will turn color from green to deep pink.

To determine the exact amount of total alkalinity in the water, the tester should slowly squeeze the reagent from a dropper bottle into the prepared sample and count the number of drops needed to change the color of the sample. Many test kits use an equivalency of 10 ppm per drop to calculate parts per million of total alkalinity. Therefore, if it were to take 10 drops to change the green sample to pink, the total alkalinity in the pool would be 100 ppm. When high disinfectant levels are found in the pool, the color change will be from blue to yellow rather than green to pink. Addition of thiosulfate before starting the test will neutralize chlorine interference. Tablets are also available for this test, but may not be as accurate as liquid reagents.

Calcium Hardness Testing

Water hardness is a familiar concept to most people, thanks to the advertising of the "Culligan Man."

While softened water is desirable for household use, a certain amount of hardness (specifically from mineral calcium) is needed in pool water for it to be balanced.

Ideally, calcium hardness levels should be maintained between 200 and 400 ppm. If below 200 ppm, pool water may be too aggressive, that is, it will seek calcium from the pool plaster, concrete, and grout, causing

damage; if above 400 ppm, the calcium hardness may produce scale, causing rough surfaces and clogging the filter, pipes, and heater. The calcium hardness test is another drop test whereby a specified volume of water is titrated with a hardness reagent.

After collecting the correct volume of water as a sample, the tester should add a pH-increasing reagent to assist in the color change and then a chemical indicator. Next, a titrant called EDTA (ethylenediaminetetraacetic acid) should be swirled into the sample and the drops should be counted. The sample will turn from red to blue, but this change occurs slowly and subtly. The reading should be taken after the change in color is complete, not when the sample begins to change color. If the tester is unsure whether the reaction has reached its end point, he or she should add one more drop of titrant. If the color remains the same, this drop should not be counted. The number of drops required to permanently and completely change the sample from red to blue should be recorded and then multiplied by the drop equivalence, often 10 ppm per drop.

Cyanuric Acid Testing

Cyanuric acid (CYA) is used for stabilizing chlorine against the damaging UV rays of the sun. The trichlor and dichlor forms of chlorine already contain CYA, or it can be added to water independently when "unstabilized chlorines" are in use (chlorine gas, sodium hypochlorite, calcium hypochlorite, lithium hypochlorite). FC will last 3 to 5 times longer in pool water containing 25 ppm of CYA than in CYA-free water when exposed to sunlight. Most states do not allow CYA levels above 100 ppm in swimming pools and significantly lower levels are suggested. If CYA levels drop below 30 ppm, its chlorine-stabilizing ability is reduced. However, some pool operators claim excellent results with as little as 5 to 10 ppm. CYA is only for outdoor pools, as degradation by sunlight is not a problem indoors. CYA should never be used in indoor pools.

A turbidimetric test is used to determine the CYA level. In this case, a reagent called melamine should be added to a water sample to create a white precipitate that clouds the water in proportion to the amount of CYA present. Then the cloudy mixture should be poured into a special view tube until a dot on the bottom becomes obscured. The tube is graded so that the stopping point can be read as parts per million CYA.

Another type of turbidity test involves lowering a marker into cloudy water until it disappears, and then making the reading at that point. CYA can also be read using a photometer or a test strip, although the strip is limited in how precise it can be.

CYA levels must not be allowed to exceed 100 ppm. Not only do most states dictate this ceiling, but also chlorine's effectiveness is reduced at this level, and in addition, ORP readings are reduced. When CYA levels climb over 70 ppm, the pool water may become dull and somewhat hazy. The only practical way of reducing CYA is to drain some of the pool water. Because cartridge filters are cleaned without being backwashed, pools employing both CYA and cartridge filters may experience a more rapid rise in CYA. Testing for CYA in warmer water becomes tricky because higher temperatures restrict the production of turbidity, leading to low readings. To prevent this, the water sample needs to cool to an ambient temperature.

Copper and Iron Testing

Testing for metals is not usually conducted routinely. However, if pool water turns a clear green, orange-brown, or purple-black, or if surface stains appear, pool operators should conduct tests for copper, iron, or manganese. If any of these metals is causing a problem, it is either present in the fill (source) water, or unbalanced pool water is attacking metal components such as copper pipes and steel fittings, or copper-based algaecide is being overdosed. Colorimetric tests, similar to those described above, are used for troubleshooting (see Figure 16.13).

Sequestering agents may be used to prevent both copper and iron from precipitating out of solution, and maintaining balanced water will prevent attacks on metal circulation components. *Note:* An aggressive trichlor tablet should never be used in a skimmer.

Testing for copper and iron is not usually conducted until a metals problem in the pool is suspected.

Bacteriological Testing

To ensure that diseases will not be transmitted through swimming pool water, bacteriological tests are required of most public pools. This is one type of test that is normally not conducted at poolside. Rather, samples must be collected and sent to a certified laboratory, where an environmental health agency supervises the test. Total plate counts and coliform counts have been the most common bacteriological tests of swimming pool water in the past, but *E.Coli* testing is strongly encouraged today because it is a better predictor of water quality. In the chlorinated environment of aquatic facilities, pool operators can expect zero fecal coliforms or *E. coli* colonies when testing the water. If low levels of fecal coliform or *E. coli* are found (1 to 5 colonies/100 ml) retesting is encouraged, and if positive results are found again, the facility should be closed. Some states require weekly bacteriological testing of swimming pools. When pool disinfectants are kept at acceptable levels, bacteria

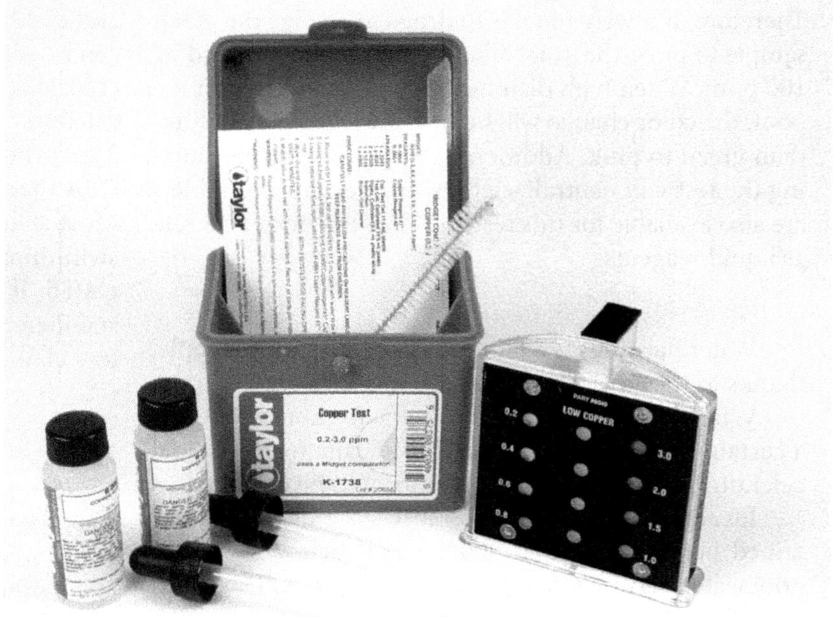

Figure 16.13. Test for copper or iron with a simple color-matching test. (Photo courtesy of Taylor Technologies, Inc.)

> **Dr. Tom's Tip**
>
> For best results, buy new reagents each and every season and replace cracked, stained, and lost parts immediately. For technical assistance, do not hesitate to call the test kit manufacturer. Some manufacturers post helpful video demonstrations on their websites as well.

proliferation should not a problem, but even the best maintained pools can become contaminated.

Sterilized bottles are used for this testing procedure, and people who handle the bottles must be careful not to contaminate the top, cap, neck, or inside of the bottle. Some labs require the sample to be refrigerated. The sample must be sent to a state-certified lab quickly (often within 24 hours).

Summary

Pool water testing, if performed properly and regularly, will help to keep the water sparkling clear, clean, and free of germs. Test kits must be stored properly, and the reagents used must always be fresh. Testing should be conducted often from several different sites around the pool (but away from return lines). All water testing records should be kept for 5 years. Before a test kit is purchased, the capabilities of several should be compared at a local pool store or dealer or online at manufacturers' websites.

Bibliography

The American Water Works Association. (1971). *Water quality and treatment* (3rd ed.). Denver, CO: Author.

Kowalsky, L. (Ed.). (1991). *Pool/spa operators handbook.* San Antonio, TX: National Swimming Pool Foundation.

Mitchel, K. (1988). *The proper management of pool and spa water.* Decatur, GA: BioLab.

Pool & Spa News, Los Angeles. www.poolspanews.com/ *Service Industry News,* Torrance, CA.

Steininger, J. (1990, June). Clean up with ORP. *AQUA.* http://aquamagazine.com

Taylor, C. (1989). *Everything you always wanted to know about pool care.* Chino, CA: Service Industry Publications.

Taylor Technologies. (2011). *Pool and spa water chemistry, testing and treatment guide with tables.* Sparks, MD: Author.

BioGuard Lab. (1981). *The pool book.* Decatur, GA: Author.

Washington State Public Health Association. (1988). *Swimming pool operations.* Seattle, WA: Author.

Williams, K. G., & Young, R. A. (Eds.). (2011). *Aquatic facility operator manual* (6th ed.). Ashburn, VA: National Recreation and Park Association.

How to Use the Treatment Tables

Once all the tests for water balance have been completed, and once the need for treatment has been determined, you can use the following tables to find the correct amount of treatment chemical to add. Turn to the appropriate table, and using the column with the correct volume of water, determine the amount of treatment chemical to add.

By using combinations of various columns, you can determine the exact amount of treatment chemical needed. For example, for a 30,000-gal pool, the column value for 20,000 plus 2 times the 5,000 gal column value will give an approximate amount of treatment chemical needed. Alternatively, the 20,000 gal column value plus 0.5 times the 20,000 gal column value will give the same result.

Treatment Table Tips

• To add chlorine products, the following products can be used:

Chlorine Products for Pools

Chlorine Product	% Available Chlorine	pH (in a 1% solution)
chlorine gas	100%	0
trichloroisocyanurate	90%	2.8–3.5
calcium hypochlorite	45–78%	8.5–11.8
dichloroisocyanurate	55–63%	6.7
lithium hypochlorite	35%	10.8
sodium hypochlorite	10–12%	11–13

(Courtesy of Taylor Technologies, Sparks, MD)

- When calculating or measuring chemicals, use the following rules to round the amount. If the last number is less than 5, round down to the nearest number. If the last number is equal to or greater than 5, round up to the next number. For example, 3.67 rounds up to 3.7, but 3.42 rounds down to 3.4.
- When converting from one liquid measure to another, use the following table:

Adjusting Treatment Levels for Different Strength Chemicals

	tsp.	TBS.	oz.	cup	pt.	qt.	gal.
tsp.	1.0	3.0	6.0	48.0	96.0	192.0	768.0
TBS.	.33	1.0	2.0	16.0	32.0	64.0	256.0
oz.	.16	.5	1.0	8.0	16.0	32.0	128.0
cup	.02	.06	.125	1.0	2.0	4.0	16.0
pt.	.01	.03	.06	.5	1.0	2.0	8.0
qt.	.005	.02	.03	.25	.5	1.0	4.0
gal.	.001	.004	.008	.06	.125	.25	1.0

(Courtesy of Taylor Technologies, Sparks, MD)

Adjusting Treatment Levels for Different Strength Chemicals

Treatment table values are based on specific strength chemicals (e.g., sodium carbonate, 100% or calcium chloride, 77%). If the specific treatment chemical used in your pool or spa is a different strength, *you must adjust the treatment amount given.*

For example, say you determine that 24 lb of calcium chloride (at 77%) is needed to increase your calcium hardness level by 100 ppm. However, by checking the label on the bag, you find that the strength is 95%—almost 24% stronger. To determine how much less calcium chloride you will need, follow the formula below:

**Treatment Table Strength ÷ Label Strength × Table Treatment Value
= Adjusted Treatment Value**

The formula with the numbers shown above:
$77 \div 95 \times 24.0 = 19.5$ lb of calcium chloride at 95% strength

Figure 16.14. Photo courtesy of Taylor Technologies, Sparks, MD

17

Pool Problems

To provide the reader with a practical troubleshooting guide for correcting common swimming pool problems, we organized this chapter differently from the others. For every pool problem presented, the following areas are discussed: cause, symptom, treatment, and prevention. By presenting material in this manner, we hope readers achieve a more comprehensive understanding of pool problems. In this fashion, readers can become more familiar with how and why pool problems arise and how to solve them. Not every pool problem is discussed in this chapter, only those that occur often and are serious in nature. The following pool problems that most often puzzle pool operators are discussed in this chapter:

- Algae
- Chlorine odor
- Discolored water
- Sand/DE in pool
- Excessive chlorine
- Foam
- Eyeburn/skin irritation
- Cloudy water
- Corrosion
- Scale
- Water loss

Algae

Cause

Although hundreds of types of algae exist, we discuss only species that affect pools. Algae grow in indoor and outdoor pools, but outdoor pools provide an ideal environment for algae growth. Therefore, the emphasis of this chapter is algae in outdoor pools, although indoor pools may also develop algae problems when windows, skylights, and exterior doors opening directly to the pool deck are present.

Algae are the simplest forms of the plant kingdom, and these microscopic, single-celled plants thrive in all bodies of water. Algae have a tendency to grow in and around swimming pools and can be found even in the best maintained aquatic facilities.

Algae growth is promoted by heat, humidity, sunlight, heavy swimmer loads, rain, and above all, insufficient disinfectant level. Dissolved minerals and scale formation also provide pool surfaces that aid algae growth and proliferation. Some pool operators claim that high CYA levels promote algae growth, but other pool operators refute this claim.

Algae itself in the pool is not harmful to swimmers. It is unsightly and gives the appearance of a poorly maintained pool. But algae growth can create other severe pool problems. Algae on pool decks and bottoms can be extremely slippery and may lead to falling accidents. If untreated, algae can also turn pool water green, reducing visibility. In addition to these problems, algae growth will attract the disinfectant's killing power, rendering the disinfectant less effective in killing bacteria and other organic wastes. Untreated algae can also harbor bacteria growth.

Whenever the disinfectant level in a pool drops and/or the pH level increases, algae may begin to flourish. This is particularly true in outdoor pools, but even more when these conditions combine with high temperatures and swimmer loads and following heavy winds and thunderstorms.

Symptoms

Algae growth is easy to detect. Pool bottoms, walls, and decks become slippery at the initial stages of algae growth and have an unsightly appearance. Algae plants come in different types, and the following colors are most often experienced at pools.

Green algae. Green algae are free-floating and can turn the most well-kept pool "pea soup" green in a matter of hours.

Green algae most often begin to grow in pools that are disinfected periodically rather than continuously. They are more likely to begin after summer storms when algae spores are blown into the pool. Once green algae begin to grow in a swimming pool, they are extremely difficult to kill.

Blue-green algae. Often called black algae, this type of algae appears to be black and typically attaches itself in cracks and on rough surfaces in pools with inadequate disinfectant levels. Blue-green algae often appear as black spots on pool bottoms and walls and in expansion joints in pool decks. If left untreated, this type of algae is not only unsightly and slippery but can also harbor bacteria such as amoebas and hookworm. Blue-green algae have a protective gelatinous sheath that protects them from disinfectants. In the case of blue-green and other surface-clinging algae, brushing is required before superchlorination.

Mustard algae. Mustard algae, which most often grow on pool walls that are shaded, are easily brushed off surfaces yet are difficult to kill. Although mustard algae may not present problems of the same magnitude as green and blue-green algae, this form of algae appears to be resistant to normal disinfectants and the addition of algaecides. Some swimming pool algae are also pink in color.

Treatment

More than any other pool problem, when it comes to algae growth, the best treatment is prevention. Regular brushing and vacuuming, along with proper chemical levels, will prevent most algae growth. Brushing not only removes algae from walls and bottoms to be better exposed to chlorine, but it also reduces the need for vacuuming. Once algae appear in a swimming pool, they must be treated with powerful chemicals to be rid of them completely (see Table 17.1). However, before we discuss specific treatments, we will discuss the difference between an algaecide and an algaestat. An algaecide is used to kill algae once they begin to grow in a pool, whereas an algaestat prevents and inhibits algae growth. Disinfectants such as chlorine and bromine are excellent algaestats. Once algae are detectable, the addition of an algaecide may be required.

Algaecides

Algae are a pesky challenge once they are established in a swimming pool. They will continue to grow and are

difficult to ameliorate with chlorine or other sanitizers. A number of specific products have been designed to eradicate algae.

Once algae are present, an algaecide is often added to the pool to remove them. Many algaecides are *quaternary ammonium compounds*, which are referred to as *quats*. Although this type of algaecide works well in killing algae and also possesses germicidal properties, quats are notorious for causing foam in pools, although this foaming may be due to overdosing. When algaecidal quats are used to fight algae growth, they should be used weekly and the manufacturer's guidelines must be followed carefully. Algaecides that have a tendency to foam should not be used in hot tubs or spas. Both quats and polyquats may slightly increase chlorine demand.

Polyquat has both algaecidal and algaestatic properties and has been used to control algae in pools, hot tubs, and spas. The major advantage of polyquat is that it does not foam. This compound also flocculates organic material, thus assisting filtration. Proper levels of polyquat must be maintained continually in the pool for it to function properly. Most experts recommend adding polyquats weekly.

Both copper- and silver-based algaecides have been used with success. Copper-based algaecides in particular can rid pools and spas of mustard algae, whereas silver-based algaecides are known to kill black algae. However, both metals have a tendency to precipitate out of the water and may cause pool stains. Many manufacturers recommend a chelating agent to prevent copper carbonate and copper oxide from precipitating onto pool and spa walls. Lowering pH has also been recommended to help prevent pool and spa staining.

The following steps should be taken when treating algae:

Table 17.1
30 ppm Shock Table for Algae Removal

% Available Chlorine*	Volume of Water						
	400 gal	1000 gal	5000 gal	10,000 gal	20,000 gal	50,000 gal	100,000 gal
5%	1.92 pts	2.40 qts	3.00 gal	6.00 gal	12.0 gal	30.0 gal	60.0 gal
10%	15.4 fl oz	1.20 qts	1.50 gal	3.00 gal	6.00 gal	15.0 gal	30.0 gal
12%	12.8 fl oz	1.00 qts	1.25 gal	2.50 gal	5.00 gal	12.5 gal	25.0 gal
35%	4.58 oz	11.5 oz	3.58 lbs	7.15 lbs	14.3 lbs	35.8 lbs	71.5 lbs
60%	2.67 oz	6.68 oz	2.09 lbs	4.17 lbs	8.35 lbs	20.9 lbs	41.7 lbs
65%	2.47 oz	6.17 oz	1.93 lbs	3.85 lbs	7.70 lbs	19.3 lbs	38.5 lbs
75%	2.27 oz	5.66 oz	1.77 lbs	3.53 lbs	7.05 lbs	17.7 lbs	35.3 lbs
90%	1.78 oz	4.45 oz	1.39 lbs	2.78 lbs	5.56 lbs	13.9 lbs	27.8 lbs
100%	1.60 oz	4.01 oz	1.25 lbs	2.50 lbs	5.01 lbs	12.5 lbs	25.0 lbs

(rev. 12/96)

% Available Chlorine	Volume of Water						
	2000 L	4000 L	20,000 L	40,000 L	80,000 L	100,000 L	400,000 L
5%	1.20 L	2.40 L	12.0 L	24.0 L	48.0 L	60.0 L	240 L
10%	600 mL	1.20 L	6.00 L	12.0 L	24.0 L	30.0 L	120 L
12%	500 mL	1.00 L	5.00 L	10.0 L	20.0 L	25.0 L	100 L
35%	171 g	343 g	1.71 kg	3.43 kg	6.86 kg	8.57 kg	34.3 kg
60%	100 g	200 g	1.00 kg	2.00 kg	4.00 kg	5.00 kg	20.0 kg
65%	92.3 g	185 g	923. g	1.85 kg	3.69 kg	4.62 kg	18.5 kg
75%	84.6 g	170 g	846 g	1.70 kg	3.88 kg	4.24 kg	17.0 kg
90%	66.7 g	133 g	667 g	1.33 kg	2.67 kg	3.33 kg	13.3 kg
100%	60.0 g	120 g	600 g	1.20 kg	2.40 kg	3.00 kg	12.0 kg

(rev. 12/96)

*NOTE: Chlorine products contain different amounts of available chlorine.

1. All pool surfaces and skimmers should be brushed aggressively with a brush compatible with the pool shell. Use of an inappropriate brush may mar the pool finish. Brushing cannot be overemphasized for both treatment and prevention of algae growth. For best results, the pool recirculation pump should be turned off during brushing so that living algae are not drawn back to the filter.
2. Affected areas can be treated with a granular disinfectant such as calcium hypochlorite or trichlor placed directly on visible algae growths. This is not recommended for liner pools because bleaching or spotting may result.
3. Superchlorination should be up to 30 ppm. Superchlorination instructions such as predissolving and diluting shocking agents must be followed so that pool finishes are protected.
4. An algaecide should be added. Quats or polyquats should be added 24 hours after superchlorination.
5. Filters should be cleaned. Filters and filter elements must also be treated because stubborn forms of algae may continue to grow there while other forms are being killed in the pool.
6. Steps 1 to 5 should be repeated as needed.

Prevention

With any pool problem, prevention is the key, and algae prevention is particularly important. Once algae get a foothold in a swimming pool, they are extremely difficult to kill completely. The following tips are key factors in preventing algae growth:

1. Disinfectant levels should be kept up. Levels of disinfectant should be increased as conditions (sunlight, high swimmer loads, rain) that promote algae growth arise. Algae usually begin in the absence of disinfectants.
2. Brush, brush, brush. All pool finishes must be brushed frequently. Skimmer baskets, gutters, water lines, and filters must also be scrubbed. Care must be taken to use strong bristle brushes that will not scratch the pool or spa finish. The manufacturer should be consulted in this case. Concrete pools usually require stainless steel brushes, whereas vinyl-lined pools require a soft nylon brush. Brushes must be cleaned and disinfected after each use. The more brushing that is done, the less vacuuming that will be needed.
3. Filters should be cleaned and backwashed regularly according to the manufacturer's recommendations. Filter elements, media, and septa must also be checked and treated for algae.
4. An algaecide should be added during prime algae growth periods. In addition to the above precautions, nonfoaming algaecides should be added when conditions are prime for algae growth. If a pool exhibits persistent algae problems, a polyquat algaecide is probably a good idea. The pool operator must follow the suggested guidelines provided on the label for all algaecides.
5. The first sign of algae growth must be responded to quickly and aggressively.

6. When and where algae are prevalent, the pool operator should experiment with placing small amounts of copper sulfate (blue stone) in skimmers and gutters to kill algae as they are brought into the pool. Placing the blue stone in socks or sacks may help to prevent children from playing with the colorful chemical.

Chlorine Odor

Cause

As mentioned previously, obnoxious "chlorine" odors are perhaps the most persistent problem in heavily used pools and should be considered the number one problem at indoor pools, particularly those with tight, energy-efficient air-handling systems. The odor to which pool patrons object is caused by too little, not too much, chlorine. Chloramines, or combined chlorine (CC), are the culprit in this case. When free chlorine (FC) combines with ammonia and other nitrogen compounds, chloramines are formed. Perspiration, urine, saliva, body oils, and lotions are a few compounds with which chlorine readily combines to form chloramines.

Symptoms

The symptoms of chloramine development are easy to detect because pungent, obnoxious chlorine odors permeate the facility. These symptoms are more noticeable in indoor than outdoor pools. Eyeburn and redness of the eyes may also accompany the chloramine odor, along with an itchy reaction of the skin. The water may also appear dull or even cloudy. Even excessively high levels of FC do not smell. Experienced pool operators agree that when they "smell" chlorine, they know it is time to superchlorinate.

Treatment

The treatment of chloramines is quick and simple. Once a combined chlorine reading is determined by proper use of a test kit, the pool water is "shocked" to an FC level that is 10 times greater than the amount of CC. For example, if a CC level of 0.4 ppm is found, the FC level must be increased 4.0 ppm. Sodium hypochlorite, calcium hypochlorite, and lithium hypochlorite work well for shocking. If the pool needs to be reopened to the public immediately after shocking, a nonchlorine oxidizer such as monopersulfate should be used. Whatever form of shocking is used, the target FC level must be reached as quickly as possible. Undershooting the target FC will actually worsen the CC problem. In indoor pools, windows and doors should be opened to allow the chloramines to be "off-gassed," and adding large "sideline" box fans during superchlorination comes highly recommended. Chapter 13 has specific instructions regarding shocking.

Prevention

One way to avoid a buildup of chloramines is to maintain disinfectants at breakpoint and to keep ammonia by-products to a minimum in the pool. Breakpoint chlorination is a maintained heightened level of disinfection whereby chloramines are unable to form. As swimmer loads increase, breakpoint levels will also have to be adjusted upward. Showering before swimming in a pool does much to prevent chloramine development. If swimmers understood this concept, they would probably shower with regularity before entering the pool. Unfortunately, many swimmers do not shower because they believe they are clean. Clean swimmers still carry body oils, lotions, perspiration, and other compounds into the water that produce CC. Showering is a good preventive measure and pool patrons must be educated to this fact.

Perhaps the best way to prevent chloramine production is adding a properly sized Ultra Violet (UV) system to supplement the primary disinfectant (chlorine). Zeolites are an excellent and inexpensive temporary fix until UV or other more prominent measures can be installed. Zeolite will hold the ammonia produced by swimmers and keep it in the filter tank. Without ammonia in the swimming pool, chloramines are unable to be produced.

Routine shocking is also a recommended practice to prevent chloramine production, particularly just before heavy swimmer loads such as swimming meets or hot, humid days. In addition to shocking, disinfectant levels should never be allowed to drop to unacceptable levels. New sanitation systems are also being introduced to assist in preventing the chloramine problem in heavily used aquatic facilities. One recently introduced computer-controlled system simultaneously adds calcium hypochlorite for disinfection and oxidation and a nonchlorine shocking agent to oxidize the chloramines.

Dr. Tom's Tip

If you have had chloramine problems in the past, experiment with raising the free chlorine levels 0.5 ppm higher than usual for several months. This may keep your water at breakpoint and may not allow chloramine formation. Better yet, add UV, zeolites, and fresh air.

Eye and Skin Irritation

Cause

Swimmer discomfort is often caused by high CC levels and can be avoided with the procedures mentioned above. However, if chloramines are not present in the pool water and discomfort is still a problem, the pH of the water may be too high or too low. Eye and skin irritation can be caused by a pH that is above 7.8 or below 7.2.

Symptoms

CC levels above 0.3 ppm can produce eyeburn. Red eyes and itching skin experienced by swimmers can also be attributed to pH levels that are excessively high or low. The CC level should be checked first, however. When the pH level becomes too high, the water will actually feel slippery.

Treatment

If swimmer discomfort is actually caused by improper pH levels, the pH must be adjusted to between 7.2 and 7.6, and even more ideally between 7.4 and 7.6. If the pH must be lowered, either muriatic acid or sodium bisulfate (dry acid) should be used. If the pH must be raised, soda ash is commonly added to the pool. If chloramines are present, shocking is required. Chapter 13 details specifics.

Prevention

Prevention in this case is simple. Constant and vigilant monitoring of pool water will help to keep the pH within its ideal range. Mandatory showers, regular shock, and zeolite filtration will assist in preventing chloramines.

Cloudy (Milky) Water

Cause

Numerous causes exist for cloudy water in swimming pools. Because several causes exist, clearing up a pool can be frustrating and challenging. The cause must be specifically identified before corrective action can be taken. The cloudy water that we discuss here is not discolored water, but rather a milky white water that has no coloration at all. We will discuss discolored (red, blue, or green) water separately.

Perhaps the leading cause of cloudy water is a lack of disinfectant, which leads to poor oxidation in the water. High pH or another chemical imbalance can also lead to cloudy water, but lack of oxidation is most often the culprit. When chlorine levels drop too low, the water turns cloudy quickly. On the other hand, once it turns cloudy under low chlorine levels, it takes hours and sometimes days to clear it up with high levels of chlorine. If a DE filter is in use, it is probably the DE leaking back into the water rather than a chemical problem. Using a good test kit, the pool operator should analyze chlorine levels. If adequate FC is found in the pool water, then pH, total alkalinity, calcium hardness, and total dissolved solids (TDS) and a saturation index should be quickly calculated. Once again, cloudy water is most often produced in the absence of oxidation due to no disinfectant in the water.

Another leading cause of cloudy water is inadequate or nonexistent filtration. If the pool water is not being filtered, it will turn cloudy quickly. First and foremost, the flow meter should be checked to ensure water is adequately circulating through the pool plant. When filtration is the cause of cloudy water, a host of additional problems may exist: the recirculating pump may not be running, the filter may need backwashing or cleaning, the hair and lint strainer may be clogged, or another obstruction may exist in the circulation and filtration system, which would all be immediately detectable by the flow meter. In sand filtration systems, unbalanced water might calcify the sand media, making water filtration impossible. Oils, hair, and lint can create mud balls that can also hinder filtration. If a DE system is in use, a ripped or torn septa might be allowing the media to pass back into the pool. Cartridge filters must be cleaned and repaired often because they can become worn or clogged quickly.

Also, in a highly saturated pool, air entering the system through a faulty hair and lint strainer cover or another location can turn a pool milky quickly. The air turning the pool cloudy may not be detected as air and may easily fool the pool operator.

This discussion assumes that the swimming pool treatment plant is filtering at proper flow rates and turnover rates and that the filtration system is properly sized. Insufficient turnover and inadequate filter size will not produce good water clarity. The filtering charts provided in Chapters 7 and 8 should be referred to when determining the proper flow rate, turnover, and filter size. If turnover rates are too slow, a new pump will probably be needed. If the filter surface area is too small, installation of an additional filter(s) may be necessary. High swimmer load, CC, and TDS levels may also cause cloudiness.

Symptoms

A pool that turns cloudy often does so slowly. As the water progressively turns from dull to cloudy, the pool operator must quickly and systematically check the above-mentioned areas of concern. Unfortunately, once a pool turns cloudy, it takes an extremely long time to clear up again.

If the cloudy water makes it difficult to observe the deepest point of the pool clearly, the pool must be closed completely until acceptable clarity is restored.

Treatment

When cloudy water first appears, the water chemistry should be checked immediately. If any chemical parameters are not within ideal ranges, adjustments should be made promptly. In the case of inadequate filtration, the flow rate meter should be checked first. Often when cloudy water appears, little or no water is moving through the filters. If no flow rate exists, the pump and hair and lint strainer should be checked. If inadequate flow rate is present, the filters may need to be backwashed. If air is in the system, it usually comes from a faulty gasket on the hair and lint strainer or a crack in a plexiglass housing or other apparatus on the circulation system. The suction side of the pump must be checked for air leaks, including valves and chemical injectors, but especially the hair and lint strainer and all lids. These items would have to be repaired or replaced. If a DE filter is in use, all elements and septa must be checked for tears or gaps where DE can be returned to the pool. When found, they need to be replaced.

If high CC levels are causing the turbidity, shocking is required. If high TDS levels are causing cloudiness, replacing some or all of the water is in order. If particles are too small for the filter to trap and remove, then the addition of clarifiers and flocculants may be used to clump these fine particles together, thus improving filtration.

Prevention

To prevent pool water from becoming cloudy, pool chemistry must be continually monitored and kept within ideal ranges or even higher. Filters must run effectively and be backwashed and cleaned regularly. When high swimmer loads and/or CC levels appear, shocking should commence. When high TDS levels occur, some or all of the water should be replaced.

Discolored Water and Staining

Cause

When pool water becomes discolored or stains on the pool shell begin to appear, the actual color exhibited can often predict the pool problem being experienced. Discoloration problems in swimming pools can be the result of high mineral content in the source water used to fill the pool or corrosive water in the pool, which erodes iron, copper, and other metals. Some copper or silver-based algaecides can also produce staining or spotting of the pool shell.

Symptoms

Green, blue-green water. If not caused by algae, green or blue-green water normally indicates copper. Algae produce cloudy green water, and copper produces clear green water. Highly aggressive, unbalanced water can corrode copper pipes and heater elements, thus turning the water green or blue-green. Source water may sometimes have a high copper content. High halogen levels will also cause this discoloration.

> **Dr. Tom's Tip**
>
> Green water that does not have good clarity and visibility is most often caused by algae. Conversely, water that is clear green is caused by high copper content.

Red or brown water. Water that is colored red or brown usually indicates iron in the water. High iron content is often found in source water, or unbalanced water may be dissolving iron pipes. An abundance of rust could also be finding its way into the water.

Blue or black water. Likewise, blue or black discolored water is caused by a high manganese content or by highly aggressive water.

Treatment

When discoloration and staining first appear, the pool operator should contact a local swimming pool supplier or pool chemical dealer to see whether they are familiar with the problem. Perhaps these experts are familiar with the source of the discoloration and can offer a quick cure to the problem. The water should be balanced immediately to ensure pool equipment is not being dissolved. Depending on the metal causing discoloration, either sequestering or chelating agents are used to combat the problem. Although these agents are slightly different, they are often used interchangeably in the swimming pool industry. Sequestering agents are most often used and hold the offending metals in solution so that they are not visible. However, if sequestering agents are used regularly, a chelating agent may eventually be required. Chelating agents bring these metals out of the solution so that they can be filtered or vacuumed from the pool. Numerous pools are plagued with high iron content, and as a result, a chelating agent must be used regularly. Stains and spots on the pool shell may require draining for acid washing. If the water has a high mineral content that creates discoloration, the discoloration is extremely difficult to prevent.

Aquatic facilities located in geographical areas with high heavy metal content (iron, copper, manganese, etc.) perhaps should install an industrial-sized cartridge filter for incoming (make-up) water only so that these metals can be filtered out before arriving at the swimming pool filters. If the facility cannot add a heavy metal cartridge filter, then purchasing a truckload of good, clear water when the pool is first filled will help to minimize the problem.

Corrosion of Pool Equipment

Cause

Corrosion is a natural process, but when swimming pool water is unbalanced, aggressive water conditions may result. Aggressive water can deteriorate many pool parts, but particularly those made of metal or copper, such as pipes, heat exchangers, ladders, and light rings. Additionally, if disinfectant levels are allowed to remain above the recommended levels for extended periods of time, the corrosion process will be accelerated. Also, when TDS levels become excessive, electrical conductivity increases, thereby promoting corrosion.

Symptoms

The malfunctioning of swimming pool heaters is often one of the first symptoms of aggressive water to appear. Because heat sinks and heat exchangers are usually made of copper and copper is susceptible to corrosive conditions, this is one of the first pool components to be adversely affected by aggressive water. As mentioned earlier, if pool water becomes colored, metals are often being dissolved. Pump impellers and other metal fixtures in contact with pool water may be eaten away. In addition, copper, iron, or manganese may begin to stain the pool walls and floors.

Treatment

Corrosive water can be corrected by balancing the water with the aid of the saturation index. Increasing pH, total alkalinity, and calcium hardness may be in order depending on the results of the saturation index. Second, disinfectant levels may have to be lowered if they are above the upper limits of the recommended ideal range. TDS levels and water temperatures may also need to be lowered. Chapter 15 details specific instructions on making water less corrosive.

Prevention

Fortunately, preventing corrosive water is simple. Water must be kept balanced by constant calculation of the saturation index. Disinfectant levels should be kept within ideal ranges except for superchlorination. TDS levels and temperatures should not be allowed to rise too high.

Sand or DE in Pool

Cause

If sand or DE finds its way into the swimming pool, it is usually caused by filter problems. In the case of sand filters, the media will be deposited on the pool bottom near inlets. Several causes exist for this. The pool pump may be oversized, pushing sand back into the pool. The laterals may be broken and need to be replaced or other parts of the manifold may be broken or missing. The filter bed may have mud balls and channeling in it and may need to be cleaned and raked or replaced. Finally, too much sand may be in the filter.

DE filters will often allow the media to enter the pool through holes or openings in the filter screens or return manifolds, and when this happens, the pool water will turn milky white. Sometimes, human error is responsible for this problem. If return valves to the pool are mistakenly left open during the backwash cycle, DE can be pushed back into the pool through inlets in white clouds.

Symptoms

Malfunctioning sand filters will deposit sand granules on the pool bottom near pool inlets, particularly right after the filters are backwashed. DE filters that do not operate properly will turn the pool water milky white.

Treatment

Treatment calls for checking the source of the problem, the filter, and correcting it. Sand filters may need new sand, new laterals, or possibly a downsized pump. Other internal fixtures might also be broken or missing in the pressure sand tank. DE filters may require the filter septa or manifold to be repaired or replaced. Close attention to backwashing procedures may also correct this problem if filter screens and manifolds are in good repair.

Prevention

Regularly scheduled maintenance to the filter, filter elements, and filter media will prevent the media from entering the pool. Unfortunately, this area is often neglected at many pools.

> **Dr. Tom's Tip**
>
> If you use sand filtration, dress up your sand once a year. By that I mean, open a port and take a close look at the top layer of sand in the filter. Use a small rake or garden tool to clean and level the surface. Add filter sand if needed. If the sand is hard, has mud balls, or is uneven, you may want to contact a filter specialist.

Excessive Scale Formation

Cause

Excessive scale formation, like many other pool problems, is caused by unbalanced water. Scale is produced when the pH, total alkalinity, and calcium hardness levels become too high. This type of unbalanced water is basic and scale-forming. Slight scale formation has positive effects because it can become a protective coating for heater elements, valves, impellers, and fittings. But when scale formation becomes extreme, it can roughen pool and spa finishes, cause filter calcification, and reduce circulation. Excessive scale can also clog pipes, tubes, injectors, and chemical feeders. In regions that have extremely hard water, even the most rigorous water-balancing programs may not prevent scale buildup.

Symptoms

Typically, excessive scale formation may slow and even stop swimming pool circulation and filtration. Roughened pool and spa finishes, filter calcification, damaged heater elements, slowed circulation, and clogged swimming pool parts are a few of the side effects caused by excessive scale formation. Scale can be observed as a hard, white precipitate.

Treatment

Treating for scale requires the pool owner or operator to return the pool water to balance by lowering pH, total alkalinity, or calcium hardness depending on which values are high. Chapter 15 details specific directions on reducing scaling properties in water. Basic water usually requires muriatic or dry acid for balancing. Using a sequestering agent (sequestrant) may also be required to inhibit scale formation. Sequestrants may be required in geographical regions with extremely high calcium hardness levels. In rare cases involving exceedingly high levels of calcium hardness, the pool water may need to be drained and refilled with freshwater low in calcium hardness. Water softeners are recommended only in extreme cases, and this method of lowering hardness is extremely expensive.

Prevention

Preventing scale formation requires balanced water. Use of the saturation index regularly will help in this regard. If scale is a constant problem, a sequestering agent may have to be added regularly.

Excessive Chlorine

Cause

Shocking, faulty chlorination equipment, or human error may cause chlorine levels to become excessively high. Above 10 ppm, chlorine can begin to cause discomfort to swimmers. Above 25 ppm or so, chlorine will start to bleach bathing suits.

Symptoms

Actually, high chlorine levels are difficult to detect without a test kit and can be tricky to test as well. As mentioned previously, when chlorine levels are high, test reagents may be bleached out, indicating no chlorine is present. In this scenario, the sample "flashes" pink when the reagent is first introduced to the vial and then quickly disappears. High chlorine levels do not permit chloramine production, and as a result, no "chlorine" odor is present. However, high chlorine levels may cause eye and skin irritation, particularly when pH levels are low.

Treatment

Sodium sulfite, sodium bisulfite, or sodium thiosulfate (the most popular) can be added to quickly reduce high chlorine levels. However, adding too much chlorine neutralizer will make it difficult and sometimes nearly impossible to return chlorine levels to acceptable ranges. Large amounts of a neutralizing agent may also significantly lower pH, so a watchful eye must be kept on this value as well. Chapters 12, 13, and 15 or a local swimming pool company can answer questions concerning high chlorine levels.

Prevention

A vigilant water testing program will ensure that chlorine levels will be kept within ideal ranges. Test reagents must be kept fresh so that faulty readings do not confuse the pool owner or operator. All chemical controllers and feeders must receive regular preventive maintenance.

Foam

Cause

Foaming water occurs more often in spas and hot tubs than in swimming pools. Although foam on the surface looks unsightly, it is not much of a problem unless it spills onto decking and creates a slip hazard or obscures a view of the bottom. Foaming pool or spa water has several causes. Soft water suds and foams easily, so low calcium hardness may promote this problem. Some algaecides, particularly quats as opposed to polyquats, cause foaming. In spas with high TDS stemming from lotions, creams, and shampoos, foaming may also be encouraged. Finally, pranksters have been known to add detergents to pools and spas.

Symptoms

Foam on a pool or spa surface is readily detectable. In severe cases, a foaming spa resembles a bubble bath.

Treatment

Although the fast-fix method of combating foam is to add a defoamer, attacking the cause of the problem is often better. Calcium hardness may have to be raised, TDS lowered, and a polyquat algaecide used instead of a quat. If foaming persists, then a defoamer may be warranted. Pranksters may sometimes add detergent to the pool or spa, in which case the vessel must be emptied.

Prevention

Residential spas and hot tubs should not be filled with treated water from a water softener. If soft water must be used to fill a hot tub, spa, or pool, the calcium hardness must be increased immediately. Showering before soaking or swimming might also reduce foaming, particularly in hot tubs and spas. Nonfoaming algaecides should be used.

Excessive Water Loss

Cause

Water loss that is excessive would be more than 1 in. in a 24-hour period. For every 1,000 sq ft of surface area, 1 in. of pool water represents 620 gal. This type of water loss is probably due to a leak rather than evaporation or splash-out. Leakage in the pool shell can occur around inlets, outlets, and copings, but most large leaks are most often detected in the main drain box. Broken or corroded pipes may also cause major water loss. Vinyl-lined pools are easily punctured by sharp objects and can cause major water loss. Vandalism can easily damage vinyl liners. Water loss occurs naturally at swimming pools through evaporation and splash-out. Pool rules controlling behavior and pool covers can help prevent natural water loss.

Symptoms

Excessive water loss is usually detected by the addition of large amounts of make-up water to keep the pool full. When large amounts of make-up water need to be added to the pool, particularly after slow periods, a leak should be suspected. Leaks in the pool shell are best detected by using a scuba diver with a syringe or squirt gun filled with dye or food coloring. By injecting this coloring in pool water near suspected leaks, the scuba diver can follow the movement of the dye to the leak. Vinyl liner pools only need to be inspected for cuts and punctures in the shell. Wet spots may also be noticed outside the pool shell on adjacent ground. Professionals may be required to detect hard-to-find leaks (see Figure 17.1).

Figure 17.1. Professionals may be required to detect hard-to-find leaks. (Photo courtesy of National Leaks Detection)

Treatment

Fixing a leak in a swimming pool is often a difficult task. If the leak is on the pool bottom, naturally the pool must be drained. Vinyl-lined pools are easily repaired as full and waterproof patch kits are available in most swimming pool stores. Scuba diving makes this chore much easier. If the leak is in the filter room or other pool plumbing, pipes and fixtures may need to be replaced. Whatever the cause, the leak may require a professional to patch or repair it.

Prevention

Whenever a pool or spa is emptied, the shell should be checked for cracks or gaps and repaired as necessary. Properly balanced water will prevent corrosion of pool pipes and parts. Sharp objects should not be allowed in a vinyl-lined pool and should be protected against vandalism.

Fecal Accidents

Solid stools in the pool water should not induce panic. Liquid diarrhea is more of a concern because of communicable diseases. Chapter 18 assists aquatic facility management with this difficult area of hygiene.

Summary

This chapter dealt with pool problems that occur most frequently in swimming pools throughout the United States. Because source water differs dramatically from region to region, when a pool problem suddenly affects a given pool, local experts should be consulted early during the troubleshooting process.

References

Mitchel, K. (1988). *The proper management of pool and spa water.* Decatur, GA: BioLab.

Bibliography

The American Water Works Association. (1971). *Water quality and treatment* (3rd ed.). Denver, CO: Author.

BioGuard Lab. (1981). *The pool book.* Decatur, GA: Author.

Kowalsky, L. (Ed.). (1991). *Pool/spa operators handbook.* San Antonio, TX: National Swimming Pool Foundation.

Mitchel, K. (1988). *The proper management of pool and spa water.* Decatur, GA: BioLab.

Pool and Spa News, Los Angeles. www.poolspanews.com/

Pope, J. R., Jr. (1991). *Public swimming pool management, I and II.* Alexandria, VA: National Recreation and Park Association.

Service Industry News, Torrance, Calif.

Taylor, C. (1989). *Everything you always wanted to know about pool care.* Chino, CA: Service Industry Publications.

Taylor Technologies. (2003). *Pool and spa water chemistry, testing and treatment guide with tables.* Sparks, MD: Author.

Williams, K. G., & Young, R. A. (Eds.). (2011). *Aquatic facility operator manual* (6th ed.). Ashburn, VA: National Recreation and Park Association.

Photo courtesy of Water Technology, Inc.

18

Recreational Water Illnesses (RWIs)

Michael Beach
contributor

Key Concepts

- Waterborne germs
- Bacteria
- Virus
- Parasite
- Cryptosporidium (Crypto)
- Shigella
- The Model Aquatic Health Code (MAHC)
- Giardia
- E. coli O157:H7
- Hepatitis A
- Pseudomonas (Swimmer's ear)
- Legionella (Legionnaires Disease)
- 12 steps for healthy swimming

Healthy Swimming: 12 Steps to Reduce the Spread of Recreational Water Illnesses (RWIs)

In 1998, national newspapers were full of reports about an outbreak of the deadly *E. coli* O157:H7 bacteria at a water park that resulted in 26 children becoming ill and one child's death. In 2000, an outbreak of *Cryptosporidium* (Crypto) at a private club pool in Ohio resulted in more than 700 people becoming ill. In 2001, a community-wide outbreak of *Shigella*, which may have started at a local city wading pool, occurred and sickened hundreds. In 2005, a public health investigation concluded 3,900 people fell ill from cryptosporidiosis as a result of recreating at a spray park in New York. One hundred thirty-four recreational water-associated outbreaks, resulting in 13,966 cases, were reported by 38 states and Puerto Rico from 2007 to 2008 (CDC, 2011). What do these outbreaks mean for pool managers and aquatic staff? In this chapter, we will discuss recreational water illnesses (RWIs), illnesses spread by swallowing, breathing, or having contact with contaminated water from swimming pools or other aquatic facilities. How are RWIs spread through pool use? What can aquatics staff do to reduce the risk of their pools spreading RWIs? How can this information be used proactively to impact decisions made by aquatic directors and their staff, health department staff, and swimmers in the United States? The primary focus will be on disinfected water venues and diarrheal illness—the most commonly reported RWI spread through swimming pool use. However, illnesses other than diarrhea (skin, outer ear, eye, urinary tract, and respiratory infections) may be spread through recreational water use. In addition, RWIs are also spread in lakes, rivers, and oceans.

Why focus on RWIs? People have been swimming for millennia, from the building of Roman baths around the world to today's multimillion-dollar water parks. However, times have changed. The setting has changed from relatively few people soaking in the water to aquatic facilities where thousands of swimmers come together in small areas and participate in a full range of aquatic activities. Over the past century, great advances have been made in enhancing swimming water quality through the introduction and use of sanitizers, filtration systems, and technology, including UV systems for swimming pools and spray parks/splash pads that help remove *Cryptosporidium*. These activities have increased the participation of all persons, sick and healthy, and the chance for full body and head immersion and water swallowing. As a consequence, the risk of spreading RWIs has increased.

When drinking a glass of water from the tap, few people ask from where that water came and how it was purified before it was sent to their house tap. They drink that water without question. If someone were to rinse his or her hands, feet, or body in that water and then hand them the glass to drink, what would be their reaction? They would likely be appalled to have been asked and would refuse to drink it. Why then is it so common to see swimming pools full of people swallowing the water as if it were drinking water? When people swim, do they think about the fact that they share the water with swimmers who have been in the pool recently? Few swimmers take an effective soapy shower before their swim (rather more like rinsing their swimsuits); many do not visit the restrooms often enough, and commonly incontinent persons, such as diaper-aged children, swim in the same pool as continent persons. Are swimmers aware of these challenges? From 1998 to 1999, the CDC conducted multiple focus group discussions with parents of young children who swam. At that time, parents had little knowledge that swimming could spread illnesses. They did not understand how illnesses could be spread or understand the concept that swimming was a "shared" or "communal" water experience. People share the water, and therefore, they can share illnesses that people bring with them, increasing the chance for spreading RWIs. Part of the reason that swimmers are unaware of RWIs is that they think chlorine kills all germs instantaneously and therefore the pool water is sterile. Despite swimming being tightly woven into the fabric of our society, these practices contribute to making recreational water an ideal place to spread RWIs. How can can people be stopped from swimming when they are ill with diarrhea? How can pool owners and operators encourage swimmers to minimize the amount of water they swallow? How can they promote a healthy swimming environment that continues to give everyone the exercise and fun that they expect while promoting good hygiene and protection of the public's health? What factors have come together to make it imperative to reduce the spread of RWIs?

Why Focus on the Spread of RWIs?

1. Waterborne germs are common.
2. Diarrheal illness is common.
3. Fecal contamination of recreational water is high.
4. Recreational water use is very high.
5. Recreational water use has been linked to the spread of a variety of illnesses.

Over the past several decades, different microbes such as the toxin-secreting bacterium *E. coli* O157:H7, the Noroviruses (Norwalk virus), and the parasites *Cryptosporidium parvum* (Crypto) and *Giardia intestinalis* (*Giardia*) have emerged as increasing causes of diarrheal illness in the U.S. population and of recreational water outbreaks. These microbes can cause severe to life-threatening illness and are well suited for being spread through water. How are diarrheal illnesses spread through water use? These microbes are found in high quantities in the stools of infected animals or people. Feces from infected people or animals can easily contaminate commonly ingested substances such as food and water, as well as

objects that children may put in their mouths. If someone with diarrhea has an "accident" in the pool and other swimmers accidentally swallow the contaminated water, then those swimmers may become ill. This continues the cycle that will allow the illness to continue to spread. Many waterborne microbes have low infectious doses, so few of them need to be swallowed to cause illness. Does the chlorine in swimming pools kill germs and sterilize the water? Although chlorine is an effective disinfectant against many germs, it takes time to kill them. Some germs are more resistant than others to the free chlorine in pools (see Table 18.1), with Crypto being so resistant that it can survive for days in a properly disinfected pool. Filtration can be effective at removing larger germs, but filtration systems and filter media vary in efficiency. Conventional pool filters are not designed to remove bacteria or viruses and are challenged by smaller parasites such as Crypto. The MAHC, USA Swimming, many health codes, and others recommend UV systems to remove *Cryptosporidium*. The Model Aquatic Health Code (MAHC) and the Centers for Disease Control and Prevention's (CDC) Healthy Swimming address reducing RWIs and should be consulted in depth.

Table 18.1

Disinfection Time for Microbes in Chlorinated Water

Microbe	Disinfection Time in Minutes (1 ppm free chlorine, 25°C)
E. coli O157:H7 Bacteria	Less than 1 min
Hepatitis A Virus	About 16 min
Giardia Parasite	About 45 min
Cryptosporidium (Crypto) Parasite	About 15,300 min (10.6 days)

Note. 1 mg/l (1 ppm) free chlorine at pH 7.5 and 25°C (77°F). These disinfectant times are only for pools that do not use chlorine stabilizers such as cyanuric acid. Disinfection times would be expected to be longer in the presence of a chlorine stabilizer. From "Healthy Swimming/Recreational Water," by Centers for Disease Control and Prevention, n.d., Atlanta, GA: Author.

Diarrheal illness is common throughout the world. In the United States, about 11% of people have had diarrhea in the past month. This means that, on average, each person in the United States has at least one bout of diarrhea each year. How does that impact pools? It means that many of the people who are swimming may be currently ill with diarrhea or have recently recovered. Surely people stop swimming when they have diarrhea, right? Not really. during one swimming pool-associated outbreak caused by Crypto, over 200 people became ill, and almost 1 out of 5 people continued to swim even though they were still ill (CDC). Even after people recovers from diarrhea, germs can still be found for weeks in their stool. These swimmers can continue to contaminate the water despite feeling better. In 1993, over half the residents of Milwaukee, Wisconsin, became ill with Crypto following an outbreak associated with the city's drinking water (CDC). After residents' diarrhea stopped and they began to feel better, they started to swim again and caused a number of satellite Crypto outbreaks associated with swimming pool use.

Education is clearly needed. Swimming is a shared water experience in which everyone is immersed in the same water as everyone else. If someone is ill with diarrhea and they contaminate the water, then everyone else using the pool could potentially become ill if they swallow the water. Hygiene is important to keeping the water clean. The average person has about 0.14 g, enough to cover the nail on your pinkie finger, on their bottom that will end up in the pool. Although this sounds like a small amount, a pool averaging 1,000 people per day could be dealing with pounds of feces each week. This uses valuable chlorine and, if some of those people have a diarrheal illness, they could spread it to others using the pool. Fecal contamination also occurs when people have "accidents" in the pool. If they are ill with diarrhea, other swimmers may not know these "accidents" have happened. With Crypto, a single fecal accident during the peak of illness is enough to contaminate even the largest pools, so swallowing a mouthful is enough for people to become ill. The ease with which fecal contamination can occur, combined with the high bather loads and the presence of incontinent swimmers (e.g., diaper-aged children), increases the risk for spreading RWIs in many pools. This supplies a strong incentive for raising awareness about RWIs with swimmers and pool staff and vigilant maintenance of high water quality. No pool should be without proper disinfectant and pH levels. No person who is ill with diarrhea should be swimming. All swimmers should minimize how much water they swallow.

The risk of becoming ill with an RWI is unknown, but it may be relatively low for individual swimmers. However, the massive number of swimming visits each year in the United States, over 360 million, means that even low-risk events are likely to occur on a regular basis. Annual tracking of diarrheal illness outbreaks associated with use of recreational water such as pools, lakes, and rivers shows that outbreaks routinely occur each year. In addition, annual reports of outbreaks of diarrheal illness associated with swimming have increased over the past 15 years. Much of this increase in the number of reported outbreaks of diarrhea has occurred in chlorinated pools. This is where Crypto's extreme chlorine resistance (Table 18.1) has made it the leading cause of outbreaks of diarrheal illness associated with swimming pool use. Other RWI outbreaks are caused by chlorine-sensitive germs such as *E. coli* O157:H7 and *Shigella*. These outbreaks clearly implicate poor pool maintenance as the culprit since proper disinfection would have prevented them.

Although we will not discuss them in detail, several illnesses can be spread through use of swimming pools and spas. Although diarrheal illness is reported most often, swimmers also can get skin, ear, eye, and lung infections by using contaminated swimming pools and spas. However, the chance of spreading illness can be dramatically reduced by maintaining good water quality.

Microbes Causing Outbreaks of Illness at Disinfected Pools

Diarrhea
Crypto, Giardia, Shigella, E. coli O157:H7,
Noroviruses (Norwalk-like virus), Salmonella,
Campylobacter, *Enteroviruses*
Skin Infections *Pseudomonas* (hot tub rash)
Outer ear infections
Pseudomonas (Swimmer's ear)
Eye infections
Adenoviruses
Respiratory infections
Legionella (Legionnaires Disease)
Hepatitis
Hepatitis A

What are the challenges that pool owners and operators face? Swimming is the second most popular exercise activity in the United States. Water-based recreation has also become the choice for family entertainment. To meet the demand for water-based recreation, more pools and larger aquatic facilities are being built. As a result, this shared water activity has also become a means for swimmers to efficiently spread the illnesses they bring to the pool. Unfortunately, diarrheal illness is common, and swimmers continue to swim despite being ill with diarrhea. At the same time, swimmers swallow pool water regularly. Chlorine clearly is a good safeguard, but it has limitations so that some germs, such as Crypto, can survive long enough to spread to other swimmers, even in a well-maintained pool. Other RWI outbreaks are caused by chlorine-sensitive microbes such as *E. coli* O157:H7 and *Pseudomonas*. They are usually a result of poor pool maintenance and a lack of understanding by pool staff that maintaining high water quality is the single greatest barrier to the spread of RWIs. Patrons' and staff's lack of awareness about RWIs only increases the risk of spreading RWIs.

12 Steps for Reducing the Spread of RWIs

How can pool operators protect swimmers from RWIs without restricting access and enjoyment? What about prevention and protection? Pool operators should consider how pool operators deal with other risks that have been identified at the pool. Problems that have been on deck for years include drowning, injuries, bad weather, and blood spills. Pool operators have adopted risk management strategies that rely on state-of-the-art safety equipment and intensive training of staff. Lifeguards are trained in drowning prevention, rescue, first aid, and policies related to weather use and injury prevention. RWI prevention is no different. It will require equipment and design improvements, new thoughts on pool policies and management, and critical training and education of staff. Where do the swimmers fit in? Pool operators also need to raise the awareness of swimmers and educate them about the necessary changes that swimmers need to make to have a healthy experience. The desirable outcome has both pool staff and swimmers realizing that they share responsibility for the quality of the pool water and health of the swimmers. Because this is such a complex problem, everyone (e.g., pool staff, swimmers, health departments) has a role to play in reducing the spread of RWIs. Integrating the following 12 steps into a risk management program should reduce the risk of a pool spreading RWIs.

12 Steps for Reducing the Spread of RWIs

Step 1:   Lead your staff.
Step 2:   Develop partnerships.
Step 3:   Educate pool staff.
Step 4:   Educate swimmers and parents.
Step 5:   Maintain water quality and equipment.
Step 6:   Evaluate aquatic facility design.
Step 7:   Develop disinfection guidelines.
Step 8:   Evaluate hygiene facilities.
Step 9:   Develop a bathroom break policy.
Step 10: Create a policy for large groups of young children.
Step 11: Post and distribute health information.
Step 12: Develop an outbreak/emergency response plan.

Step 1: Lead Your Staff

Every aquatic facility is different. Each facility has different priorities and bottom lines that have to be juggled on a daily basis with limitations on staff and resources. However, all aquatic facilities make safety and health a top priority. Making a choice to integrate an RWI protection plan into the facility's risk management plan is the single greatest decision a pool operator can make to protect swimmers from RWIs. Pool operators should take the lead, outline their vision, show their commitment to their staff, and put themselves at the forefront of the aquatics field. They need to decide that RWI protection is a priority and back it up with resource investment and commitment, and that will set the tone for the rest of the staff. The following recommendations can be implemented in a facility with available resources. Investing heavily after the outbreak occurs, a common occurrence, is great, but it would have been better for the public's health and more cost effective if this were done before the outbreak occurred.

Step 2: Develop Partnerships

What is the role of the community health department and pool operators? What should they do when they hear there is a Crypto or *Shigella* outbreak in town? A Crypto outbreak in 2000 that sickened over 200 people started out at one pool. When it was discovered, the pool was shut down for hyperchlorination to stop the outbreak. Did it work? No. Swimmers went to other pools and spread the illness to people using the other pools. The net result was that the outbreak(s) spanned most of the summer until the pools closed at the end of the swim season. What lessons can be learned from this? It comes down to networking and communicating with other groups in the community. Building a communication bridge to the health department and other aquatic facilities is a great way to obtain information about other outbreaks occurring in the community. If pool operators hear about outbreaks associated with other pools, day cares, schools, and so forth where their swimmers attend, then they can take proactive measures and demonstrate increased vigilance to protect their pool. Staff, swimmers, and visiting day care groups need to be educated. If a pool closes because of a suspected outbreak, that does not mean that all the swimmers should descend on another pool without being educating about RWIs. Pool operators should work with their health department to spread the word when a potential RWI outbreak in the community is occurring. One message to send out whenever a diarrheal outbreak is occurring is, do not swim if ill with diarrhea. Pool operators can use communication networks and the media to alert patrons that they should not be swimming if they are ill with diarrhea. Pool operators who protect their facility, make contacts early, and build a communication network will be aware of the health status of their community at all times.

Step 3: Educate Pool Staff

From ensuring proper pool maintenance to educating swimmers, pool staff are critical to preventing the spread of RWIs at the pool. The pool operator should take a standardized training course from trained aquatics professionals and spread this information to other staff members who need to know. The six "P-L-E-As" for Healthy Swimming and RWI awareness should be integrated into staff training, and staff should promote good hygiene and safety around the pool by integrating these messages into interactions and discussions with swimmers. All staff should know the critical role of water testing, proper testing methods, and how to respond if a problem occurs. Swimmers need to know that unhealthy behaviors at poolside and elsewhere can spread illness and are no longer acceptable. Parents told the CDC during focus group discussions that they wanted to be able to rely on the lifeguards for help and enforcement of these principles. Staff should be trained sufficiently so that they can explain, in a way that is unoffensive and acceptable to parents, why behaviors such as using public tables and chairs for diaper changing is a health risk. This may require a more mature staff member with toddler experience be assigned to the "kiddie" pool where these behaviors are more likely to occur.

Step 4: Educate Swimmers and Parents

Educated patrons are the key to knowing what is going on around a pool. Will this scare them off? The U.S. Air Force decided to get serious about protecting their users against RWIs and required that all facilities worldwide start to educate and promote RWI prevention. Did patrons stop swimming? No. The feedback from users underscored that swimmers continued to use the facilities but greatly appreciated being educated, being able to make informed choices, and the staff's commitment to protecting their health. The CDC's focus group discussions with swimmers also highlighted that swimmers wanted to be educated so that they could make informed choices about swimming; they were actually angry that pool operators were not making an effort to inform them about RWIs. Does the pool have season pass holders? Season pass holders are likely to feel stronger ownership of a facility because they spend so much time onsite and have a greater stake in keeping RWIs out of the

Six "P-L-E-A-s" to Reduce the Spread of RWIs

- Please do not swim when you have diarrhea. This is especially important for kids in diapers. You can spread germs into the water and make other people sick.
- Please do not swallow the pool water. In fact, try your best to avoid even having water get in your mouth.
- Please wash your hands with soap and water after using the toilet or after changing diapers. You can protect others by being aware that germs on your body end up in the water.
- Please take your kids on bathroom breaks often. Waiting to hear "I have to go" may mean that it is too late.
- Please change diapers in a bathroom and not at poolside. Germs can spread to surfaces and objects in and around the pool and spread illness.
- Please wash your child thoroughly (especially the rear end) with soap and water before swimming. We all have invisible amounts of fecal matter on our bottoms that end up in the pool.

facility. Pool operators should sell your RWI protection plan to them and ask for their support and assistance by integrating RWI prevention information and materials into their orientation packet and newsletters. Pool opertors can raise awareness and educate patrons by distributing brochures and fact sheets throughout their facility to alert them about the issues. People care about their health, so a lead-in might be, "To ensure the health and safety of all our visitors, we ask that you remember to follow these six easy 'P-L-E-As' for Healthy Swimming." For season pass holders or large groups, pool operators should consider implementing a short safety and RWI orientation when they buy a pass or before they enter the

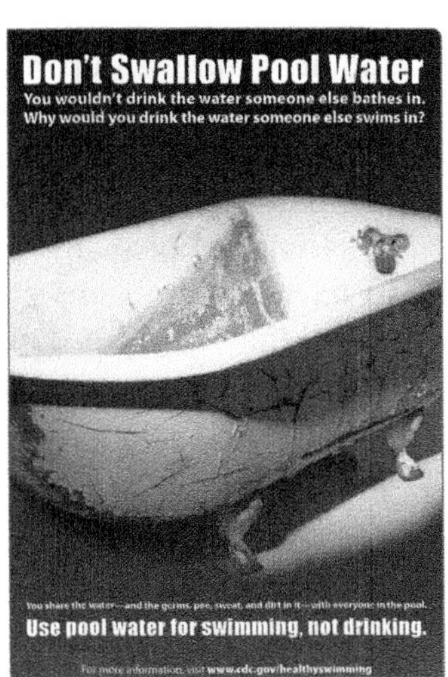

pool complex. This could be particularly important for groups with young children (see Step 10).

Step 5: Maintain Water Quality and Equipment

Maintaining pool water quality according to existing public health requirements will prevent the spread of most RWIs such as *E. coli* O157:H7. Regular and thorough maintenance of the recirculation and filtration equipment will provide maximum filtration. Chemical feed equipment should be maintained and chemicals should be kept at optimal levels within state and local government regulations and the MAHC. This includes maintaining disinfectant at regulated levels, optimal pH (7.2 to 7.8), alkalinity (80 to 120 ppm), calcium hardness (200 to 400 ppm), and total dissolved solids (below 2500 mg/l). Pool staff should understand that they are the greatest barrier to the spread of most RWIs. Poor pH control can compromise the effectiveness of chlorine as a disinfectant, so the pool operators should not assume that their staff understand the link between pH and the effectiveness of the disinfectant; staff need educated need to know that poor maintenance of disinfectant and pH levels can cause serious health consequences for swimmers. Chlorine should be monitored regularly where the chlorine is needed—at poolside. If staff regularly monitor chlorine and check the pump house and systems, pool operators should be able to reduce the risk of an RWI outbreak by preventing their pool from running out of chlorine. Pool operators should never rely totally on automated systems to work 24-7 without regular checks by pool staff. They should keep good records of water quality measurements, major equipment repairs or changes, fecal accident occurrences, and so forth. To stop rashes or ear infections caused by the bacteria *Pseudomonas*, the pool and spa should be cleaned often. These bacteria are normal contaminants in the environment, but they do not need to take up permanent residence in a facility. The scum layer that can form at the tile–water interface should be broken up regularly. Germs can bury themselves in this scum layer, which can serve as a protective shield even if the germs are normally chlorine sensitive. Recurring skin infections in a pool or spa indicate problems with pool maintenance and disinfection. Failure to fix these problems could cause contamination with germs that may cause much more severe or life-threatening illness such as *E.coli* O157:H7. Is it worth the risk?

Step 6: Evaluate Aquatic Facility Design

Some pools and water parks have already started to redesign their facilities for the purpose of RWI prevention. Before building a new facility, pool operators should seek feedback from industry colleagues and public health experts about the safety and protection features they need to consider in the design stage. Splash pads and spray parks have gained popularity, but are especially prone to RWIs. Specific regulations for disinfection and secondary sanitizers including UV for these features

Fernley Swimming Pool Spray Park, Nevada

are included in the MAHC. Pool designers will respond to pool operators, their customer, if they are clear that their public health needs are a high priority and they consider it an investment in safe operations. First, the filtration system needs to be evaluated. If the kiddie pool filtration system is connected with other pools, this increases the chance that fecal contamination can be dispersed from the kiddie pool or splash pads to the other pools. The best situation is one in which the kiddie pool and splash pads have a separate filtration system. Diaper- and toddler-aged children should be kept in pools specifically designated for them. Water turnover rates in kiddie pools and splash pads should be increased; it may decrease the length of time that swimmers are exposed to contaminating germs.

Pool operators should make this decision in collaboration with state and local regulators, the MAHC, and design consultants to avoid causing suction injuries. This will require installation of anti-vortex drain covers (with no top openings and automatic cutoff valves) that are Virginia Graeme Baker Pool and Spa Safety Act (P&SS Act) compliant. Filtration can help to stop the spread of some illnesses, but completely filtering the pool takes substantial time.

Second, the form of disinfection needs to be evaluated. There is a great deal of interest in new technologies that disinfect pool water such as ultraviolet (UV) irradiation, ozone, and mixed oxidants, and they look promising. In fact, many agencies now strongly recommend UV to eliminate chlorine-resistant microorganisms. Experts will have the latest information, and a residual disinfectant will still need to be used in the pool with ozone and UV. Third, hygiene is important. Restrooms and diaper-changing areas (see Step 8) need to be convenient, clean, safe, and ready to use so that waste goes in the toilet, not the pool. Facility staff should consider having hot water available in shower facilities that swimmers use. Swimmers need to be encouraged to shower with soap and water before entering the pool. This could reduce the risk of pool contamination by removing invisible fecal matter from their bottoms before they enter the pool. A quick rinsing over a swimsuit with cold water does not do much good.

Step 7: Develop Disinfection Guidelines

Fecal accidents are a concern and an inconvenience to both pool operators and patrons. Should all fecal accidents be treated the same? A diarrheal fecal accident is a higher risk event than a formed stool accident. With most diarrheal illnesses, the number of infectious germs found in each bowel movement decreases as the diarrhea stops and the person's bowel movements return to normal. Therefore, a formed stool is probably less of a risk than a diarrheal accident. A formed stool may contain no germs, a few, or many that can cause illness. The germs that may be present are less likely to be released into the pool because they are mostly contained within the stool. However, formed stool also protects germs inside from being exposed to the chlorine in the pool, so prompt removal is necessary. Should a formed fecal accident be treated as if it may contain Crypto? The CDC tested fecal accidents collected from aquatic facilities for Crypto and *Giardia*. None of the 293 fecal accidents collected tested positive for Crypto, but *Giardia* was found in 4.4% of the samples collected. These results suggest that formed fecal accidents pose a small Crypto threat that would require extensive hyperchlorination, but should be treated as a risk for spreading other moderately chlorine-resistant germs such as *Giardia*. The CDC fecal accident response recommendations can be found in Appendix 1. These recommendations do not replace state or local regulations, so pool operators should first check with a local pool inspector for requirements.

Staff should be trained how to explain to patrons the facility's policy on responding to fecal accidents. Pool staff should carefully explain to swimmers that for their own health and safety, the pool needs to close in response to a fecal accident. Understanding that pool closure is necessary for proper disinfection and protection of swimmers' health is likely to promote support rather than frustration. Pool closures allow chlorine to do its job and protect swimmers from RWIs. However, proactive is better than reactive. Having a written fecal accident response policy and records of all fecal accidents and the procedures used to disinfect (date, time of event, formed stool or diarrhea, chlorine levels at the time or observation of the event, pH and free chlorine levels before reopening, the procedures followed in response to the fecal accident, and the contact time) is important. This should help pool operators to respond more efficiently to problems. They may have little control over a toddler contaminating a kiddie pool, but they do have control over how they document and respond to this occurrence.

What about other body fluids that can contaminate the pool water? Vomiting while using swimming pools appears to be a common event. Often, people vomit when they swallow too much water, and the vomit is probably not infectious if it is just water. However, if the full contents of the stomach are vomited, then the CDC's recommendations for disinfecting a formed fecal accident or guidelines from a state or local regulatory group and the MAHC should be followed. The time and chlorine level combinations needed to disinfect a formed stool should also be adequate to disinfect the germs found in vomit.

Coming in contact with blood in pool water is unlikely to spread illness. Germs (e.g., Hepatitis B virus or HIV) found in blood are spread when infected blood or certain body fluids enter the body and bloodstream (e.g., by sharing needles and by sexual contact). The CDC is not aware of these germs being transmitted to swimmers from a blood spill in a pool. These germs do not survive long when diluted in properly chlorinated pool water. Swimmers may want action to be taken after a blood spill, so should the pool be closed for a short period of time? There is no public health reason to recommend closing the pool after a blood spill. However, some pool staff choose to do so temporarily to satisfy patrons. Blood spills on the deck or on surfaces are a different problem and require prompt cleanup and disposal.

Step 8: Evaluate Hygiene Facilities

In the CDC's interviews with parents, they uniformly said they changed diapers at poolside because changing rooms were unclean, were poorly maintained, and/or had inadequate diaper-changing facilities. The goals for RWI protection are to stop swimmers from urinating, which uses needed disinfectant, and defecating in the pool, which could spread RWIs. In addition, patrons need to change diapers in a hygienic and safe location where they can clean themselves and their children after use. Based on the CDC's discussions with parents, asking the following questions and responding to the feedback could improve the use of restroom and diaper-changing facilities:

1. Do you have an adequate number of restrooms?
2. Are the facilities close to the pool?
3. Are the restrooms well maintained (stocked and cleaned)?
4. Is your diaper-changing area big enough to hold older children?
5. Does the diaper-changing area have a surface that is easily cleaned? Are disposable barrier materials available that could be discarded each time?

6. Does the diaper-changing area have waste containers and hand-washing capacity right next to it so people can clean up after use without leaving the child unattended?

7. Is a washing area attached so parents can clean their children?

The bottom line is, would you walk barefoot into diaper-changing facilities as your patrons do? The best way to find out about facility use and the needs of patrons is to ask. Pool operators should survey swimmers periodically to obtain feedback and should make the improvements they suggest. This should enhance restroom and diaper-changing area use. If the facility is large enough, pool operators should determine the utility of hiring a person to maintain the restrooms or consider remodeling the diaper-changing stations. Both improvements may be good investments if they increase the number of parents and children who use them. Installing diaper-changing cabanas with soap and running water close by the kiddie pools could discourage parents from changing diapers on tables or lounge chairs. It can also help mothers who are also keeping an eye on other children and do not feel they can leave the pool. Train staff to recognize risky behavior such as changing a child on public tables or chairs. Have them educate patrons about why this is a health risk.

Remember the fecal matter that people carry into the pool? It could add up to pounds per week! Convincing your patrons to take a cleansing shower before they swim could reduce the risk of RWIs and, as a bonus, save disinfectant. Pool operators should encourage swimmers to shower with soap and water before entering the pool. Facilities should have hot water and soap available in shower facilities to make it more likely that swimmers will take a true cleansing shower rather than the usual quick swimsuit rinse. This could reduce the risk of pool contamination and decrease disinfectant use by removing invisible fecal matter from their bottoms before they enter the pool.

Step 9: Develop a Bathroom Break Policy

Regular chlorine testing, fecal accidents, and appropriate disinfection guidelines are worrisome to pool operators. The chance of fecal accidents can be reduced by staff helping parents get their children to the bathroom before they contaminate the pool. An hourly break or "adult swim" can be used for combined disinfectant testing and bathroom use. Staff should inform patrons that this break provides optimal timing for bathroom use. Additionally, to prevent the spread of germs, bathrooms should be clean, stocked with toilet paper, and have ample soap for hand washing. If parents ask, staff should tell them this policy reduces not only fecal contamination but also the amount of urine in the pool that uses up disinfectant that could be killing germs.

Step 10: Create a Special Policy for Large Groups of Young Children

For large groups of diaper- and toddler-aged children in the pool (e.g., from day care centers), a required RWI orientation training can inform care providers and ensure they understand that the pool, like most day care centers, excludes children ill with diarrhea. Also, pool operators should consider a policy to keep diaper- and toddler-aged children in pools specifically designated for them.

Step 11: Post and Distribute Health Information

Posting and distributing information throughout a facility on RWI prevention that stresses the "Six P-L-E-As for Healthy Swimming" is important. Information can be handed out at the entrance and posted around the pool. These messages can be reinforced by being posted in the restrooms and inside bathroom stalls. Postings should be moved around so that people continue to read them. Orientation times, meetings, and newsletters can be used to spread the word that RWI protection plans have a role and a benefit for everyone. Health department inspection reports and pool chlorine and pH readings can be posted to show swimmers that pool operators are serious about their RWI protection plan and stand behind the water quality they provide.

Step 12: Develop an Outbreak/Emergency Response Plan

The best advice is to be prepared. Most pool staff already have a risk management plan for injuries and drowning, but many do not have plans for managing an RWI outbreak or other emergency situation. A policy should be put in place to follow in the event that the public calls the pool facility for information or that the health department starts an investigation. Part of this plan should include a strategy to communicate with the local health department and media. A designated spokesperson will ensure that a consistent response is given to outside sources (callers, media, health department, and others) and that these sources have a clear contact person. Pool operators should talk to their colleagues who have experience. If they are not ready when an outbreak occurs, speaking with reporters can be difficult. If the situation arises, pool operators should collaborate with their local health department. A thorough investigation may find that the illness is unrelated to the pool. If the outbreak is associated with using the pool, then the investigation will often reveal how and why the illness was spread. This information leads to better RWI prevention strategies that can help everyone.

RWI protection plans can be integrated into everyday operations as a part of a risk management and communication plan. Where can more information be found to protect swimmers from RWIs? The CDC's Healthy Swimming website (www.healthyswimming.org) has brochures, fact sheets, frequently asked questions, prevention information, posters, pool staff newsletters, disinfection guidelines, and further technical information on RWI outbreaks. These materials were made using information from focus group discussions with swimmers and input from national and community level public health, recreation, and aquatics staff to develop community-based materials for distribution to swimmers and pool staff. Raising awareness and expanding education efforts, improving management policies and practices, upgrading facilities and equipment, and building communication networks should reduce the risk of future RWI outbreaks in pools and communities.

Summary

Many different and varied recreational illnesses can be encountered by patrons when appropriate measures are not taken by pool operators. Clear water is not necessarily clean water. It is important to follow the CDC's Healthy Swimming resources and the MAHC for guidelines to inhibit Cryptosporidium and other microorganisms that can cause Recreational Water Illnesses. Healthy Swimming also provides many materials to educate both patrons, lifeguards, facility operators.

References

Centers for Disease Control and Prevention. (2009–2010). Cryptosporidiosis surveillance—United States. *Morbidity and Mortality Weekly Report, 61*, 1–12.

Centers for Disease Control and Prevention. (2008). Violations identified from routine swimming pool inspections—Selected states and counties, United States. *Morbidity and Mortality Weekly Report, 59*, 582–587.

Centers for Disease Control and Prevention. (n.d.). Healthy swimming/recreational water. Retrieved from www.cdc.gov/healthywater/swimming/

Centers for Disease Control and Prevention. (2001a). Prevalence of parasites in fecal material from chlorinated swimming pools—United States, 1999. *Morbidity and Mortality Weekly Report, 50*, 410–412.

Centers for Disease Control and Prevention. (2001b). Protracted outbreaks of cryptosporidiosis associated with swimming pool use: Ohio and Nebraska, 2000. *Morbidity and Mortality Weekly Report, 50*, 406–410.

Centers for Disease Control and Prevention. (2001c). Responding to fecal accidents in disinfected swimming venues. *Morbidity and Mortality Weekly Report, 50*, 416–417.

Centers for Disease Control and Prevention. (2001d). Shigellosis outbreak associated with an unchlorinated fill-and-drain wading pool. Iowa, 2001. *Morbidity and Mortality Weekly Report, 50*, 797–800.

Centers for Disease Control and Prevention. (2011). Surveillance for waterborne disease outbreaks and other health events associated with recreational water: United States, 2007–2008. *Morbidity and Mortality Weekly Report, 60*(ss12), 1–32.

Gerba, C. P. (2000). Assessment of enteric pathogen shedding by bathers during recreational water activity and its impact on water quality. *Quantitative Microbiology, 2*, 55–68.

Gilbert, L., & Blake, P. (1998). Outbreak of Escherichia coli O157:H7 infections associated with a water park. *Georgia Epidemiology Report, 14*, 1–2.

Goodgame, R. W., Genta, R. M., White, A. C., & Chappell, C. L. (1993). Intensity of infection in AIDS-associated cryptosporidiosis. *Journal of Infectious Disease, 167*, 704–709.

Gradus, M. S., Blair, K. A., Peterson, D. E., Kazmierczak, J. J., Addiss, D. G., Fox, K. R., . . . Davis, J. P. (1994). A massive outbreak in Milwaukee of cryptosporidium infection transmitted through the public water supply. *New England Journal of Medicine, 331*, 161–167.

MacKenzie, W. R., Kazmierczak, J. J., & Davis, J. P. (1995). An outbreak of cryptosporidiosis associated with a resort swimming pool. *Epidemiol Infect, 115*, 545–553.

Lee, S. H., Levy, D. A., Craun, G. F., Beach, M. J., & Calderon, R. L. (2002). Surveillance for water-borne-disease outbreaks—United States, 1999–2000. *Morbidity and Mortality Weekly Report, 51*(SS-8), 1–47.

Mac Kenzie, W. R., Hoxie, N. J., Proctor, M. E., Gradus, M. S., Blair, K. A., Peterson, D. E., Kazmierczak, J. J., Addiss, D. G., Fox, K. R., & Rose, J. B. (1994). A massive outbreak in Milwaukee of cryptosporidium infection transmitted through the public water supply. *New England Journal of Medicine, 331*(15): 1035.

Mead, P. S., Slutsker, L., Dietz, V., McCaig, L. F., Bresee, J. S., Shapiro, C., . . . Tauxe, R. V. (1999). Food-related illness and death in the United States. *Emergency Infectious Disease, 5*, 607–625.

U.S. Census Bureau. (1995). *Statistical abstract of the United States* (115th ed.). Washington, DC: Author.

www.cdc.gov

www.cdc.gov/healthywater/swimming/

Appendix 1

Healthy Swimming

Fecal Incident Response Recommendations for Pool Staff*

What do you do when you find poop in the pool?

*Check for existing guidelines from your local or state regulatory agency before use. CDC recommendations do not replace existing state or local regulations or guidelines.

- These recommendations are for responding to fecal incidents in chlorinated recreational water venues.

- Improper handling of chlorine-based disinfectants can cause injury. Follow proper occupational safety and health requirements when following these recommendations.

- **Pool Closures:** Fecal incidents are a concern and an inconvenience to both pool operators and patrons. Pool operators should carefully explain to patrons why the pool needs to be closed in response to a fecal incident. Understanding that pool closure is necessary for proper disinfection and protection of the health and safety of swimmers is likely to promote support rather than frustration. Pool closures allow chlorine to do its job — to kill germs and help prevent recreational water illnesses (RWIs).

w w w . c d c . g o v / h e a l t h y s w i m m i n g

What do I do about...

formed stool in the pool?

Formed stools can act as a container for germs. If the fecal matter is solid, removing the feces from the pool without breaking it apart will limit the degree of pool contamination. In addition, RWIs are more likely to be spread when someone who is ill with diarrhea has a fecal incident in the pool.

diarrhea in the pool?

Those who swim when ill with diarrhea place other swimmers at significant risk for getting sick. Diarrheal incidents are much more likely than formed stool to contain germs. Therefore, it is important that all pool managers stress to patrons that swimming when ill with diarrhea is an unhealthy swimming behavior.

---

1. **For both formed-stool and diarrheal fecal incidents,** close the pool to swimmers. If you have multiple pools that use the same filtration system — all pools will have to be closed to swimmers. Do not allow anyone to enter the pool(s) until the disinfection process is completed.

2. **For both formed-stool and diarrheal fecal incidents,** remove as much of the fecal material as possible (for example, using a net or bucket) and dispose of it in a sanitary manner. Clean and disinfect the item used to remove the fecal material (for example, after cleaning, leave the net or bucket immersed in the pool during disinfection).

VACUUMING STOOL FROM THE POOL IS NOT RECOMMENDED.

---

3. Raise the free chlorine to 2 parts per million (ppm), if less than 2 ppm, and ensure pH 7.5 or less and a temperature of 77°F (25°C) or higher. This chlorine concentration was selected to keep the pool closure time to approximately 30 minutes. Other concentrations or closure times can be used as long as the contact time (CT) inactivation value* is achieved (see next page).

4. Maintain free chlorine concentration at 2 ppm and pH 7.5 or less for at least 25 minutes before reopening the pool. State or local regulators may require higher

free chlorine levels in the presence of chlorine stabilizers,[†] which are known to slow disinfection. Ensure that the filtration system is operating while the pool reaches and maintains the proper free chlorine concentration during the disinfection process.

3. If necessary, before attempting the hyperchlorination of any pool, consult an aquatics professional to determine the feasibility, the most optimal and practical methods, and needed safety considerations.

4. Raise the free chlorine concentration to 20 ppm[¶,§] and maintain pH 7.5 or less and a temperature at 77°F (25°C) or higher. The free chlorine and pH should remain at these levels for at least 12.75 hours to achieve the CT inactivation value of 15,300.[**] **Crypto CT inactivation values are based on killing 99.9% of Crypto. This level of Crypto inactivation cannot be reached in the presence of 50 ppm chlorine stabilizer, even after 24 hours at 40 ppm free chlorine, pH 6.5, and a temperature of 77°F (25°C).[††] Extrapolation of these data suggest it would take approximately 30 hours to kill 99.9% of Crypto in the presence of 50 ppm or less cyanuric acid, 40 ppm free chlorine, pH 6.5, and a temperature of 77°F (25°C) or higher.**

5. Confirm that the filtration system is operating while the water reaches, and is maintained, at the proper chlorine level for disinfection.

6. Backwash the filter after reaching the CT inactivation value. Be sure the effluent is discharged directly to waste and in accordance with state or local regulations. Do not return the backwash through the filter. Where appropriate, replace the filter media.

7. Allow swimmers back into the water only after the required CT inactivation value has been achieved and the free chlorine and pH levels have been returned to the normal operating range allowed by the state or local regulatory authority.

Establish a fecal incident log. Document each fecal incident by recording date and time of the event, whether it involved formed stool or diarrhea, and the free chlorine and pH levels at the time or observation of the event. Before reopening the pool, record the free chlorine and pH levels, the procedures followed in response to the fecal incident (including the process used to increase chlorine levels if necessary), and the contact time.

---

* CT inactivation value refers to concentration (C) of free chlorine in ppm (or mg/L) multiplied by time (T) in minutes at a specific pH and temperature.

[†] Chlorine stabilizers include compounds such as cyanuric acid, dichlor, and trichlor.

[¶] Many conventional test kits cannot measure free chlorine levels this high. Use chlorine test strips that can measure free chlorine in a range that includes 20–40 ppm (such as those used in the food industry) or make dilutions with chlorine-free water when using a standard DPD test kit.

[§] If pool operators want to use a different free chlorine concentration or inactivation time, they need to ensure that CT inactivation values always remain the same (see next page for examples of how to accomplish this).

[**] Shields JM, Hill VR, Arrowood MJ, Beach MJ. Inactivation of *Cryptosporidium parvum* under chlorinated recreational water conditions. J Water Health 2008;6(4):513–20.

[††] Shields JM, Arrowood MJ, Hill VR, Beach MJ. The effect of cyanuric acid on the chlorine inactivation of *Cryptosporidium parvum*. J Water Health 2008; 7(1): 109–114.

Pool disinfection time...

How long does it take to disinfect the pool after a fecal incident? This depends on what type of fecal incident has occurred and at which free chlorine levels you choose to disinfect the pool. If the fecal incident is formed stool, follow Figure 1, which displays the specific time and free chlorine levels needed to inactivate *Giardia*. If the fecal incident is diarrhea, follow Figure 2, which displays the specific time and free chlorine levels needed to inactivate Crypto.

Figure 1 *Giardia* Inactivation Time for a Formed-Stool Fecal Incident

Free Chlorine Level (ppm)	Disinfection Time*
1.0	45 minutes
2.0	25 minutes
3.0	19 minutes

* These closure times are based on 99.9% inactivation of *Giardia* cysts by chlorine at pH 7.5 or less and a temperature of 77°F (25°C) or higher. The closure times were derived from the U.S. Environmental Protection Agency (EPA) Disinfection Profiling and Benchmarking Guidance Manual. These closure times do not take into account "dead spots" and other areas of poor pool water mixing.

Figure 2 Crypto Inactivation Time for a Diarrheal Fecal Incident

Free Chlorine Level (ppm)	Disinfection Time*[†]
10	1,530 minutes (25.5 hours)
20	765 minutes (12.75 hours)
40	383 minutes (6.5 hours)

* Shields JM, Hill VR, Arrowood MJ, Beach MJ. Inactivation of *Cryptosporidium parvum* under chlorinated recreational water conditions. J Water Health 2008;6(4):513–20.

[†] At pH 7.5 or less and a temperature of 77°F (25°C) or higher.

The **CT inactivation value** is the concentration (C) of free chlorine in ppm multiplied by time (T) in minutes (CT inactivation value = C x T). The CT inactivation value for *Giardia* is 45 and the CT inactivation value for Crypto is 15,300 (pH 7.5 or less and a temperature of 77°F [25°C] or higher). If you choose to use a different free chlorine concentration or inactivation time, you must ensure that the CT inactivation values remain the same.

For example, to determine the length of time needed to disinfect a pool after a diarrheal incident at 15 ppm, use the following formula: C x T = 15,300.

Solve for time: T = 15,300 ÷ 15 ppm = 1020 minutes or 17 hours. It would take 17 hours to inactivate Crypto at 15 ppm.

Cleaning Up Body Fluid Spills on Pool Surfaces

Body fluids, including blood, feces, and vomit are all considered potentially contaminated with bloodborne or other germs. Therefore, spills of these fluids on the pool deck should be cleaned up and the contaminated surfaces disinfected immediately.

Appropriate Disinfectants

Bleach

One of the most commonly used chemicals for disinfection is a homemade solution of household bleach and water. Since a solution of bleach and water loses its strength quickly, a fresh mixture should be made before each clean-up to make sure it is effective.

> **Recipe for Bleach Disinfecting Solution**
>
> 9 parts cool water
>
> 1 part household bleach
>
> Add the household bleach to the water. Gently mix the solution.

Other Disinfectants

A listing of other approved commercial disinfectants can be found at www.epa.gov/oppad001/chemregindex.htm and www.fda.gov/cdrh/ode/germlab.html. These disinfectants are effective when used according to the manufacturer's instructions.

Clean-up Procedure Using Bleach Solution

1. Block off the area of the spill from patrons until clean-up and disinfection is complete.
2. Put on disposable gloves to prevent contamination of hands.
3. Wipe up the spill using paper towels or absorbent material and place in plastic garbage bag.
4. Gently pour bleach solution onto all contaminated areas of the surface.
5. Let the bleach solution remain on the contaminated area for 20 minutes.
6. Wipe up the remaining bleach solution.
7. All non-disposable cleaning materials used such as mops and scrub brushes should be disinfected by saturating with bleach solution and air dried.
8. Remove gloves and place in plastic garbage bags with all soiled cleaning materials.
9. Double-bag and securely tie-up plastic garbage bags and discard.

Healthy Swimming

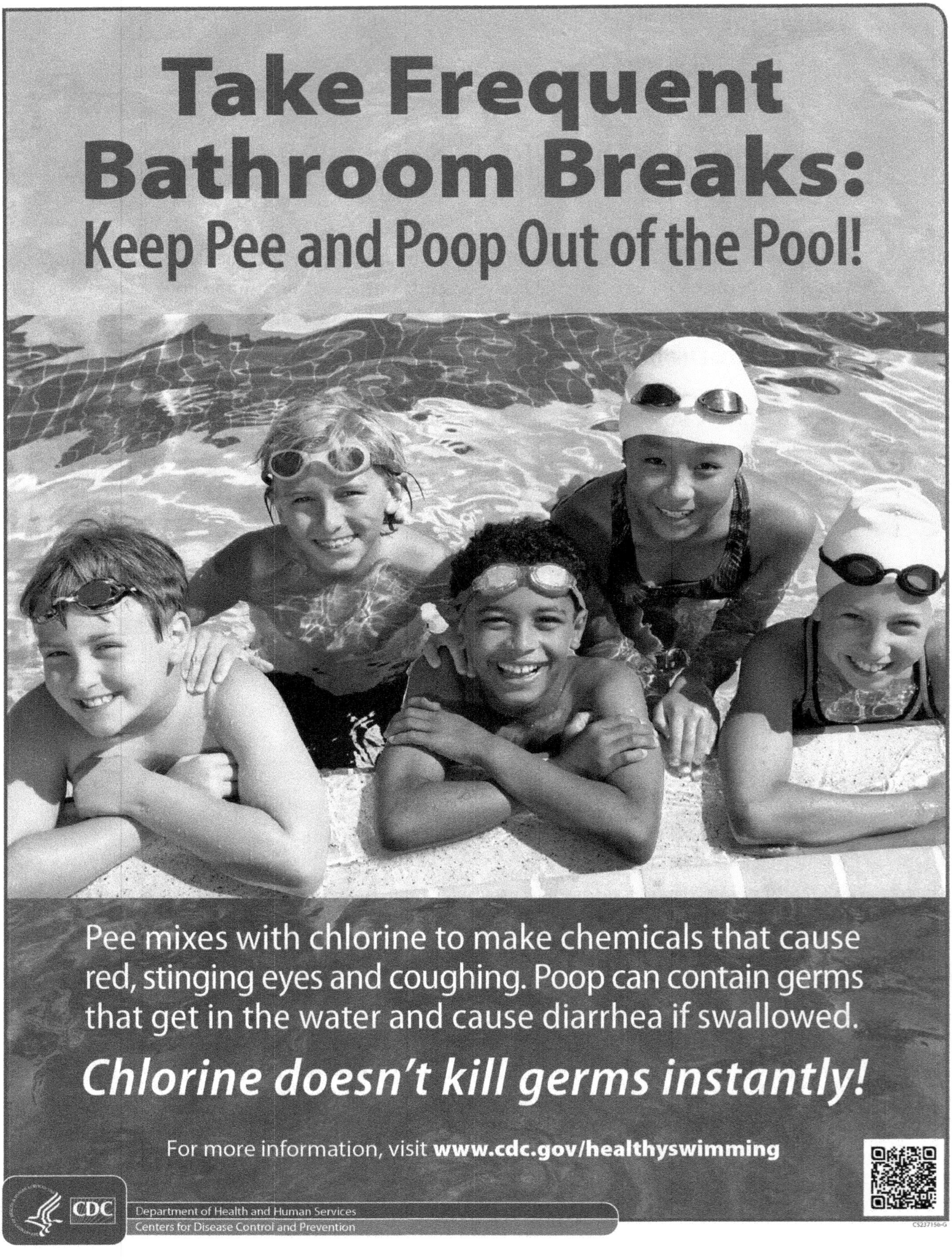

Take Frequent Bathroom Breaks:
Keep Pee and Poop Out of the Pool!
Pee mixes with chlorine to make chemicals that cause red, stinging eyes and coughing. Poop can contain germs that get in the water and cause diarrhea if swallowed.
Chlorine doesn't kill germs instantly!
For more information, visit www.cdc.gov/healthyswimming
CDC
Department of Health and Human Services
Centers for Disease Control and Prevention
CS237150-G

Section IV

Specialty Pools

This section concentrates on pools and topics that are slightly different from the standard residential or public pool. Chapter 19 discusses hot tubs and spas, which is probably the fastest growing area in the swimming pool industry. Of particular interest in this chapter is "hot water chemistry." The reader will find that as water temperature increases, so do the challenges for the hot water pool owner or operator. Typically, hot tubs and spas require higher levels of disinfectant and much more attention to water balance. TDS is also a problem in this environment. Many different safety concerns are also outlined in this chapter.

Chapter 20, Waterparks, presents a wealth of information that will assist the reader in establishing a risk management program for waterparks. Waterparks entertain many more patrons than standard pools and thus require closer supervision. These parks also offer tremendous variety in their attractions. Rides, special park procedures, and guarding techniques are discussed in detail.

Chapter 21 concentrates on winterizing procedures for seasonal pools. Both residential and public pools are considered in this discussion. The underlying theme of this chapter is that winterizing is important and must be taken seriously. More damage can occur to a swimming pool and its equipment during the off-season than during the hottest summer months. It is also emphasized that organization is the key to good winterizing.

Photo courtesy of Water Technology Inc.

19

Hot Tubs and Spas

Key Concepts

- Hot tubs
- Spas
- Chemical standards
- Soaker loads
- Heaters
- Safety
- Timers
- Filtration

Hot tubs and spas are considered separately in this text because they have unique problems apart from swimming pools. In fact, some spa specialists strongly believe that spas are not swimming pools and therefore should not be treated as such. Although spas and hot tubs are the fastest growing facilities in the swimming industry, and although they offer hours of relaxation, recreation, and therapy, unique challenges are associated with their use.

Hot water soaking has been a popular form of relaxation and therapy for centuries. The Romans, Japanese, and other cultures have enjoyed the benefits of hot water immersions. Soaking in a hot tub or spa relaxes tired muscles, promotes circulation, and relieves mental stress.

According to the Arthritis Foundation (2008), about 46 million Americans, or 1 in 5, have arthritis. By 2030, about 67 million Americans 18 and older are projected to have doctor-diagnosed arthritis (*Arthritis & Rheumatism*, 2006). Although there are many kinds of arthritis, most forms are characterized by inflammation. A hot tub or spa can provide the warmth, hydrotherapy, and buoyancy needed to relax and exercise the affected joints and muscles of the body in the convenience of one's own home. The warm water allows muscles to relax, which in turn makes exercising and daily tasks easier to perform. Arthritics should consult their personal physicians before purchasing or exercising in a spa. If treatment is the primary reason for purchasing a hot tub or spa, all or part of the purchase may qualify as a medical expense and tax deduction. To receive this deduction, the owner should consult a doctor, lawyer, and accountant.

Today as many as 4 million hot tubs and spas are in the United States, and nearly 3 million can be found in private residences. More than one third of privately owned hot tubs and spas are located in California. Soaking in a hot tub or spa produces benefits that many swimming pools cannot. These benefits can be physical, psychological, or both. Physical benefits include reducing muscle soreness as well as aches and pains. Of course, the reduction of modern-day stress and tension and the promotion of overall relaxation are achieved through the combination of hot water and hydrojet action of the water in a hot tub or spa. As a result, hot tubs and spas have become vital components for health clubs, hotels, hospitals, rehabilitation clinics, housing developments, and private residences.

Water temperatures in hot tubs and spas should range from 98° to 104°F. These high water temperatures, coupled with relatively high soaker loads and organic debris, make spa maintenance troublesome in some cases. The warmth and moisture offer an ideal breeding ground for bacteria, algae, and fungi. Four people in a 500-gal spa is equal to 160 people in a 20,000-gal pool. Heavy soaker loads plus the heat and moisture promote problems that must be controlled through proper chemical disinfection. So although the advantages of owning and operating a hot water spa are many, upkeep for the spa can be overwhelming because the volume of water is relatively small, whereas the pollution contributed by soakers is relatively high.

Definitions

Hot tub, spa, whirlpool, Jacuzzi, and *therapy pool* are terms that have been used interchangeably throughout the years. Although steam rooms and saunas are closely related to the hot water pools mentioned, they are not considered in this discussion because they do not offer

Photo courtesy of Water Technology Inc.

body immersion in water. This discussion is limited to hot tubs and spas that have chemically treated water. Jacuzzi is a brand name of hydrotherapy jets and related pool equipment, whereas whirlpools and therapy pools are often associated with athletic training rooms and rehabilitation hospitals. Hot tubs and spas use several pumps for different functions. Separate pumps are required for filtration, water jets, and air jets.

Hot Tubs

California probably made hot tubs popular in the United States because of the availability of redwoods and the wine industry making these barrels plentiful. For the purposes of this book, hot tubs refer to wooden barrels or tubs that have hot water and hydrotherapy jets associated with them. In addition to redwood, hot tubs can also be made of mahogany, teak, cedar, and other woods. Hot tubs are found in residences rather than commercial establishments. Basically, if it is made of wood, it is a hot tub; if it is not, it is a spa!

New wooden hot tubs, when first filled, may turn the water brown. Rust- or coffee-colored water is caused by nontoxic tannic acid leeching out of the wood. The water should be replaced frequently during the first four to six weeks, but eventually the discoloration of the water decreases with time. High water temperatures, high chlorine levels, and low pH levels increase the leeching process. A similar concern of wooden hot tubs is the bleaching of the wood that occurs as the lignin, or natural cellulose glue, present in woods reacts with sanitizers.

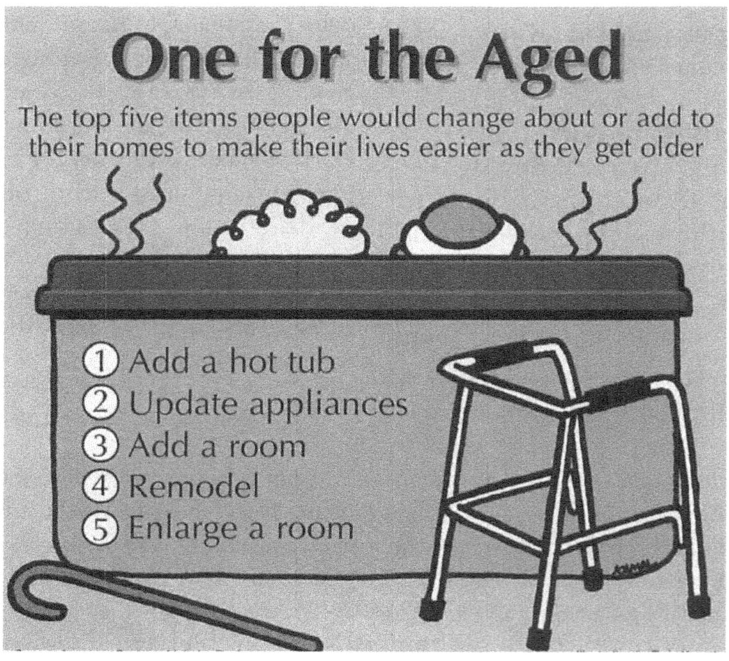

When first filled with water, hot tubs may leak until the wood swells and becomes watertight.

Wooden hot tubs should be emptied periodically to remove stubborn stains. Commercial cleaners and fine sandpaper should be used, but never acid. However, wooden hot tubs should not be drained and left empty for long periods of time. When this occurs, the hot tub may shrink, causing leaks. The grain of the wood in hot tubs may also provide more breeding grounds for bacteria to flourish. Hot tubs made of wood appear to be more suitable for residential rather than public use.

Spas

A more recent version of the wooden hot tub is a fiberglass, acrylic, or stainless steel prefabricated shell that is available in several shapes, sizes, colors, and seating arrangements. Spas can be installed inground or aboveground, inside or outside. Aboveground spas are less expensive and movable, which is a big advantage. Larger spas are often inground models made of gunite or concrete, and many of these are tiled. Fiberglass and acrylic spas should be much easier to clean than wooden hot tubs.

Hot Water Chemistry

As mentioned earlier in this text, increased water temperatures create interesting challenges in water chemistry. Disinfection and water balance are much more difficult to maintain in hot water than in normal swimming pool water (78° to 84°F). Perhaps the greatest challenges for hot tub and spa owners are the production of chloramines and the increasing level of total dissolved solids (TDS). Bacteria growth is also an ever-present concern.

One problem that hot water chemistry poses is increased bacteria proliferation. Many bacteria thrive and reproduce better in warm water. Therefore, it is not surprising that as the popularity of hot tubs and spas has increased, so has the number of outbreaks of dermatitis and folliculitis resulting from exposure to *Pseudomonas aeruginosa*. Pontiac fever, or Legionnaires' disease, has also been associated with hot water pools. Considering that *Pseudomonas* thrive and may even double in number every 20 minutes in water temperatures between 100° and 105°F, hot tubs and spas make a perfect home for these rod-shaped bacteria. *Pseudomonas* also enjoy smooth surfaces such as fiberglass, acrylic, and PVC pip-

ing that accompany hot tubs and spas. Associated with the increased bacteria proliferation in hot water pools are high water temperatures that tend to dilate the pores of the body and water jets that can "jackhammer" bacteria into the skin, making soakers more susceptible to bacteria. This is why soap showers are recommended before and after hot tub or spa use.

Compounding this problem are disinfectants that are less effective at higher temperatures. Because of reduced killing power at higher temperatures, more chemicals must be added to a hot tub or spa to keep it clean, clear, and bacteria free.

Soakers in hot tubs and spas perspire much more than in pools, and therefore, more chloramines are produced. Additional chemicals are required to burn out the chloramines, and as more chemicals are added, TDS levels also rise. In addition, as temperatures increase, calcium carbonate becomes less soluble and precipitates out of solution. As a result, water chemistry in hot tubs and spas must be continually monitored and adjusted. Recommended chlorine and bromine residuals are much higher than in standard pools.

Another problem associated with hot tubs and spas is the turbulence of the water created by the hydrojets. This water agitation increases evaporation of both water and chemicals. Chemical levels in these hot water pools must be checked hourly. It is especially difficult to keep sufficient amounts of disinfectant in the water in public spas with high soaker loads.

For the reasons mentioned, hot tubs and spas require a tremendous amount of disinfectant, which in turn results in significant TDS production. Hot tubs and spas are also a good place to experiment with alternative sanitizers in an attempt to avoid chloramine and TDS buildup. Both ozone and potassium monopersulfate show promise in this regard. Of the halogens, bromine is preferred over chlorine because it tends to be more stable at higher temperatures and bromines are effective sanitizers, whereas chloramines are not. Dichlor, the stabilized chlorine, is also becoming popular with hot tub and spa users, but because it contains cyanuric acid (CYA) to protect chlorine from the damaging effects of ultraviolet (UV) rays in the sun, it should not be used indoors. Trichlor, another stabilized chlorine, should not be used in hot tubs or spas because it is too acidic. Trichlor in hot water pools may lower the pH sufficiently to cause damage to both the equipment and the shell.

- Check local building and safety codes and, if required, obtain permits before starting installation.
- Make sure the hot tub will be placed on a level spot on structurally sound material, such as concrete, treated wood, or manufactured support pads. For deck installation, check for adequate deck supports.
- Make sure the chosen installation site is not too close to trees or foliage, where falling leaves or brush may fall into the hot tub or where roots may cause problems.
- Check for adequate water runoff and drainage. Do not install a hot tub where it will block a designed runoff area.
- Make sure tub and equipment sites are accessible and properly ventilated.
- Determine the direction of the prevailing wind. If the hot tub is not protected from the wind, operating expenses for heating will go up.
- Check for overhead wires.
- Check for underground cables, septic tanks, and water and gas lines.
- Check for ease of access from the house to the tub.
- Check any gates that provide entry. Gates must be self-latching and self-closing.
- Check for proper fencing, if required.
- Check for privacy from surrounding areas.
- Check that required permits are in order, or make appropriate additions.
- Make sure there is access to electrical service and that there is available power. Electrical service must have a proper disconnect box.

Figure 19.1. Hot Tub Installation Site Checklist. ©2011 The Association of Pool & Spa Professionals

Photo courtesy of Water Technology, Inc.

Because water chemistry changes rapidly in hot tubs and spas, disinfectants should be added by reliable and accurate automatic controllers rather than manually. Particularly for hot tubs and spas with high soaker loads, proper disinfection and oxidation may be impossible to maintain if disinfectants are added manually. Too often in the case of hot tubs and spas, proper chemistry cannot be maintained for long periods, and the only solution is to empty the tub or spa. "Dumping" a hot tub or spa is an unavoidable ritual that should be performed on public spas with higher soaker loads according to this formula:

$$\frac{\text{days between}}{\text{drainage}} = \frac{\frac{1}{3} \text{ volume in gallons}}{\text{maximum no. of daily users}}$$

Bimonthly dumping is recommended for moderately used spas and hot tubs. Well-maintained residential hot tubs and spas with low soaker loads do not need to be dumped as frequently. Shocking hot tubs and spas should also be a regular practice. Public spas should probably be shocked daily, preferably at the end of each day.

But dumping and refilling these hot water vessels frequently is perhaps the best preventive maintenance that can be offered.

Chemical Standards

The Chemical Operational Parameters in Table 15.11 (Ch. 15, p. 165) are recommended by The Association of Pool & Spa Professionals for hot tubs and spas.

Soaker Loads for Hot Tubs and Spas

Because hot tubs and spas can quickly become overburdened with too many people, resulting in excessively high soaker wastes, many states suggest using the following formula to calculate soaker loads for hot tubs and spas. Basically, the area of the hot tub or spa divided by 10 dictates the number of people allowed in the spa at a given time. The formula for the area of a circle (most hot tubs and spas are circlular) is $A=\pi r^2$, where $\pi = 3.14$. If a spa has a 12-ft diameter, the radius is half of the diameter, or 6 ft. The soaker load of this 12-ft spa is determined by the following formula:

$$\pi r^2 \div 10 = \text{soaker load}$$

$$3.14 \times 6^2 \div 10$$

$$3.14 \times 36 \div 10 = 11 \text{ soakers}$$

In the case of a rectangular or square spa, the area is determined by multiplying length times width, and that total is divided by 10. Soaker loads for hot tubs and spas must be monitored aggressively. If recommended soaker loads are exceeded, the water chemistry and balance likely will become even more difficult to control.

Filtration

Good filtration is also extremely important for hot tubs and spas. Although many public and private pools have 6- to 8-hour turnovers, hot tubs and spas must turn over their pool capacity every 30 minutes or less. In fact, in heavily used public hot tubs and spas, complete turnovers will occur every 5, 10, or 15 minutes. In addition to quick turnovers, the filtration systems must have superior ability to trap dirt and body oils. Hot tubs and spas should also provide at least 5 times the filter area for the hot water pool as for an equivalent amount of swimming pool water. Sand filters often become ineffective in hot tub and spa applications because oils, grease, and a high mineral content eventually clog the sand media, which must then be replaced. Regenerative DE filters seem to work well in hot water environments, and cartridge filters may also do a good job if the owner or operator is willing to purchase new cartridges frequently. Because

rapid buildup of body oils on the filter medium and septa is a constant problem associated with hot tubs and spas, these filter elements must be cleaned and degreased more often than traditional swimming pool filters. A watchful eye must be kept on all flow gauges, and strict enforcement of the shower rule will aid in effective filtration.

Public spas should be filtered 24 hours a day, although many owners and operators do not follow this guideline to conserve energy. This is a questionable practice because these hot water pools require more time to regenerate after large soaker loads. Owners of residential hot tubs and spas may turn off heaters and filters for long periods of time for energy conservation, but it is a good idea to filter for at least 2 to 4 hours before and after each use. Once again, good water balance must be maintained in hot tubs and spas so that the filter medium and related equipment can run effectively. In addition, several filter aids and clarifiers such as enzymes and organic polymers are available for hot tubs and spas.

Heaters

Regardless of what type of heater is used for a hot tub or spa, a quality cover, preferably a hard, tight-fitting cover, should be used. When not in use, the tub or spa needs to be covered so that heat and the energy used to produce that heat can be preserved. This cover will also protect children from climbing or falling into the hot tub or spa. Heat loss, of course, is more of a problem for outdoor installations. Proper insulation of the shell is also recommended whenever possible.

Before a heater is purchased, several types and models should be researched. Spa specialists should be consulted for their recommendations. Several pros and cons accompany each heater. Fuel source and heater size in British thermal units (BTU) should be discussed fully with pool suppliers. Hot tub and spa heaters should have an automatic high temperature shutoff switch so that excessive temperatures do not become a problem.

Photo courtesy of Water Technology Inc.

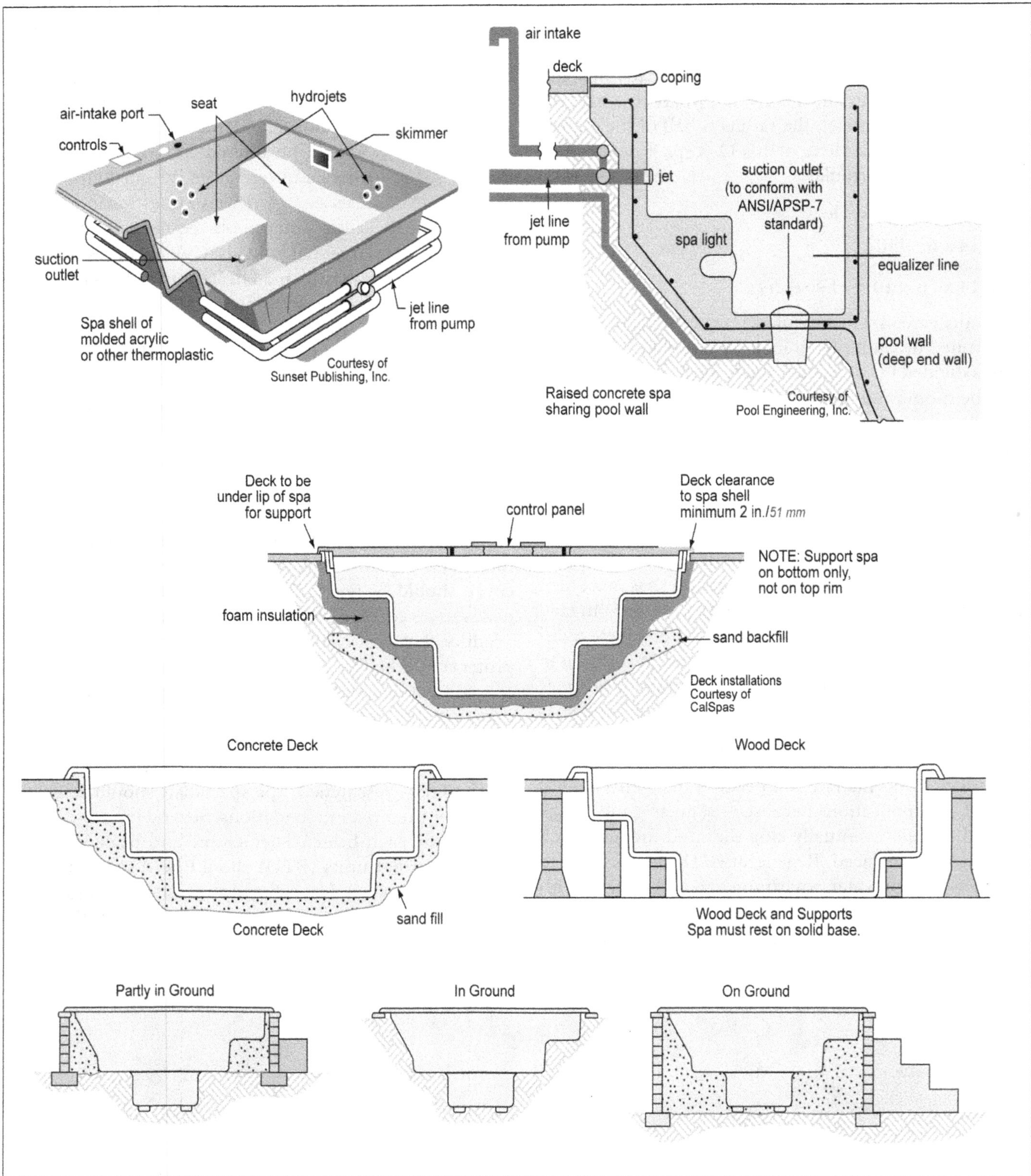

Figure 19.2. Inground spa installations. (Courtesy of The Association of Pool & Spa Professionals, 2014)

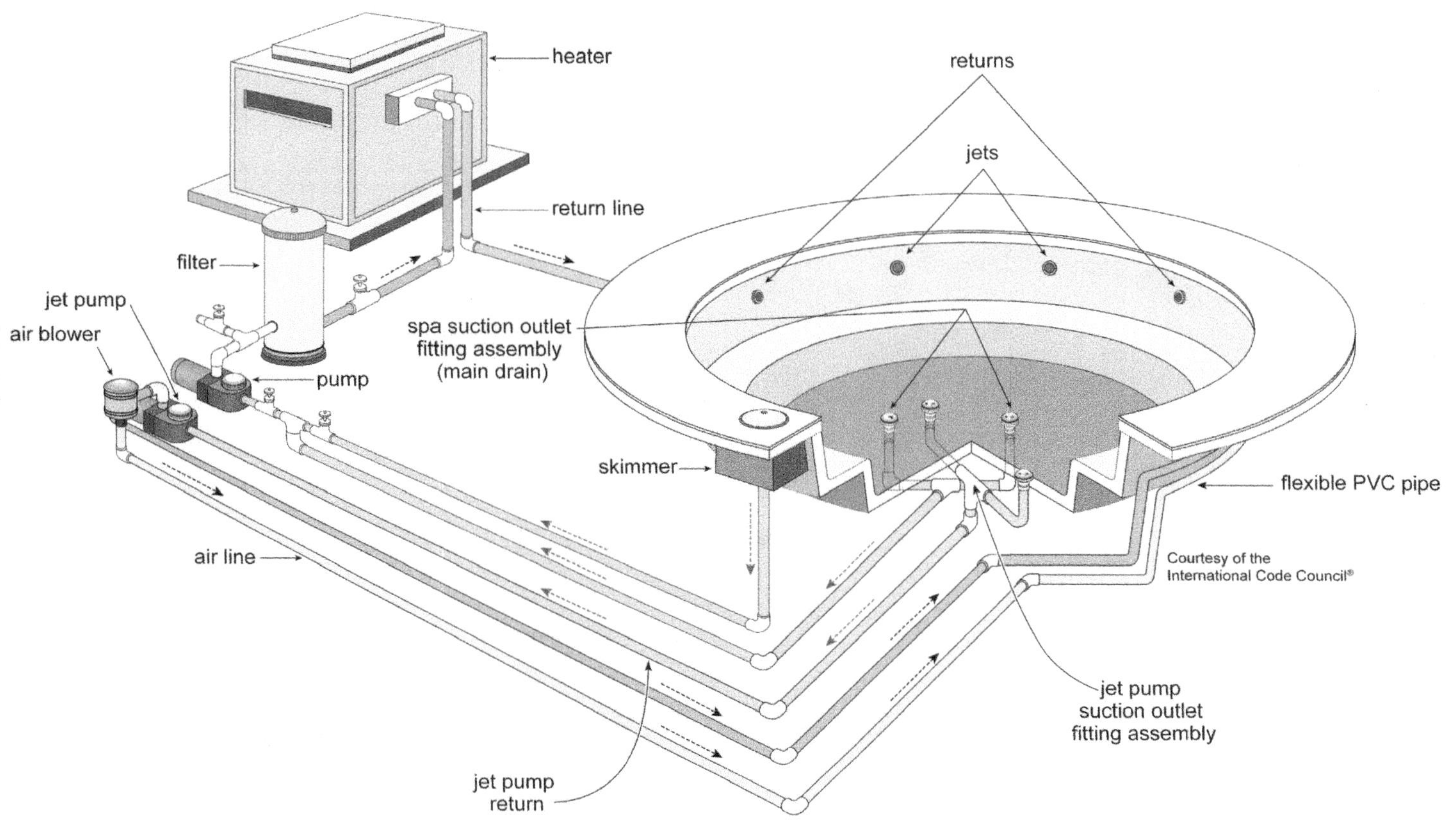

Figure 19.3 This schematic clearly illustrates all of the essential components of a hot water spa. (Courtesy of International Code Council©)

Water balance is of paramount importance to the functioning and longevity of the heater. Unbalanced water that is aggressive corrodes heater elements. Most heater components are made of copper, which is sensitive to low pH values. When hot tubs and spas are installed in homes with a water softener, adjustments must be made to keep calcium hardness levels up, otherwise the pool heater and other components will be destroyed quickly. Conversely, highly basic water with an elevated pH forms calcium deposits in the heater, making the system inefficient and unable to produce sufficient heat. Because the heater contains the hottest water in the system and calcium carbonate is less soluble at higher temperatures, it is likely that calcium buildup will occur. Many hot tubs and spas have continual heater problems because water balance goes unchecked. Water balancing is more important and more difficult to maintain in hot water pools than in standard pools.

Safety

Elevated water temperatures found in hot tubs and spas can create physiological changes in users, which can lead to accidents. Hot tubs and spas are not intended for use by everyone and have numerous restrictions. At higher temperatures (104°F) and for extended stays (greater than 15 minutes), hot water can elevate the core temperature of the body and produce hyperthermia. Hyperthermia can be accompanied by drowsiness and elevated blood pressure. Alcohol can exaggerate this condition. Researchers at Boston University found that pregnant women who used spas, hot tubs, and saunas during the first eight weeks of pregnancy were 3.5 to 7 times more likely to deliver a baby with birth defects. Therefore, the following conditions should preclude individuals from using a hot tub or spa and may lead to serious injury:

1. hypertension (high blood pressure),
2. children under age 12,
3. use of prescription medication,
4. pregnancy,
5. heart disease,
6. diabetes,
7. epilepsy,
8. use of alcohol or recreational drugs, and
9. body infections or open sores.

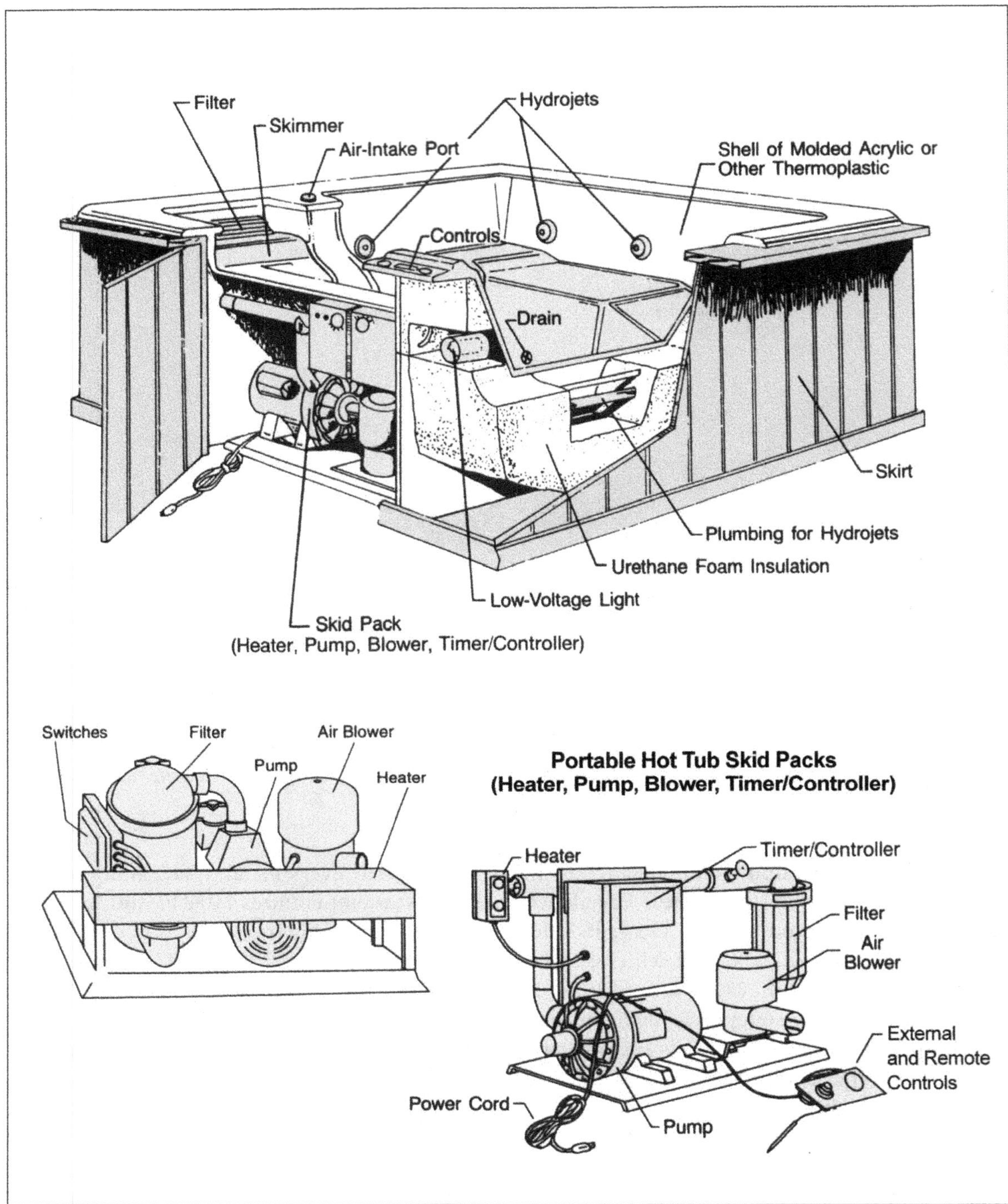

Figure 19.4. Components of a hot water spa. (Courtesy of The Association of Pool and Spa Professionals)

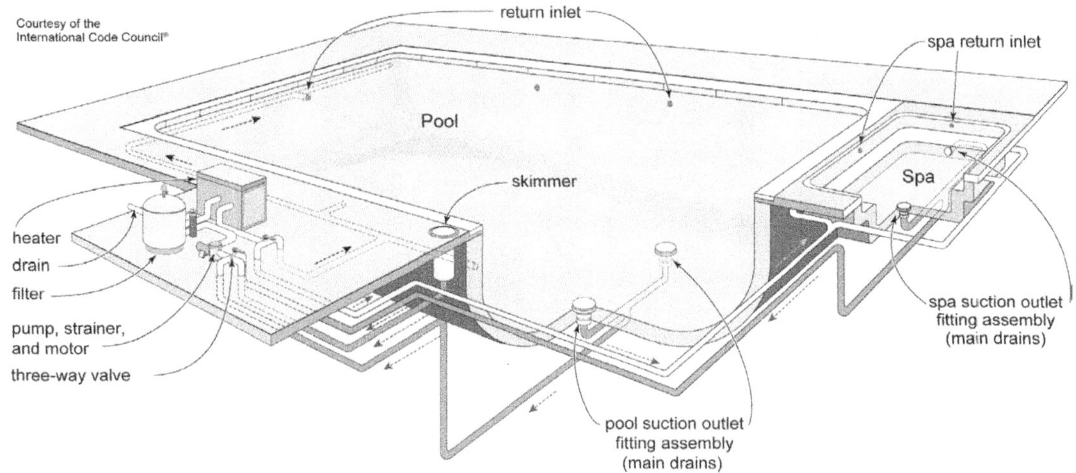

Figure 19.5. A schematic of a hot water spa incorporated to a swimming pool. (Photo courtesy of the International Code Council)

Whenever doubts remain about the above concerns or other concerns, a physician should be consulted (Sidebar 19.3).

Other rules and regulations should be followed to ensure the safety of hot tub and spa users:

1. a 15-minute time limit;
2. a maximum temperature of 104°F;
3. no use of tub or spa if bottom cannot be seen clearly;
4. a soap shower before and after entry;
5. no diving, handstands, or underwater swimming;
6. no use alone;
7. only slow, stretching exercises allowed;
8. no lotions of any type permitted;
9. no use of electrical appliances in or around hot tubs and spas (radios, hair dryers, and other appliances have caused extreme electrical shocks); and
10. the head and face should be kept above the surface of the water to prevent hair entanglement as well as waterborne infections.

Drain Covers

Another area of concern with hot tubs and spas is drains and drain coverings (Figures 19.6 and 19.7).

Orifices not properly covered have been known to keep victims submerged long enough to drown them. The suction in this case can be extremely strong, and an emergency cutoff for the pump should be readily accessible to all hot tub and spa users. Each pumping system should have at least two suction orifices. Every drain or suction orifice must be covered with an anti-vortex plate to prevent entrapment or entanglement and must be Virginia Graeme Baker Pool and Spa Safety Act (P&SS Act) compliant (Figure 19.8). The P&SS Act was initiated after a young girl, Virginia Graeme Baker, drowned from a suction entrapment in a hot tub drain. The statute was signed into law by President Bush in 2007 and includes requirements for drains, drain covers, and automatic shutoff valves. The P&SS Act, commonly know as VGBA (Virginia Graeme Baker Act), will be discussed in more depth in Chapter 27. If any drain or suction orifice is not properly covered, the hot tub or spa should be closed. Individuals with long hair must keep it either covered or up off the shoulders, and hair should not be allowed underwater. Entanglement and entrapment accidents have occurred in hot tubs and spas, but misuse and alcohol have usually been linked to these occurrences.

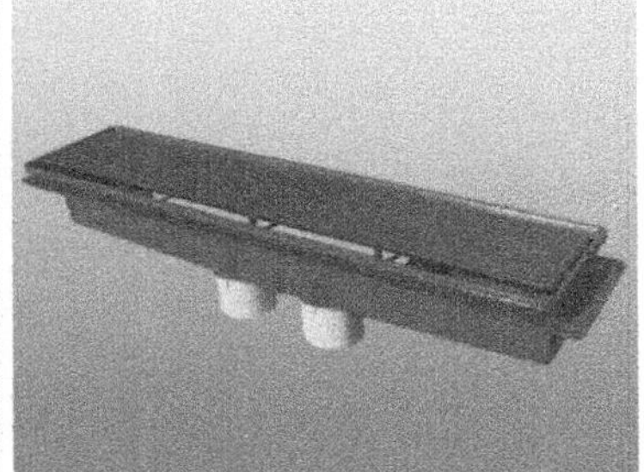

Figure 19.6. Anti-entrapment covers. (Courtesy of The Association of Pool & Spa Professionals 2014)

Figure 19.7. A well-marked and VGBA protected hot water spa. (Photo courtesy of Aquatic Safety Research Group)

TOO HOT TO HANDLE

Although spa use clearly has its benefits, there are some people for whom the physiological changes a spa causes can be too taxing. As a result, medical and allied experts caution people with the following conditions to consult their physician before soaking:

- **High or low blood pressure.** A doctor needs to determine in these cases whether the patient can withstand the sudden (albeit temporary) changes in blood pressure that hot water causes.
- **Heart disease.** Medical experts agree that the heart cannot handle the stress presented by the rise in blood pressure that comes with soaking in hot water, although recent studies see some benefit. The best advice is to consult a doctor.
- **Lung disease or illness.** This category includes patients with emphysema and bronchitis whose lungs would not be able to accommodate increased blood flow and heart rates.
- **HIV-positive blood.** In advanced stages, these patients are generally too weak to withstand the hot water and its effects. (It should be noted that there is no medical evidence that the AIDS virus is transmitted through spa water.
- **Multiple sclerosis.** The muscle-weakening effects of the spa sap too much strength from these patients.
- **Thermal-nerve deficiency.** This causes inability of sufferers to recognize when they are being burned or to monitor their temperature.
- **Asthma or allergies.** The sudden change in temperature may be hazardous for these patients.
- **Seizures.** The effects of hot water may affect the brain in a way that could bring on seizures.
- **Diabetes.** Soaking in a spa or hot tub can affect consumption of insulin, and the body may not be able to take the change in activity within the body.
- **Pregnancy.** Fetuses exposed to hot water in the first month of pregnancy are more vulnerable to spina bifida and other neural-tube defects.
- **Acute or new injury.** In most cases, an injury is going to be swollen for a couple of days; this swelling indicates that there's quite a bit of blood circulation occurring in that area, and hot water may serve to aggravate the injury.
- **Lost sensation.** It's important that spa users be able to tell whether they are too hot, so people who have a loss of feeling should consult with their doctor before soaking.

Patients with certain other conditions should also consult practitioners before using a spa, including those with vascular disease, kidney disease, open wounds or pressure sores, skin infections or contagious rashes, malignant or active tuberculosis, acute fever, or impaired balance. In addition, obesity and incontinence can be factors precluding spa use. It should also be noted that discretion should be used in deciding whether infants and very young children should soak at all because their bodies are not yet sufficiently developed to regulate their own temperature. And, of course, users need to be warned not to use the spa after taking prescription drugs that affect the body's heart rate, blood pressure, or its ability to regulate temperature. Finally, those who are using alcohol (or recovering the morning after) should stay away from spas. Alcohol and certain drugs have several of the same effects on the body as hot water, thus amplifying the effects of both; at the same time, those substances impair the body's temperature-regulating mechanisms.

Sidebar 19.1

Figure 19.8. P&SS Act-compliant, also commonly VGB-compliant, drain cover in a spa. (Photo courtesy of Aquatic Safety Research Group)

Foaming

Several factors contribute to foaming of the water in hot tubs in spas. High TDS is a major contributor to foaming and sudsing. Low calcium hardness levels also contribute to this condition. In addition, soaps, body oils, and suntan lotions tend to foam quickly. The air jets that are powered by pool pumps cause these materials to foam readily. Not only are these suds unsightly, but they also smell, create a bathtub ring, and can also create slippery, unsafe conditions. Defoamers are often used by hot tub and spa owners, but controlling TDS and calcium hardness levels, banning oils, and requiring showers also keep foam to a minimum.

Ventilation

Good ventilation is a must for rooms that contain hot tubs and spas. Gases must be pulled from the area during superchlorination, which is done often in these specialty pools. Also, as chloramines develop, symptoms of exposure are reduced with good ventilation. Because heat and humidity are extremely high in this environment, it would be wise to have quick air changes to protect equipment and appliances in the room.

Signage

Rules and regulations must be clearly posted around hot tubs and spas. Because hot tub and spa use involves many precautions, a lot of information needs to be presented. "No Diving" signs must be posted both vertically (on walls) and horizontally (on floors). "No Diving" signs on the deck should be within approximately 18 in. of the edge of the spa. Water depths should also be clearly marked. It is also imperative that all horizontal deck markings be slip resistant. In addition to the signage required, a staff member should check the spa regularly to ensure patrons are following the rules. Although lifeguards are not normally assigned to hot tubs and spas, someone on staff should check on the patrons periodically to make sure they are fine. When a new hot tub or spa is installed, the placement of the spa should be considered. A location where it can be visually monitored from adjoining areas is ideal. Closed-circuit television coverage of hot tub and spa use may also be a good idea in some instances. These precautions should apply to residential hot tubs and spas as well as public facilities.

Timers

Installation of a 15-minute timer is highly recommended to prevent prolonged immersions in hot tubs and spas that may lead to hyperthermia and related problems. This timer switch should be designed to turn off the hydrotherapy jets every 15 minutes and should be located at least 10 ft away from the water. If someone is using a hot water pool alone (which is not recommended), the timer switch will force the soaker to leave the water at least every 15 minutes, thus providing a moment for patrons to cool off. The emergency shutoff switch should also be located in this area.

Accidents

The majority of accidents occurring in and around hot tubs and spas are alcohol related. Most adults injured in these specialty pools are legally drunk at the time of the accident. The combination of hot water immersion and alcohol consumption can cause drowsiness, weak-

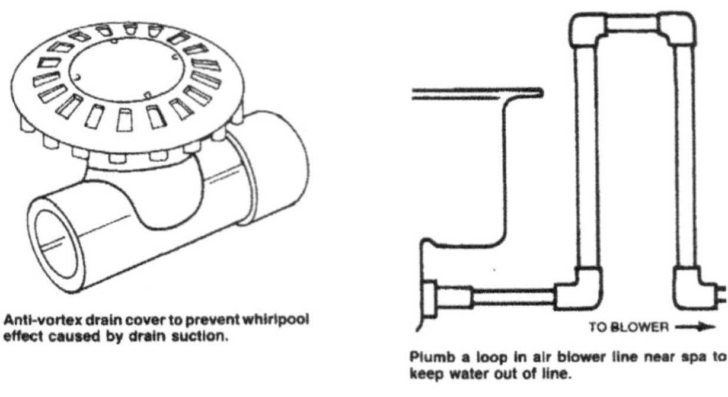

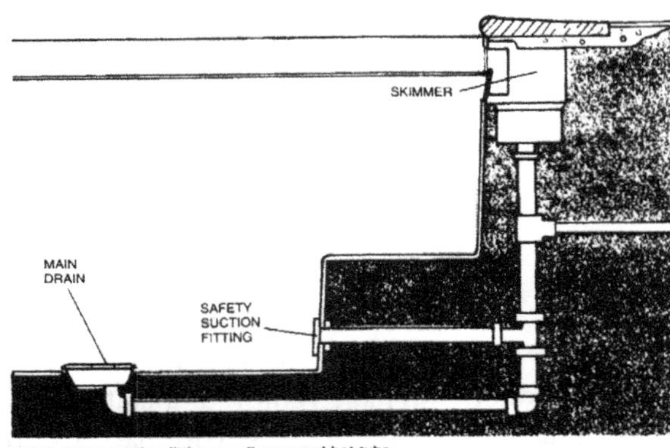

Figure 19.9. Anti-vortex plumbing solutions to prevent suction entrapments. (Courtesy of The Association of Pool and Spa Professionals)

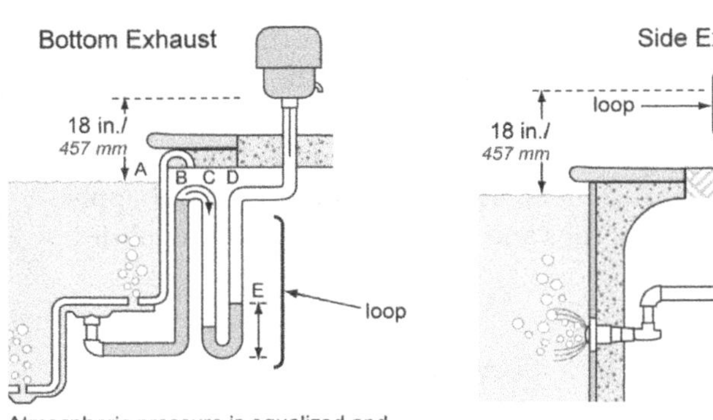

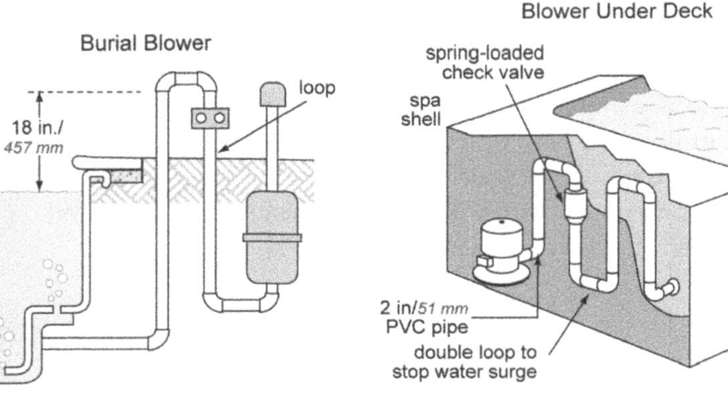

Figure 19.10. Air-blowers for hot tub and spa jets. (Courtesy of Association of Pool and Spa Professionals, 2014)

ness, and irregularities in the heart. Drownings are often the result of an intoxicated person slipping, tripping, or falling in this environment. In addition, accidental electrocutions occur in hot tubs and spas because patrons misuse electrical appliances such as radios, televisions, VCRs, and hair dryers. All electrical appliances should be kept away from this environment, and GFI outlets are a must. Alcohol consumption should be discouraged before and during hot tub use. Patrons should also be checked on periodically.

Younger children, particularly those with long hair, have become entangled with drains and grates. As mentioned previously, children under age 12 should not use hot tubs or spas. If a younger person is allowed to use a hot tub or spa, an adult should supervise the child.

Summary

Hot tubs and spas are perhaps the fastest growing appliances in the swimming industry. Some experts believe they are the most popular request for home improvements. Not only do hot tubs and spas provide hours of recreation and relaxation, but they also provide hydrotherapy for many individuals. Hot tubs and spas require special attention because of the hot water they use and because not everyone can use a hot tub safely. The Association of Pool and Spa Professionals (APSP) publishes consumer tips for buying a spa or hot tub. They also have a comprehensive list of dealers selling these hot water pools. For further information, visit www.apsp.org.

References

Arthritis Foundation. (2008). *Arthritis prevalence: A nation in pain.* Atlanta, GA: Author.

Kowalsky, L. (Ed.). (1991). *Pool/spa operators handbook.* San Antonio, TX: National Swimming Pool Foundation.

National Spa and Pool Institute. (1992). *Pool and spa market study for the year 1991.* Alexandria, VA: Author.

The Association of Pool and Spa Professionals. (2014). Retrieved from www.apsp.org

Bibliography

Arthritis & Rheumatism. (2006). 54(1), 226-229. [Data Source: 2003 NHIS]

BioGuard Lab. (1981). *The pool book.* Decatur, GA: Author.

BioGuard Lab. (1991). *The spa book.* Decatur, GA: Author.

Kowalsky, L. (Ed.). (1991). *Pool/spa operators handbook.* San Antonio, TX: National Swimming Pool Foundation.

Mitchel, K. (1988). *The proper management of pool and spa water.* Decatur, GA: BioLab.

National Spa and Pool Institute. (1988). *Maintaining your spa or hot tub: How to protect your investment.* Alexandria, VA: Author.

Osinski, A. (1992, September/October). Safe and clean: Amenities need special care to ensure guest satisfaction. *Aquatics International, 4*(5), 20–28.

Pool & Spa News, Los Angeles, CA. Retrieved from www.poolspanews.com/

Taylor, C. (1989). *Everything you always wanted to know about pool care.* Chino, CA: Service Industry Publications.

Taylor Technologies. (2011). *Pool and spa water chemistry: A testing and treatment guide with tables.* Sparks, MD: Author.

Walsh, D. (1992). *Spa troubleshooting.* Torrance, CA: Service Industry News.

Williams, K. G., & Young, R. A. (Eds.). (2011). *Aquatic facility operator manual* (6th ed.). Ashburn, VA: National Recreation and Park Association.

(Photo courtesy of Water Technology, Inc.)

20
Waterparks

P. J. Heath
World Waterpark Association
Contributors

Key Concepts

- Pricing, operational costs, and expenditures
- Children's flumes and play areas
- Standard ride flumes
- Innertube rides
- Rapids rides vs. slow rivers
- Wave pools

Evolution and Attendance

Since their inception, waterparks have evolved from a small group of entrepreneurial waterslide facilities to a worldwide recreation industry serving over 70 million visitors each year. What began as homebuilt concrete flumes has become the diverse and highly segmented, family-focused water leisure industry. Today's water leisure industry represents, in addition to the traditional independent waterpark, the emerging indoor and resort waterpark segment, the rapidly growing public facility segment, the large corporate chain segment, the combination wet–dry family entertainment center segment, and an international segment.

Waterparks are expanding the most rapidly in the United States. However, waterparks are increasing in numbers throughout the world. For example, the waterpark industry is increasingly cultivated in Asia with many resort areas adding indoor and outdoor waterparks (Themed Entertainment Association/Economics Research Associates' Attraction Attendance Report, 2007).

According to Coy (2013), in the United States in 2007, 40 new waterparks opened, which was a record high. In 2010, 20 new waterparks opened; in 2011, 27 opened, and in 2012, 21 new waterparks opened. Although newly constructed waterparks are not at an all-time high, resort acquisitions and expansions are on the rise because they are currently less expensive and easier to finance (Coy, 2013).

The industry's World Waterpark Association now represents more than 1,100 members from more than 40 countries around the world. Taken together, these various segments have made the waterpark as familiar as amusement parks to today's families.

Facility Admission Pricing

A 2010 survey by the World Waterpark Association (WWA) found that

- 72% of all parks offer an afternoon discount,
- 82% of all parks offer an annual or season pass,
- 90% of all parks offer discounted child admission,
- 94% of all parks offer free admission to toddlers,
- 78% of public parks offer a group discount, and
- 100% of private parks offer a group discount.

Based on the WWA survey, the average adult admission price for a public facility is $9.40 and the average adult admission price for a private facility is $32.30.

Facility Operating Expenses

Because of the varied operating requirements of different waterpark segments, it is difficult to provide a detailed breakdown of expenses by category that applies to all waterpark facilities, but guidelines are available that operators can use to increase the efficiency of their operation.

Generally accepted operating expense guidelines by category are

- seasonal staff—24%,
- full-time staff—13%,
- marketing—11%,
- supplies—9%,
- maintenance—8%,
- utilities—8%, and
- insurance—5%.

Personnel

The WWA (2010) data show the following:

- 77% of waterparks start seasonal employees at or near federal minimum wage, with front gate and merchandise employees typically at minimum wage and lifeguards and food service workers slightly higher, and
- 91% of seasonal waterparks have a structured wage administration program that offers returning employees a wage increase between $0.25 and $0.50.

High-Risk Locations

Running is the number one cause of accidents in waterparks. Another area of trouble occurs with one guest colliding with another on a waterslide. We discuss other potentially hazardous areas later in this chapter.

Waterpark Attractions

In this section, we discuss information about waterpark rides and attractions in general and generic terms. (*Note:* Lifeguards should understand the manufacturer's specific operating guidelines for each attraction or ride they are operating.) Every facility should check state and local codes and regulations to ensure compliance.

A good operating routine does not mean a waterpark can avoid all hazards or risk of injury. However, such routines can reduce and maintain injuries at minimum levels. Lifeguards are responsible for making considerable efforts to lessen guest injury during normal use.

Lifeguards cannot predict or foresee all of the guests' personalities, behaviors, or physical abilities. This creates the possibility (not probability) that injury will happen as the result of inappropriate or abusive guest activity.

The following section pertains to seven common attractions and rides. Safety considerations are presented in a "fact sheet listing" for easy and quick reference. The safety considerations are not inclusive because of the special considerations of every attraction or ride.

As with most areas of aquatics, it may become critical to meet or exceed the recommendations by the Model Aquatic Health Code (MAHC). States can adopt the MAHC. Even in states that do not adopt the code, the MAHC might be considered a model to follow nationally.

Children's Flumes

Children's flumes are short-length flumes with an uncomplicated design that controls rider speed (to some extent) and allows each rider to clear the ride with little or no risk of injury (under normal use and supervision; Figure 20.1).

Safety Considerations
Staff
1. Staff oversee the flume area.
2. Staff demonstrate skill at working with young children.
3. Staff are aggressive and continuously talk and physically move people away from the slide discharge area.
4. The staff's areas of responsibility for this attraction comply with the "10/20" rule. The 10/20 protection standard is the Ellis & Associates International Lifeguard Training Program guiding principle for life-

Figure 20.1. Children's flume slide. (Photo courtesy of Water Technology, Inc.)

guards in charge of aquatic facility safety. The 10/20 protection standard provides 10 seconds to recognize a guest in distress and an additional 20 seconds to reach the guest and begin rendering aid. (Ellis & Associates, 2007).

Attraction

5. Flumes are smooth on the slide surfaces to eliminate exposure to skin abrasions.
6. The main drains incorporate covers with openings no smaller than ⅜ in. in diameter and no longer than 1 in.
7. Depth markings are placed on the deck near the edge of the pool (or on the coping of the pool) and on the interior wall of the pool except in rimflow or deck-level pools where the wall is below the water level.
8. The deck and step surfaces are nonslip.
9. All ledges in the splashpool are painted a contrasting color.
10. All gates to flumes, splashpools, and doors contain self-closing and positive self-latching mechanisms at a height above a toddler's reach (minimum of 4 ft).
11. Flumes are "locked" when not in use.
12. The deck surface can be completely drained.
13. Appropriate precautions are taken to prevent slips and falls in the approach and entry areas.
14. Water flow rate down the flume conforms with the manufacturer's recommendations.

15. The splashpool or water run is of adequate depth and conforms with the manufacturer's recommendations.

Guests

16. U.S. Coast Guard-approved life jackets are available to those who are required to or wish to wear one.
17. Children are not engaged in "uncontrolled play."
18. Strict rules to educate children and parents against running, horseplay, and other risks of slipping are maintained.

Children's Play Areas

Play areas vary in design and attraction content (Figure 20.2). Items that may exist in play areas include "climb-on" apparatus, small straight slides, water fountains, wall falls, rope swings, water guns, small tunnel chutes, small obstacle mazes, themed characters, and landscaping.

Safety Considerations

Staff

1. Staff oversee the play area. Staff are attentive to activity and potential accidents.
2. Staff are positioned to continuously monitor the play area. Staff are located in effective vantage points that allow the entire play area to be monitored.
3. Staff demonstrate skill at working with young children. Staff demonstrate friendly, firm behavior that

Figure 20.2. Children's play areas. (Photo courtesy of Aquatic Safety Research Group)

is effective in communicating with children; children listen and obey a large majority of staff instructions.

4. Staff conduct daily cleaning and checks for broken glass and other litter.
5. Staff do not permit too many children on the same piece of equipment at the same time.
6. The staff's areas of responsibility for this attraction comply with the 10/20 rule.
   Attraction
7. Concrete pool bottom surfaces are slip resistant by providing adequate barefoot friction to prevent falls but not cause injury to feet.
8. Surfaces intended for guest activity are slip resistant and moderate in slope and elevation changes.
9. Pool drains are equipped with multiple anti-vortex-drains or suction inlets to pumps (Virginia Graeme Baker Pool & Spa Safety Act Compliant).
10. Steps and ledges are painted a contrasting color.
11. Tubing has no exposed ends that should be covered by plugs or caps.
12. Equipment has no accessible sharp edges or points.
13. Equipment has no broken or missing rails, steps, rungs, or seats.
    Guests
14. Strict rules to educate children and parents against running, horseplay, and other risks of slipping are maintained. Rules are stated clearly and briefly, prevent or deter hazardous or risky behavior, and are consistently enforced.
15. Children are not engaged in "uncontrolled play."
16. Children are not permitted to use damaged equipment.
17. U.S. Coast Guard-approved life jackets are available to those who are required to or with to wear one.

Standard Ride Flumes

Standard ride flumes are usually serpentine (winding) structures that feature a slide path with an appropriate mixture of straight and drop sections (Figure 20.3). These rides generally expel a slider at an exit speed of approximately 30 ft/s or less (about 20 mph) and are characterized by short drop sections and winding paths rather than spiral, whip, or straight slide paths.

Safety Considerations

1. The chief risk in standard ride flumes and splashpools is the possibility of guest collisions. Other potential risks to guests include the following:
   - slips and falls in approach and entry areas,
   - impact with flume sidewalls,
   - impact with splashpool water surface or floor,
   - abrasions to skin from sidewalls and slide bottom,
   - ejection from flumes in turns, and
   - falls and collisions within the waterslide run.
2. Lifeguards are the key to minimizing guest risk and injury. Therefore, lifeguards must be alert and aware of the waterslide activity.
3. Guests travel at different speeds because of differences in body weight, friction from swimming apparel, and rider position or posture.
4. When guests slide on mats with low water flow, the loss of mats may slow their progress, requiring the next guests to delay their starts. The lifeguard or attendant needs to be constantly aware of slider progress.
5. On "no mat" slides, lifeguards need to be aware that materials such as denim cause the rider to slide more slowly than synthetic materials.
6. Restrictions on guest dress should be clearly posted.

Figure 20.3. Inground standard flume slide. (Photo courtesy of Water Technology Inc.)

7. On slides designed for multiple sliders or use with sleds for multiple sliders, lifeguards should follow manufacturer's guidelines.
8. Collisions primarily occur in the splashpool area.
9. Sliders have a tendency to watch for their friends coming down behind them or they become confused and disoriented on entry into the splashpool. Lifeguards must be aggressive and continually talk and physically move people away from the slide discharge area.
10. Another hazard at the splashpool exit is the improper storage of mats. Mats on walk paths present serious fall hazards to spectators and sliders.
11. No sliding in the standing position is allowed.
12. No backward sliding is allowed on any standard waterslides or chutes.
13. Only specifically designed slides should allow headfirst sliding. However, headfirst sliding may be possible on slides that have landing flaps or decelerating run-out sections as a braking mechanism or in conjunction with a splashpool.
14. Headfirst sliding on "no mat" slides requires special slider instructions.

Innertube Ride—Chute and Pool Rides

This type of ride is primarily serpentine and features a slide path that allows innertube access through a combination of turns with an appropriate mixture of straight and drop sections and intermittent splashpools (Figure 20.4).

Safety Considerations

1. The chief risk on innertube chute and pool rides is the collision hazard at the bottom or splashpool area of each chute.
2. Guest exposure to concrete sidewalls can produce skin abrasions.
3. Improper or uncontrolled guest access to the slide chute presents a risk of collision or injury. Lifeguards should patrol and monitor chute access.
4. Intermediate pools should be of sufficient depth to permit rollovers without injury to the rider.
5. Generally, the tube style does not present a safety hazard.
6. Water flow rate down the chute should conform to the manufacturer's recommendations.
7. Concerning water flow rate, the following may occur: Extremely low water flow or barely wet surfaces (0 to 150 GPM) result in high rider speeds. An increase in water flow (up to 600 GPM) decreases the rider speed. Further water flow increases (up to 1,500 GPM) decrease rider speed. At a water flow rate greater than 1,500 GPM, the rider speed tends to equal the speed of the water. High flow rates tend to decrease the differences in acceleration and exit speed among various guests.
8. Lifeguards should be aware of the design of their facility's innertube chute because some designs result in whirlpools and back eddies.

Innertube Ride—Rapids Rides

Rapids rides are identified by an innertube slide path that is continuous or nearly continuous. The path may

Figure 20.4. Innertube slide. (Photo courtesy of Water Technology Inc.)

be designed in a random serpentine, curved, or "stream" shape. This ride can include devices that cause "choppy water" and obvious bumps in the slide path.

Safety Considerations

1. The splashpool approach and design should give the rider a balanced entry, producing a landing pattern that allows minimal risk for rider turnovers and in-pool collisions.
2. A facility should have a procedure that allows guests to release their tube and exit the pool without diverting attention to tube recovery.

Innertube Ride—Slow Rivers

Slow rivers are a popular attraction in a waterpark. They are usually a flat circuitous stream moved by booster pumps providing a riverlike flow rate (under 5 mph) in which riders are transported on various flotation devices or by body floating or walking (Figure 20.5).

Safety Considerations

1. The entry and exit locations in a slow river require consideration of the potential for rider impact with rails, stairwells, and ramp ways.
2. Tunnels, bridges, waterfalls, and other features should have adequate clearance to ensure that riders can avoid a collision.
3. Rivers flowing faster than 5 mph need special provisions for guest entry and exit to provide convenience and to ensure safety.

Wave Pools

Wave pools (Figure 20.6) are classified into two general categories: wave action and solitary transitional.

Wave Action

Wave action (WA) pools have a motion that is oscillating (seesaw motion) or standing (no rolling waves). These pools produce waves by cyclic pulsing; therefore, WA pools cause little cross flow. As a rule, waves are generated in cycles of approximately 3 seconds and produce a crest to valley depth of 4 ft or greater. This type of wave pool usually operates several minutes "on," followed by a period of calm or greatly reduced water action. Wave patterns will vary among facilities depending on experience and manufacturer's recommendations. In some facilities, WA pools have special equipment to generate waves in patterns and heights to allow bodyboard and boogie board riding, rafting, and exhibition surfboarding.

Solitary Transitional

Solitary transitional (ST) wave pools create waves that make a moving wall of water that runs the total length of the wave pool. Provided the ST wave pool has the equipment and design, waves 6 ft high or greater can be generated for a few seconds to several minutes. In ST wave pools the waves are controlled by the design of the pool bottom. Characteristically, ST wave pools develop flow (wave) patterns below the average water level of the pool. This information is outlined in the manufacturer's operating procedures.

Figure 20.5. Innertube ride—slow river. (Photo courtesy of Water Technology, Inc.).

Figure 20.6. Wave pool. (Photo courtesy of Water Technology, Inc.)

Safety Considerations

1. Generally, the same local codes and health department requirements for water quality, signage, depth markers, and other parameters apply to wave pools and standard pools.
2. All walkways should have slip-resistant surfaces.
3. Slips and falls are most likely to occur in shallow areas (0 to 24 in.) of the wave pool.
4. Underwater currents and falls can occur in wave pools that have significant undertows and backflow.
5. ST pools have strong backflows or cross flows of water after passage of the main wave.
6. Pool grab rails and ladders should be inspected daily for tightness.
7. Signs should be visible from the pool and deck, stating that only strong swimmers should proceed beyond a designated point.
8. Signage should be posted noting that small children must be under continuous adult supervision while in the wave pool.
9. The use of mini-surf, surf, and boogie boards may be permitted only when the manufacturer has designed the wave pool for these activities. The manufacturer's guidelines for the operating procedures, emergency procedures, crowd control, and rules for use during these activities should be followed.
10. Masks, fins, and snorkels should not be permitted in wave pools during wave action periods.
11. Lifeguards should be alert to tired guests and novice or weak swimmers.
12. Lifeguards should have overlapping areas of responsibility to scan.
13. When a lifeguard determines a swimmer is being placed in danger, voice or whistle commands should direct the swimmer to shallower water.
14. A signal or warning should be sounded or seen before resuming wave action. Lifeguards should be aware of guests running from the deck to "hit the waves" when the signal is given.
15. It is important that lifeguards be rotated from station to station and to other assignments to break boredom and increase alertness.
16. Signs should warn guests that waves can be overpowering and that collision and falls are possible.
17. ST pools are tiring. Lifeguards should scan the pool after the wave action has stopped to pick out guests who should exit or move to shallower water to rest.
18. Collisions generally occur during the wave cap; in shallow water, scraping the bottom is possible. Lifeguards should respond immediately to signs of guest distress.

Speed Slides

Speed slides are identified by chutes or roller tracks that may be straight, serpentine, helical, or whiplike and that have long or steep drops (Figure 20.7). These slides exit sliders into a splashpool or run-out at speeds of approximately 20 mph or greater. Depending on slide design, guests may be positioned on the slide in a number of ways. Guests may be seated in a chain of four or be lying feetfirst or headfirst on sleds and mats according to the manufacturer's recommendations. Many speed slide designs permit sliding without mats or sleds.

It is important for every speed slide to have an exit system that safely decelerates (slows down) the guest, who may be traveling at a speed of 40 mph. In addition, the guest's body position (attitude) must be correct during the entry into the splashpool. A speed slide may use one of the following exit systems: run-out (trough lane), direct to splashpool, landing flap to splashpool, or combination run-out and pool. The combination run-out and splashpool is a longer, somewhat level continuation of the slide trough containing water. The slider's speed is reduced by pushing against this water with the body, creating a braking action.

Safety Considerations

1. Only one slider enters at a time.
2. Lifeguards need to consider the rider's height, weight, and age against the slide design and operational limits.
3. Absolutely no headfirst sliding is allowed except where approved by the manufacturer's and/or park safety supervisor's instructions.
4. Sliding feetfirst on the back is usually the best position.
5. Depending on the speed of the slide, legs may need to be crossed at the ankles and arms crossed over the chest.

Figure 20.7. Speed slide. (Photo courtesy of World Waterpark Association, Inc.)

6. Lifeguards should not dispatch the next slider until the first slider is out of the run-out and moved from the flume exit center line.

7. Any slider who appears to be under the influence of drugs or alcohol should not be permitted to use the speed slide. (This rule should apply to all activity-oriented attractions in the facility.)

8. Good instructional signage informing the guest what to expect and how to slide and exit safely on the speed slide is extremely important.

9. Guests who may not be suited for speed slide use include the following:
   a. guests who are frail due to age,
   b. pregnant guests,
   c. young children without supervision,
   c. guests who are obese (overweight),
   d. physically challenged guests or guests wearing a prosthesis,
   e. guests who have demonstrated previous horseplay, and
   f. guests with a history of heart condition, back problems, or fear of heights.

Lifeguarding at a Waterpark

Lifeguarding is the development and application of the skills and techniques necessary to control and prevent aquatic accidents (Figure 20.8). It is demanding, monotonous at times, and tiring. Lifeguarding is not as glamorous as portrayed on television and in motion pictures. However, lifeguarding is challenging and can be personally rewarding.

The major responsibility of the lifeguard is to prevent accidents and to respond in the event of an emergency. No people are in a better position to prevent accidents in a waterpark than alert lifeguards sitting and standing in position watching their areas of responsibility. Lifeguards act as human radar, constantly scanning their areas of responsibility for potential problems.

Figure 20.8. Lifeguard on duty at wave pool. Photo courtesy of World Waterpark Association.

Over the past decade, a demand for new standards of training for lifeguards has developed with the emergence of waterparks. In the past, any student who completed a lifesaving course was considered a qualified candidate to hold a lifeguard position. Several authorities in the aquatic industry contend that lifeguards should be skilled beyond the competence of an advanced lifesaver.

When a drowning or serious injury occurs, the performance of the lifeguard becomes the issue, and in a court of law, the training and certification of the lifeguard is closely examined. Therefore, trained professional lifeguards are a necessity and not a luxury, regardless of the type or size of the waterpark.

Although traditional swimming pools and waterparks have similarities, they also have significant differences. According to Ellis & Associates, many waterparks encounter more patrons in one summer season than many traditional pools see in several years. In addition, it appears that although waterpark rides are exciting and challenging, many visitors are not skilled or prepared to handle the waves, currents, "white water," and hydraulics that many waterparks provide. In addition, some waterparks are profit driven rather than service driven, so management of the park is also different. Management and lifeguards cannot run a waterpark safely and efficiently armed with only traditional pool rules and skills.

Several differences exist between lifeguarding at a waterpark and lifeguarding at a public swimming pool. The differences include the following:

Waterparks

1. Draw new guests every day
2. Have a greater number of lifeguard staff
3. Draw a larger number of guests
4. Have large expense attractions
5. Are operated for profit
6. Have frequent water rescues daily
7. Have greater news media coverage
8. Attract the recreational swimmer

Public Swimming Pools

1. Draw same guests from local community
2. Have only a few rescues per season
3. Are funded by local government or are nonprofit
4. Offer aquatic education programs
5. Attract swimmers of all types and for different reasons

The Job of the Lifeguard

Lifeguards at waterparks may be called on to fill different roles while on duty. They may find themselves in the roles of host, friend to a lost child, provider of first aid treatment, disciplinarian, referee of human behavior, complaint manager, or a professional who is "coolheaded" in an emergency. Lifeguards must be authority figures who are respected for their knowledge and skills (Figure 20.9).

The romantic or glamorous status of the lifeguard is only imagined in the minds of uninformed employers, swimmers, and inexperienced lifeguards. The truth is that a lifeguard's job is full of serious responsibilities. Although a lifeguard's responsibilities and duties are different among facilities, the primary responsibilities remain the same:

1. the prevention of accidents through assuming responsibility for the guests in the facility and
2. the immediate response to an emergency requiring the technical skill and knowledge of a trained lifeguard and the administration of appropriate emergency care.

Figure 20.9. Lifeguard assisting tube riders. (Photo courtesy of World Waterpark Association)

The basic premise of lifeguarding is that preventing accidents is more desirable than performing successful rescues. Therefore, lifeguards should keep guests from getting into dangerous situations.

Knowledge of and adherence to the following principles indicates that the lifeguard has accepted responsibility for the safety of the guest:

1. Danger areas of waterpark attractions should be continuously and closely supervised. Lifeguards should anticipate problems by watching guests closely. In a waterpark, high-risk areas include the following:
   a. physical hazards—for example, shallow water, underwater steps, deep water, slippery surfaces, cloudy water, algae, and objects floating in the water;
   b. chemical hazards—for example, chlorine gas, acid, and cleaning chemicals;
   c. environmental hazards—for example, lighting in and around a water attraction and glare on water surface from sunlight or artificial light; and
   d. behavioral hazards—for example, running, pushing people, throwing people, riding a slide in the wrong position, horseplay, and swimming in or around a splashpool
2. Rules should be enforced tactfully and consistently. (Rule enforcement is covered in detail later.)
3. Lifeguards should be heard and seen by facility guests. The use of a whistle and uniform are universally recommended for lifeguards. A bright colored uniform will help guests spot the lifeguard quickly.

Being seen also includes remaining in the assigned location that is visible to all guests. Lifeguards should realize that a quick response is expected when the situation warrants. Therefore, uniforms that include laced shoes or pullover sweatshirts could hamper a rescue effort.

Personal Health Hazards of Lifeguarding

Lifeguards face several health hazards while performing their duties (Figure 20.10). Lifeguards should know what hazards exist and how to protect themselves from harm. As a rule, the supervisor does not have the time to constantly remind the lifeguards to protect themselves. Each lifeguard is responsible for taking care of himself or herself. The following hazards are caused by the environment and/or weather. (The following are universal suggestions and are not intended as individual prescriptions for prevention. A doctor should be consulted for medical advice.)

Skin Hazard

Although it is fashionable to have a rich, dark, deep suntan, roasting the epidermis to get that "fashionable look" has a cost. The cost may result in the skin cancer known as melanoma. Scientists have correlated other hazards to sunlight, including a suppression of the immune system (a possible contributor to other forms of cancer) and damage to skin cells that causes the cells to lose their soft, pliable properties. The prudent lifeguard avoids the concentrated ultraviolet (UV) radiation of the sun that occurs between 11 a.m. and 3 p.m.

The closer a person gets to the equator, the more intense the UV rays of the sun. The risk of skin cancer doubles about every 300 miles a person travels toward the equator, so the "sun time" and sunscreen strength should be adjusted accordingly. The intensity of the rays also increases with altitude, so necessary precautions should be taken when applicable.

Lifeguards should wear protective clothing, stay under a sun umbrella if possible, or wear sunscreen. There are two basic types of sunscreens. Physical blockers such as zinc oxide or titanium dioxide block all light rays. Chemical blockers found in lotions, creams, and ointments selectively absorb UV radiation before it can affect the skin. When using chemical blockers, lifeguards should pay attention to the sun protection factor (SPF). The SPF is a number on a scale of 2 or higher that tells how long a person can extend exposure time in the sun by using a particular sunscreen. A product with SPF 8 will increase the time it takes for a person to turn red by a factor of 8. The following are tips for selecting a chemical blocker sunscreen:

Figure 20.10. Alert Lifeguard properly stationed in the water at the bottom of a tube slide. (Photo courtesy of Water Technology, Inc)

- Light-skinned persons should use a sunscreen with an SPF of at least 6 and possibly 15 or higher.
- A sunscreen with two or more UV-absorbing ingredients should be selected.
- A long-lasting formula that penetrates or clings to the skin and is not rinsed off easily should be selected. A water-in-oil lotion is a good example. (Lifeguards should not apply coat after coat, which may prevent perspiration and increase the risk of heatstroke.)
- People who are allergic to certain diuretics, sulfa drugs, or hair sprays may develop rashes as a reaction to PABA. If a reaction occurs, a doctor should be consulted regarding the use of a PABA-free sunscreen.
- Lifeguards should apply a sunscreen 30 minutes to 2 hours before sun exposure to give the sunscreen time to penetrate the outer layer of skin. Another skin hazard of which a lifeguard should be aware is the development of skin irritation from wearing a wet swimsuit for an extended period. Lifeguards should remove wet suits when possible and use talcum or baby powder with cornstarch to dry out moist body areas.

Eye Hazard

Good sunglasses can provide safe, comfortable vision, especially while a person is around water. The main purposes of sunglasses are to reduce the amount of vision light and provide protection from glare and UV rays.

Sunglasses should block out 75% to 90% of visible light. Some sunglasses carry a tag stating their "transmission factor" (the amount of light that can pass through). Unless specially treated, few sunglasses provide protection from UV rays. UV rays can damage the retina of the eye; however, sunglasses with a special clear coating can block a large percentage of UV rays from reaching the eye. Lifeguards should wear UV-protected sunglasses because of the amount of time spent in the sun and the constant watch over the water surface.

Dark lenses that do not have a UV coating can harm the eye. They will cause the pupil to dilate, exposing the retina to more UV rays than usual. A burning or gritty feeling in the eye after exposure to bright sunlight may be a sign of eye sunburn, which requires prompt treatment from an ophthalmologist.

Dehydration Hazard

To avoid dehydration, lifeguards should drink plenty of water over an extended time and stay in the shade to avoid profuse sweating and excessive loss of body fluid. In short, they should protect their bodies as much as possible.

Guest Relations

Positive guest relations can only be achieved by having waterpark employees who are courteous and tactful to the guests in the park. The importance of positive guest relations is twofold. First, the guest has bought the right to have an enjoyable time (Figure 20.11). This right includes exceptional treatment from the staff. Second, the best defense against a potential lawsuit is positive guest relations. A well-treated and respected guest will respond positively to most situations, whereas a guest who is treated poorly or neglected is more likely to become mad and file a lawsuit.

All waterpark employees should encourage guests to voice their opinions about the facility and its operation. This is not an easy task because guests generally do not like to complain and employees do not like to hear it. In a survey conducted by the World Waterpark Association, only about 4% of guests voiced a complaint; the other 96% voted with their money by not coming back to the facility. Eight out of 10 unsatisfied guests told their friends about "unhappy experience" at the facility. Employees should give the guests the opportunity to tell them about an "unhappy experience" so that the employee can help make it happy.

Figure 20.11. Lazy rivers are tons of fun for everyone! (Photo courtesy of World Waterpark Association)

Your best defense against a lawsuit is positive guest relations. Give guests the opportunity to tell you about an "unhappy experience" so that you can help make it happy. The staff should implement the following to facilitate positive guest relations.

Media

The waterpark should have a plan of action to follow when the media are inquiring about an incident or accident. The plan should designate a facility spokesperson to handle questions the media may ask. All other staff should direct the media to the spokesperson and refrain from commenting. Staff should never say, "I have no comment." This statement can be construed as implied fault with an attempt to cover it up. The media are the waterpark's only link to "future guests," and the impression given could affect guest attendance and ultimately the employee's job.

Guest Complaints

All complaints should be received in an appreciative manner, and necessary action should be initiated as soon as possible. The guest can provide the staff with valuable insight and constructive criticism that may prevent a potential accident or disaster. Regardless of how valuable or constructive a guest's comment may seem, the guest has bought the right to voice dissatisfaction with a product or service. Staff are obligated to listen with interest and concern.

Lost and Found

The facility should have a policy and location for lost and found items and persons. If an item is found by or turned in to an employee, that employee is responsible to see that the proper owner has an opportunity to claim the item. The old rule of "finders keepers" does not apply. A guest has paid not only for use of the facility but also for honest, customer-oriented service that respects guest property. In addition, the facility should have a plan of action for lost or missing persons. Lost children must be taken under the guardianship of the staff until the parent or responsible adult is found.

Park Information

Staff are responsible for knowing all waterpark information or the person who can answer a guest's question. It is frustrating to the guest to be led on a "wild goose chase" to find the answer to a simple question. Employees should know the correct answer or know who will have the correct answer.

Correcting Guests

Employees cannot treat all guests the same. The approach and delivery of a corrective statement differs from child to adult and from child to child. In general, use positive commands that show concern and respect for the guest. Employees must remember that they are not only in the business of preventing accidents and saving lives but also promoting goodwill between the guests and the waterpark.

Enforcement of the Rules

The first point that employees must understand is that they are symbols of authority and, as such, must demonstrate respect for authority by personally adhering to all park rules and policies (Figure 20.12). It is difficult to expect guests to comply with rules designed for their safety if employees are not held to the same rules. When enforcing the rules, employees should consider several points.

Consistency

To be consistent means to enforce the same rule in the same way every time. Uniform rule enforcement means that if two guests are violating a rule, both should be stopped. Rules should be fair for everyone.

Delivery/Demeanor

Employees should try to explain to the guest the reasons for rules when enforcing them. An employee should correct guests, not punish them. The delivery of the message is crucial. For example, read the following two statements and decide which statement is most effective:

1. "Mister, you can't bring that bottle in here."
2. "Excuse me, sir. For your safety, bottles are not allowed in the pool. Broken glass in the pool is almost impossible to find and clean up. You can get a paper cup at the concession stand."

Employees should use a little diplomacy when explaining the rules. Diplomacy can be defined as telling guests to do something in such a way that they actually look forward to following the instruction. The second statement is by far the better of the two. It states the rule, explains why, and offers a solution while using diplomacy. In contrast, the first statement is condescending and abrupt. The old saying "you can catch more flies with honey than vinegar" has merit and application here.

Education of Guests

Because most accidents occur when employees are not present, employees must interject safety education at every opportunity. It is important that the employee explain why certain actions are dangerous and why other actions are desirable.

Figure 20.12. Lifeguard enforcing the rules. (Photo courtesy of World Waterpark Association)

Adults vs. Young Children

In general, adults and children differ in their motivations and experiences. Children are accustomed to being told what to do. Adults are more self-directed. Children are not likely to be interested in the reasons for a rule, whereas adults want to know immediately what the reason is for the rule. The reason a child is running through the park will usually be different from the reason the adult is running across the park. Thus, the employee should adapt corrections to the age level of the guest.

The Out-of-Control Guest

An effective way to deal with an out-of-control guest is for the employee to remain in control. The emotions of rage, hostility, and anger usually need "fuel" to keep them alive. An out-of-control employee will serve as that fuel, whereas an employee who remains calm and calls for assistance will not encourage the rage and anger to continue. Another out-of-control guest is the one who ignores and/or defies the rules and authority of the employee. The employee should use the same principles as stated above.

You Should Remember

Do not expect guests to comply with rules designed for their safety if you do not obey the same rules. Enforce the same rules in the same way every time. Remember that you are correcting guests, not punishing them.

Guests' Safety Perceptions

Every guest in a facility begins to form a mental impression about the park and the staff on duty. These mental impressions or perceptions can be positive or negative depending on the appearance and condition of the park and staff. The environment should look safe and be safe.

Signs, safety equipment, and other equipment (e.g., trash cans) should be available for guests and employees. The park should look clean and neat, with everything in its assigned place. Every staff member is responsible for the appearance and condition of the park. If something is out of place or out of order, staff should correct it.

Employees are an important part of the facility team and contribute to the total environment. If employees look and act like professionals, the park looks like a well-run park. Employees are "on stage," and the guests watch what employees do and do not do. Therefore, employees must not only be professionals but also look like professionals at all times.

Some employees may be talented enough to effectively watch an attraction or ride and carry on a conversation with two of their friends. However, the perception in the mind of the guest is that the employee is not paying attention. Why should employees care what a guest's perception is, as long as they are doing their jobs? The reason is that every guest is a potential witness in a court of law.

If the guest carries a negative impression of the employee on the witness stand, this will weaken the employee's defense. Perceptions are received at face value and not judged as right or wrong. The fact that the employee was talking to friends is the fact that will remain in the guest's mind and the jury's mind, regardless of whether the employee was also performing other duties. A prosecuting attorney will focus on the fact that the employee was supposed to be giving the attraction or ride total attention to do the job correctly.

Employee Operations of a Waterpark

Chain of Command

A chain of command is the ranking of employees in the order of superiority or command within the organization. The ranking structure is usually mapped out in a diagram. The basic concept behind the chain of command is that someone is in charge and thus is ultimately responsible for the facility operation. All employees should know the chain of command so that they understand who has the responsibility and authority to make decisions at the various levels of the command. It is extremely important that the chain of command is used effectively to ensure the smoothest facility operations possible.

Rotation System

Although ride operations are not physically demanding, the sun, heat, humidity, and crowd noise produce stress-induced fatigue and subsequent drowsiness. Employees should remain at a station for no more than 20 to 30 minutes. A change of location can boost the alertness and attentiveness of employees. Rotations can be organized to include a combination of time at attraction one, followed by walking duty through the park, time at attraction two, a "little patrol" or miscellaneous assignment, and then completion of the rotation cycle with a break period.

Uniforms

Facility employees need to be clean and neat in appearance for guest relations purposes, and all employees should be outfitted in a uniform. The uniform may consist of specified pants, shirt, jacket, whistle, hat with a visor, and sunglasses. The hat, pants, and jacket are necessary for quick identification by both employees and guests. It is often difficult to tell employees from guests on peak attendance days without employees wearing a visible uniform.

Rescue Equipment

Rescue equipment for waterparks may be specified in the local and state codes. The park should adhere to these codes as a minimum acceptable standard. Each employee should be aware of the location and use of the rescue equipment.

Equipment that may be used or needed includes megaphones or bullhorns, whistles, warning signs, emergency lighting, backboard, stretcher, first aid kit, blankets, rescue tubes, ring buoys, and resuscitator or resuscitation mask.

Communications

It is important that each employee learn the signals and communication system used at the park. The communication must be simple, clear, and easily understood to be effective in an emergency. In many facilities, a "10-code" system (e.g., "10-4" means "OK" or "I read you"; "10-20" means "state your location") is established and used to communicate during operations. All employees should know the communication system used in their park.

Telephone

A telephone should be available for use in an emergency. If possible, one phone should be designated only for official business and emergencies. It is recommended that a verbal code be established to aid in quick communication of common information. If such a code is used in a park, it should be explained in the emergency action plan. The telephone numbers for emergency services should be posted near the phone and should be easily readable.

Electronic Devices

Technology continues to advance and allows communication systems to improve in the delivery, speed, and accuracy of information. Some of the electronic devices used are walkie-talkies, lights (stop and go), electronic gates, buzzers, and public address systems. If modern technology is not available, flags can be used.

For example, flags can be used to dispatch guests down the slide when the landing is clear of sliders.

General Ride Operating Procedures

Large waterpark facilities, commonly known as theme parks, may have carnival amusement rides at the facility. The following procedure applies to this type of ride.

When operating any ride or attraction, the employee's primary concern should be guest safety. A vast majority of park rides are automatic. Therefore, the attendant's job is to make sure that guests are able to make the transitions from ride entrance to ride unit and from ride unit to ride exit in absolute safety. To ensure this safety, the ride attendant must remain alert and be prepared for unexpected problems that may occur during operation. Due to automation and modern technology, some rides are easy to operate, and attendants are tempted to neglect their duties and responsibilities. However, each employee is personally responsible for the safety and welfare of the guests and must constantly be conscious of those duties.

Opening Procedures

Each ride operator should complete the following opening procedure or equivalent procedure before allowing guests to use the ride:

1. Operators should check in with their supervisor or at the main office to obtain new information or working material needed for their shift.
2. They should visually inspect the ride to ensure that no one is working on it and make sure all moving units have a clear path to operate.
3. They should start the ride two or three times and listen for strange noises that may be mechanical problems. They should test brakes and make sure all gauges register properly.
4. They should inspect all safety straps and bars to ensure that they are properly operating.
5. They should complete the necessary checklist or documentation to verify completion of opening procedures.
6. They should notify their supervisor of ride status and open the ride to guests at the appropriate time.

Loading and Unloading Procedures

Because guests are only in the park for a relatively short period of time, it is extremely important that ride attendants attain the highest capacity that is safely possible for their ride. Profit is just as important as safety, but profit should never overrule safety procedures. The following is a general guideline for loading and unloading procedures:

1. After collecting the ticket from the guest, attendants should direct him or her to the ride unit.
2. They should provide assistance to guests who need help and always instruct guests to keep their hands and legs inside the ride unit.
3. Guests should not be allowed to eat or drink on or during the ride.
4. The attendant should review the rules with the guests to ensure a safe ride.
5. They should load guests in numbers closest to the maximum comfortable load per ride unit. If there is not a line, it may be best to allow guests to ride separately to distribute or balance weight, depending on the attraction or ride.
6. They should check all safety belts or straps to ensure they are properly fastened around each guest.
7. They should dispatch the unit or start the ride when all waiting guests are clear and all riding guests are secure and ready.
8. After the ride has completed its normal "trip time," attendants should help guests out and direct them to the exits.
9. Last, they should show positive guest relations by wishing guests "a great day" or "a good time" while visiting the park.

Closing Procedures

Each ride operator should complete the following closing procedure or equivalent procedure before leaving the facility:

1. After the guests are clear of the ride, ride operators should clean all ride units and pick up litter around the ride.
2. They should bring the ride to the "night storage" position.
3. They should turn off all appropriate power switches and lights.
4. They should cover any ride units if necessary.
5. They should take all working materials to the main office and report any maintenance that needs to be done before the next operating day.
6. They should check with the supervisor about new information and check out for the day.

You Should Remember

The opening and closing procedures for rides may vary. Therefore, you should know the procedures for the rides in your area of responsibility.

General Waterpark Lifeguard Operating Procedures

Operating procedures are designed to give an overall view of the lifeguard position at a facility. The procedures and training, combined with the employee's common sense and good judgment, will aid him or her in being successful as a lifeguard. The following are examples of opening, operating, and closing procedures for lifeguards. The procedures may vary among waterparks. Therefore, the following is an example and not a recommendation for any specific waterpark. The waterpark management team must develop procedures that suit its facility.

Opening Procedures

Each day, lifeguards have opening procedures. The number of lifeguards may vary because of attendance levels at various times of the season. However, each of the following opening procedures is completed before the gates are opened to guests regardless of the number of lifeguards on duty.

1. Lifeguards check in and advise supervisors that they are present and starting work.
2. Lifeguards check the communications system to determine proper operations. Problems are reported to the supervisor.
3. All furniture is arranged in an orderly manner and cleaned as needed.
4. The pools are vacuumed or brushed.
5. All sidewalks, stairs, and pool decks are swept.
6. All tables, trash cans, and urns are cleaned and put in position.
7. Guard stand safety equipment is cleaned and checked for proper function. All equipment is positioned for rescue use. (The facility's opening procedures explain exactly where the equipment is to be located and positioned for rescue use.)
8. All items such as brooms and pans are stored out of sight of guests. Each broom should be returned to its original storage location.
9. All lifeguards are in their duty stations in proper uniform when the gates open at 11 a.m.

Operating Procedures

Operating procedures should be explained for each attraction that requires a lifeguard. This example is for a wave pool:

1. Lifeguards are responsible for the safety of each guest in their area of responsibility.
2. Lifeguards should be constantly alert for weak swimmers. The deeper water is only for strong swimmers during the wave action.
3. Guests are not allowed to hold on to ladders during the wave action or at any other time.
4. Lifeguards should watch for nonswimming guests on rafts. Rafts are not personal flotation devices designed to keep a swimmer afloat.
5. Lifeguards should watch for guests entering the wave pool with floating devices. Only Coast Guard–approved life jackets are allowed. Ring buoys, inflated rubber boats, and water wings are not allowed in the wave pool. Lifeguards should tell guests where they may use the items safely.
6. No masks, fins, or snorkels are allowed in the wave pool. Lifeguards should tell the guests that masks are permitted at the shallow end of the activity pool if the mask is made of tempered glass or has a plastic faceplate.
7. No pushing or horseplay is allowed in the pool or on the deck area.
8. No one may jump or dive into the pool. Guests may enter the pool only through the shallow end.
9. No running is allowed in the pool or on the surrounding deck area.
10. Guests should keep off the buoy lines.
11. All lifeguards stand at their assigned positions during the wave action.
12. Available lifeguards on duty cover the assigned positions or stand while the duty lifeguard makes the rescue and returns.

13. Lifeguards are required to wear rescue tubes while in the watch position.

Closing Procedures

The manager on duty notifies the lifeguard or attendant to close the attraction or pool. Once the lifeguard has been instructed to close, the following procedure begins:

1. Lifeguards should clear guests from the pool by use of the whistle and by announcing that the pool is closed and all guests should exit.
2. Lifeguards clean the bathroom nearest their attraction.
3. Furniture is stacked and put in night storage.
4. Pool decks and sidewalks must be swept.
5. Rental tubes left out by guests are returned to the tube rental stand and counted.
6. Trash cans and cigarette urns are emptied.
7. Assigned personnel clean the parking lot of trash and debris.
8. Lifeguards squeegee all decks of excess water.
9. Lifeguards are responsible for collecting life jackets around their areas of responsibility.
10. The supervisor inspects each area and clears lifeguards to clock out. Lifeguards should remember to sign their time card. No signature means no pay.

> ### You Should Remember
>
> Operating procedures are designed to give an overall view of the employee position at your facility. The operating procedures and training, combined with your common sense and good judgment, will assist you in being a successful employee.

Thunder and Lightning Storms

At least 100 Americans are killed by lightning each year, which is more deaths than caused by tornadoes, hurricanes, or floods. However, to keep things in perspective, the chances of dying in a drowning accident are 50 times (5,000%) greater. When lightning strikes a person, the person generally goes into cardiac arrest and/or respiratory failure. The prudent employee can understand that lightning is too fast, too powerful, and too unpredictable to risk the chance of allowing guests to use the facilities during a thunderstorm.

Action Procedures During Thunderstorms

Definitive information as to when guests may return to activities once a storm has ended does not exist from any authoritative agency or organization. Therefore, the employee needs to refer to the supervisor's judgment and the park policies. The judgment of the supervisor and the park policy should consider several points in determining when to clear the facility and when to resume activity.

Evacuating Park Guests From the Facility

All guests should evacuate the surrounding area at the first sound of thunder. The criterion for this action is not based on the sighting of lightning but rather on the sound of thunder because thunder occurs as a result of lightning.

The employee who hears the first sound of thunder should implement the park's emergency action plan for evacuation. This may mean that a supervisor is advised of the situation and begins the evacuation procedure. Because lightning is attracted to the tallest object in the area, guests and staff should not congregate under umbrellas, trees, or other tall objects. All persons in the facility should go indoors or take cover in their automobiles.

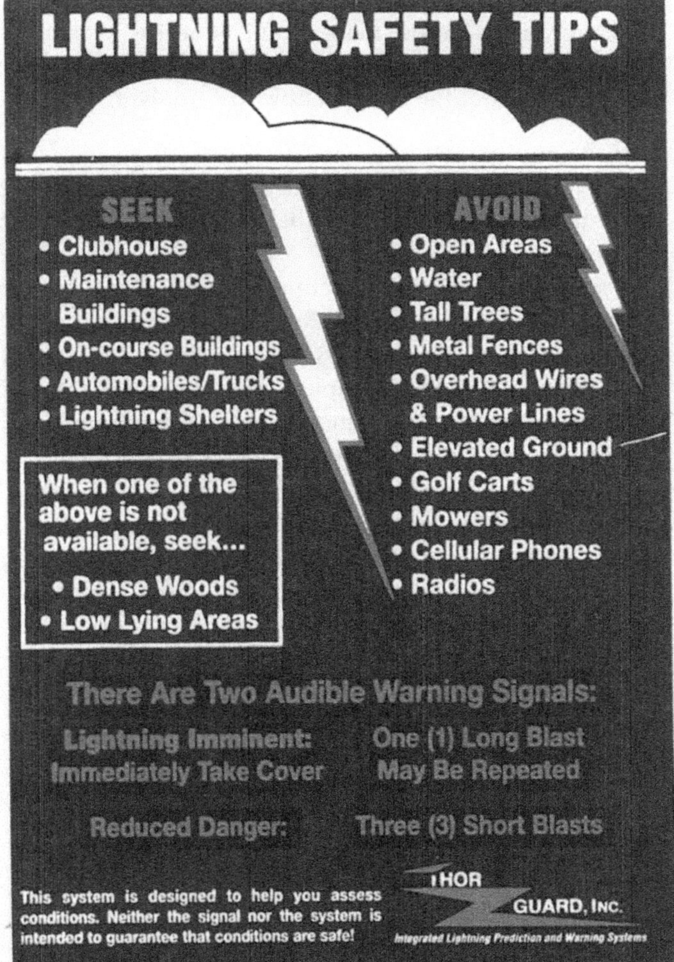

Return to Normal Operations

The National Weather Service does not consider a thunderstorm "over" until there has been no sound of thunder for at least 15 minutes. However, an additional factor to consider is whether the sky is dark and threatening. Unless there are obvious signs of clearing, a thunderstorm should not be considered "over." It may be necessary for supervisors or employees to consider an additional 5- to 15-minute safety margin before allowing guests to return to park activities.

Park Policy

All facilities should state their activity rules and regulations in writing for guests to see before using any attraction. It seems prudent to state that the facility will be cleared at the first sound of thunder and that guests will not be allowed to reenter the ride or attraction area until 15 to 30 minutes after the last sound of thunder is heard.

The Americans With Disabilities Act

Many waterparks in the past were not accessible for people with physical challenges. In 2010, the Americans With Disabilities Act (ADA) was expanded to require aquatic venues to provide a means of access to their facilities. See Chapter 6, Americans With Disabilities Act, for details about the Act and how to comply it.

Staff Training

Careful training can modify behavior and develop new attitudes in recognizing the abilities of persons with disabilities. The most effective training should include some element of experimental learning according to Chesnut (1992), author of *Breaking Down Barriers: A Complete Guide to Business Relationships With People With Disabilities*. For example, a requirement of training may be for staff to be confined to a wheelchair or become a person with sight impairment. Staff would remain in this condition throughout the day and would be required to function in the normal environment of the facility or show. Staff with the disability would experience barriers in pathways such as furniture, steps, curbs, and power cords. Through this experimental learning, staff have opportunities to experience the challenges and frustrations that persons with disabilities or physical impairments experience and therefore have a greater understanding of persons with disabilities.

It is not too late to begin a formal in-service training program with staff. In-service training topics or activities related to persons with disabilities may include the following:

1. Proper etiquette when dealing with a person with a disability can be discussed.

2. The most updated ADA requirements for aquatic facilities (see Chapter 6) can be discussed. What does it mean to this facility?
3. Staff can discuss impairments and disabilities such as Alzheimer's disease, amputees, aphasia, arthritis, cerebral palsy, cerebrovascular accident, epilepsy, mental illness, mental retardation, multiple sclerosis, and muscular dystrophy.
4. Staff can discuss special situations at the facility (e.g., certain amusement rides or attractions may not be "reasonably safe" for persons of selected disabilities).
5. Staff can write or review a standard operating procedure guide for handling persons with disabilities.
6. Staff can evaluate their ability to accommodate persons with disabilities.
7. Management can ask a local community expert to speak about selected topics regarding persons with disabilities, for example, a physical or occupational therapist.
8. Management can have a person with a disability speak about a selected topic at the in-service training.

A critical area for training is helping employees understand company policies regarding hosting guests with disabilities. For example, safety considerations may prevent certain guests from using a ride. Obviously, employees must know how to handle a situation or contact a supervisor if questions arise. This type of training is ongoing as new attractions are opened. For example, if a ramp to allow wheelchairs is added to a gift shop, employees of the shop need to learn about how to assist guests in wheelchairs.

Bloodborne Pathogens and Waterpark Personnel

The Occupational Safety and Health Administration (OSHA) has issued regulations to protect people from the hazards of blood-borne pathogens such as human immunodeficiency virus (HIV) and hepatitis. This regulation was primarily intended for emergency evacuation teams, hospital employees, and others who deal with the injured; the regulations also appear to apply to employees who are likely to come into contact with human blood. The legislation may apply to first aid personnel and lifeguards.

The regulations have a number of requirements such as protective gear, information and training, record keeping, and the administration of preventive injections to appropriate personnel. The regulations are found in 29 Code of Federal Regulations (CFR) 1910.1030. If employees are likely to encounter human blood because of their job duties, an attorney or the OSHA office should be contacted to determine exactly what the regulations require.

What Are Waterparks to Do?

There are four steps the standard of care requires employers to take regarding the prevention of transmission of bloodborne pathogens:

1. Waterpark staff who are at risk of exposure to bloodborne diseases must be identified (e.g., first aid personnel, emergency medical technicians, registered nurses, and possibly lifeguards).
2. An infection-control plan should be activated to reduce exposure to blood. For example, first aid personnel should be supplied with resuscitation masks, protective eyewear, and latex or nitrile gloves.
3. Hepatitis B vaccinations should be offered to staff who are occupationally exposed to blood and other body fluids on a regular basis. A regular basis may be as regular as once a month.
4. Staff who have occupational exposure should attend a mandatory training program about bloodborne diseases and precautions against them. Mandatory training is primarily important because so many people are ignorant about how HIV and AIDS are transmitted and how they can be prevented. It is important that documentation be maintained. Waterparks should have or begin maintaining the following documents: annual training of staff, employee request to receive the hepatitis B vaccination, hepatitis B vaccination refusal form, the blood-borne pathogen exposure medical follow-up form, and program audit forms such as engineering controls needed, protective equipment, work practices, housekeeping and laundry, biohazard labeling, medical waste, and program audit summary. To research this subject further, the U.S. Public Health Service, the Centers for Disease Control, or local or state OSHA agencies should be contacted.

Are Waterparks Targets for Terrorism?

Unfortunately, terrorism involving chemical, explosive, or biological weapons is not news. The recent past reveals instances of the use of these weapons. The question is, how ready is the waterpark's emergency response system to deal with an incident involving threats of terrorism. The first line of defense against terrorism is intelligence gained by law enforcement agencies. An established, effective communication with the local city/county police and other law enforcement agencies could prove valuable in detouring or preventing a terrorist incident. The intelligence that law officials can provide is what will forewarn emergency responders that an unusual incident may occur. Other indications or clues may influence the forewarning of emergency responders.

Managing unfortunate incidents is difficult at best. Properly trained incident management officials can control changing situations and working forces in a coordinated, efficient manner. During a terrorist incident, success of managing these forces is contingent on the level of training and pre-incident planning.

Trained waterpark management should involve police, fire, and emergency medical services in preplanning efforts, as well as during a terrorist incident. Park management staff and these agencies need to present an integrated/unified command system from the onset. Management of an incident also depends on rapidly identifying hazards and implementing appropriate solutions to deal with the hazards.

Obviously, extreme loss of life and mass casualties are possible with the use of weapons of mass destruction. Terrorist events, historically, have not created large death ratios in the United States. Even internationally, most past terrorist events have not involved a huge loss of life and have deliberately avoided children and women. Events such as the Pan Am flight crash in Lockerbie, Scotland, where hundreds of innocent people died as the result of a bombing are rare events. Terrorists' intentions seem to have been to strike areas that would attract media coverage and incite fear in targeted populations, but not necessarily murder legions of innocent people. However, in the recent past, the incidents appear to be changing. The federal building in Oklahoma City bombing and the World Trade Center airplane attacks were deliberately designed to kill multitudes of people. The sarin subway incident in Tokyo, Japan, was largely unsuccessful but had the capability to kill thousands. It is apparent that motive of operation in recent attacks have changed. This new pattern of attacks includes striking with the motive to end many lives without regard to gender or age.

The speed and effectiveness of incident responders and efficiency are paramount to limiting the loss of life and important property. Terrorist activities often target loss of human life; therefore, the focus of response must be aimed at the life and health consequences of the terrorist attack. A waterpark's incident management team should consider the following when planning countermeasures to minimize the effects and/or chance of an incident.

The waterpark's incident management team should develop integrated training and exercise activities that include fire, police, emergency medical services, hospital, health departments, emergency management organizations, and local and state agencies.

The incident management team should promote integrated planning with regional response teams that include the following:

- metropolitan medical strike teams, which are being developed, funded, and trained by the federal government to assist local response agencies immediately;
- local police department;
- FBI field office; and
- fire department special operations.

The incident management team should ensure access to sufficient medical supplies, personal protection equipment, decontamination equipment, evidence recovery equipment, and stress debriefing to responders, affected staff, and hospitals for use during and after the incident. The incident management team should develop integrated informational intelligence systems between local and state officials.

The following preparation procedures and documents can guide staff members in the event of an act of terrorism. Park management should customize the following sections with detailed instructional information using community resources.

Assessment of Potential Threat

Park management should conduct an analysis of the type of threat, the probability of each type, and high exposure times for each threat.

Administrative Review

Management should review the park's strengths, weaknesses, and opportunities to deal with the threats. Areas that should be reviewed include the following:

- insurance coverage,
- media response plans,
- security procedures and capabilities,
- park restricted area access procedures,
- terrorism threat potential for the community, and
- internal and external response capabilities.

Emergency Response Agencies and Park Cooperation

Park management should consider inviting local and/or state emergency response agencies to review and/or endorse the park's preparations and plans for dealing with terrorism. Their experience will be valuable and may defer criticism if an event unexpectedly "sours" the plan.

Crisis Media Response Plan

The key to an effective media response plan is careful development and frequent implementation rehearsals. As a rule of thumb, the response plan should cover the following:

- crisis management philosophy;
- mission statement;

- assignment of staff duties;
- how, who, when, and where response plan steps should be activated;
- staff member crisis team recall roster, including name, home and cell phone, radio call numbers, fax number, and address; and
- community authorities notification roster, including name, phone, fax, and address.

Crisis Management Planning

The crisis management plan should delineate responsibilities and the chain of command to be followed during an incident. The responsibilities should be unambiguous, no matter who is leading the response to an incident.

Staff Training

Obviously, no plan can be effective if staff are not trained on the plan procedures and responsibilities. Effective training is essential because the park will be remembered by how the staff reacted to the incident, not how well they planned to react.

It is obvious that terrorism is a major and real threat in today's world. Therefore, waterparks should consider appropriate preparations to effectively handle the "unthinkable" terrorist encounter. Consultants can be used to provide specific guidance on preparations, training, and incident operations.

The Paperwork—Plans, Procedures, and Record Keeping

Waterparks should have a system for reporting and recording park activity. Adequate types and amounts of records should be retained for an appropriate period of time. Park management can consult with legal counsel and/or the insurance carrier to determine a record retention policy. The purpose is to provide vital data for future reference, such as data for market response evaluations, accurate facts for claims and lawsuits, required wage and hour records, records of unusual circumstances, and records of maintenance activity. In conjunction with the manufacturer's recommendations of attractions/rides, a record-keeping system should be established to include at least the following documents.

Preoperations Inspections

Prior to opening the park, staff should complete a walk-around assessment of conditions such as housekeeping, maintenance, structural conditions (i.e., cracks, loose fasteners, or loose joints), and quality of park appearance.

Operation Spot Checks

A condensed "spot-check" version of the preoperations inspection should be completed at reasonable intervals of the operating day. This will help ensure that standards are being maintained.

Inspection Reports

Operation and maintenance reports should have a uniform format with an area for handwritten notes. The primary notations in these reports will be variances from normal operation and the action(s) taken to address the variant. The park should consider the advantages of maintaining daily, weekly, and monthly inspection reports.

Emergency Plans and Procedures

The document is an action plan for foreseeable emergencies. A detailed procedure should be developed for each foreseeable emergency to direct the actions of park employees.

Maintenance Records

These records detail corrective action, routine, or preventive maintenance done on equipment and/or attractions and rides.

Staff Records

Because of high seasonal employment turnover, it may be wise to only maintain information required by local and federal wage, hour, and labor laws after each operating season. There may be exceptions to this such as staff data incorporated in specific incident reports or employee records of returning staff members.

Training

This is documentation of a training occurrence that includes the date, time, instructor, participants' names, employee ID number, and topic covered.

Incident Reports

These reports include first aid requests, customer complaints, and "unusual occurrence" reports.

Manager's Log

This log is a daily report showing the day's weather conditions, staffing levels, ride and attraction start and shutdown times, and other unusual occurrences of the operating day.

Supervisor's Report

This daily report or log by supervisors informs management of details of the day's operation.

Government Regulations

As required by law, documentation should be kept on the following procedures and/or programs. (Local-ity of the park may necessitate other and/or additional documentation.)

- federal and state labor laws governing minors,
- federal OSHA programs and/or state OSHA programs (when and where applicable),
- hazard communication,
- OSHA Injury/Illness Log 300,
- blood-borne pathogens,
- Americans With Disabilities Act,
- confined space,
- personal protective equipment,
- hearing conservation program,
- lockout–tagout program, and
- other requirements of 29 CFR 1910.

Note: The law is specific in its requirements and it calls for proper organization, record keeping, and compliance procedures. Violation fines are sizable and few penalties are being abated.

Reducing Liability at Waterparks

The following is a list of questions for pool operators to consider when reviewing the overall operation of their waterpark. Unique or special areas at a waterpark can be added to this list.

Operations: Personnel and Ride Areas

1. What are the preemployment testing procedures the park uses in selecting its staff?
2. What are the preemployment training procedures the park uses to train its employees before their first day on the job?
3. What are the ongoing training procedures and meetings the park uses throughout the season? Is the documentation of these trainings current and well stated?
4. Are copies available of all management and employee documents that are a part of the training process? This will include employee handbooks, newsletters, standards of performance, job descriptions, operating procedures, bulletins, and training manuals.
5. Does a staff member spend time observing the employees in action?
   a. How do they enforce rules?
   b. Are they consistent?
   c. Are the employees alert?
   d. Do they conduct themselves in a professional manner?
   e. Do they present a positive image of the park?
   f. Do they know how to handle typical emergency situations?
6. Does the park have a first aid room and an injury treatment system? Where is the nearest ambulance service? Hospital? Does the park have a backboard?

Are staff well trained in the use of the backboard? Does the park have a communication system for emergencies?

7. Is the management team well trained? Can they handle the employees? What is management's training and background? Can management handle emergencies?

8. What formal training is required by the park for its various employees? Is all the training approved through a national certifying agency? Do all employees have cardiopulmonary resuscitation (CPR) and first aid training?

9. Are maintenance workers provided with funding to attend operator and equipment maintenance workshops? If not, what measures are taken to train these people?

10. Is there a standard form and system for reporting accidents?

11. Are emergency and accident management procedures written and rehearsed to ensure a prompt, organized response to an accident?

12. Have emergency and accident management procedures been reviewed by an attorney, local paramedics, and/or hospital officials?

13. Are emergency and accident management drills conducted at least twice a month, one of those times during peak facility use?

14. Is current safety literature available to staff?

15. Are all accidents carefully investigated and reviewed with the proper authorities and is corrective action taken?

16. Do staff members complete safety checks of facilities and equipment weekly, with the report or check sheet filed in the appropriate office?

17. Are staff familiar with all local, county, state, the MAHC, and professional safety and health standards that may affect the operation of the facility?

18. Do staff carefully inspect equipment each day before use to ensure its safe use? Is a report filed?

19. Are potentially hazardous conditions or areas marked with proper signage?

20. Is the current ride or attraction permit on file if applicable in your state?

21. Is the electrical inspection up to date?

22. Are pool operations reports maintained and submitted to the health department when required?

23. Is a bacteriological analysis conducted weekly on any pools?

24. Are chlorine and pH tests conducted as required?

25. Is the water turnover rate maintained at an acceptable rate that meets local health standards?

26. Are SCBA masks available and in working condition?

27. Is water clarity maintained as required by law (usually measured by a 6-in. black disk being visible on the bottom from anywhere on the deck around the deep end)?

28. Is the water level maintained above gutter or skimmer level?

29. Is a test kit available with fresh chemicals?

30. Are depth markings the proper size and at the correct locations (usually 4-in. numbers written in red or black and located wherever depth changes 1 ft or every 25 ft)?

31. Does management keep a detailed maintenance and repair record?

32. Are staff aware of what activities are considered to be high risk?

33. Is a positive morale held by employees? What is done to maintain a positive morale?

34. Do staff have a room or area that is a comfortable atmosphere to relax when off duty?

35. Are the filter and mechanical equipment rooms secured and kept in a clean and accessible condition? Is there adequate lighting for clear visibility of each equipment component and gauge for maintenance purposes?

36. Are the components of the pool bathhouse (clothes storage space, dressing areas, shower room, drying room, toilets, and lobby) in clean operating condition?

37. Are employees routinely evaluated and praised for the duties they perform?

Physical Environment

1. Are walkways safe and well maintained?

2. Is there adequate instructional signage throughout the park? Is the signage clear in its intended meaning? Is it informative, professionally produced, and well maintained?

3. Are the buildings and other areas to which the guests have access free of hazards? Are the buildings and structures well maintained? Do they enhance the overall appearance of the park?

4. What is the condition of ramps and stairs? Are they slippery, do they have adequate handrails, and can small children slip through the rails?

5. Are the rides and attractions safe and in good working order? Are the rides and attractions causing injuries? If so, why? How can this be prevented?

6. Does the overall physical appearance of the park reflect a caring management attitude and attention to detail? Does the park appear to be professionally operated?

7. Where are chemicals and equipment stored? Is the storage area off limits to unauthorized personnel?

8. Is the snack bar or food service area clean and properly maintained according to local health department regulations?

9. Does the park have sufficient lighting for night operations (overhead and underwater lighting)?

10. Do warning signs accomplish the following three basic objectives?

    a. to tell people about a threat to their well-being posed by dangerous conditions or products,

    b. as a safety measure to change people's behavior so that they act safely, and

    c. to remind people of *a* and *b*.

11. Are signs posted to warn guests of the physical, chemical, environmental, and behavioral hazards?

Summary

Waterparks are always evolving and growing, seemingly becoming bigger and better throughout the years. With the popularity of waterparks, the size, and diversity of these facilities, it is important to understand special issues that are involved in waterpark operation. This includes safety considerations and rules for each diverse ride and attraction from slow lazy rivers to speed slides and tube rides. With such a diverse environment, waterparks also entail special guest, media, and employee relations, as well as education about safety threats such as lighting and even terrorism. Specific Emergency Action Plans (EAPs) for waterparks should also be implemented, documented, and practiced. Waterparks can be a fun environment for guests and staff alike, when waterpark-specific planning, rules, education, and considerations are developed.

Bibliography

Bureau of Business Practice. (1992). *1992 safety manager's guide.* Englewood Cliffs, NJ: Prentice-Hall.

Chesnut, A. (1992). *Breaking down barriers: A complete guide to business relationships with people with disabilities.* Hackett, AK: Trio Research Services.

Clayton, R. D., & Thomas, D. G. (1989). *Professional aquatic management* (2nd ed.). Champaign, IL: Human Kinetics.

Coy, J. (2013). Waterpark development: Not a bad year for resort and hotel owners. *Resort + Recreation.* http://www.resort-recreation.com/

Davy, M. (2013, June 28). Getting your feet wet at water parks. *The New York Times.* Retrieved from http://www.nytimes.com/

Ellis & Associates. (2007). International lifeguard training program (3rd ed., p. 7). Burlington, MA: Jones and Bartlett publishers.

Gabrielsen, M. A. (Ed.). (1989). *Swimming pools: A guide to their planning, design, and operation* (4th ed.). Champaign, IL: Human Kinetics.

International Association of Amusement Parks and Attractions. (1992, February). *Funworld* [1991 amusement industry abstract]. Retrieved from http://www.iaapa.org/ Alexandria, VA: Author.

International Association of Amusement Parks and Attractions. (1992, July). *Funworld.* Retrieved from http://www.iaapa.org/ Peter Herschend, Alexandria, VA: Author.

Paulozzi, L. J., McKnight, B., & Marks, S. D. (1986). A cluster of injuries at a water slide in Washington state. *American Journal of Public Health, 76,* 284.

Peterson, J. A. (1987). *Risk management for park, recreation and leisure services.* Champaign, IL: Management Learning Laboratories.

Pope, J. R., Jr. (1989). *Public swimming pool management II.* Ashburn, VA: National Recreation and Park Association Printing Office.

Smith, D. S., & Smith, S. J. (1987). *Water wise.* Charlevoix, MI: Smith Aquatic Safety Service.

Themed Entertainment Association/Economics Research Associates' Attraction Attendance Report. (2007). Retrieved from http://www.teaconnect.org

University of California. (1985). Buying guide: Sunscreens. *Berkeley Wellness Letter, 1,* 3.

University of California. (1988). Buying sunglasses: The eight key questions. *Berkeley Wellness Letter, 4,* 3.

U.S. Department of Transportation. (1987). *Emergency action guide for selected hazardous materials* (8th ed.). Washington, D.C.: U.S. Department of Transportation.

World Waterpark Association. (1989). *WWA considerations for operating safety.* Overland Park, KS: World Waterpark Association.

World Waterpark Association. (2013). www.waterparks.org

Evergreen Wings & Waves Waterpark in which waterslides dispatch in the belly of an Evergreen International Aviation B747-100 aircraft. (Photo courtesy of Counsilman-Hunsaker)

21

Winterizing

Key Concepts

- Emptying the pool
- Propylene glycol
- Decks
- Equipment
- Security
- Circulation equipment
- Filtration equipment
- Winter covers
- Utilities

Most pools in the United States are outdoor pools. A significant number of these pools are located in cooler portions of the country and, as a result, must be winterized to protect them and their parts, particularly the plumbing, from freezing water. Moisture destroys pool equipment, particularly when the pool is not in use. If equipment cannot be protected from moisture, it should be removed to a dry environment during the off-season. Winterizing pools means different things to different people depending on where the pool is located. The colder the climate, the more involved winterizing is. In the United States, pools above the Mason-Dixon Line call for much more winter protection than facilities south of the line. Many pool service companies can provide excellent winterizing services for $150 to $450 depending on the size of the pool.

Winterizing is basically a prevention program. When a seasonal pool is winterized, the most important areas of concern are the following:

1. preventing damage to the pool shell caused by hydrostatic pressure,
2. preventing rust and other deterioration,
3. preventing vandalism,
4. preventing spring start-up problems by an organized and systematic closing procedure, and
5. preventing unauthorized entry that could lead to drowning.

Whether to empty the pool or keep it full during the winter months is a popular topic of discussion with many pool experts. For many reasons, many individuals favor a "full" pool. Regardless of how winterizing is approached, if done correctly and completely, it will be easier to open the pool the following summer. In addition, more damage can be done to a pool in the off-season than during the peak summer months. This chapter begins by illustrating the disadvantages of emptying pools in freezing climates. The discussion of winterizing then progresses from the pool shell, to the deck, and finally to the surrounding buildings.

Emptying the Pool

Although some individuals empty the pool to be certain to prevent damage caused by the expansion of freezing water in pipes, this practice is not recommended, particularly in colder climates. Perhaps the most serious result of emptying the pool is "floating" a concrete pool, which can occur if the surrounding water table is high and the hydrostatic pressure relief valves are either clogged or insufficient in number. The hydrostatic relief valves can normally be found in the main drain boxes and allow surrounding groundwater to enter the pool harmlessly rather than damaging the pool shell.

In this case, when the water with all its weight is removed from the pool, the shell of the pool becomes relatively light compared with the weight of the surrounding groundwater. As a result, the pool "pops" out of the ground, damaging both the shell and the piping. This can occur whenever the level of the water in the ground is higher than the water level in the pool. This is a serious concern in colder climates.

Emptying a vinyl-lined pool can also create problems. Shrinkage and wrinkling can occur to the liner in a vinyl-lined pool.

Another problem associated with an empty pool is that even if small amounts of water are left between tile joints, cracks in concrete, and coping, tremendous damage can result because of the "freeze–thaw" cycle.

An empty pool can also be hazardous to both humans and pets. Particularly in the early spring, children can be attracted to the rainwater that collects in the empty pools. During the fall, skateboarders and in-line skaters are tempted by the dry, large, flat surfaces. The diving area becomes particularly attractive for advanced tricks. As the popularity of skateboarding, in-line skating, and BMX biking increases, so will the difficulty of keeping these tricksters out of an empty pool. This may be the primary reason for not emptying the aquatic facility during the off-season.

One advantage of emptying a pool before winter is that pool personnel can inspect the condition of the pool shell. Cracks, joints, and blemishes can be both inspected and repaired easily in an empty pool. Many individuals question whether this advantage outweighs the risks associated with emptying the pool, however.

Winterizing a "Full" Pool

Many aquatic experts agree that keeping the pool full or nearly full is the best way to winterize a pool with some precautions. Not only is it safer for the plumbing, but also a full pool is actually safer to people and pets, particularly when a safety mesh cover is used to keep people, pets, and trash out.

Dr. Tom's Tip

Please cover your winterized pool with a safety cover. As an expert witness, I have seen too many children drown in pools during the off-season. Even if you empty your pool completely, large amounts of water will collect in swimming pools during the fall, winter, and spring. If left uncovered, many children will find this standing water and may fall into it, often with tragic results.

Although costly, some pools are winterized by covering them with a security cover. This is done more often in climates that do not experience harsh winters. The pool is kept completely full, and water is circulated and heated slightly only when the temperatures reach the single digits. The movement of the water for the most part prevents it from freezing, and the heater can be turned on when the temperatures become extreme. Even if water freezes in the pool, most of the expansion occurs upward rather than sideways, so damage does not occur. Placing logs or tires in a winterized pool that is full is no longer recommended. Little chlorine is needed because

sunlight and swimmers do not use it up. Although utilities (water and electric) must be paid during the winter months, some pool operators argue that when a pool is winterized in this fashion, there are few summer start-up costs. The million-gallon Olympic-sized outdoor pool at Penn State University has been winterized in this fashion for more than 50 years.

When most pools are winterized, the water level is lowered about 16 in. or to just below the inlets. Although the recommended water level varies with each pool, at least 1 ft of water should always cover the shallow end floor. The cover used may determine what water level is most appropriate. There are two reasons for slightly lowering the water level in the pool. First, sufficient water in the pool remains to protect the pool shell from floating and prevents the pools sides and bottom from "frost heaving." Second, it allows the skimmers and other supply lines to be drained so that they can also be protected from freezing.

The water level in a winterized pool should never be allowed to reach the tile edge that surrounds some pools because if freezing occurs, ice can either crack the tile or damage the coping.

Because the pool should be vacuumed thoroughly and the filters cleaned before winterizing, both vacuuming and backwashing should be performed to "waste" so that these maintenance functions and the lowering of the water level are completed simultaneously.

Once the pool level is lowered to the desired level, one of two precautions should be taken to protect these lines. Antifreeze should be added to the skimmers and other lines that cannot be kept dry during the winter. But care must be taken to use a recreational antifreeze such as propylene glycol, which is a biodegradable, recreational antifreeze. Automotive antifreeze should never be used in a swimming pool application. Automotive antifreeze is toxic, whereas recreational antifreeze is nontoxic. Antifreeze is usually preferred in extremely cold climates because even small amounts of water left in lines can freeze and cause significant damage.

Some pool technicians prefer to blow lines dry with small compressors or reversing industrial vacuums rather than using antifreeze. Care must be taken to rid the lines of all water when lines are blown and to make sure that valves and fittings are airtight so that water does not find its way back into the lines. Special plugs are inserted in the outlets to ensure that these lines remain dry. Although skimmers should be plugged, it is difficult to keep rain or melted snow from reentering skimmer boxes, so antifreeze still may be required in skimmers even though the lines have been blown dry. Another option is to place expansion bags or bottles in the skimmer to protect them.

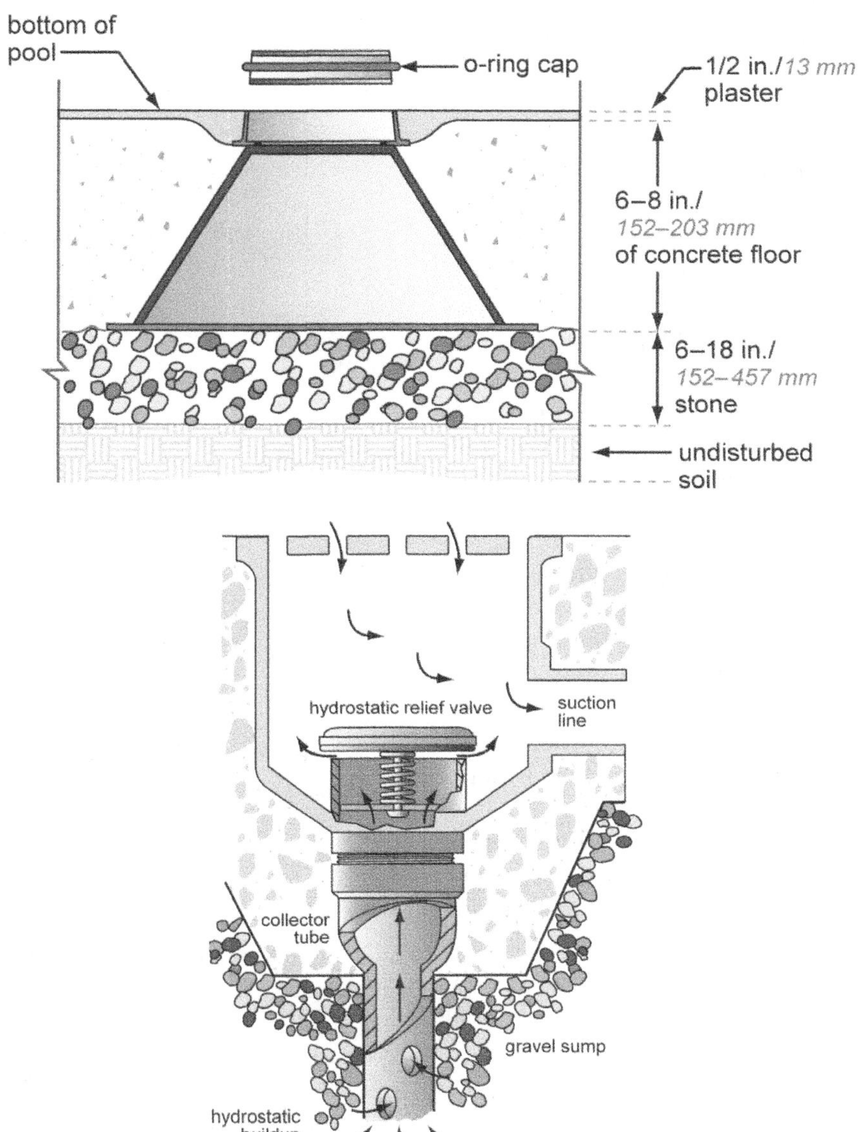

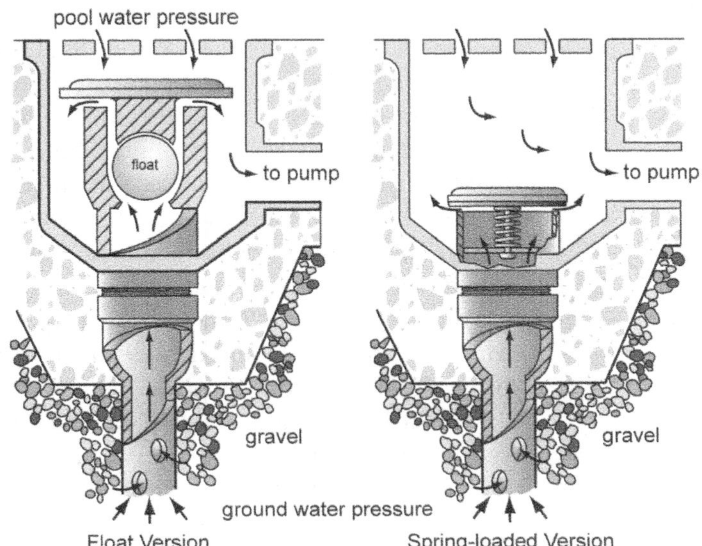

Figure 21.1. Hydrostatic pressure relief valves to protect pools surrounded by high water tables. These hydrostatic pressure release valves allow external ground water to enter the pool when emptied without damaging the pool shell. (Courtesy of Rizzo Pool Construction, Aquatic Consultants)

Blowing lines dry has become an area of expertise in the pool industry. Pool technicians isolate equipment and lines throughout the circulation system and then systematically drain and blow them dry. Although some technicians cap or plug all lines and close all valves, some experts prefer to leave valves returning to the filter room equipment open to allow invading water room to move in case it freezes. This process usually begins in the filter room where the filter, heater, and pump are drained with drain plugs remaining open. The lines are usually blown dry from the filter room back to the pool, and this includes the main drain line.

When a vinyl-lined pool is winterized, the risk of "floating" is not as great as with a concrete or fiberglass pool, but vinyl-lined pools should still remain nearly full during the winter. If vinyl-lined pools are emptied completely, the liner can shrink, wrinkle, or crack. Another precaution must be taken when "shocking" the pool for winter. Postseason shocking with sanitizer is recommended to prevent algae growth, but if the sanitizer level becomes too high in a vinyl pool, the liner can be bleached or damaged. Some experts recommend keeping shocking levels below 6 to 8 ppm, whereas others urge the use of lithium hypochlorite, which is not as harsh on liners as other sanitizers.

The water should be balanced for the winter in the same fashion as for the summer. The only other precaution that should be taken is the addition of an algaecide. Although a winterized pool does not have much light or warm water, the water will remain stagnant for long periods, so algae growth can become a problem in the fall and spring if an algaecide is not added.

Figure 21.2. Pool chairs in desperate need of cleaning. (Photo courtesy of Casual Refinishing)

Pool Decks and Equipment

After the pool shell has been winterized, attention must be turned to the pool deck and its equipment. Once the deck has been completely cleaned, of utmost concern is protecting the pool deck from the damage inflicted by freezing water. All construction joints, expansion joints, and other areas where two solid materials meet should be carefully protected with quality caulking or other long-lasting sealants. If water enters these joints or other cracks and then freezes, the pool deck will deteriorate rapidly.

While the pool deck is being protected, all deck equipment should also be cared for. Ladders, diving boards, lifeguard chairs, pool furniture, and safety equipment should be removed from the pool deck and stored indoors if possible. Any nuts, bolts, and washers used to secure these items in place should also be stored, but only after heavy lubrication to prevent rust and corrosion. The winter months are a great time to refurbish lawn furniture. Some companies now pick up pool furniture during the fall and refurbish, re-strap, and repaint it, store it for the winter, and then return it during the late spring, all for a reasonable price.

When ladders and handrails are removed, the anchors, cups, and bolts should be placed in a bag and tied to the ladder or handrail so that they are not misplaced.

Chemicals Commonly Used for Winterizing

Winterizing chemicals fall into four major categories:

- Sanitizers: Calcium hypochlorite (cal hypo), lithium hypochlorite (lithium hypo), sodium dichlor, sodium hypochlorite (liquid chlorine), gas chlorine, nonchlorine microbicide (Baquacil), and bromine (activated by addition of a high level of oxidizer such as chlorine, ozone, or potassium peroxymonosulfate)
- Algaecides: Copper, silver, quats, polymers, herbicides, chlorine enhancers, and algae inhibitors
- Stain and scale preventers: Sequestering agents, chelating agents, and pH adjusters
- Maintenance chemicals: Antifreeze, tile cleaner, cover cleaner and protectant, polish, clarifier, filter cleaner, and enzymes (Courtesy *Service Industry News*)

The same is true for lifeguard stands. Diving board bolts must be greased and stored with the board.

Water fountains should have the supply water turned off and should be drained, removed, and stored in a warm, dry place.

Circulation and Filtration Equipment

To prevent rusting and overall deterioration of circulation and filtration equipment, special care must be taken to protect it during the winter. Basically, all equipment should be drained of water, cleaned, lubricated, and removed to a warm, dry place. Any parts that show signs of rust should be scraped and painted with a rust retardant. Each of the following items must be carefully protected.

The Pump

The power to the pump should be turned off and the terminal box should be weatherproofed. All water must be drained from the pump. If the pump is left outside and water remains inside the pump, the freezing water could cause it to crack. Whenever possible, the pump should actually be removed to a warm, dry place. If the pump cannot be removed, it should be cleaned, lubricated, and then covered. When pumps and motors are covered for the winter, they should not be completely sealed because condensation that forms will not be allowed to escape, thus damaging the pump. The lid and basket for the hair and lint strainer should also be removed. The strainer basket is an ideal place to keep freeze plugs and other pool parts. A light coating of grease should be applied to the hair strainer lid and pot. The off-season is a good time to have the pump sent out for inspection, overhaul, or repairs.

The Filters

All filters should be backwashed and cleaned before the winterizing process begins. The pressure relief valves should be opened on pressure systems and drain plugs removed so that all water is removed. Sand beds should be inspected and cleaned as needed, and in the case of diatomaceous earth (DE) filters, the filter elements should be removed, inspected, cleaned, and repaired. They should also be covered to protect them from rodents and debris.

Pipes and Plumbing

All water must be turned off. All drain plugs should be removed, lubricated, and stored in a safe place. Standing water cannot be allowed to remain in the pipes. Experts should be consulted if questions arise concerning winterizing pipes and plumbing. All valves should be opened and kept open during the winter unless the system is below the normal operating water level of the pool. Opening the valves allows the water to drain from them, particularly if a poolside plug is dislodged.

Chlorinators and Chemical Feeders

Chlorinators and chemical feeders must be drained of water and cleaned for the winter. Parts such as injectors, diaphragms, and check valves must be cleaned carefully and lubricated. Whenever possible, chlorinators and feeders should be moved to a warm, dry place. Chlorinators should be kept dry during the winter to prevent corrosion. The off-season is perhaps the best time to overhaul or repair this equipment.

Pressure Gauges and Flow Meters

Both pressure gauges and flow meters should be unscrewed, have water removed, be dried, be lubricated, and be stored in a safe place. All small parts should be bagged and marked. Many pool operators tie these bags to the hair and lint strainer or another larger associated apparatus.

Chemicals

Chemicals must be dealt with during the colder months. If possible, chemicals should be returned to the supplier. Dry chemicals must be tightly sealed and kept dry and off the ground. Liquid chemicals and reagents must not be allowed to freeze. It is important to know the shelf life of each of the remaining chemicals as the end of the season approaches. For example, sodium hypochlorite has a short shelf life, and storing it over the winter will only result in wasting the chemical. Sodium hypochlorite must be ordered conservatively at the end of the season. If liquid chlorine is still remaining when the pool closes, it should be used in the pool for superchlorination or other pool sanitation chores. Empty chlorine gas cylinders should be returned to the chemical supplier. Test kits and reagents should be moved to a warm, dry, safe environment, but it may be wise to discard reagents at the end of the season and to purchase fresh reagents at the beginning of the next season. Algaecides should be kept on hand during the off-season in case warm periods are experienced while the pool is closed.

Other Equipment

Pool Heater

The power source to the heater must be turned off. The water must be drained and the heating elements should be cleaned according to the manufacturer's recommendations.

Pool Lights

Pool lights must be protected from freezing water. Power to the lights must be turned off at the circuit box. Wet niche lights should be removed from a full pool that is being winterized. Once out of the water, lights should be inspected for damage and leakage, repaired, and then lubricated. The gaskets require special attention. Whenever possible, lights should be boxed or wrapped and kept in a warm, dry place. If lights are left on the pool deck, vandalism must be prevented. Another approach to dealing with underwater lights is to weigh them down after removing them from their niche and to sink them to the pool bottom after weighting them with a brick. Extra care must be taken to avoid cracking the lens when lowering them to the bottom of the pool.

Safety Equipment

All safety equipment must be moved indoors and kept dry. Self-contained breathing apparatus (SCBA) systems need to be stored indoors, protected from the weather and vandalism. First aid kits should be inventoried and stocked with replacement items before the winter. If this is done, fewer tasks will be required in the spring. Ring buoys, reaching poles, rescue tubes, and other equipment should be covered, stored indoors, and kept together. All ropes and lines should be neatly coiled and stored to save hours of work untangling them in the spring.

Maintenance Equipment

All cleaning and maintenance equipment should be stored together and organized. Tool boxes should be cleaned out and replacement tools purchased in the fall. All brushes, poles, vacuums, hoses, and other cleaning tools should be inspected, repaired, and replaced as needed. Again, the off-season is when these time-consuming tasks must be completed, not during the preseason.

Equipment needs should be evaluated as the pool is being winterized while these needs are still fresh in the minds of the pool operators. In many respects, running a seasonal swimming pool is like farming. A successful summer season often depends on how much effort is exercised in the off-season. A slow, organized winterization program in the fall will most certainly lead to an easier and safer opening of the pool during the upcoming season.

Locker Rooms

Locker rooms deserve special attention, particularly because of the risk of frozen pipes leading to showers, sinks, and toilets. All lines should be drained and blown dry to prevent freezing. Mirrors should be covered with cardboard to prevent breakage, particularly if pool equipment is to be stored in the bathhouse during the off-season. The locker rooms should be protected against rodents and vandals; doors and windows must be locked securely. After the locker rooms have been thoroughly winterized, the water must be turned off for the winter.

Pool Covers

Many covers are available for the winterization of swimming pools. The most commonly used covers are winter covers and safety covers. Winter covers are large, solid, vinyl fabric covers that are held down with sandbags or water bags (Figure 21.3). The purpose of the winter cover is solely to keep debris such as leaves and dirt from entering the pool. They are often held down with water bags or sandbags, but the trend is moving toward a strap or cable locking system that anchors these covers to the pool deck because the weighted bags often break. One disadvantage of the solid cover is that large amounts of water can collect on the surface, making it difficult to remove during the spring. One advantage of the solid vinyl winter cover is that it is relatively inexpensive.

Figure 21.3. Large winter cover. (Photo courtesy of Penn State University)

Figure 21.4. Security cover used in winter.

Safety covers are strong polypropylene mesh covers that can support people and pets that might mistakenly wander onto the cover. They are anchored to the pool deck with a cable system and can withstand a great amount of weight (Figure 21.4). They allow rain and melted snow to pass through the cover, but they keep all solid objects out of the pool. Safety mesh covers are used for winterizing but also provide a large margin of security. Another advantage of these security covers is that glass bottles tossed into the pool bounce harmlessly on the cover without breaking on the bottom of the pool.

Dr. Tom's Tip

I now recommend security covers for all outdoor pools during the off-season. Not only will these covers save you a lot of money in springtime cleaning, but they will save you significant worries as well; they are real lifesavers.

Some automatic pool covers are solid pool covers that secure the pool at night during the season, but they can also be used to winterize the pool.

Superchlorination or heavy algaecide use may damage some pool covers. If water chemistry is going to change drastically when a pool is covered, the manufacturer's recommendations must be followed closely. In addition, regardless of the type of cover used, the perimeter must be fastened down sufficiently to prevent the wind from getting under the cover and displacing it.

Perimeter Security

The perimeter of the pool must be securely fenced in before the pool is closed for the winter. The fence should be at least 8 ft tall, but many aquatic facilities have taller fences. All holes, gaps, and other points of unauthorized entry must be sealed. Locks should be checked to ensure that they are in working order. The police should be notified when the pool is closed, and their advice should be sought for protecting the property against trespassers. Although chain-link fence is perhaps the most popular and practical exterior fence for aquatic facilities, some suggest that it offers handholds and footholds, making it easy to climb. If affordable, a tall vertical slat fence may be superior to a chain-link fence.

In addition to fencing, lighting is important. Mercury vapor or other bright lights should be installed. A security system should be considered if fencing is inadequate. Electronic or battery-operated appliances should also be removed from the pool premises and secured in a warm, dry, safe environment. This includes walkie-talkies, bullhorns, radios, televisions, VCRs, computers, and cash registers.

Utilities

The last step in the winterizing process is the cancellation of utilities, including water, gas, and electric. Although water should be turned off, some swimming facilities have electricity maintained in the filter room and bathhouses so that they can be checked during the off-season. Also, if the electricity is left on, heat bulbs can be controlled with a timer to control moisture. This is particularly true in the filter room.

Summary

Too often, when aquatic facilities (small or large) close for the winter, the owners or operators do not take sufficient time to winterize properly. All pools should be closed for the off-season slowly, deliberately, and completely to protect against cold, moisture, insects, rodents, and vandalism. Lack of use, particularly in a moist, cold environment, often destroys pool equipment prematurely. Opening an aquatic facility for the summer is also a comprehensive task. But the harder one works in closing a pool for the winter, the easier it will be to open for summer. Above all, the aquatic facility and the vessel itself must be protected from unauthorized entry. Drowning should never happen during the off-season at an aquatic facility, but unfortunately it does because facilities closed for the winter are not adequately protected.

Dr. Tom's Tip

If you have drained your aquatic facility in the past years, consider winterizing with a full pool this upcoming season. Take note of your repairs and expenses between an empty pool and a full pool. You may be surprised at the results.

References

Herman, E. (1991). *Pool and Spa News,* Los Angeles. Retrieved from www.poolspanews.com/

Walsh, M. (1992). *Aquatics International, July/August,* 17–21. Retrieved from www.aquaticsintl.com/

Bibliography

Aquatics International, Communications Channels, Atlanta. Retrieved from www.aquaticsintl.com/

Association of Pool & Spa Professionals. (2014). www.APSP.org

Gabrielson, A. M. (1987). *Swimming pools: A guide to their planning, design, and operation* (4th ed.). Champaign, IL: Human Kinetics.

Kowalsky, L. (Ed.). (1991). *Pool/spa operators handbook.* San Antonio, TX: National Swimming Pool Foundation.

Pool and Spa News, Los Angeles. Retrieved from www.poolspanews.com/

Pope, J. R., Jr. (1991). *Public swimming pool management: I and II.* Alexandria, VA: National Recreation and Park Association.

Williams, K. G., & Young, R. A. (Eds.). (2011). *Aquatic facility operator manual* (6th ed.). Ashburn, VA: National Recreation and Park Association.

Appendix 1: APSP Winterizing Tips for Pools, Spas, and Hot Tubs

Retrieved from www.deschutes.org

APSP Bulletin: Winterizing Tips for Pools, Spas, and Hot Tubs

Off-Season Maintenance in Mild Climates

In mild climates during the off-season, pool and spa operations should be maintained at all normal levels. These include maintaining the water level, continuing regular sanitizer schedules, and retaining proper pH, total alkalinity, and calcium hardness levels. Circulating unheated water through the entire system will generally keep the equipment reasonably free of problems, even during occasional freezing periods.

The entire system can be operated intermittently, or on a timer set for when the sun is down or the weather is cooler. Make sure that the timer can be overridden if there is any danger that the equipment might freeze.

Twice-a-month cleaning is recommended for optimum care; at least once a month is the minimum. Uncovered pools and spas must be kept free of debris, such as leaves and other materials.

Winterizing a Pool in Severe Climates

In climates where freezing temperatures are normal, a pool or spa should be completely winterized by cleaning, treating water (if left standing), and protecting the pool/spa and equipment from weather-related problems. It is necessary to winterize the plumbing, equipment, and pool structure before they freeze. Check the structure and all equipment to make sure everything is in safe and proper working order. Have repairs made during the off-season. Standard procedures for winterizing are provided below, but not every type of equipment is covered. Be sure to check the manufacturer's product information.

1. Water Cleaning: Vacuum thoroughly. Vacuum wastewater to the appropriate location. If the filter does not have a "waste" position, vacuum on "filter" position only. Where appropriate, use a portable pump to vacuum directly to waste.

2. Water Treatment: Test the water. Balance the pH, calcium hardness, and total alkalinity. Chemically treat the water with sanitizer, stabilizer, and algaecide just as you would at other times, or treat with a proper amount of special winterizing chemicals. This treatment is important so that water will not become corrosive when the temperature reaches the freezing point. Depending on the chemicals, some are added before draining, and some are added just before putting on a cover.

3. Lower Water Level: Here are suggested winter water levels for different types of pools, with or without solid material covers or mesh covers. Consult your cover manufacturer's literature.

a. <u>Vinyl-lined:</u> 1 inch/2.5 cm below skimmer mouth, but lower in areas of heavy rain and snow precipitation.

b. <u>Plaster finish with solid material cover:</u> 1 to 6 inches/2.5 to 15 cm below the skimmer mouth or tile line, whichever is lower.

c. <u>Painted or natural finish with solid material cover:</u> 6 inches/15 cm below skimmer mouth.

d. <u>With mesh cover or no cover:</u> 18 to 24 inches/45 to 61 cm below skimmer mouth.

(Cont.)

Appendix I (Cont.)

e. <u>With automatic covers:</u> water level should not be lower than bottom of skimmer mouth.

Hydrostatic pressure can destroy a drained concrete pool if proper precautions are not taken (e.g., leaving the bottom drain valves open). If in doubt, it is best to leave the pool almost full of water.

4. Piping and Valves: Drain and blow water out of all piping, and fill pipes with a pool-winterizing antifreeze solution. This includes skimmer and main drain lines, return lines, and lines to solar heaters, cleaners, chlorinators, and other accessories. The pump, filter, and heater will also be drained. To blow water out of circulation piping, use a tank vacuum cleaner on reverse flow or an air compressor. A non-toxic antifreeze solution of one part propylene glycol to two parts water should protect water from freezing to 10°F/-12°C and allow for possible dilution by water still left in the pipes. Never use an automobile antifreeze.

Valves must be thoroughly drained and kept water-free. Be sure that any valves below the water level are sealed securely. Any lines below water level that are exposed to freezing but cannot be drained or filled with an antifreeze solution must be protected with an electric heat tape. Follow the manufacturer's instructions.

5. Accessory Equipment: Remove ladders, diving boards, and handrails. Rinse with clear water. Store in a cool, dry place. Diving boards should be stored flat, if possible.

6. Lights: Remove pool lights from their niches if they have less than 18 inches/45 cm of water over them. Either cover them with plastic and place on the deck, or weight them, if necessary, and lower to the bottom of the pool. Make sure that the breaker is turned off or that the fuse is removed so that the light cannot be turned on accidentally.

7. Pumps and Motors: Drain the pump by removing drain plugs provided for this purpose. These plugs should be left out so that condensation cannot build up within the casing and freeze in cold weather. Another method is to remove all water from the pump housing and strainer compartment using a wet/dry shop vacuum and add ½ cup to 1 cup/0.12 to 0.24L of antifreeze to the housing without removing the drain plugs. Then replace the strainer/pump lid.

Disconnect the power that leads to the motor if you are removing the motor. In northern climates, the motor is often removed from the pump housing and stored in a warm, dry location.

If there is a timer, be sure to remove the timer lugs and set to the "off" position. The circuit breaker should be turned off, or the fuses should be removed from the pool circuit.

When winterizing cast iron pumps, coat all drain-hole threads with the proper lubricant to prevent corrosion during the winter.

8. Filters: In general, all filters should be thoroughly cleaned before shutting them down. Do not leave water in any filter, and make certain that the open valves cannot leak water into the filter.

a. Backwash sand filters three to five times longer than normal. This can be done as the water is lowered, but not while vacuuming. A sand cleaner can be used during this process. Remove the drain plug and open any drain cocks, as well as the air relief on top of the filter. Then put the multi-port valve in the "winter" position. Inspect the sand bed and complete repairs, if needed. This requires removing the lid from the filter. Put the lid back on the filter, but do not seal it. Leave the air relief valve open.

b. Backwash DE filters, drain them, take out the elements, and check them. These elements need to be soaked in a special cleaning solution. This cleaning process may reveal small tears in the fabric. After cleaning the inside of the tank, re-install the elements or store them indoors. In either case, reassemble the filter body, and do not fully tighten the filter lid. This will relieve pressure on the gasket during the winter.

(Cont.)

Appendix I (Cont.)

c. With vacuum-type DE units, the drain should be left partially open. For pools located outside hard-freeze areas, the filters can be cleaned in the spring since they will be used occasionally in the off-season.

d. With cartridge filters, remove the cartridge, clean it, and store it where it can dry out. Then drain the cartridge filter body (tank) and leave the filter cap loosely attached to the filter body. As an alternative, remove water from the filter body with a wet/dry shop vacuum, add ½ cup to 1 cup/0.12 to 0.24L antifreeze, and reinstall the cartridge in the filter body.

All filters should be drained completely after winterizing the lines and pump. Leave drain plugs out, but grease the threads with a heavy grease to avoid rusting or corrosion.

Winterizing an Inground Spa

In general, do not leave an inground spa empty for the winter, as hydrostatic pressure in the ground can damage or destroy it. Following are normal procedures for winterizing an inground spa.

1. Drain the Spa Completely: Follow all regulations regarding disposal of spa water. Check local codes. Be sure to turn on the blower to get all water out of the air channel. You may have to use a wet/dry vacuum or sponge.

2. Blow out all Plumbing Lines and Piping.

3. Non-toxic Antifreeze: Add a non-toxic antifreeze solution—such as one part propylene glycol to two parts water—to all pipes and blow lines until it appears at spa fittings. *Never* use toxic automobile antifreeze. Then plug the lines and install a quart-sized (liter-sized) bottle filled with sand or gravel in the skimmer. Fill skimmer body with antifreeze. Remove the weir.

4. Beware of Hydrostatic Ground Pressure: Inground spas are not left empty in areas where hydrostatic ground pressure may pop an empty inground spa out of the ground. Place vinyl or black poly sheeting, at least 6 mils/15mm thick, in the bottom of the spa to form a liner. Fill the spa with water to the bottom of the skimmer. This liner equalizes pressure and keeps water out of the pipes.

5. Drain Filter Pumps, Air Blower, and Heater: Follow the appropriate winterizing procedures for all equipment. Always check the manufacturer's product manual. Remove and store in an area safe from freezing.

6. Keep Water Below Skimmer: If water builds up in the spa before freezing weather, pump it out to keep water just below the skimmer. If you will not be checking the spa periodically, leave the spa empty enough to accommodate some build-up of water.

(Cont.)

Appendix I (Cont.)

Winterizing a Hot Tub

Following are steps for winterizing a manufactured hot tub.

1. Power off: Turn off the circuit breaker for the hot tub's electrical line or, if possible, unplug the unit.

2. Drain the Hot Tub: Remove the cover and drain the hot tub. Use the hot tub drain line and/or a submersible pump to be sure you get all the water out. If you use a submersible pump, be sure to open drains you can find once the hot tub is empty.

3. Clean the Filters: Remove and clean the filters. Have the owner store them in his/her basement or garage.

4. Check the Blower for Water: If the hot tub has a blower, turn it on when the hot tub is empty to clear out any water in the air channel.

5. Remove Standing Water: Vacuum or mop out any standing water. Use a wet/dry shop vacuum to suck or blow any water out of the jets, skimmers, and suction fittings.

6. Use Non-toxic Antifreeze: Pour non-toxic antifreeze that does not contain ethanol into the skimmer, and try to get it into as many jets and suction fittings as you can. (Check the ingredients carefully—ethanol can damage rubber or synthetic seals, yet some swimming pool antifreeze products contain it.) You can use the wet/dry shop vacuum to blow the antifreeze through the plumbing.

7. Winterize the Equipment Area: Check the pumps for drain plugs, heaters, and any places water might gather. Loosen the unions of pumps and heaters. Remove any drain plugs that may be on the pump housing. If you are in a particularly difficult environment, you may want to remove the pumps for storage in a less-exposed place, such as a basement or garage.

8. Use a Cover: Cover the hot tub with the cover; strap in place. Check that the cover is in good shape and not leaking water into the hot tub. The cover's surface should repel water, and its shape should slope toward the outside to shed rainwater or snow.

9. Secure the Hatch Door: Close and secure the equipment hatch door. Vermin will often try to nest inside hot tub cabinets over the winter. If they gain access, they can chew wires and cause expensive damage. Products are available to discourage rodents from entering the hot tub enclosure.

To return the hot tub to service, simply reverse the winterization process, being careful to purge the plumbing lines in the process.

For more information about servicing manufactured hot tubs, contact APSP (**memberservices@APSP.org**) to order a copy of the *APSP Hot Tub Technician Manual.* For information about servicing pools and spas, order a copy of the *APSP Service Tech Manual.*

Section V
Safety, Supervision, and Risk Management

Although the chapters in this section appear to be quite different, the major theme is preventing accidents and lawsuits by promoting education and safety. Chapter 22 deals with the psychological aspects of lifeguarding, which is rare to find in other texts and sets this book apart. This chapter includes a new introduction by Daniel Simons, adding a cognitive psychologist's perspective on lifeguarding. Specifically, this chapter deals with the psychological aspects of lifeguarding that have been largely ignored by the training agencies. Maslow's Heirarchy of Needs, Flow Theory, and other proven psychological concepts will be discussed, along with their pertinence to lifeguarding. This information is meant to supplement, not replace, the lifeguarding texts.

Chapter 23 emphasizes the importance of proactive prevention through mindful, active lifeguarding over reactive resuscitation that often comes too little too late. The information on preventive lifeguarding offers a unique approach to lifeguarding education. Rather than discussing skills and knowledge that lifeguards should possess, this chapter concentrates on the art of lifeguarding—particularly vigilance, surveillance, scanning, and mindfulness—not often mentioned in other texts. An emphasis of this chapter will also be placed on the supervision of lifeguards. This chapter should be beneficial to lifeguards wishing to improve their supervision of swimmers and managers wishing to improve their supervision of lifeguards. An important distinction is made here between life saving and guarding. Special topics such as the lifeguard blindness, the RID factor, the 10/20 rule, the five-minute scanning strategy, high-risk patrons, and motivating lifeguards are also discussed. Again, this chapter should be viewed as a supplement to the existing lifeguarding texts.

Much of the information contained here cannot be found elsewhere. Chapter 24, Shallow Water Blackout, could possibly be the most important addition in the third edition. The extensive, in-depth discussion informs readers how to prevent this death in good swimmers in their aquatic facilities. When it comes to competitive, repetitive, and prolonged breath-holding and underwater swimming in your aquatic facilities, just don't allow it! Chapter 25 informs the reader about the latest advances in warning signage. Readers should find the Five Cs of signage helpful yet easy to accomplish. Chapter 26 is perhaps the most comprehensive treatment of headfirst entries and specifically deals with accidents caused by headfirst entries into shallow water and springboard diving. The thrust of this chapter is not to encourage pool owners and operators to remove their diving boards from their facilities, but rather to show them how to make diving safer. However, we now know that headfirst diving requires much deeper water than was initially thought. It is very difficult to dive safely in most residential pools. If pool personnel could prevent all adults from entering headfirst into less than nine feet of water, headfirst entries would no longer be much of a risk at swimming facilities. Poor judgment, a lack of common sense, and alcohol consumption often contribute to neck injuries at swimming pools. This chapter stresses the value of education, effective signage, and supervision in preventing these catastrophic accidents. When it comes to existing 3m boards, however, they must either be removed or renovated to make them fall-proof onto the deck below.

Chapter 27 is another new and important chapter that explains in detail the Virginia Graeme Baker Pool and Spa Safety Act, which illustrates the hazards of unprotected drains and outlets in all types of pools and tubs. Speaking in terms of cold, hard cash, a drowning could cost an aquatic facility up to $1 million; a catastrophic neck injury could reach up to a $9 million verdict, whereas an entrapment accident could result in a financial award of between $29 million to $35 million! Following the requirements of the VGBA, however, will eliminate all worries of accidents and liability when it comes to suction entrapments.

Chapter 28 takes a quick, common-sense look at practical risk management, including the Seven Deadly Sins of Aquatic Facilities. In Chapter 29, Gareth Hedges from the Redwoods Group explains in detail the importance of insurance and risk management services as it relates to accident prevention and liability. The Redwoods Group is a Risk Management company with proactive strategies for preventing drowning and child sexual abuse. They consult and insure many swimming pools and waterfronts around the country, especially for YMCAs and JCCs. Shawn DeRosa's comprehensive treatment of legal liability and risk management is found in Chapter 30, and is an especially valuable contribution to this book. This chapter educates readers regarding the legal aspects of aquatics, how to safeguard guests, and how to prevent lawsuits, in simple understandable terms.

Chapter 31 deals with planning and coping with emergencies at your aquatic facility. It not only informs how to react to emergencies before they happen but what explains what to do after the emergency, particularly if and when employee stress becomes a problem. Chapter 32 is all about routine operations. This discussion includes daily, weekly, and monthly procedures. Although checklists are a major part of routine operations, much information is offered concerning the philosophy of organized operations, the value of written records, and the importance of a common-sense approach to pool safety and operations. Chapter 33 is a vitally important treatment of safe chemical handling by Dr. Kerry Hoffman Richards, and goes more in-depth than other discussions of safe chemical handling. There is so much to read and learn from just what's on the chemical label!

22

The Psychology of Lifeguarding

Key Concepts

- Internal noise
- Lifeguard distractions
- Lifeguard thoughts and emotions
- The RID Factor
- The Inverted U Hypothesis
- Flow theory
- Hierarchy of Needs

Chapter Introduction by Daniel Simons

Lifeguards have a nearly impossible task. They have to scan a large area while distinguishing the relatively rare event of a child drowning from far more common events that look a lot like drowning, such as swimming underwater, resting on the bottom of the pool, floating on the surface, splashing frantically, and so on. Lifeguards use scanning strategies designed to help them survey the pool and regularly take breaks and change viewing stations to help maintain their vigilance. But even best practices cannot override what are largely structural limits on how individuals see the world.

People think that important events, such as a child in trouble, will automatically grab their attention. In reality, they often do not. The problem is that *looking* is not the same as *seeing*. Airport baggage scanners know exactly where illicit objects might appear, but they regularly miss them. Lifeguards have a much more challenging situation; a child in trouble could be anywhere in the pool. Just because lifeguards' eyes are focused in the right part of a pool does not mean that they will see what is there. And even if they do see what is there, that does not guarantee that they will interpret what they are seeing correctly!

Lifeguards simply cannot see everything. And, as long as they persist in the mistaken belief that important events automatically capture attention, they will continue to pursue strategies that will have minimal benefit. But if they account for these limits, they can begin to develop ways to compensate for the limits of human perception and attention.

—**Dan Simons** is a professor in the Department of Psychology and the Beckman Institute for Advanced Science and Technology at the University of Illinois. His research explores the limits of our own minds and the reasons why we often are unaware of our limits. His first book, *The Invisible Gorilla*, was coauthored by Christopher Chabris and was published in 2010 (by Crown).

Although much has been written on the physical skill and knowledge required of lifeguards, little has been offered in the way of the psychological effects of lifeguarding. Starting more than a century ago, both the American Red Cross and the YMCA of the USA have offered excellent lifeguard training programs. The United States Lifesaving Association likewise has been accrediting primarily safe surf beaches that follow its training programs and has a wonderful safety record at its open-water facilities. More recently, Ellis and Associates and StarGuard, among others, have developed lifeguarding programs to improve water safety through better lifeguard training, and as expected, the competition between training agencies has improved lifeguarding programs and lifesaving techniques. With the skills and knowledge available to lifeguards today, the actual job of lifeguard surveillance can be boring and tedious. Thus, many well-trained and well-intentioned lifeguards can easily become distracted and miss victims in trouble because it is nearly impossible for humans to remain vigilant for long periods of time, particularly young teenagers. Until now, little information has been available to lifeguard instructors and lifeguard candidates regarding the role of psychology in reducing boredom while increasing attention, concentration, and vigilance on duty. This information, although not new, is perhaps new to the water safety world. If reviewed objectively, this information will undoubtedly help lifeguards to increase vigilance and reduce boredom and fatigue, ultimately saving lives. In 2012, groundbreaking research was conducted on the effects of internal noise on lifeguards. Internal noise is cognitive and/or emotional interference, which can distract an individual from a task, especially a task such as lifeguarding. In addition to the other psychological research presented, this research illustrates significant ways lifeguards may not maintain vigilance or mindfulness. This chapter presents important aspects of the psychology of lifeguarding from many perspectives, including external distractions and physiological factors that may produce challenges for lifeguard surveillance.

Lifeguarding: A Paradoxical Profession

Lifeguarding is a peculiar profession. Although lifeguards perform a serious task, for the most part, they are underpaid and overworked. To be a lifeguard requires special training; first aid certification, cardiopulmonary resuscitation (CPR) certification, and lifeguarding certification are usually minimal requirements before potential lifeguards are considered for employment. Rigorous skill tests and on-the-job training often begin once a lifeguard is hired. Most aquatic professionals agree that today's lifeguards are highly trained emergency care professionals, not babysitters. Lifeguarding has many responsibilities associated with it, although financial rewards may not be great. Aquatic facility lifeguards, possessing three certifications and being responsible for protecting and saving lives, often make less money than their peers working in fast-food restaurants. Many areas of the United States have been experiencing lifeguard shortages. This is because better paying jobs are available that do not require as much training to obtain the job, and then once the individual is hired, he or she does not carry the burden of responsibility that comes with lifeguarding. The possibility of being sued in a court of law and contracting communicable diseases are deterrents for young people who at one time thought about becoming lifeguards. Although many water safety professionals encourage increasing the pay and professionalism of lifeguards, in reality, this is not an easy task because most lifeguards are young, seasonal, part-time employees, making it more difficult to increase benefits, pay, and commitment by employees who only work 3 months a year.

Compounding this situation are the many lifeguards, although highly trained and extremely competent in water rescues, who are distracted from watching swimmers in the water. One study of beach lifeguards found that lifeguards focused on swimmers only 51% of the time while on duty. Nearly half of the time on duty, the lifeguards in this study were found looking away from their areas of responsibility. Poseidon Technologies and Ellis and Associates found that lifeguards took an average of 1 minute, 14 seconds to detect a motionless mannequin placed underwater directly in front of them. For the most part, lifeguarding is boring and tedious. In another series of lifeguard surveys conducted at Penn State University (1995), lifeguards responded that one of their greatest challenges was preventing boredom and making the time pass quickly while on duty. Bored lifeguards often become mesmerized with one person or object in or out of the pool and ignore everyone else. This type of tunnel vision in lifeguards is not acceptable and jeopardizes safety of the pool patrons. Most recently, a study was published in the *International Journal of Aquatic Research and Education* (R. Griffiths & Griffiths, 2013) that showed the internal noise lifeguards face while on duty. The study uncovered what lifeguards thought and felt while they were on duty providing patron surveillance.

The International Internal Noise Study

R. Griffiths and Griffiths' (2013) study published in the *International Journal of Aquatic Research and Education* is the first of its kind to discover internal noise that lifeguards face while on duty. The study is consistent with many of the findings revealed in the previous studies mentioned in this chapter. Findings from "Internal Noise Distractions in Lifeguarding" (R. Griffiths & Griffiths, 2013) follow.

Distraction is defined as an "involuntary division of attention" (Sen, 1983, p. 53). External distractions are stimuli originating from an individual's outside environment. Internal noise is more difficult to recognize and more challenging to manage than external distractions. Internal noise is stimuli from thoughts and emotions that can distract an individual from a task. Internal noise can easily distract a lifeguard from focusing on patrons in the water. At the same time, internal noise often cannot be easily detected. When lifeguards have their eyes

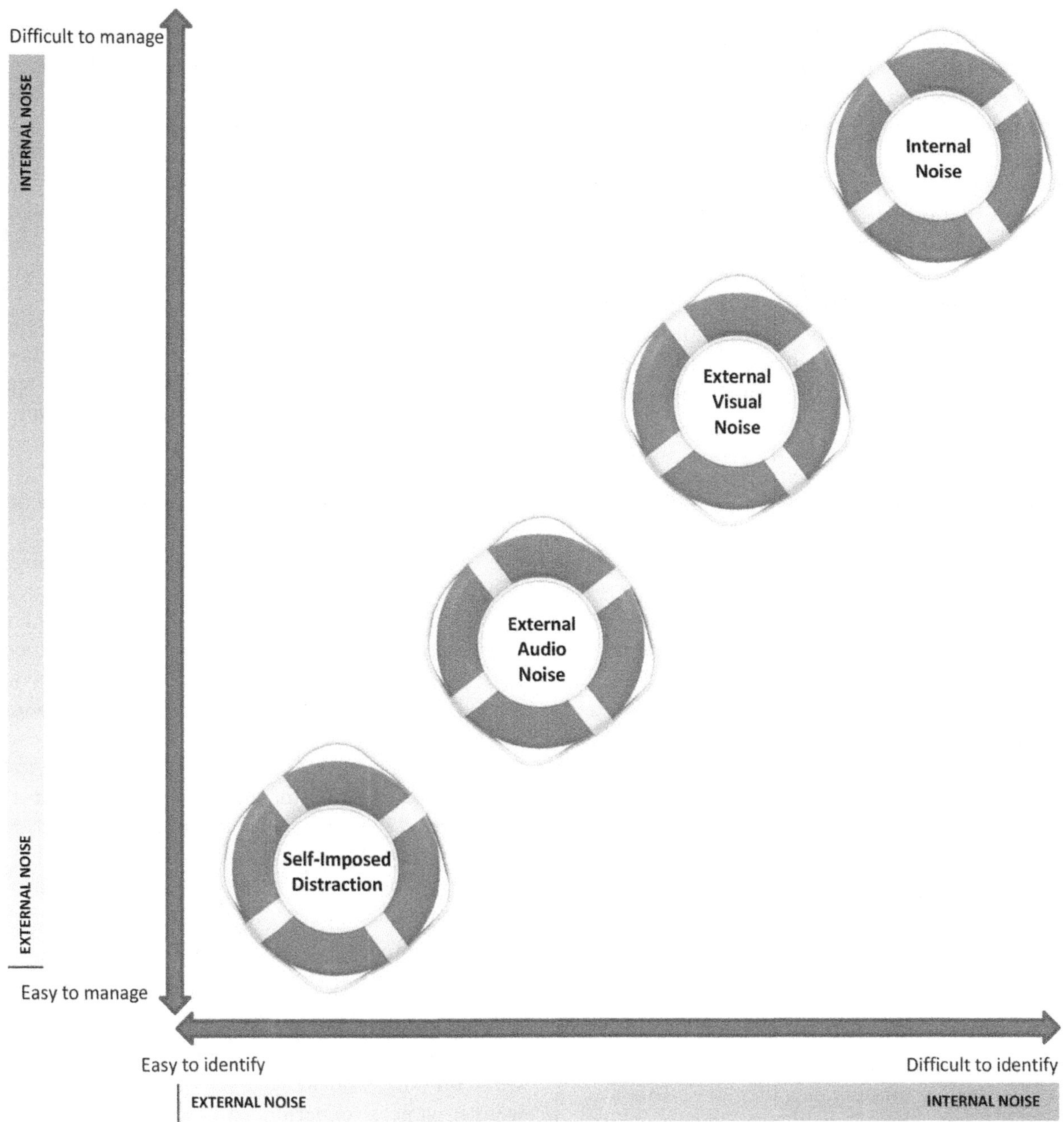

Figure 22.1. External and internal noise distractions ranging from easy to identify and manage to difficult to identify and manage. (© 2013 *International Journal of Aquatic Research and Education*)

on the water, it seems like they are watching the water, both from their own perspective and from others'. Many lifeguards do not realize their own thoughts and emotions may blind them from "seeing." This study explored the degree to which lifeguards reported and experienced internal noise while on duty.

Internal noise is a major distraction because it can significantly reduce focus and mental concentration. "Any drop in mental focus during the performance of safety-sensitive, high risk, or repetitive tasks can result in serious human and financial consequences, includ-

ing death" (Beder & Webb, 2011). Additionally, The National Safety Council (2010) reported that the ability to multitask is a myth. The human brain only processes one stimulus at a time. Even though multitaskers perceive they are effectively engaged, they are less engaged and less effective (Beder & Webb, 2011).

Internal noise is difficult to recognize because lifeguards are constantly experiencing distracting thoughts and emotions. It is difficult or sometimes impossible for an individual to recognize when his or her own thoughts and feelings start to deter from the task at hand and turn into a distraction. It is also challenging for a supervisor or an individual other than the lifeguard to identify whether a lifeguard is mentally disengaged or distracted.

A moderate amount of anxiety enhances performance. On the contrary, too much anxiety can lead to performance detriment (Beder & Webb, 2011). If individuals are anxious about performing a job, they can experience hesitation and uncertainty (Beder & Webb, 2011). In the context of lifeguarding, hesitation can be the difference between life and death when a victim is in the water. Drowning is unique depending on the person and can happen in a matter of seconds. Internal noise can lead to disbelief, denial, and hesitation when a distressed swimmer is present. Delay in turn can lead to drowning or death.

Habits

If focusing on the water is left to automatic behavior, the mind often be distracted by internal noise. "When a habit emerges, the brain stops fully participating in decision making. It stops working so hard or diverts focus to other tasks" (Duhigg, 2012, p. 20). Habits such as scanning and keeping eyes on the water are necessary for lifeguards to know what to do while on duty. However, these habits can also result in excess internal noise. If individuals are lifeguarding solely out of automatic habit, their vigilant behaviors become automatic and may leave space for their minds to think unrelated thoughts. It is paramount to understand, acknowledge, and directly address the type and frequency of internal noise that lifeguards actually face.

Results of the International Internal Noise Study

Thoughts

Participants were asked to list five topics they think about while they are on duty as a lifeguard. This was an open-ended question to which respondents could reveal thoughts that cross their minds while lifeguarding. A text analysis was conducted to decipher the most prevailing thoughts lifeguards had while on duty. The most prominent word participants expressed (239 responses) they thought about while on duty lifeguarding was *pool*. The next most common responses were *relationships* (184 responses), *patrons* (115 responses), *family* (111 responses), *plans after work* (108 responses), *weekend plans* (91 responses), and *doing after work* (76 responses) (Figure 22.2).

Emotions

Lifeguards were asked to describe emotions they feel when they supervise the pool as a lifeguard. This was an open-ended question. A text analysis revealed lifeguards most commonly responded they felt *bored, happy, nervous, calm, responsible, stressed, worried, confident*, and *anxious* while lifeguarding.

Survey participants expressed a wide array of emotions (see Figure 22.3). These were the most explicated from the respondents and revealed that although lifeguards felt positive emotions such as confidence, happiness, and a sense of pride while lifeguarding, many also had dissonant feelings of anxiety, stress, and nervousness. The majority of individuals who felt nervousness or anxiety while lifeguarding were worried about having to make a rescue or missing a victim. For example, specific responses included "When I supervise the pool I feel nervous sometimes because I do not want to let anyone drown" and "I feel nervous; these people are relying on me to keep them and their loved ones safe." Many lifeguards also reported feeling tired, preoccupied, and daydream while on duty.

Phone Use

Figure 22.4 shows how often lifeguards reported talking on the phone while lifeguarding. Figure 22.5 shows the the frequency that lifeguards reported texting while on duty. Considering the participants in the study were in general experienced lifeguards, the number of lifeguards who text while on duty is likely higher than the number captured in the study. The texting while on

Figure 22.2. What lifeguards report thinking about while lifeguarding. (©2013 *International Journal of Aquatic Research and Education*)

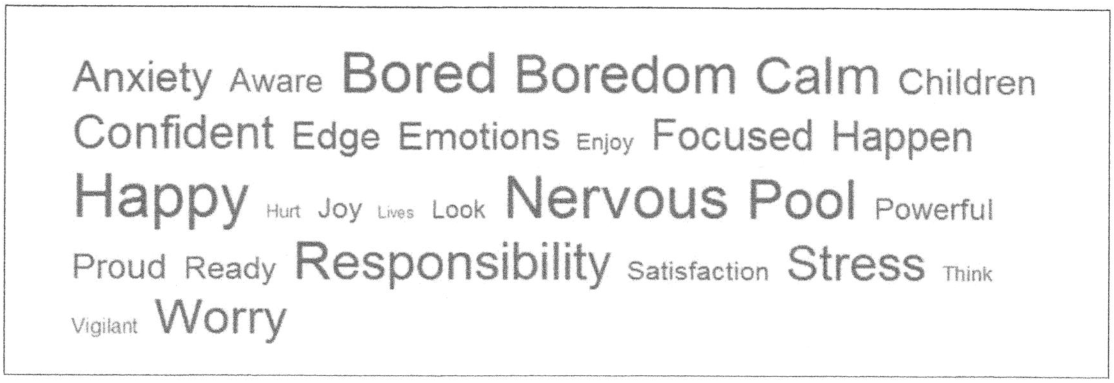

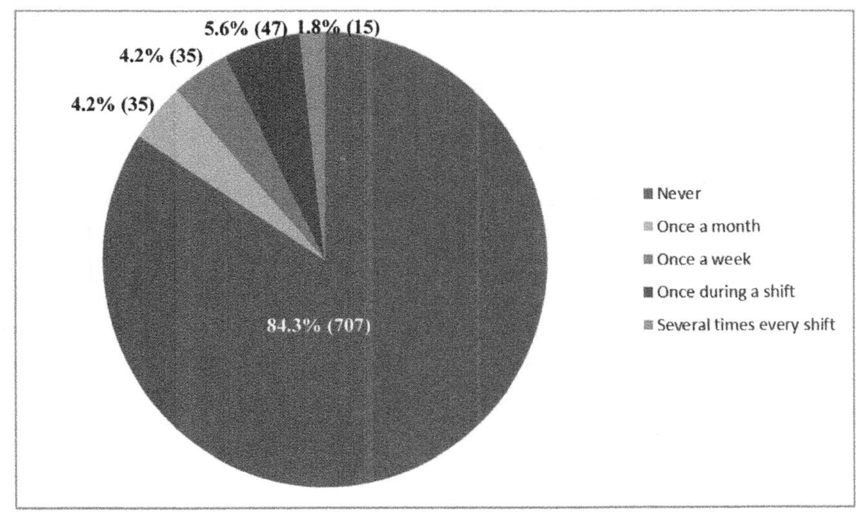

Figure 22.3. What emotions lifeguards report feeling while lifeguarding. (© 2013 *International Journal of Aquatic Research and Education*)

duty findings pose a paradox as well. When the subject of rules regarding cell phone use at work while lifeguarding were addressed in the aquatic professional community, most of the supervisors purported a zero tolerance rule. To address this issue, it would be interesting to discover how the lifeguards are obtaining the access to text while on duty.

Lifeguards should be trained to aggressively scan and maintain mindfulness. Systematic scanning is one of many defensive lifeguarding techniques that should be mastered to be an effective lifeguard. Lifeguards must be trained to expect the unexpected and to make every attempt to prevent accidents instead of making rescues. Making the time meaningful while on duty is important to lifeguards and their supervisors. Strategies will be discussed in Chapter 23.

The RID Factor

Frank Pia studied films of hundreds of near-drowning victims at Orchard Beach on Long Island Sound in New York to help develop his RID theory of unwitnessed drownings (Pia, 1974). He contended that unwitnessed drownings are caused by one or more of the three factors discussed.

Recognition

Pia (1984) claimed that many drownings go unnoticed because lifeguards' perception of how a drowning victim acts on the surface is significantly different from what actually occurs. Victims may hardly struggle. The arm stroke can be similar to a breast stroke or dog paddle and may actually resemble play in the water. They cannot cry out for help because all their effort is spent on breathing. The "struggle" may last between 20 and 60 seconds. Although the image of a drowning victim shifted from the belief a victim would splash erratically and yell for help to a quick, quiet, and subtle victim, recent security camera video footage reveals drowning scenarios that are diverse. Victims may also splash across the pool, bobbing up and down, appearing to be swimming, or may quietly slip beneath the surface without struggle, or may lie face down horizontally in the water and struggle to lift their heads.

Despite these facts, many lifeguards still expect troubled swimmers to display a frantic fight on the surface with plenty of splashing, "white water," and cries for help. On the other hand, if lifeguards are taught to look for a vertical drowning posture exclusively, with little or no movement, with the victim's head tilted slightly

Figure 22.4. Frequencies lifeguards reported talking on the phone while on duty lifeguarding. (© 2013 *International Journal of Aquatic Research and Education*)

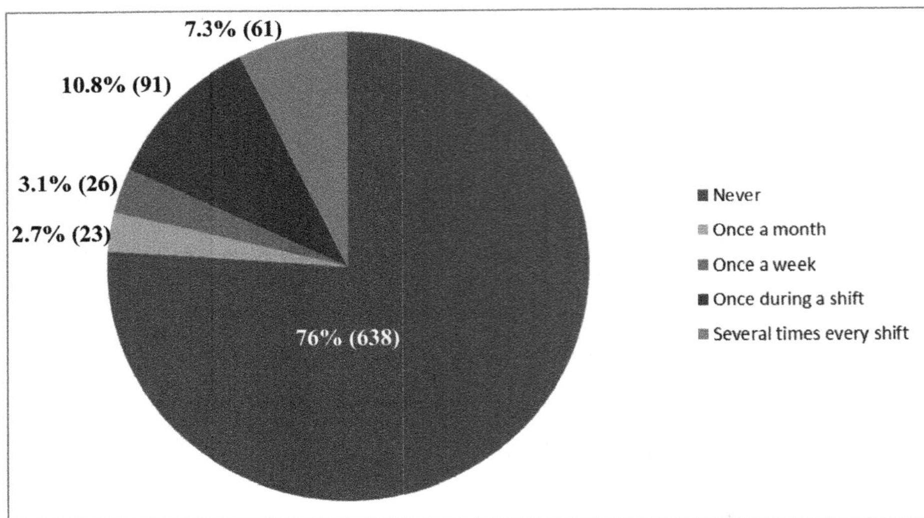

Figure 22.5. Frequencies lifeguards reported texting while on duty lifeguarding. (© 2012 *International Journal of Aquatic Research and Education*)

backward, they may miss victims that either float horizontally on the surface or make erratic forward progress. Perhaps neither should be taught as to "what drowning looks like" because the truth is drowning does not have a certain "look." True, drowning can be quick and quiet, but it is also unpredictable. Security camera footage clearly illustrates to lifeguards ways in which distressed swimmers act in the water. Lifeguards should know that drowning does not necessarily occur in one way. Drowning can vary greatly, and the warning signs are still extremely difficult to detect. The more footage that is viewed of drownings, the more it becomes apparent that "what drowning looks like" may not be able to be communicated to lifeguards. Drowning can be quick, quiet, and subtle, but can be significantly different. Whenever in doubt, lifeguards need to check them out.

Intrusion

Many lifeguards are not able to watch those in the water carefully because they are asked to perform additional tasks unrelated to preventive lifeguarding. This is particularly common at swimming pools. Their eyes are diverted from the water because maintenance tasks such as water testing, backwashing filters, deck cleaning, and other pool maintenance chores are performed while lifeguards are on duty. If lifeguards are expected to safeguard those in the water, they cannot be given tasks that divert their attention away from these swimmers. Pool management often compromises good preventive lifeguarding by asking too much of the lifeguard by overburdening the guards with too many tasks unrelated to water safety. Conversely, lifeguard experts now suggest if lifeguards on duty are not allowed to talk during surveillance or are required to remain still and stoic while working, this can quickly lead to monotony and boredom, thereby reducing vigilance.

Distraction

Perhaps more than any other factor, distractions play a major role in producing poor preventive lifeguarding. Boredom sets in easily for most lifeguards, and when this occurs, their attention tends to drift away from the swimmers in the water. Socializing, horseplay with peers, and generally goofing off can occur in an attempt to cope with boredom. Lifeguards cannot afford to be distracted. To prevent distractions, lifeguards should use systematic scanning techniques that include frequent and regular safety checks to ensure that all patrons are being monitored. Lifeguards must also be supervised while on duty to be certain that they are focused, on target, and continually scanning.

The RID²

In addition to the information from Pia's original RID factor, it is imperative to integrate more recent research, including internal noise. The RID² (see Figure 22.6) is the original RID factor multiplied by "failure to recognize internal distractions." Thoughts and emotions (internal noise) that distract a lifeguard from really seeing the patrons in the water must be understood and considered as significant intrusions and distractions, in addition to external intrusions and distractions.

The Inverted U Hypothesis and Arousal

Since the early 1900s, scholars have known that there is an optimal level of psychological arousal for different physical and mental tasks. In 1908, the Yerkes-Dodson law was formulated that graphically showed very high and very low levels of arousal could be used to predict poor performances. Simply stated, moderate levels of arousal produce the best performances in most cases, and this has been proven to be the case in competitive sports as well. Excessively high levels of arousal produce catastrophic performances, panic, and choking, whereas very low levels of arousal lead to lackadaisical and unmotivated performance (see Figure 22.7).

Many lifeguards feel stressed and anxious at times while lifeguarding, but also feel bored and tired other times. For optimal performance in many simple motor skills and vigilance tasks, there is a happy medium level of arousal. Since the inception of the Yerkes-Dodson law, thousands of articles and books have been written on controlling excessive arousal and anxiety for optimal or peak performance. Staying focused and relaxed in a stressful environment is important to success. The task of lifeguarding often becomes mindless. Mindlessness is an inattention to the present moment that leads to feelings of dullness and boredom. In lifeguarding, it also can lead to delay in an emergency. Lifeguarding training should emphasize shifting from mindless scanning and lifeguarding to mindful scanning and lifeguarding. Mindfulness entails focus in the present moment while minimizing "drifting off." Mindfulness training also is used in many companies to increase productivity among staff. In the field of psychology, mindfulness training can help in many therapies from children with attention deficit disorder to adults with depression. An emphasis on mindfulness rather than mindlessness is important for both improved performance and increased enjoyment for lifeguards.

For activities such as competitive swimming, diving, football, basketball, and golf, a little bit of nervousness is helpful, but too much nervousness is bad and can quickly lead to "choking." Aquatic professionals have asserted for years that a moderate amount of swimmers and/or activities in the aquatic facility produces the best conditions for vigilance, but both very slow days and very busy days can lead to poor lifeguarding performance and a decrease in vigilance. Although conditions with moderate swimmers and/or activities may still be better for vigilance, aquatic professionals now realize that in any situation if scanning becomes too habitual, proactive thinking, judgment, and decision-making skills for victim recognition may decrease.

Lifeguards as Athletes

Although sports psychologists and psychophysiologists have dealt primarily with overarousal and high anxiety in athletes, many lifeguards and their supervisors grapple with low levels of arousal caused by long periods of uneventful surveillance without any hint of "potential drownees." Certainly, low levels of arousal

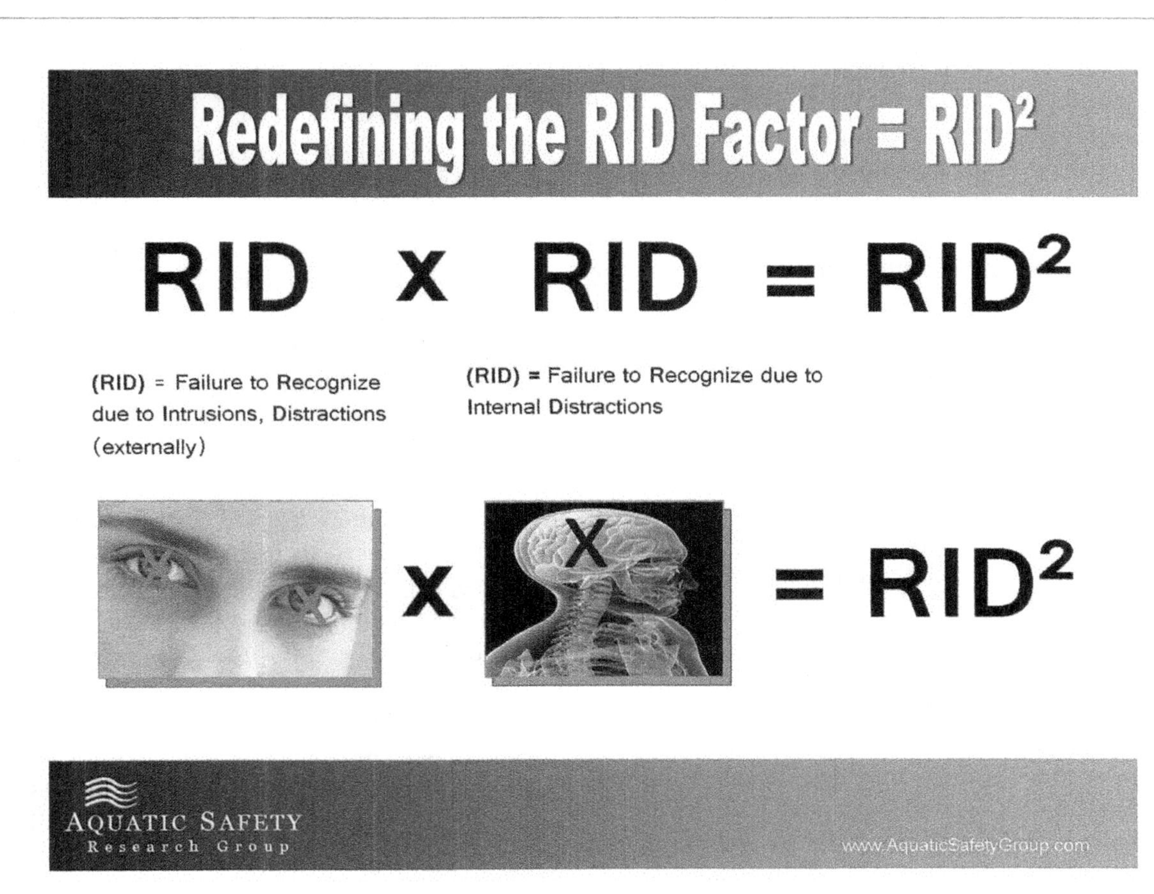

Figure 22.6. The RID factor renewed and revitalized. (© 2013 Aquatic Safety Research Group)

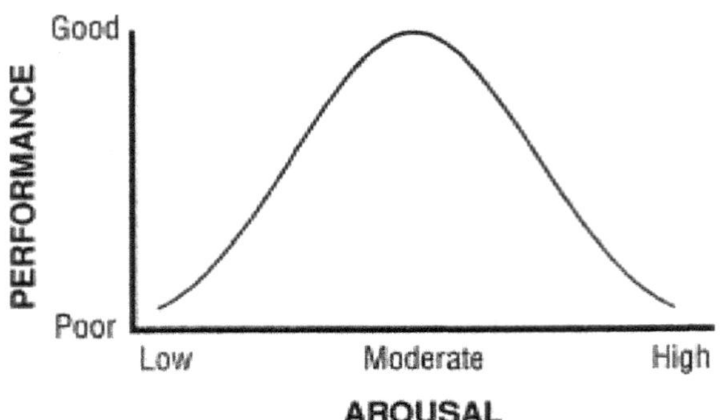

Figure 22.7. Yerkes-Dodson model of performance and arousal.

are not the norm for most ocean guards or lifeguards at busy waterparks with many and varied stimuli, but for the thousands of guards scanning the boring rectangular pools with low attendance in the United States (schools, parks, neighborhoods, hotels, and YMCAs), this is a problem. This can also be a significant problem for ocean and waterpark lifeguards on slow days. The key to effective lifeguarding is constant vigilance and mindfulness, but vigilance and mindfulness are difficult to maintain in a boring, uneventful setting. According to Pieron (1979), "vigilance is the ability to detect unforeseeable and slightly suprathreshold signals." Monotony leads to boredom, which in turn leads to a lack of vigilance, one of the biggest problems in lifeguarding today. Ellis and Associates (2001) performed approximately 500 tests in 90 pools during the summer of 2001. Even though Ellis and Associates lifeguards are comprehensively trained in the "10/20 patron protection rule" requiring 10 seconds to detect a person in trouble and an additional 20-second response time, the average time to detect a lifelike mannequin placed on the bottom of the facility for these well-trained guards was 1 minute, 14 seconds. In this case study, the mannequin was placed directly on the bottom of the pool. Although Ellis and Associates lifeguards have a reputation for being vigilant and for strict adherence to the 10/20 rule, the lifeguards in this study who appeared to be scanning may have been mistakenly concentrating on the surface. The results of this study detected a problem in Ellis and Associates' scanning process that they are now attempting to remedy. During the summer of 2002, the detection time improved to just under 1 minute on average, but this is still too slow for Ellis and Associates lifeguards.

In 2012, the City of Phoenix changed its lifeguard audit system from using staff as victims to mystery shoppers in order to audit lifeguards. The mystery shopping assessments entailed four adolescents who were trained to be unconscious victims in order to test lifeguards' recognition times and rescue skills. For the lifeguard assessments, the "victims" lay face-down on the surface of the water, breathing through a straw until a lifeguard or another person retrieved them from the water. Three lifeguards out of 32 recognized the victim within 10 seconds, most of the lifeguards recognized the victims after 45 seconds, and five never did.

The problem of vigilance is not exclusively a lifeguarding phenomenon, but also afflicts pilots, automobile drivers, and other surveillance personnel. Since there has been more research conducted in these other areas of surveillance, it may be prudent to apply these findings to lifeguards on duty.

Flying and Driving

While much has been written and researched on high states of arousal, little has been conducted on low levels of arousal and boredom, and even less has been written about lifeguard vigilance. At low levels of arousal during any surveillance task, it is almost impossible to maintain attention, concentration, and vigilance for extended periods of time. Most of what aquatic professionals know about lifeguard vigilance is inferred from research results compiled in other fields of study.

During World War II, studies on vigilance and sustained attention began out of necessity. The Royal Air Force commissioned psychologist Norman Mackworth to study a dangerous phenomenon: Airborne radar operators were missing important blips on their screens after short periods while performing this simple surveillance task. It was thought that if radar operators could easily miss German submarines on their screens, control tower personnel and airport security (and lifeguards in our case) may be experiencing the same problems while on duty. Numerous studies confirmed that half of the vigilance decrement was occurring during the first 30 minutes on watch, but some decrements also started as early as 15 minutes into surveillance. Another aspect of these studies deals with the complexity or difficulty of the task being performed. For optimal performance, a higher level of arousal or activation is needed for simple tasks and a lower level of arousal is needed for more difficult tasks.

Scientists then learned that physiological strategies could be used to increase vigilance. Mild physical exercise, sensory stimulation, and even changes in environmental temperatures may increase attentiveness of individuals performing simple surveillance tasks. Using nuclear station control room operators, Coblentz and Cabon (1994) found in 1992 in Paris, France, improvements in vigilance when operators worked in teams of two and alternated between active and passive surveillance with frequent changes in activities. This finding may be beneficial in some lifeguarding situations. In his 1970 book, *Vigilance and Attention,* Mackworth found that frequent short breaks and even changes in activities can lead to increased vigilance. Other studies also found that the more noncritical signals observers must examine over a long period of time, the less likely they are to detect the critical signs. Of course, this would likewise be true for lifeguards working at slow pools with few accidents or rescues. Jerison and Pickett discovered in 1964 that vigilance actually increased with the frequency of critical signals detected and as noncritical signs decreased. This information is important to lifeguards, particularly those working at traditional yet boring swimming pools.

Temperature can also have a negative effect on vigilance. In separate studies, both Mackworth (1945) and Pepler (1953) found that when air temperatures rose above 84°F, performance decrements became appreciable. This fact is double trouble for lifeguards because as the temperature climbs higher and their vigilance drops, attendance at the aquatic facility usually increases. Therefore, dipping into the water while rotating to a new position or using a water-misting bottle when stationary may keep lifeguards cool and more attentive as temperatures rise. Increasing shade and the consumption of ice cold water may also help lifeguards to maintain vigilance when the weather becomes warmer.

Studies involving automobile drivers find similar results to the pilot studies. Additionally, drivers who drive frequently for long stretches on monotonous highways or rural roads are at an increased risk for drowsy driving (University of Maryland Medical Center, 2014). Apparently, long, straight, boring roads do not provide enough variety, stimuli, or arousal, just like boring rectangular swimming pools on slow days. It may be hypothesized, then, that ocean and waterparks lifeguards tend to be more vigilant than traditional pool lifeguards, and even pool lifeguards claim to be more vigilant when they are busy. The AAA Foundation for Traffic Safety also surveyed thousands of drivers and found the most effective ways reported of overcoming driving boredom were rotating drivers, talking with someone in the vehicle, pulling off the road to exercise, singing, and washing the face with cold water. No behavioral countermeasures in these studies were as effective as sleep, either before a road trip or at a rest stop during a trip.

Many lifeguards have appreciated that movement and mild exercise during surveillance tasks can stimulate the muscles and increase the blood flow that oxygenates the brain. Although the explanation for this phenomenon is complex, the reasoning should be stated. Specifically, human attention requires stimulation of two major areas of the brain to function properly according to Plum and Posner (1972) in their neurophysiology text *The Diagnosis of Stupor and Coma*:

1. the ascending reticular activating system (ARAS) in the upper brainstem and
2. areas of the cerebral cortex.

The ARAS receives additional pathways from and is stimulated by every major somatic (organ) and every sensory (nerve) pathway. Simply stated, visual stimuli as well as stimuli from muscle groups centers from respiration, and increased sympathetic tone from even minimal exertion feeds into the ARAS. This area then primes the brain cortex for stimulus reception that in turn focuses this arousal energy for heightened arousal. The prefrontal cortex of the dominant right hemisphere helps maintain attention and the parietal cortex plays a role in shifting attention. These zones with their limbic connections are the "attentional gate" or "environmental monitor" for sensory stimulation back to the thalamic portion of the brain. This complicated and sophisticated input/feedback system requires the individual to be well rested and not overly stimulated to maintain a higher level of alertness and vigilance. This explanation also helps to illustrate why moderately increased movement, respiration, and heart rate of the lifeguard serve to stimulate the neurological pathways for improved attention and concentration.

Baseball and Lifeguarding

Playing baseball is in many ways like lifeguarding. Although the game can be exciting and the outcome can be decided in seconds, many players experience long stretches of inactivity. Hours can pass without engaging certain players, particularly outfielders, in any action. This can lead to a lack of vigilance that can adversely affect performance. Baseball players are often thought of as superstitious. Although this may be true, their daily rituals are actually focusing mechanisms that remind them to keep active both mentally and physically in what can be an important yet boring game for many of the participants. These seemingly unimportant and even silly routines they follow remind them to stay on their toes during a long yet important game and keep their bodies in a state of readiness. Warming up between innings, tapping the glove, repeatedly talking nonsense to others, stretching, and jogging in the field are all mechanisms to keep them alert and vigilant because the next ball might be coming their way. To be effective, however, these routines must be purposeful and systematic, specifically designed to help the athlete/lifeguard to direct his or her energy and focus to the task at hand. Additionally, lifeguards can also incorporate positive self-talk that athletes from many sports use to sustain their intensity of focus. Similarly, lifeguards may want to use predetermined cue words or positive self-talk every 5 minutes to help maintain focus.

While playing sports and while lifeguarding, athletes and lifeguards should experience improved vigilance by reducing negative self-talk. Another appropriate analogy is driving a car. At boring facilities on slow days, lifeguarding is like sitting in an idling car. Certainly, sitting in an idling car for hours would lead to boredom and inattentiveness. If an accident should occur while on duty, that lifeguard must put the pedal to the metal, 0 to 60 mph in seconds flat. If the lifeguard is not mentally and physically prepared, slow and/or inappropriate action may occur and the lifeguard may even become injured during the course of the rescue because the body is not warmed up. Waterpark and ocean guards are often mentally more ready to make a rescue because their environments are more stimulating and even entertaining at times. The trick for many underaroused (bored) lifeguards is to create mental and physical drills while on duty and to mentally rehearse rescues before going on duty so they do not miss important water safety cues and they are physically able to respond safely and appropriately when an emergency occurs.

How the Media Keep Viewers' Attention

Today's news show no longer has a professional-looking anchorperson alone on the screen telling the news in a professional manner. Now this announcer makes up less than one third of the screen and the rest is used to bombard viewers with a bevy of attention-getting news leads. The weather, sports, business, and other informational stimuli are constantly being beamed into homes while the announcer, who is now more of an entertainer, goes on with the "show." This is done purposefully to keep viewers' eyes focused on the television and to keep their attention longer, and it also attracts a younger audience. The same type of strategies may have to be used to keep lifeguards alert.

Maturation and Motivation of Lifeguards

Most lifeguards in the United States are young teenagers. Motivating this group to come to work and continually keep their focus to prevent accidents is important, particularly when many of them believe that water accidents are not likely to happen. Mihaly Csikszentmihalyi, former chairman of the School of Psychology at the University of Chicago, has written many books on his flow theory. Flow theory can be applied to all walks of life, and although the theory is not written specifically for lifeguards, the information provided in his books about the theory shows readers how to bring meaning and significance to the most boring of tasks. This is extremely important for lifeguards who face many hours of

boredom and tedium. Flow theory shows people how to use energetic focus and creative concentration to get the most out of their jobs (see Figures 22.8 and 22.9). The theory also illustrates how to balance periods of boredom with the challenges of anxiety and stress. If this theory was applied by young lifeguards, perhaps they would enjoy their jobs more and at the same time apply these suggestions to their full-time careers after they graduate from lifeguarding.

In almost all walks of life, including lifeguarding, people find their jobs too boring, too challenging, or just right—the perfect fit. Lifeguards often do not return the following season because they found the job to be too boring or too stressful. For example, The Pool Management Group based in Atlanta, Georgia, discovered that the primary cause of lifeguarding attrition in their company (3,000 lifeguards in 14 cities) was prompted by a conflict between the lifeguard and an adult at the facility. This is usually caused by teenage lifeguards not having the skills to deal with an upset adult, and that describes the essence of flow theory: for optimal performance and experience, individuals must possess the skills and abilities to meet the challenges of the job or sport. For lifeguards to be happy and effective, they must learn to maintain a challenge–skills balance. This is not only true in lifeguarding but also in sports and in all walks of life. Perception of the skills an individual possesses is almost as important as the skills themselves. Flow theory teaches individuals to use creative concentration and energetic focus to bring significant meaning to their jobs and lives and to concentrate on the task at hand.

In summary, when challenges become greater and more stressful, skills must be improved. When the skills are present and abilities are good, increased challenges are needed for an individual to remain focused.

Maslow's Hierarchy Of Needs

With the vast majority of lifeguards in the United States being teenagers, it is often difficult to determine what motivates them to perform in a mature, safe, and efficient way day in and day out, on busy days as well as slow days.

Perhaps it is best to study Maslow's hierarchy of needs to understand where young lifeguards are in their maturation and motivation process. Maslow's hierarchy of needs (see Figure 22.10) is a pyramid of eight separate needs that humans experience with deficiency needs on the base of the pyramid and growth needs at the top.

The **deficiency needs** are found in the first four levels:

1. physiological: hunger, thirst, bodily comforts, and so forth;
2. safety and security: protection from harm;

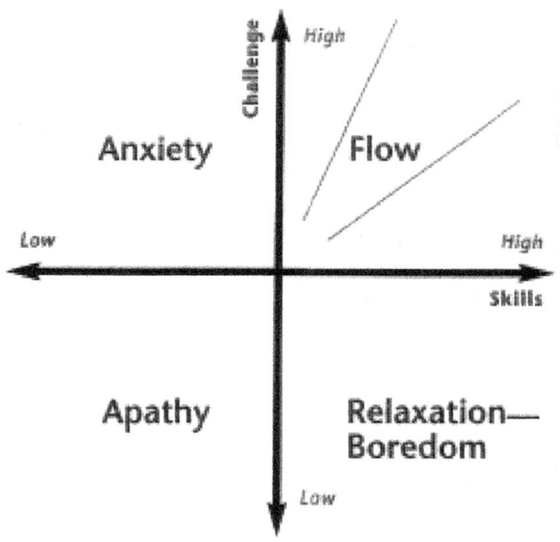

Figure 22.8. Flow theory.

needs until the deficiency needs are met. So how does this affect aquatic facilities? Many of the owners, managers, and supervisors who work with lifeguards have already satisfied their own deficiency needs and are now working on their growth needs that (1) are problem focused, (2) incorporate an ongoing freshness and appreciation of life, (3) are concerned about personal growth, and (4) are concerned with the ability to have peak experiences. The problem is that although employers are approaching self-actualization (the top half of the pyramid), most lifeguards are still working on their deficiencies (the bottom half of the pyramid), that is, fulfilling their physiological and safety needs as well as the need to belong, to be loved, and to have positive self-esteem. Teenage lifeguards cannot be expected to be mature, self-actualized adults in a work environment when it takes years to pass through the deficiency stages.

3. belongingness and love: affiliate with others, be accepted; and
4. esteem: to achieve, to be competent, to gain approval and recognition.

The **growth needs** are found on the top four levels:
1. cognitive: to know, to understand, and to explore;
2. aesthetic: symmetry, order, beauty;
3. self-actualization: to find self-fulfillment and realize one's potential; and
4. transcendence: to help others find self-fulfillment and realize their potential.

According to Maslow (1954), all humans must satisfy each of the needs at the lower level before moving to the next level. People are not able to act upon the growth

As individuals become more self-actualized and transcendent, they become wiser and almost automatically know what to do in a variety of situations. Isn't that what aquatics professionals want lifeguards to be? But this takes time and supervision. This means that teenagers are exactly that, teenagers, and they must be supervised more often. Supervision of lifeguards should be more about coaching and mentoring and providing for socialization in acceptable ways to make progress fulfilling their deficiency needs. Although adults tend to criticize children today for being kids, the maturation process takes time and requires more than a summer or two. As aquatic professionals work with lifeguards, they must realize that lifeguards are still growing and are impressionable and that they can make a difference. The top of the pyramid is "transcendence"; the responsibilities at that level include helping others to be "self-actualized."

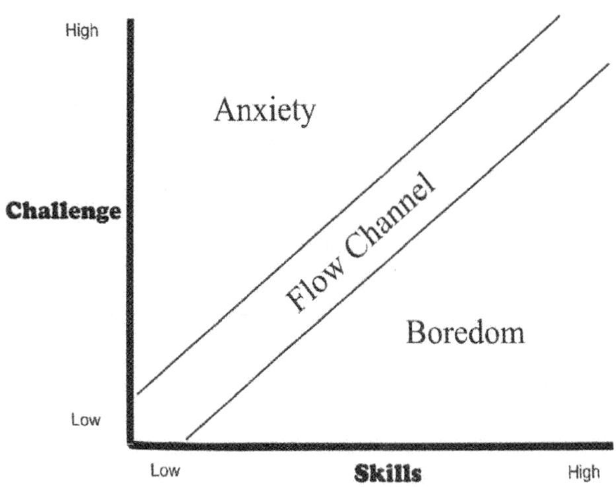

Figure 22.9. The flow. From *The Flow,* by M. Csikszentmihalyi, 1990, p. 74.

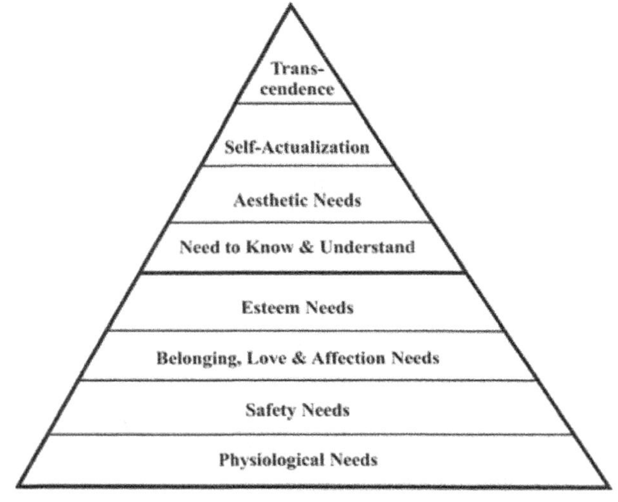

Figure 22.10. Maslow's Hierarchy of Needs.

Summary

In summary, this chapter examined several psychological principles that have been used successfully for many years in various fields and recent research regarding internal distractions in lifeguarding. The newer research applying physiological principles specifically to lifeguarding is a novel body of research and should be expounded upon with additional research in the field of aquatics in the coming years. It is hoped that the theories and principles presented will make lifeguards more vigilant and conscientious.

References

AAA Foundation for Traffic Safety. (2014). Retrieved from www.aaafoundation/ resources/index/

Aquatics Safety Research Group. (2014). Retrieved from www.aquaticsafetygroup.com

Beder, B., & Webb, P. (2011, June). Improving organizational and safety performance by addressing human error (Session No. 510). Technical presentation at the conference of the American Society of Safety Engineers Conference, Chicago, IL.

Coblentz, A., & Cabon, P. (1994). Effets de la monotonie et de l'organisation des horaires de travail sur la vigilance et la performance des opérateurs – Paris : Editions Techniques. (Encyclopédie Médico-Chirurgicale:Toxicologie-Pathologie profession-nelle, 16-784-A-10).

Csikszentmihalyi, M. (1990). *Flow: The psychology of optimal experience.* New York, NY: Harper and Row.

Ellis and Associates. Retrieved from www.jellis.com/news/o1news/december/vigilanceby jeff.html

Griffiths, R. C., & Griffiths, T. (2013). Internal noise distractions in lifeguarding. *International Journal of Aquatic Research and Education, 7*(1), 56–71.

Griffiths, T. (1987, July 19). Do lifeguards do what they're are paid to do? *The New York Times*, p. 22.

Griffiths, T. (1998, July/August). All along the watch tower. *Aquatics International*, 14.

Griffiths, T., Chambers, V. & Steel, D. (1995). Survey results: Systematic scanning for lifeguards. *Parks and Recreation Magazine, 30*(2), 40–47.

Griffiths, T., Steel, D., & Vogelsong, H. (1996, April). The 1995 national lifeguard survey: How waterpark lifeguards fared. *Splash Magazine*, 26–28.

Griffiths, T., Steel, D., & Vogelsong, H. (1999). Lifeguarding behaviors and systematic scanning strategies. In J. Fletemeyer, F. Freas, F. (Eds), *Drowning: New perspectives on intervention and prevention* (pp. 267–279). New York: CRC Press.

Griffiths, T., Vigelsong, H., & Steel, D. (1997). Results of the 1996 national lifeguard survey. *Parks and Recreation Magazine, 32*(11), 62–68.

Griffiths, S., Vogelsong, H., & Steel, D. (2000). Results of the 1998 lifeguard survey—Keeping their guard up. *Aquatics International, 12*(6), 36–38.

Jerison, H. J., & Pickett, R. M. (1964). Vigilance: The importance of the elicited observing rate. *Science, 113*, 970–971.

Mackworth, N. H. (1950). *Researches in the measurement of human performance* (Medical Research Council Special Report Series 268). London, England: His Majesty's Stationery Office.

Mackworth, J. F. (1970). *Vigilance and attention.* New York: Penguin Books.

Maslow, A. H. (1970). *Motivation and personality.* New York: Harper and Row.

National Safety Council. (2010). Understanding the distracted brain [White Paper]. Retrieved from http://www.nsc.org/safety_road/Distracted_Driving/Documents/Dstrct_Drvng_White_Paper_Fnl(5-25-10).pdf

Pepler, R. D. (1953). *The effects of climatic factors on the performance of skilled tasks by young European men living in the tropics: 4. A task of prolonged visual vigilance* (MRC-156/53). Cambridge, UK: Medical Research Council, Apply Psychology Unit.

Pia, F. (1974, July). Observations on the drowning nonswimmers. *Journal of Physical Education.* Warsaw: Indiana: The YMCA Society of North America.

Pia, F. (1984, June). The RID factor as a cause of drowning. *Parks & Recreation.* Ashburn, VA: National Parks & Recreation Society.

Pieron H. (1979). *Vocabulaire de la psychologie* (6e ed.). Revue et augmentée. Paris, PUF.

Pigeau, R. A., Angus, R. G., O'Neill, P., & Mack, I. (1995). Vigilance latencies to aircraft detection among NORAD surveillance operations. *Human Factors, 37*(3), 622–634.

Plum, F., & Posner, J. (1972). *The diagnosis of stupor and coma.* Philadelphia, PA: F.A. Davis.

Sen, A. (1983). *Attention and distraction.* New York: Sterling Publishers.

Yerkes, R. M., & Dodson, J. D. (1908). The relation of strength of stimulus to rapidity of habit-formation. *Journal of Comparative Neurophysiological Psychology, 18*, 459–482.

Aquatic Safety Research Group. (2014). Retrieved from www.aquaticsafetygroup.com

Simons and Chabris. (2010). Retrieved from www.theinvisiblegorilla.com/

www.viscog.com/

Bibliography

AAA Foundation for Safety. (2010). *Asleep at the wheel: The prevalence and impact of drowsy driving.* Washington, DC: AAA Foundation for Safety.

Aquatic Safety Research Group. Retrieved www.aquatic-safetygroup.com

Griffiths, R. C., & Griffiths, T. (2013). Internal noise distractions in lifeguarding. *International Journal of Aquatic Research and Education, 7*(1), 56–71.

Mackworth, N. H. (1945). *Effects of heat and high humidity prolonged visual search as measured by the clock test.* London: Med. Res. Council.

Maslow, A. (1954). Motivation and personality. New York, NY: Harper.

Pepler, R. D. (1953). The effect of climatic factors on the performance of skilled tasks by young European men living in the tropics. *Rep. Clim. Efficiency Subcomm.,* RNPRC, T.R.U. 3(51).

Poseidon Technologies. (2014). Retrieved from www.poseidon-tech.com/us/ lifeguarding.html

University of Maryland Medical Center. (2014). *Drowsy Driving.* Retrieved from www.umm.edu

www.circadian.com/learnin

www.theinvisiblegorilla.com/

Retrieved www.viscog.com/

23

Preventive Lifeguarding

Key Concepts

- Lifeguard effectiveness
- The Complex Quadriplex of Lifeguard Blindness
- Drowning Ds
- Lifeguarding
- Lifesaving
- Scanning
- Sweeping
- 10/20 rule
- Five-Minute Scanning Strategy
- High-risk guests
- Emergency action plans
- Evaluating lifeguards
- Junior lifeguards
- Job descriptions
- Rules and regulations
- Guard stations
- Uniforms
- Communications
- Motivation

Lifeguard Effectiveness

According to the Centers for Disease Control (CDC, 2001), most drownings are preventable through a variety of strategies, one of which is to provide lifeguards in public areas where people are known to swim and to encourage people to swim in those areas protected by lifeguards. The CDC strongly states that trained, professional lifeguards have positively affected drowning prevention in the United States. Apparently, lifeguards on duty make a difference in saving lives.

Historically, by the early 1900s, as many as 9,000 people in the United States drowned each year (American Red Cross, 1995). Concerned with this high number of drownings in the United States, Commodore Wilbert E. Longfellow began an aggressive crusade of water rescue and safety around the country. In 1910, he became the commander in chief of the U.S. Lifesaving Corps and established the nationwide American Red Cross Lifesaving Corps in 1914. The Commodore personally trained thousands of lifeguards and instructors throughout the country and convinced owners and operators of pools and beaches to staff their facility with his well-trained professionals. Largely through his efforts, the drowning rate in the United States began to drop dramatically.

In 1914, the drowning rate was 10.4 deaths per 100,000 participants (International Swimming Hall of Fame, n.d.). By 1947, this number was halved to 5.2 per 100,000 participants. By 1990, the drowning rate had been reduced to 1.9 per 100,000. This drastic reduction in drowning deaths is attributed to the Longfellow and the American Red Cross swimming and water safety courses that have been popular in the United States. The YMCA of the United States has also had a rich and successful tradition of water safety and lifeguarding programs. Figure 23.1 shows a summary of aquatic safety developments. On a yearly basis through the 1970s and 1980s, the drowning rate held at around 7,000 to 8,000 drownings annually. Since the mid-1990s, the annual

Royal Humane Society (1774)
Massachusetts Humane Society (1786)
U.S. Coast Guard Lifesaving Service (1871)
YMCA entrance into teaching (1885–1890)
Lifesaving Program, Springfield College (1911)
National YMCA Lifesaving Service (1912)
First American lifesaving text (1913)
Red Cross lifesaving training (1914)
YMCA Lifesaving and Swimming Manual (1929)
Cureton-Silvia test text (1939)
YMCA Lifesaving and Water Safety Instructor's Text (1940)
Silvia's *YMCA Lifesaving and Water Safety Today* (1965)
New YMCA Aquatic Safety and Lifesaving Text (1974)
YMCA Aquatic Safety and Lifesaving Program (1979)
On the Guard: YMCA Lifeguard Manual (1986–present)
American Red Cross Lifeguarding Manual (1994-Present)
International Lifeguard Training Program, Ellis & Associates (1999-present)
StarGuard Best Practices for Lifeguards (1999-present)
The National Aquatic Safety Company (NASCO) (1999-present)

Figure 23.1. Aquatic Safety Developments

drownings dipped below 5,000. Some suggest a significant portion of this reduction is due to responsible drinking around the water.

Approximately 60% of drowning deaths among children occur in swimming pools. Although more Americans gravitate to the water for increasing opportunities in aquatic recreation, the drowning rate continues to decline. According to the National Center for Health Statistics (2000), the incidence of drowning in the United States declined from 6,300 persons in 1981 to about 4,000 persons in 1998. From 2005 to 2009, the CDC reported an average of 3,533 fatal unintentional drownings (not including boating-related drownings) annually in the United States—about 10 deaths per day. The number of drownings can be reduced further by improving the training and supervision of lifeguards. Both supplementing supervision and strengthening supervision are vital to reduce the risk of drowning. Supplementing supervision, including life jackets for all nonswimmers, has been detailed in previous sections of this book. This chapter is devoted to strengthening supervision through preventive lifeguarding techniques rather than water rescue practices and procedures. In addition, this chapter concentrates on swimming pool and waterpark lifeguards rather than surf or beach lifeguards, although concepts introduced here apply to both. *Better Beaches*, published by the National Recreation and Park Association, and *Safer Beaches,* published by Human Kinetics, are excellent reference texts for operators running flat water and/or surf beaches. Surf beaches, particularly those that are guarded by United States Lifesaving Association Lifeguards, have a tremendous safety record. Proper lifeguarding attitudes and philosophies are examined here instead of specific training techniques and skills, but perhaps the most important aspect of this chapter is aimed at increasing vigilance and mindfulness through increasing attention and concentration and reducing boredom on duty. When someone drowns in a guarded facility, it is often not caused by the poor swimming ability of the lifeguard or an improper rescue technique, but rather a lifeguard who missed the distressed swimmer due to boredom, inattentiveness, distraction, or intentional or unintentional lapses in supervision (internal noise, stimulus habituation, denial, disbelief, etc.). Too often, another patron or a family member finds the victim on the bottom of the pool. Therefore, vigilance and mindfulness are key.

The American Red Cross, national YMCAs, Ellis and Associates, the Star Guard program, the United States Lifesaving Association, and other training agencies have excellent books and courses available to train lifeguards. Regardless of the training agency used, aquatic facility managers and water safety personnel should become familiar with other lifeguard training organizations and their educational materials; they have much to offer. This chapter is intended as a supplement to those training texts and courses. Local lifeguarding requirements are available through the regulatory agencies in charge of pools in specific geographical regions, but in many regions, it is hoped that aquatic facilities exceed the minimum standards imposed. Lifeguards should be qualified in addition to certified. Being qualified exceeds the minimum standards required by the certification. This includes thorough and diverse in-service trainings; supplementary materials including educational sessions and DVDs that illustrate not only the importance of rescue and resuscitation but also the challenges lifeguards face such as the Complex Quadriplex of Lifeguard Blindness (c) (CQLB); and methods to help lifeguards overcome these challenges.

Lifeguard training in the past emphasized swimming rescues and water skills. In fact, over the years, even the names of the Red Cross courses have changed dramatically. The "Junior and Senior Lifesaving" course became the "Advanced Lifesaving" course that was eventually transformed into "Lifeguarding." Although today's lifeguards receive extensive training in the water, water safety awareness and accident prevention is emphasized. Before the 1970s, it was commonly believed that the lifeguards with the most rescues were the most competent. Today, the trend has been reversed. Many experts believe those with the fewest rescues are the most vigilant

Lifesaving versus Lifeguarding

Lifesaver	Lifeguard
Reacts to an accident, acting after the fact	Acts to first prevent the accident, does react to emergency
Reacts from a moral principle only	Acts under a moral and legal duty
May be covered by the Good Samaritan Laws	Can be found liable and negligent in a court
Does not need certification	Must be certified by an accredited agency as required by law in some states or qualified and trained by an individual in that facility or setting
Has general training and is an amateur	Is a professional with specific training for specific locations, with specific procedures for emergencies
Usually has no special equipment available	Has specific rescue equipment for that aquatic setting

Figure 23.2. Lifesaving vs. Lifeguarding

in their supervision of swimmers, because this indicates they are more proactive rather than reactive. Water rescues are risky for both the victim and the rescuer. It's safest to prevent accidents and drowning before they occur. The YMCA provides an excellent explanation describing the difference between lifesavers and lifeguards (see Figure 23.1). They claim that although the words *lifesaver* and *lifeguard* share the same prefix, the areas of responsibility they share are dissimilar. A lifesaver is an amateur who stumbles on an aquatic emergency and accidentally becomes involved in the water rescue. Conversely, lifeguards are trained professionals who have accepted the responsibility of protecting swimmers at a specified place and time. Lifeguards have a moral, professional, and legal responsibility to prevent accidents by enforcing rules and regulations of the aquatic facility and to respond correctly to aquatic emergencies should they occur.

But parents must also be reminded to watch their children, even when lifeguards are on duty, and that not all aquatic accidents can be prevented even under the best circumstances. Furthermore, the box shows comparisons from the YMCA that distinguish lifesaving from lifeguarding.

The Drowning Ds During Supervision

The Drowning Ds (see Figure 23.3) during supervision illustrate six contributing factors why lifeguard supervision and adult supervision fail. These include *dereliction, distraction, disguise, disbelief, denial,* and *delay*. All of these can lead to death, which can be, but is not necessarily, caused by drowning.

Additionally, the Drowning Ds fall under three categories: lack of supervision, child neglect, or a lapse in supervision.

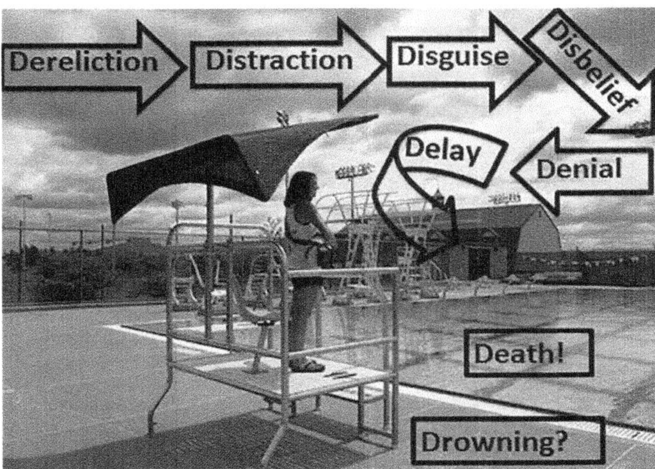

Figure 23.3. The Drowning Ds. (Photo courtesy of Aquatic Safety Research Group)

Dereliction

Dereliction often is neglect. This includes leaving the pool deck to answer a phone call, go to the bathroom, or go to the pump room. Dereliction of duty is the easiest to avoid. For example, maintaining vigilance; providing active supervision; effectively scanning; and fulfilling the duties of a responsible, qualified lifeguard are not dereliction.

Distraction

Distraction during lifeguarding can be fatal because drowning can happen in a matter of seconds. External distractions include noise from the street, a birthday party on the pool deck, or talking to patrons. Internal noise can be just as distracting, if not more distracting, and is difficult to recognize and difficult to manage. Internal noise includes thoughts, emotions, and daydreams (see internal noise study in Chapter 22).

Disguise

Disguise of a victim is the third D of drowning. A drowning victim often becomes disguised once he or she submerges underneath the water. When a drowning victim is beneath the surface of the water, body blindness causes that person to be completely invisible. Water ripples and glare can cause a body on the bottom to become invisible. The video *Disappearing Dummies* (Griffiths, 2008) demonstrates how water disguises victims by showing dummies on the bottom of the pool disappearing to the human eye as a result of ripples on the surface of the water, reflection, or glare.

Disbelief

Disbelief is not uncommon for individuals to experience, especially during tragic events. People will not see what they do not want to see. In the internal noise distractions while lifeguarding survey (Griffiths & Griffiths, 2012), see internal noise survey Chapter 22), lifeguards most often expressed feeling *happiness, nervousness, boredom, responsibility, stress, worry,* and *anxiety*. This internal noise, especially when nervous about lifeguarding, can lead a person's mind to not see a drowning victim, in disbelief.

Denial

Denial includes thoughts or feelings, consciously or subconsciously, in alignment with the mind-set "this cannot be happening to me." For example, many times lifeguards have watched people drown thinking the person was holding his or her breath underwater. In some cases, the mind is in denial and convinces the lifeguard that the person is "fine," "holding their breath," or "playing." Similar to disbelief, denial often occurs in tragic events, such as drowning. Additionally, when lifeguards feel an immense responsibility and/or are stressed, anxious, or scared, they can experience denial.

Delay

Dereliction, distraction, disguise, disbelief, and denial all lead to delay. Even a short delay can lead to death or drowning at an aquatic facility.

The Complex Quadriplex of Lifeguard Blindness

The Aquatic Safety Research Group (ASRG, 2013) developed The Complex Quadriplex of Lifeguard Blindness (CQLB) (see Figure 23.4), which covers the four most significant challenges lifeguards face: (1) external distractions, (2) physical body blindness, (3) cognitive body blindness, and (4) internal noise.

External Distractions

The first quadrant is external distractions. This includes the RID factor and other external distractions, such as noise, socialization, and phone use.

Physical Body Blindness

The second quadrant in the CQLB is physical body blindness. Physical body blindness is the second "blindfold" lifeguards wear. Physical body blindness includes the three Rs and Glare:

Reflection. Reflection on the surface of the water can prevent any human from seeing beneath the surface of the water. Even when a lifeguard is looking directly at a person under the water in a pool, reflection of the sun or an object on the surface of the water can effectively hide the person under the water.

Refraction. Refraction of the water can bend, skew, and also make a body under the surface of the water un-

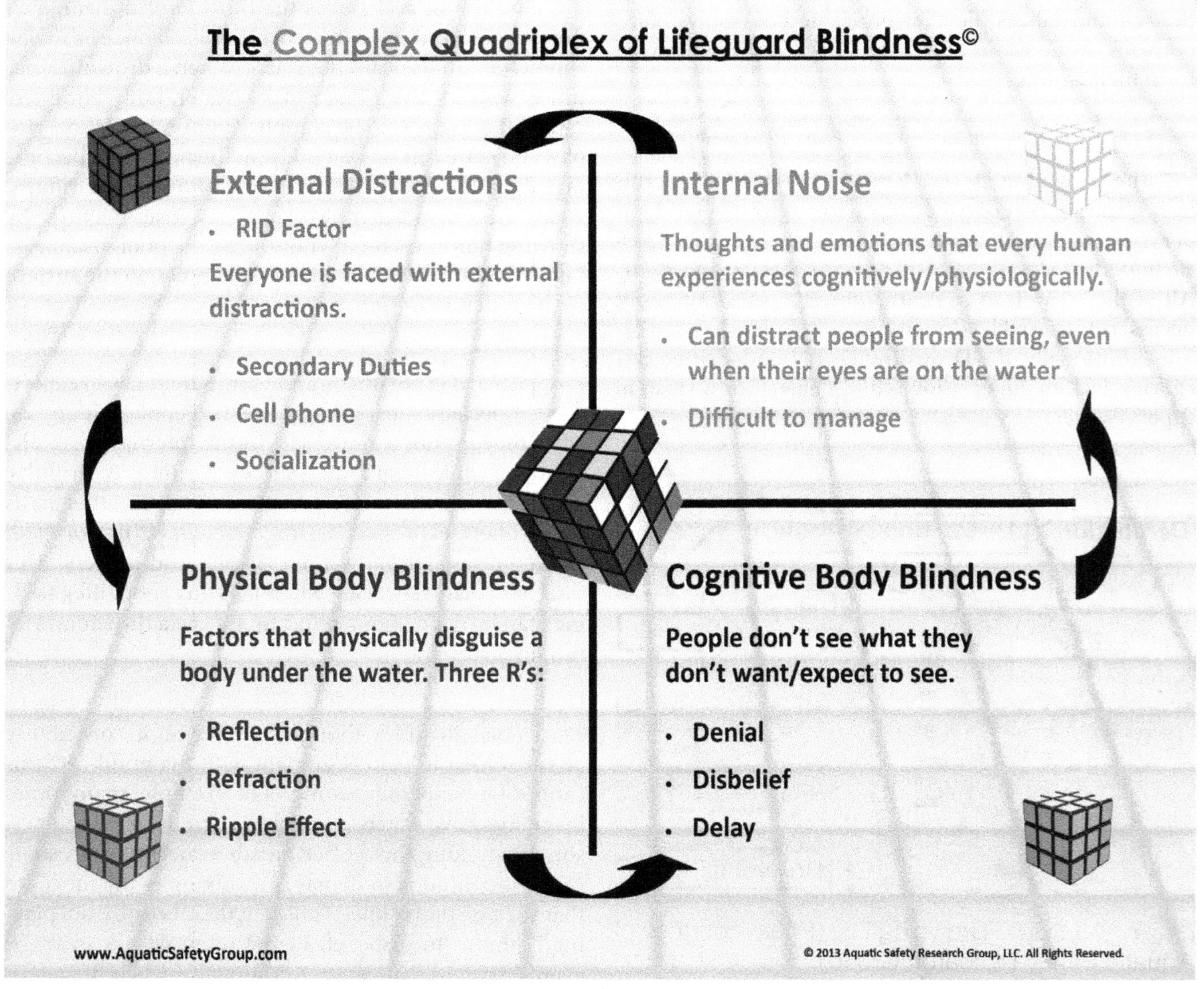

Figure 23.4. The Complex Quadriplex of Lifeguard Blindness©. (Courtesy of Aquatic Safety Research Group)

noticeable or even make a body disappear to the human eye.

Ripple effect. Water agitation from splashing or people swimming causes ripples that can make seeing beneath the surface of the water difficult or impossible. Spotting a victim underneath the surface of the water is difficult or impossible due to physical body blindness, and further challenging is how quickly and quietly a victim can slip beneath the surface and "disappear."

Glare. Glare is bright, strong light that may cause difficulty in sight.

Cognitive Body Blindness

The third quadrant in the CQLB is cognitive body blindness, or perceptual body blindness. This includes denial and disbelief and in turn leads to delay when lifeguarding. People do not see what they do not want to see or do not expect to see.

Internal Noise

Fourth, internal noise is cognitive and/or emotional interference and can be just as distracting as external noise, but is often more difficult to manage. Emotions are especially blinding and can prevent certain stimuli from being processed in the brain.

The RID² emphasizes the importance of integrating the knowledge of the four lifeguard blindnesses, into aquatic research and lifeguard training to further improve lifeguard supervision. In addition to supplementing supervision, strengthening supervision is vital due to critical challenges lifeguards face in the CQLB. Myriad existing strategies as well as recently developed strategies to improve lifeguard vigilance and mindfulness are explicated here. Lifeguard supervisors, managers, and staff are encouraged to use strategies presented in this chapter and to build upon these methods to find the most effective practices for specific aquatic venues.

The 10/20 Rule

The 10/20 rule, developed by Ellis and Associates, dictates that every lifeguard on duty must be able to detect a swimmer in distress within 10 seconds and make contact with the victim within the next 20 seconds. Ellis and Associates established this timeframe because it is possible for a person, particularly a child, to disappear under the water in less than 30 seconds. To apply the 10/20 rule, lifeguards must be vigilant in their supervision, lifeguard stations must be appropriately placed for proper coverage, and lifeguards must be monitored continually to ensure they are watching patrons in and around the water. Lifeguards must also receive instructions concerning which are the most hazardous areas within the swimming pool complex and which patrons are high-risk swimmers. Although this is a good life-guarding goal, in reality, the 10/20 rule is difficult, if not impossible, to achieve, particularly as the number of swimmers and the size of the zone increases. Lifeguards certified and audited by Ellis and Associates should naturally be more able to achieve the 10/20 patron protection rule than lifeguards trained by other agencies. In a summer of 2001 study conducted by Ellis and Associates in cooperation with Poseidon Technologies, Ellis and Associates lifeguards, who are required to detect a distressed swimmer in just 10 seconds, on average took 1 minute, 14 seconds to detect a lifelike mannequin on the bottom of the pool. During the summer of 2002, Ellis and Associates lifeguards improved their detection time to just less than 1 minute, but this is still far from the 10-second ideal. This suggests that even lifeguards aggressively trained and audited regularly on the 10/20 patron protection rule do not see victims in a timely fashion.

The Five-Minute Scanning Strategy

To be effective in preventing accidents, lifeguards should develop systematic scanning techniques. Regardless of what scanning technique is chosen, lifeguards should check each patron within their area of responsibility regularly and often. Many good lifeguards use individualized techniques they have personally developed, but now a standardized system has been developed that is research based and field tested.

After years of research conducted at Penn State University, Tom Griffiths, EdD, along with help from Sport Psychologist Donald Steel, PhD, from the University of Maryland and Hans Vogelsong, PhD from East Carolina University, developed the Five-Minute Scanning Strategy for lifeguards. The Five-Minute Scan is a practical preventive guarding technique and is based on research conducted with thousands of lifeguards around the world. This technique was also piloted with almost 3,000 lifeguards in the United States. Thousands of lifeguard in the United States now use this simple yet effective technique to increase attention, concentration, and overall vigilance while reducing distractions and boredom while on duty. The StarGuard program (starting in 2000) and Ellis and Associates (starting in 2003), along with many other agencies, organizations, and programs, subscribe to the Five-Minute Scanning Strategy.

Physiological and psychological research has shown that after 15 minutes of performing a simple task, a person's performance on that task worsens. The Five-Minute Scanning Strategy was developed to help lifeguards stay alert while performing the task of watching people in the pool. The strategy is based on physiological and psychological responses and what research shows many experienced lifeguards have already been doing to stay alert. The Five-Minute Scanning Strategy helps lifeguards stay physically more awake by promoting a slightly higher respiratory rate and helps them stay mentally more alert by changing the mental process every 5 minutes. It is also supported by years of research on circadian rhythms. Figure 23.5 shows a lifeguard stand designed for the Five-Minute Scanning Strategy, with a wide platform to assume different positions throughout a shift in addition to sitting.

Figure 23.5. Paragon® Griff's Vision Guard Station with two additional places to stand while in the station. (Photo courtesy of Pentair Aquatic Systems)

Circadian Rhythms

It has been known for centuries that human beings, like plants and animals, have biological clocks that detect levels of alertness and fatigue with both levels fluctuating significantly throughout the day. What is troublesome for aquatic professionals is that peaks in alertness do not usually coincide with busy times at the facility. Most people experience a natural cycle of peak alertness in the early to midmorning hours and again in the late afternoon. Between noon and the early hours of the afternoon, most people sense more fatigue, and this is certainly not good news for lifeguards and aquatic administrators. The Circadian Learning Center offers Nine Switches of Human Alertness that should help lifeguards combat their natural body shifts into fatigue.

Interest, Opportunity, a Near Miss, Sense of Danger

Nothing pulls people out of a drowsy state faster than a threat or a danger, whether real or imagined. This is why unannounced audits and rescue drills effectively keep lifeguards alert.

Muscular Activity

Muscular activity, such as walking or stretching, triggers the sympathetic nervous system, which helps to keep people alert. Conversely, sitting in a chair makes staying alert difficult. This is another reason why the Five-Minute Scanning Strategy is highly recommended.

Time of Day or Circadian Clock

Midnight to dawn and the hours following lunchtime produce the lowest levels of alertness. Knowing this, lifeguards and aquatic professionals need to use more alertness switches during these times.

Sleep Bank Balance

Sleep deprivation for several days creates a "sleep debt" that leads to dangerously low levels of daytime alertness levels. For teenagers lifeguarding during the summer months, lack of sleep can be dangerous.

Ingested Foods and Chemicals

Some substances (such as caffeine) temporarily increase alertness, and others (warm milk, turkey, bananas, sleeping pills) induce sleep. Education and wise decision making should be discussed with lifeguards so they do not ingest the wrong substances prior to working.

Environmental Light

Bright light tends to increase alertness, and dim light leads to drowsiness. Lifeguards might need to use alertness strategies on cloudy, dreary days and in the evening hours.

Temperature

Cool, dry air, especially on the face, helps to keep people alert, and heat and humidity make people drowsy. Naturally, this area is a concern for lifeguards and must be dealt with appropriately using a combination of shade, hats, fans, misting, and cold water. Dipping into the water also comes highly recommended.

Sound

Constant sounds such as rolling waves or the hum from machines cause drowsiness, and irregular sounds such as radio, talking, horns, bells, or whistles promote alertness. This is why intermittent talking (not long conversations) is now recommended for lifeguards, provided their eyes are not diverted from the water.

Aroma

Smells such as peppermint promote alertness, whereas smells such as lavender promote drowsiness.

Finally, comfort is often incompatible with alertness. To be fully alert, many lifeguards need to be a little uncomfortable. Too often, lifeguards performing important surveillance techniques try to make themselves comfortable and turn off many of the alertness switches. When this happens, catastrophic results can happen.

Summing it up, it appears from the research findings that

- circadian rhythms should be studied and understood to determine how to improve alertness and combat fatigue;
- some vigilance decrements occur after only 15 minutes of observation, with significant decrements occurring after 30 minutes of surveillance;
- mild exercise and/or sensory stimulation may improve attention, especially when low levels of arousal and stimuli are present;
- surveillance breaks every 15 to 20 minutes and changes in activity should be helpful in maintaining vigilance;
- keeping cool when on duty, either by dipping into the water or using shade may improve vigilance, particularly when the ambient temperature climbs above 84°F, and drinking cold water may also help alertness; and
- guarding in pairs may also be of assistance, provided that the lifeguards do not distract one another from surveillance.

Many of the research findings and suggestions of the past were also reported more by actual lifeguards surveyed by Griffiths, Vogelsong, and Steel between 1996 and 2001 and published in *Aquatics International, Parks and Recreation,* and *Splash* magazines. The results of their research have led to the development of the Five-Minute Scanning Strategy, which is a practical and effective system of lifeguard scanning to prevent boredom.

An excellent and comprehensive review of the literature dealing with vigilance, attention, and concentration and its relevance to lifeguarding can be found through the Poseidon website (http://www.poseidon-tech.com/us/vigilanceStudy.pdf). This research compilation was collected and published by Applied Anthropology in Paris, France, in September 2001.

The Five-Minute Scanning Strategy technique was designed to improve concentration and attention while reducing boredom. In light of the significant challenges that lifeguards face, techniques to reduce mindlessness and increase energized focus and mindfulness are especially important. Finally, using this technique can be fun for the guards. The next section explains a handout used by the Pool Management Group based in Atlanta, Georgia, with 3,500 lifeguards in 14 U.S. cities. The purpose is to teach new guards how to use the Five-Minute Scan at its pools and is required by all Pool Management Group lifeguards.

How to Perform the Five-Minute Scanning Strategy

When on Duty Watching the Pool, Make a Major Change in Posture Every 5 Minutes as Follows:

1. Sit in the lifeguard stand for 5 minutes.
2. Stand on the footboard of the lifeguard stand or on the deck next to the lifeguard stand for 5 minutes.
3. Then, stroll (walk) one time around your zone. On slow days, walking for 5 minutes may be more effective.

This is referred to as the "Sit, Stand, and Stroll" variation of the Five-Minute Scanning Strategy.

*At some pools it may not be practical to get out of the stand, in which case the lifeguard may choose to sit and then stand, but not stroll or sit, stand, and "stretch."

During the stroll, lifeguards must keep their eyes on the people in the water. Lifeguards must also carry the rescue tube while they keep moving and should not stop for prolonged periods. Lifeguards are urged to stay along the edge of the pool within approximately 2 to 3 ft of the edge of the water. Lifeguards are also encouraged to greet people during patrol but should not stop for extended conversations or divert their attention from the water.

Lifeguard patrols or "strolling" should not be encouraged when the pool deck is crowded because visual obstructions will occur and rescues could be slowed. It is important to remember that the people in the pool area must be able to spot the lifeguard immediately. When the lifeguard is in the stand, this is easy, and when the lifeguard is walking, it must be clear that they are "on duty," performing surveillance tasks and not socializing. If patrons try to engage the lifeguard in lengthy conversation, the lifeguard should be taught to use statements such as the following:

- "I'm sorry I cannot stop and talk now, but I will be glad to talk to you during the next safety break."
- "I'm sorry, but I cannot stop and talk now. Please walk with me as I go back to the stand."
- "I need to keep my eyes on the pool while we talk, but I can listen to what you are saying as we walk."

Variations of the Three Ss of Major Change in Posture

Option 1
1. Sit in the lifeguard stand for 5 minutes.
2. Stand on the footboard of the lifeguard stand or on the deck next to the lifeguard stand for 5 minutes.
3. Then, stroll (walk) one time around your zone.

Option 2
1. Sit in the lifeguard stand for 5 minutes.
2. Then, stroll (walk) one time around your zone.

3. Stand on the footboard of the lifeguard stand or on the deck next to the lifeguard stand for 5 minutes.
4. Then, stroll (walk) one time around your zone.

Option 3
1. Sit in the lifeguard stand for 5 minutes.
2. Stand on the footboard of the lifeguard stand or on the deck next to the lifeguard stand for 5 minutes.

Change Scanning Pattern Every 5 Mintues (Every Time You Change Posture) Remembering to "Visually Touch People"

The facial expression on people's faces is most important for lifeguards. When lifeguards look for facial expressions, they can detect signs of fear or concern. To do this, the head must move often. As a result, good lifeguard scanners are sometimes referred to as "swivel heads."

Whatever the Scanning Pattern, the Head Must Move
- Eyes become less fatigued when the lifeguard moves the head, instead of just moving the eyes.
- People can only see details in the center of their field of vision. Lifeguards need to see the details of people's faces.
- The lifeguard has an obligation to assure people; parents get assurance from seeing the lifeguard's head move.
- Supervisors are obligated to assure that the lifeguard is scanning. Supervisors have to be able to see the lifeguard's head move since they cannot see the eyes move from behind the lifeguard or if the lifeguard is wearing sunglasses. Supervisors must watch the lifeguards watch the water, but can never assume the lifeguards are actually seeing the most important cues. It may be best for supervisors to actually test lifeguards on duty by questioning them about specific populations and activities in the zone of coverage.

Examples of Scanning Patterns
- Watch faces of patrons in the pool.
- Cluster people into groups, center on a focal person (unique) in the group, and change the focal person with leapfrog centering.
- Connect the dots (people)
- Scan vertically.
- Scan horizontally.
- Scan in a circular pattern (see Figure 23.6).
- Do not forget to look under the water and on the bottom of the pool.

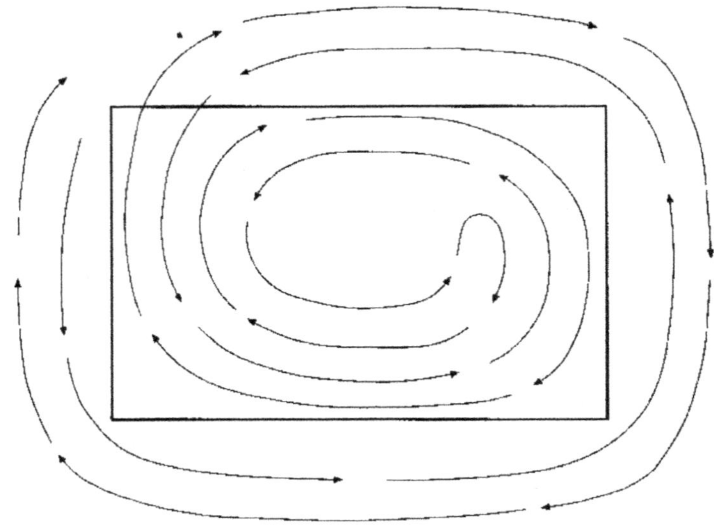

Figure 23.6. Circular scanning.

Count the People in Your Zone at the End of Each 5-Minute Period

All lifeguards are expected to use the Five-Minute Scanning Strategy. The three steps in the Five-Minute Scanning Strategy cycle are as follows:

1. Change posture every 5 minutes (the three Ss).
2. Change scanning pattern every 5 minutes.
3. Count the people in your zone every 5 minutes.

Note: Optimal communication and responding to patrons need for help requires the lifeguard to have a rescue tube and whistle at all times.

Another way of thinking of the Five-Minute Scan is to emphasize the four Ps required by the strategy:

> Every 5 minutes change the four Ps:
>
> 1. Posture change
> 2. Position change
> 3. Pattern change
> 4. Patron count

Note: The success and popularity of the Five-Minute Scanning Strategy led to the development of Griff's Guard Stations™, which include standing platforms and lifeguard seats. With steps up the front of the station instead of ladders on the back, Griff's Guard Stations promote the use of the Five-Minute Scan. Griff's Guard Stations are manufactured by Pentair Aquatic Systems in LaGrangeville, New York. A videotape of the Five-Minute Scan is available through the Aquatic Safety Research Group LLC, 1632 Glenwood Circle, State College, PA 16803 or call 814.234.0313, www.aquaticsafetygroup.com.

Another scanning technique that may be incorporated into the Five-Minute Scan is the monitoring of hazardous areas in order of priority from most hazardous to least hazardous. The lifeguards prioritize the most dangerous facilities or equipment in their zone and then scan each item and the people around it before checking on the next area. For instance, a lifeguard may check the diving boards first, the pool decks second, the ladders third, under the lifeguard chairs fourth, and the lap swimming lanes last. It is important to keep in mind and regularly check "blind spots," such as directly beneath the lifeguard, shadowed areas, or areas with reflection on the surface of the water. Lifeguards should look for areas of which they do not have clear vision and move around the visual obstructions and challenges (glare, reflection, refraction, shadows) to see spots that may be slightly (or significantly) hidden. The stroll and head movement segments of the Five-Minute Scanning Strategy should also assist with gaining different vantage points of the pool.

People watching is another technique whereby lifeguards check all children first, senior citizens next, young adults next, and so on. Lifeguards should, of course, check on the high-risk patrons first. A helpful way of keeping track of all swimmers in a particular zone for the lifeguard is to periodically guess the number of patrons and then count them individually. Again, this should occur every 5 minutes.

Preventive lifeguarding techniques require lifeguards to scan their areas of responsibility systematically so that boredom and distractions will not divert their attention. Lifeguards should be trained in scanning techniques, and they must also be monitored while on duty. It is also important for water safety personnel to differentiate between a sweep and a scan. As the developer of the Five-Minute Scan, I define *scanning* as a system or strategy of visual observation that lasts 5 minutes. A *sweep,* on the other hand, is one visual trip through the lifeguard's zone of coverage and should last just seconds.

CQLB
The WHY of Scanning

10/20
The WHEN of Scanning

Five-Minute Scanning Strategy
The HOW of Scanning

Reactive Response vs. Proactive Prevention

In recent years, with new technologies and advances available to water safety personnel, many good protocols have been added to lifeguard training, particularly in the medical science areas. Lifeguards can now use CPR, deliver oxygen, use automated external defibrillators (AEDs), backboard victims, use bag valve masks, all while protecting themselves from blood-borne pathogens. These positive and necessary advances not only protect lifeguards but also increase the success rates of rescue and resuscitation efforts. With these advances come disadvantages, however. It will take time for lifeguards to learn, become familiar with, and be assimilated to these new devices and technologies. In addition, these new skills and technologies must be incorporated into in-service training. Hopefully lifeguard training is not overemphasizing rescue and resuscitation while minimizing prevention. After all, it was only in the 1980s when the name changed from lifesavers to lifeguards. With all the time and effort spent on all aspects related to the emergency action plans, it seems that reactive response is being stressed more heavily than progressive prevention. Not that less skill or technology in rescue and resuscitation is needed, but a move back to basics and reemphasis of the scanning process is certainly warranted.

Available today is a new computer-based technology that has been introduced to aquatics as "the lifeguard's third eye." Underwater television cameras and computers are now being manufactured to assist lifeguards with their scanning, particularly in boring rectangular pools. Although lifeguards are trained to scan, rescue, and resuscitate, too many motionless bodies are still being discovered on the bottom of guarded facilities. This technology will be more vigilant than lifeguards because it cannot, and will not, succumb to environmental conditions that produce low levels of arousal and vigilance in humans. Technology developed by Poseidon (see Figure 23.7) and other companies certainly brings hope for the future in reducing the drowning rate worldwide.

To reduce drownings with lifeguards on duty, water safety professionals need to systematically study what happens to lifeguards at low levels of arousal and how to maintain moderate levels of arousal in lifeguards. Before this can be accomplished, however, the definition of the scanning process must be refined. Lifeguard scanning is more than just the physical process requiring constant eye and head movement around the aquatic facility. To define the scanning process, it should be assumed that lifeguard scanning is an interactive process that includes physical, mental, and psychological aspects. The act of

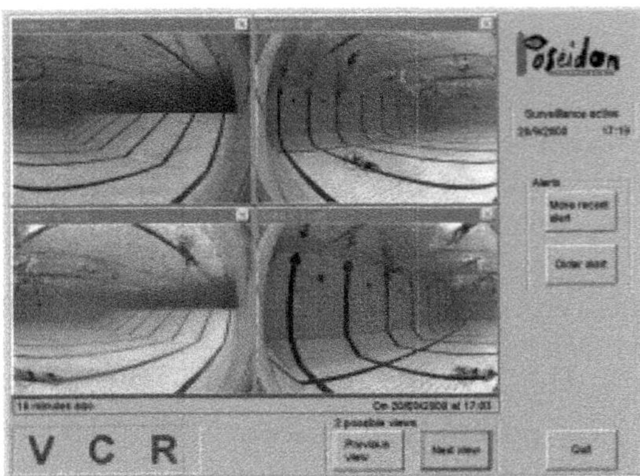

Figure 23.7. Underwater video of actual drowning victim that signaled lifeguards to initiate rescue. (Photo courtesy of Poseidon Technologies, Inc.)

scanning is simple, but the process of scanning and remaining vigilant is a comprehensive and vitally important task. For starters, I recommend defining each individual visual trip through the lifeguard's zone of coverage as a sweep. A scan is a process of repeated sweeps. As the components of scanning are examined, the inverted U hypothesis should be applied. Although instinctively and intuitively aquatic professionals realize that many physical and psychological tricks can be used to increase vigilance, careful study of the cause and effects of these scanning tips is important. The psychophysiology of lifeguarding should be applied to the scanning process to increase vigilance in the future.

High-Risk Guests

Each facility should determine which patrons are high-risk guests. Once these individuals or groups are determined, the lifeguard must be made aware of these findings and then taught how to best safeguard these individuals. For example, children ages 1 to 4 have the highest drowning rates, males are at greater risk for drowning than females, and the drowning rate for African Americans is significantly higher than that of whites (CDC, 2010). Additionally, for individuals with seizure disorders, drowning is the most common cause of unintentional injury death (CDC, 2010). Elderly guests are also at risk of dying in the swimming pool as a result of medical conditions, such as cardiac arrest.

Responding to Emergencies

Too often when lifeguards must respond to an emergency, they either do not respond properly or injure themselves in the process. Another advantage of the Five-Minute Scan is that the body is relatively warmed up physically and mentally in case an aquatic emergency arises. When an emergency response arises, the lifeguard must not panic or react too quickly without

thinking about what options are available. Emergency action plans should be established and practiced at every aquatic facility. Depending on the design of the facility and other factors such as proximity of the emergency medical systems, emergency action plans may vary. Lifeguards must know, understand, and practice the facility emergency action plan.

When an aquatic emergency arises, lifeguards must be trained to resist the temptation of overreacting by responding too quickly. Lifeguards are usually talented and gifted athletes. Quick reactions are a part of their training and within their capabilities. But some lifeguards react emotionally to a crisis and act before thinking rationally. Every lifeguard should be trained to stop and think the situation through clearly before taking action. Reacting hurriedly to an emergency often leads to an inefficient rescue attempt or an injury. On the opposite end of the continuum, some lifeguards choose not to respond at all when faced with an emergency, probably because they do not want to admit that an accident has happened.

Once an emergency is spotted, a predetermined emergency signal should be used to initiate the emergency action plan, but the first responder should stop and think clearly before taking action. If this process is followed, more lives could be saved and fewer injuries could occur to lifeguards.

Evaluating Lifeguards

One of the most significant contributions of Ellis and Associates to the lifeguarding profession is lifeguarding audits. Ellis and Associates trains, certifies, and supervises its lifeguards, most of whom work at waterparks. This lifeguard training agency uses unannounced lifeguarding audits to spot-check facilities and guards. Unannounced videotaping of guards is a common and effective practice. Audits not only check to see that lifeguards are doing what they are supposed to be doing on duty but also evaluate the guards on surprise simulated emergency situations. Lifeguard audits and facility inspections are a portion of a total risk management program. One problem of unannounced audits is that lifeguards can actually fake scanning by moving their head through choreographed patterns to pass the audit. To avoid this, auditors might ask lifeguards to turn their backs on the zone of coverage and ask how many people are in their area. To pass an audit, the lifeguard can use the Five-Minute Scanning Strategy, which requires at least significant body movement every 5 minutes to ensure the lifeguard is not dozing off, and a safety check is also required during this time. Counting of patrons is also encouraged when possible. Many professionals who use the Five-Minute Scan suggest that it serves as a lifeguard audit every 5 minutes, especially if counting or a similar safety check is used. Ellis and Associates now subscribes to the Five-Minute Scanning Strategy.

Any aquatic facility can conduct its own lifeguard audit, but sometimes having an unbiased and objective outsiders perform this important evaluation is beneficial. The American Red Cross now offers certified aquatic examiners who are trained to professionally audit aquatic facilities for safety. In-house audits can be accomplished simply, however. A colored ball can be subtly placed into the water to determine how long it will take the lifeguard on duty to spot it, or the lifeguard can be recorded while on duty for objective data that can be used to constructively criticize the lifeguard. Another supervisory technique is to record the amount of time spent looking away from the area of observation. Perhaps the best evaluation is to ask the lifeguard to turn his or her back on the water, with the supervisor taking over surveillance and asking the lifeguard exactly what he or she saw. Some pools make the use of a problem–incentive log that not only records lifeguard and facility deficiencies but also allows the supervisor to praise the lifeguard for a job well done (Figure 23.8).

P. J. Heath (2003) recommends developing data-based evaluation methods at swimming pools so that lifeguard evaluations can be made accurately, consistently, and reliably. Too often, lifeguard supervisors criticize their staff in vague, opinionated, and emotional terms. Heath urges lifeguard supervisors to use coding sheets that analyze on-task and off-task behaviors. Off-task behaviors include activities such as social talking, non-attentive behavior, and insufficient scanning. By calculating the percentage of time spent on task and off task, supervisors can easily and objectively rate the lifeguard. (See Figures 23.9 and 23.10 for examples of Heath's coding sheets and summary reports.)

PROBLEM/INCENTIVE LOG

DAY: M T W TH F S S	DATE:
POOL:	CODE:

POOL OPENED LATE	LIST TIME:
GUARD ARRIVE LATE	LIST TIME:
POOL CLOSED EARLY	LIST TIME:
HEALTH INSPECTION	PASS OR FAIL
GUARD NOT IN CHAIR/WATCHING POOL	
GUARD NOT IN UNIFORM	
FAIR OR POOR ON FIELD REPORT	
FAIR OR POOR ON EVALUATION	MIDSEASON END
FAILURE TO OBTAIN SUB FOR TIME OFF	
ASSISTED STAFFING	
OTHER/COMMENTS	
EMP#:	NAME
EMP#:	NAME
EMP#:	NAME
EMP#:	NAME

COMPLETED BY:	ENTERED BY:

Figure 23.8. Lifeguard summary report. (Courtesy of P. J. Heath)

SUMMARY REPORT

Employee: Dan Stevens Location: WOSSC

Date: 8-3-13 Position: P-3

Time Started: 1:36pm Ended: 1:48pm Evaluator: PJH

Time/Task Analysis Results of Employee Behavior

Total Time ON-TASK	6:20-380 SEC	
Scanning Time	4:20-230 SEC	Comments:
Rescue Time	0:00	
Discipline Time	1:10-70 SEC	Total Time -
Managerial Time	:50-50 SEC	8 MIN
Percent of Time ON-TASK	79%	280 SEC
Scanning Time	54%	
Rescue Time	0%	
Discipline Time	14%	
Managerial Time	10%	
Total Time OFF-TASK	1:10-100SEC	
Talking Time	1:10-70 SEC	Comments:
Non-Attentive	:50-50 SEC	
Off Ready Position	:30-30 SEC	
Poor Vantage Point	0:00	
Inappropriate behavior	0:00	
Percent of Time OFF-Task	:20-20 SEC	
Talking Time	4:20-230 SEC	
Non-Attentive	21%	
Off Ready Position	10%	
Non-Attentive	6%	
Off Ready Position	0%	
Poor Vantage Point	0%	
Inappropriate Behavior	4%	

ON-TASK - 79%
OFF-TASK - 21%

Figure 23.9. Lifeguard summary report. (Courtesy of P. J. Heath)

LIFEGUARD EVALUATION CODING SHEET

LB	S	S	S	S	NA	NA	S	S	D	D	S	S	3 MIN.
PC	F/M/LO												

LB	S	S	D	D	S	S	T	T	T	T	T	NA	3 MIN.
PC	F/M/M												

LB	IB	IB	S	S	S	S	S	D	D	D	M	M	3 MIN.
PC	F/M/LO												

LB	M	S	S	S	S	S	S	S	S	S	M	M	3 MIN.
PC	F/M/LO												

Pool Climate
Patron Load
Heavy (H)
Fair (F)
Light (L)

Type of Activity
Organized Play (OP)
Lap Swim (LS)
Free Play (FP)
Mixed (M)

Level of Activity
High (HI)
Medium (M)
Low (LO)

Lifeguard Behavior
On-Task Behaviors
Scanning (S)
Rescue (R)
Discipline (D)

Off-Task Bahaviors
Talking (T)
Non-Attentive (NA)
Poor Vantage Point (PP)
Off Ready Position (RP)
Inappropriate Behavior (IB)

Figure 23.10. Lifeguard evaluation coding sheet. (Courtesy of P. J. Heath)

Job Description

Every lifeguard needs a job description to outline specific duties and responsibilities. Without a job description, pool employees are often confused. Lifeguards should be responsible for water safety and accident prevention only when on duty at poolside performing surveillance. If given other tasks, lifeguards must accomplish them only when not stationed at the facility on surveillance duty. Whenever possible, personnel other than certified lifeguards should be assigned pool operation and maintenance tasks. Job expectations must be spelled out clearly in the job description. Behaviors that are not acceptable should also be highlighted in the job description. The chain of command is also important and should be illustrated in the job description. It is a good idea to have each lifeguard sign and date a lifeguard pledge, which can be customized for each pool (Figure 23.11).

Rules and Regulations

Lifeguards must know, understand, and enforce all rules and regulations adopted by the pool. These rules should be posted conspicuously at the pool and passed out to the patrons if possible. When a patron violates a swimming pool rule, pool staff should point out the rule and explain the rationale for obeying the rule to the violator. Yelling and screaming at misbehaving patrons is often counterproductive. Rules and regulations are established to safeguard the swimmers by preventing accidents. Ignoring pool rules, on the part of either the swimmer or the lifeguard, can lead to accidents. Lifeguards must be taught how to speak with adults, particularly regarding rules and regulations. One of the primary reasons for lifeguard attrition is a conflict with a parent, and these often occur over pool rules, so this type of training is particularly important at each aquatic facility.

Today's Date: __/__/__

"AS A PENN STATE LIFEGUARD AT THE McCOY NATATORIUM INDOOR POOL, OUTDOOR POOL OR WHITE BUILDING POOL, I WILL…"

- Continually scan the water so that everyone in my zone is checked.
- Always guard the pool from the lifeguard chair or stand/walk at the pool's edge. Never anywhere else.
- Never leave the pool unattended, even for as little as 5 seconds.
- Never read, study, write or sleep on duty.
- Always know and enforce all pool rules.
- Always be currently certified in lifeguarding and CPR.
- Always wear the Penn State lifeguard uniform (no sneakers or sweats).
- Always by punctual. On time at Penn State means reporting to the pool operator 15 minutes early.
- Always follow the emergency action plan described in the PSU lifeguard manual.
- Always watch out for "HIGH RISK" patrons (senior citizens, children, and minorities).
- Always report problems to Tom Griffiths or the pool operators.
- I have read and completely understand the lifeguard manual.

Print Your Name: _______________________________________

Sign Your Name: _______________________________________

Figure 23.11. Lifeguard pledge. (Courtesy of Tom Griffiths)

Lifeguard Stations

Some states require lifeguards on duty to be in elevated lifeguard chairs, but most states require that the lifeguard on duty be stationed at poolside. Ironically, numerous accidents are caused by the lifeguard climbing in or out of the lifeguard stand, particularly during a crisis. Fortunately, a growing trend is for creating lower elevated lifeguard stations that provide additional safety to the lifeguard as well as the patron. Lifeguard stations that are shorter and wider allow not only for easy, safe access in and out of the stations, but also for changes in position of the lifeguard while on duty in the station. Some states require that a lifeguard be stationed at poolside. Portable lifeguard stations are much preferred than permanently installed lifeguards stations because the movable stations can be placed to avoid glare from the sun and more strategically regarding groups and activities. If possible, ladders should be avoided on lifeguard stations. Vertical ladders are too difficult to climb up and down, particularly in an emergency, and may even be dangerous to the lifeguard in wet conditions. Sitting in lounge and deck chairs intended for patrons should be avoided. Because they are low to the ground, visual obstructions may occur, and the perception that the lifeguard is relaxing rather than working is always a problem. Lifeguard chairs and stations should be fully equipped with the recommended rescue and communication equipment and should also provide shade and water. Although the required equipment varies with each state, the minimum equipment expected for a lifeguard would probably be the following:

1. a rescue tube or can (depending on which type is preferred);
2. a long, light reaching pole or shepherd's crook;
3. a ring buoy with throwing line attached;
4. whistle and bullhorn;
5. shade; and
6. water to drink and to spray for cooling off.

Lifeguards should be cautioned about the causes, symptoms, treatment, and prevention of heat stress and skin cancer. The lifeguard station is an ideal place to provide protection from the sun, including shade and cold water. The local chapter of the American Cancer Society is a great source of sun protection information. Equipment to protect lifeguards from the hazards of blood-borne pathogens such as HIV, hepatitis, and others as specified by the Occupational Safety and Health Administration should also be accessible at the lifeguard stations. Some lifeguards carry protective equipment (pocket masks, shields, latex gloves) in fanny packs so that they are never without this vital protection. Walk-

ing or standing at poolside, although not without drawbacks, is often an effective lifeguard station.

Lifeguard Communications

Lifeguards can communicate in several ways. Clear communication becomes especially important during an aquatic emergency. Some forms of communications include the following:

- whistles,
- flags,
- hand signals,
- bullhorns,
- telephones,
- walkie-talkies, and
- other electronic devices.

Regardless of what form of communication is selected for lifeguards, both lifeguards and patrons must fully understand the language to be used for discipline and aquatic emergencies. Signals and their meanings should be posted near the entrance of the pool or the lifeguard stations.

Uniforms

Lifeguard uniforms are important not only to gain the attention and respect of the pool patrons but also to protect guards from the elements. Regardless of what type of apparel is chosen for the employee, "Lifeguard" or "Guard" should appear boldly on the front and/or back (Figure 23.12). Brightly colored lifeguard shirts, shorts, and hats are common at pools and beaches. Pool managers and supervisors would be more successful getting their staff to wear uniforms if the staff had input into the design and selection of the uniforms. Lifeguard hats and umbrellas should also be supplied by the pool when possible. All staff should be encouraged to wear hats and quality sunglasses that block ultraviolet rays and to apply generous amounts of sunscreen.

Motivating Lifeguards

Motivating lifeguards is often a problem because lifeguarding is not as glamorous as many perceive, and it becomes boring and tedious quickly. In-service training conducted periodically is highly recommended to prevent staffing problems and to keep motivation high. In-service training should be reserved not only for refining lifesaving water skills but also for motivating guards by rewarding the good guards and improving communications in weak areas. It is important to allow the guards to have input during in-service training and throughout the season. Lifeguards can also be beneficial in establishing policies, rules, and regulations. As much as possible, lifeguards should be an important part of the decision-

Figure 23.12. Lifeguards should be on duty even for swim team practices. (Photo courtesy of Aquatic Safety Research Group)

making process at aquatic facilities. Team-building activities are deemed to be vitally important when attempting to increase lifeguard morale and motivation. Because most lifeguards are teenagers, socialization should be encouraged during the day and after hours, provided it is appropriate and does not detract from their lifeguarding responsibilities.

When working with lifeguards, supervisors will find it helpful in many situations to frame areas in need of improvement as learning opportunities and teaching moments rather than to express the need for improvement negatively. Additionally, intermittent rewards or random rewards are known scientifically to be the most motivating reward system. Intermittent rewards, also referred to as random rewards, are rewards that are not expected and are not routine. Rewards can include positive feedback, small rewards, or empowering opportunities, such as planning an activity for the next in-service training. Intermittent rewards can be carried out effectively, can become motivating, and can increase stimulation for on-duty lifeguards.

Lifeguard competitions are a good way of honing swimming and rescue skills, improving camaraderie and team spirit, and increasing fun at the workplace. Lifeguard competitions are becoming increasingly popular in the United States and abroad. There are even international lifeguarding competitions which are fun events for lifeguards to participate in and audiences to watch. Businesses in the local community usually appreciate supporting the lifeguard competitions by donating valuable prizes. Of course, lifeguard parties are a great way to show appreciation to the lifeguards. If held at the pool, extreme caution must be exercised because lifeguards can injure themselves while showing off or competing. Awards can also be given at these parties to lifeguards who have given outstanding service to the facility.

In addition to in-service training, it is advisable to offer continuing education whereby lifeguards can obtain additional training beyond what they receive at their facility. Providing release time for continuing education and even paying for courses that lifeguards take is beneficial and appreciated by lifeguards. Continuing education need not be an elaborate program. Setting a schedule for visiting other pools and offering additional training with accompanying certifications can be helpful to the staff.

Junior Lifeguarding Programs

In the past, junior lifesaving courses were taught to youngsters aged 11 to 15. Because it was feared that

Figure 23.13. A vigilant lifeguard performing the Five-Minute Scanning Strategy.© (Photo courtsy of Aquatic Safety Research Group)

many junior lifesavers would misuse their skills by attempting to make rescues, the program was changed to basic water safety courses.

However, many youngsters aspire to be lifeguards and have tremendous swimming ability, and it is no secret that the United States is experiencing a lifeguarding shortage. Junior lifeguard programs of today are a great way to recruit potential lifeguards, but more important, they provide another set of eyes and ears to help safeguard swimmers. After completing successful "internships" at local aquatic facilities, they often have a job waiting for them when they reach lifeguarding age. Although junior lifeguards cannot make rescues, they can help with equipment and communications. Junior lifeguards can be invaluable during an emergency situation when the emergency medical services system must be activated. They can also provide supervision on decks, in wading pools, at slides, around obstructions, and inside buildings that lifeguards may have trouble covering, particularly when busy. Junior lifeguard programs are a great way to combat the lifeguarding shortage without incurring great expense.

Youngsters are not the only ones who can assist lifeguards at swimming pools. Senior citizens who enjoy the water and who have extra time can also provide another layer of supervision at pools. Senior citizens, like junior lifeguards, are not trained to make water rescues, but they can assist. Senior citizens may even be more effective than lifeguards in enforcing rules and regulations and carrying out disciplinary actions. Most pool

lifeguards are between ages 15 and 21. For the most part, they are single and do not have children. Senior citizens, on the other hand, are often grandparents. They have a lifetime of experience dealing with children and people in general and understand how quickly young children can get into trouble. They can assist swimming pool staff in several ways, and some senior citizens have even been known to work for pool privileges rather than wages. Senior citizens are another source to assist the lifeguards and safeguard the pool.

Figure 23.14. Resting in between events at a Junior Lifeguarding Competition. (Photo courtsy of Aquatic Safety Research Group)

How Many Lifeguards?

How many lifeguards should be on duty is an often-asked question that is extremely difficult to answer. And no single answer is correct. The number of lifeguards required will not only vary with geographical location but with the facility and the guests engaging in water activities.

Local bathing codes and swimming pool ordinances must be consulted to determine what type of lifeguards are required and how many should be on duty at any time, but again, local bathing codes often offer minimum standards. Some states require one lifeguard per 50 swimmers, and other ordinances state that one lifeguard must be on duty for every 2,000 sq ft of water surface area. Many other lifeguard standards exist as well. However, for busy public pools with a mixed clientele, one lifeguard for every 25 swimmers may be required. But these ratios can be troublesome. If a 1:50 lifeguard-to-swimmer ratio is established, does having 51 people in the water mean that the facility is unsafe?

More important, pool staff must evaluate the swimming facilities and patron types to determine specific lifeguard requirements. Whenever the number of swimmers exceeds a predetermined limit placed on certain sections of the pool, additional guards should be added. For instance, in a diving well, two guards may be required when more than 10 people are using that specific facility. Having one criterion for all pools in the same geographical region is not a good idea because of the variety that exists among pools. Guarding 50 lap swimmers in a rectangular shallow water pool without obstructions is likely to be much safer and easier than guarding 50 people in a deep water wave pool with some obstructions. Rapid response time must be considered when determining lifeguard numbers. A lifeguard-to-square-footage-of-water-surface-area ratio may be preferred to a lifeguard-to-patron ratio because the square footage ratio remains the same and does not fluctuate daily.

Minimum age and special certification requirements may also be placed on lifeguards. For most public pools, the following lifeguard requirements may exceed local pool codes and are strongly recommended:

1. at least 16 years of age,
2. current lifeguarding certification from a nationally recognized agency or equivalent,
3. current CPR certification, and
4. current first-aid, AED certification.

In addition to the above requirements, the employer should test each lifeguard on rescue skills, lifeguarding knowledge, verbal skills, and situational problems that might arise.

Some risk managers state that at least two lifeguards must be on duty for all pools at all times. Although this is recommended for most public pools, it can be cost prohibitive and unrealistic for small private or semipublic pools. Because the second lifeguard on the scene of an accident often assists the primary rescuer by calling 911 or other emergency numbers and clearing the pool of other swimmers, exceptions might be made for small pools. These secondary tasks may be assigned to other staff who are not lifeguards, provided they are mature and well trained in their jobs. This should only be done when a minimum of two staff members are on duty when the pool is open (one lifeguard and one assistant to the lifeguard). This procedure must also be written into the job description and emergency action plan. Desk attendants are the most obvious candidates for assisting lifeguards in emergency procedures at small pools.

Some states require lifeguards to be in elevated lifeguard chairs, but others do not. In some cases, a roving lifeguard is more effective than one who sits in an elevated chair. Perhaps the best combination is to have some lifeguards stationed in elevated chairs and one or more lifeguards roving. The keys to positioning lifeguards include the following:

1. not being distracted by patrons,
2. no sight obstructions or glare,
3. able to respond quickly and safely to a distressed swimmer, and
4. able to see all patrons.

In determining the appropriate number and placement of lifeguards, supervisors must apply common sense. Questions such as "Can I see everyone in my zone?" and "Can I reach everyone in my zone quickly and safely?" must be answered before deciding how many lifeguards must be on duty at a given time and where these lifeguards should be placed. Lifeguards should rotate every 15 to 20 minutes to prevent boredom and should receive a rest break from surveillance every 1 to 2 hours.

Summary

Certified lifeguards are most often well trained and highly competent. It must be emphasized, however, that the purpose of having lifeguards at poolside is first to prevent accidents and second to respond to emergencies promptly and properly. Lifeguards must be specifically trained for the facility at which they will be working and must be continually supervised. Motivating currently employed lifeguards and recruiting potential lifeguards are important challenges that must be done continually. Many lifeguards are guilty of not watching the people in the water continuously. The key to running a safe aquatic facility is not necessarily the lifeguards, but perhaps more appropriately the supervision of the lifeguards.

Lifeguards in general are young considering the importance of the job and therefore must be mentored and monitored regularly. Finally, even when lifeguards are present, parents must be strongly urged to watch their children.

References

American Red Cross. (1992). *Swimming and diving.* St Louis: Mosby.

American Red Cross. (2009). *Swimming and water safety. StayWell.* Yardley, PA: Author.

Branche, C. M., & Stewart, S. (Eds.). (2001). *Lifeguard effectiveness: A report of the working group.* Atlanta: Centers for Disease Control and Prevention, National Center for Injury Prevention and Control.

Ellis and Associates. (1990). *National pool and waterpark lifeguard training manual.* Houston: Author.

Fenner, P., Lealhy, S., Buhk, A., & Dawes, P. (1999). Prevention of drowning: Visual scanning and attention span in lifeguards. *The Journal of Occupationnal Health and Safety, 15*(1), 61–66.

Griffiths, R. C., & Griffiths, T. (2013). Internal noise distractions in lifeguarding. *International Journal of Aquatic Research and Education, 7*(1), 56–71.

Griffiths, T. (July 19, 1987). Do lifeguards do what they get paid to do? *The New York Times.*

Griffiths, T., Steel, D., & Vogelsong, H. (1999). Lifeguarding behaviors and systematic scanning strategies. In J. Fletemeyer, F. Freas, F. (Eds), *Drowning: New perspectives on intervention and prevention* (pp. 267–279). New York: CRC Press.

Heath P. J. (Jul/Aug 1991). *Splash,* pp 35–36.

Pia, F. (1974). Observations on the drownings of non-swimmers. *Journal of Physical Education,* 164–167.

Pia, F. (June, 1984). *Parks & Recreation,* pp. 52–67.

www.aquaticsafetygroup.com

www.circadian.com/learning

www.poseidon-tech.com/us/lifeguarding/html

Bibliography

American Red Cross. (1992). *Swimming and diving.* St Louis: Mosby.

American Red Cross. (1990). *Lifeguarding.* Washington, D.C.: The Red Cross.

American Red Cross. (1995). *Lifeguarding today.* St. Louis, Missouri: Mosby Lifeline.

Branche, C. M., & Stewart, S. (Eds). (2001). *Lifeguard effectiveness: A report of the working group.* Atlanta: Centers for Disease Control and prevention.

Centers for Disease Control and Prevention. (2010). Wide-ranging OnLine Data for Epidemiologic Research. Retrieved form http://wonder.cdc.gov/mortsql.html

Center for Disease Control and Prevention (2010). Unintentional Drowning: Get the Facts. Retrieved from http://www.cdc.gov/

Clayton, R. D., & Thomas, D. G. (1989). *Professional aquatic management* (2nd ed.). Champaign, IL: Human Kinetics.

Ellis and Associates. (1990). *National pool and waterpark lifeguard training manual.* Houston: Author.

Griffiths, R. C., & Griffiths, T. (2013). Internal noise distractions in lifeguarding. *International Journal of Aquatic Research and Education, 7*(1), 56–71.

Griffiths, T. (1998). "All Along the Watch Tower, *Aquatics International,* p. 14.

Griffiths, T. (1999). *Better beaches.* Hoffman Estates, IL: NRPA.

Griffiths, T. (2008). *Disappearing Dummies* [DVD]. State College, PA: Aquatic Safety Research Group.

Griffiths, T., Chambers, V., & Steel, D. (1995). "Survey Results: Systematic Scanning For Lifeguards." *Parks and Recreation Magazine, 30*(2) pp. 40–47.

Griffiths, T., Steel, D.. & Vogelsong, H . (April 1996). The 1995 National Lifeguard Survey: How Water Park Lifeguards Fared. *Splash Magazine,* pp. 26–28.

Griffiths, T., Steel, D., & Vogelsong, H. (1999). Lifeguarding behaviors and systematic scanning strategies. In J. Fletemeyer, & F. Freas, F. (Eds), Drowning: *New perspectives on intervention and prevention* (pp. 267–279). New York: CRC Press.

Griffiths, T., Vigelsong, H., & Steel, D. (1997). Results of the 1996 National Lifeguard Survey. *Parks and Recreation Magazine,* pp. 62–68.

Griffiths, T., Vogelsong, H., & Steel, D. (2000). Results of the 1998 Lifeguard Survey—Keeping their Guard up. *Aquatics International,* pp. 36–38.

Heath, P. J. (1992). *Basic risk management for water parks.* San Antonio: Glynn Barclay.

International Swimming Hall of Fame. Commodore Wilbert E. Longfellow (USA): 1965 honor contributor. (n.d.). Retrieved from www.ishof.org/65clongfellow.html

National Center for Health Statistics. (2000). *Vital Statistic of the United States: Mortality, Underlying and Multiple Causes of Death.* Public Use Files. Hyattsville, Maryland: NCHS.

Pia, F. (1984). The RID factor as a cause of drowning. *Parks & Recreation,* 19, pp. 52–67.

The YMCA of the USA. (1986). *On the guard: The YMCA lifeguard manual.* Champaign, IL: Human Kinetics.

Torney, J. A., & Clayton, R. D. (1970). *Aquatic instruction, coaching and management.* Minneapolis: Burgess.

www.circadian.com/learning

24

Shallow Water Blackout

Key Concepts

- Hyperventilation
- Recovery time
- At-risk swimmers
- Genetic drowning triggers

Shallow water blackout (SWB) is not a new phenomenon. Medical researchers, divers, and physicists began studying SWB in the 1940s. However, much attention has never surrounded SWB. Obtaining evidence that shows the prevalence of SWB is difficult for several reasons. First, when a victim is unconscious in the water, it is often coined a *drowning*. The cause of unconsciousness underneath the surface may have been SWB, but it is most often not labeled as SWB. Thus, in these cases, SWB is not documented. Second, obtaining witnesses that watched an individual succumb to SWB from the start is difficult. For example, a swimmer may be practicing extreme breath-holding techniques, but a lifeguard may not see the swimmer until he or she is passed out on the bottom of the pool or other body of water. Third, a lifeguard or another individual may not be with a swimmer when they succumb to SWB to know if the swimmer was practicing extreme breath-holding, or breath-holding after strenuous exercise or hyperventilation. Fourth, if a swimmer has an underlying genetic drowning trigger, it may be completely undetected before or even after the SWB event. Because of these reasons and others, illustrating the prevalence of the problem in "hard evidence" is difficult. In spite of these challenges, we do know that SWB is a problem; it does occur; and it continues to happen, causing many deaths. The good news is that awareness is greater than ever. Greater awareness brings more questions as well. To address these questions, the culture of SWB awareness is beginning to shift.

History

In the 1960s, Craig published research on the dangers of prolonged breath-holding and began raising awareness of SWB (Figure 24.1). The traditional definition of SWB in scuba diving and free diving manuals includes ascending from depths to shallow water and involves the lowering of the partial pressure of oxygen. Breath-holding and hyperventilation also are included in this definition. The swimming pool definition of SWB is competitive, repetitive, or prolonged breath-holding that

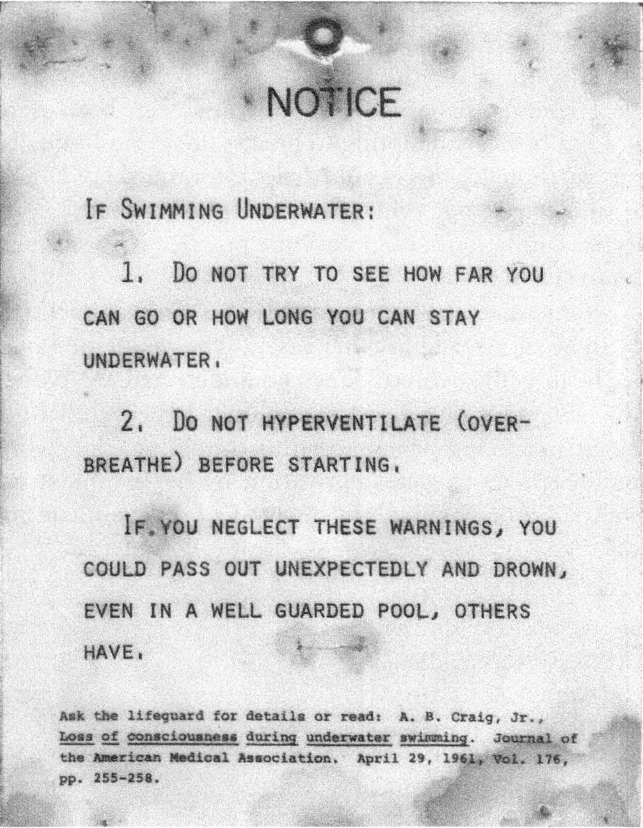

Figure 24.1. This warning was posted at the Penn State University Natatorium in 1985.

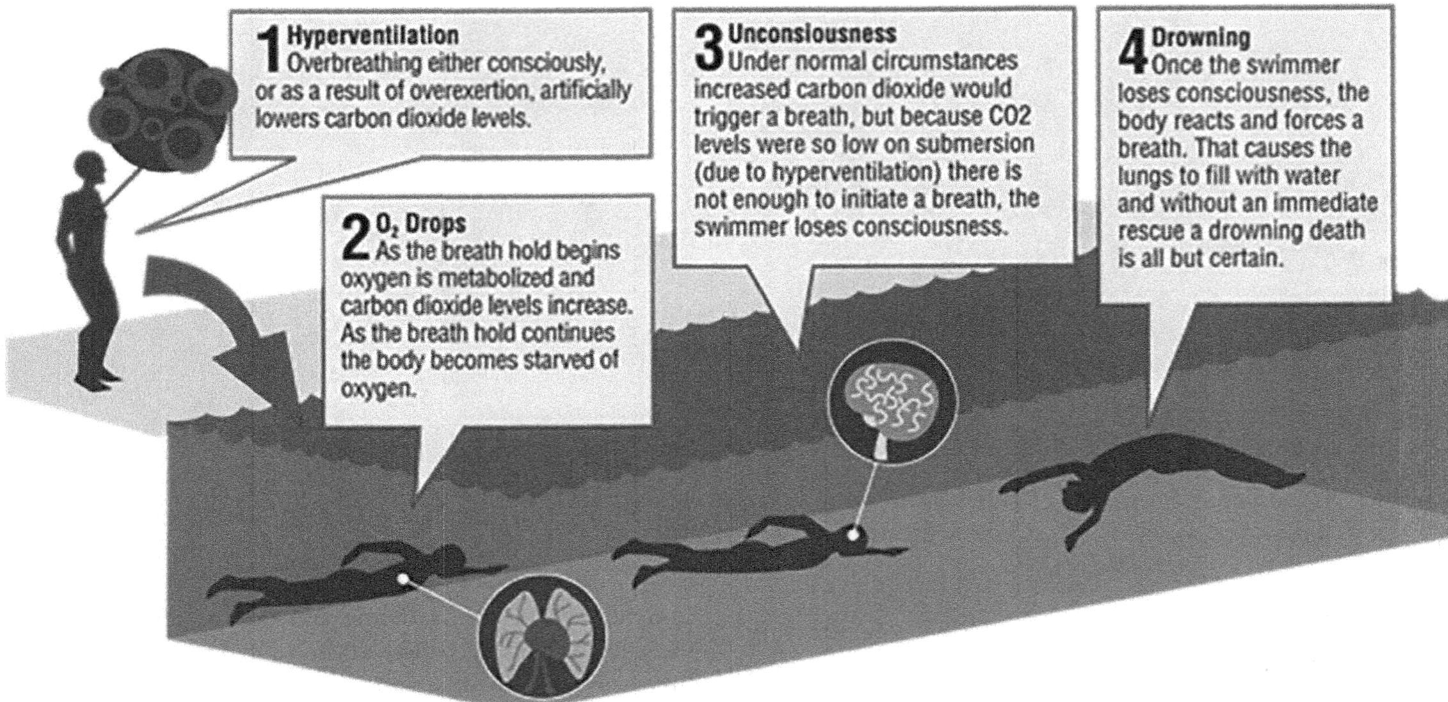

Figure 24.2. Shallow water blackout. (Aquatics International, 2011)

can include hyperventilation, resulting in an individual blacking out under the water.

Hyperventilation is taking rapid, deep breaths in and out before attempting to breath-hold. Traditionally, people thought this would help swimmers hold their breath longer, but evidence does not exist that it does. Hyperventilation should never be practiced. It can cause hypoxia and SWB.

Sometimes the hyperventilation is overt, sometimes it can be subtle, and in other cases, hyperventilation may not be directly involved or can go undetected. SWB does not always involve overt intentional hyperventilation. When practicing prolonged breath-holding, the swimmer reacts to oxygen deprivation by hyperventilating, even if he or she did not intend to hyperventilate for

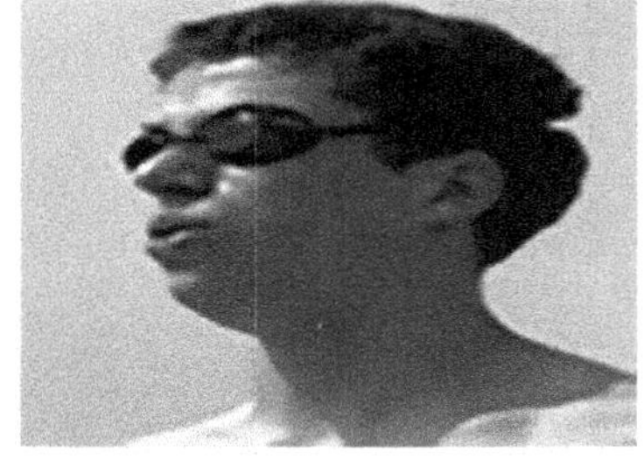

Figure 24.3. A swimmer hyperventilating prior to entering the water. (Photo courtesy of *Shallow Water Blackout* [DVD], Griffiths, 2008)

training. In other words, unintentional hyperventilation or strenuous exercise can lead to SWB. It is important to understand that many individuals have died while training hypoxically without signs of hyperventilation (www.shallowwaterblackoutprevention.org).

SWB occurs when a person holding their breath underwater, usually following intentional or unintentional hyperventilation or strenuous exercise, passes out underwater. SWB also has been described as "fainting underwater." In the simplest terms, a swimmer loses consciousness underwater from lack of oxygen. Often, the unconscious individual aspirates water, and drowning or sudden death from underlying medical maladies underwater occurs. Craig (1961), however, believed breath control could be practiced safely. A general rule of thumb is "One Breath, One Time, One Length, One Time."

Hypoxic training became even more popularized in the 1970s, with the book *Swimming Fastest* by Ernest W. Maglischo, which encouraged hypoxic training to improve performance. Since Craig's original warnings, there still have been far too many victims and far too many deaths (United Educators, 2005). Some coaches believe that elite athletes should practice hypoxic training and hyperventilation and that these athletes can handle it. This has never been proven.

Genetic Drowning Triggers

In addition to SWB, holding one's breath and/or hyperventilation may trigger underlying disorders (genetic "drowning" triggers), such as long QT syndrome, RYR2, and seizure disorders, which also can lead to sudden cardiac arrest (Griffiths, 2006). Many of the underlying medical maladies, which competitive, repetitive, and/or prolonged breath-holding could preclude are even unknown to the individual. Without comprehensive genetic testing, a swimmer may not know they have a genetic drowning trigger. This is an important reason competitive, repetitive, and prolonged breath-holding should be banned.

Case Studies

SWB deaths do not seem to be subsiding. The following are just a few victims of SWB.

Two 21-year-old boys, Bohdan Vitenko and Jonathan Proce, died while doing a Navy SEAL training exercise. Proce and Vitenko were found unconscious in 3 ft of water in a Staten Island public pool on Wednesday July 13, 2011. The pair was doing breath-holding exercises similar to those used in military training, authorities said. Vitenko died at the site of the incident, and Proce, who was a certified lifeguard, later died in the hospital after going into a coma.

Athleticism is a common trait for SWB victims. Another athletic boy, Gene Whitner Milner III, was 23 years old when he died tragically from SWB in his family swimming pool on April 17, 2011. He was practicing his breath-holding and was found in the position he assumed when practicing prolonged breath-holding.

Education is extremely important, as 12-year-old Jack Alexander Kevin MacMillan's mother found out. She always supervised her children in the water, but was unaware of SWB, and she watched Jack die of SWB as it took his life quickly and silently. He was also an athletic boy. He lost his life while he was practicing breath-holding in the shallow end of his family's swimming pool. His mother was close by, as she never left him or his sisters unattended while they swam. However, he succumbed to SWB quickly and silently, with no warning to the victim or those around him.

In 2012 and 2013, a string of swim team members passed out while practicing "breath-control," or trying to swim as far as possible without taking a breath. Traditionally, this practice has been encouraged by swim coaches. Evidence does not exist of benefits to extreme breath-holding, yet there continues to be many victims. All children should learn to swim. Often, however, SWB victims who have already learned to swim and are in fact accomplished swimmers are not educated about SWB.

Too often, good swimmers are encouraged to engage in competitive, repetitive, and prolonged breath-holding.

Media

Often, media glorify extreme dangerous breath-holding, such as David Blaine on the Oprah Winfrey show in 2008 holding his breath underwater for 17 minutes, 4 seconds. Material online and in magazines instructs how to hold one's breath longer, many times without noting the dangers. Some big wave surfing writers also encourage extreme breath-holding practice for amateurs in swimming pools. Breath-holding contests, games, competitions, and training are extremely popular, accepted, and ingrained in society for recreation and thrill from an early age. However, no advantages are evident and the stakes are high—unconsciousness underwater, which can lead to death.

Prevention

When individuals are taught to swim, relaxed breath-holding is key. Humans cannot descend under the water without holding their breath. Breath-control is needed for children to learn to swim, as well as for experienced swimmers. However, when this is taught, it should be relaxed with plenty of rest in between and under close supervision.

SWB occurs as a result of competitive, repetitive, and/or prolonged breath-holding. This may include a swim coach having swim team members swim multiple 50 yards holding their breath with little rest in between, Navy SEALs conducting a brick walk for training, or teenagers competing against one another in breath-holding contests. These are just a few examples of competitive, repetitive, and/or prolonged breath-holding activities.

When competitive swimmers are training, restricted breathing exercises should only be practiced one drill at a time and with plenty of rest. Restricted breathing can be instructed under close supervision, such as breathing every fifth stroke. However, if the swimmer is unable to accomplish this, they should not be pushed past their limits and should NEVER be encouraged to resist the urge to breathe. Coaches should never give rewards, have contests, or encourage swimmers to resist the urge to breathe through prolonged breath-holding. If a facility is going to host a sport or activity that requires breath-holding, these activities should be conducted with extra supervision and either before or after the pool is open to the public. A waiver would also be helpful for these activities.

SWB was orginally emphasized as occurring only after overt hyperventilation. Now, medical experts assert that intentional hyperventilation is not necessarily involved. Thus, the key is to minimize extreme/prolonged breath-holding. Another reason extreme and prolonged breath-holding must be warned against is because often lifeguards, parents, and other supervisors actually watch children and others drown, thinking they were holding their breath. Not allowing competitive, repetitive, and prolonged breath-holding would eliminate this delay that many lifeguards have in recognizing a drowning victim. Additionally, a myriad of underlying medical maladies can be spurred by long underwater breath-holding activities, including long QT syndrome, RYR2, and seizure disorders.

Organizations such as the American Red Cross and the YMCA of the USA ban prolonged breath-holding and breath-holding games within their respective programs. USA Swimming has warnings regarding hypoxic training. In addition, some of these organizations have issued position statements that highlight the dangers of engaging in prolonged breath-holding activities.

Sidebar 24.1

MY HOPE IS THAT WE SAVE A LIFE

College Pool

Night after night, she's passed the indoor pool,
promising herself she'll never look, but tonight
she turns her head, her resolve not to bring it
back, broken.
She sees a young man like her son dive in
and begin swimming.
She wants to run in and whistle him out.
Doesn't he know he wouldn't be seen in those black
trunks by the black line if he slipped under?
She wants to tear the goggles from his face.
Doesn't he know they'd leave
engravings to the end?
She wants to ask where all his buddies are,
she wants to towel him dry, she wants to say go home.
Instead, she stands silent at the wall of glass,
sees ancient wailing women beating their
breasts, long black braids trailing down their backs.

Coming Home

On my lap, our son's blanket
too bulky to pack, the smell of strawberry shampoo.
Beside us, his belongings in carry-on bags.
We are crying.

"I travel light now," he bragged, going back to
school two weeks ago, leaving bike and stereo
behind.

We are two hours ahead of time in the boarding
area, we misread the tickets.

The security lady kneels by my husband, apologies
for making him open the bags, says she also lost
a child, a little girl, a hit and run.

A man from the Piedmont counter
speaks of a support he attends,
quietly maps out grief

where we are, where we must go,
how to get there.

I cannot follow the low tones
as he tells our other sons how it affects
schoolwork how he lost his son.

I cannot breathe,
I am drowning too.

On the plane I read the paper a teacher gave me
at the memorial service. "There's nothing special
about me," our son wrote.

I begin a eulogy, writing on bags from the seat
pockets–the stewardess brings paper.

We carry home the weight, and in the hold of
the plane, his body.

Shells

In and out the sea breathes green
against the shore, a beach
all mine this December day.

I find a mussel shell; blue, hinged, an empty house.
I press it closed, hold the bivalve in my hand,
keep the halves together. Seven years since we
were broken open.
Death came as still water in a college pool,
found you son, holding your breath
that final lap in the seventh lane.

Now behind the dunes I step around
a cover of hudsonia. Heathlike
the undershrub holds fast
despite its fragile roots—will live
some 70 years if undisturbed.

(A mother's poem tribute to her son, Stephen Prainser, a collegiate tri-athlete at the University of North Carolina-Wilmington, who died in 4 ft of water during public swim hours at his University pool.)

Figure 24.4. Effective SWB signage cones in English and Spanish. (Sign design ©Clarion Safety Systems. All rights reserved)

Aggressive signage in warning colors, shapes, and symbols banning prolonged breath-holding and warnings are needed at all swimming pools—residential, public, and semipublic.

Swim coaches, aquatic staff, and the public must be educated about the dangers of extreme breath-holding practices. The nonprofit organization Shallow Water Blackout Prevention tracks case studies of fatal and nonfatal SWB events and spreads education to prevent SWB. If individuals wish to engage in extreme underwater breath-holding sports, they must become aware of the risks and gain the proper training and education. For recreational and competitive swimmers, competitive, repetitive, and prolonged breath-holding must be banned.

ABC for SWB

A Breathing Continuum for Shallow Water Blackout (ABC for SWB; Aquatic Safety Research Group, 2012) illustrates a range of safer breath-holding activities through more risky breath-holding activities. This continuum is only a guideline, but can help decipher relaxed breath-holding for learning to swim versus risky behaviors that could lead to SWB and should be discouraged. The ABC for SWB can be downloaded for free at www.aquaticsafetygroup.com. For education and information about SWB prevention and case studies, visit www.ShallowWaterBlackout.org.

Summary

It is important for anyone managing an aquatic facility to be aware of Shallow Water Blackout and appropriately warn against dangerous breath-holding. Even the very best of swimmers succumb to SWB, not often weak or novice swimmers. Therefore, potential SWB victims are difficult to detect. Prevention programs and signage must be both vigilant and aggressive. The tragedy of Shallow Water Blackout is after teaching these individuals to swim to prevent drowning, they end up killing themselves unwittingly in the water because we did not provide adequate education and warning to them.

References

Craig, A. B. (1961). Loss of consciousness during underwater swimming. *Journal of the American Medical Association, 176*, 155–178.

American Red Cross. (2008). *Safety training for swim coaches.* Retrieved from http://www.redcross.org/images/MEDIA_CustomProductCatalog/m4240201_TrainingforSwimCoaches.pdf

Griffiths, T. J., & Griffiths, W. (2005). Dying for air. *Aquatics International.* Retrieved from www.aquaticsintl.com

Griffiths, T. J. (2008). *Shallow water blackout* [DVD]. Available from Aquatic Safety Research Group website: http://www.aquaticsafetygroup.com/booksandDVDs.html

Johnson, A., Erb, M.W., & Mahoney, J. (2009–2010). Shallow water blackout: Not just a summertime hazard. *Sea and Shore, 12*(1), pp 2–7.

Sperling, J. (2008, February). Coming up for air. *Aquatics International.* Retrieved from www.aquaticsintl.com/2008/feb/0802_rm.html

YMCA of the USA. (2011). *Unsafe breath holding practices* [Aquatic Safety & Risk Education]. Chicago, IL: Author.

United Educators. (2005). *Risk research bulletin: Buildings and grounds.* United Educators. Retrieved from www.ue.org

USA Swimming. (2009). *Safety loss/control manual.* Retrieved from Shallow Water Blackout Prevention website: www.shallowwaterblackoutprevention.org

ABC for SWB©

A Breathing Continuum for Shallow Water Blackout

HYPERVENTILATION AND/OR STRENUOUS EXERCISE PRIOR TO BREATH-HOLDING CAN BE DEADLY.

Swimming Activities

Limited Breath-Holding

Breath-holding for breath-control and relaxation during instruction (10-20 seconds). *Not resisting the discomforting urge to breathe.* *Swimmers will not necessarily experience an urge to breathe.

Includes (but not limited to): Retrieving an object from bottom, bobs, breath-control in learning to swim, blowing bubbles. These should always be practiced with plenty of rest in between (minutes, not seconds) and under close, continuous supervision.

Restricted Breathing

Incremental breathing exercises *on the surface* of the water. *Not resisting the discomforting urge to breathe.* *Swimmers will not necessarily experience an urge to breathe.

Includes (but not limited to): breathing every 5 strokes or every 7 strokes or training with a reduced orifice snorkel. This can be practiced for swimmers on a team, for short periods of time, and under close, continuous supervision of coaches and others.

Hypoxic Training

Attempts to increase amount of time a swimmer can hold his/her breath *underwater*. *Resisting the discomforting urge to breathe.* *Swimmers will not necessarily experience an urge to breathe.

Includes (but not limited to): intense restricted breathing exercises, 10 x 25 yard lengths with no breaths and little rest in between. Dangerous. Not Recommended.

Prolonged Breath-holding & Breath-holding Contests

Competitive, repetitive, prolonged breath-holding (more than 20-30 sec.), *resisting the discomforting urge to breathe.* *Swimmers will not necessarily experience an urge to breathe.

Includes (but not limited to): breath-holding contests, breath-holding for time, distance and/or training, swimming three lengths of the pool without breathing, "over unders," brick walk, strenuous exercise prior to breath-holding. Dangerous. Not Recommended.

GUIDELINE ONLY

Water Sports

Snorkeling/Skin Diving

With proper education and training and use of the buddy system and/or under close, continuous supervision. *Not resisting the discomforting urge breathe.* *Swimmers will not necessarily experience an urge to breathe.

Synchronized Swimming and Underwater Hockey

With proper education and training and use of the buddy system and/or under close, continuous supervision. *Not resisting the discomforting urge to breathe.* *Swimmers will not necessarily experience an urge to breathe.

Recreational Free Diving & Spearfishing

With proper education and training and use of the buddy system and/or under close, continuous supervision. *Not resisting the discomforting urge to breathe.* *Swimmers will not necessarily experience an urge to breathe.

Intense Competitive Free Diving and Spearfishing

Not recommended for the general public. *Resisting the discomforting urge to breathe.* **Extreme sports participants with proper education, training, certifications, adhering to strict protocols and at your own risk. Dangerous.** *Swimmers will not necessarily experience an urge to breathe.

***This is only a guideline.**

Figure 24.5. ABC for SWB (@2012, Aquatic Safety Research Group)

25

Rethinking Pool Signage

When the first edition of this book was written, safety signage was addressed only intermittently throughout the book. By the writing of the 2nd edition, signage had become much more important than it was a decade ago. More recently, the aquatics industry has begun applying strong safety signage that has been around for decades in other industries, such as highway safety, to the pool. Today, we know even more about factors for effective and conspicuous water safety signage from warning experts. One reason for the increased emphasis on signage may be the increased lawsuits against aquatic facilities accusing management of a "failure to warn." Although this chapter is not lengthy, it describes important treatment of safety signage. Rather than discussing and explaining the principles of effective signage, this chapter attempts to illustrate good examples of appropriate aquatic facility signage with an emphasis on safety signage. This chapter begins with the assumption that aquatic professionals have not done an especially good job of using effective signage to prevent accidents.

The four Cs of good signage include signs that are *clear, concise, consistent,* and *conspicuous,* but I would suggest that it is time to make aquatic signs more *creative* in order to gain the attention of pool guests.

Clear

The message should be accurately conveyed to the guests without ambiguity. Large letters in contrasting colors are best.

Concise

The message should be as brief as possible and to the point. Too much information will require too much time to read and may also confuse the reader. Plus, too much information provided may provide instruction for how to perform an unsafe activity.

Consistent

Signs should be consistently done. Although warning signs should look significantly different than informational signs, within these two categories the themes, colors, shapes, and sizes should be consistent. In other words, all warning signs should have similar shapes and colors, and although informational signs would be different than warning signs, they would be similar.

Conspicuous

If signs are to be effective, they must be conspicuously placed and designed to attract attention. Placement, color, size, shape, and creativity make signs more conspicuous.

Creative

Signs that are creative, use a sense of humor, and better relate to the locals attending the facility are much more likely to be noticed and followed. In addition, many facilities have been using the same signage for the past 50 years without any creativity or additional attention-getters added to them.

Aquatic facilities have many rules and regulations that should be posted, but too often good behavior and housekeeping rules are mixed with more important safety rules. When this happens, the important messages are often buried in less important information. The primary purpose of aquatic facility signs should be to warn and educate guests about risks and hazards inherent in the facility without sacrificing aesthetics. It is also important to increase safety and enjoyment for patrons without producing sign pollution. To accomplish this, a new scheme or strategy may be necessary to highlight the most important safety messages and to reduce in size and frequency information that is needed but not as important.

General information, directions, locations, and regulations are valuable information for pool signs to convey, but not at the expense of important safety signs. Another way of characterizing signage is grouping it into areas of patron importance:

1. information that is nice to know (Figure 25.1),
2. information that should be known, and
3. information that MUST be known.

For starters, aquatic facility managers should stress color-coding signs by the messages they convey. This would be helpful for guests attending the facility.

For instance, the three general categories of signs, which are not only colored differently but also sized differently, are listed from least important to most important:

TYPE	SIZE	COLOR
Informational/ Directional (nice to know)	small	Brown & white Green & white
Regulatory (should know)	medium	Black & white
Safety Signs (must know)	large	Red & white Black & white

Informational/Directional Signs

Informational/directional signs provide information and/or directions concerning restrooms, snack bars, telephones, and other information. The color scheme should be softer than the hard, contrasting colored warning or danger signs. The shape should also be different, and perhaps a horizontal rectangular-shaped sign is best for this purpose.

Regulatory Signs

Regulatory signs should be black and white, placed on a vertical rectangular sign and have the code or ordinance number that empowers the regulation on the bottom of the sign. An example of a regulatory sign would be "Pets Are Not Allowed in This Facility" or "Smoking Is Banned in This Facility."

Safety/Warning

Safety/warning signs should be the largest and most dramatic signs in the facility. Red and white is usually preferred, but red and white signs in outdoor facilities will not last nearly as long as black and white signs. Diamond-shaped black on yellow signs also clearly connote danger because these danger signs are easily recognizable. Perhaps the best combination would be a red and white or black and white sign with safety verbage and a

Figure 25.1. Examples of signage displaying information that is "nice to know." (Photos courtesy of Water Technology, Inc.)

diamond-shaped yellow and black sign with the universal DO NOT symbol added to it.

The most important warning signs at most aquatic facilities are "No Diving," "No Long Breath-Holding," "Watch Your Children," and "Nonswimmers Should Wear Life Jackets" (see Figure 25.2).

Highway Signs

Another philosophy to consider is to use attention-getting highway signs for the most important messages. Red and white octagonal stop signs and yellow and black diamond-shaped warning signs can be used to attract attention to the most vital warnings (Figure 25.3).

Three Strikes and You're Out!

For the most important messages, posting signs in three areas may be beneficial, for instance, at the entrance, in the bathhouse, and at poolside or at the lifeguard chair. This strategy gives the patron three opportunities to read about the risks involved and to help them avoid the hazard. With the warning posted three times, it is difficult to blame the facility for failure to warn.

Figure 25.2. The four most important warning signs at most aquatic facilities are (1) "No Diving," (2) "No Long Breath-Holding," (3) "Watch Your Children," and (4) "Nonswimmers Should Wear Life Jackets." (Sign design Clarion Safety Systems©)

Figure 25.3. Photos courtesy of Clarion Safety Systems©

Creating a Safety Signage System

by Geoffrey Peckham, Chair
ANSI Z535 Committee, CEO
Clarion Safety Systems LLC

Safety signs posted in a pool area are critically important for pool users and facility owners and must meet three conditions:

1. Safety signs must convey critical safety information so accidents and injuries are avoided.

   Without question, this is the number one goal and everything else is subordinate to the objective of protecting people from possible tragedy.

2. Safety signs must fulfill the facility's legal duty to warn so that if an accident occurs, the facility is better protected from liability exposure.

3. Last, safety signs must meet applicable local, state, and federal sign requirements.

Safety signs are a "system" of signs that work together to accomplish the above objectives. The bar for safety communication in the United States and abroad is rising, meaning that people have higher expectations regarding being warned about potential hazards so they can avoid injury. When people are not warned and an accident occurs, liability lawsuits often result, lawsuits based on "inadequate warnings" or failure to warn that seek awards from property owners and product manufacturers for not having done the job right. The expense of specifying and installing a good safety sign system will be far less than the time and money that will be spent defending the aquatic facility if the owner is sued for failure to warn or is found to have posted inadequate warnings. Both of these allegations are commonly found in today's liability lawsuits and make well-designed safety sign systems a requirement for practically every aquatic facility.

Separating and Defining Sign Content

With the understanding that pool safety signs must function as a system that teaches people how to remain safe while in an aquatic facility, the aquatic facility manager's first task is to decide what guests need to be warned about. From the start, the list of safety messages will eventually be prioritized and placed into three general buckets:

- Things that could seriously injure or kill a person.
- Things that could cause a minor (recoverable) injury.

- Things that pertain to preventing recreational water illnesses (RWIs).

The major flaw with many facilities' pool safety signage is that their safety signs are nothing more than a list of rules that mix up all three buckets of safety messages. The resulting mostly text-only signs treat every rule the same, using the same type size, font, and color. No one message is emphasized more than another (see Figure 25.4).

The problem with the vast majority of pool safety signage is that critical safety messages (that is, those that could result in serious injury or death if not obeyed) are lost in between messages such as "No Running" and "Return Used Towels to the Bin." The first step in defining an effective pool safety sign system is to separate safety and safety-related messages into these buckets. But first, the right method to convey safety information on signs must be discussed.

ANSI Sign Standards

New ANSI Z535-1998 standards modernize the hazard alert system that uses various signal words and colors

Figure 25.4. Typical pool rules sign. (Photo courtesy of Clarion Safety Systems©)

to distinguish between levels of hazards. Aquatic facility operators may want to use these researched standards to provide more uniform visual communications that promote recognition and avoidance of hazards.

Sign Design Considerations

In the United States, ANSI Z535.2 Environmental and Facility Safety Signs (2011) is the voluntary consensus standard that defines the "state of the art" for safety sign design. This standard, revised every 5 years, defines the general design rules for safety signs to be placed in public and private facilities and environments. It uses text and/or graphics to convey hazard and hazard avoidance information. The formats prescribed by this standard use an innovative combination of color-coding, the safety alert symbol (a triangle with an exclamation mark in it), and specifically defined signal words to communicate varying degrees of risk and/or the actual type of safety sign. This sounds confusing, but it will be easy to understand with examples.

In the fall of 2013, the Occupational Safety and Health Administration (OSHA) revised its general workplace (1910) and construction (1926) safety standards to include references of the 2011 ANSI Z535.2 Standard for Environmental and Facility Safety Signs. This update, long expected, allows property owners and employers to use the newer ANSI standard instead of the 1968-era standard OSHA has had in its regulations since it was first published in 1971. The acceptance by OSHA of the newer sign formats (which, as we've seen, typically contain more substantive content and graphical symbols), reinforces the pool owner's need to use this standard's safety sign design principles to improve safety.

OSHA's acceptance of the ANSI Z535.2-2011 standard makes an even more powerful case for the pool owner to use these signs, not only for their safety communication benefits, but because their use should add to the owner's defense position should an accident occur and a lawsuit arise. Use of the new signs should help eliminate "failure to warn" and "inadequate warnings" allegations, as such allegations will likely be difficult to prove by plaintiff's experts given that the newer sign formats are endorsed by OSHA.

The first type of ANSI Z535.2 sign is a *hazard alerting sign*. The signal word definitions and colors for hazard alerting signs follow.

Danger

Danger (white letters on a red background) is used to indicate a hazardous situation, which will result in death or serious injury if not avoided. This signal word is to be limited to the most extreme situations (Figures 25.5 and 25.9).

Figure 25.5. Photo courtesy of Clarion Safety Systems©

Warning

Warning (black letters on an orange background) is used to indicate a hazardous situation, which could result in death or serious injury if not avoided (Figures 25.6 and 25.7).

Caution

Caution (black letters on a yellow background) is used to indicate a hazardous situation, which could result in minor or moderate injury if not avoided.

Notice

The next type of ANSI Z535 sign is a notice sign. These signs use the signal word *Notice* (white italicized letters on a blue background) without the safety alert symbol to communicate nonpersonal injury-related safety information and safety policy information.

Safety Instruction

The final type of ANSI safety sign is a safety instruction sign. These signs convey specific safety-related instructions. The signal phrase *Safety Instructions* (white letters on a green background) can be used, or the phrase can be changed to better describe the content of the sign, such as *Pool Hygiene Rules* (Figure 25.13).

Now with this understanding of ANSI Z535.2 safety signs, safety messages can be divided into the bucket that

Figure 25.6. Photo courtesy of Clarion Safety Systems©

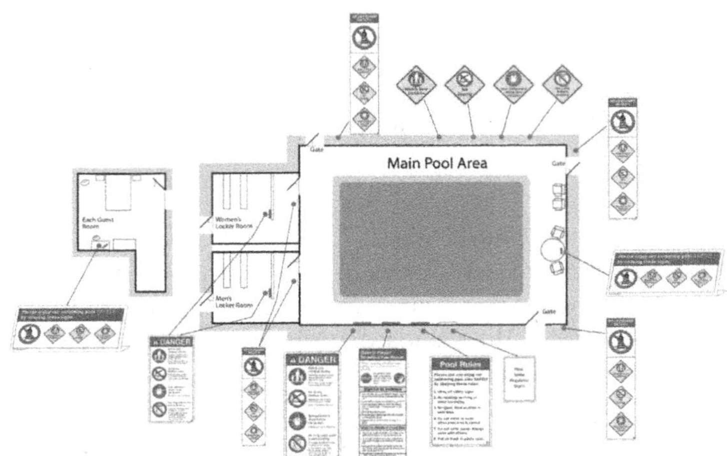

Figure 25.8. Sample location plan for signage around the aquatic facility. (Photo courtesy of Clarion Safety Systems©)

Figure 25.9. Depth marker warning tile embedded in coping. (Photo courtesy of Clarion Safety Systems©)

Figure 25.7. Photo courtesy of Clarion Safety Systems©

Figure 25.10. Highly visible poolside warning cones in English and Spanish. (Photo courtesy of Clarion Safety Systems©)

Figure 25.11. Desk placard recommended for unguarded hotel, motel, and resort pools. (Photo courtesy of Clarion Safety Systems©)

Figure 25.12. Excellent signage for an unguarded pool. (Photo courtesy of Clarion Safety Systems©)

Figure 25.13. Photo courtesy of Clarion Safety Systems©

is most appropriate for each sign: *Danger, Warning, Caution, Notice,* or *Safety Instructions.*

Proper use of ANSI Z535 standards will allow signs to fit into a nationally recognized system of safety communication. This is good from a viewer's perspective because consistency in the presentation of safety information is meant to make it easier for people to recognize and understand safety signs. But it is also good from the standpoint of the facility's liability and loss control prevention program. Since ANSI Z535 is the standard that U.S. courts recognize as setting the benchmark for defining the proper content and formatting of an adequate warning, intelligently using them for pool safety signs should significantly help if a lawsuit occurs and a facility owner needs to defend the decisions he or she made with regard to the warnings provided.

Text

When it comes to hazard alerting signs, the ANSI Z535.2 standard advises explaining the nature of the hazard, the consequence of inaction with the hazard, and how to avoid the hazard. Why? Because human factors experts and legal court cases have found that this is the information people most often need to know to avoid hazards. But it is also true that people tend to ignore lengthy word messages. So herein lies the problem: Signs need to be brief yet convey enough information to provide an adequate warning. Fortunately, words are not the only communication tool.

Symbols

The world of safety signs is changing. The standards that define the state of the art for safety signs (ANSI Z535, OSHA, and NFPA in the United States and ISO and IEC internationally) now emphasize and encourage the use of graphics. The overall theory behind this evolution in safety sign design is that symbols have the ability to communicate across language barriers and to communicate to children and people with cognitive difficulties. In practice, this is only true when the symbols are well-designed and legibly reproduced. Plenty of poorly drawn symbols are out there, doing more harm than good because they cause confusion rather than comprehension. So a portion of the responsibility for the communication effectiveness of a sign can be placed on using well-designed graphics, either to reinforce the text or to replace the text.

Graphics serve another key purpose, one that is absolutely necessary if a safety sign is to have any chance at being effective. Symbols can draw attention to the sign. *Noticeability* is the term that best describes this trait. A safety sign that goes unnoticed is useless when it comes to protecting people. Graphics, along with color, size, and placement of signs, help to achieve noticeability.

Putting the Pieces Together

Now the aquatic facility manager must match up safety messages with the signal words, choice of text, and symbols to fit within the confines of a series of signs that should be properly placed, each in a location where it will have the best opportunity to do its job of communicating its intended message (Figure 25.8). For the most important messages, those trying to prevent serious injury or death, the aquatic facility manager should consider repeating these messages within the sign system in uniform ways so people have more than one opportunity to see them (Figure 25.12).

For example, the most important safety messages could be displayed in the form of signs and stand-up desk placards. They could be located in guest rooms and on registration desks (at a hotel), in locker rooms, on entry doors, on poolside walls or fences, on floors, on pool decks, or on bright yellow safety cones (Figure 25.10). The possibilities are varied. It is worth placing some creativity into the display of the most critical safety messages because seeing this information could mean the difference between life and death for patrons of the facility.

Code-Mandated Signage

Many states in the United States have pool safety signage codes with which aquatic facilities must comply. These requirements typically call for large-lettered "No Lifeguard on Duty" signs and various health and hygiene-related messages to be conveyed near the pool or spa. As such, these signs must be incorporated into the overall sign system. Although the requirements are almost always for text-only signs, graphics can supplement the text so the signs better convey their intended messages and fit into the overall sign system (Figure 25.14).

Summary

It is hoped that by reading this short chapter, those running aquatic facilities will be a little more creative and stimulated to attempt to warn guests of the risks at their facilities more effectively. Whenever new signs are developed, they should be field tested first before they are permanently affixed in the facility. Before drastically changing existing signs, aquatic facility managers should consult with legal counsel first. The three challenges for signs are preventing accidents from occurring, protecting the facility from liability, and meeting code regulations. Using the ANSI standards, using well-designed graphics, clearly defining and communicating the content, and choosing the ideal placement locations are key to an effective pool safety sign system.

References

American National Standards Institute. (2011). *ANSI Z535.2: American National Standard for Environmental and Facility Safety Signs.*

International Organization for Standardization. (2011). *ISO 3864-1 Graphical Symbols: Safety colours and safety signs, Part 1: Design principles for safety signs in workplaces and public areas.*

National Fire Protection Association. (2012). *NFPA 170 Fire Safety and Emergency Symbols.*

Occupational Safety and Health Administration. (2013). *CFR 1910.145, Specifications for Accident Prevention Signs and Tags, 1971.*

For information about the Center for Disease Control efforts to combat recreational water illnesses, see www.cdc.gov/healthywater/swimming/rwi/

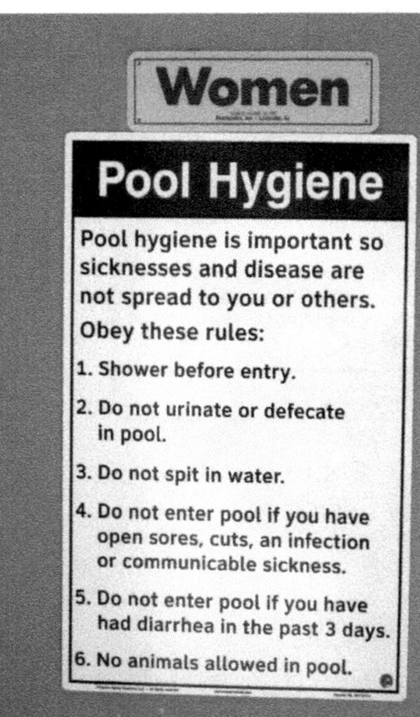

Figure 25.14. Photo courtesy of Clarion Safety Systems©

26

Diving and Other Headfirst Entries

Key Concepts

- Diving versus headfirst
- Spine
- Diving victim
- Safe diving envelope
- Residential pools
- Public pools
- Starting blocks
- Diving boards
- Signage
- Shallow water

Headfirst entries can cause catastrophic injury whenever shallow water is present. Traumatic spinal cord injuries often result in permanent paralysis. Perhaps the most tragic fact about catastrophic headfirst entries is that the injured party can be rendered quadriplegic in less than one second; a quick mistake in judgment can mean a lifetime of paralysis. Headfirst entries into shallow water continue to be one of the leading causes of sport-related spinal cord injuries (Boden & Jarvis, 2008). Of these injuries, 95% occur in less than 5 ft of water, 5% occur in between 5 and 8 ft, and virtually no injuries occur in water depths greater than 9 ft. Although spinal cord injuries most often occur in shallow water, they rarely occur from diving boards, particularly those placed in pools that meet competitive diving standards. The sport of springboard diving is one of the safest sports in existence. In the history of competitive diving, USA Diving, the National Collegiate Athletic Association (NCAA), and the National Federation of State High School Associations (NFSHA) have no reports of fatalities or catastrophic injury from competitive diving. The main water-related cause of spinal injury is during recreational use of water (World Health Organization, 2014). On average, more than 6,500 children and adolescents are treated for diving-related injuries annually in the United States (Day, Stolz, Mehan, Smith, & McKenzie, 2008). Catastrophic neck injuries usually occur in the shallow end of the swimming pool rather than the deep end. Most headfirst entry injuries (approximately 50% to 60%) are alcohol related.

Although most serious neck injuries occur in open water (beaches, lakes, and quarries), this discussion is limited to swimming pools and waterparks. Some aquatic facilities present more risk than others when it comes to injuries because of inadequate dimensions and bottom contours, but lack of supervision and inadequate warnings also play a role in diving (headfirst) injuries. Safe diving depths and distances are perhaps the most controversial topic in water safety circles. The purpose of this discussion is not to propose diving depths and distances that will guarantee safety, but to reveal facts and opinions surrounding the diving controversy that will assist aquatic professionals in developing safe diving and headfirst entry policies that will prevent accidents in their facilities.

In 2012, Brown, Penn State University springboard diving coach, timed headfirst and feetfirst entries from the side of the swimming pool and from the 3-m diving board, simulating the amount of time it takes for a fall, jump, and dive to occur (Popke, 2012). Headfirst dives from the pool deck (Figure 26.1) with push-offs into the water ranged from .68 to .82 seconds from the time the subjects' feet left the pool deck until the time the feet disappeared under the water, replicating the point at which the head would hit the bottom of the pool (dives and falls were conducted in water depths of 10 to 14 ft to avoid injury to the participants). The falling dive (simulating a headfirst fall) for 50 dives from the 3-m diving board and step-off (simulating a feetfirst fall) for 50 step-offs into the water occurred between .47 and .49 seconds and .56 and .58 seconds, respectively. The significant finding of this study is that headfirst entries into shallow water occur *in less than a second*. This makes it impossible for any person to intervene and stop the dive from happening once it is initiated. Headfirst entries into shallow water must be prevented by all means possible, especially aggressive "No Diving, Shallow Water" signs posted clearly and conspicuously in and around shallow water. A red warning stripe around the pool that reads "No Diving" on the perimeter of shallow water is effective. In addition, vertical and horizontal depth markings and "No Diving" signage is a must to prevent catastrophic diving injuries and death.

A study by DeVivo (1997) provided case study information that is specific to spinal cord injuries in pools. The study identified 1,106 persons injured in headfirst (diving) accidents. Of these, 631 were injured in open water and 341 were injured in swimming pools. One hundred ninety-six of the 631 injured in swimming pools completed the survey supplied by DeVivo. All spinal injuries occurred between C4 and C6. The acute care and rehab costs for those injured was about $192,414 each. The information gleaned from these accidents confirmed accident trends found in other studies:

- In the United States, the most common cause of spinal injuries in pools is from diving into the upslope of the pool bottom or into shallow water (World Health Organization, 2000).
- 64% occurred in inground swimming pools and 36% occurred in aboveground pools.
- The majority of injuries occurred in private residential pools.
- Only 8% occurred in public pools and only 4% in semipublic pools and clubs.
- Most injuries occurred in less than 4 ft of water; few spinal injuries occurred in water greater than 8 ft deep.

- In 44% of the cases, the injury occurred in the person's first visit to the pool.
- In 28% of the cases, the injury occurred during the person's first dive into that pool.
- Approximately 70% of all injuries were a result of ordinary dives. Unusual dives accounted for 17%, and 6% of the injuries were caused by swimmers being pushed into the pool.
- Almost half of the injuries occurred during a party, and half of the injuries involved alcohol.

The following conditions existed at the facilities where the accident occurred:

- No warning signs were posted in 87% of the cases (Figure 26.2).
- No depth markers were posted in 75% of the cases.
- No lifeguard was on duty in 94% of the cases.
- Dives occurred from the sides of the swimming pool rather than the diving board.
- No artificial lighting was available in 53% of the time; when lighting was provided, it was inadequate in half of the cases. (DeVivo, 1997)

Definitions

Before discussion of diving injuries, the term *diving* must be clearly defined. Too much blame is being placed on diving boards when headfirst entries into shallow water from decks, docks, and other platforms are the real culprits resulting in traumatic injuries.

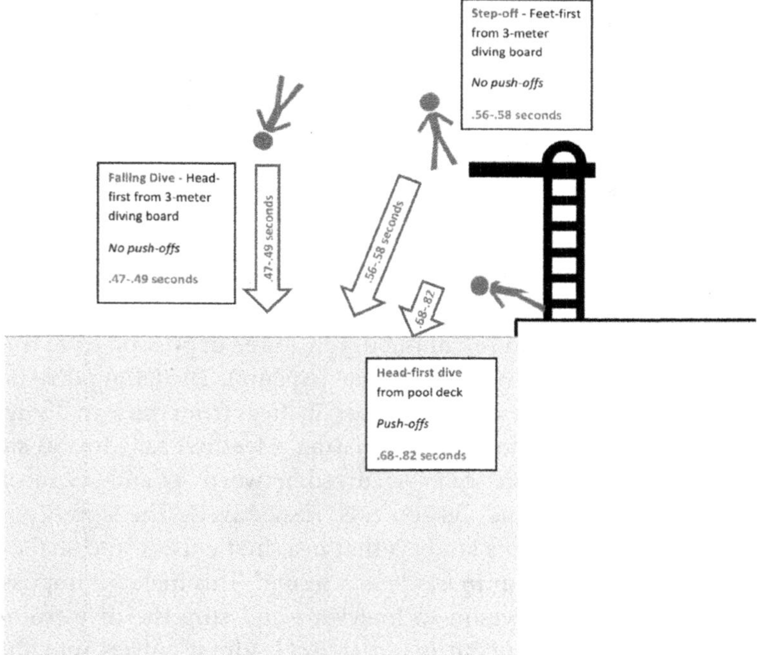

Figure 26.1. In less than a second...

50 dives - All subjects hit the water in LESS THAN A SECOND

Figure 26.2. A conspicuous "No Diving" warning. (Photo of Aquatic Safety Research Group)

Springboard diving is the sport of entering the water headfirst from a diving board. Diving requires formal training from a qualified instructor or coach. Many springboard divers compete in springboard diving events, which is referred to as the sport of competitive springboard diving. All competitive diving should be supervised. Traumatic springboard diving injuries are extremely rare, particularly when the activity is supervised. As mentioned in Chapter 3, no catastrophic diving injuries have occurred in NFSHSA-, NCAA-, or USA Div-ing–sanctioned pools. This is true for both competitive and recreational springboard divers. The NFSHSA has allowed diving competitions in as little as 10 ft of water with no catastrophic injuries.

Headfirst entries closely resemble dives but are initiated by untrained, unsupervised individuals from decks, docks, or platforms other than diving boards. Diving authorities refer to this as recreational diving, but the term *headfirst entry* is preferred to clearly distinguish the two distinctly different activities. Headfirst entries may sometimes be referred to as *diving* in this text when they are not related to competitive springboard diving.

Racing starts are long, shallow, streamlined dives that are performed in competitive swimming from either blocks or decks (Figure 26.3). Training and supervision should be required for all racing starts. Competitive swimmers use starts for water entries on both the front and the back. Improper racing starts have caused traumatic neck injuries, mostly to recreational swimmers going off the blocks without adequate training or supervision. The Model Aquatic Health Code (MAHC) may suggest a minimum depth of 6 feet, 7 inches. The finalized MAHC will be important to follow. A 5-ft minimum height is strongly recommended regardless of the height of the block (Figure 26.4).

National YMCAs already require a minimum of 5 ft under all competitive swimming starting blocks. Because more individuals are experiencing catastrophic spinal injuries from competitive starting blocks than from competitive springboards, deeper depths are recommended for racing starts from platforms. Recommendations for the use of starting platforms are found later in this chapter. The Model Aquatic Health code should be followed for safe diving depths and swimming pool construction.

Figure 26.3. Photo courtesy of Counsilman-Hunsaker.

Figure 26.4. Photo courtesy of Counsilman-Hunsaker

pool construction.

These distinct features of springboard diving, headfirst entries, and racing starts are important. Too often diving boards are removed from swimming pools after an intoxicated trespasser is injured entering the shallow end headfirst while showing off. Perhaps one of the most difficult issues in this area is determining what pool dimensions are required for safe springboard diving in private pools. Most residential pools do not have adequate depth or distance to permit safe springboard diving. It is impossible to determine safe diving depth and dimensions that will guarantee safety for everyone because most catastrophic injuries are the result of reckless, improper diving. However, if the design of swimming and diving pools only allowed for headfirst entries into at least 10 ft of water, regardless of where the diver initiated the dive, catastrophic head and neck injuries would be rare.

The Spine

The spine is a strong yet flexible column that supports the head and trunk and also protects the spinal cord. The spine is composed of individual vertebrae that are cushioned by a layer of cartilage called intervertebral disks. The spinal cord is made up of a bundle of nerves and runs through the center of the vertebrae (Figure 26.5).

Injuries to the spine include fractures, dislocations, sprains, and compressions. Any of these injuries can cause damage to the spinal cord, resulting in temporary paralysis, permanent paralysis, or even death. Although these injuries can occur anywhere on the spine, most diving injuries damage the cervical region. Paralysis re-

sults from the point of trauma downward. Trauma to C7 downward usually results in paraplegia, whereas damage to C4 through C6 often results in quadriplegia. Many diving accidents result in complete quadriplegia.

The Typical Diving Victim

Unlike drowning, which affects all ages, sizes, and ability levels, spinal injuries most often affect a certain group of swimmers. Although some females suffer severe spinal trauma, headfirst victims are more often male. The National Spinal Cord Injury Statistical Center, Birmingham, Alabama (2013) found that 80% of all spinal cord injuries reported were male. Male victims of spinal injury are usually between 5 ft 7 in. and 6 ft tall and weigh between 145 and 185 lb. This group is at risk because they tend to be athletic and strike the bottom with great force. The victims are usually between 18 and 31 years of age and are generally athletic. Youth under age 13 rarely suffer from severe headfirst accidents because they do not possess sufficient size and weight to strike the bottom forcefully enough to damage the spinal cord. Headfirst victims often injure themselves on their first entry during their first visit to the pool. When these accidents occur, supervision, "No Diving" signs, and warnings are usually missing and the depth of water is less than 5 ft. Often when a severe spinal injury occurs, the water has poor visibility and the bottom lacks markings, making depth perception difficult. Many headfirst accidents occur during a pool party where alcohol is consumed in the late evening or early morning hours. Before discussing the types of pools and equipment most likely to be involved in spinal injuries, we will discuss the safe diving envelope first.

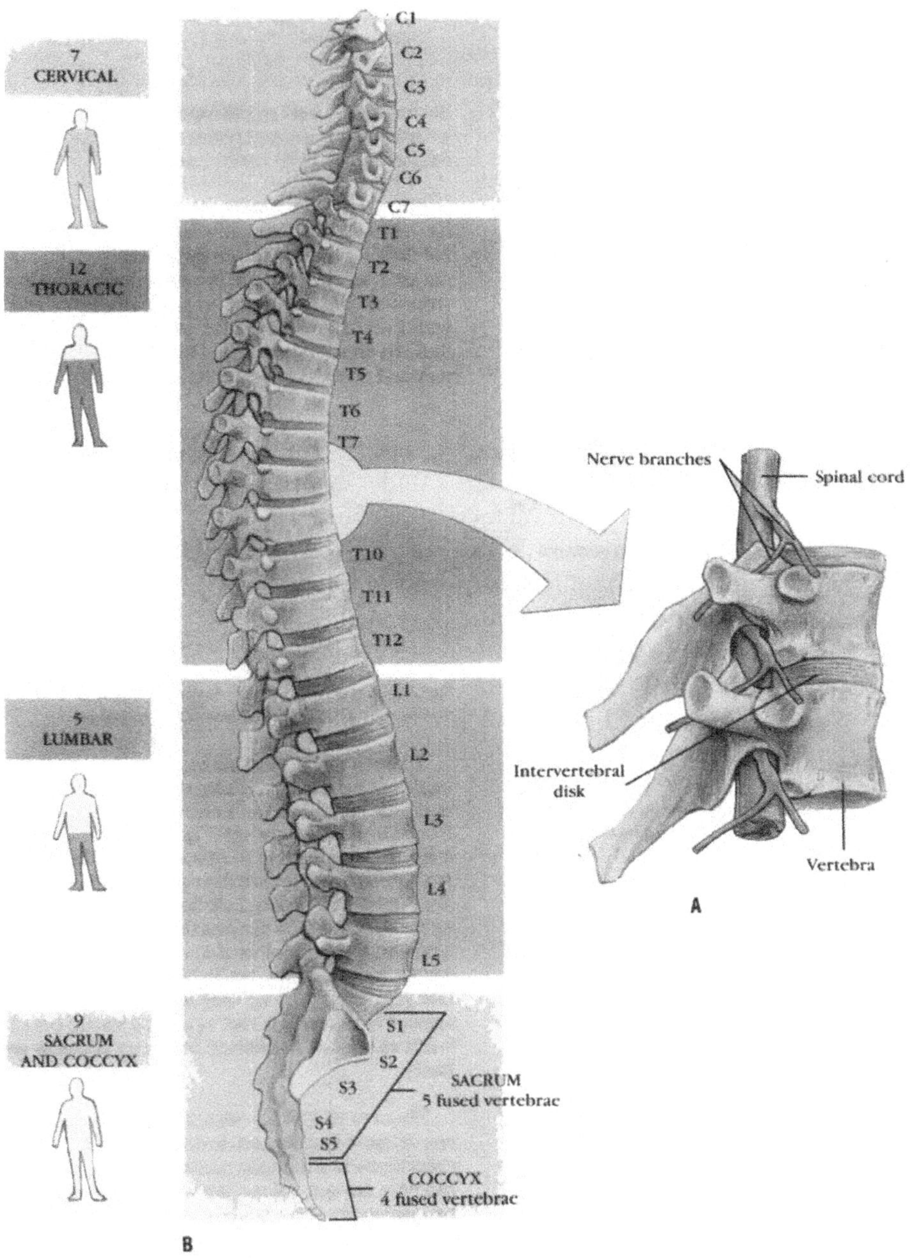

Figure 26.5. Vertebrae are separated by cushions of cartilage called disks. The spine is divided into five regions. (From *Swimming and Diving*, by the American Red Cross, 1992, St. Louis, MO: Mosby.)

The Safe Diving Envelope

According to the American Red Cross (2009), the safe diving envelope is the underwater area of a swimming pool into which a diver can enter headfirst safely without touching the sides, slope, or bottom. A depth of 9 ft should be encouraged whenever headfirst entries are allowed from a pool deck; unfortunately, many pools allow headfirst entries in only 5 ft of water. Swimming pool staff and signage must encourage patrons to enter headfirst into deep water only and to use feetfirst entries for shallow water. Underwater ledges, steps, and other obstructions should not be found in the diving envelope.

When a diving board is available, the safe diving depth must be present not only directly under the end of the board (plummet) but also in front of the board and on either side of the diving board. This text suggests a minimum diving depth of 11 ft, but between 12 and 12.5 ft is strongly preferred for 1-m (low) competitive diving boards. Deep, flat bottom, constant depth areas are safest for diving activities, but unfortunately these pools are not as common. Some pools that have diving boards have hopper bottoms or spoon-shaped bottoms. Although the depth for diving directly under the tip of the board is often sufficient, too often the shape of the pool bottom and sides does not allow for safe diving forward or to the sides of the plummet. The chance of hitting the upslope or sides of the pool is increased when swimmers diving into a hopper bottom or spoon-shaped pool. In both types of pools, the bottom angles or slopes up sharply on all four sides from the deepest point to the breakpoint for shallow water.

Unskilled, impromptu dives from a diving board by untrained individuals into a spoon or hopper bottom pool can be risky. The depth posted often refers to the plummet depth only. Some recreational divers travel forward rather than upward when diving. Conversely, competitive divers tend to achieve more height than distance from the board. Therefore, a recreational diver diving into this facility may strike the upslope, which is significantly more shallow than the posted depth. Hopper bottoms and spoon-shaped bottoms are found in residential pools, hotel and motel pools, and even older (more than 25 years) larger public pools.

Many residential and hotel and motel pools do not have sufficient size and depth to allow diving boards. Before a diving board is placed in a spoon-shaped or hopper bottom pool, all conditions must be considered when evaluating whether a diver may hit the bottom. If any chance exists of a diver hitting the bottom or slopes from a diving board, diving equipment should be prohibited. When a diving board already exists in such a pool where depths and distances are marginal, the diving board should be completely removed. One trend today is to replace the diving board with a drop slide. This is a safer alternative in regard to serious neck injuries (provided, of course, sliders go down feetfirst!), but may also tempt nonswimming children to slide into deep water. Supervision is key when a drop slide becomes a replacement for a diving board. Also gaining popularity, aquatic climbing walls can be a safer alternative to diving boards. Some pool operators have suggested keeping the diving board in place and establishing a policy allowing only children under age 12 to use the boards with direct supervision. But many risk managers consider diving boards to be an attractive nuisance for all age groups, so a lawyer should be consulted before establishing this type of policy. Also, the diving board in a pool with marginal distance to the slope must be low to the water and short and stiff. This rigid board is less likely to propel the diver as far out into the pool as longer, higher, or more flexible boards. In this case, a safe diving envelope would exist for children but not adults. If adults cannot be prevented from using the board, even when they are trespassing, the diving board should be removed. These considerations do not guarantee headfirst injuries will not occur. Another word of caution, when the diving board is removed from older, smaller pools, a dangerous deep "hole" is left in the pool where nonswimmers could end up if not careful.

THE DROWNING POOLS *by Tom Griffiths*

Sidebar 26.1

Shortly after World War II, with a strong economy and returning soldiers who had a better appreciation of aquatics, the United States experienced a construction boom in the swimming pool arena. Many smaller pools were constructed in neighborhoods, clubs, private residences, apartments, townhomes, hotels, motels, and resorts. However, to make these smaller pools more attractive, "big pool" amenities such as slides and diving boards were added. Not until the 1980s did we tragically discover that most of these smaller private and semiprivate pools with diving hoppers could not safely support the diving board. We now know that springboard diving requires significantly greater depths and distances than what was thought earlier when smaller residential pools were constructed. During the mid-1980s and early 1990s a proactive safety decision was made by those managing these smaller pools to remove the diving boards to eliminate the deadly dangerous activity. That is the good news.

The bad news is that today we are stuck with thousands of smaller pools with nearly half of the water being dedicated to the deep end of the pool. Most of these pools have between 8 and 9 ft of water at the deepest point, and they create real drowning pools because careless nonswimmers unexpectedly and abruptly find themselves in water over their heads. This occurs because, although these pools are small, the slope from the shallow area to the deep end is necessarily great. But the depth of the pool is not the only culprit. Too often these pools also suffer from a lack of water clarity created by the combination of overloading by guests and low levels of chlorine. To make matters worse, lifeguards are not typically stationed at these pools and parents do not watch their children adequately. Adults can also act irresponsibly concerning their own behavior. So what can be done with older, smaller, deceptively deeper pools with more than their share of drownings? PLENTY!

cont.

AFO/CPO/LAFT

First of all, a certified Aquatic Facility Operator (AFO), Certified Pool Operator (CPO), or Licensed Aquatic Facility Technician (LAFT) needs to be assigned to these pools, whether guarded or unguarded, to ensure the water stays clear and is adequately disinfected and the pool is properly marked, and well equipped. Certified Operators tend to be good risk managers. Ron Gilbert, an attorney who specializes in aquatic liability, stated on these very pages years ago (*Aquatics International*, 1994) that the lack of an AFO or CPO at an aquatic facility was both an accident waiting to happen and an easy way to win a lawsuit.

DO AWAY WITH THE DEEP END

Although costly, whenever possible the pool should be completely renovated by eliminating the deep end and creating a shallow pool ranging from 3 to 4 ft deep in the shallow end to a maximum of 5 ft at the deepest end. I firmly believe that whenever we restrict the depth of water to 5 ft in our facilities, we reduce the risk of drowning significantly. Although people, particularly children, can still drown in 5 ft of water or less, it is much less likely because the slope is made gradual and subtle and rescue in 5 ft becomes achievable by even nonswimmers. If nothing else, shallow pools are more popular and entertaining than deep pools. But eliminating the entire deep end of the pool is expensive and sometimes unrealistic. However, when filling in the deep end is too costly, I recommend the following upgrades to increase the safety at these pools.

CREATIVE SIGNAGE

Although I did not think much of safety signage earlier in my career, I now believe it is of the utmost importance not only for improving safety but also in defending lawsuits. The problem with most aquatic safety signage in the United States is that it is not effective as printed, yet we continue to use the same, tired statements such as "Swim at Your Own Risk." We can do better than that. We need more signage that gets the point across such as the following:

"Parents PLEASE Watch Your Children....It only takes seconds to drown!"

"Parents: If you're more than an arm's length away.....you've gone too far!"

"Parents: There is absolutely no substitute for your close, vigilant supervision!"

"This pool is unguarded and unsupervised.
You alone are responsible for your safety."

"Have fun but PLEASE be careful. Exercise caution and common sense when around the pool."

"Nonswimmers should wear life jackets."

Keep in mind, no matter how creative, bold, and conspicuous, signs will often be ignored by adults.

SAFETY EQUIPMENT

Forget about small white ring buoys with 50 ft of twisted, tangled line attached. In an emergency, no one is going to notice them, let alone know how to use them. Instead, purchase the huge, obnoxiously orange ring buoys you have seen hanging on the sides of the Queen Mary, but do not attach any line. Mount these huge ring buoys (2 to 3 ft across) up high on every side of the pool. Not only will everyone see them, but they will also support up to four adults in the water when used. However, even the biggest, brightest ring buoy does not mean that it will be used in an emergency. Also, create an emergency station painted in red on a wall or kiosk where the 911 phone, shepherd's crook, and emergency action plan are prominently displayed.

THE LIFELINE

This buoyant line suspended on the surface of the water separating the shallow end from the deep end is by far the most problematic piece of equipment at smaller aquatic facilities. Although it is recommended that these lines stretch across the width of the pool to prevent nonswimmers from slipping down the slope into the deep end, we have no proof that this line will accomplish that. Also, when this line is in place, it renders the pool useless for lap swimming, water jogging, and other activities requiring the length of the pool. In addition, this lifeline is often broken because children love to sit on this suspended "water swing," either pulling the hooks off the rope or the eyelets out of the pool sides. To supplement the lifeline, we need painted lines on the pool bottom and the deck indicating that the water is deep. "DANGER! Deep Water" should probably be printed on the pool deck in a red or black stripe surrounding the deeper portion of the pool. Naturally, depth markers and breakpoint lines should also be in place, but again, they are not guaranteed to make a difference.

ELECTRONIC SURVEILLANCE

Particularly when unguarded, smaller pools should be monitored electronically. This can be accomplished by closed-circuit television played at the front desk or in the manager's office, or better yet, the latest in computerized underwater vision security system can be installed. Regardless of what procedures and protocol are used to improve

cont.

Aboveground Pools

Although not true in all cases, generally speaking, the smaller the pool, the more likely a neck injury will occur. Aboveground pools are smaller, temporary pools that can be removed and stored and have average depths of 4 ft (Figure 26.7). Headfirst entries must never be allowed in aboveground pools. Instead, aboveground pools should encourage slow, gentle feetfirst entry only. Depths in an aboveground pool range from 3.5 to 4.5 ft, but the water depth in any particular aboveground pool is usually constant. The aboveground pool presents increased risks for headfirst entries not only because the water is shallow but also because in many instances headfirst entries can be performed from platforms or decks above the surface of the water. Aboveground pools with soft sides may encourage teenagers and young adults to dive over the sides and into the pool. Pool ladders, decks, fences, and rooftops are platforms from which the unwary have initiated dives that have resulted in catastrophic injury. Therefore, aggressive "No Diving" signs and warnings are needed.

Forward rolls and somersaults must also be banned in aboveground pools as these have caused catastrophic neck injuries in the past. Also, aboveground pools are more suitable for children than adults because of the size and depth constraints.

Aboveground pools are inexpensive and allow families to enjoy swimming in the privacy of their backyards. But when an aboveground pool is installed, every precaution must be taken to prevent headfirst and other risky entries. Effective "No Diving" warnings must appear conspicuously on the pool itself, on the pool ladder, and anywhere else in close proximity to the pool (Figure 26.6). Homeowners must warn visitors that headfirst entries are strictly prohibited. Aboveground pools must never have diving boards or jump boards, and if they have a slide, only small children with supervision should use it. Adults should not use slides in an aboveground pool, and all sliders must go down feetfirst. Some newer aboveground pools are inflatable and soft to the touch. These types of pools can inadvertently promote diving into the pool from the yard because the sides and top of the pool are soft rather than hard.

Inground Residential Pools

Although many inground residential pools have diving boards, few, if any, have a safe diving envelope into which a safe headfirst entry can be made. A 1-m residential diving board should have sufficient depth (at least 10 ft) in any direction and must allow divers to maneuver safely underwater without forcefully striking underwater surfaces. This is difficult to guarantee. Also, continuous depth in front of the board is more critical than more depth. The 10-ft NFSHSA requirement might be safe, but only if this depth extends far enough forward to ensure that divers will land in this depth. Again, many residential pools cannot safely accommodate diving from a springboard.

Figure 26.6. "No Diving" signs on aboveground pools.

Figure 26.7. This pool especially warrants aggressive "No Diving" signs because the soft-sided pool tempts teenagers and young adults to run on the lawn and dive over the soft, forgiving pool walls. Headfirst entries must never be allowed in an aboveground pool and "No Diving" warnings and symbols are a must. (Photo courtesy of SOFPOOL)

If a diving board is removed in an inground pool to prevent spinal injuries, additional safety precautions must be added to protect against drowning. A lifeline or safety line should be added across the pool where the breakpoint starts from shallow to deep water. This device is intended to prevent nonswimmers from unknowingly entering the deep water, but no one knows whether it works. Depth markings, diving rules, regulations, and warnings should be conspicuously placed around the pool, but these alone do not guarantee diving safety.

Serious neck injuries are not caused only when a diver hits a pool bottom. Several individuals have suffered paralyzing neck injuries while attempting to dive through an inner tube from a diving board in a backyard pool. Landing on other swimmers is also a serious problem. The results of these injuries are just as tragic as hitting the bottom of the pool. This illustrates that the water depth is not the only concern regarding diving boards.

Another way for adults to suffer a catastrophic neck injury is to go down a slide headfirst into the pool. This happens more than it should. The slider comes off the slide with tremendous force, causing severe impact with the bottom. Additionally, many neck injuries are caused in private and semipublic pools that try to offer "big pool" attractions in a small pool. To make matters worse, these pools often lack proper signage and supervision.

Public Pools

Many public pools offer springboard diving equipment, a safe diving envelope, and supervision. As a result, public pools should have fewer diving injuries than residential or semipublic pools. However, not all public pools have safe springboard diving facilities.

Perhaps one of the greatest fears in a diving facility is the patron hitting the board. Today's springboards are flexible and forgiving when divers accidentally strike them. Hitting the board happens occasionally, but this rarely results in serious injury. Hitting a springboard rarely, if ever, causes traumatic injuries, whereas striking the bottom of the pool or pool deck can be debilitating.

To prevent hitting the bottom during diving and other headfirst entries, children must be taught the concept of steering to the surface after entering the water. Steering to the surface is an important diving skill that should be emphasized in all water safety and learn-to-swim programs (Figure 26.8). Keeping both hands extended above the head is also extremely important.

Public pools should adhere to the standards of one of several competitive diving organizations. The NCAA, Fédération Internationale de National Amateur (FINA), USA Diving, and NFSHSA provide recommended dimensions for safe springboard diving. **Additionally, be sure to consult finalized Model Aquatic Health Code (MAHC).** National YMCAs and the American Red Cross also offer instruction in safe diving techniques. Serious diving accidents have never occurred in facilities sanctioned by the competitive diving organizations listed above.

Public pools usually offer 1-m springboards (low diving boards) and/or 3-m diving boards (high diving boards). Although some pools have higher diving platforms (5, 7.5, and 10 m), these are often closed to the public. Many 3-m boards have been and are being removed because of fear of accidents, but when accidents occur from 3-m boards, the cause of injury is not hitting the bottom of the pool, but rather falling off the board or

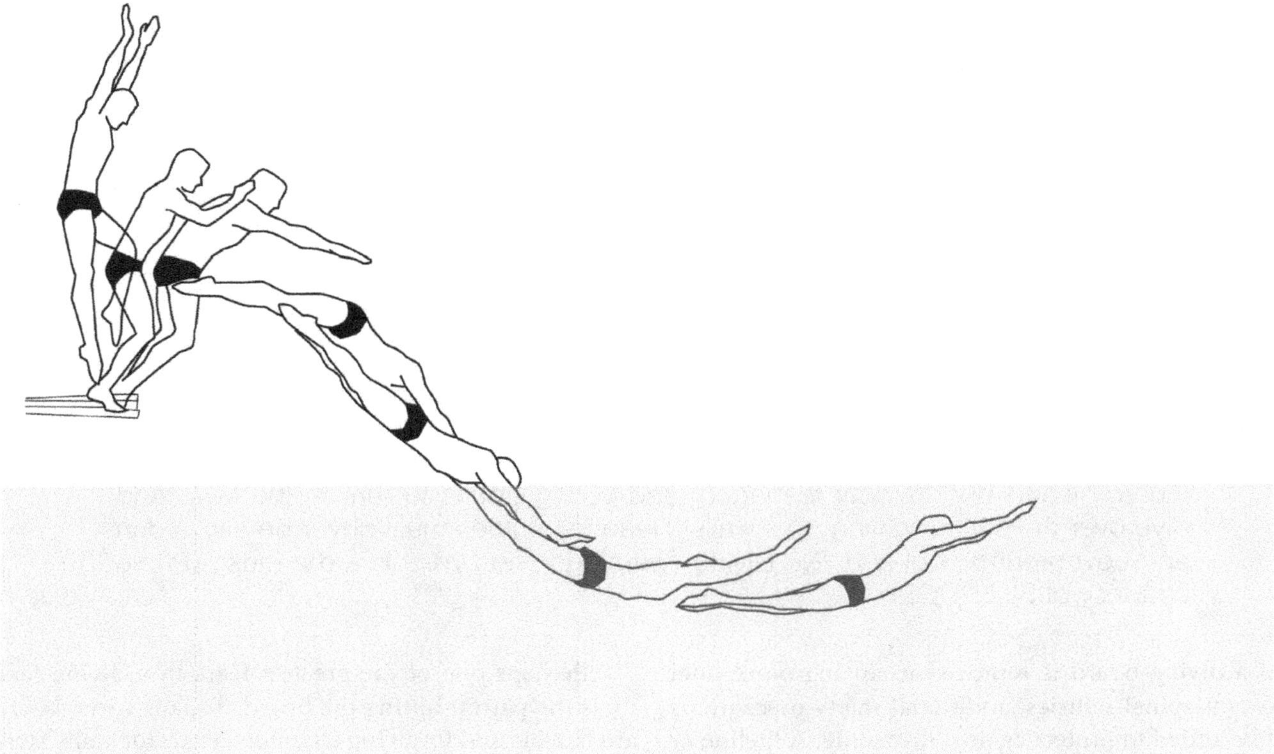

Figure 26.8. This photo demonstrates safely "steering up" from a head-first dive as suggested by APSP. While this maneuver is highly recommended, it usually requires coaching and practice to master. (Photo courtesy of The Association of Pool & Spa Professionals©, 2014)

ladder onto the concrete pool deck. When 3-m boards remain in use, extended railing systems and an enclosed stairway are preferred to a ladder with a handrail. The problem with the use of 3-m boards is that soft landing areas under the board, enclosed ladders and stairways to the board, and extended and enclosed rails on the board are not used as they are for playground safety.

When 5-, 7-, and 10-m platforms are open to the public, similar yet more stringent safety rules apply. The pool dimensions required for 1- and 3-m diving boards are described. Although diving organizations provide information on required depth and distances, the following information summarizes the most important figures:

Depth of Water at Plummet

- 1-m board: minimum 11 ft, 12 to 12.5 ft preferred
- 3-m board: minimum 12.5 ft, 13 ft preferred
- Distance to the upslope: 16.5 ft to 20 ft
- Distance to sidewall:
  - 1-m board: 8 ft
  - 3-m board: 10 ft

Pools with diving areas should display the rules on or near the diving equipment. Posting the rules alone is not sufficient; they must be strictly enforced. Typical rules include the following:

- Handrails must be used when climbing the stairs and while walking on the board.
- Only one diver is allowed on the diving board at a time.
- Only one bounce on the end of the board is allowed.
- The area must be clear before diving or jumping.
- Divers must dive or jump directly ahead.
- After each entry, divers should exit quickly to the nearest ladder.
- Divers should not attempt new dives or tricks unless under the direct supervision of a teacher or a coach.
- The hands must enter the water first on all headfirst dives.

When diving facilities are in use at a pool, a lifeguard should be specifically stationed there to manage the activity. In addition to enforcement of diving regulations, safety equipment for treatment of spinal injuries must be kept by the diving area. This includes a spine board, straps, and cervical collars. Lifeguards must also observe all diving rules when they are diving. All diving equipment, including boards and stands, should be checked daily. Diving boards should be used only when the proper facility dimensions are available.

3-Meter Diving Boards

Brown (2012) shows in his study that dives and falls from the pool deck and from a 3-m diving board take less than 1 second to occur. Two major problems occur with diving activities in aquatic facilities nationwide. The first is entering water headfirst in shallow water depths that are less than 5 ft. The other is falling from 3-m boards (high diving boards). The sport of springboard diving has a surprisingly clean safety record. However, 3-m boards open for recreational use pose danger. Somewhat surprisingly, the problem with the 3-m board usually is not striking the pool bottom, landing in the water, or hitting the board, but rather falling to the concrete deck. The seriousness of falls to the deck from 3-m boards cannot be overstated; death or permanent paralysis is often the result. Many coaches, safety advocates, and diving equipment manufacturers call for increased supervision to prevent shallow water dives and falls from 3-m boards. However, the results of the study strongly suggest that these two activities are difficult, if not impossible, to supervise. These accidents occur quickly and without warning. A lifeguard takes at least 10 seconds visually sweep a pool once. Falling to the deck from a 3-m diving board is 20 times quicker. Therefore, lifeguards sweeping their eyes horizontally to scan the pool have an immense supervision challenge and are likely to miss these potential catastrophic events. Furthermore, if a vigilant lifeguard spots someone slipping or diving, stopping the incident would be nearly impossible in less than 1 second. When the head strikes the pool bottom or deck, regardless of the height of the starting platform, most of the damage is immediate and permanent.

Three-meter diving boards must be *renovated* or *removed*. They are especially dangerous for several reasons:

- vertical ladder,
- 10 ft over concrete,
- wet environment,
- too few rails at board level,
- railings not extending over the edge of the water,
- bare feet, and
- excited or nervous children.

For 3-m diving boards to be used safely in a recreational facility, they must be made fall-proof.

Although this may sound complex, it is not. Facilities wanting 3-m boards need to follow the example of playground planners by eliminating ladders and replacing them with safer stairways with landings and using complete railing systems. Falling from the ladder leading to the 3-m diving board or from the diving board itself onto the pool deck can result in death, paralysis, or traumatic brain injuries. If existing 3-m boards are to be used safely for recreation, the railings must be ex-

panded and extended. Likewise, the ladders should be replaced with stairways and railings. If existing 3-m diving boards are not renovated for safety, their use must be restricted to trained, competitive springboard divers in the presence of a certified springboard diving coach.

When 3-m board injuries occur, the victim's family is often awarded millions because diving boards are an invitation to dive. Climbing to a height of 10 ft, in a wet environment over concrete is not acceptable for children, regardless of the activity. To allow children to climb high over concrete in a wet environment in aquatic facilities is irresponsible.

Only hypervigilant supervision combined with better and safer engineering will make 3-m diving boards safer.

To prevent injuries from 3-m boards, two clear choices are available: renovate or remove the structures. Even with improved safety features added to the diving board structures, specialized supervision is still required. If 3-m diving boards are to remain, a variety of strategies should be used:

- The horizontal rails at the diving board level should be increased in number and extended to a foot or more beyond the swimming pool edge in a fall-proof fashion.
- The ladder should be replaced with a stairway with horizontal landings and safety spindles (Figure 26.9).

Figure 26.9. Good 3-m diving board design with safer stairway. (Photo courtesy of Aquatic Safety Research Group)

- When a new 3-m board is going to be installed in an aquatic facility, the safest design is to mount the board on a wide concrete platform rather than a metal stand. Access to the 3-m board should be by stairway, not ladder.
- Three-meter diving boards should be in a designated diving area with water depth of at least 12.5 ft.
- Soft padding should be placed throughout the entire landing area in the drop zone.
- If the existing 3-m diving board cannot be safely renovated, it should be removed.
- Safer alternatives are climbing walls and slides because participants enter the water feetfirst and they are engineered in such a way as to prevent falls to the deck (Figure 26.10).

Figure 26.10. Climbing walls are a safer alternative to 3-m diving boards for recreational use. Feetfirst entry and engineered angling over the water prevent falls to the deck. (Photo Courtesy of Everlast Climbing, A PlayCore Company)

High boards should not be an endangered species. Springboard diving will hopefully flourish, not decline. Diving equipment manufacturers, aquatic facility managers, and springboard diving associations should follow the suggestions for 3-m board removal or renovation.

Starting Platforms

Another area of potential for spinal injuries is the starting blocks or platforms. Both competitive and recreational swimmers have sustained traumatic neck injuries while performing racing starts from starting platforms. One explanation for the neck injuries to the competitive swimmers is the increased popularity of the pike or scoop racing dive that carries the swimmer deeper into the water. However, poor teaching progressions have been a big problem in this area, and some swim coaches have actually caused catastrophic neck injuries to their swimmers while teaching them competitive starts. Teaching these dives should be reserved for deep water, and teaching tricks such as diving over poles or through hoops should be discouraged. Regarding recreational swimmers and starting block catastrophes, unsupervised dives and general misbehavior have been the usual causes of these types of mishaps.

Every attempt should be made to locate starting blocks in the deep end of the pool where water depth is at least 9 ft. When the pool does not have a deep end, at least 5 ft of water should be available, and many organizations now prefer at least 6 ft. Many competitive swimming agencies are now moving toward a deeper requirement because deeper water is safer when it comes to diving and in particular racing starts. When not in use by team members, diving platforms should preferably be removed or covered so that they cannot be used when it is impractical to move them (Figure 26.11). Signs warning swimmers of the danger associated with diving from these blocks should also be posted.

Figure 26.11. Starting platforms safety covers. (Photo courtesy of Pentair Aquatics Systems)

Signage

Proper signage is especially important to safeguard patrons from injuring themselves by entering shallow water headfirst. But "No Diving" signage should probably be larger and more creative than signs used in the past. Special attention should be given to the shallow (less than 5 ft) areas of the pool (see Figure 26.12).

Patrons must also be warned of attempting headfirst entries in water depths between 5 and 9 ft. A variety of signs and warnings are available, but it is best to warn all patrons of dangerous diving areas as they enter the facility. This may be best accomplished by creating and illustrating no diving zones in the swimming pool. As guests enter the pool, graphics or statements should alert them as to where they can and cannot enter headfirst.

Additional signs are needed on pool walls and fences. A new trend is to paint a stripe around the pool deck delineating the no diving zone. "No Diving" ceramic tiles are available in letters and graphics. Graphic "No Diving" signs may be more effective in multicultural, bilingual localities. "No Diving" warnings should be conspicuously placed in warning shapes, symbols, and colors (Figure 26.13). Although "No Diving" signs should be used at pools, a totally effective diving warning has not been developed.

> **Dr. Tom's Tip**
>
> When warning patrons against the catastrophic headfirst entry, post warnings in at least three separate areas: (1) when they first enter the facility, (2) before they leave the locker room, and (3) when they reach the pool deck. All warning signs should include the five Cs of signage: CLEAR, CONCISE, CONSPICUOUS, CONSISTENT, and CREATIVE.

Summary

To prevent serious neck injuries at swimming pools, patrons must be effectively and repeatedly warned of the serious consequences resulting from entering shallow water headfirst. This may be accomplished through effective and creative signage and supervision. Water less than 5 ft deep must be particularly guarded from headfirst entries, but depths between 5 and 9 ft should also contain warnings. Special precautions must be taken to prevent headfirst entries at parties, in the evening, and when alcohol is served. Whenever possible, individuals should be encouraged to jump rather than dive, particularly the first time they enter a facility. Steering to the surface immediately following each headfirst entry is a skill that must also be mastered.

Although most aquatic organizations concur that competitive diving should have a minimum depth of 11 ft and preferably 12.5 ft, they do not agree on a safe diving depth for noncompetitive recreational diving. Some water safety experts disagree with the minimum requirements in the Association of Pool and Spa Professionals standards and suggest that diving pools be deeper and longer than the minimum standards required.

Whenever pool patrons enter the water headfirst, they take a risk. All pool professionals must be aware of the risks associated with diving and other headfirst entries and develop a comprehensive plan to safeguard these individuals without eliminating the sport of springboard diving. For springboard diving into a safe diving envelope, the emphasis on safety should be to protect divers from falling onto the deck or jumping or diving onto other swimmers. Finally, it takes less than one second for a person to render himself or herself quadriplegic because of a misjudged headfirst entry, so

Figure 26.12. Effective warning tiles embedded into pool deck.

Figure 26.13. Two layers of protection—a vigilant lifeguard and an effective "No Diving" warning cone. (Sign design Clarion Safety Systems©)

aggressive prevention in this area is important. Aggressive precautions against diving into shallow water should be taken at all costs, but just because patrons are warned against diving does not mean that they will refrain from this dangerous activity.

References

American Red Cross. (1990). *Lifeguarding.* Washington, DC: Author.

American Red Cross. (1992). *Swimming and diving.* St Louis, MO: Mosby.

DeVivo, M., & Sekar, P. (1997). Prevention of spinal cord injuries that occur in swimming pools. *Paraplegia, 35,* 509–515.

Gabrielsen, A. M. (1984). *Diving injuries: A critical insight and recommendations.* Indianapolis, IN: Council of the National Cooperation in Aquatics.

National Spinal Cord Injury Statistical Center. (March 2013). *Facts and Figures At a Glance.* Birmingham, AL: University of Alabama at Birmingham.

Bibliography

American Red Cross. (1992). *Swimming and diving.* St Louis, MO: Mosby.

American Red Cross. (2009). *Swimming and water safety.* Yardley, PA: Staywell.

Boden, B. P., & Jarvis, C. G. (2008). Spinal injuries in sports. *Neurologic Clinics, 26*(1), 63–78.

Figure 26.14. Photo courtesy of Counsilman-Hunsaker.

Day, C., Stolz, U., Mehan, T. J., Smith, G. A., & McKenzie, L. B. (2008). Diving-related injuries in children <20 years old treated in emergency departments in the United States: 1990–2006. *Pediatrics, 122*(2), e388–e394.

DeVivo, M. J., & Sekar, P. (1997). Prevention of spinal cord injuries that occur in swimming pools. *National Center for Biotechnology Information, 35*(9), 509–515.

Gabriel, J. (1992). *Diving safety: A position paper.* Indianapolis, IN: U.S. Diving.

Gabrielson, A. M. (1984). *Diving injuries: A critical insight and recommendations.* Indianapolis, IN: Council for the National Cooperation in Aquatics.

Gabrielson, A. M. (1987). *Swimming pools: A guide to their planning, design, and operation* (4th ed.). Champaign, IL: Human Kinetics.

National Federation of State High School Associations. Retrieved from www.nfhs.org

Popke, M. (2012). Extra vigilance necessary with 3-meter diving boards. *Athletic Business.* Retrieved from www.athleticbusiness.com

World Health Organization (WHO). (2000). *Guidelines for Safe Recreational-Water Environments: Swimming pools, spas and similar recreational-water environments.* Retrieved from www.who.int/water_sanitation_health/diseases/spinal/en/

World Health Organization (WHO). (2014). *Water sanitation health: Water-related diseases.* Retrieved from http://www.who.int/water_sanitation_health/diseases/spinal/en/

(Photo courtesy of Aquatic Safety Research Group)

Photo courtesy of David Monk with Neptune-Benson.

27

Virginia Graeme Baker Pool and Spa Safety Act and Body, Hair, and Limb Entrapments

Key Concepts

- Entrapments
- Entanglements
- Eviscerations
- Compliant covers

When the first edition of this book was published in 1994, not much was known about suction entrapment hazards on pool and spa bottom outlets. Then the summer of 1996 arrived, and today it is still often referred to as the summer when suction entrapments in aquatics facilities captured national exposure and concern. On Saturday, May 25, 1996, 16-year-old Tanya Nickens was pulled onto at 12 in. x 12 in. flat floor grate on the bottom of a large hot water spa in New Jersey when she submerged herself to wet her hair. At that moment, everything that could go wrong did go wrong. No emergency shutoff switch was available for the powerful pump, although multiple bottom outlets were piped to individual pumps, and finally, a host of strong adult males could not pull her off the shallow water drain. That is when the U.S. Consumer Product Safety Commission (CPSC) became involved to avert future senseless tragedies.

Since the second edition of this book, perhaps the most significant development in prevention of suction entrapment in spas, hot tubs, and swimming pools occurred. In June 2002, 7-year-old Virginia Graeme Baker, granddaughter of former Secretary of State James Baker III, became stuck to a hot tub drain. Neither she nor her mother was able to pull Graeme free from the voracious suction of the drain. Two men eventually pulled hard enough for the faulty drain cover to break, but it was too late. She died from drowning as a result of a faulty drain cover. Following this tragedy, the Virginia Graeme Baker Pool and Spa Safety Act (P&SS Act), also commonly known as the VGB Act, was signed into law by President Bush in 2007 and enacted in December 2008. The P&SS Act requires antientrapment drain covers and other safety devices as needed to prevent suction entrap-

ments in hot tubs, spas, and swimming pools. Along with the P&SS Act, CPSC launched *Pool Safely: Simple Steps Save Lives*, a national public education campaign to raise public awareness about drowning and entrapment prevention, support industry compliance with the P&SS Act's requirements, and improve safety at pools and spas in the United States. According to the P&SS Act, "under the law, all public pools and spas must have ANSI/ASME A112.19.8 performance standard, or the successor standard ANSI/APSP-16 2011 compliant drain covers installed and a second anti-entrapment system installed, when there is a single main drain other than an unblockable drain."

Aquatics professionals must not only fully understand the P&SS Act, but must closely follow the requirements for drain covers and antientrapment systems, as the P&SS Act is currently the only federal law in the swimming pool industry. That means aquatic facilities must comply with the P&SS Act specifications for drain covers and that antientrapment systems are required, not optional. Noncompliant drain covers and systems are disobeying the law. Therefore, drain covers and systems must be compliant with the P&SS Act to avoid legal ramifications and also to prevent dangerous suction entrapments. Pool Safely (www.poolsafely.gov/pool-spa-safety-act/) provides information about the P&SS Act, interpretations and staff guidelines, up-to-date requirements, and more. P&SS Act compliance is a must to operate an aquatic facility.

What follows in this chapter are various recommendations and warnings for preventing deadly suction entrapments in aquatic facilities. This chapter is written with the goal of identifying and eliminating dangerous entrapment and entanglement hazards. Although often in the United States too much attention is paid to lawsuits and legal settlements, some generalities about aquatic lawsuits can put entrapments into better perspective. When someone drowns at an aquatic facility, if negligent, the facility could lose upwards of $1 million. If someone breaks their neck while entering shallow water headfirst, if negligent, the facility could pay the plaintiff up to $10 million. When a child sits on an unprotected bottom outlet (drain) and becomes disemboweled, the payoff is often between $29 million and $35 million. This is often because this type of accident is easy to avoid and the medical care to keep the child alive and well for the rest of his or her life is astronomical. Now, this situation also violates federal law.

This discussion can be confusing and comprehensive particularly for readers who lack plumbing and mechanical training, but we will attempt to keep it simple. Even the smallest of pool pumps can create catastrophic suction entrapments. Four major types of entrapments exist:

1. hair entanglement,
2. limb and finger entrapment,
3. body vacuum entrapment, and
4. disembowelment (evisceration).

In the vast majority of cases, the bottom outlet or drain causing the problem is piped directly to the pump so that this outlet serves as the single suction point for the pump. With the exception of hair entanglement, the outlet in question is often unprotected by a grate or anti-vortex cover. The combination of these two conditions creates this dangerous situation. Conversely, the prevention of these entrapments is simple; dual drains with secure covers would prevent almost all injuries of this kind.

Hair Entanglements

More specifically, hair entanglements occur particularly when a person with longer hair drops underwater and the hair is sucked into an outlet grate or anti-vortex plate. This type of entanglement is most commonly occurs to young females with longer hair in older spas that do not meet today's standards. When hair strands are drawn through drain gratings, hair entanglement may follow by the knotting or wrapping mechanisms as illustrated in Figure 27.1.

Figure 27.1. Hair entanglement

Body Vacuum Entrapments

Body vacuum entrapments typically happen when a person submerges and covers the unprotected outlet with the buttocks, back, or front of the torso. Vacuum entrapment can and will occur if every aperture on a drain cover is blocked by a por-

tion of a swimmer's body while the pump is working (Figure 27.2). On at least one occasion (Tanya Nickens), body entrapment has occurred on the grate covering the outlet.

Limb Entrapment

Limb entrapment is similar to body entrapment with one important exception.

In the case of limb entrapment, the arm or the leg is sucked into the unprotected pipe in the pool, spa, wading pool, or similar type of bottom outlet. Limb entrapments usually occur in larger pipes, that is, plumbing greater than 2 in. in diameter. The added problem with a limb entrapment is that the suction immediately engorges and enlarges the extremity because body fluids are being pulled by the pump inside the limb, and even after the pump is turned off, the limb remains stuck because it has become a "cork in the bottle." Finger entrapment can also occur and be just as deadly (Figure 27.3).

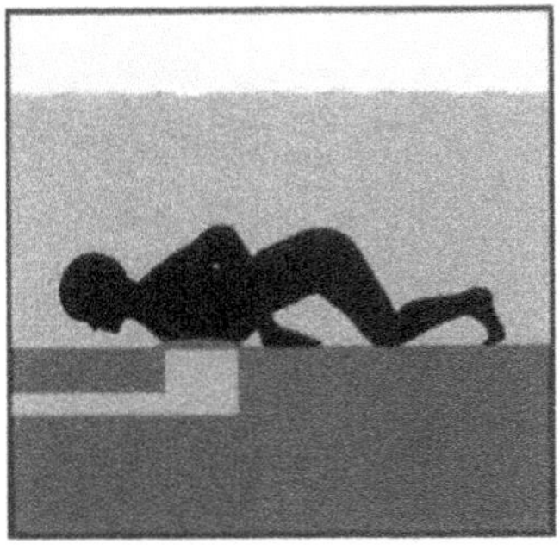

Figure 27.2. Body entrapment

Figure 27.3. Finger entrapment

Disembowelment

One of the worst entrapment scenarios is disembowelment (evisceration), which most often happens to small children aged 3 and 6 years who sit on an unprotected bottom outlet (drain). In this case, the lower intestines are pulled out of their body through the anus (Figure 27.4). Not a pleasant thought. Although this tragedy does not often result in death like drowning does, the child lives but requires many surgeries and transplants to restore quality of life.

Solutions

The solutions for preventing entrapments in all aquatic facilities can be divided into three major categories:

1. design solutions,
2. protective measures, and
3. warnings.

Figure 27.4. Evisceration

The design solutions are probably the most effective in preventing entrapments because with dual suction outlets on all recreational water vessels, the vast majority of suction problems will be eliminated. Simply stated, in a dual suction situation, if a swimmer obstructs one outlet, the suction is quickly diverted to the other open outlet, thus eliminating the problem. Because the single suction outlet is the primary cause of all entrapments, creating two outlets in all pools prevents most injuries. Covering and protecting these outlets at the same time almost always guarantees safety (see Figure 27.5). The covers should be P&SS Act compliant and should not be removable except by a certified technician with tools.

Another design safeguard for bottom outlets is to ensure that the flow rate is less than 6 ft per second. At this low flow, suction is not sufficient to cause entrapments. In the rare event that one of two outlets in a dual suction system is blocked, the slow flow rate would not be strong enough to entrap someone. Still another protective measure is to have the two outlets at least 3 ft apart so that both drains cannot be obstructed simultaneously.

Including these safety design concepts on new construction is easy and relatively inexpensive. Retrofitting these plumbing changes on existing pools is more complicated and expensive. However, the physical and financial costs could be catastrophic if the design problem is not corrected. Children in wading pools pose the greatest risk because the water is so shallow they can sit directly on top of the drain. Wading pools should be retrofitted to have two bottom outlets at least 3 ft apart with secure anti-vortex grates in place. This renovation should cost less than $2,000 in most localities.

Wading pools must also follow the P&SS Act requirements, including ANSI/ASME A112.19.8 performance standard or successor standards approved by the CPSC.

Protective Measures

Protective measures specifically deal with covers and or grates; most of the suction entrapments occur in the absence of a protective grate or anti-vortex cover over the bottom outlet. Too often the cover is missing and has gone unnoticed by lifeguards and managers until it is too late. Because of this, aquatic professionals should check that all grates and covers are securely in place and show no signs of wear, corrosion, or other abnormalities. The cover should be unable to be removed without the use of tools. All anti-vortex covers should be labeled with the appropriate marking for maximum flow rates and labeled as compliant with the ANSI/ASME A112.19.8 performance standard, or any successor standard, and requirements in the P&SS Act. If the cover does not carry this marking, the pump should be turned off and the cover replaced with an appropriately tested and labeled cover that is compliant with the P&SS Act. Spas and hot tubs manufactured prior to 1982 should be inspected because they probably were installed with inferior, nonprotective covers.

New anti-vortex grates are a huge safety improvement that can even prevent hair entanglements. The vertical dimensions of new style grates have collimated gratings to protect against entanglements by increasing "critical length." Shorter, conventional grates can cause the lasso effect on longer hair.

Figure 27.5. Two bottom drains with appropriately fitting P&SS Act-compliant drain covers. (Photo courtesy of Aquatic Safety Research Group)

Sidebar 27.1

The Virginia Graeme Baker Pool & Spa Safety Act (P&SS Act)

If a public swimming pool or spa has a single main drain other than an unblockable drain, the P&SS Act requires at least one of the following devices:

- Safety vacuum release system—must be tested by an independent third party and conform to ANSI/ASME standard A112.19.17 or ASSTM standard F2387.
- Suction-limiting vent system
- Gravity drainage system
- Automatic pump shutoff system
- Drain disablement
- Other systems—any other system determined by the CPSC to be equally effective as or better than the systems listed above at preventing or eliminating risk of injury or death associated with pool drainage systems.

P&SS Act (A) (ii) http://www.poolsafely.gov/pool-spa-safety-act/read/ See the full Act for further information.

Even though turning off the pump may be too late in the case of disembowelments, safety shutoffs should be clearly marked and located near all aquatic facilities. In the event of a hair entanglement or limb entrapment, many lives could be saved by turning off the pump. Additional technology in the way of automatic cutoff switches is also available. Automatic shut-off valves may be required. Consult the P&SS Act and the MAHC. This is accomplished by adding a vacuum switch to the pump. When the switch senses a sudden increase in vacuum pressure because of an obstruction, it immediately shuts down the pump. This could prevent drowning deaths because of hair entanglements, bodily entrapments, and limb entrapments, but probably not disembowelments. This horrific injury occurs in just fractions of a second before the pump automatically switches off.

Warnings

Finally, appropriate warnings and signage may increase awareness and change behavior, particularly where parents and small children are involved. In the case of hot water spas, all soakers should be advised to keep their head and hair above the surface of the water. With all drains, parents should be told to keep their children away from them.

Educating people who install, repair, and manage pools is also important. One source of guidelines for this information is found in *Guidelines for Entrapment Hazards: Making Pools and Spas Safer* (CPSC, 2005). Most important, the P&SS Act and the Pool Safely: Simple Steps Save Lives campaign provide information to operate a safer swimming pool.

Summary

Disembowelment (evisceration) can occur in a fraction of a second. Four hundred to 600 lb of suction force must be overcome to lift an entrapment victim from a circular drain. Safety innovations are becoming available that meet and exceed the ANSI/ASME A112.19.8 performance standard or the successor standard ANSI/APSP-16 2011, which require compliant drain covers and a second antientrapment system installed, when there is a single main drain other than an unblockable drain. Like other safety issues, "layers of protection" are important, particularly to prevent entrapments and entanglements. It is a federal requirement for every facility to be P&SS Act compliant.

Bibliography

http://www.poolsafely.gov/pool-spa-safety-act/

Steinike, J. (2001, March). Mandating safety. *Aqua Magazine.*

The entrapment solution. (1997). *Aquatics International.* (Reprinted from *Pool and Spa News,* 1996, November 20)

U.S. Consumer Product Safety Commission. (2005). *Guidelines for entrapment hazards: Making pools and spas safer* (Publication #363 009801). Washington, DC: Author.

Virginia Graeme Baker Pool and Spa Safety Act Title XIV. (2007). Retrieved from http://www.poolsafely.gov/pool-spa-safety-act/

28

Practical Risk Management

- Elements of risk management
- Walkabouts
- Four Ps of risk management
- Seven deadly sins

Before the excellent and comprehensive Chapters on Insurance and aquatic risk management by Gareth Hedges (Chapter 29), legal liability and risk management (Chapter 30), and legal liability and risk management (Chapter 30) by Shawn DeRosa, we will review common sense and extremely practical aquatic risk management techniques. Although textbooks usually define risk management as the identification, evaluation, and control of loss to personal and real property with loss further defined as injury, death, destruction of property, financial loss, or harm by reputation, some aquatic professionals say that risk management is structured, organized common sense. The practical risk management section will focus on safety and the reduction of accidents.

All recreational activities have risks, but risks are especially notable in aquatics. Accidents can and do occur at aquatic facilities despite efforts to avoid them. Preventing all accidents is impossible, and when they occur, a lawsuit will often follow. Victims and their families often seek compensation through lawsuits, which can threaten the financial well-being of the facility, its owners, and employees and damage their reputations. This chapter and Chapters 29 and 30 will better prepare aquatic facility managers to not only avoid accidents but also better defend resulting lawsuits. Identifying risks, taking reasonable steps to reduce them, and notifying guests of unusual or hidden risks that cannot be ameliorated will go a long way in preventing accidents and lawsuits.

The point of aquatic risk management should be to control these risks, to make aquatic facility users aware of these risks, and to attempt to transfer the responsibilities for accepting these risks to aquatic facility patrons. Aquatic risk management should not be about eliminating all risks, but rather controlling and reducing these risks whenever possible. No Risk = No Fun. With a systematic approach to identify, evaluate, and control risks, aquatic facilities can become safer and more enjoyable.

One user friendly way of approaching aquatic management in an organized, structured way is to use the analogy of a baseball diamond (Figure 28.1). This approach is a practical way of "covering all your bases" when it comes to total and practical aquatic risk management.

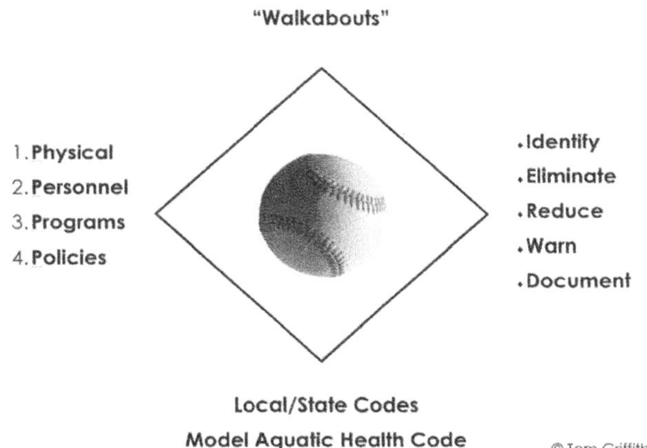

Figure 28.1. This baseball analogy simplifies and explains numerous Risk Management Concepts as the reader rounds the bases.

Home Base

At home base, aquatic facility managers must have in their possession two copies of the local codes and standards that directly govern their facility; one copy to post and the other to keep as a reference in a safe place. The local or state code is law. Facility managers must know the codes and follow them as best as possible. Local codes and standards provide facility managers with minimum requirements that safeguard aquatic facility patrons. Much miscommunication and misunderstanding revolves around local codes. That is why having a recent copy of the local pool ordinance at the facility and readily available for review is important. Too often, critics will adamantly espouse certain sections of the code which either were never in the code or were removed from the code. No excuse exists for not knowing, understanding, and having the local pool code at the aquatic facility. The Model Aquatic Health Code (MAHC) also must be understood and followed. The MAHC is a guidance document that can help local and state authorities make swimming and other water activities healthier and safer. More specifically, the MAHC is a model and a guide for local and state agencies during the process of updating or implementing swimming pool and spa code, rules, regulations, guidance, law, or standards governing the design, construction, operation, and maintenance of aquatic facilities including swimming pools, spas, and hot tubs (CDC, n.d.).

First Base

At first base, the basic elements of risk management should be understood: identifying hazards, eliminating hazards if possible, and reducing hazards whenever possible, particularly when they cannot be removed. When eliminating and reducing hazards are not possible and the facility must be kept open, then warning the patrons is important. Finally, as management progresses through these steps of *identifying, eliminating, reducing,* and *warning of hazards*, documenting in writing the steps taken is important. Documentation of this risk management progression will be invaluable when defending a lawsuit.

Second Base

Perhaps the best and most practical method of developing solid risk management practices is by conducting regular audits. Daily audits through simple walkabouts are perhaps best and should be accomplished at least three times per day. A walkabout is strolling throughout the entire facility looking for problems with water clarity, trip hazards, electrical problems, improperly stored chemicals, and more. The walkabout is intended for a quick walk-through, taking minutes rather than hours to complete. At this time, the manager can identify hazards and check up on personnel and guests. Carrying a small pocket-sized spiral notepad is excellent for jotting down reminders. Walkabouts work most effectively when they are completed first thing when the facility opens, last thing at night when the facility closes, and at least once during the day. Actually, at facilities that are heavily used and where management is housed in the aquatic facility, a walkabout every 30 minutes is highly recommended. More comprehensive audits can be performed by outside auditors on a seasonal basis.

Third Base

Third base in this risk management paradigm includes the five Ps of risk management: *physical aspects, policies and procedures, personnel,* and *programs.*

This is a simple way of remembering important areas to investigate when auditing an aquatic facility.

Physical Aspects

Of primary importance to aquatic facility patrons are the physical attributes of the facility, particularly in terms of hazards and cleanliness. Water clarity is one of the most important physical factors that is most often cited in serious accidents and lawsuits. Unmarked areas of shallow water can also produce catastrophic neck injuries. Uncovered and unprotected bottom outlets and drains can also produce catastrophic injuries. Entrance and exits to facilities and locker rooms should also be checked for damage and trip, slip, and fall concerns. Once again, the facility should meet all local, state, and regional codes, including those for the building, such as electrical, fire, and lighting standards. In areas where codes are not in existence, other agencies, municipalities, or experts should be consulted about the physical aspects of the facility.

Policies and Procedures

Patron rules should be reviewed regularly to ensure they are realistic, legally enforceable, and fair. For example, a common pool rule is no street shoes on the deck. However, if this rule is never enforced and guests and employees are constantly walking on the deck with shoes, perhaps it is time to reexamine the rule. Large groups of children are often taken to aquatic facilities for class trips and outings. These groups can inundate and quickly overburden lifeguards on duty. Too many aquatic facilities lack written group use policies that would better protect individuals coming as a group, so policies and procedures in this regard are needed. Policies and procedures for both employees and guests should be in writing, readily available, widely known, and most important, regularly enforced. Employee handbooks are a must today and should include all policies and procedures including expected behavior, appearance, attendance, and alcohol and drug abuse. Due process systems should also be explained in writing to all employees and participants. After reading employee manuals and documents, employees should sign and date them.

Emergency action procedures (EAP) are an expected standard for every aquatic facility, and having a written copy of the EAP alone is not sufficient; it must be practiced regularly by employees. The site-specific EAP must be in effect for severe injuries, drownings, heart attacks, fire, fights, robbery, vandalism, bomb threats, severe weather, and similar problems. Again, the EAP must not only be readily available and posted, but must also be practiced and refined regularly. The EAP is an excellent component for in-service training.

Personnel

Aquatic facility managers should be aware of professional certifications and training available to all pool personnel. Certifications are merely the first step in providing a safe facility. Especially for lifeguards and managers, achieving certifications is no longer a choice, but rather an obligation and responsibility. Conversely, certification does not necessarily mean qualification. In cases when local or state codes require certifications, these certifications must be checked frequently and kept on file. But certifications alone are not the only prerequisite or job requirement. All employees, particularly lifeguards, must be assessed of their knowledge and skills regularly. In addition to the job descriptions mentioned previously, lifeguards must complete pre-job orientations and in-service training. A Penn State study (Griffiths, 1994) indicated that approximately 95% of lifeguards surveyed stated that they completed both pre-job training and in-service training when employed as a lifeguard. Close supervision is required of all lifeguards, and continual supervision helps to prevent personnel issues as well. Personnel must also be protected against blood-borne pathogens with appropriate training and equipment. Perhaps it is helpful to consider personnel in three large categories:

- employing, evaluating, and terminating;
- employee education; and
- evidence and content of staff training.

Accidents sometimes happen involving employees when they act in a manner outside the scope of their training, whether due to recklessness or a genuine need to accomplish a task that they are inadequately prepared to perform. Ensure employees have adequate training for all tasks to which they are likely to be assigned (routine and emergency) and that they do not engage in activities for which they are untrained.

Programs

Finally, all programs should be inspected periodically for course content, participant safety, instructional sequencing, and potentially dangerous activities. It is helpful to have programs under the jurisdiction of an activity coordinator or program coordinator. Aquatic facilities should have regularly scheduled safety meetings involving the entire staff. The entire aquatic facility staff should be instructed in the basics of risk assessment and taught to identify the potential for injury and accidents.

Supervision of programs is key for managing risks. Many accidents can occur, and some lawsuits result when supervision for an activity is either absent or in-adequate. Aquatic facility managers should determine the standard of care for their programmed activities. In many instances, a signed waiver, warning, or release statement from program participants is required. Many adults, being made fully aware of the risks involved with a program or activity, can contract away their rights to be reimbursed for injuries that may result. Children cannot contract away their rights and parents cannot contract away their child's rights, but they can contract away their right as a parent.

Risk management must be a comprehensive and organized system of identifying, evaluating, and controlling risks. If the four broad areas addressed are kept in mind while checking the pools and surrounding areas, most concerns will be addressed. Included in this system should be an examination of other industry and agency standards that may be applied to an aquatic facility. All aquatic facility employees should be included on the risk management team, not just lifeguards.

Seven Deadly Sins

Another risk management idea is to remind all aquatic staff of the catastrophic risks that could occur and must be avoided at all costs. Each facility can come up with its Seven Deadly Sins that might keep employees focused on the most important issues.

Managing an aquatic facility requires safeguarding guests, and this task can appear burdensome and overwhelming to many aquatic facility managers. But as I review accidents and court cases throughout the United States, it becomes apparent that a few recurring lapses often result in catastrophic accidents and lawsuits. Although this list does not cover all the accident possibilities and is certainly not a complete risk management guide, at least it is a quick list of significant flaws that still exist in many aquatic facilities. Although each of these safety violations may not result in death or drowning, they could adversely affect a facility.

Lack of a Certified Aquatic Facility Operator (AFO), Licensed Aquatic Facility Technician (LAFT), or Certified Pool Operator (CPO)

The missing link in successful trials is the lack of a certified AFO/CFO or LAFT on duty at the time of the accident. It is apparent that the AFO/CPO/LAFT is much more of a risk manager than the lifeguards on duty and that he or she appreciates the consequences of breaches in safety and the standard of care.

Lack of a Group Use Policy

Many groups (church, school, civic) are attracted to aquatic facilities because they provide certified lifeguards who not only protect guests, but also provide free baby-sitting and a break for teachers, parents, and counselors.

When lifeguards see these groups coming, they tend to relax because they assume the adults will be watching the children. This is a major miscommunication: The adults expect the lifeguards to be watching the children, and the lifeguards expect the adults to be watching the children, so rather than having double coverage, there is double trouble. Group use policies should include adult-to-child ratios, U.S. Coast Guard-approved life jacket use, swimmer and nonswimmer rules, and so forth. Note & Float™ is a surefire group use policy. Although Note & Float™ should be used for all nonswimmers all the time, if a pool does not have Note & Float™ program regularly at the facility, they should at least have and use a Note & Float™ for groups.

Failure to Warn Against Headfirst Entry

Only deep water can prevent catastrophic head and neck injuries whenever a swimmer attempts headfirst entry at an aquatic facility. The magic depth for safety when attempting any dive is at least 9 ft, regardless of the height from which the dive is attempted. Signs, graphics, and warnings must be aggressively and creatively used to prevent headfirst entries from the side of the pool in all aquatic facilities. The following facts are important to remember: It takes less than a second to render a patron quadriplegic in aquatic facilities, but at the same time, springboard diving has never had a safety problem in the United States. Dumb headfirst entries are dangerous, not springboard diving. Even the most aggressive campaign to stop diving into shallow water may not be successful, but at least defensive strategies will assist an aquatic facility operator in a court of law.

Failure to Warn Against Breath-Holding and Underwater Swimming

Competitive, repetitive, and prolonged breath-holding drills and games are extremely dangerous and must be curtailed in all bodies of water. Although the physiology of the underwater event is complicated, the results are simple: death by drowning, cardiac arrhythmia, or cardiac arrest. Breath-holding and underwater swimming cause accidents with better swimmers, so they often go undetected when problems arise. When it comes to prolonged breath-holding in the water, the rule is simple and clear: Just Don't Do It!

Failure to Guard Children of Tender Years

Seventy percent of all preschoolers who drown are in the care of one or both parents at the time of the accident. Parents typically are distracted from watching their children at facilities and are unable to recognize when their children are at risk or in trouble. Children under age 7 must be vigilantly supervised, even in shallow water. Parents must also be reminded to watch their children. Where parents and toddlers congregate, shal-low water lifeguards or safety lookouts can be used when fully certified lifeguards are not adequate in number. All nonswimmers should wear U.S. Coast Guard-approved life jackets.

Failure to Protect Against Entrapments and Entanglements

Any drain or outlet can cause a severe entrapment or entanglement risk in aquatic facilities, particularly those that have single outlets leading to a circulation pump. A variety of strategies must be used to prevent these injuries, including intact grates, anti-vortex covers, multiple outlets, and emergency shutoffs. Pools should be compliant with the Virginia Graeme Baker Pool and Spa Safety Act.

Failure to Post and Follow a Fecal Accident Policy

The best advice to follow when a fecal accident occurs is to simply refer to the CDC Healthy Swimming website (https://www.cdc.gov/healthywater/swimming/aquatics-professionals/fecalresponse.html).

Summary

Hopefully the tips and suggestions will make aquatic facilities safer and more enjoyable for guests and employees. The next chapter looks in-depth at aquatic liability from a legal perspective.

Bibliography

Berry, W. D. (1992). *Managing change: City, state, and federal regulations related to liability and changing regulations.* Unpublished manuscript, Washington College, Chestertown, MD.

Clement, A. (1997). *Legal responsibility in aquatics.* Tallahassee, FL: Sport and Law Press.

Clement, A. (1988). *Law in sport and physical activity.* Ann Arbor, MI: Benchmark Press.

Griffiths, T., Steel, D., & Vogelsong, H. (1997). Results of the 1996 lifeguard survey. *Parks and Recreation Magazine, 32*(11), 62–68.

References

Centers for Disease Control and Prevention. (n.d.). Model Aquatic Health Code (MAHC): A national model swimming pool and spa code. Retrieved from http://www.cdc.gov/healthywater/swimming/pools/mahc/

Note and Float Life Jacket Fund - www.NoteandFloatLifeJackets.org

Virginia Graeme Baker Pool and Spa Safety Act. (2007). Retrieved from www.poolsafely.gov/pool-spa-safety-act/

29

Insurance and Aquatic Risk Management

By Gareth Hedges, The Redwoods Group

Key Concepts

- Liability
- Insurance
- Test, mark, protect
- Serving others
- Risk management matrix

As is clear in this book, risk is ever present in aquatic facilities, and aggressive risk management must be a key priority for all who operate a swimming pool. Unfortunately, risk management and its insurance component are often not well understood. This chapter will give a general overview of both insurance and operational risk management specific to aquatic facilities. This is most important for the person responsible for the facility's risk management plan, but is also valuable information at all levels of the organization because creating a culture of safety requires everyone to manage risk.

Although the first thing that may come to mind in risk management is "insurance," the insurance transaction is only a small piece of an organization's risk management system. Risk management entails identifying risks, analyzing and prioritizing risks, developing and implementing risk management strategies, and financing the pecuniary aspect of those risks through retention, contract, or most commonly, insurance.

Insurance

In the insurance transaction, the insured facility transfers its risk of specific financial losses to the insurer in return for a set payment (the premium). If a covered loss occurs to an insured facility, the insurer is required to indemnify, or pay, the insured for the loss, up to the limits of the insurance policy. This transaction allows individual entities to spread the risk of loss among all the insured entities in return for a predictable and affordable payment. In this manner, an insured entity can have the financial security needed to run a business that has

risks—such as the risk of death due to drowning—that it otherwise could not afford.

The following are the most common commercial insurance policies that insured facilities obtain and what those policies cover. This is only a general overview of each type, but as policies can differ, insured entities should discuss the specifics of their policies with their insurance partner and insurance broker.

Property

Property insurance covers real property such as building structures, fixtures, and the pool itself, as well as business property such as machinery, equipment, and furniture, from covered causes of loss. The policy may also include business interruption coverage that will pay for lost income when the property is unusable.

For a pool operator, the following are important considerations to discuss with an insurer and broker in obtaining property coverage:

1. **Is there a deductible?** A deductible is the limit of money up to which the insured is responsible to pay before the insurer is responsible. For example, if an insured has a $500 deductible, then it is responsible for the first $500 of a loss, and the insurer is only responsible above that amount. A deductible is often obtained to receive lower premium payments.

2. **How is the property valued?** The insured may be given several valuation options at different prices:
   a. *Replacement cost:* replaces damaged property with new replacement property without deduction for depreciation.
   b. *Actual cash value:* replacement cost less depreciation. For older properties, this valuation may not cover the cost needed to replace damaged property with new.
   c. *Functional replacement cost:* allows the insurer to replace damaged property with a functional

equivalent. For example, expensive locker room fixtures may be replaced with basic models.

d. *Market value:* the price that would be paid for the property based on free market conditions. Market value is not commonly offered, but local market conditions may make this an option.

e. *Co-insurance:* A provision that allows the insured to carry insurance limits equal to a specified percentage of the property's actual cash value (ACV) in return for a reduced premium rate. Many policies include a clause that requires at least 80% of the ACV to be insured to receive a full payment in the event of a loss. This is important if the value of the property increases as the insured may not receive full payment if the insured amount is less than 80% of the ACV. An "agreed value" option may be used to remove the co-insurance requirement, and the insurer will cover losses at the agreed value.

3. **Is the facility covered for the most likely risks?** The insured should evalutate its risks and compare them with its insurance coverage. For example, property coverage commonly excludes flood damage (which may be unavailable or available only through a federal program), earthquakes, and landslides, among others, and may have increased deductibles for windstorms such as tornadoes or named hurricanes. If these are likely risks, the insured should discuss available options with an insurance broker.

General Liability

General liability covers an insured's liability to third parties for bodily injury and property damage. The policy may also provide coverage for personal and advertising injury (e.g., liability for defamation or false advertising) or provide no-fault medical payment coverage for program participants.

As with property coverage, aquatic facility operators must address specific questions when obtaining general liability insurance:

1. **Are my limits high enough?** Put simply, does the insurance amount ensure that the organization can continue to operate in the event of a devastating loss such as the death of a child by drowning? Although most losses are low in value, a death in a swimming pool can often subject the facility to millions if not tens of millions of dollars of liability. The policy should provide sufficient coverage for the riskiest aspects of the operation. Umbrella policies—which provide coverage for losses in excess of the primary limits of the general liability policy—may also be purchased. The policy may exclude coverage for punitive damages.

2. **Who is covered?** Generally, a liability insurance policy covers the organization and its employees. Volunteers are often included, but may not be covered. If the organizations has volunteers, both the organization and the volunteers should know whether they are covered.

3. **What is covered?** "All risk" commercial general liability coverage is broad. It covers losses from any event, unless specifically excluded. However, certain risks are commonly excluded from commercial general liability policies. For example, in some policies, liability due to sexual abuse and molestation may not be included without an endorsement to the policy. Additionally, liability from certain types of pollution may be excluded, and the insured may need an endorsement to cover liability due to the leaking of chemicals commonly used in pool disinfection. Other common exclusions also include liability due to the sale of liquor, injury to employees, and injuries caused by the use of trampolines. Supplemental policies or endorsements may be purchased to protect against these individual risks, and it is important for the insured to ensure it has the coverage that it needs for its specific operations.

Automobile

As with a personal car, all business automobiles that will be operated on public roads will need to be insured. Due to the dangerous nature of specific automobiles, insurance coverage may be unavailable or expensive. For example, 12-passenger and 15-passenger vans—the traditional favorites of traveling swim teams—should be insured due to the increased rollover risk and structural instability of the vehicles. Even if insurance is available, driving a larger minibus or bus (using a commercial driver may be necessary) or using several minivans instead of these vehicles is recommended.

Workers' Compensation

This is a statutorily required form of no-fault insurance that all employers are required to purchase to cover employees for injuries they receive in the course and scope of their employment. Workers' compensation provides a sole remedy for these injuries that compensates injured workers and protects employers from lawsuits.

Directors and Officers

This type of policy protects the leaders of an organization from several liability losses including employment discrimination and statutory violations such as claims made under the Americans With Disabilities Act (ADA).

Although the above policies may provide the financial security for a facility, insurance is only a financial risk transfer device, not a substitute for an aggressive risk management program. In addition to financial responsibilities, pool operators have both business and moral responsibilities to provide a safe environment for their community. Insurance can indemnify a financial loss, but it cannot restore the reputation of a business or the life of a child following a tragic loss.

Operational Risk Management

We will now explore these elements in regard to the specific operational risks of an aquatic facility. Of course, the risks will differ depending on the facility. A homeowners' association pool has different risks than a water park; a YMCA pool in Nebraska may have different risks than a YMCA pool in Pennsylvania. In addition to different risks, aquatic facilities also have different purposes, missions, and reasons for being. Risk management cannot occur in a vacuum; pool operators must understand their facility's purpose to determine whether a particular risk or risk management solution is acceptable. During every stage of the process, pool operators should ask, "Does this further our mission?"

Additionally, no facility can address every risk it identifies immediately with limited resources: time, money, and staff. It is important to prioritize risks and target mitigation strategies that will be most effective. A primary way to prioritize risks is to analyze risks with regard to their frequency and severity.

Frequency

Frequency is the likelihood that a particular event will occur. Pool operators should evaluate frequency over the long term, not the immediate future, to ensure they are evaluating the probability of occurrence "at all" not "tomorrow."

Severity

Severity is the projected amount of damage that the event will cause. In its simplest form, severity can be evaluated in dollars and can be put into the perspective of the organization's overall financial stability and appetite for risk. A more dynamic evaluation, however, will consider not only the financial severity but also the severity of loss of reputation, goodwill, ability to continue to serve the community, and moral obligation to provide a safe environment.

By evaluating by frequency and severity, pool operators can prioritize the risks they address, as pictured in Figure 29.1.

Clearly, the most important risks to address are those with both the highest severity and the highest frequency—catastrophic losses that are almost certain to happen. Again, frequency should be thought of not as "likely to happen tomorrow" but as "likely to happen ever." Below, several risks familiar (or possibly unfamiliar) to aquatic facilities are placed in the grid as an example. Risks and their placement may differ due to the specifics of the facility, and some risks may be difficult to accurately place due to the complexity of the risk (see Figure 29.2).

With this analysis in mind, and in evaluating the most severe pool-related incidents handled by Redwoods, we focus on two of the most severe yet different risks that swimming pool operators face: drowning and child sexual abuse.

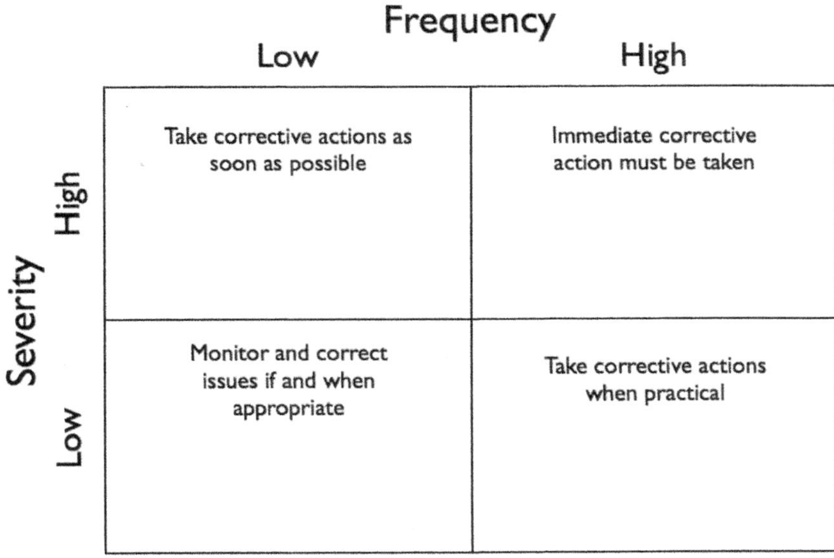

Figure 29.1. Risk management matrix.

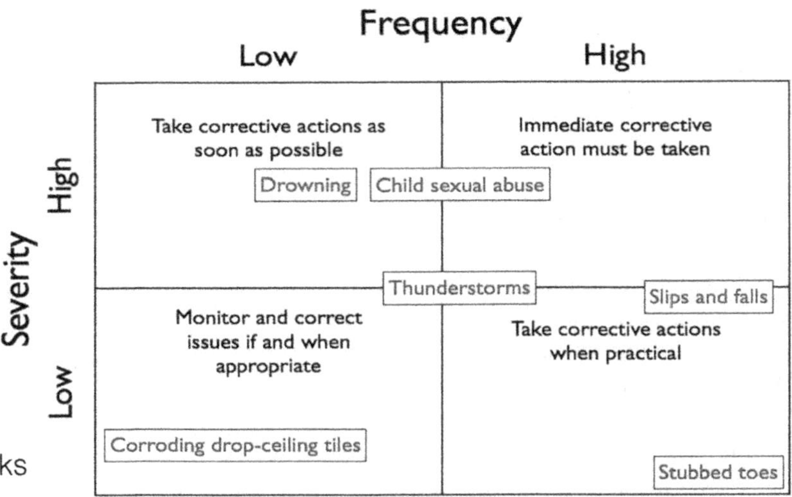

Figure 29.2. Examples of risks at swimming pools.

Drowning

Of course, the most obvious risk associated with a swimming pool is the risk of injury or death by drowning. Although it is often stated that "anyone can drown"—and this is technically true—specific factors clearly increase a person's likelihood of death or injury by drowning. Age (younger children), gender (male), and race/ethnicity (African American and Hispanic) are demographic factors tied to higher drowning rates. But the number one risk factor in drowning in swimming pools is swimming skill, or more specifically, a lack of swimming skills. Contrary to popular misconception, the vast majority of swimming pool drowning injuries that Redwoods has investigated have occurred in shallow water less than 5 ft deep (see Figure 29.3).

To eliminate injury and death by drowning at a pool, the first step is to implement a comprehensive nonswimmer protection plan that ensures that no one uses the pool without the benefit of multiple layers of protection.

One of the most important layers of protection is effective lifeguard surveillance. The topic of effective lifeguards is addressed extensively in this book and in other available resources such as those published by the

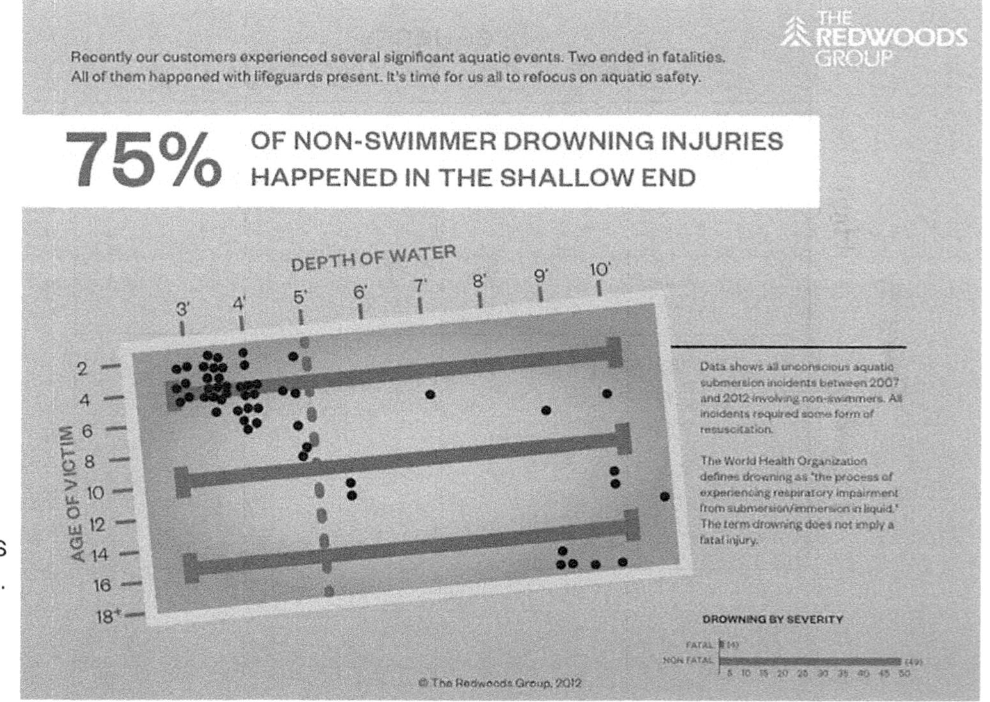

Figure 29.3. The Redwoods Group drowning data.

American Red Cross, YMCA of the USA, Ellis and Associates, and many others. For that reason, we will not discuss the topic at length, but there are two important points about lifeguards.

First, lifeguards are extremely important to operating a safe swimming pool. In fact, at The Redwoods Group, we think lifeguards are so important that we will not partner with an organization that has any aquatic activity that lifeguards do not actively supervise. It is a black-letter prerequisite for our insurance program.

Second, as crucial as lifeguards are, they are humans, often teenagers, and they are not perfect. Humans have lapses in attention and judgment; they make mistakes. Lifeguards cannot be the only layer of protection. Lifeguards must be supported by systems and technology that allow them to better perform their jobs and that protect nonswimmers by adding layers of redundancy in case a lifeguard does not identify or respond to an emergency quickly enough.

The Redwoods recommended aquatic safety plan for all pool and waterfront use is as follows:

For all children entering the water, including all children and adults that are part of an outside group (rentals, special events, birthday parties, etc.):

- **Test:** Swim test to determine swimming ability. Users who do not take the test or children under age 7 years may be automatically designated as nonswimmers.
- **Mark:** Clearly mark all users to identify swimming ability.

- **Protect:** Most aquatic incidents happen in shallow water (3 to 5 ft). Protect nonswimmers, especially younger children, by restricting them to the shallow end and adding additional layers of protection, including the following:
  - (a) the nonswimmer is actively engaged in a swim lesson or activity with staff;
  - (b) the nonswimmer is actively supervised, within arm's reach of an adult parent or caregiver; or
  - (c) the nonswimmer is wearing a properly fitted U.S. Coast Guard-approved life jacket (see Figure 29.4).

Although the aquatic safety plan above is simple and any aquatic facility can adopt it, the particulars of how it is implemented will vary depending on the facility and its users. For example, administering a swim test to children in a YMCA day camp may be no problem, but administering the same test to children that visit a public waterpark may not be practical. The organization may need to offer the swim test only at designated times or for features that have deep water. Or, as many waterparks now do, the organization may regard all children as nonswimmers and require direct parental supervision and/or life jacket use.

Child Sexual Abuse

Possibly a less obvious risk to pool members and guests, and a risk to the reputation if not the continued existence of the facility, is child sexual abuse. Although child sexual abuse is not a problem unique to aquatic

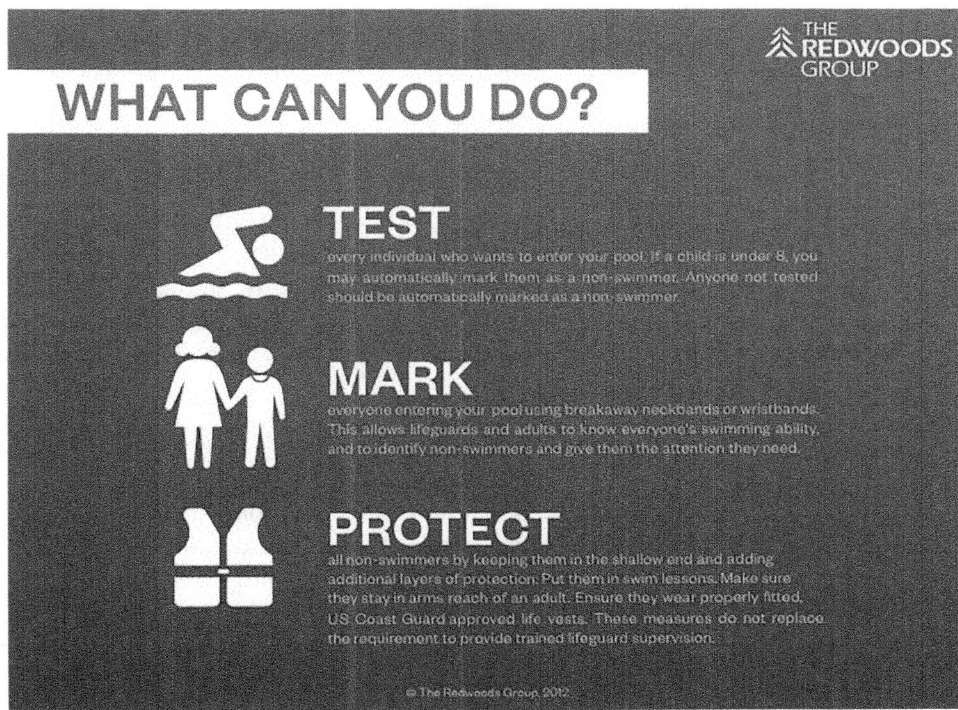

Figure 29.4. Test, Mark, Protect developed by the Redwoods Group.

facilities, but a community-wide issue, aquatic facilities and programs often pose a greater risk of child sexual abuse and present unique challenges to combat the problem.

According to the Centers for Disease Control and Prevention (2005), 1 in 4 girls and 1 in 6 boys in the United States are abused as children. These numbers are likely low, as the majority of incidents of child sexual abuse go unreported because of the psychological and social damage that often accompany child sexual abuse. Abusers may be adults—most commonly a close family member, friend, coach, counselor, or other adult in a position of trust—or other children.

A comprehensive review of the dynamics of child sexual abuse is beyond our scope; for more information, see the references section at the end of this chapter. However, at Redwoods, our claims data show that the risk of child sexual abuse increases whenever water is present. Locker rooms, bathrooms, and swimming pools are high-risk areas for child sexual abuse to occur on-site because of the private nature of the settings and often a lack of clothing. Additionally, several high-profile cases of child sexual abuse have occurred in coach–athlete and teacher–student relationships, both of which are risks pool operators face in regard to competitive swim teams and swim lessons.

Although every case is different, child sexual abuse tends to follow patterns, and it is from these patterns that we and other organizations have developed guidance to combat child sexual abuse. Below are examples of common patterns of abuse.

Red Flags

The grooming process for a preferential pedophile child abuser tends to be almost the same every time. We do not catch abusers abusing, we catch them breaking the rules. These red flags should be reported:

- **Inappropriate touching or tickling.** Abusers touch or handle children in ways that are inappropriate to test limits and push boundaries.
  - *What should you do?*
    Clearly define the rules for touch within the organization. If you see someone violating these rules, stop it and report it. Train your staff to watch for this behavior from any adult who comes in contact with children.
- **Gifts or preferential treatment.** Abusers single out children that might be susceptible and offer them gifts to gain trust and favor and set expectations that gifts could go away.
  - *What should you do?*
    Do not allow staff to give gifts that show preference of one child over others. Every child demands a different level of care and attention, but

when a caregiver expresses favoritism for one or more children, take corrective action.

- **Creating one-on-one time.** Abusers create opportunities where they have time alone with children at the facility.
  - *What should you do?*
    Make sure any one-to-one time is in a public, observable space, such as in the front lobby or entrance to the building. Choose group situations when possible. Set a good example by avoiding one adult–one child situations with children other than your own.
- **Opportunities for outside contact.** Abusers seek privacy to abuse children, and privacy is easier to get off-site, such as the abuser's or the child's home.
  - *What should you do?*
    Have and enforce strict policies prohibiting outside contact with children, including prohibiting staff from transporting or babysitting children in your program. Explain to parents why you have these policies. Also, help them understand that offenders often earn the trust of parents. Their vigilance is crucial to keeping children safe.

The Facts

- **Child abuse is pervasive.** Experts estimate that 1 in 4 girls and 1 in 6 boys are sexually abused before they are 18.
- **Trust is involved.** In more than 90% of sexual abuse cases, the child and the child's family know and trust the abuser.
- **Avoid the one to one.** More than 80% of sexual abuse cases occur in one adult–one child situations.

For pool operators, the chances are high that the facility will attract children. For parents, the risk of child sexual abuse is present and high. Therefore, pool operators have an obligation—both legal and moral—to proactively prevent child sexual abuse in their organization and in their community. The following are key areas for an organization to address to create a safe environment.

Screening and Hiring

At a minimum, a criminal background check should be performed on all staff that work with children. Best practice is to perform a comprehensive background check on all staff, volunteers, and contractors that will be working with or around children. A comprehensive background check includes a local, state, and national criminal background check (depending on availability and local legal requirements), a sexual offender registry check, and a social security trace. Additionally, an organization's commitment to child sexual abuse prevention should be made clear to a potential employee at the application stage. The application should contain a statement of the organization's child protection policy. It should require an applicant's prior employment history and personal and professional references. All items should be checked prior to hire, and an application should be returned for clarification or rejected if it is incomplete or inconsistent.

Training

All staff, volunteers, and contractors should be required to sign a code of conduct that contains the organization's child protection policies. Additionally, staff, volunteers, and contractors should be required to be trained specifically on the risk of child sexual abuse, including the organization's policies, red flag behaviors, and reporting requirements. Many organizations such as YMCA of the USA, Praesidium, The Redwoods Group's Redwoods Institute, and USA Swimming offer video and/or online training programs that can supplement an organization's specific policies. It is important to train staff, volunteers, and contractors who will work directly with children, as well as those who supervise or may interact with those who work with children.

Staff Expectations and Operational Procedures

A few key policies can greatly reduce the risk of child sexual abuse, both adult to child and child to child. The implementation of these policies may differ by facility and program, but the core policies described should be strictly enforced.

- An adult should never be alone and unsupervised with a child: Sexual abuse rarely occurs in the open; an abuser exploits private areas to commit the physical act of abuse. This policy often presents a unique challenge for competitive swim teams and private swim lessons where one-on-one interaction may be integral to the program. These interactions can occur provided they are in full public view. For example,
  - all individual meetings between coaches and athletes should occur in public areas, such as on the bleachers, on the pool deck, or in an open lobby—individual meetings in an office, or "behind closed doors," are never allowed;
  - parents should be invited to attend all lessons, practices, and meetings and should be encouraged to drop in at any time; and
  - staff should be trained to move to a public or supervised area if a one-on-one situation occurs, such as when a swimmer arrives early or is picked up late from practice.

- Outside contact between staff and participants should be prohibited, or allowed only if scheduled, approved, and supervised.
  - Private practices, individual training sessions, or other off-site or unscheduled practices for individual or small groups of athletes should be prohibited or closely monitored.
  - "Away" swim meets, especially for small groups or individual elite swimmers, may pose a risk for unsupervised outside contact. Coaches should be mindful never to be alone and unsupervised with athletes. They should never share a hotel room, should encourage parental supervision and participation, and should avoid situations such as social outings that could place the coach and athlete in one-on-one situations.
  - Staff should never transport participants in their own vehicles.
  - Staff should not babysit or provide other unrelated outside services (e.g., private swim lessons in a backyard pool) to children they meet through the facility's programs.
- Staff should be trained in appropriate touch when working with children. Appropriate physical contact is necessary for coaching, instructing, and the emotional development of children, and what is appropriate will differ by the age of the child and the type of interaction. Some guidelines are as follows:
  - Children should never be touched in private areas (generally areas covered by a swimsuit).
  - Avoid frontal hugs, tickling, lap-sitting, and physical horseplay.
  - Swim instructors and coaches should clearly communicate how and where they will touch a child prior to doing so, and as best practice, should ask permission. For example, "To help you float on your back, I am going to place my hand on your lower back as you rest on it to help keep you up. Is that OK with you?" The instructor should speak loudly enough for a parent watching to hear.
- To prevent child-to-child sexual abuse, children should be actively supervised. The facility and/or program will determine what type of supervision is appropriate. For example, a 6-year-old child in a day camp program is expected to be supervised 100% of the time. A 16-year-old swim team member that drives herself to practice before school has different supervision expectations—she will be supervised at practice, but it is not likely expected that she will be supervised in the locker room or in the parking lot. In evaluating supervision of children, pool operators should pay attention to supervision strategies for the highest risk areas: bathrooms and locker rooms.

Reporting

Clear reporting guidelines for reports of abuse or violations of policy are important; we do not catch abusers abusing, we catch them breaking the policies. For staff, clearly outlined steps for reporting allegations to supervisors or local authorities and reporting agencies are important considering staff may be mandated by state law to report abuse.

Often employees are reluctant to report for fear of making a false allegation. Reporting should be safe and encouraged. It is not an employee's role to determine whether abuse has occurred, only to report the facts or allegation. Multiple paths for reporting are important so that employees can report even if they are not comfortable reporting to a designated person.

The code of conduct should be public, and parents and children should be encouraged to report rule violations or allegations of abuse.

After a report has been made, a clear plan is needed for following up on the report, including

- reporting the allegation to the police or the reporting agency;
- suspending the alleged perpetrator from the facility pending the investigation; and
- contacting the insurance and risk management partner for assistance in
    - communicating to the board of directors, staff, and/or membership,
    - communicating with the community,
    - handling media requests, and
    - cooperating with investigations and/or performing an internal investigation as necessary.

Community Engagement

No matter how aggressively pool operators work to prevent child sexual abuse in their facilities, as long as it is prevalent in the community, they remain at risk. The final step in preventing abuse in a facility is to become active in preventing it in the community. Like children are taught to swim to keep them safe when they come to a pool, families can be taught to keep their children safe from abuse both at an aquatic facility and away from it. The organization's mission, its place in the community, and its resources will determine the extent to which the pool operator can be an activist for child sexual abuse prevention. These basic steps can be followed:

- Parents should be provided with the facility's code of conduct and basic child sexual abuse prevention training. If parents know the rules—no private swim practices, for example—they can help to enforce them.
- Parents should be encouraged to talk to their children about their experiences at a facility and about appropriate behavior in general.

- Parents should be provided clear reporting paths to report policy violations or allegations of abuse.
- Children should be taught about appropriate behaviors and expectations. The content will differ with the age of the children and with the program. For example, young children in a swim lesson may be told to keep their hands to themselves and to tell the teacher or their parents if anyone touches them in a bad or uncomfortable way. A teenager on the swim team may have clearer rules about one-on-one situations, outside contact with staff, and reporting inappropriate behavior.

The risk managers job does not end by drafting a policy in a manual. In most incidents and accidents, the policies and protocols that are written in the book are fine, but the practices—what is actually happening on the pool deck—do not match. A gap exists between protocols and practices, and accidents happen in that gap. In that gap, children drown or are abused.

Operational risk management does not end once the risks are identified and the plans are written. There must be action that changes the operating behavior into safer behavior, which allows the industry as a whole to reduce injuries and save lives. The safer facilities are collectively, the more they grow. The more they grow, the more aquatic professionals learn about keeping patrons safe. At Redwoods, we call this model the "Virtuous Cycle," and it can apply both collectively as the aquatic industry and individually as a single organization (Figure 29.5).

Figure 29.5. The Redwoods Group Virtuous Cycle.

Summary

Risks and hazards are present at aquatic facilities, from drowning and injury to child sexual abuse. This chapter explains the role and need for insurance in conjunction with training and education in all aquatic facilities and programming. When considering insurance and aquatic risk management, it is important to weigh the risks and hazards against benefits. The risk management models presented help decide how to identify, eliminate, reduce, warn, and insure against aquatic accidents.

References

Centers for Disease Control and Prevention, www.cdc.gov

Centers for Disease Control and Prevention. (2005). *Adverse Childhood Experiences Study: Data and Statistics.* Atlanta, GA: Centers for Disease Control and Prevention, National Center for Injury Prevention and Control. Retrieved from www.cdc.gov.

Darkness to Light, www.d2l.org

National Alliance for Insurance Education and Research, www.scic.com

Praesidium, www.praesidiuminc.com

The Redwoods Group, www.redwoodsgroup.com

USA Swimming, www.usaswimming.org

YMCA of the USA, www.ymca.net/

Figure 29.6. Photo courtesty of Shawn DeRosa.

Photo courtesy of Water Technology, Inc.

30

Legal Liability and Risk Management

by Shawn P. DeRosa, JD, EMT

Key Concepts

- Negligence
- Duty
- Breach
- Causation
- Degrees of negligence
- Contributory vs. comparative
- Immunity

Aquatic recreation is among the top recreational activities worldwide. Whereas swimming pools were once designed primarily as competitive venues, recent changes in customer expectations have required a new approach to aquatic facility design. In many instances, gone are the traditional rectangular pools with a shallow and a deep end and in their place are free-form shallow water play areas with slides, play structures, and other attractions. Waterpark features once reserved to the private or commercial sector are now common among public entities. Indoor waterparks have grown in popularity, allowing for year-round use even in colder climates. These changes bring new risks and require managers to adapt or develop new injury prevention strategies.

With any aquatic activity, participants should expect a certain level of risk. Although catastrophic injuries at aquatic facilities are not numerous, when they occur, the injured party incurs significant expenses, including medical costs, long-term rehabilitation costs, and legal expenses. Aquatic managers should conduct a thorough risk assessment of their facility, including an evaluation of the physical elements, individual programs, personnel practices, and policies and procedures. During the assessment, aquatic managers should identify and then implement strategies to reduce the risk of injury and resultant economic costs.

Figure 30.1. Photo courtesy of Counsilman-Hunsaker.

The growing presence of shallow water presents a risk for facility management. Not only are head, neck, and spine injuries reasonably foreseeable in this environment, but also the public's perception of "shallow water" as "safe water" presents a risk. For example, although 4 ft of water may be considered shallow to an adult, it would be considered deep to a young child. During a thorough risk assessment, aquatic managers would identify this perception as a risk to be managed and would then consider strategies to eliminate or reduce this risk. Because this risk involves public perception, creating a water safety educational strategy that informs adults of the importance of staying within arm's reach of young children may be needed to help change public perception. Additionally, the facility could implement swim tests and require the use of life jackets for all nonswimmers, again emphasizing safe use of the facility. Lifeguards could be required to provide patrons friendly reminders about the importance of close, active supervision of children whenever around the water. Together, these steps provide an example of managing a common risk at an aquatic facility.

With the popularity of water-based recreation, it is reasonable to assume that aquatic facility managers will, at some point in their careers, be involved in an incident that results in litigation. Although drowning prevention remains a priority, a number of claims arise out of slips and falls. These claims are generally considered premise liability claims; that is, some condition of or on the property contributed to the plaintiff's injury. Other claims involve allegedly negligent behavior of facility staff, such as failure to warn against headfirst entries or failure to supervise. We will explore these common causes of action (premises liability and negligence) and defenses that may relieve an aquatic service provider from liability. We will also explore the basics of employment law, an often overlooked area of risk for aquatic facilities.

Negligence

Negligence occurs when a person, owing a duty of care to another, fails to act reasonably in fulfilling that duty, thereby causing harm. Negligence can be in the form of *misfeasance*, doing something that a reasonably prudent person in a similar situation would not have done, or *nonfeasance*, failing to do something that a reasonably prudent person would have done under similar circumstances. The majority of negligence claims arise out of unintentional acts resulting from carelessness or inattention to one's duties. If an injured person believes the negligence of another person caused his or her injuries, he or she will file a civil lawsuit seeking monetary damages to compensate him or her for his or her injuries. *Malfeasance* (intentionally doing something that is deemed unlawful) or acts done with gross or reckless disregard for safety may also result in criminal liability or punitive damages. The elements of a negligence claim that a plaintiff must establish include duty, breach of duty, damages, and causation.

Duty

Under the law, a *duty of care* is an obligation to conform to a certain standard of conduct or performance.

Figure 30.2. Photo courtesy of Counsilman-Hunsaker.

The proper discharge of one's duties should protect others against the foreseeable risk of unreasonable harm. Whether a duty exists is a question of law for a judge to decide. Judges will typically find a duty of care where it seems reasonable that one should exist. A duty can arise out of contract, wherein the parties agree in advance to the duties each owed to one another, or out of a special relationship between the parties (e.g., parent–child, employer–employee, pool manager–patron). In some cases, a duty may be voluntarily assumed even when one would not otherwise exist under the law, such as when a Good Samaritan stops at the scene of an accident to provide first aid. Aquatic facility managers and staff have a duty to protect patrons from the foreseeable risks of unreasonable harm. *Foreseeability* is a critical aspect of a negligence action. There is no duty to protect against consequences that are not reasonably foreseeable. However, as society changes, courts are now finding more consequences to be reasonably foreseeable, including the criminal acts of third parties. Thus, for sound risk management practices, aquatic facility managers would need to take reasonable steps to protect against foreseeable harm.

In determining whether a duty has been fulfilled, courts will ask whether the conduct in question met the applicable *standard of care*. Generally, standard of care can be classified in three ways. The lowest standard is that of the *reasonable person—"What would the reasonably prudent person do in the same situation?"* Where a special relationship exists between the parties (e.g., inn keeper and guest), the law will require a slightly elevated standard. Last, the highest standard of care is owed by professionals and thus has been named the *professional standard.* Lifeguards have to meet the highest standard of care; that is, they are expected to act as other reasonably prudent professional rescuers (lifeguards) would act under similar circumstances. Should an injury occur at an aquatic facility, actions of staff will be compared to applicable codes, standards, and best practices to determine whether the defendants met the standard of care or performance required under the circumstances.

Expert witnesses may be asked to explain to the jury the applicable professional standards. These individuals, who by their specialized knowledge, skills, experience, or training have expertise in a particular area, will look to state laws and local regulations to explain the standards that apply given the facts of the case. Position statements and manuals from professional groups and training organizations may also help form part of the standard of care. Similarly, voluntary consensus standards such as the *ANSI/NSPI-1 Standard for Public Swimming Pools* may be considered in defining the standard of care. Although in many cases compliance with ANSI standards is voluntary, some states and the federal government have adopted by regulation certain ANSI standards. In these instances, compliance with the ANSI requirements can then be enforced by state or federal authorities. In the absence of state adoption of such standards, the reasonably prudent aquatic manager would nevertheless rely upon the result of the consensus standard process as an example of commonly accepted best practices in the industry. These best practices, in turn, help define the standard of care owed to patrons.

Breach

The second element in a negligence claim is a breach of duty. A breach occurs when facility staff fail to meet their duties and obligations under the law, that is, when they fail to uphold the applicable standard of care. Facility staff can breach their duty of care in many ways, such as a pool manager failing to properly supervise staff, failing to provide lifeguards facility-specific training, or failing to provide warning signs regarding known dangerous conditions on the premises. Lifeguards can become inattentive, thereby failing to provide adequate supervision over pool patrons. A lifeguard who fails to provide safety instructions or to enforce facility rules, such as a "no diving in shallow water" rule, may amount to a breach of the duty to provide safe facilities. Facility maintenance staff can fail to properly inspect and maintain play structures and equipment, thus breaching the duty to provide safe equipment. Not every breach results in a finding of negligence.

Causation

For a negligence finding, the defendant's breach of duty must have caused or significantly contributed to the plaintiff's harm. Some sort of direct causal relationship between the breach and the harm suffered must be established. The court must consider whether the defendant's negligence caused the plaintiff's injuries. The more distant the defendant's actions are from the plaintiff's injury, the less likely the court will find the defendant negligent. If the injury would have occurred irrespective of the defendant's actions, then no causal connection would exist and the defendant would not be found negligent. A court will also consider whether the harm that the plaintiff suffered was the reasonably foreseeable result of the defendant's actions. The law only requires aquatic facility managers to take steps to protect patrons from reasonably foreseeable injuries. One way to determine what injuries are reasonably foreseeable is to look at prior incident reports, first aid reports, and even newspaper articles. Remaining abreast of incidents and injuries occurring at similar facilities is also important. Just because an injury has not yet occurred at a facility does not mean that it is not foreseeable.

Harm/Damages

It is often said that where there is no harm, there is no foul. In the context of a negligence claim, this is true. Essential to any claim for negligence is the element of damages or harm. Damages include physical, financial, or emotional injuries that the plaintiff suffered. In the aquatic environment, damages can be physical (e.g., lacerations; broken bones; head, neck, or spine injuries; or drowning) or financial (e.g., medical and rehabilitation expenses, lost wages, or diminished earning capacity). Plaintiffs expect to be compensated for these injuries, as well as for pain and suffering they may have experienced. *Compensatory damages* are intended to compensate an individual for his or her injuries. Lost wages, medical expenses, and restitution for damages to property are common examples of compensatory damages.

Because water recreation activities involve some degree of contact with equipment such as a slide or diving board and even the pool surface itself, minor scrapes and bruises are not considered significant enough to warrant legal action. Courts consider the risk of injuries such as these as inherent in almost any sport. These types of injuries do not rise to the level of unreasonable harm, and therefore, liability would not attach. However, if staff members fail to provide proper care for injuries that a patron sustained while on the premises and those injuries then become more severe requiring medical attention, liability could be a concern. In some states, emotional harm such as loss of consortium or companionship is also actionable. *Punitive damages* are awarded over and above compensatory damages. Punitive damages are designed to punish the wrongdoer financially to discourage the same harmful behavior in the future. Punitive damages are often reserved for extreme cases where the defendant's behavior is so outrageous that it shocks the conscience of the court.

Negligence Per Se

The law, in certain circumstances, may hold a defendant liable for damages resulting from the violation of a safety regulation or law provided that the plaintiff is within the class of persons the law was designed to protect. This concept is called *negligence per se*. For example, federal law governs swimming pool drains. With the enactment of the Virginia Graeme Baker Pool and Spa Safety Act, every public pool and spa in the United States is required to be equipped with antientrapment drain covers that comply with the ANSI/ASME A112.19.8 performance standard. Assuming that a public pool or spa did not have a compliant drain cover, and further assuming that a child were to become entrapped on the drain and suffer injury or death, the pool operator or owner could be held liable under the doctrine of negligence per se. In this example, the safety law the defendant is alleged to have breached was designed to protect against the very injury that the plaintiff suffered.

Degrees of Negligence

The seriousness of a defendant's negligence is often categorized by degrees of negligence. *Ordinary negligence* is the lowest form of negligence, and often amounts to an inadvertent mistake. Under the ordinary negligence standard, a defendant is responsible for using reasonable (ordinary) care to protect the plaintiff from reasonably foreseeable injuries. Examples of ordinary negligence include failing to properly supervise staff or failing to secure the facility at the end of the day. Liability for ordinary negligence is usually limited to compensatory damages. Depending upon state tort laws, public recreation providers or nonprofit entities may be immune from negligence suits unless the plaintiff can establish a degree of negligence beyond ordinary negligence.

Gross negligence is conduct that goes beyond accident, inadvertence, oversight, or mistake. Gross negligence is analogous to intentional failure to fulfill one's legal duties with utter disregard for the consequences. Gross negligence can be described as unreasonable conduct that is known, or reasonably should be known, to have the potential for unreasonable injury. Examples of gross negligence may include failure to provide adequate safety equipment despite the presence of known dangers or the failure to close a swimming pool when water clarity is compromised. In these cases, the risk of danger to patrons is extreme and the likelihood of injury is reasonably foreseeable. In cases of gross negligence, a court may allow for punitive damages.

Conduct that is so unreasonable that it is said to be in flagrant disregard of safety standards or needlessly endangering life and limb is termed *willful, reckless,* or *wanton misconduct.* For conduct to be considered reckless or wanton, the court must generally find that the defendant knew of the dangerous consequences of his or her actions yet proceeded to act despite the known risk of injury. In cases of willful, reckless, or wanton conduct, the court may impose criminal liability.

Defending Negligence Claims

Aquatic managers should anticipate lawsuits alleging negligent behavior and should employ strategies designed to minimize not only the risk of patron injuries, but also the likelihood of a successful negligence claim. Agreements to participate and waivers can be used to educate patrons of the risks involved in a given activity and also can transfer liability for injuries onto the patron. Waivers become particularly important for instructional programs (e.g., swimming lessons, scuba) or special activities (e.g., facility rentals, nontraditional events).

Some jurisdictions allow the defendant to limit liability by showing that the plaintiff assumed a risk of injury by voluntarily participating in the activity. Known as the "assumption of risk" doctrine, the defendant must show that the plaintiff *understood* the risks inherent in the activity and that he or she *voluntarily* agreed to assume those risks. The defense of assumption of risk is predicated upon communicating to participants the risks of injury that are reasonably foreseeable. Many recreational service providers use *agreements to participate* to communicate to participants the reasonably foreseeable risks of injury inherent in an activity.

Primary assumption of risk was, at one point, considered a complete bar to recovery, as it removed the defendant's duty to provide care. With the adoption of comparative fault schemes in many jurisdictions, the defense of assumption of risk begins to lose its teeth as the issue of the plaintiff's ability to protect himself or herself becomes more of a question of whether the plaintiff contributed to his or her own injury. If a plaintiff contributed to his or her own injury, there could be either a complete bar to recovery or a reduced award for damages based on the plaintiff's own percentage of fault.

In the aquatic realm, many patrons lack swimming ability and/or experience and may not fully appreciate the risks or the dangers involved in water-based recreation. Warning signs, placards, symbols, educational material, and agreements to participate may inform patrons of the dangers of specific attractions or activities and may encourage appropriate behavior. Educating patrons about safe use of the facility should be a goal of any aquatic recreation provider. Although the law expects swimming pool patrons to use due care to avoid self-injury, what is reasonable in any given situation may depend upon the knowledge, skill, and ability of the person involved. A person with years of swim team experience will be held to a higher standard of self-protection while swimming at a pool than someone who has never visited a swimming pool before. Given this, a wise risk management strategy would be to educate all patrons about the safe use of the facility and its attractions.

Contributory and Comparative Negligence

A plaintiff may be found to have contributed to his or her own injury when his or her conduct fails to meet the standard of self-protection expected of persons with similar skill and experience. *Contributory negligence* is conduct by the plaintiff that helps bring about his or her injuries and acts as a complete bar to recovery. If the plaintiff's own actions played a significant role in causing his or her own injuries, the defendant would not be liable even where the defendant's negligence may also have played a role in causing the injury. In the five states (Alabama, District of Columbia, Maryland, North Carolina, and Virginia) that still allow the affirmative defense of contributory negligence, any contributory negligence on the part of the plaintiff, even 1%, will be a complete bar to recovery. This approach is often considered to be a harsh position as any negligence on the part of the plaintiff prevents recovery.

Most states have adopted a form of *comparative negligence* wherein the plaintiff's recovery will be reduced by his or her own percentage of fault. In *pure comparative* jurisdictions, even if a plaintiff is 80% responsible for his or her own injury, he or she will nevertheless recover a judgment for his or her injuries, reduced then by his or her own degree of fault. For example, if the plaintiff were awarded $100,000 in damages, the judge would reduce recovery by the percentage of the plaintiff's own fault (80%). In this example, damages owed to the plaintiff would be reduced to $20,000. States following a doctrine of pure comparative negligence include Alaska, Arizona, California, Florida, Kentucky, Louisiana, Mississippi, Missouri, New Mexico, New York, Rhode Island, South Dakota, and Washington.

Another form of comparative negligence is *modified comparative fault*. Under this scheme, if a court determines that the plaintiff's percentage of fault reaches a certain threshold (typically 50% or 51%), the plaintiff cannot recover anything at all. In concept, if the plaintiff contributed equally to his or her injuries or if the plaintiff was more at fault than the defendant, the plaintiff should recover nothing at all. States that follow the *50% Rule,* which bars recovery if the plaintiff is 50% responsible for his or her own injuries, include Arkansas, Colorado, Georgia, Idaho, Kansas, Maine, Nebraska, North Dakota, Oklahoma, Tennessee, Utah, and West Virginia. In contrast, states following the *51% Rule* (prohibiting recovery if the plaintiff is more responsible for her own injuries than the defendant) include Connecticut, Delaware, Hawaii, Illinois, Indiana, Iowa, Massachusetts, Michigan, Minnesota, Montana, Nevada, New Hampshire, New Jersey, Ohio, Oregon, Pennsylvania, South Carolina, Texas, Vermont, Wisconsin, and Wyoming.

Governmental Immunity

The doctrine of *sovereign immunity* has historically afforded government agencies protection from liability for acts for which a private entity would be held liable. The Federal Tort Claims Act of 1946 (FTCA; 28 U.S.C. § 2674) brought about change; through this Act, Congress authorized the "government to be sued when the government engaged in activities in competition to private enterprise." The FTCA specifically allowed for monetary damages from the federal government where personal injury, property damage, or death was caused by the negligent acts of federal employees acting within the scope of their employment. Today, all states have enacted some sort of tort reform allowing government agencies to be sued under certain circumstances, for instance, the negligent operation of public facilities.

Even with federal and state tort reform, the right to sue the government is not absolute. Policy decisions, as well as those related to the allocation of public resources, cannot be the subject of a lawsuit. For example, in the absence of a law or regulation mandating lifeguard coverage at swimming pools, the decision whether to provide lifeguard services at a city-owned or city-operated swimming pool may be protected as a *discretionary function* and therefore immune from suit. However, should a government agency decide to provide lifeguard services and then fail to adequately train or supervise lifeguard staff or otherwise fail to operate the pool in accordance with applicable standards of care in the industry, resulting in injury, a lawsuit would be allowed.

Good Samaritan Statutes

Good Samaritan statutes provide liability protection to individuals who *voluntarily* and *in good faith* render care at the scene of an emergency. These laws, which vary from state to state, are based on public policy. It is in society's best interest to encourage volunteers to render care without the fear of a lawsuit acting as a barrier to involvement. Once a bystander offers to render care, the bystander voluntarily assumes a duty of reasonable care. Because most Good Samaritan statutes provide protection from claims of ordinary negligence, the risk of liability does not exist as long as the Good Samaritan acts reasonably.

In contrast, persons such as lifeguards or police officers act not voluntarily but rather out of an employment obligation. Because these individuals are compensated for their work and have a legal duty to act, they are not considered to be acting voluntarily. That said, some states have enacted separate laws to limit liability of on-duty rescue workers such as emergency medical technicians, doctors, and nurses. A competent defense attorney would research the state's Good Samaritan laws to determine whether liability protections may apply to the facts of the case.

Premises Liability

Under the theory of premises liability, landowners are liable for injuries sustained by persons coming onto their property in varying degrees based upon the status of the land entrant. The duty of care owed to patrons may vary depending upon the character and intended use of the property. In the swimming pool environment, much of the protections that might exist if the property were in its natural, undeveloped condition do not apply. Unlike a natural water body such as a lake or a pond, a swimming pool is a man-made creation. The landowner decided to alter the land, such as by excavating the earth and pouring a concrete basin that then formed a swimming pool. Similarly, adding an aboveground swimming pool to the property also changes the nature of the land. Where man-made alterations exist, the landowner has created a hazard that did not exist prior to construction or installation. In this case, where the landowner has created the risk, the duty of care owed might be slightly elevated and may vary depending upon the status of the land entrant and intended use of the property.

Trespassers

Trespassers enter upon land for their own purposes without the knowledge or permission of the landowner. Many landowners mistakenly believe that they owe no legal duty to protect trespassers from injury. The law states otherwise. Landowners owe a minimal level of care to trespassers; landowners must refrain from intentionally or recklessly injuring trespassers. As to trespassers, landowners generally have no duty to inspect their premises, provide warnings, or otherwise make their property safe. However, where a landowner has knowledge of trespassers, such as known after-hours use of the aquatic facility, the landowner then owes a duty of reasonable care to warn of dangerous conditions on the premises including ongoing projects. Moreover, where children of tender years (often defined as 6 years and under) trespass onto a landowner's property, the landowner may be deemed to have a slightly elevated duty of care, particularly where a condition of or on the property, such as a swimming pool, may be construed as an *attractive nuisance*. Where the property is found to attract children, landowners should take reasonable steps to restrict access to dangerous areas to help prevent injury. Failure to do so may result in liability.

At least one court found no liability under the state attractive nuisance statute where a 16-year-old trespasser suffered severe injury after diving from a slide into shallow water and striking the bottom of the pool (*Christopher Davidson v. Metropolitan District Commission et al.*, 1997). The rising high school senior entered the "pool either through a hole in the fence or through a gate with a broken lock; after midnight; when he knew the pool was closed; when he could see that no lights were on; when he knew or should have known that no lifeguards were on duty." The agency operating the pool knew that the fences were subject to repeated attacks by vandals overnight, and evidence was offered that employees repaired the pool fence on each occasion. Moreover, the court established that the teenager had prior swimming experience and appreciated the dangers of swimming pools including the risks involved in diving into shallow water. Given the foregoing, the court found that the statutory requirements of the state's attractive nuisance law were not met. Specifically, the "Plaintiff was not a child who, because of his youth, did not discover the condition or realize the risk involved in the activity he rashly undertook. Put very simply, Plaintiff injured himself because he engaged in activities that, according to ordinary norms of human behavior, society expects mentally sound 16-year-olds to avoid."

Figure 30.3. Photo courtesy of Water Technology Inc.

Although landowners must avoid intentionally or recklessly harming trespassers, industry standards and state codes often require landowners to take reasonable steps to keep trespassers away from swimming pools. Construction codes and standards such as ANSI/NSPI-1 often require fences with self-closing and self-latching gates to surround outdoor swimming pools. Failure to adequately secure the premises at the end of the day could give rise to liability even to trespassers. However, where the landowner can prove that the facility was properly secured, liability would not likely attach.

Licensee

Unlike a trespasser who has no permission to be on the property, a *licensee* enters the property for his or her own personal interest or gain with the landowner's permission. At swimming pools where no admission fee is charged, patrons would be considered licensees. Aquatic facility managers owe a duty of *reasonable care* to protect licensees from known hazardous conditions that pose an unreasonable risk of harm. The landowner must repair dangerous conditions on the premises that he or she knows about or should reasonably know about. If dangerous conditions cannot be removed or repaired, the landowner is obligated to provide adequate warnings to protect patrons from injury. Warnings and instructions

related to water depth, diving safety (e.g., "No Diving – Shallow Water"), and safe use of equipment and attractions are well advised. Although these are generally required by code and included in industry standards, they nevertheless demonstrate reasonable steps in providing patrons notice of known dangerous conditions. The failure to provide adequate warnings could result in liability.

Invitees

Land entrants that are present for the benefit of the landowner, such as when an admission fee is charged, are said to be business *invitees*. Where the landowner stands to benefit from use of his or her property, the law imposes an elevated duty of ordinary care. Not only must the landowner take reasonable steps to protect patrons from known dangerous conditions on the premises, but also the landowner must protect against dangers of which he should reasonably be aware. In other words, landowners owe invitees a duty to inspect the premises for dangerous conditions, to remove or repair those that are found, and to provide adequate warnings of dangers that cannot be removed or repaired. Furthermore, landowners should consider foreseeable uses and activities by patrons and take reasonable steps to protect patrons from foreseeable harm.

Aquatic managers at facilities that charge membership fees, daily admission, season passes, and so forth should conduct and document daily inspections of the premises as one method of establishing a reasonable approach to managing the property. Even then, daily inspections may not be enough, particularly at high-volume waterpark facilities. Ongoing inspections throughout the day, properly documented, would go a long way in showing that the landowner made reasonable attempts to inspect the facility for dangerous conditions.

Current Trend

Some courts now blur the distinction between licensees and invitees holding that landowners owe a duty of reasonable care to all persons lawfully on their premises, irrespective of classification as licensees or invitees (see *O'Sullivan v. Shaw*, 2000). This duty of care includes an obligation to maintain one's property "in a reasonably safe condition in view of all the circumstances, including the likelihood of injury to others, the seriousness of the injury, and the burden of avoiding the risk" (*Mounsey v. Ellard*, 1978) and "to warn visitors of any unreasonable dangers of which the landowner is aware or reasonably should be aware" (*Davis v. Westwood Group*, 1995). Given this, aquatic facility managers should take reasonable steps to identify, eliminate, and control hazardous conditions on the premises. This is a sound risk management strategy that would apply equally to all classifications of land entrants. By protecting all people from known hazards, as well as by making and documenting reasonable inspections of the premises, aquatic managers demonstrate their reasonable approach to managing risks at their facilities.

Recreational Use Statutes

Most states have enacted recreational use statutes to encourage landowners to open their land to the public for recreational purposes. These statutes, which have been interpreted to include liability protection for public landowners such as municipalities and state governments, limit a landowner's responsibility for injuries to persons who use the landowner's property for recreational purposes. Each state's statute may differ in the level of protection offered. Aquatic professionals must understand the recreational use statute in their jurisdiction.

A fundamental component of most recreational use statutes is the requirement that landowners not charge for use of their property. Charging an admission fee may remove any liability protection that would otherwise be provided under the recreational use statute. Fees not tied to land use, however, may be permissible. One commonly cited example is a fee for parking. In this case, protection from liability for injuries sustained while recreating outside of the parking area would apply.

Some states do allow landowners to charge a fee for land use, but set a limit on the maximum amount of money a landowner may charge annually before losing the protections afforded by the statute. The Wisconsin Recreational Use Statute (Chapter 895.52), for example, also allows property owners to collect up to $2,000 in aggregate annually from persons using the property for recreational use before statutory protections are lost. The same statute also provides that organized team sports that the landowner sponsors (e.g., swim team) do not qualify for liability protection. In all cases, recreational use statutes will not protect against willful, wanton, or reckless conduct by landowners, including the failure to warn against known hazardous conditions on the property.

Risk Management

Risk management is the process of identifying, evaluating, and controlling risks of injury or financial loss through a systematic analysis of all aspects of an aquatic program. Having a risk management plan demonstrates management's intent to operate the aquatic facility in a reasonable manner. Moreover, empowering employees to implement the plan reduces risks and increases safety, thereby minimizing the likelihood of a lawsuit. A comprehensive plan might uncover potential areas of legal exposure that had not previously been considered, in-

cluding human resource issues such as wrongful termination and sexual harassment.

Although many textbooks offer detailed steps to create a risk management plan, swimming pool operators need practical advice on how to address risks common in the industry. The risk management process proposed involves the following:

- identifying risks,
- eliminating risks whenever possible,
- evaluating the likelihood and frequency of occurrence and the potential severity of the risk,
- selecting steps to minimize the risk,
- documenting the process, and
- using insurance and other risk allocation devices, specifically waivers and releases.

Risk Identification

All aquatic facility staff should be trained to constantly assess risks as they walk about the facility. Managers or their designees should inspect the premises routinely and identify conditions that could result in physical injury or financial loss. The use of opening and closing checklists is one way to document facility inspections. Additionally, maintenance logs document steps to inspect and maintain equipment, including pumps, motors, slides, diving boards, and ladders.

As part of the risk assessment, managers should note any *dangerous staff practices* that could result in injury or financial loss. Managers never want employees to become injured while on the job, so they must foster a culture of safety wherein staff recognize their cooperative role in helping to avoid injury. In addition to the obvious physical harm that can occur, on the job injuries may also lead to workers' compensation claims and, in some cases, OSHA (Occupational Safety and Health Administration) inspections, warnings, and fines. The following are examples of dangerous or risky staff practices:

- failure of lifeguards to wear the rescue tube;
- failure to use personal protective equipment while handling chemicals;
- failing to call for backup during a potentially violent situation;
- intervening physically during fights among patrons;
- leaving the guard stand without being properly relieved;
- asking inappropriate questions during an interview that reveal protected class status;
- failing to administer a swim test, thereby allowing nonswimmers into deep water;
- one-on-one contact with children in isolated areas such as offices, cars, or locker rooms; and
- telling inappropriate jokes, particularly jokes with sexual undertones.

In addition to considering employees' behaviors that could lead to injury or a lawsuit, managers should evaluate the potential *risky behaviors of patrons*. What are patrons likely to do that could cause injury? How have patrons been injured in the past? The following are examples of risky behaviors:

- headfirst entries into shallow water,
- underwater breath-holding competitions for time or distance,
- failing to stay within arm's reach of young children, and
- failing to follow posted safety instructions for use of equipment.

Understanding the risky behaviors of patrons allows managers the opportunity to develop reasonable rules and regulations to control these behaviors. Water safety information and facility rules and regulations can be made available online, in addition to being reinforced by facility staff.

A facility's *policies and procedures* are also important. Are these reviewed regularly to ensure they are consistent with state, federal, and local laws and regulations? Are there new policies that require background checks or mandated reporter training? Are all policies and procedures in writing and available to employees either through an employee handbook or another similar resource? Policies with respect to appropriate behavior, appearance, attendance, and the use of alcohol and/or drugs before or during work should be periodically reviewed to ensure they are consistent with relevant laws and judicial decisions. Most important, policies must be enforced uniformly. A facility's policies and procedures can create an expectation that such policies and procedures will be followed. When they are not followed and injury results, liability can attach.

While conducting this risk audit, managers should walk about their facility and note potential risks from possible code violations. Good managers are familiar with local, state, and federal laws and regulations that relate to various functions within the facility. Copies of relevant health codes, state statutes, and the like should be kept on file and shared with the management team. At a minimum, swimming pool operators should receive copies of regulations governing water quality, lifeguard managers should receive copies of regulations governing lifeguard operations, and concession or food and beverage staff should have copies of regulations governing the storage and serving of food items.

Does the facility comply with all of the applicable OSHA or state-OSHA requirements, including training and documentation requirements (e.g., blood-borne pathogens training, training on the Hazardous Communication standard)? Have managers reviewed the ANSI standards for public pools, spas, or other aquatic recreation facilities and taken steps to align operations with the standards therein? Do managers know whether the ANSI standards have been specifically adopted by their state?

Policies for inventory of equipment are also important. Do staff routinely inventory assets and document value in case of future loss from theft, vandalism, or fire? Have buildings and equipment been inspected for deterioration and have needed repairs been identified? Have capital investments been prioritized in part based upon safety considerations? Is rescue equipment inspected daily to ensure that it is in good condition and ready for use? Is there a plan to take defective equipment out of service without interrupting facility operations?

Although managers have many risks to consider at an aquatic facility, the simple approach to risk identification is to always ask, *"What if?"* What if a swim team were to practice underwater breath-holding drills? What if someone were to dive headfirst into shallow water? What if a parent were to fail to actively supervise a young child? What if staff were to spill chemicals onto themselves without wearing appropriate protective equipment? By asking this question, pool managers identify areas of risk that they can address with their risk management plan.

Eliminate Risks

Once a risk has been identified, it should be eliminated if it is possible to do so without ruining the activity. For example, if broken glass is on the pool deck, it should be quickly and carefully removed to prevent lacerations. Defective equipment should be taken out of service and then repaired or replaced. In the recreational setting, many risks cannot be completely eliminated. If a risk cannot be removed, then careful evaluation of the risk is needed to determine how to best manage the risk to minimize the risk of injury to patrons or staff or of financial loss to the facility.

Risk Evaluation

Risks that cannot be removed should be evaluated as to frequency of occurrence and severity of outcome. Pool managers are most concerned with risks that are likely to result in moderate to severe outcomes. Examples of these risks are spinal and submersion injuries. These risks require substantial management as part of the organization's risk reduction strategy. Similarly, risks that may result in less severe injury or financial loss yet occur frequently may also require substantial management. Small but frequent payouts over time add up to significantly larger amounts. To avoid long-term expenditures, it may be necessary to more aggressively manage the high-frequency yet low-impact risks. Once each risk is evaluated as to its likelihood of occurrence and its potential severity or outcome, managers should consider what level of management is needed to reduce the likelihood of occurrence or to avoid the risk altogether.

Managers can use a risk evaluation matrix, such as the one in Figure 30.4, to determine the extent of management effort needed for a given risk. As the severity of impact and/or the frequency of the risk increases, more management of the risk is required. A risk matrix can also be used to guide managers in deciding whether certain risks should be accepted, avoided, or transferred to a third party.

		Severity of Outcome / Impact		
		Minor	**Moderate**	**Severe**
Frequency or Likelihood of Occurrence	**High**	Manage and monitor risk	Significant management and monitoring of risk *required*; Avoid risk	*Extensive management of risk critical*; Avoid risk
	Medium	Accept or transfer risk and monitor	Management of risk beneficial	*Substantial management and monitoring of risk required*; Avoid risk
	Low	Accept or transfer risk	Consider accepting or transferring risk	*Considerable management of risk required; Prevention critical*

Figure 30.4. Risk management table.

Insurance may be particularly beneficial for risks that the pool manager is not willing to accept because either the severity of impact is too great or the frequency of occurrence is too high. See Chapter 29 for further information about insurance.

Minimize Risks

In the aquatic arena, many risks cannot be eliminated. The risk of drowning is ever present; the only way to remove the risk is to remove the water from the pool. Clearly, this is not possible without ruining the activity. Although the frequency of drowning is low, the severity or impact is high, thus requiring considerable management of the risk. With any risk that cannot be eliminated, managers should identify action steps to minimize the risk of occurrence or severity of impact. Consider for a moment the risk of drowning. What can be done to minimize the risk of drowning? Should lifeguard services be offered? Should life jackets be required for all nonswimmers? How will the staff determine who is a nonswimmer? Will the facility provide life jackets free of charge? Should a shallow water play area be defined with a buoyed rope to help prevent young children from going too deep into the water? Is this life line, as it is commonly called, required by code?

Deciding how to best minimize risks takes careful thought and consideration of the many options available to the facility manager. Facility operators would be well advised to consult with professional colleagues to learn how others manage the risks identified. Networking with other pool operators locally or through national associations is a good way to stay informed and to develop the connections needed to address risks in accordance with best practices in the industry.

Documentation

Documentation is a critical step in the risk management process. The axiom "if it was not documented, it was not done" is often the case in the eyes of the law. From the defense perspective, a risk management plan supported with proper documentation of the preventive steps taken to reduce the risk of injury goes a long way to establishing reasonableness in managing the facility. Standard business records such as opening and closing checklists, incident and injury reports, employee certifications, in-service training records, and performance audits records are essential in establishing before the jury a well-managed facility. An attorney's advice should be followed with regard to routine documentation and retention guidelines. The absence of routine documentation, or documents that other facility operators would have on file as a matter of standard operating procedure, creates the appearance of impropriety.

Another benefit of maintaining accurate records regarding a preventive maintenance program is that many product warranties require certain inspection and maintenance cycles. For repairs or replacement to be covered under a warranty, it is often incumbent upon the owner to provide documentation that the product has been maintained according to the manufacturer's recommendations. Failure to provide evidence of required maintenance may nullify a warranty. This becomes particularly important for the high-value items such as pumps, motors, and ultraviolet light disinfection systems.

Risk Transfer

Transferring risk is commonly done by contract. Many aquatic facilities could not afford to pay a large verdict or settlement without risking going out of business. Catastrophic injuries, such as quadriplegia or disembowelment, can result in jury verdicts worth millions of dollars. Insurance is used to transfer the financial risk associated with large verdicts or with frequently occurring low payout claims to a third party, typically an insurance company or risk pool. An insurance agent should be consulted to determine the extent of coverage recommended for a facility.

Waivers of Liability

A waiver is a contract, signed prior to participation, in which the participant agrees to relinquish the right to sue for injuries resulting from *ordinary* negligence in exchange for the ability to participate. Many courts will uphold a properly worded waiver against adult participants. Because of this, waivers form an essential part of a risk management strategy. Waivers must be carefully worded so they are clear and unambiguous. Plain language that is easily understood should be given preference to legal jargon. Ambiguity will be construed against the party creating the waiver and may be grounds for invalidating the waiver in its entirety. Additionally, any verbiage that courts in a given jurisdiction require must be included in the document, or the waiver may be found invalid. All waivers should be written or reviewed by competent legal counsel in the appropriate jurisdiction.

A waiver that is valid in one state may not be recognized by courts in another. A minority of jurisdictions will uphold waivers signed on behalf of minor children, under age 18 years. In these states, a parent/guardian may give up his or her own right to sue for his or her child's injuries in addition to the child's right to sue for his or her own injuries. However, the majority of states do not allow parents to give up their child's right to sue for injury. Some states disallow waivers completely, holding that they violate public policy. If a waiver is not recognized by the court, the organization is essentially in the same position it would have been in had the waiver never been signed. Because of this, waivers come strongly recommended as one part of a risk management strategy. At best, waivers may protect the organization from liability. At worst, even if a court ultimately found a waiver invalid, its mere existence may unto itself serve to discourage a lawsuit from being filed.

Release of Liability

A release of liability is, in many jurisdictions, the same as a waiver; it releases the service provider from liability for ordinary negligence. In fact, the terms *waiver* and *release* are often used interchangeably. In some states, however, a subtle distinction is found between a release and a waiver. In these states, a release is considered a contract in which one party relinquishes existing claims against another, often in exchange for a settlement. In these states, releases are signed following injury as part of the settlement of a claim rather than prior to participation. Competent legal counsel in the appropriate jurisdiction should review release of liability forms to ensure proper use.

Human Resources

Aquatic facility managers should have a basic understanding of the legal issues surrounding employment relationships. Although many organizations have a human resource office to guide employment questions, many supervisors often receive little to no training in the human resource function, including employment of minors, contract law, and of course, civil rights law. Anyone who supervises employees should become familiar with the basics of employment law.

Employee or Independent Contractor?

There are generally two types of employment relationships: "regular" employees (either at will or contracted) and independent contractors. The latter are not employees of the organization, but rather are under contract with the organization to perform certain services. The contracting "employer" does not control the work of the contractor beyond mere oversight. Instead, independent contractors direct the manner and means of their own work with guidance from the "employer." The more control an organization exerts over the work of an independent contractor, such as telling the contractor specifically how to perform a job, the more likely courts will find that an employment relationship exists rather than a contractual one. This raises many issues, including concerns for workers' compensation, overtime pay, and tax withholding in addition to potential liability for the actions of the contractor/employee.

The Internal Revenue Service (IRS) uses a 20-factor test, often called the "right-to-control test," to determine whether a worker is truly independent or whether an employment relationship exists. Among the factors to be considered are the level of instruction/control the company exerts over the worker, the amount of company-specific training required, whether the company or the worker controls assistants, the requirements of reports, the method of payment (hourly, weekly, monthly, or upon completion of the project), and the payment of business or travel expenses.

The Fair Labor Standards Act of 1938 (FLSA; 29 U.S.C. Chapter 8) requires employers to pay covered employees at least the federal minimum wage and overtime pay of 1.5 times the regular rate of pay. This law also establishes guidelines for the employment of minors. Executive employees may be exempt from overtime requirements. Because independent contractors are not considered employees, they are exempt from the FLSA requirements.

Most aquatic facility employees will be considered *regular* employees. This means that the employer, in exchange for payment of wages or salary, has the right to control the employee's daily work duties and assignments. *Volunteers* are also treated in many regards like employees, even though they do not receive compensation. The employer is obligated to provide a nondiscriminatory work environment, safe working conditions, and the equipment and supplies employees need to perform their work. Employers are also liable, under the doctrine of vicarious liability, for all employee actions that are within the scope of their employment. Organizations may also be liable for negligent hiring or failing to terminate employees that pose a risk to others. A thorough background check of potential employees is strongly recommended to protect against a claim for negligent hiring. State and federal criminal background checks, as well as state-specific checks of child welfare and/or sexual offender registries, should be conducted. Hiring managers should always check applicant references. Keeping notes of reference checks will demonstrate the manager's due diligence in researching each potential new hire.

At-Will and Contracted Employees

Most workers are considered at-will employees. An at-will employee may be terminated without cause or for any nondiscriminatory reason. When terminating an at-will employee, many employers thank the worker for their service and inform them that their services will no longer be needed. Although employers are encouraged to provide routine, ongoing feedback and coaching to struggling employees prior to ending the employment relationship, no such requirement exists under the law. Although it is preferred that an employee never be surprised by a termination, the employer is not obligated to provide the employee a reason for the termination. Providing workers an employee manual that explains a progressive discipline process leading up to termination may create an expectation of continued employment ab-

sent stated discipline. In these cases, managers would be well advised to follow the process of progressive discipline explained in the employee manual prior to terminating an employment relationship.

Contracted employees are those who receive a contract explaining the terms and dates of employment, the rate of pay, and the reasons that the agreement may be terminated before the end of the contracted term. Members of an employment union, often called "union employees," are a form of contracted employees. The terms of their employment are explained in a collective bargaining agreement (contract). Managers who supervise contract employees should become familiar with the terms of the employment contract and be certain to follow requirements for progressive discipline.

Employment of Minors

Many aquatic facility employees, including lifeguards and concession workers, begin their employment prior to having reached age 18. These employees fall under the Department of Labor's rules for child employment. The FLSA regulates the hours that children may work during the school year and limits the jobs that minors can perform. Furthermore, the FLSA establishes safety standards prohibiting minors from using certain powered tools while on the job. Additionally, state-specific laws and regulations may be more restrictive than federal child labor laws. Employers of children must be familiar with their state's requirements in addition to the requirements of the FLSA. Violations of child labor laws, including inadvertent violations, often carry heavy penalties.

Figure 30.5. A well-designed family aquatic center. (Welch Community Swimming Pool, State College, PA)

Summary

Effective aquatic managers have a general awareness of legal issues and an appreciation of the critical role a risk management plan plays in reducing liability. Pool managers who act reasonably in protecting against foreseeable risks may avoid lawsuits based upon theories of negligence or premises liability. Moreover, implementing a risk management plan that includes consistent use of waivers, releases, and agreements to participate may not only remove liability for ordinary negligence, but also discourage injured parties from filing suit. Aquatic facility managers, particularly those without the support of a human resource office, should familiarize themselves with basic concepts of employment law to avoid liability for issues such as wrongful termination, discrimination, and violation of child labor laws. A commitment to safety and a commonsense approach to managing risks is the foundation of any well-administered aquatic program.

References

Americans with Disabilities Act of 1990, 42 U.S.C. § 12101 (1992).

Americans with Disabilities Act Amendments Act of 2008, Pub. L. No. 110-325 (2009).

Carpenter, L. J. (2000). *Legal concepts in sport: A primer* (2nd ed.). Urbana, IL: Sagamore.

Christopher Davidson v. Metropolitan District Commission et al., 8 Mass. L. Rep. 36 (1997).

Fair Labor Standards Act of 1938, 29 U.S.C. § 201 *et seq.*

Hronek, B., Spengler, J., & Baker, T., III. (2007). *Legal liability in recreation, sports, and tourism.* Urbana, IL: Sagamore.

Peterson, J. A., Hronek, B. B., & Garges, J. R. (2008). *Risk management for park, recreation, and leisure services* (5th ed.). Urbana, IL: Sagamore.

Prosser, W. L., & Wade, J. W. (Reporters). (1965–1979). *Restatement Torts, Second* (Vols. 1–4). Philadelphia, PA: The American Law Institute.

Sharp, L., Moorman, A., & Claussen, C. (2007). *Sports law: A managerial approach.* Scottsdale, AZ: Holcomb Hathaway.

Wisconsin Recreational Use Statute, Wis. Stat. § 895.52 (1997).

Figure 30.6. Photo courtesy of City of Phoenix Aquatics.

Photo courtesy of City of Phoenix Aquatics.

31

Preparing for and Coping With Emergencies

by Shawn P. DeRosa, JD, EMT

Key Concepts

- Emergency action plan (EAP)
- Critical incident
- Stress
- Defusing
- Debriefing
- Critical Incident Stress Debriefing (CISD)

Swimming pools offer myriad safe and healthy opportunities for recreation, fitness, and therapy. Unfortunately, along with the many positive aspects of swimming pools come real dangers. Drowning and other catastrophic injuries, such as injuries to the head, neck, and back, can and do happen at aquatic facilities. Although lifeguards and facility staff can take many steps to prevent such emergencies from arising, the fact remains that should a patron require emergency assistance, facility staff must be properly prepared to manage the incident. Although much of the focus of emergency preparedness often falls upon lifeguards, all staff, including managers, must understand their role in a facility's emergency action plan (EAP).

Figure 31.1. Tandem Tube rides are extremely popular but rider misbehavior should be eliminated through supervision, education, and warning. (Photo courtesy of Water Technology, Inc.)

An EAP is a well-thought-out guide to responding to emergencies. Facilities may develop EAPs for emergencies on land or in the water. Plans may also be developed to guide staff in responding to a particular threat, such as a weather-related emergency requiring sheltering in place or facility evacuation. To be effective, an EAP must not only be facility specific, but also regularly practiced using a variety of scenarios that could be expected to occur. A plan that exists on paper but is not brought to life by regular practice may be conceptually accurate but, in practice, ineffective.

Lifeguards and facility staff must not only understand the facility's EAP, but must be ready to implement the plan almost instinctively. Experience shows that this level of performance only occurs at facilities where scenario-based training wherein the EAP is fully implemented regularly occurs. Management's role is to ensure that staff practice the EAP before an emergency occurs and to remain alert for signs of critical incident stress that may occur following an emergency. EAPs have four key priorities: (1) caring for the health and safety of patrons, (2) protecting the health and safety of staff, (3) minimizing damage to the facility itself, and (4) minimizing disruption of normal service delivery.

To ensure that these four priority areas are addressed, management must create EAPs that define the role each staff member plays during an emergency. Lifeguards are taught to follow EAPs provided by their employers. Unfortunately, many aquatic managers are not well versed in creating EAPs, and others are under the mistaken impression that lifeguards themselves will know what to do in an emergency. Both of these can lead to tragic consequences. The manager's responsibility is to ensure that lifeguards and staff receive training on the EAP before assuming patron surveillance responsibilities.

Assessment

The first step in creating an EAP is to conduct a thorough assessment of the emergencies likely to occur. Aquatic facility managers should assemble a diverse team of individuals to conduct the assessment, examine records and reports from prior incidents at the facility, speak with colleagues from neighboring facilities to see what incidents they have experienced, and consider the emergencies that may be possible given the facility and its geographic location. Potential emergencies may include the following:

- drowning,
- spinal injury,
- violence/fights,
- loss of electricity,
- lost child,
- medical emergencies (heart attack, stroke, allergic reactions),
- abduction,
- weather emergencies (thunderstorms, lightning, heavy rain, hail, snow),
- chemical leaks/spills,
- sexual assault,
- bomb threats, and
- fire.

After identifying potential emergencies, managers should compile research and data from reputable sources specific to each emergency. Potential information sources include the American Red Cross, the National Weather Service, and local police and fire departments. Other aquatic facilities can be contacted for samples of their EAPs. This information can be used to develop a facility-specific EAP.

Develop the Plan

To develop the EAP, management and workers at all levels should be involved to ensure a cooperative response to the event. Many facility-specific factors must be considered when developing an EAP, such as the size and layout of the facility; the recreational amenities present; the number of lifeguards and other staff on duty; and the rescue equipment that is available, such as rescue tubes, backboards, and emergency oxygen. Another consideration is whether trained emergency medical staff is on-site, which may be the case at a waterpark, or local emergency medical services will need to be summoned to assist with medical care.

As team members develops the EAP, they should consider the following:

- Once an emergency is recognized, how will the EAP be activated? Will staff use an air horn or push-button alarm? Is there a specific whistle signal that will be used to initiate a response? Are hand signals incorporated into the EAP? These visual signs could become useful when ambient noise makes it difficult for lifeguards to communicate verbally. Whatever signals are used, all staff must understand how to activate the facility's EAP.
- The general steps to follow during the emergency should be outlined, including providing backup coverage whenever a lifeguard must leave his or her station to render assistance.
- Each staff member should be assigned a specific job to perform during an emergency. For example, one staff member will be responsible for getting the first aid kit and one will wait for EMS responders and direct them to the scene. It is best to assign responsibilities during an emergency by job category or position rather than by employee names. The plan may need to be practiced multiple times to work out issues that become more apparent when bringing the plan to life. The plan can be adjusted as needed.
- Smaller facilities might need to rely upon patrons for assistance with routine tasks (e.g., waiting for the ambulance to arrive and assisting with crowd control).
- A specific employee should be responsible for contacting the local emergency services number.
- Another staff member should be "incident commander" and coordinate the overall response and determine whether the attraction or facility needs to be closed as part of the emergency response. This is often a senior staff member or supervisor. This individual may also determine whether to reopen the facility following the emergency.
- All emergency exits and evacuation routes should be identified.
- A general meeting area needs to be defined in the event of an evacuation.
- How will the chain of command be notified of an emergency? A designated person in the plan, typically a supervisor, will notify managers at the appropriate time.
- A media spokesperson should be designated to handle media inquiries, an inevitable result of a major aquatic emergency. Generally, the media spokesperson is a management level employee with specific training in how to properly respond to media inquiries to minimize legal exposure.
- What information needs to be gathered during the emergency (e.g., witness contact information), and what information can be gathered post-incident (e.g., staff incident reports)?
- A risk management agency and the local police department can help determine who should capture witness statements following a major emergency. An investigation could be compromised if untrained individuals such as lifeguards attempt to conduct witness interviews. In recent years, the growing trend

has been to investigate drowning deaths to rule out criminally negligent behavior of lifeguards and facility management. Given this, witness statements are often best handled by police or those trained to conduct investigations. However, in situations where no police investigation will occur, managers, or perhaps even lifeguards, may collect witness statements.

- Trained mental health professionals in the community who could assist following an emergency need to be identified. When an incident occurs, these professionals should be involved as soon as possible.
- Proper documentation of the incident is an important part of the EAP. The plan should define who completes incident reports, what forms must be completed, and where the forms should be submitted or filed. In cases of major emergencies, it may be necessary for all staff involved to complete separate statements. Again, consulting with a risk manager or legal counsel may determine what documentation is required.
- If rescue equipment was used during the emergency, all equipment must be in proper supply and working order before returning to normal operations.
- If equipment such as the facility's backboard is taken by EMS responders to the hospital, will they leave their backboard behind so that the facility can remain open?
- Staff should be provided time to discuss the emergency response post-incident. The staff debriefing, sometimes called an "operational debriefing," allows staff to assess the overall efficacy of the EAP and to identify areas for improvement. This debriefing is not intended to assign blame for the incident, but rather to evaluate the facts that caused the incident and the manner in which staff responded. This allows managers to evaluate whether modifications to the EAP are necessary and to observe possible signs of stress reactions among staff.

Rehearse the Plan

After a plan has been developed, managers must communicate the plan to staff and rehearse the plan as part of a pre-service training program. When lifeguard services are offered, the standard of care dictates that the moment the lifeguard assumes patron surveillance duties that he or she knows how to properly respond to emergency situations following the prescribed EAP. During pre-service training, the plan should be practiced daily, or more frequently, until it runs smoothly. At that point, regular practice of plans is recommended. EAP drills can be conducted at least monthly, with varying emergency scenarios each month so that staff are continually reminded of their responsibilities during an emergency. The importance of rehearsing the EAP until

it runs smoothly cannot be overemphasized. During an emergency situation, staff should follow the plan almost instinctively, as during crisis events, people react according to what they are familiar with. Emergency responders such as lifeguards should act in accordance with the specific training provided.

For EAP rehearsals, the following should be considered:

- One person should be an observer, carefully watching the events as they unfold, timing the response at appropriate intervals and recording notes to review with staff following the rehearsal.
- Outside agencies should be involved in the emergency response rehearsal. Ideally, members of these agencies were involved in developing the plan and will be eager to participate in a mock incident.
- If mock drills are conducted during times the facility is open to the public, patrons need to be informed so as not to cause panic.
- If drills are conducted while the public has access to the facility, patrons will see both the good and the not-so-good elements of the practice sessions. If staff are weak in their emergency response skills, members of the public could notice this and lose confidence in the staff's abilities to handle emergency situations. For revenue-generating facilities, this could translate into loss of income from patrons choosing not to use the facility.
- If the staff's emergency response skills are strong, inviting local media outlets to cover the mock rescue could be valuable, particularly when local EMS is involved. This will generate free publicity and lend credibility to the program.
- EAP drills should be part of the facility's pre-service training program, yet they should also be included as a routine part of an ongoing in-service training program. This keeps the plan "fresh" and enhances the likelihood of a positive response.
- Each mock rescue or EAP drill needs documented as part of the facility's ongoing risk management plan. In the event of litigation, this documentation will show that staff were properly trained to handle emergencies.

Implement the Plan

The last step of the process is plan implementation. Accidents can occur even in the most well-managed facilities. Staff members that are well prepared by having practiced their emergency response procedures, will be best positioned to respond appropriately during an emergency. An EAP that is well rehearsed and properly implemented helps to minimize legal exposure, provided that proper documentation of all training programs exists. Of course, following any emergency, managers should review the response and determine whether the EAP should be updated. Any changes to the EAP will require retraining and additional practice to ensure that the new steps are properly implemented.

Critical Incident Stress

Following emergency situations, managers should be alert for possible negative stress reactions among staff. Stress is a physical and psychological response to actual or perceived threats, challenges, or demands. Everyone has suffered from stressful moments at some point. However, following critical emergencies, stress reactions can become unhealthy. Critical incidents are often defined as those incidents that cause unusually strong emotional responses in the emergency responders. In the aquatic environment, lifeguards and other staff involved with the emergency may suffer from such an emotional response. Critical incident stress can interfere with a lifeguard's ability to function normally, either at the scene of the emergency or at a later date.

Critical incident stress is likely to arise when

- the incident is unexpected;
- staff are not properly trained to respond;
- the event endangers the life of the rescuer or someone known to them, including coworkers;
- a child is involved;
- death occurs;
- multiple victims are involved; or
- whenever intense media coverage of the event exists.

People experience stress reactions to events differently. What might be a critical incident for one lifeguard may be considered an unfortunate but expected part of the job for a more experienced lifeguard. If lifeguards feel responsible for the incident, such as for not having seen a child submerge, their emotional response may be intense even if they did everything they were supposed to do. Helping prepare staff for the realities of the job, properly rehearsing the EAP, and educating staff about critical incident stress can prevent adverse stress reactions. These efforts may develop resilience among staff and give them the tools needed to cope with the crisis with their own internal resources.

Stress reactions may not be immediate. Staff members may appear in control of their emotions immediately following an emergency, but may begin to experience signs and symptoms of critical incident stress later that night or over the course of the days or weeks following the incident. Supervisors should remain alert for signs that may indicate an employee is in need of assistance.

Signs of Adverse Stress Reactions

Signs of critical incident stress may manifest in four general areas: cognitive, behavioral, emotional, and physical. Staff should be familiar with the signs and symptoms of critical incident stress and should feel comfortable in seeking help when needed.

Cognitive
- Seeing the event over and over again
- Nightmares or intrusive images
- Placing blame for the event
- Acutely increased or decreased awareness of one's surroundings
- Confusion
- Poor attention and/or concentration
- Feelings of insanity ("Am I going crazy?")

Behavioral
- Withdrawal from family and/or friends
- Crying
- Extreme hyperactivity (e.g., pacing)
- Insomnia (loss of sleep)
- Increased smoking or alcohol consumption
- Intensified "startle reflex"

Emotional
- Anger
- Anxiety
- Depression
- Fear
- Guilt
- Irritability
- Panic reactions
- Wanting to die
- Inappropriate emotional responses

Physical
- Difficulty breathing*
- Chest pain*
- Excessive vomiting
- Headaches
- Grinding teeth
- Fatigue
- Disturbed sleep
- Diarrhea
- Nausea

indicates a need for immediate medical intervention.

Managers should be prepared to offer assistance to staff members exhibiting signs of a unhealthy stress reaction. These signs are likely to intensify over the first few weeks following an emergency, but should fade with time. Watch for the following additional clues that a staff member may be suffering from critical incident stress:

- excessive tardiness or absence following an emergency;
- apprehension over participating in training programs, moving to the back of the line, excessive reports of minor illness and/or injury to avoid training; and
- excessive time preparing for a shift, such as checking equipment or making many adjustments.

Meeting With Staff Following an Emergency

Managers can play a key role in preventing adverse stress reactions among staff. In addition to providing proper training and preparation, managers should remind staff that stress is a normal response to a crisis situation. While meeting with staff following an emergency, managers should assess whether lifeguards are ready to return to work or whether they should be relieved from duty for the remainder of the shift. It may be necessary to close the facility and seek the assistance of the trained mental health workers identified in the EAP.

Before staff are sent home for the day, they should be reminded of the following tips to minimize the likelihood of suffering from critical incident stress:

- Maintain a normal routine
- Eat healthy meals
- Alternate exercise with relaxation techniques
- Get plenty of rest
- Maintain a sense of humor
- Spend time with others
- Talk with friends and family
- Keep a journal—this may help get through sleepless hours
- Do things you enjoy to refocus away from the incident
- Avoid major life decisions

- Allow yourself time to adjust to the situation
- Seek professional help if needed—stress is a normal reaction, not a sign of weakness

Critical Incident Stress Debriefing (CISD)

Growing in popularity in the 1980s, critical incident stress debriefing (CISD) sessions were adopted by many emergency response agencies, including law enforcement, fire, rescue, and military personnel. It was believed that the CISD process, led by trained mental health professionals, would help participants express their feelings about the event in a supportive and nonthreatening atmosphere and reduce the likelihood of post-traumatic stress disorder (PTSD).

Over the past decade, the efficacy of CISD and critical incident stress management has been debated. Several studies have questioned the value and safety of CISD, with some studies finding that CISD is harmful to some participants, forcing them to relive the stressful event. The American Red Cross (2006) has taken a position against CISD: "There is no convincing evidence that psychological debriefing or group debriefing are effective in reducing PTSD. There is evidence that the CISD process may have deleterious effects...In addition, studies have shown that those who do not participate in CISD actually have greater reduction in symptoms than those who do participate...As such the CISD process should not be used for rescuers following a traumatic event."

Given the foregoing, aquatic managers would be well advised to meet with mental health professionals in advance of an emergency to determine the most appropriate course of action to assist aquatic staff in the event of a death, drowning, or other catastrophic injury. At a minimum, trained mental health professionals should be identified so that if staff need counseling following an emergency, they can be referred to appropriate mental health professionals.

Figure 31.2. Courtesy of Water Technology, Inc.

Summary

Reading and understanding this book will go a long way in helping you prevent serious aquatic accidents. But even the best managed and operated aquatics facilities can have emergencies. This specific chapter has demonstrated how to be best prepared for emergencies and how to respond to them.

Additionally, although Critical Incident Stress Debriefing (CISD) has been encouraged in the past, it is now discouraged. However, dealing with stress of staff following critical incidences is imperative. When it comes to emergencies, planning and rehearsal prior to emergencies is the key.

References

American Red Cross. (2012). *Lifeguarding*. Yardley, PA: StayWell.

American Red Cross Advisory Council on First Aid, Aquatics, Safety, and Preparedness. (2010). *ACFAS scientific review: Critical incident stress debriefing*. Washington, D.C.: Author.

Hafen, B., & Karren, K. (1992). *Prehospital emergency care and crisis intervention* (4th ed.). Upper Saddle River, NJ: Brady/Prentice Hall.

Mitchell, J. T. (1988). Stress: The history, status and future of critical incident stress debriefings. *Journal of Emergency Medical Services, 11,* 47–52.

Rabstejnek, C. V. (n.d.). *Evaluating the efficacy of critical incident stress debriefing: A look at the evidence.* Retrieved from http://www.houd.info/articles.htm

Figure 31.3. Courtesy of Water Technology, Inc.

Figure 31.4. Courtesy of Water Technology, Inc.

32

Routine Operations: Daily, Weekly, Monthly

Key Concepts

- Recordkeeping
- "Walkabouts"
- Opening pools
- Closing pools
- Maintenance
- Daily routines
- Weekly routines
- Monthly routines

Many important tasks must be performed by pool owners, operators, and managers. For experienced pool operators, many of these duties become habit and are an integral part of a daily, weekly, or monthly routine. It must be emphasized throughout this chapter, however, that checklists and records must be kept for up to five years on all operational tasks. If a lawsuit is brought against the facility, facts and figures regarding the condition of the pool provide valuable information for the defense. Written procedures are also important because if the primary pool operator is unable to work due to illness or vacation, an assistant or lifeguard can perform these routines easily and correctly. Whenever any of these procedures are completed, the date, time, and initials of the person completing the job should be recorded alongside the task on a checklist.

The Pool "Walkabout"

Perhaps the most beneficial practice a pool owner or operator can perform is to evaluate the entire facility the first thing in the morning before the pool actually opens and the last thing at night after all patrons have left. This should be done slowly and carefully, without distractions. Carrying a clipboard to take notes at this time is helpful. Residential pool owners should also make this a practice.

"Walkabouts" should also be conducted during the day when the pool is in use, but it is normally easier to spot deficiencies when the facility is quiet and calm. In addition, it allows the owner or operator more time to take corrective measures. Unfortunately, too many pool personnel rush through morning and evening procedures to simply open and close the pool on time. When this occurs, deficiencies often go unnoticed. The priorities when conducting the walkabout should be the pool water first, the filter room second, and the locker rooms and support facilities last.

Opening Procedures

Opening routines are critical, particularly at public pools. Bathing codes and local ordinances often supply lists of what must be done before opening and closing pools. Similar to the walkabouts, when the pool is opened, the first thing to be checked is the pool water, followed by a trip to the filter room, and finally the locker rooms and other facilities.

The first priority when any swimming pool or spa is opened should be the condition of the water. "Is the water clear?" is the question all good pool operators should ask themselves on arriving at the facility. If a six-inch black disk or the main drain cannot be seen from everywhere on the pool deck, the pool or spa must not be opened. This particular water clarity standard is fairly consistent throughout the United States. If the water is not clear, corrective measures must be taken immediately so that clarity can be restored and the pool opened. The filtration and chemistry must both be checked in this case (Chapters 8 and 15).

Another priority is water chemistry. All chemical parameters should be within ideal ranges before the pool opens. If it is an outdoor pool and a hot, humid day is predicted, higher levels of free-available chlorine (FC) should be established earlier in the day so that when the sun and the swimmer loads are at their peaks, sufficient chlorine will be available. Particularly with chlorine and pH levels, it is important to get these readings where they should be before pools open, because once swimmers are in the pool, these levels are more difficult to control and adjust.

The water level is also an important factor when opening the pool. The level of the water should be sufficient to allow for a continuous skimming action either through skimmers or gutters. Water should be added immediately to ensure proper skimming action, and the amount of water should be recorded. This information is valuable when leaks are suspected. Skimmer baskets should be emptied before opening the pool or spa. The skimmer weirs, baskets, equalizer lines, and other associated parts should also be checked at this time.

All drain covers and anti-vortex plates must be in place. The general condition of the bottom is also important. Is algae growth visible? Is there any debris or discoloration in the water? The pool bottom should be checked for these concerns, even though vacuuming may not be scheduled for that particular day.

One chore that must be completed before opening is vacuuming the pool bottom (Figure 32.1). This task must be done after the water has been still for several hours so that particulate matter not oxidized or filtered can sink to the bottom. If performed in the evening shortly after the pool closes, dirt that has been disturbed by swimmers will still be suspended in the water. Although vacuuming is not required daily in many pools, it must be performed regularly and should follow a predetermined schedule. Many pools have a slow day, one in which the facility opens late or fewer patrons attend. This "off day" or slow day, which is often Sunday, may allow sufficient time for proper vacuuming. Busy days may not provide adequate time for complete vacuuming.

Brushing the pool is almost as important as vacuuming and also should be done daily. Brushing is one of the best defenses against algae development in outdoor pools.

Once the pool water is monitored, the filters should then be checked. When the filter room is entered, the floor should be checked for standing water to ensure that filters and related equipment are not leaking. The flow meter should be checked and the flow rate recorded. If the flow rate is insufficient to provide the required turnovers, corrective measures should be taken immediately. When pressure filter systems are used, the pressure differential must be recorded daily, and this is best done before the pool opens. When the pool pump is checked, the noise and temperature of the pump are important. The pump should not be too hot or noisy. The pressure gauges on all pressure filters should then be checked to determine whether backwashing is needed. While backwashing, the hair and lint strainer should always be cleaned and checked. A clean, spare basket should always be immediately available, and the gasket and O-rings should always be checked during backwashing. The hair and lint strainer is perhaps the most overlooked piece of equipment in the filter room and for best filtering results, the hair and lint basket should be checked daily.

Cleaning or backwashing the filters should be done when swimmers are not in the water. It is best to perform this important function when the pool is closed so that distractions and people are not present. This is not always possible, however. Some experts prefer doing this chore in the evening. After the water filtration and chemistry is corrected or adjusted, the pool deck, lifeguard stands, pool equipment, and safety equipment should be readied for opening. The pool deck should be clear of water, obstructions, and other debris. Rescue equipment such as reaching poles, ring buoys, and rescue tubes, must be put into place before the pool opens.

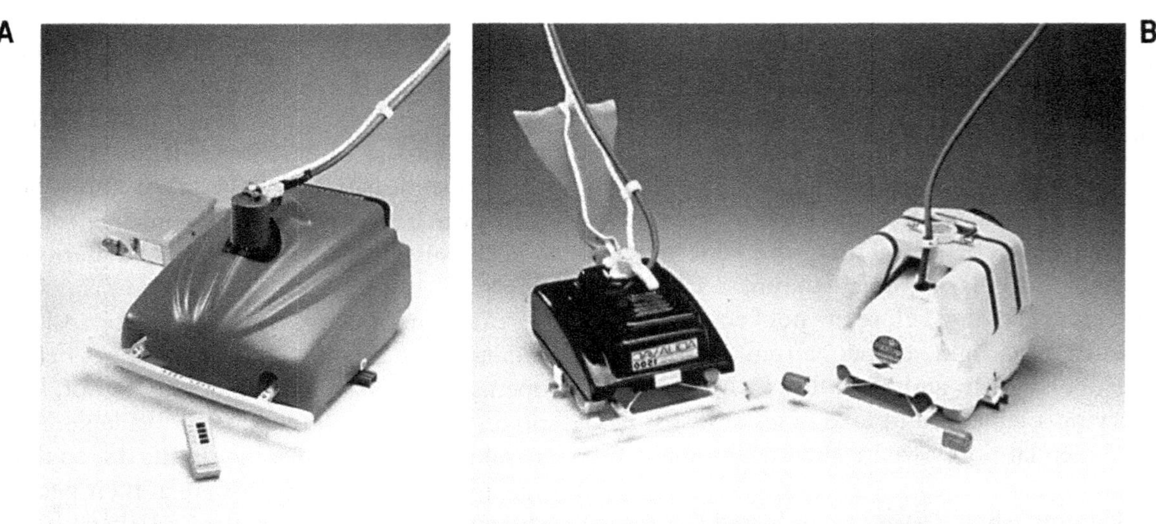

Figure 32.1. A, remote control pool vacuum for large public pool. B, Electric pool vacuum for residential pools. (Photo courtesy Aqua Vac Systems, West Palm Beach, FL)

Bathhouses, locker rooms, entrances, and other facilities also need special attention before opening the pool. These areas might be better prepared by a staff member who does not have water safety duties, although this might be financially imposing. These areas are best cleaned during the evening to allow adequate time for the floors to dry. Before the pool is opened, however, these areas must be carefully checked for standing water, debris, slippery spots, and adequate supplies.

Daily Routines

Once the pool is open, numerous tasks must be performed so that the pool and its equipment can be continually monitored. Of course, water chemistry must be checked diligently. Ideal ranges for any pool must agree with the swimming pool ordinances or bathing codes.

These ideal ranges should be posted and printed on test kits, reports, and records so that anyone taking these readings will know whether they need to increase or decrease chemical levels. Typical chemical standards for swimming pools are as follows:

pH	7.2-7.8
FC	2.0-4.0 ppm
Total available chlorine (TC)	No higher than 0.2 ppm above FC
Combined Chlorine (CC)	Less than 0.3 ppm
Oxygen reduction potential (OPR)	650-750 mv
Cyanuric acid (CYA)	20-30 ppm, no higher than 100 ppm (outdoor pools only)

The above readings should be taken hourly at busy public pools and perhaps every two hours at other pools. Water temperature, water clarity, weather conditions, and number of swimmers must also be recorded daily.

Although there are other chemical parameters that must be monitored, such as calcium hardness, total alkalinity, and the saturation index, they do not need to be measured daily because these values do not fluctuate as quickly. These measurements should be taken weekly at most pools.

Other daily tasks include the filtration process. The flow rate should be checked daily to ensure the proper turnovers. The filters must also be checked daily to see whether they require cleaning. Backwashing and other filter cleaning should be kept on the daily log along with the chemical readings.

Skimmers must be checked daily. However, depending on the season and geographical location of the pool, some skimmer baskets need to be emptied more frequently. When much organic debris is dropping into the pool, such as leaves or grass clippings, the skimmer baskets will need to be emptied several times each day.

The swimming pool deck should be cleaned daily. This may be done with a high-pressure washer or hose that not only does a superior job but also saves time. Decks are most often cleaned either before the pool opens or after the pool closes. Deck cleaning is performed at these times so that conflicts with swimmers and sunbathers can be avoided. Locker rooms, showers, and bathrooms must also be cleaned daily, but as mentioned earlier, these jobs are best performed before the pool opens. Deck furniture, lifesaving equipment, and any other associated apparatus must also be arranged before the opening of the pool.

Figure 32.2. Proper maintenance keeps the pool water, the pool bottom, and the pool deck clean and safe for guests. (Photo courtesy of Aquatic Safety Research Group)

Closing Routines

A walkabout is also strongly recommended shortly after the pool has closed for the day and all patrons have left. All rooms should be checked, and the doors locked to be certain that no one is remaining in the facility. Bathroom stalls should be carefully checked to ensure that potential trespassers are not hiding there. Security lights must be turned on and all doors and gates must be locked. Both chemical readings and filtration readings should be taken for the last time. Chlorinators must be turned down or off, depending on the situation. All safety and programming equipment should be picked up and locked inside. Water temperature and clarity should also be recorded at this time, and the pool should be re-filled with water as needed so that proper skimming action is maintained during the evening. All standing water, whether it be on the pool deck, in the locker rooms, or in the filter room, should be squeegeed off so that it does not create a problem for the morning shift. The flow rate should be recorded at this time, along with the pressure differential. Backwashing after the pool closes is a good idea. All debris, including litter and lost and found articles must be removed after closing.

Weekly Routines

Water balancing should be a weekly routine. In addition to the daily chemical readings, total alkalinity and calcium hardness measurements must be taken each week. The saturation index should also be computed when these two values are found. The index should be recorded and corrective measures should be taken as soon as possible. The saturation index is perhaps one of the most overlooked tasks at pools (see Chapter 15).

In addition to balancing the water, most states require a weekly bacteriological analysis of the water. The water sample must be sent to a certified laboratory and may not exceed 200 bacteria/mm3 in a standard plate count, and the total coliform count should not exceed 2.2/100 ml.

Another weekly duty is the sanitization of the pool deck and similar surfaces such as diving boards and locker room floors. Each of these surfaces can become very slippery if not disinfected regularly. When algae growth is a real problem, sanitizing these surfaces may be required more than once a week. However, if done well, weekly disinfecting should suffice.

In heavily used pools, shocking may occur once a week. This may be done either with a chlorine or non-chlorine shocking agent. It must be emphasized, however, that an accurate chloramine count is the only way to determine when shocking is needed. Shocking cannot take place with swimmers in the water.

A scum line or "bathtub" ring develops quickly around outdoor pools because of the large amounts of suntan lotion used. As a result, this line that occurs at the water level on the pool walls must be scrubbed regularly. The frequency of this chore varies with different pools, but typically, outdoor pools are scrubbed weekly, whereas indoor pools are scrubbed monthly. Spas and hot tubs, however, may have to be cleaned more often than once a week. Pool cleaners that will not scratch or destroy the finish of the pool must be used. Pool operators must be careful when selecting cleaners for this purpose; the cleaner must match the finish.

Any swimming pool apparatus that is secured to the deck or similar structure must be checked for sturdiness at least once a week. This includes diving boards, ladders, lifeguard chairs, and anything else that is bolted down. For instance, shaky ladders can easily cause accidents and lawsuits. At outdoor pools, umbrellas can become airborne during heavy winds. Because they can cause serious injuries, umbrellas must be tightly secured in place.

The filter room, guard room, first-aid room, front office, and similar facilities should be cleaned and organized at least once a week. Supplies that are missing and need to be replaced should also be noted. First-aid kits should also be replenished weekly. Lifeguard audits should also be conducted weekly.

Bulletin boards, phone recordings, and other information sources should be checked at least once a week to be certain that the data displayed are current.

Monthly

Unfortunately, many monthly tasks are often perceived as routines that should be done if time permits but in reality never get done. Monthly tasks should be assigned a specific date such as the 1st or 15th of every month or the first Monday of every month.

Chemical feeders should be cleaned monthly. Particularly when pumping sodium hypochlorite or soda ash, chemical feeders tend to clog quickly. Gas chlorinators should also be checked. Manufacturer's recommendations for cleaning feeders must be followed. A common way of cleaning chemical feeders is as follows:

1. The feeder is turned off.
2. The foot valve and strainer are removed from the chemical solution it is pumping.
3. This assembly is placed in fresh water and pumped for five minutes to remove all chemicals.
4. The foot and strainer are placed in a 10% solution of muriatic acid, the pump is turned on, and at least a pint of the acid is run through the unit.
5. The assembly is removed from the acid solution and placed once again in fresh water to remove all acid from the unit. Pumping fresh water for at least five

minutes should remove all acid before returning the unit to its original chemical solution.

Lighting should be checked at least once a month, as well as GFIs and fire extinguishers.

The filter media must also be checked monthly. If a sand filter is being used, the sand should be checked for mud balls or channeling or any other abnormality that may occur. Raking the sand clean and adding or replacing sand may also occur if the filter bed is inadequate. If a D.E. filter is used, the filter septa must be checked for tears or holes and repaired if necessary. When cartridge filters are used, they should be soaked at least once a month in a cleaner to remove excess oils.

Security checks of the facility are often conducted monthly. However, where security and vandalism are problems, this important routine may be done weekly or even daily. At outdoor pools, fences and gates are particularly important. Every barrier must be checked to be certain that trespassers cannot enter under or through gaps in the barrier. Doors, locks, and latches must also be checked regularly to ensure that they are in good working order. All security lights must be checked, as well as any electronic surveillance equipment.

Staff meetings, orientations, and review of emergency procedures should occur at least monthly. At crowded public pools, this important training procedure should be conducted more frequently. Whenever such a meeting takes place, attendance should be taken and a written record of the agenda should be kept for five years. This important information is critical during a lawsuit, because it shows that the pool owner or operator kept the staff current with emergency procedures.

Typical topics to be covered during staff meetings are the following:

1. Problem areas that have recently arisen and review of customer complaints
2. Review of emergency procedures, which should include simulated rescues and backboarding procedures
3. Input from the staff regarding safety improvements and working conditions at the pool

MSDS sheets, first-aid kits, SCBA units, backboards, cervical collars, lifeguarding equipment, and similar safety apparatus should be checked between weekly and monthly depending on the type of pool.

Summary

This chapter has attempted to cover some of the more important routines that should be conducted at aquatic facilities. Not all operational procedures are covered in this section. Each pool is different. Therefore each pool needs specific routines that are customized. Using the checklists provided in the back of this book will help, but unique procedures and routines should be added. All records, logs, and check lists used at a pool should be kept for a minimum of five years in case an insurance claim or lawsuit is brought against the facility.

Bibliography

American Pool Service. (1990). *Pool operations manual.* Lanham, MD: The Service.

Association of Pool & Spa Professionals. (2014). www.APSP.org

Clayton, R. D., & Thomas, D. G. (1989). *Professional aquatic management* (2nd ed.). Champaign, IL: Human Kinetics.

Gabrielson, A. M. (1987). *Swimming pools: A guide to their planning, design, and operation* (4th ed.). Champaign, IL: Human Kinetics.

Kowalsky, L. (Ed.). (1991). *Pool/spa operators handbook.* San Antonio, TX: National Swimming Pool Foundation.

NSPI. (1983). *The sensible way to enjoy your pool.* Alexandria, VA: The Institute.

Williams, K. G., & Young, R. A. (Eds.). (2011). *Aquatic facility operator manual* (6th ed.). Ashburn, VA: National Recreation and Park Association.

Figure 32.3. Photo courtesy of Water Technology, Inc.

33

Safe Handling of Pool Chemicals

by Kerry Hoffman Richards

Key Concepts

- Understanding the label
- Types of pesticides
- Signal words and symbols
- Storage and handling
- Direction for use
- Toxicity and exposure

Pesticides need to be biologically active, or toxic, to be effective against the pests they are intended to control. *Toxicity* is a measure of their capacity to cause injury; it is a property of the chemical itself. *Hazard*, or risk, on the other hand, is the potential for injury, or the degree of danger involved in using a pesticide under given circumstances. Hazard depends on both the toxicity of the pesticide and the risk of exposure to harmful amounts of the chemical. Many pesticide accidents can be traced to applicator carelessness or misuse as well as improper storage of pesticides. These accidents can damage plants and wildlife and, more important, endanger the health of the user or other people.

The best way to avoid or minimize accidents associated with the hazards of pesticide use is to know the chemical being used and how to use it. This means the user must read the label carefully and follow instructions. The attitude of the user is important. If users mistakenly think they know exactly how to use a pesticide, or if they do not care what precautions should be taken, accidents are more likely to occur. People must realize their legal and moral obligations when using pesticides. By taking adequate precautions and practicing good management with safety in mind, users should experience few accidents from pesticide use.

In this section, we will review the many facets of pesticide toxicity, health, safety, and storage. Proper understanding of these concepts is essential for the safe handling and use of swimming pool chemicals. Any chemical can be poisonous or toxic if absorbed in excessive amounts, even common table salt if too much is consumed. The toxic effects of a pesticide depend on both the toxicity of the chemical and the amount the body absorbs following exposure. One of the more important tools for the safe and effective use of pesticides is the product label. Pesticide manufacturers are required by law to put certain information on the label, information that when not heeded and followed can result in a pesticide accident and legal action against the violator. Labels are legal documents that provide directions on how to mix, apply, store, and dispose of a pesticide product.

Labels are not exclusive to pesticide chemicals. Most products purchased and used daily (including breakfast cereal, furniture polish, mouthwash, laundry detergent, paints, and food items) bear labels that identify the product, its purpose, details on use, the manufacturer, and other information.

The label is the main means available to the manufacturer to communicate information about the product to the user.

The Background of the Label

To appreciate the value of the information on a pesticide label, the time, effort, and money spent in gathering it must be considered. The information on a product label is the result of years of research by scientists from laboratory and field tests. This information takes a minimum of 6 years to obtain and costs a chemical company millions of dollars. Chemical companies continually make new compounds and then screen them in the laboratory for possible pesticide use. For each material that finally meets the standards of a potential pesticide, thousands of other compounds are screened and discarded. When a promising pesticide is discovered, its potential use must be evaluated. If the company believes it has a worthwhile product and the possibility for a significant sales market is strong, widescale testing and label registration procedures begin. In the development and labeling of a pesticide, scientists and registration specialists are interested in proving that the chemical not only will control pests but also will not cause unreasonable adverse effects.

Many carefully controlled tests must be done to determine the effectiveness and safety of each pesticide under a range of environmental conditions.

Toxicity and Toxicological Tests

How poisonous or dangerous is a pesticide to humans, wildlife, and other organisms? Does the chemical cause any long-term or chronic effects? Will the test chemical cause any skin or dermal reactions? To determine these and other health effects, the pesticide is administered at different dosages to test animals, usually rats and mice. These toxicological tests alone often cost the company several million dollars to complete.

Efficacy or Performance Tests

Does the pesticide control the target pest? The company must have performance data to show that the pesticide will control a particular pest or group of pests on one or more hosts or sites, including plants, animals, soil, and structures. Data must show that the pesticide, when used for its intended purpose and according to directions, is a useful product.

Degradation and Mobility

What happens to the pesticide after it is applied? A series of studies is needed to show how long it takes for the compound to break down (degrade) into harmless materials under various conditions.

Effects on Wildlife and Environment

The chemical company must determine the effects of applications of the pesticide on wildlife and the environment. Potentially harmful effects on wildlife and the environment that are recognized during these studies must be included in the environmental impact statement submitted to the Environmental Protection Agency (EPA).

EPA Label Review

The chemical company is now ready to take data to the EPA for review. The chemical company asks for pesticide "use registrations" on as many crops, animals, or other application sites as it has pest management test data to support its claims. The EPA must approve the label before a product can be marketed.

Parts of the Label

Some labels are easy to understand; others are complicated. The user is responsible for reading and understanding the label before buying, using, storing, or disposing of a pesticide. Each label must include the following:

- directions for use,
- the phrase "keep out of the reach of children,"
- name and address of the manufacturer,
- percentage of each active ingredient, and
- EPA registration number.

Each of the label components will be discussed in this section.

Trade, Brand, or Product Names

Every manufacturer has trade names for its products. Most companies register each trade name as a trademark and will not allow other companies to use that name without permission. Different trade names are used by different manufacturers, even though the products contain the same active ingredient. The brand or trade name shows up plainly on the front panel of the label and is the one used in advertisements and by company salespersons. For example, calcium hypochlorite is sold under the trade names HTH, Repak, and Pitchlor, among others.

Ingredient Statement

Every pesticide label must list every active ingredient and its percentage on the container. Inert ingredients are not usually named, but the label must show what percentage of the total contents they comprise. The ingredient statement must list the official chemical names and/or common names of the active ingredients. For example, Olin's HTH has a label that lists the following:

Active ingredient:
Calcium hypochlorite......65%
Inert ingredients...............35%

Because chemical names are usually complex, many are given a shorter common name. Only common names that the EPA has officially accepted may be used in the ingredient statement on the pesticide label. The official common name is usually followed by the chemical name in the list of active ingredients. The common name for HTH is calcium hypochlorite, which is often referred to as cal hypo. By purchasing pesticides according to the common or chemical names, the user will certainly get the right active ingredient, no matter what the brand name or formulation.

Use Classification Statement

The EPA classifies every pesticide product as either *restricted use* or *unclassified/general use*. Every pesticide product that is federally classified as restricted use must include the following statement in a prominent place on the front panel of the pesticide label.

Restricted use pesticides are for retail sale to and use only by certified applicators or persons under their direct supervision and only for those uses covered by the certified applicator's certification.

Pesticides labeled for restricted use warrant special attention. Many pesticides are designated as restricted use products if reasons exist that they could harm humans, livestock, wildlife, or the environment, even when used according to label directions. Persons using these products need special training and a certain level of competence to ensure they can handle these pesticides properly. The restricted use statement may indicate why the pesticide has been classified as such.

Type of Pesticide

The type of pesticide is usually listed on the front panel of the pesticide label. This short statement indicates in general terms what the product will control. Examples include the following:

- algaecide for control of algae or
- bactericides for control of unwanted bacteria.

Net Contents

The front panel of the pesticide label shows how much product is in the container. This is expressed as pounds or ounces for dry formulations or as gallons, quarts, or pints for liquids. Liquid formulations may also list the pounds of active ingredient per gallon of product. Many labels now also include metric units (grams, kilograms, liters) as part of the contents information.

Name and Address of the Manufacturer

The law requires that the manufacturer or formulator of a product put the name and address of the company on the label.

Emergency Telephone Number

Many pesticide manufacturers include an emergency telephone number on their product labels. These companies are ready to assist anyone in the event of an emergency (poisoning, spill, fire) involving their product.

Registration Numbers

An EPA registration number (e.g., EPA Reg. No. 3120-280) must appear on pesticide labels. This indicates that the pesticide product has been registered and that the EPA has approved its label. In cases of special local

needs, pesticide products may be approved for use in a specific state. An example of such a registration is EPA SLN No. PA-910002. In this case, SLN indicates "special local need" and PA means that the product is registered for use in Pennsylvania.

Establishment Numbers

An EPA establishment number (e.g., EPA Est. No. 5840-AZ-1) must also appear on the pesticide label to identify the facility that produced the product. This is necessary in case a problem arises or the product is adulterated in any way.

Signal Words and Symbols

Every pesticide label must include a signal word. This important designation gives the user an indication of the relative acute toxicity of the product to humans and animals. Signal words are established based on the LD_{50} value of the chemical. This is the amount or concentration of a toxicant (i.e., pesticide) required to kill 50% of a test population of animals under a standard set of conditions. LD_{50} values of pesticides are recorded in milligrams of pesticide per kilogram of body weight of the test animal (mg/kg) or in parts per million (ppm). For example, a LD_{50} of 135 means that it would take approximately 135 mg of a chemical for each kilogram of an animal's body weight to kill one half of the test animals in a population. LC_{50} values of pesticides are recorded in 

milligrams of pesticide per volume of air or water (ppm). To put these units into perspective, 1 ppm is analogous to 1 in. in 16 miles or 1 minute in 2 years.

LD_{50} and LC_{50} values are useful in comparing the toxicity of different active ingredients and different formulations of the same active ingredient. The lower the LD_{50} value of a pesticide, the less it takes to kill 50% of the population, and therefore the greater the acute toxicity of the chemical. Pesticides with high LD_{50} values are considered the least acutely toxic to humans when used according to the directions on the product label.

Acute toxicities are the basis for assigning pesticides to a toxicity category and selecting the appropriate signal word for the product label.

The signal word must appear in large letters on the front panel of the pesticide label along with the statement "Keep Out of Reach of Children." The following signal words may be found on pesticide labels:

- DANGER-POISON—skull and crossbones symbol. These words and symbol must appear on products that are highly toxic by any route of entry into the body. *Peligro*, the Spanish word for danger, must also appear on the label. LD_{50} values for these chemicals range from a trace to 50 mg/kg.
- DANGER—Products with this signal word can cause severe eye damage or skin irritation.
- WARNING—This word signals that the product is moderately toxic either orally, dermally, or through inhalation or causes moderate eye and skin irritation. *Aviso*, the Spanish word for warning, must also appear on the label. LD_{50} values for these chemicals range from 50 mg/kg to 500 mg/kg.
- CAUTION—This word signals that the product is slightly toxic either orally, dermally, or through inhalation or causes slight eye and skin irritation. LD_{50} values for these chemicals are above 500 mg/kg.

Signal words can be used to choose the least toxic chemical that will give the desired level of pest control.

Precautionary Statements

Pesticide labels contain additional statements to help applicators decide what precautions to take to protect themselves, their employees, and other persons (or animals) that could be exposed. Sometimes these statements are listed under the heading "Hazards to Humans and Domestic Animals." They may be composed of several sections.

Routes of Entry Statements

These statements indicate which route or routes of entry (mouth, skin, and lungs) are particularly hazardous. Many pesticide products are hazardous by more than one route, so these statements should be studied carefully. A DANGER signal word followed by "May be fatal if swallowed or inhaled" gives a far different warning than DANGER followed by "Corrosive—Causes eye damage and severe skin burns."

Typical DANGER label statements include the following:

- Fatal if swallowed.
- Poisonous if inhaled.
- Extremely hazardous by skin contact—rapidly absorbed through skin.
- Corrosive—causes eye damage and severe skin burns.

Routes of entry statements are not uniform on all labels and many variations are found. More than one or even all four precautions may be stated on a label.

Typical WARNING label statements include the following:

- Harmful or fatal if swallowed.
- Harmful or fatal if absorbed through the skin.
- Harmful or fatal if inhaled.
- Causes skin and eye irritation.

Typical CAUTION label statements include the following:

- Harmful if swallowed.
- May be harmful if inhaled.
- May irritate eyes, nose, throat, and skin.

Specific Action Statements

These statements usually follow the route of entry statements. The specific action statements recommend specific precautions to take and protective clothing and equipment to wear to reduce exposure to the pesticide. These statements are directly related to the toxicity of the pesticide product (signal word) and the routes of entry.

DANGER labels typically contain statements such as the following:

- Do not breathe vapors or spray mist.
- Do not get on skin or clothing.
- Do not get in eyes.

Typical WARNING labels combine specific action statements from DANGER and CAUTION labels.

CAUTION labels generally contain specific action statements that are less threatening than those on the DANGER label, indicating that the toxicity hazard is not as great:

- Avoid contact with skin or clothing.
- Avoid breathing dust, vapors, or spray mists.
- Avoid getting in eyes.

Protective Clothing and Equipment Statements

Pesticide labels vary in the information they contain on protective clothing and equipment. Some labels do not contain such a statement. Other pesticide labels fully describe appropriate protective clothing and equipment. A few list the types of respirators that should be worn when handling and applying the product; others require the use of a respirator but do not specify a type or model. Advice on protective clothing or equipment that appears on the label should be followed. However, the lack of such a statement or the mention of only one piece of equipment does not rule out the need for additional protection. The proper type of protective clothing and equipment needed can be determined with the signal word, the route of entry statements, and the specific action statements.

Other Precautionary Statements

Labels often list other precautions that should always be followed when handling the product. These are self-explanatory:

- Do not contaminate food or feed.
- Remove and wash contaminated clothing before reuse.
- Wash thoroughly after handling and before eating or smoking.
- Wear clean clothes daily.
- Not for use or storage in and around a house.
- Do not allow children or domestic animals into the treated area.

These are commonsense statements. The absence from the label of such statements does not indicate that these precautions should be ignored.

Statement of Practical Treatment

This section lists first aid treatments recommended in case of poisoning. Typical statements include the following:

- In case of contact with skin, wash immediately with plenty of soap and water.
- In case of contact with eyes, flush with water for 15 minutes and get medical attention.
- In case of inhalation exposure, remove victim from contaminated area and give artificial respiration if necessary.
- If swallowed, induce vomiting.

All DANGER labels and some WARNING and CAUTION labels contain a note to physicians describing the appropriate medical procedures and antidotes for poisoning emergencies. The label should always be available in emergencies.

Environmental Hazards

Pesticides can be harmful to the environment. Some products are classified restricted use because of their environmental hazards. The label may have special warning statements concerning hazards to the environment.

Special Toxicity Statements

If a particular pesticide is especially hazardous to wildlife, it will be stated on the label:

- This product is toxic to fish.
- This product is highly toxic to bees.
- This product is toxic to birds and other wildlife.

These statements alert pesticide users to the special hazards that a product poses. They should help applicators choose the safest product for a particular job and remind them to take extra precautions.

General Environmental Statements

Some of these statements appear on virtually every pesticide label. They are reminders to follow certain commonsense procedures to avoid contaminating the environment. The absence of any or all of these statements does not indicate that adequate precautions do not need to be taken. Sometimes these statements follow a "specific toxicity statement" and provide practical steps to avoid harm to wildlife. Examples of general environmental statements include the following:

- Do not apply when runoff is likely to occur.
- Do not apply when weather conditions favor drift from treated areas.
- Do not contaminate water by improperly disposing of rinse water and other pesticide wastes.
- Do not apply when bees are likely to be in the area.

Physical or Chemical Hazards

This section of the label describes any special fire, explosion, or chemical hazards the product may pose:

- Flammable—Do not use, pour, spill, or store near heat or open flame. Do not cut or weld container.
- Corrosive—Store only in a corrosion-resistant tank.

Hazard statements (hazards to humans and domestic animals, environmental hazards, and physical or chemical hazards) are not located in the same place on all pesticide labels. Some labels group them under the headings listed above. Other labels list them on the front panel beneath the signal word. Still other labels list the hazards in paragraph form somewhere else on the label under headings such as "Note" or "Important." Prior to use, the label should be examined carefully for these statements to ensure that the product is handled properly and safely.

Storage and Disposal

Pesticide labels contain general instructions for the appropriate storage and disposal of the pesticide and its container. State and local laws may vary considerably, so specific instructions usually are not included. One or more statements may appear in a special section of the label titled "Storage and Disposal" or under headings such as "Important," "Note," or "General Instructions." These include the following:

- Store oxidizers away from incompatible chemicals and petroleum products.
- Store at temperatures above 32°F (0°C).
- Do not reuse container; render unusable.
- Do not contaminate water, food, or feed by storage or disposal.

- Triple rinse and dispose in an approved landfill.

Advice should be sought if needed to determine the best storage and disposal procedures for a particular business or location.

Directions for Use

These instructions provide the directions on how to use the product. The following will be listed on the use instructions:

- the pests that the manufacturer claims the product will control,
- the proper mixing instructions,
- how much to use (rate) and how often, and
- where and when the material should be applied.

It is illegal and considered a misuse to use registered pesticide in a manner inconsistent with its labeling. Examples of pesticide misuse include applying a pesticide to a site that is not listed on the label, applying a pesticide at a higher-than-labeled rate, and handling a pesticide in a manner that violates specific label instructions (i.e., storage near food or water, improper container disposal). In some instances, however, use of a pesticide in a manner that the label directions do not describe is allowable and not considered a violation of the label.

Many terms are used on labels to describe when and how to use pesticides. Many technical terms are also found in leaflets and bulletins from local cooperative extension offices, land-grant universities, or other agencies. The applicator's understanding of these terms will help him or her to obtain maximum results from pesticide applications. If applicators do not understand the directions on a label, they should check with their pesticide dealer or salesperson. The label provides a wealth of information. Failure to follow the instructions on a pesticide label can result in a serious pesticide accident and constitutes a legal violation subject to civil or criminal prosecution. The label is a legal document. The user is liable for personal injury, crop damage, or pollution incurred through misuse of a pesticide.

When to Read the Label

Before buying a pesticide, the applicator should read the label to determine the following:

- whether it is the pesticide needed for the job,
- whether the pesticide can be used safely under the application conditions,
- whether the proper application equipment is available for the job,
- whether the necessary protective equipment is available,
- how much pesticide is needed, and

- whether restrictions exist for use of the pesticide.

Before mixing the pesticide, the applicator should read the label to determine the following:

- what protective equipment should be used,
- how much pesticide to use, and
- the mixing procedure.

Before applying the pesticide, the applicator should read the label to determine the following:

- what safety measures to follow,
- when to apply the pesticide, and
- how to apply the pesticide.

Before storing or disposing of the pesticide or pesticide container, the applicator should read the label to determine the following:

- where and how to store the pesticide,
- how to dispose of the pesticide container, and
- where and how to dispose of surplus pesticide.

In addition to the pesticide label, manufacturers often provide supplemental labeling information. These materials (e.g., pamphlets, brochures, information sheets, and advertising) complement the product label, but they do not legally substitute for the label.

Protect Yourself From Pesticides

The greatest risks arise in handling concentrates, especially when mixing, loading, or applying them. Although a dilute chemical is generally less hazardous than a concentrate, the hazard increases when significant drift occurs or when appropriate safety and application procedures are not followed. Danger of exposure also exists when cleaning up spills or repairing equipment or entering treated areas prematurely. The risk associated with pesticide use can be expressed with the following equation:

> **Risk = Toxicity Exposure**

Understanding and controlling the toxicity of the pesticide being used and/or the exposure to that pesticide is critical to reducing risk to the applicator or bather in areas treated with pool chemicals.

Toxicity and Potential Health Effects of Pesticides

As we discussed earlier, the toxicity of a pesticide is its capacity or ability to cause injury or illness. The toxicity of a pesticide is determined by subjecting test animals (usually rats, mice, rabbits, and dogs) to different dosages of the active ingredient and each of its formulated products. Two types of toxicity are acute and chronic.

Acute Toxicity

Acute toxicity, based on a single, short-term exposure, is determined by at least three methods:

- dermal toxicity is determined by exposing the skin to the chemical,
- inhalation toxicity is determined by the test animals breathing vapors of the chemical, and
- oral toxicity is determined by feeding the chemical to test animals.

Harmful effects that occur from a single exposure by any route of entry are termed *acute effects*. The effects of acute pesticide poisoning usually occur within minutes or hours after exposure. In addition, the effect of the chemical as an irritant to the eyes and skin is examined under laboratory conditions.

Acute toxicity is usually expressed as LD_{50} (lethal dose 50) or LC_{50} (lethal concentration 50). As discussed earlier, this is the amount or concentration of a toxicant (i.e., pesticide) required to kill 50% of a test population of animals under a standard set of conditions. The lower the LD_{50} value of a pesticide, the less it takes to kill 50% of the population, and therefore the greater the acute toxicity of the chemical. Pesticides with high LD_{50} values are considered the least acutely toxic to humans when used according to the directions on the product label.

Chronic Toxicity

The chronic toxicity of a pesticide is determined by subjecting test animals to long-term exposure to the active ingredient. Harmful effects that occur from small doses repeated over a period of time are chronic effects. Suspected chronic effects from exposure to certain pesticides include birth defects (teratogenesis); fetal toxicity (fetotoxic effects); production of tumors (oncogenesis), either benign (noncancerous) or malignant (cancerous/carcinogenesis); genetic changes (mutagenesis); blood disorders (hematoxic effects); nerve disorders (neurotoxic effects); and reproductive effects. As a consequence, a number of pesticides include chronic toxicity warning statements on the product label. The chronic toxicity of a pesticide is more difficult to determine through laboratory analysis than acute toxicity.

Pesticide Poisoning

The symptoms of pesticide poisoning can range from a mild skin irritation to coma or even death. It is important that pesticide users and handlers learn to recognize the common signs and symptoms of pesticide poisoning.

The effects, or symptoms, of pesticide poisoning can be broadly defined as being either topical or systemic. Topical effects generally develop at the site of pesticide contact. Topical effects from exposure to pesticides are a result of either the irritant properties of a chemical in a pesticide formulation (an active or inert ingredient) or an allergic response by the victim. Dermatitis, or inflammation of the skin, generally is accepted as the most commonly reported topical effect associated with pesticide exposure. Symptoms of dermatitis range from reddening of the skin to blisters or rashes. Some persons may be allergic to pesticide chemicals. Symptoms of an allergic reaction range from reddening and itching of the eyes and skin to respiratory discomfort often resembling an asthmatic condition.

Systemic effects are different from topical effects. They often occur away from the original point of contact as a result of the pesticide being absorbed into and distributed throughout the body. Systemic effects often include nausea, vomiting, fatigue, headache, and intestinal disorders.

Different classes or families of chemicals cause different symptoms. Individuals also vary in their sensitivity to different levels of these chemicals. Some people may show no reaction to a dose that causes severe illness in others. Early recognition of symptoms and an immediate appropriate response may save a life. However, the development of certain symptoms is not always the result of exposure to a pesticide. Common illnesses such as the flu, heat exhaustion or heat stroke, pneumonia, asthma, respiratory and intestinal infections, and even a hangover from overindulgence can cause similar symptoms. Some individuals exhibit allergic reactions when using pesticides or when these materials are applied in or around their homes or places of work. When symptoms appear after contact with a pesticide, medical attention should be sought immediately. The label or, if necessary, the container, should be taken to the hospital, but not in the passenger section of a vehicle. The doctor needs to know what the product ingredients are, and an antidote is often listed on the label. If the material safety data sheet (MSDS) is available, this should be taken to the hospital too, as it frequently contains information for the doctor in the event of an emergency.

For persons who handle pesticides or reside near areas where they are used, the name and number of the National Poison Center should be readily available. These centers are staffed on a 24-hour basis.

For pesticide emergencies, the National Pesticide Information Center (NPIC) is also available. The NPIC toll-free telephone number, 1-800-858-7378, provides a variety of information about pesticides to anyone in the United States.

Emergency numbers should be readily available next to the telephone and in service vehicles involved in transporting pesticides. Warehouses and retail outlets should list these numbers along with other emergency numbers near telephones to enable any employee to use them in an emergency.

Applicator Exposure: How Pesticides Enter the Body

Four routes by which a pesticide can enter the human body include

- the skin (dermal),
- the lungs (inhalation),
- the mouth (oral), and
- the eyes.

Dermal

In most pesticide exposure situations, the skin is the most important route of entry into the body. Evidence indicates that about 97% of all body exposure to pesticides during an application is through skin contact. Dermal absorption may occur as the result of a splash, spill, or drift when mixing, loading, applying, or disposing of pesticides.

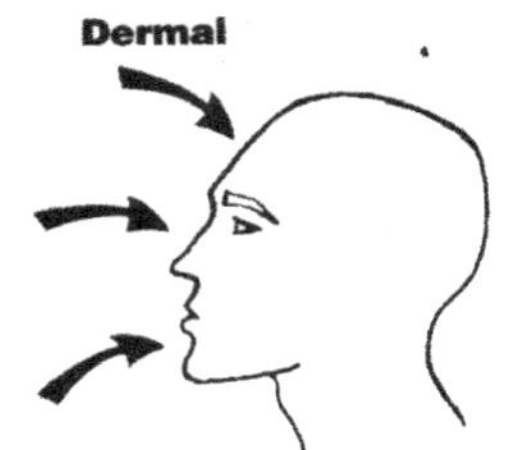

Even if only a small amount of chemical remains on the skin, it can be absorbed into the body, and the person can be poisoned. Different parts of the body vary in their ability to absorb pesticides. Research with certain pesticides has found that the scrotal area and the head are absorptive, although cuts, abrasions, and skin rashes can enhance absorption in other parts of the body. Pesticide formulations vary in their ability to be absorbed through the skin.

Inhalation

Protection of the lungs is especially important when pesticide gases, vapors, or small spray droplets can be inhaled during mixing, loading, or application. If breathed into the lungs, pesticides can enter the bloodstream rapidly and completely. If inhaled in sufficient amounts, pesticides can also cause damage to nose, throat, and lung tissue.

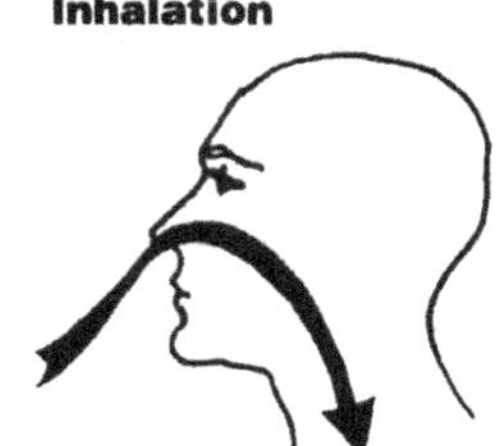

Oral

Accidental oral exposure occurs most frequently when pesticides have been taken from the original labeled container and put into an unlabeled bottle or food container. Unfortunately, children are the most common victims in these situations.

Oral exposure also occurs when liquid concentrates splash into the mouth during mixing or while cleaning equipment. The mouth must never be used to begin siphoning a pesticide from a tank or container. Chemicals can also be swallowed when eating, drinking, smoking, or even persons licking their lips. Since many pesticides are rapidly and completely absorbed by the intestinal tract, it is essential that an applicator always wash hands and face thoroughly before eating, drinking, or smoking.

Eyes

Under certain conditions and with certain pesticides, absorption through the eyes can be significant and particularly hazardous. Eyes are sensitive to many pesticides and considering their size are able to absorb surprisingly large amounts of chemical. Serious eye exposure can result from a splash or spill, from a drift, or by rubbing the eyes with contaminated hands or clothing.

The best way to minimize exposure to pesticide is by selecting the proper protective clothing. Specific protective clothing may not be specifically listed on the label. However, protection may be needed to reduce the risk of chemical contact. Similarly, a statement specifying only one piece of safety equipment does not rule out the need for additional protection.

Clothing

For typical pesticide applications, protective clothing includes a clean long-sleeved shirt and long trousers made of a tightly woven fabric or a water-repellent material. However, swimming pool pesticide application may require less protective clothing to minimize exposure. The same basic principles for selecting the proper protective clothing still apply.

Gloves

Wear unlined, waterproof, chemically resistant gloves when handling or applying pesticides. Gloves should be long enough to cover the wrist and should not have a fabric wristband. Gloves are made from many materials, but current information indicates that nitrile, butyl, and neoprene provide the best protection for liquid and dry pesticide formulations. Natural rubber gloves are recommended only for dry formulations. Leather or fabric gloves should not be used because they tend to absorb pesticides and transfer them to the skin. Decontamination is virtually impossible once leather and fabric gloves have become saturated; disposal is the only option. Gloves should be approved for use with the chemicals that will be used. Some rubber products react with certain solvents and become sticky as the rubber dissolves. If this occurs, dispose of these gloves and use gloves approved for use with pesticides. Gloves can be checked for holes by filling them with water and

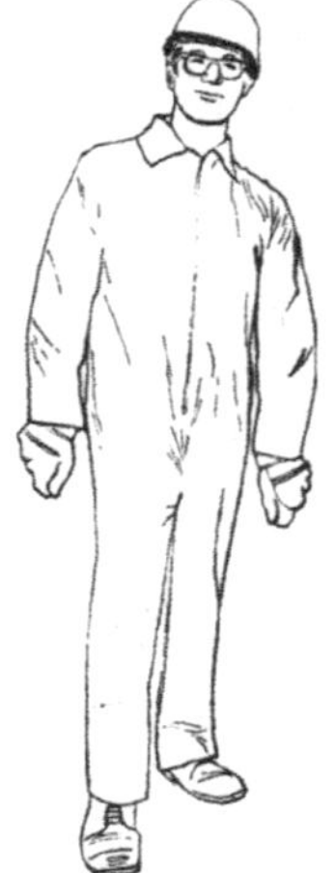

squeezing; damaged or leaking gloves should be discarded. To further reduce the possibility of skin contamination, gloves should be washed with soap and water before taking them off.

Goggles or Face Shield

Tightly fitting, nonfogging goggles or a full face shield should be worn when the pesticide has any chance of getting in the eyes. This is especially important when pouring or mixing concentrates or handling dusts or toxic sprays. Those who wear contact lenses may want to consult an eye doctor prior to using pesticides.

Goggles and face shields should be kept clean at all times. They can be washed with soap and water and sanitized by soaking equipment for 2 minutes in a mixture of 2 tablespoons chlorine bleach in 1 gal of water. Then they should be rinsed thoroughly with clean water to remove soap and sanitizer and wiped with a clean cloth and allowed to air dry. Attention should be paid to goggle headbands because they are often made of absorbent material that needs to be replaced regularly.

Respirators

For many toxic chemicals (e.g., chlorine gas), the respiratory (breathing) system is the quickest and most direct route of entry into the circulatory system. From the blood capillaries of the lungs, these toxic substances are rapidly transported throughout the body.

Respiratory protective devices vary in design, use, and protective capability. In selecting a respiratory protective device, the user must first consider the degree of

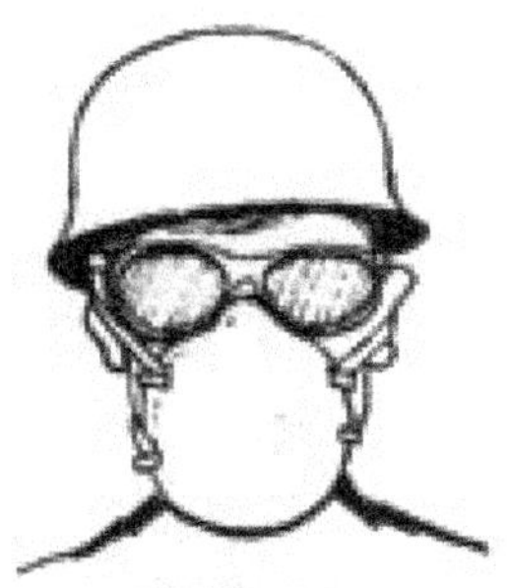

hazard associated with breathing the toxic substance and then understand the specific uses and limitations of the available equipment. The user should select a respirator that is designed for the intended use and should always follow the manufacturer's instructions concerning the use and maintenance of that particular respirator. Different respirators may be needed for application of different chemicals or groups of chemicals. Select only equipment approved by the National Institute of Occupational Safety and Health (NIOSH) and the Mine Safety and Health Administration (MSHA). The NIOSH/MSHA approval numbers begin with the letters *TC*.

Laundering Pesticide-Contaminated Clothing

Protective clothing and equipment should be washed at the end of each day because the concentration of pesticide in the fabric tends to build up with successive exposures. The more concentrated the pesticide in the fabric, the more difficult it is to remove during laundering. Contaminated clothing should be stored and washed separately from the family laundry. Pesticides can be transferred from one garment to another in the wash water. Cases have been reported in which several family members developed skin rashes after wearing clothes that were washed in the same water as pesticide-contaminated clothing. Waterproof gloves should be worn when handling contaminated clothing, and the product label should be checked for specific laundering instructions. Clothing that has become saturated with a product concentrate should be discarded.

Some residues may be removed by presoaking the contaminated clothing in an appropriate container or by using a prewash cycle on the washing machine. A prewash product should always be used in any pretreatment process. Washing in hot water at full water level removes more pesticide from clothing than washing in colder water temperatures—the hotter, the better; cold water might save energy, but it is relatively ineffective in removing pesticides from clothing. Washing clothes more than once should increase the amount of pesticide removed, but it may not remove all residue.

Most laundry detergents are effective in removing pesticides from fabric. However, heavy-duty liquid detergents typically have better oil-removing ability and therefore are more effective than other detergents in removing emulsifiable concentrates. The ease of pesticide removal through laundering does not depend on toxicity but rather on the formulation of the pesticide. Bleach or ammonia may help in the removal or breakdown of certain pesticides, but they should never be mixed together because they react to form chlorine gas, which can be fatal.

After the clothes are washed, the washing machine should be rinsed with an empty load using hot water and the same detergent. Line drying of clothing is recommended for two reasons. First, it eliminates the possibility of residues collecting in the dryer. Second, residues of many pesticides break down when exposed to sunlight.

Storing Pesticides Safely

Proper pesticide storage helps prolong chemical shelf life and protects the health of people, animals, and the environment. The product label can be consulted for specific storage information. Basic guidelines that are essential for safe pesticide storage are presented in the following section.

Storage Area

Pesticides should be kept out of reach of pets, livestock, children, and irresponsible people. A storage facility must be secured against theft, vandalism, and unauthorized access. Pesticides should be stored in a locked place such as a separate building, room, or cabinet. For storage outdoors, a security fence should be erected.

The storage facility should be located where water damage is unlikely to occur. Soil and land surface characteristics should be considered when selecting a storage area or constructing a storage facility to prevent contamination of surface water or groundwater from runoff, leaching, or drainage. The floor in a storage facility should be free of cracks and have an impermeable surface that can be cleaned and decontaminated if a spill occurs. A floor that is sloped into a containment system or recessed below the level of the doors will help to keep pesticides within the restricted area. In certain situations, diking or another containment structure may need to be constructed around the storage facility.

In addition, the following guidelines should be observed:

- Highly visible warning signs should be placed on walls, doors, and/or windows to indicate to anyone attempting to enter the facility that pesticides are stored there. "No Smoking" signs should be displayed. Fireproof construction is best.
- Pesticides should be stored in an area away from food, feed, potable water supplies, and protective equipment. This prevents contamination from vapors, dusts, or spills and reduces the likelihood of accidental human or animal exposure.
- A well-ventilated storage area can prevent the accumulation and movement of vapors and dust into work areas. Temperature extremes should be avoided. Very high or low temperatures can cause pesticide deterioration. Exhaust fans directed to the outside will reduce temperatures and remove dust and vapors from the storage facility.
- Pesticide containers should be kept out of direct sunlight to prevent overheating.

Pesticide Containers

- Pesticides should be stored only in their original containers. Soft drink bottles, fruit jars, fuel cans, and other nonpesticide containers should never be used. Besides the fact that such storage is illegal, serious poisonings could result from using the wrong container because children, as well as most adults, associate the shape of a container with its contents.
- The original label should be attached to the container. To keep a label legible, it can be protected with transparent tape or lacquer. The label is the most important safety factor in the use of pesticides. It should not become damaged or destroyed.
- Bulk tanks should be placed on an impermeable surface. Diking around a tank will keep spilled or leaking pesticide inside a restricted area and will also prevent damage to the tanks from vehicles and equipment. A dike should be large enough to contain the volume of the liquid in the tank plus at least an additional 10%. Valves and pumps should be within the diked area. Drains within the dike should be connected to a holding tank.
- Pesticide products should never be stored in unmarked or unlabeled containers. Pesticide users should not rely on verbal directions.
- Containers should be closed securely when not in use. Dry formulations tend to cake when wet or subjected to high humidity. Opened bags of wettable and soluble powders, dusts, and granules can be placed into sealable plastic bags or other suitable containers. This reduces moisture absorption by the material and prevents a spill should a tear or break occur.
- Liquid formulations and small containers of dry formulations should be stored on metal shelving. Metal shelving will not absorb spilled chemicals and is easier to clean than other surfaces.
- Liquids and heavier containers should be stored on the lower shelves. Containers should not extend beyond shelving where they could be bumped or knocked off. Shelving should be tested to ensure it will be able to handle the quantity and weight involved.
- Larger metal drums and nonmetallic containers should be placed on pallets.
- Volatile oxidizers should be stored separately to avoid possible cross contamination of other pesticides or chemicals.
- Containers should be checked regularly for leaks, breaks, rust, and corrosion. If a leak or break occurs, the container should be placed inside another container or the contents should be transferred to an empty container that originally held the same material and has the same label attached.

Safety

- Duplicate copies of labels should be available for the products currently being used. These will be needed in case of an emergency. A material safety data sheet should also be available for every hazardous chemical in the storage facility.
- Appropriate protective clothing should be worn when handling pesticide containers.

- Items used for handling pesticides (measuring utensils, protective equipment, etc.) should be labeled to prevent their use for other purposes.
- Clay, pet litter, fine sand, activated charcoal, vermiculite, diatomaceous earth, or similar commercially available absorbents can be used to clean up spills or leaks. Hydrated lime and bleach should be available for decontamination of spill surfaces, but these two materials should never be used together. A shovel, broom, and heavy-duty plastic bags are also needed for spill containment and cleanup.
- Plenty of soap and water should be available in or close to the storage facility. A fire extinguisher, first aid equipment, and emergency telephone numbers should also be readily available.

Shelf Life of Pesticides

Pesticides in storage should be inventoried, and each container should be marked with the purchase date. Some products have an effective shelf life recorded on the label. If there are questions about the shelf life of a product, the dealer or manufacturer should be contacted. Pesticide deterioration may be indicated during mixing by excessive clumping, poor suspension, layering, or abnormal coloration. Sometimes, however, pesticide deterioration from age or poor storage conditions may be apparent only after application as indicated by poor pest control. For example, even when stored under ideal conditions, sodium hypochlorite has a shelf life of approximately 6 months.

To minimize storage problems, large quantities of pesticides should not be stored for long periods. Records of previous usage will help with estimating future needs. Only as much as will be needed should be purchased for the season; recommendations may change by next season.

Reporting Requirements

Title III of the Federal Superfund Amendments and Reauthorization Act of 1986 (SARA Title III) is also called the Emergency Planning and Community Right-to-Know Act. The act requires the reporting of inventories of certain pesticides if the amount stored is greater than a "threshold planning quantity (TPQ)." Facilities that produce, use, or store, at any time, a designated substance above a specific TPQ must notify the State Emergency Response Commission (SERC) and possibly a county Local Emergency Planning Committee (LEPC).

The local fire department should be informed of any chemicals being stored. Chemical fires often cannot be extinguished by ordinary means, and the smoke from the fire can be extremely hazardous to firefighters. The fire department must be properly prepared in the event of a chemical fire.

Mix and Load Pesticides Safely

The most hazardous activities involving pesticides are mixing and loading of concentrates. Adequate protective clothing and equipment should be available and put on before handling or opening a pesticide container. A respirator or an appropriate form of eye protection should be worn if the chance of pesticide inhalation or eye exposure exists. The user should never eat, drink, or smoke while handling pesticides. Reading the label before opening the container allows the user to become familiar with mixing and usage directions.

If work must be done indoors or at night, adequate ventilation and light is important. Clean water and soap should be available, and if possible, the user should not work alone.

Paper containers should not be torn open, but rather they should be opened with a sharp knife or scissors. When pouring chemicals from a container, users should keep the container at or below eye level and avoid splashing or spilling chemical on their faces or protective clothing. Users should never use their mouths to siphon a pesticide from a container. Users should stand upwind so the wind does not blow the pesticide toward them. If an accident occurs, it should be attended to immediately. Any contaminated clothing should be removed immediately, and the user should wash thoroughly with soap and water. Spills should be attended to promptly.

Label instructions should be followed, and only the amount the user plans to use immediately should be mixed. The effectiveness and safety of an application are jeopardized if too much or too little chemical is used. Measuring devices such as "tip and pours" help in handling small amounts of concentrate. Measuring devices (e.g., spoons, cups, scales) should be kept in the pesticide storage area and never used for other purposes. Label them accordingly to prevent their use for anything else. Measuring cups should be rinsed and the rinsate put into the pool. Pesticide containers should be triple rinsed as soon as they are emptied because residues can dry and become difficult to remove later. The rinsate should be poured into the pool to avoid disposal problems and wasting product. Containers should be closed tightly and returned to the pesticide storage area.

Apply Pesticides Safely and Effectively

The safety and effectiveness of a pesticide application hinge largely on using the correct amount of pesticide and an appropriate application method. This assumes, however, that the pest problem has already been correctly diagnosed and monitored and the pesticide has been carefully selected to consider performance, worker safety, cost, water balance, and compatibility with other chemicals.

Before Application

Before a pesticide is applied, the product label should be read. For safety precautions, an inexperienced person should not apply pesticides alone.

Correct handling procedures require that clean clothing and proper protective equipment be worn. Respiratory protection may be essential when using chlorine gas or other respiratory irritants.

Users should never eat, smoke, or drink while handling pesticides or even carry food or smoking items. Fresh water, soap, and paper towels should be available to allow for quick removal of pesticide contaminants from the body in the event of a spill or exposure. A first aid kit and a plastic, flushing action eyewash bottle are also good precautions, particularly in service vehicles.

Dispose of Pesticides Safely

The pesticide user is responsible for properly disposing of pesticide wastes such as unused chemicals and empty pesticide containers. Improperly disposed pesticide wastes can create serious hazards for both humans and the environment.

It makes good business sense to deal with pesticide wastes properly and safely. The following guidelines should be observed:

- Disposal problems associated with excess pesticide can be avoided by purchasing only the amount needed for one season. Product registrations may change, and new chemicals may be better than old ones. A long storage period may also exceed the effective shelf life of the product.
- The label is the first source of disposal information. However, the label may not always give clear, practical guidance. And, if the product is old, the label recommendations may be outdated and no longer appropriate.
- During disposal of unwanted pesticides or containers, appropriate protective clothing and equipment should be worn.
- Clothing and protective equipment to be discarded, contaminated soil, and materials used to clean up spills should be considered pesticide waste and handled as such.
- Federal and state laws regulate the disposal of containers and other pesticide wastes. the regional office of the U.S. Environmental Protection

An important part of managing pesticide waste is waste reduction. Reduction in the amount of waste generated can reduce disposal problems and costs. Reducing pesticide waste requires careful planning of purchases and careful handling and application of pesticides.

Pesticide Concentrates

Label instructions should be read carefully for storage requirements. Some pesticides are destroyed by freezing temperatures. Once frozen, they often cannot be used and become a disposal problem. Similarly, pesticide containers can corrode, and some pesticides are destroyed if they become wet. If a pesticide container does not have a legible label, it cannot be identified and therefore cannot be used. The container now becomes a disposal problem for the applicator.

The safest means of disposal for pesticide concentrates is to use the product in a manner consistent with its label. If this is not possible, it should be returned to the dealer or manufacturer or offered to another qualified applicator. If no disposal option is available, then the user can check with a regional office of the Pennsylvania Department of Agriculture (PDA) or the regional chemist in a regional Department of Environmental Protection (DEP) office.

Certain pesticides may be disposed of through a municipal refuse collection service; others may require more stringent and costly disposal procedures such as the need to hire a licensed hazardous waste transporter.

Applicators should be aware of the current hazardous waste guidelines established under the Resource Conservation and Recovery Act (RCRA) and comparable state hazardous waste statutes and regulations. They should be thoroughly familiar with the guidelines prior to disposing of pesticide wastes. For instance, pesticide wastes classified as hazardous require special disposal and record-keeping practices.

Equipment Rinsates

Rinsates must be handled carefully to avoid water contamination or injury to nontarget plants and animals.

Pool rinsate should not enter a sewer or a drain that leads to a water or sewage treatment system. When possible, rinsate should be poured into the pool.

Pesticide Containers

Properly rinsing glass, metal, plastic, and even some heavy paper containers effectively removes most pesticide remaining in the container. Rinsing not only saves the applicator money by using the rinsate but also allows disposal of the containers as nonhazardous waste. Rinse containers as soon as they are empty. Some pesticide residues become difficult, if not impossible, to remove after they dry. Rinse containers using either the triple-rinse method or an equivalent procedure such as pressure rinsing. The triple-rinse method requires the following steps:

- The concentrate should be drained from the pesticide container into the pool for at least 30 seconds after the flow begins to drip.
- Approximately one fourth of the container volume should be filled with water or an appropriate solvent, the cap replaced, and the container rotated so all of the interior surfaces are rinsed.

Triple rinse containers

- The rinsate should be poured into the pool and allowed to drain for at least 30 seconds after the flow begins to drip.
- This procedure should be repeated two more times.

Triple-rinsed or pressure-rinsed containers that are being held for disposal at a later date should be marked with the date to indicate that rinsing has been done. Containers that cannot be recycled through a recycling facility or the dealer should be rendered unusable by being pierced or crushed. Pesticide containers should not be reused. Containers should be kept in a locked storage facility until disposal and away from possible contact with children and animals.

Few disposal options exist for empty pesticide containers. Municipal sanitary landfills are not required to accept pesticide containers, but at this time, rinsed containers are still being accepted at many licensed municipal landfills. It is a good policy to check with the local solid waste authority prior to discarding pesticide containers this way.

Triple-rinsed or pressure-rinsed containers should be recycled whenever feasible. For information on recycling facilities, local solid waste disposal authorities or the regional resource recovery and planning coordinator at a regional DEP office or regional PDA office should be consulted.

Combustible containers can be burned only if permitted by the instructions on the label and by local and state ordinances and policies. Those planning to burn combustible containers should contact the Bureau of Air Quality at a regional DEP office.

Although accidents and emergencies involving pesticides are rare, unfortunately they do occur. Manufacturers, transporters, dealers, and users of pesticides must be prepared to respond to emergencies promptly and correctly.

Fires

Pesticide products vary significantly in their flammability and storage hazard. Those requiring extra precautions usually include the label statement "Do not use or store near heat or open flame." Because they present an increased fire hazard, pesticides containing oils or petroleum solvents and oxidizers are most likely to have these warnings. Certain dry formulations also present fire and explosion hazards.

Potential problems associated with pesticide fires include the following:

- The pesticides may be highly flammable or explosive (e.g., oxidizers, aerosols, solvents, dusts, or powders).
- The pesticides may give off vapors or smoke that is highly toxic to firefighters, nearby residents, and animals (e.g., organochlorine pesticides and certain solvents).
- Some products may give off vapors or smoke that is toxic to plants (phytotoxic; e.g., vapors from some herbicides).
- Pesticides may be present in the debris and soil.
- Runoff from the fire site is likely to contain highly toxic chemicals.

Precautions to Reduce Fire Hazards

With certain fundamental safety precautions, the threat of a serious pesticide fire can be reduced or even eliminated. Whenever possible, the following precautions should be observed:

- Storage facilities should be located as far as possible from where people and animals live.
- Storage facilities should be locked at all times.
- Signs should be posted that indicate combustible materials are stored in the facility.
- Combustible materials should be stored away from steam lines and other heating systems.
- Glass or pressurized containers should not be stored in sunlight where they can concentrate heat rays and possibly explode or ignite.
- Fire detection systems should be installed in large storage areas.
- Foam-type fire extinguishers that are approved for chemical fires should be kept in storage areas.
- The servicing fire company should be notified of the location and contents of the storage facility. It may save their lives and the lives of others if a fire were to occur.
- An emergency plan should be developed, and workers should be trained in its execution.
- A written inventory of the pesticides held in storage should be kept, and the list should be filed away

from the main office. If a fire occurs during nonbusiness hours, emergency personnel will need to know what chemicals are present.

Action in the Event of a Fire

Prompt and responsible action is essential in the event of a toxic chemical fire. Emergency (or contingency) planning prior to the occurrence of a fire or other catastrophe is the cornerstone of a responsible action plan. Details on how to respond to a fire should be coordinated with local emergency response officials and reviewed at least annually. Then the following actions can be taken promptly with a minimum of confusion if a toxic chemical fire were to occur:

- The premises should be evacuated.
- The fire department should be notified and informed of the nature of the pesticides involved. Firefighters should be warned of the dangers from exploding containers, chemical vapors, smoke, runoff, and debris. Material safety data sheets provide technical and emergency information.
- People should be kept away.
- If significant smoke is generated, people and animals in the vicinity should be evacuated to a location upwind of the fire.
- A doctor and/or ambulance should be on standby at the site.
- Firefighters must wear protective clothing and use a self-contained breathing apparatus. Other respirators will not provide adequate protection. Smoke and water should be avoided even when wearing full protective gear.
- Eating, drinking, or smoking during firefighting operations should be avoided—they increase the danger of exposure to hazardous chemicals.
- Fire can be fought with fog, foam, or dry powder. If only water is available, it should be used as a fine spray or fog. Water jets should not be used because they can break bags and glass containers.
- Water and spilled chemicals need to be contained. Only as much water as absolutely necessary should be used.
- If runoff occurs or dangers arise from exploding containers, withdrawing and allowing the fire to burn out is an option. Dikes should be built to contain the runoff.
- Persons exposed to pesticide vapors or smoke or to splashing chemical and persons showing signs of illness, dizziness, or unusual behavior should be relieved from duty and placed under medical care. Poisoning by pesticides can be mistaken for heat exhaustion, smoke inhalation, or physical stress. Contaminated clothing should be removed immediately.

- On completion of activities, equipment and clothing should be cleaned and personnel involved should take showers.

After the fire, cleanup and salvage operations should not be attempted until the area has cooled, and then under expert supervision only.

Pesticide Spills

As careful as most people try to be, pesticide spills still occur. The spill may be a minor one involving only a few leaking containers, or it may be a major accident where a piece of equipment malfunctions and releases its contents or where a tank truck or railcar overturns and spills its cargo. Users of hazardous chemicals should be thoroughly familiar with the laws and guidelines governing chemical spills. Their inability to respond properly to such an emergency, no matter how minor, could seriously endanger public health and environmental quality.

The suggested guidelines in the event of a hazardous chemical spill are included under the "three C" program: CONTROL the spill, CONTAIN it, and CLEAN it up.

Control the Spill

Immediate steps should be taken to control the flow of the liquid being spilled. If a sprayer has tipped over, or if a hazardous chemical is leaking from a damaged tank truck, or if a 1-gal can on a storage shelf has rusted through and is leaking, the leak or spill should be safely stopped immediately. For instance, smaller containers can be put into larger containers to prevent further release of the chemical. Stopping larger leaks or spills often is not so simple.

Do not expose yourself unnecessarily to the leaking chemical. Protective equipment should be worn when attempting to control the leak. Also, charging in blindly if someone is injured is not a good idea; again, proper protection is important.

Get help. The state and local police should be alerted if the spill occurs on a public highway. In certain cases, it may be necessary to alert the fire department, but they should be cautioned not to wash down the spill until advised to do so. At times, contacting public health officials and the nearest hospital emergency room may also be necessary.

Isolate the area. The contaminated area should be roped off; people should be kept at least 30 ft away from the spill. Contact with any drift or fumes that may be released should be avoided. Road flares should not be used if the leaking material is flammable. At times, evacuating people downwind from the spill may be necessary, either to an upwind location or completely away from the area.

The spill site should not be left unattended. Someone should be present at the spill site continuously until the chemical is cleaned up and the danger is removed.

Contain the Spill or Leak

At the same time the leak is being controlled, the spilled material should be contained in as small an area as possible. In some situations, a shovel or power equipment may be used to construct a dam. The important thing to remember is that the spilled material should never get into any body of water, including storm sewers, no matter how small the spill.

Discharge of chemical substances into waterways must also be reported to the EPA under the authority of the Clean Water Act (National Response Center, 1-800-424-8802). The authorities should notify downstream users as soon as possible to prevent accidental poisoning of livestock and to avoid contamination of irrigated crops and soil.

Liquid spills can be further contained by spreading absorbent materials such as fine sand, diatomaceous earth, vermiculite, clay, or pet litter over the entire spill. However, several manufacturers now have nonselective, universal sorbents packed in porous fabric pillows. These pillows or "tubes" can be placed directly on the spill or used to dike around the spill area. Waste disposal is also simplified since the contaminated pillows can be placed into heavy-duty disposal bags without dust or spillage.

The spread of dust or granular material can be reduced further by lightly misting the material with water or covering the spill with a plastic cover. However, this cover is now contaminated and should be discarded after use.

Disposal of hazardous wastes must be done in strict accordance with state and federal (RCRA) laws. This applies to any pesticide spill.

Clean Up the Spill

Absorbent material should be added to the contaminated area until the liquid is soaked up and then swept up. Material from small spills may be applied according to label directions. Larger spills should be placed in a steel or fiber drum lined with a heavy-duty plastic bag. Once the spill has been cleaned up, decontaminating or neutralizing the area may be necessary.

Ordinary household bleach in water (approximately 30%) or hydrated lime can be used to decontaminate or neutralize the area. Protective equipment should be worn. Bleach and lime should not be used together. This cleaning material should be worked into the spill area with a coarse broom. Fresh absorbent material should be added to soak up the now contaminated cleaning solution. This material should then be swept up and placed in a plastic bag or drum for disposal. This procedure should be repeated several times to ensure that the area has been thoroughly decontaminated.

Clean the equipment and vehicles. Vehicles and equipment that were contaminated either as a result of the original accident or during the cleanup and disposal procedures must be cleaned. However, before beginning, the cleaner should be properly clothed and protected to avoid contact with the chemical. Ordinary household bleach in water (approximately 30% bleach) or an alkaline detergent (dishwasher soap) solution can be used to clean equipment. Bleach and alkaline detergent should not be mixed together.

Porous material and equipment such as brooms, leather shoes, and cloth hats cannot be effectively decon- taminated and must be discarded or destroyed. Also, disposable garments and gloves or badly contaminated clothing should not be saved but rather disposed of properly immediately after cleanup.

Follow Up

For legal protection, it is advisable to keep records of activities and conversations with regulatory authorities, emergency response personnel, and the general public when dealing with a pesticide spill. Photographs help to document damage and the cleanup process. The spill should be reported to the appropriate regulatory agencies.

SARA Title III also requires the reporting of certain pesticide spills if the amount spilled is greater than the "reportable quantity" for that chemical.

Discharge of chemical substances into waterways must also be reported to the EPA under the authority of the Clean Water Act.

Spill Prevention and Preparation

A key to preventing pesticide spills is to properly maintain vehicles and application equipment. Leaks and drips from cracks or loose fittings in equipment are indications of potential trouble. An understanding of how application equipment works, especially chlorine gas equipment, is often essential to controlling the flow of a product and minimizing equipment damage should a problem occur.

Knowing how to safely handle pesticide spills and leaks is as important as knowing how to correctly apply the material. Facilities in which pesticides are handled should have a complete listing of emergency telephone numbers readily available. The user should always carry the product label! A material safety data sheet for every pesticide on the premises is a must. Proper equipment and supplies for cleaning up spills are essential in every storage establishment.

Persons using or transporting pesticides and other hazardous chemicals have a responsibility to protect the public and the environment. Doing everything possible to avoid spills and adhering to a few basic guidelines when handling spills and leaks can help these persons to meet that responsibility.

Many reasons exist for using pesticides properly and safely. The misuse of pesticides can have immediate, as well as long-term, effects upon humans, pets and wildlife, structures, and the environment. Misapplication can also waste considerable time and resources and result in failure to control the pest.

Pesticides must be used correctly to ensure the continued availability of a full range of products in the future. Every time an incident occurs through either misuse or carelessness, the future availability of pesticides is jeopardized. Prudent and safe use will help to minimize adverse regulatory actions.

There are important commonsense principles for the safe and effective use of pesticides. Some of the principles that were discussed throughout this section are listed below:

- Pesticides should be used only when necessary.
- The user should be familiar with current federal, state, and local pesticide laws and regulations.
- The label should be read to ensure a labeled site is being treated at the proper time and application rate.
- Children should not be allowed to play around pesticide application equipment or mixing, storage, and disposal areas.
- Pesticides should be locked in their original labeled containers inside a properly marked cabinet or storeroom, away from food and feed.
- Where possible, users should work in pairs when applying highly toxic pesticides.
- Only as much pesticide should be mixed as is intended for use.
- Appropriate protective clothing and equipment should be worn.
- The user should never eat, drink, or smoke while handling pesticides.

- Pesticide application equipment should be properly maintained and calibrated.
- Drift and/or runoff to nontarget areas should be avoided.
- Spilling pesticides on skin or clothing should be avoided.
- Should an accident occur, the user should wash immediately with soap and water. A clean water source and first aid supplies should be available at all times.
- If pesticide poisoning is suspected, the National Poison Center—(800) 222-1222, hospital emergency room, or a physician should be contacted. The product label should be taken to the hospital.
- Empty containers should be disposed of according to the label, in a manner that does not endanger humans, animals, or the environment.
- The user should bathe or shower after handling pesticides or pesticide-contaminated equipment. Clothes should be washed after applying pesticides; until laundered, such clothing must be handled with the same caution as the pesticides themselves. Pesticide-contaminated clothing should be kept separate from the family wash.

Summary

A variety of swimming pool chemicals is needed to keep your aquatic facility both safe and clean. What you have just read is perhaps the most comprehensive discussion on the safe handling of swimming pool chemicals.

Improper handling and storage of swimming pool chemicals cannot only cause damage and personal injury, it can ruin the reputation of your aquatic facility. Knowing the information will keep your facility, staff, and guests safe and sound.

Appendix A

General Information

A1
Resources

American Academy of Pediatrics	www.aap.org
American Association of Poison Control Centers	www.aapcc.org
American Alliance for Health, Physical Education, Recreation & Dance	www.aahperd.org
American Camping Association	www.acacamps.org
American Cancer Society	www.cancer.org
American Chemisty Council	www.c3.org
American National Standards Institute (ANSI)	www.ansi.org/
American Physical Therapy Association	www.apta.org
American Public Health Association	www.apha.org
American Red Cross	www.redcross.org
American Safety & Health Institute	www.hsi.com
American Swimming Coaches Association	www.swimmingcoach.org
American Swimming Pool and Spa Association	swimmingpooloperator.com/
American Wood Protection Association	www.awpa.com/
AMSE	www.asme.org/
Association of Aquatic Professionals	www.aquaticpros.org/
Aquatic Exercise Association	www.aeawave.com
Aquatic Safety Research Group	www.aquaticsafetygroup.com
Aquatic Therapy & Rehab Institute	www.atri.org
Aquatic Resources Network	www.aquaticnet.com
Aquatics International	www.aquaticsintl.com
Association of Pool & Spa Professionals	www.theapsp.org
ASTM International	www.astm.org/
Boys and Girls Club of America	www.bgca.org
Canadian Standards Association (CSA)	www.csa.ca
Centers for Disease Control and Prevention	www.cdc.gov/healthyswimming/
Consumer Product Safety Commission (CPSC)	www.poolsafety.gov, www.cpsc.gov
DeRosa Aquatic Consulting	www.derosaaquatics.com/
Disabled Sports USA	www.dsusa.org
Diversity in Aquatics	www.diversityinaquatics.com/
Ellis & Associates	www.jellis.com/
Every Child a Swimmer	www.everychildaswimmer.org
Federation Internationale de Natation	www.fina.org
Foundation for Aquatic Injury Prevention	www.aquaticisf.org
Foundation for Spinal Cord Injury Prevention	www.fscip.org
IDEA - Health and Fitness Association	www.ideafit.com
IHRSA - International Health, Rquet & Sportsclub Association	www.ihrsa.org
Independent Pool and Spa Service Association, Inc. (IPSSA)	www.ippsa.com
International Academy of Aquatic Art (IAAA)	www.aquatic-art.org
International Association for Sports & Leisure Facilities	www.iaks.info/en/iaks-actual/
International Association of Amusement Parks & Attractions	www.iaapa.org
International Journal of Aquatic Research and Education	journals.humankinetics.com/ijare
International Lifesaveing Federation	www.ilsf.org
International Recreational Water Professionals	www.irwp.org

IPFA - International Physical Fitness Assocation	www.ipfa.us
International Spa Association	www.experienceispa.com
International Swimming Hall of Fame	www.ishof.org
Jeff Ellis & Associates, Inc.	www.jellis.com
Jewish Community Centers Association	www.jcca.org
MSDS Hyper Glossary	www.ilpi.com/msds/ref/
National Aquatic Safety Company (NASCO)	nascoaquatics.com/
National Drowning Prevention Alliance (NDPA)	www.ndpa.org
National Electrical Manufacturers Association (NEMA)	www.nema.org
National Electrical Code - National Fire Protection Association (NFPA)	www.nfpa.org/
National Poison Control Center	www.poison.org
National Recreation and Park Association	www.nrpa.org
National Safe Boating Council	www.safeboatingcouncil.org
National Safety Council	www.nsc.org
National Safety Education Center	www.nsc.org/osh/oshtrain.htm
National Spa & Pool Institue of Canada	www.nspi.ca
National Sporting Goods Association	www.nsga.org
National Swimming Pool Foundation	www.nspf.org
New England Aquatics, Inc	www.newenglandaquatics.com
NIRSA National Intramural Recreational Sports Association	www.nirsa.org
NSF - The Public Health and Safety Company	www.nsf.org
Occupational Safety & Health Administration	www.osha.gov
Physical and Health Education Canada	www.phecanada.ca
Pool Management Group	www.poolmanagementgroup.com/
Professional Pool Operators of America	www.ppoa.org
Resort and Commercial Recreation Association	www.rcra.org/
Shallow Water Blackout Prevention	shallowwaterblackoutprevention.org
Special Olympics International	www.specialolympics.org
Starfish Aquatics Institute	www.starfishaquatics.org
Swim Lessons University	www.swimlessonsuniversity.com/
Texas Public Pool Council	www.tppc.org
The Chlorine Institute	www.chlorineinstitute.org
The Y	www.ymca.net
Underwriters Laboratories (UL)	www.ul.com
United States Diving	www.usdiving.org
United States Access Board	www.access-board.gov
United State Consumer Product Safety Commission	www.cpsc.gov
United Statees Environmental Protection Agency (EPA)	www.epa.gov
United States Lifesaving Association	www.usla.org
United States Masters Swimming	www.usms.org/
United States Olympic Committee	www.usoc.org
United States Swim School Association	www.usswimschools.org
United States Synchronized Swimming	www.usasynchro.org/
United States Water Fitness Association	www.uswfa.com
USA Swimming	www.usa-swimming.org
USA Water Polo	www.usawaterpolo.org
World Aquatic Babies & Children Newtwrk	www.wabcswim.com/
World Health Organization (WHO)	www.who.int
WHO Regional Office for the Americas	www.who.paho.org
World Swimming Coaches Association	www.swimmingcoach.org/wsca/
World Waterpark Association	www.waterparks.org

A2
Pool Sizing and Mathematical Conversion Charts

Pool Sizing

Proper determination of pool capacity is critical to how well you run your pool. Pool capacity tells you how much water balance, shocking, and problem treatment chemicals are required for your pool.

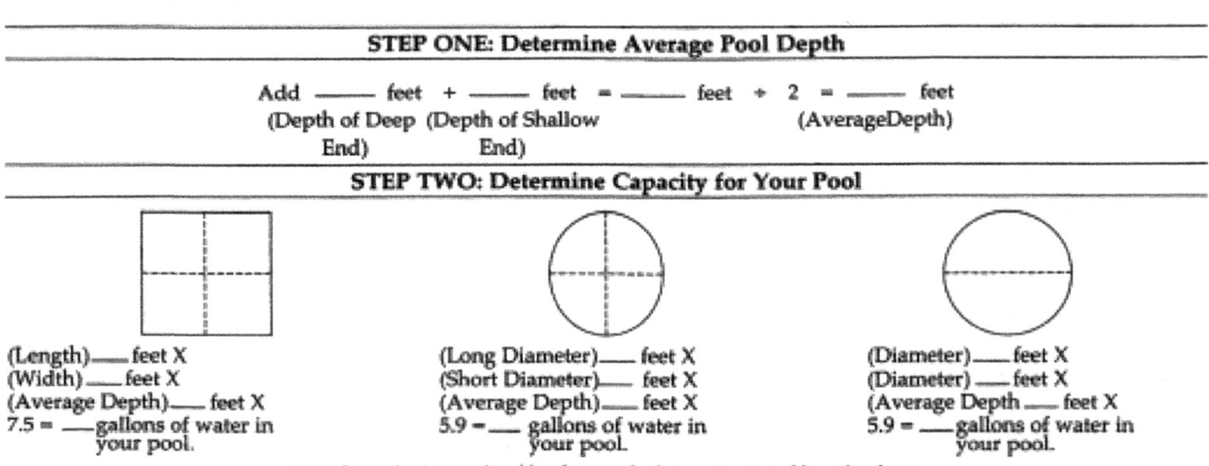

Using the two-step procedure below, one can quickly and easily determine pool capacity.

Pounds	X	0.454 =	Kilograms
Kilograms	X	2.205 =	Pounds
Ounces	X	28.35 =	Grams
Grams	X	0.0353 =	Ounces
Feet	X	0.305 =	Meters
Meters	X	3.729 =	Feet

U.S. Gallons	X	3.785	=	Liters
Liters	X	0.264	=	U.S. Gallons
U.S. Gallons	X	0.0038	=	Cubic Meters
Cubic Meters	X	264.2	=	U.S. Gallons
U.S. Gallons	X	0.833	=	Imperial Gallons
Imperial Gallons	X	1.201	=	U.S. Gallons

Mathematical Conversion Chart

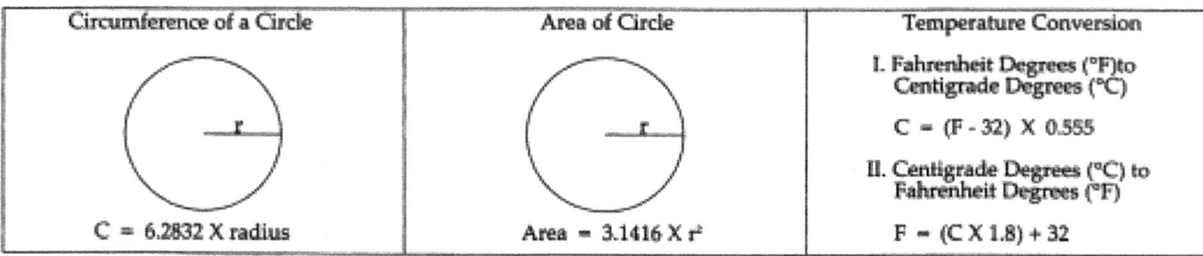

Courtesy BioLab, Decatur, Ga.

Pool area (sq ft)	Capacity (gal X 1000)	High-rate sand filters			Pressure DE filters			Cartridge filters		
		Filter area (sq ft)	GPM	Pump HP	Filter area	GPM	Pump HP	Filter area	GPM HP	Pump
<375	<15	1.4	25-30	$\frac{1}{2}$	15	25-30	$\frac{1}{2}$	45	30	$\frac{1}{2}$-$\frac{1}{2}$
375-600	15-25	2.2	30-45	$\frac{3}{4}$	20-25	35-50	$\frac{1}{2}$-$\frac{3}{4}$	70	50	$\frac{1}{2}$-$\frac{3}{4}$
600-850	25-35	3.1	45-60	$\frac{3}{4}$-1	30-35	55-70	$\frac{3}{4}$-1	100	75	$\frac{3}{4}$-1
850	35-45	4.9	75-95	1-1$\frac{1}{2}$	35-40	70-80	1-1$\frac{1}{2}$	135	95	1-1$\frac{1}{2}$

[1]Average depth 5.5 feet, turnover rate 8 hours. May vary from manufacturer to manufacturer.

Useful Mathematical Equations

Type Filter	Filter/Backwash Rates (GPM/sq ft filter area)		Filter additive	Notes
Slow rate/gravity (vacuum)	$\frac{1}{2}$-1	8-10	Alum (2 oz/sq. ft.)	Backwash one tank (or pit) at a time to achieve backwash rate.
Rapid rate sand	2-5	12-15	Alum (2 oz/sq. ft.)	(Same as preceding)
High rate sand	15-25[2]	15-25[2]	None	[2]20 GPM is recommended by most manufacturers. It is ineffective to run at a filter or backwash rate more or less than the recommended rate.
Pressure DE	1-2	1-2	DE (1$\frac{1}{2}$ oz-2$\frac{1}{2}$ oz/ 1 sq ft) or continuously feed 1-4 oz 1000 GPD	Backwash multiple tanks separately. Filtering at excessive flow shortens filter run.
Vacuum DE	2-3	External washing	Same as preceding	Above level tank requires 2 pumps. Filtering at excessive flow rate shortens filter run.
Cartridge surface	0.375-1	External	Small amounts of DE	The lower filter rate is required for public.

Courtesy of The Association of Pool & Spa Professionals

A3
Filtration System Sizes

Suggested Computations for Minimum Heights for Message Panel Wording Over Viewing Distances and Lighting Conditions

Safe Viewing Distance	Minimum Letter Height for FAVORABLE Reading Conditions	Minimum Letter height for UNFAVORABLE Reading Conditions
Less than 24 inches	$Ht\ (in) = \dfrac{View\ Distance}{150}$	$Ht.\ (in.) = \dfrac{View\ Distance}{75}$
24 to 96	$Ht\ (in) = \dfrac{View\ Distance}{300}$	$Ht.\ (in.) = \dfrac{View\ Distance}{150}$
Greater than 96 inch	$Ht\ (in) = \dfrac{View\ Distance}{400}$	$Ht.\ (in.) = \dfrac{View\ Distance}{300}$

NOTE: (1) For purposes of computation, use of upper case letter height is acceptable. Final computation of letter height for viewing distances close to 24 inches and 96 inches can be based on either formula as long as readability can be demonstrated. (2) Letter height values derived from the above computations are not absolute due to variables that affect readability such as letter style, letter weight, contrast, and illumination. Final determination of letter height should be based on a visual examination of the composed word message in the reasonably expected environment of the use or one very similar to the expected environment of use. (3) Letter heights minimums indicated for favorable reading conditions may, in some instances, be reduced further for application to small products, products containers, or products having limited surface area on which to apply the message. However, a lower case letter height of .05 in (1.2 mm) or 6-pt. type is approaching the lower limits of legibility and should be considered as the minimum height for safety messages.

From McCormick EJ: *Alphanumeric and related displays*, Human Factors in Engineering and Design 88-97, McGraw Hill, Inc. 1976.

A4
Barriers for Pools, Spas, and Hot Tubs

Application

The provisions of this document shall control the design of barriers for residential swimming pools, spas, and hot tubs. These design controls are intended to provide protection against potential drownings, and neardrownings of children under the age of five by restricting access to swimming pools, spas, and tubs.

Requirements

Section I. Outdoor Wwimming Pool

An outdoor swimming pool, including an inground, or on-ground pool, hot tub, or spa shall be provided with a barrier which shall comply with the following:

1. The top of the barrier shall be at least 48" above grade measured on the side of the barrier that faces away from the swimming pool. The maximum vertical clearance between grade and the bottom of the barrier shall be four inches measured on the side of the barrier that faces away from the swimming pool. Where the top of the pool structure is above grade, such as an above-ground pool, the barrier may be at ground level, such as the pool structure, or mounted on top of the pool structure. Where the barrier is mounted on top of the pool structure, the maximum vertical clearance between the top of the pool structure and the bottom of the barrier shall be four inches.

2. Openings in the barrier shall not allow passage of a 4" diameter sphere.

3. Solid barriers that do not have openings, such as a masonry or stone wall, shall not contain indentations or protrusions, except for normal construction tolerances and tooled masonry joints.

4. Where the barrier is composed of horizontal and vertical members and the distance between the tips of the horizontal members is less than 45", the horizontal members shall be located on the swimming pool side of the fence. Spacing between vertical members shall not exceed 1 3/4" in width. (This section is not intended to regulate fencing on top of above-ground/ on-ground pools where the pool structure forms a barrier at least 48" above grade.)

5. Where the barrier is composed of horizontal and vertical members and the distance between the tops of the horizontal members is 45" or more, spacing between vertical members shall not exceed four inches. Where there are decorative cutouts within vertical members, spacing within the cutouts shall not exceed 1 3/4" in width. (This section is not intended to regulate fencing on top of above-ground/on ground pools where the pool structure forms a barrier at least 48" above grade.

6. Maximum mesh size for chain-link fences shall be a 1 1/4" square unless the fence is provided with slats fastened at the top or the bottom which reduce the openings to no more than 1 3/4".

7. Where the barrier is composed of diagonal members, such as a lattice fence, the maximum opening formed by the diagonal members shall be no more than 1 3/4".

8. Access gates shall comply with the requirements of Section I, Paragraphs one through seven, and shall be equipped to accommodate a locking device. Pedestrian access gates shall open outward away from the pool and shall be self-closing and have a self-latching device. Gates other than pedestrian access gates shall have a self-latching device. Where the release mechanism of the self-latching device is located less than 54" from the bottom of the gate, (a) the release mechanism shall be located on the pool side of the gate at least 3" below the top of the gate and (b) the gate and barrier shall have no opening greater than 1/2" within 18" of the release mechanism.

9. Where a wall of a dwelling serves as part of the barrier, one of the following shall apply: (a) All doors with direct access to the pool through that wall shall be equipped with an alarm that produces an audible warning when the door and its screen, if present, are opened. The alarm shall sound continuously for a minimum of 30 seconds immediately after the door is opened. The alarm shall

have a minimum sound pressure rating of 85 dBA at 10'. and the sound of the alarm shall be distinctive from other household sounds such as smoke alarm, telephones and doorbells. The alarm shall automatically reset under all conditions. The alarm shall be equipped with manual rest means, such as touch pads or switches, to temporarily deactivate the alarm for a single opening from either direction. Such deactivation shall last for no more than 15 seconds. The deactivation touch pads or switches shall be located at least 45" above the threshold of the door. (b) The pool shall be equipped with a power safety cover that complies with ASTM F1346 listed below. (c) Other means of protection, such as self-closing doors with self-latching devices, which are approved by the governing body, shall be acceptable so long as the degree of protection afforded is not less than the protection afforded by (a) or (b) described above.

10. Where an above-ground/on-ground swimming pool structure is used as a barrier or where the barrier is mounted on top of the pool structure and the means of access is a ladder or steps that (a) the ladder or steps shall be capable of being secured, locked, or removed to prevent access or (b) the ladder or steps shall be surrounded by barrier that meets the requirements of Section I, Paragraphs 1(a) through 1(h). When the ladder or steps are secured, locked, or removed, any opening created shall not allow the passage of a 4" diameter sphere.

Section II. Indoor Swimming Pool
All walls surrounding an indoor swimming pool shall comply with Section I, Paragraph 9.

Section III. Prohibited Locations
Barriers shall be located so as to prohibit permanent structures, equipment or similar objects from being used to climb the barriers.

Section IV. Exemptions
A spa with a safety cover that complies with ASTM F1346 listed below shall be exempt from the provision of this-document. ASTM F1346 New Standard Performance Specification for Safety Covers and Labeling Requirements for all Covers for Swimming Pools, Spas and Hot Tubs.

Endorsed by U.S. Consumer Products Safety Commission and NSPI: Approved by the NSPI Executive Committee: July, 1991. Issued by CPSC Staff: 4-5-91.

A5
Cover and Pool Definitions

Covers: Something that covers, protects or shelters, or a combination thereof, a swimming pool, spa, or hot tub.

Hard-top cover: A cover used on pools, spas, or hot tubs that rests on the lip of the pool or spa deck (not a flotation cover) used as a barrier to users, for maintenance and thermal protection.

Winter cover: A cover that is secured around the perimeter of a pool or spa that provides a barrier to debris when the pool or spa is closed for the season.

Solar cover: A cover that, when placed on a pool or spa surface, increases the water temperature by solar activity and reduces evaporation.

Thermal cover: An insulating cover used to help prevent evaporation and heat loss from pools or spas.

Safety cover: As defined by ASTM F1346, Performance Specification for Safety Covers and Labeling Requirements for All Covers for Swimming Pools, Spas and Hot Tubs, a barrier (intended to be completely removed before entry of users), for swimming pools, spas, hot tubs or wading pools, attendant appurtenances and/or anchoring mechanisms which will—when properly labeled, installed, used and maintained in accordance with the manufacturers' published instructions—reduce the risk of drowning of children under 5 by inhibiting their access to the contained body of water, and by providing for the removal of any substantially hazardous level of collected surface water. These covers may be power or manual.

Pools

Permanently installed swimming pool: A pool that is constructed in the ground or in a building in such a manner that it cannot be readily disassembled for storage (refer to NSPI-1 Standard for Public Swimming Pools or NSPI-5 Standard for Residential Swimming Pools as applicable).

Above-ground pool (Type 0): A removable pool of any shape that has a minimum water depth of 36" and a maximum water depth of 48" at the wall. The wall is located on the surrounding earth and may be readily disassembled or stored and reassembled to its original integrity. Diving and the use of a water slide are prohibited. (Refer to NSPI-4 Standard for Above-ground Residential Swimming Pools.)

On-ground residential swimming pool (Type 0): A removable pool package whose walls rest fully on the surrounding earth and has an excavated area below the ground level where diving and the use of a water slide are prohibited. (Refer to NSPI-4 Standard for Aboveground Swimming Pools.) The slope adjacent to the shallow area shall have a maximum slope of 3:1, and the slope adjacent to the shallow area shall have a maximum slope of 3:1, and the slope adjacent to the side walls shall have a maximum slope of 1:1.

Inground swimming pool: Any pool whose sides rest in partial or full contact with the earth. (Refer to NSPI-5 Standard for Residential Swimming Pools or NSPI-1 Standard for Public Swimming Pools, as applicable.)

Residential pool: A residential pool shall be defined as any constructed pool, permanent or nonportable, that is intended for noncommercial use as a swimming pool by not more than three owner families and their guests and that is over 24" in depth, has a surface area exceeding 250 square feet and/or a volume over 3,250 gallons. (Refer to NSPI-5 Standard for Residential Swimming Pools.) Residential pools shall be further classified into types as an indication of the suitability of a pool for use with diving equipment.

Type 0: Any residential pool where the installation of diving equipment is prohibited.

Types I-V: Residential pools suitable for the installation of diving equipment by type. Diving equipment classified at a higher type may not be used on a pool of lesser type (i.e., Type III equipment on a Type II pool).

Commercial/public pool: Any pool, other than a residential pool, which is intended to be used for swimming or bathing and is operated by an owner, lessee, operator, licensee, or concessionaire, regardless of whether a fee is charged for use. References within the standard to various types of public pools (refer to NSPI-1 Standard for Public Swimming Pools) are defined by the following categories:

Class A (Competition pool): Any pool intended for use for accredited competitive aquatic events such as Federation Internationale De Natation Amateur (FINA), U.S. Swimming, U.S. Diving, National Collegiate Athletic Association (NCAA), National Federation of State High School Associations (NFSH-SA), etc. The pool may also be used for recreation.

Class B (Public pool): Any pool intended for public recreational use.

Class C (Semi-public pool): Any pool operated solely for and in conjunction with lodgings such as hotels, motels, apartments, condominiums, etc.

Class D (Other pool): Any pool operated for medical treatment, therapy, exercise, lap swimming, recreational play and other special purposes, including, but not limited to, wave or surf action pools, activity pools, splash pools, kiddie pools and play areas. These pools are not intended to be covered within the scope of NSPI standards. Public pools may be diving or non-diving. If diving, they shall be further classified into types as an indication of the suitability of a pool for use with diving equipment.

Types VI-XI: Public pools suitable for the installation of diving equipment by type. Diving equipment classified at a higher type may not be used on a pool of lesser type (i.e., Type VIII equipment on a Type VI pool).

Type N: A non-diving public pool (no diving allowed).

From ANSI/NPSI: Standard for public swimming pools, 1991, The Institute.

Appendix B
Pool and Spa Care and Maintenance

B1
Important Phone Numbers

Poison Control Center ____

Ambulance Service ____

Nearest Hospital ____

Family Doctor ____

Pool Dealer ____

Plumber ____

Electrician ____

Fire Department ____

B2
Your Pool Profile

Pool

Type of finish _______________________   Capacity in gallons _______________________

Shape _______________________   Dimensions (length x width x depth) _______________________

Piping size type _______________________   Date pool completed _______________________

Builder (name, address, telephone, email) _______________________

____

Heater

Type _______________________   Serial number _______________________

Make/model _______________________

Filter

Type _______________________   Make/model _______________________

Backwash pressure _______________________   Clean start-up pressure _______________________

Pump

Make _______________________   Motor make _______________________

Time clock (hours of operation) _______________________   Horsepower _______________________

Chlorination equipment   **Automatic pool cleaner**

Make/model _______________________   Make/model _______________________

Diving board

Length _______ Make/model _______   Diving depth _______

What else makes your pool different?

(Trees nearby, windy site, heavy use, small children, etc.) _______________________

____

Courtesy BioLab, Inc., Decatur, GA

B3
Your Pool Capacity

AVERAGE POOL DEPTH

Your pool capacity will determine the initial amount of sanitizer, stabilizer and other chemicals you might need. Use the easy formulas that follow to determine your pool capacity.

Depth of deep end   +   Depth of shallow end
=   total feet   ÷   2   =   AVERAGE POOL DEPTH

POOL CAPACITY FORMULAS

Oval Pool

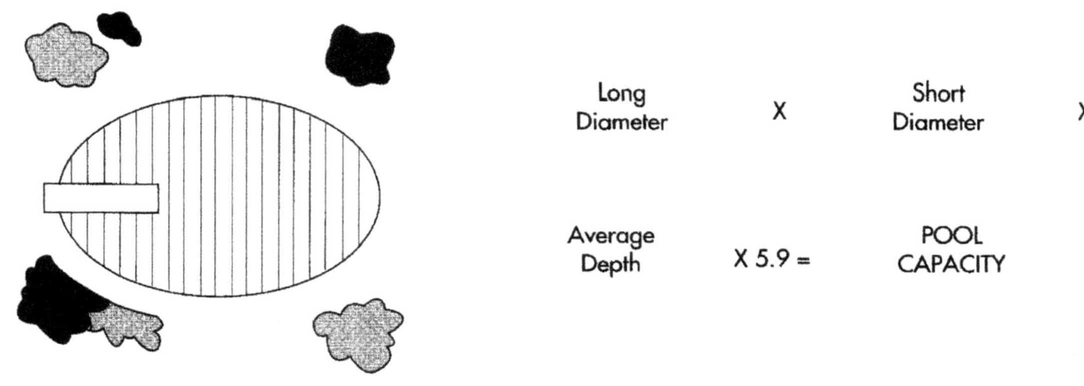

Long Diameter   X   Short Diameter   X

Average Depth   X 5.9 =   POOL CAPACITY

Rectangular/Square Pool

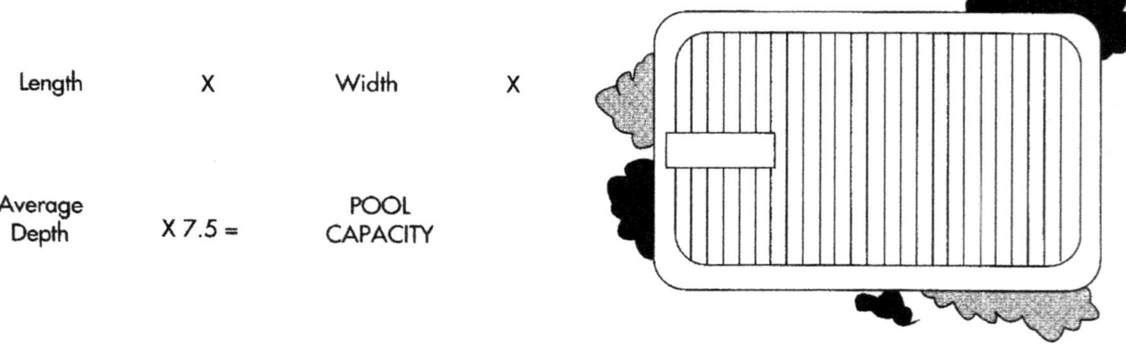

Length   X   Width   X

Average Depth   X 7.5 =   POOL CAPACITY

Circular Pool

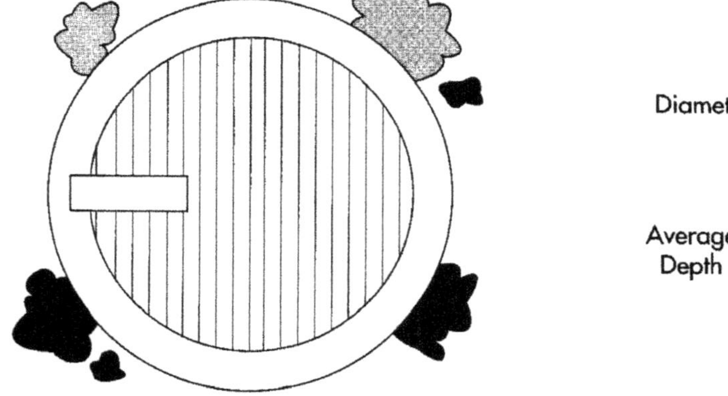

Diameter   X   Diameter   X

Average Depth   X 5.9 =   POOL CAPACITY

B4
Service Technician's Record Form

Customer name ___________________________________							
Pool volume ___________________________________							
Technician ___________________________________							
Initial observations:							
Date							
Time							
Weather							
Water level							
Inlet check							
Debris in pool							
Algae							
Water chemistry measurements:							
Water temperature							
pH							
Total alkalinity							
Calcium							
Cyanuric acid							
Saturation index							
Chemical adjustments made:							
Add chlorine							
Automatic feeder setting							
Add sodium bicarbonate							
Add cyanuric acid							
Add algicide							
Other							
Maintenance:							
Skim							
Brush							
Vacuum							
Scrub tile							
Empty skimmer baskets							
Empty filter strainer							
Empty pump lint trap							
Filter PSI							
Filter backwash							
Pump primed							
Add/drain water							
Water leaks							
Notes:							

B5
Problem/Incentive Log

DAY: M T W T F S S		DATE:
POOL:	CODE:	
	POOL OPENED LATE	LIST TIME:
	GUARD ARRIVED LATE	LIST TIME:
	POOL CLOSED EARLY	LIST TIME:
	HEALTH INSPECTION	PASS OR FAIL
	GUARD NOT IN CHAIR/WATCHING POOL	
	GUARD NOT IN UNIFORM	
	FAIR OR POOR ON FIELD REPORT	
	FAIR OR POOR ON EVALUATION	MIDSEASON END
	FAILURE TO OBTAIN SUB FOR TIME OFF	
	ASSISTED STAFFING	
OTHER/COMMENTS:		
EMP #:	NAME:	
EMP #:	NAME:	
EMP #:	NAME:	
EMP #:	NAME:	
COMPLETED BY:	ENTERED BY:	

Courtesy American Pool Service, Beltsville, Md.

B6

Swimming Pool Opening Record Form

☐ Review the pool's winterizing record form and any recommendations made during winterizing service.
☐ Remove pool cover, clean cover, treat with cover conditioner and store.
☐ Note condition of cover: ____
☐ Storage Location: ____

1. Pool structure check:
☐ Surface interior finish—plaster
☐ condition & stains
☐ Liner condition
☐ Title & grouting

☐ Coping
☐ Deck
☐ Drains
☐ Fence/gate
Notes: _______________________

Notes: _______________________
____

2. Drain & flush lines remove plugs from plumbing:
☐ All pipes & hoses
☐ Skimmer line
☐ Main drain line
☐ Return lines

3. Drain & flush equipment; replace equipment drain plugs:
☐ Pump
☐ Filter
☐ Heater

☐ Other accessories: ___________
____
____

4. Electrical preparations:
☐ Install GFCI's
☐ Replace pool light in housing
☐ Check electrical panel & grounding
☐ Replace electrical fuses
☐ Turn on electricity

5. Opening preparations:
☐ Fill pool with water to skimmer level
☐ Reinstall skimmer basket
☐ Reinstall pump motor (or remove weatherproof cover)
☐ Turn on LP gas
☐ Set pool heater for thermostat

☐ Set pool timer for filtering.

6. Start & check all equipment:
☐ Motor
☐ Pump
☐ Filter
☐ Heater (check for air locks)
☐ Time clock
☐ Automatic cleaning equipment
☐ Piping/valves

7. Install accessories:
☐ Ladder
☐ Hand rails
☐ Diving board
☐ Safety line
☐ Ropes
☐ Safety equipment
☐ List equipment for repair:
____
____

8. Clean pool:
☐ Skim/net
☐ Brush
☐ Vacuum
☐ Scrub tile
☐ Backwash filter if needed
☐ Acid wash if plaster is excessively stained
☐ Replace test reagents to ensure accurate results

9. Test water chemistry:
☐ pH
☐ Total chlorine (bromine etc.)
☐ Free chlorine
☐ Cyanuric acid
☐ Total Alkalinity
☐ Calcium hardness
☐ Total Dissolved Solids

10. Add chemicals:
☐ Chlorine (Bromine, etc.)
☐ Cyanuric acid
☐ Sodium bicarbonate
☐ Algicide or shock treatment
Others: _______________________

NOTES:
____
____
____
____
____
____

B7
Water and Energy Conservation Checklist

TO SAVE WATER AROUND YOUR POOL AND YARD

☐ 1. **Repair any leaks.** Even a small leak in either the equipment or the structural shell can cause substantial water. Just 1-1/2 inches a day in a 15-by-30 foot pool wastes approximately 102,000 gallons per year!

☐ 2. **Buy and use a cover.** Covers reduce water loss due to normal evaporation.

☐ 3. **Clean your filter.** If possible, manually clean your filter. You'll do a more thorough job and use much less water. The average backwash uses between 250 and 1,000 gallons of water—without completely cleaning your filter.

☐ 4. **Prohibit diving, splashing, and water fights.** Boisterous play causes a large amount of water loss from "splash-out."

☐ 5. **Control filter cycle and chemical use.** Use the least possible filtration time and test/treat chemically frequently. Regular care will keep the pool/spa cleaner and will avoid the need to drain and refill to correct conditions caused by neglect.

☐ 6. **Reduce heater temperature.** If you have a heater, reduce the pool/spa heater temperature because warmer water evaporates more quickly.

☐ 7. **Plug the overflow line when swimming.** If your pool is equipped with an overflow line, this prevents water loss through the line when the pool is in use.

☐ 8. **Watch when filling.** Keep an eye on the water level when filling the pool/spa. Forgetting to shut off the water can cause costly waste.

☐ 9. **Turn off tile-spray on automatic pool cleaner.** This device's splashing causes water loss by evaporation. Overspraying can send water right out of the pool.

☐ 10. **Plant drought-resistant native trees and plants in the yard.**

☐ 11. **Water early and late.** If allowed, watering of lawns should be done in the early morning or evening, when evaporation is at a minimum.

☐ 12. **Sweep instead of hosing off.** Sweep decks, patios, driveways, and sidewalks instead of hosing.

TO CONSERVE HEAT:

☐ 1. **Cover your pool.** The proper cover, kept in place when the pool is not in use, will significantly reduce water lost to evaporation. Also, it cuts heat loss by 50-70 percent. Check with your local NSPI member for the most effective cover for your needs.

☐ 2. **Swim at 78° F.** The ideal swimming temperature for recreational purposes is 78°. If you have requirements that call for a warmer temperature, such as children or elderly people using the pool, adjust the temperature to those specific needs, but no higher. Lowering the water temperature from 82° to 78°—a mere 4°—will reduce energy consumption by 40 percent, with a corresponding cost savings.

☐ 3. **Only heat when you use.** If you use your pool only on weekends or special occasions, don't heat between uses. Turn your heater off or set your thermostat at 68° or lower depending on the period between uses. Turn your heater on the night before or the morning of the day of use depending on the heat use. If you go away on a trip, turn your heater off.

☐ 4. **Shelter your pool.** Protect the surface of your pool from wind—but not from sunlight— by careful positioning of trees, plantings, fences, and cabanas. The difference between a fully sheltered pool and one exposed to a "mild breeze" of seven miles per hour can be 400 percent higher energy usage.

☐ 5. **Maintain your heater.** Have your pool service company do an annual heater inspection. A properly maintained heater is an energy-efficient appliance. Have your pool site inspected to see if an active solar collector system should be a good investment for you.

☐ 6. **Backwash only when needed.** Be sure to follow your filter manufacturer's instructions concerning backwashing. Backwashing more frequently than necessary wastes water while failing to backwash when needed wastes energy.

TO CONSERVE ELECTRICITY

☐ 1. **Use a time clock.** Use a time clock to manage the daily operating period of the circulation pump and of the pool cleaner booster pump.

☐ 2. **Control filtration.** Reduce filtration time to six hours per day. Depending on your previous usage, this can save you 50 percent or more of the energy used for filtration. If your water should lose clarity, increase filtration time in one-half-hour increments until the pool water is sparkling.

☐ 3. **Control use of automatic cleaner.** As with filtration, establish a minimum cleaning time (two to four hours daily) and expand this time on unusually heavy load situations. Be sure to run the cleaner only when the filter is running. If you have a pool cover, follow the pool cleaner manufacturer's instructions about operating the cleaner in conjunction with a cover.

☐ 4. **Clean strainer frequently.** Be sure to remove foreign matter from the pump strainer baskets and the skimmer regularly. Water will circulate more efficiently.

☐ 5. **Use pool lighting when needed.** Lighting should always be used for safety—when people are in and around the pool after dark. Use of pool and patio lighting "just for atmosphere" should be reduced.

TO CONSERVE CHEMICALS

☐ 1. **Disinfect in the evening.** Add chlorine or other disinfectant in the evening while the filter is operating. With reduced filtration time, it is particularly important to maintain an adequate disinfectant residual at all times.

☐ 2. **Keep chemistry balanced.** Keep pool water chemistry in balance and check regularly. Maintain pool pH between 7.2 and 7.8. Maintain spa pH between 7.2 and 7.6.

☐ 3. **Stabilize outdoor pool water.** Keep outdoor pool water stabilized to reduce chemical consumption. Maintain a minimum of 30 ppm of stabilizer.

☐ 4. **Trim foliage.** Trim back excess foliage around pool and keep deck areas clean to reduce chemical and filtering requirements.

Courtesy of The Association of Pool & Spa Professionals

B8
Water Loss Procedure Checklist

SIGNS AND SYMPTOMS OF SWIMMING POOL/SPA LEAKS

Normal water loss will occur from evaporation due to wind and heat. If your pool or spa loses 1/4" of water or more from its normal level in 24 hours you may have a leak.

To detect water loss, the pool/spa should be set to its normal operating level, marked with a permanent pen, and then checked in 24 hours. To prove that your water loss is not due to evaporation, do this simple check. Place a bucket of water (from the pool) in the pool, mark the water level in both, and leave for 24 hours. If the water level in the pool drops more than the bucket's, you have a leak.

High water bill (if pool has an automatic refill).

Algae or discoloration in the pool or spa water. This indicates an imbalance in the chemicals. This can occur then the water level doesn't stay constant, due to a leak. Consult a local pool service expert.

Loose or falling tiles or cracking of the cement pool deck indicates a possible leak because the surrounding ground is becoming unsettled.

Pool settling into the ground, cracks or gaps in bond beam.

If the pool has an automatic filler that is constantly releasing water.

You notice standing water, soft mushy spots, or uneven grass growth around the pool area.

Poor suction and/or bad circulation may indicate a leak.

NORMAL ACCEPTED LOSS & EVAPORATION: (1 to 1-3/4" per week, depending on region & pool/spa situation.)

ESTIMATED LOSS: Per day:

                        Per week:

WATER BILL REFLECTS: Gallons per Month:

                        Est. Domestic Use:

                        Est. Pool Loss:

POOL BUILDER:

APPROX. YEAR BUILT:

SIZE: Depth: Gallonage:

Concrete: Vinyl: Fiberglass:

ANY PREVIOUS LEAKS?

WHERE:

ANY CRACKS IN POOL SHELL, TILE, SKIMMER, GROUTING:

WHERE:

AT WHAT LEVEL IN THE POOL DOES THE WATER STOP:

IS THERE HYDROSTATIC PRESSURE UNDER THE POOL:

ESTIMATE TO REPAIR LEAKS ARE STRICTLY ON A TIME AND MATERIAL BASIS. OUR LABOR CHARGE IS $____________PER TRIP AND/OR PER HOUR PER WORKER. ANY CHECKING THAT YOU CAN DO INITIALLY WILL DECREASE THE COST. REMEMBER, YOU MAY HAVE MORE THAN ONE LEAK. WE CANNOT GUARANTEE THAT THE REPAIR OF THE OBVIOUS LEAK WILL INCLUDE REPAIR OF EVERY LEAK.

Courtesy of The Association of Pool & Spa Professionals

B9
Lifeguard Application

Name:____   Social Security#_______-_______-_______
Address:____Phone #:____________________________

Required Certifications	issued at	expiration date
Lifeguarding (ARC/YMCA/other)	____________________	____________________
CPR (NSC/ARC/AHA)	____________________	____________________
First Aid Training (type:__________)	____________________	____________________
Lifeguard Training (ARC/YMCA)	____________________	____________________

Supplemental Training		
CPO (NSPF/YMCA)	____________________	____________________
WSI (ARC/YMCA)	____________________	____________________
SCUBA (PADI/YMCA/NAUI)	____________________	____________________
OTHER: ______________________	____________________	____________________
______________________	____________________	____________________
______________________	____________________	____________________

PREVIOUS LIFEGUARDING/SUPERVISION EXPERIENCE

position	place	supervisor	date
______________	______________	______________	______________
______________	______________	______________	______________
______________	______________	______________	______________

Reference Listing

Name	Title	Phone
______________	______________	______________
______________	______________	______________
______________	______________	______________
______________	______________	______________

Interviewed by:_______________________________________   date:____________________________

Applicant Status: hired (full time):__________hired (substitute):__________
          pending:__________stipulations:____________________________

Courtesy Berry Associates, Chestertown, Md.

B10
Lifeguard Evaluation

Personnel: Lifeguard/Lifeguard Supervisor

Lifeguard being evaluated_________________________ by_______________________________Aquatic Coordinator

Observation Period:________________to__________ Date of Evaluation____

Key: "OK" = Satisfactory   "X" = Needs Improvement

CATEGORIES	RATING	COMMENTS
I. PERSONALITY	_________	
A. Exercises prudent judgment _______		
B. Maintains personal hygiene _______		
C. Maintains poise and composure _______		
D. Maintains a professional attitude _______		
II. PREPARATION	_________	
A. Holds current ALS certificate _______		
B. Holds current CPR certificate _______		
C. Holds current FA certificate _______		
D. Holds current Lifeguard Training certificate _______		
E. Attends all in-service meetings _______		
III. TASK RELATED SKILLS	_________	
A. Communicates with peers _______		
B. Communicates with superiors _______		
C. Operates within the framework of the CSC Policy Manual _______		
D. Understands emergency procedures and is able to execute them _______		
E. Keeps abreast of current safety techniques _______		
IV. SAFETY SKILLS	_________	
A. Demonstrates an advanced level of fitness _______		
B. Demonstrates an ability to perform rescue techniques _______		
C. Demonstrates an advanced level of CPR and resuscitation ability _______		

Courtesy Berry Associates, Chestertown, Md.

B11
Lifeguard Daily Activity Sheet

Submitted by________________________________ To:__________________________________

Date:__________________________________

Swim Center Staff	Position	Hours on Duty
___________________	___________________	___________________
___________________	___________________	___________________
___________________	___________________	___________________
___________________	___________________	___________________
___________________	___________________	___________________
___________________	___________________	___________________

Chemical Readings

Ideal	9am	11am	1pm	3pm	5pm
pH 7.2-7.8	______	______	______	______	______
FAC 1.0-1.5	______	______	______	______	______
TA 80-120ppm	______	______	______	______	______
CH 150-300ppm	______	______	______	______	______
H2o Temp. 26c/80f	______	______	______	______	______

Programming/Pool Load

Hour	Activity	Guests	Classes	Events	Members	Total
7am						
8am						
9am						
10am						
11am						
12n						
1pm						
2pm						
3pm						
4pm						
5pm						
6pm						
7pm						
8pm						
9pm						
Program Totals						

Special Events:

B12
Aquatic Staff In-Service Training Form

Date:_____________________________Time:_______________________________Group: (circle one)

lifeguards
instructors
management

In service topic:____

Staff Present: ____________________   ____________________   ____________________
                  ____________________   ____________________   ____________________
                  ____________________   ____________________   ____________________
                  ____________________   ____________________   ____________________
                  ____________________   ____________________   ____________________

In-Service Trainers Present:____

Specific Topic Areas/Skills:
____
____
____
____
____

Comments:

B13
Accident Report Form

DIRECTIONS: Fill out both sides this form completely and accurately. Place this copy on the Aquatic Director's desk. Copies will be made and sent to the offices checked below.

Personal Information:

1. Name: ____ Age:_____________________
   Home Address: ____
   Phone:____

2. In Guest: Sponsor's Name:____

3. Date of Accident:_____________________________________ Time:_________________________

4. Pool activity at time of accident: mark with an (X)
   Sport practice_______________________   Recreation Swim_____________________
   Activity Class (name)____________   Pool load at time of accident:_________

5. What specifically was the person doing at the time of the accident?
   ____
   ____

6. Was there supervision at the time of the accident?   yes____________   no____________
   By whom?____

7. Part of the body injured:____
   ____

8. Type of injury sustained: ____

9. Detailed description of accident: ____

10. What First Aid was administered?____

11. Was EMS notified?   yes______________   no______________

12. Person taken to hospital: yes____________   no____________   Taken by:_________________

13. Did person refuse medical assistance? If yes, Victim's signature________________________________

14. Did person return to activity?   yes____________   no____________   Time____________

Report submitted by:_______________________________________   Title:_________________________

Report received by: ______________________________________   Title: Aquatic Coordinator

Courtesy Berry Associates, Chestertown, Md.

B14
Training Form

OSHA Bloodborne Pathogens Standard

In the fall of 1991, OSHA enacted regulation 29 CFR 1910.1030 Bloodborne Pathogens. The OSHA regulation endeavors to appreciable diminish occupationally acquired infections with Hepatitis B Virus (HBV), Human Immune Deficiency Virus (HIV), and other bloodborne diseases that have public health significance. The effective date of the new regulation was June 15, 1992 with various provisions phased in within 60 to 120 days following that date. The following, summarizes the major requirements.

Scope of the Regulation

Public Swimming Pools are impacted by this regulation, specifically employees whose work duties may reasonably be anticipated to involve skin, eye, mucous membrane, or parenteral contact with blood or other potentially infectious materials.

HBV vaccination, and post-exposure evaluation/follow-up

Public Swimming Pools must make HBV vaccination available free of charge to all employees considered immediate care first aid responders under the scope of the regulation. This fee is to be absorbed by the employing facility or firm for lifeguards. These entities must provide such vaccination within 10 working days of initial job assignment, unless the employee has already received HBV vaccine. Because of an array of privacy and religious concerns, OSHA does not mandate that the employee receive the vaccination, however, employees declining the vaccination must sign the official HBV Vaccine Declination. The employee may relinquish the declination at any time, and then the employing facility or firm must provide HBV vaccine at no cost to the employee.

Employees reporting an exposure incident (specific eye, mouth, other mucus membrane, non-intact skin, or parenteral contact with blood or other potentially infectious material that resulted from the performance of job duties) are to be provided free of charge a confidential post-exposure medical evaluation and subsequent medical follow-up including port-exposure prophylaxis and counseling. Public swimming pools must provide for collection of blood to establish HBV and HIV serological status from the exposed employee and, if applicable, the source individual.

Exposure Control Plan

Public Swimming Pools must establish and begin implementation of a written Exposure Control Plan by June 15, 1992.

Information and Training Requirements

All lifeguards, swim coaches or other employees falling under the scope of the regulation must participate in a training program ASAP and at least annually thereafter. After that date new employees must receive training at the time of initial assignment.

By signing this information form, the following employees acknowledge that they have read the OSHA Bloodborne Pathogen Standard and further understand their rights and limitations as employees who may be impacted by this regulation.

Date of Training Session:_________________________________   Session Leader:_________________________________

Employee:____   Date:_______________________

Employee:____   Date:_______________________

Employee:____   Date:_______________________

Employee:____   Date:_______________________

Courtesy Berry Associates, Chestertown, Md.

B15
Swimming Pool Emergency Phone List

_____________________________   Aquatic Coordinator_____________________________

_____________________________   Facility Manager _____________________________

_____________________________   Owner/Operator _____________________________

Emergency Medical System Dial 911

Local Police   _____________________________

<u>Special Situation Procedures</u>

Situation: Intoxicated person.
Procedure: Ask the person to leave the pool area. Call local police.

Situation: Thievery.
Procedure: Call local police immediately.

Situation: Indecent exposure.
Procedure: Diplomatically suggest covering up or leaving the pool area.
                In the event of willful exposure, call local police immediately.

Situation: Abuse, disorders.
Procedure: In the event that a patron loses control and uses physical or verbal abuse, call local police and have the
                individual removed from the pool.

Situation: Fire.
Procedure: Pull the fire alarm, evacuate the pool area and locker rooms and dial 911 to report the fire.

Situation: Power failure (evenings).
Procedure: Clear the pool area and check the pool bottom. If normal power is not restored in 10 minutes call the
                Coordinator to help secure the facility.

Situation: Electrical Storms (summer).
Procedure: Prohibit access to pool until storm passes.

Courtesy Berry Associates, Chestertown, Md.

B16
Employee MSDA Training

Date:_________________________________   Trainer/Instructor:___________________

____

Topics:

- Special handling procedures for swimming pool chemicals

- Storage practices for swimming pool chemicals

- Potential health related hazards

- Swimming pool chemical interactions
        Common swimming pool chemicals
                Sodium Hypochlorite
                Calcium Hypochlorite
                Bromine
                Muriatic Acid
                Sodium Bisulfate
                Sodium Bicarbonate
                Sodium Bicarbonate
                Test Kit reagents

- General Protection Practices

- Emergency Care

Employees present for training session:

____________________________________   ____________________________________
____________________________________   ____________________________________
____________________________________   ____________________________________
____________________________________   ____________________________________

Training Verified by:____Date: ______________

Forward one copy to your insurance carrier

Courtesy Berry Associates, Chestertown, Md.

B17
Hot Tub Installation Site Checklist

☐ Check local building and safety codes and, if required, obtain permits, before starting installation.

☐ Make sure the hot tub will be placed on a level spot on structurally sound material, such as concrete, treated wood, or manufactured support pads. For deck installation, check for adequate deck supports.

☐ Make sure the chosen installation site is not too close to trees or foliage, where falling leaves or brush may fall into the hot tub, or where roots may cause problems.

☐ Check for adequate water runoff and drainage. Do not install a hot tub where it will block a designed runoff area.

☐ Make sure tub and equipment sites are accessible and properly ventilated.

☐ Determine the direction of the prevailing wind. If the hot tub is not protected from the wind, operating expenses for heating will go up (see *Chapter 8-1: Heaters*).

☐ Check for overhead wires (see *Chapter 4-6: Electrical Safety Requirements*).

☐ Check for underground cables, septic tanks, and water and gas lines.

☐ Check for ease of access from the house to the tub.

☐ Check any gates that provide entry. Gates must be self-latching and self-closing (see *Chapter 1-1: Drowning and Accident Prevention*).

☐ Check for proper fencing, if required.

☐ Check for privacy from surrounding areas.

☐ Check that required permits are in order, or make appropriate additions.

☐ Make sure there is access to electrical service and that there is available power. Electrical service must have a proper disconnect box (see *Chapter 4-4: Basic Terms/Components Used in Actual Circuits*).

Courtesy of The Association of Pool & Spa Professional, 2011

B18
Spa Service Record Form

Customer name____

Customer address____

Spa volume____

Initial observations:

Date	
Time	
Technician	

Water chemistry tests:

Water temperature	
pH	
Sanitizer level	
Ozone	
Total dissolved solids	
Iron	
Copper	
Other	

Chemical adjustments:

Add sanitizer	
Automatic feeder setting	
Add sodium bicarbonate	
Add cyanuric acid	
Add calcium	
Add mineral remover	
Add calcium remover	
Add algicide	
Shock treatment	
Other	

Maintenance:

Vacuum spa	
Clean tile	
Backwash filter	
Change filter cartridge	
Clean filter	
Drain/refill spa	
Clean/polish spa	

Equipment check:

Spa Pac	
Pump/motor	
Filter	
Heater	
blower	
Jets	
Chemical feeder	
Ozonator	
Control Panel	
Timer	
GFCI	
Light	
Cover	

Notes:________

Appendix C
Pool Chemistry

C1
Tests

IMPORTANT NOTES

1. Rinse sample tubes thoroughly before and after each test.
2. Obtain sample approximately 18" below surface of water.
3. Hold bottle vertically when dispensing.
4. Protect kit from direct sunlight and temperature extremes.
5. Read precautions on all labels carefully. KEEP OUT OF REACH OF CHILDREN.

Free Chlorine (FC) Test

1. Fill test cell to mark with water to be tested.
2. Add five drops R-0001 DPD Reagent #1 and five drops R-0002 DPD Reagent #2. Cap and mix.
3. Wipe dry and place in comparator WITH FROSTED SIDE FACING OPERATOR.
4. Match color in test cell with a color standard. Record as parts per million (ppm) free chlorine (FC).
5. Save sample for total chlorine (TC) test.

Total Chlorine (TC) Test

1. Use treated sample from FC test.
2. Add five drops R-0003 DPD Reagent #3. Cap and mix.
3. Wipe dry and place in comparator WITH FROSTED SIDE FACING OPERATOR.
4. Match color. Record as ppm total chlorine (TC).

Combined Chlorine (CC) Test

1. Subtract FC from TC. Record as ppm combined chlorine(CC). Formula: TC-FC = CC. Refer to Chlorine Tables for adjustment.

NOTE: Use test cell #4025 for high chlorine (to 10 ppm).

Bromine Test

1. Fill test cell to mark with water to be tested.
2. Add five drops R-0001 DPD Reagent #1 and five drops R-0002 DPD Reagent #2. Cap and mix.
3. Wipe dry and place in comparator WITH FROSTED SIDE FACING OPERATOR.
4. Match color in test cell with a color standard. Record as parts per million (ppm) bromine. Refer to manufacturer's instructions for proper adjustments.

NOTE: Use test cell #4025 for high bromine (to 10 ppm).

pH Test

1. Fill test cell (#4024) to 11.5 mL mark with water to be tested.
2. Using a 1.0 mL pipet (#4030), add 0.5 mL R-1003J Phenol Red Indicator. Cap and mix.
3. Wipe dry and place in comparator WITH FROSTED SIDE FACING OPERATOR.
4. Match color in test cell with a color standard. Record as pH units. If sample color is between two values, pH is average of the two.
5. Save sample for either acid demand test (if pH needs to be LOWERED), or base demand test (if pH needs to be RAISED).

Acid Demand Test

1. Use treated sample from pH test.
2. Add R-0853 Acid Demand Reagent dropwise, mixing and comparing after each drop, until desired pH is reached on comparator. Keep count of drops added. Refer to Acid Demand Tables for correct amount of acid to add to LOWER pH.

Base Demand Test

1. Use treated sample from pH test.
2. Add R-0862 Base Demand Reagent dropwise, mixing and comparing after each drop, until desired pH is reached on comparator. Keep count of drops added. Refer to Base Demand Tables for correct amount of soda ash to add to RAISE pH.

NOTE: pH Indicator, Acid Demand and Base Demand Reagents used for Midget and Slide Comparator Systems are not inter changeable with 2000 Series Comparator Blocks. That is: reagent R-0004, R-0005, and R-0006 cannot be substituted for reagents R-1003J, R-0853, and R-0862.

Total Alkalinity Test

1. Fill sample tube (#9198) to 25 mL mark with water to be tested.
2. Add two drops R-0007 Thiosulfate N/10. Swirl to mix.
3. Add five drops R-0008 Total Alkalinity Indicator. Swirl to mix. Sample should turn green.
4. Add R-0009 Sulfuric Acid .12N dropwise, swirling and counting after each drop, until color changes from green to red.

5. Multiply drops in Step four to 10. Record as parts per million (ppm) total alkalinity as calcium carbonate. Refer to Total Alkalinity Tables for adjustment.

Calcium Hardness Test

1. Fill sample tube (#9198) to 25 mL mark with water to be tested.
2. Add 20 drops R-0010 Calcium Buffer. Swirl to mix.
3. Add 5 drops R-0011L Calcium Indicator Liquid (or 1 level dipper R0011P Calcium Indicator Powder). Swirl to mix. Sample will turn red if calcium hardness is present.
4. Add R-0012 Hardness Reagent dropwise, swirling and counting after each drop, until color changes from red to blue.
5. Multiply drops in Step four by 10. Record as parts per million (ppm) calcium hardness as calcium carbonate. Refer to Calcium Hardness Tables for adjustment.

Total Hardness Test

1. Fill sample tube (#9198) to 25 mL mark with water to be tested.
2. Add 10 drops R-0854 Total Hardness Reagent. Swirl to mix. Sample should turn red.
3. Add R-0012 Hardness Reagent dropwise, swirling and counting after each drop, until color changes from red to blue.
4. Multiply drops in Step three by 10. Record as parts per million (ppm) total hardness as calcium carbonate.

Magnesium Hardness Test

1. Subtract CH from TH. Record as ppm magnesium hardness (MH). Formula: TH-CH=MH.

Cyanuric Acid Test

1. Fill CYA dispensing bottle (#9194) to 15 mL mark with water to be tested.
2. Add R-0013 Cyanuric Acid Reagent to neck. Cap and mix for 30 seconds. Sample will turn cloudy if cyanuric acid is present.
3. Slowly transfer cloudy solution to CYA view tube (#9193), while looking down through solution, until black dot on bottom of CYA view tube just disappears.
4. Read CYA view tube at liquid level. Record as parts per million (ppm) cyanuric acid.

Copper Test

1. Fill 11.5 mL test cell (#4024) to 11.5 mL mark with water to be tested.
2. Using a 1.0 mL pipet (#4030), add 0.5 mL R-0860 Copper Reagent #1. Using a separate 1.0 mL pipet, add 0.5ml: R-0861 Copper Reagent #2. Cap and mix.
3. Wipe dry and place in comparator WITH FROSTED SIDE FACING OPERATOR. WAIT FIVE MINUTES.
4. Match color in test cell with a color standard. Record as parts per million (ppm) copper.

Iron Test

1. Fill 11.5 mL test cell (#4024) to 11.5ml mark with water to be tested.
2. Using a 1.0 mL pipet (#4030), add 0.5 mL R-0851 Iron Reagent #1. Cap and mix. WAIT TWO MINUTES.
3. Using a separate 1.0 mL pipet, add 1.0 mL R-0852 Iron Reagent #2. Cap and Mix.
4. Wipe dry and place in comparator WITH FROSTED SIDE FACING OPERATOR.
5. Match color in test cell with a color standard. Record as parts per million (ppm) iron.

Courtesy Taylor Technologies, Sparks, Md.

C2
Certified Maintenance Specialist

SAMPLE CHEMICAL OPERATIONAL PARAMETERS [1]				
Parameter	Minimum	Ideal	Maximum	Comments
1. DISINFECTANT LEVELS				
Free Chlorine, ppm				
All public pools, except as listed below	1.5	1.5–3.0	5.0	In a pool, hot weather/heavy use may require operation at or near maximum levels.
Spas	3.0	3.0–5.0	10.0	
Activity/Interactive/ Wading pools	3.0	3.0–5.0	10.0	Regular superchlorination is recommended. (See Remedial Practices below.)
Continuous water course "rivers"	2.0	2.0–5.0	5.0	
Dual use pools	2.0	2.0–5.0	5.0	In a spa during hours of operation, test the water hourly and record results. Maintain this range continually and shock treat at the end of the daily use period.
Falling entry (Beach entry) pools	2.0	2.0–5.0	5.0	
Wading pools	3.0	3.0–5.0	10.0	
Wave pools	2.0	2.0–5.0	5.0	
Water attraction pump reservoirs	3.0	3.0–5.0	10.0	
Zero-depth pools	3.0	3.0–5.0	10.0	
Free chlorine in stabilized pools	3.0	3.0–5.0	10.0	
Combined Chlorine, ppm				
Public pools and spas	None	None	0.2	High combined chlorine reduces chemical efficacy. Take remedial action to establish break point chlorination. (See Remedial Practices below.) Other signs of combined chlorine: • Sharp chlorine odor • Eye irritation • Algae growth
Bromine, ppm				
Public pools	2.0	3.0–5.0	8.0	In a spa, during hours of operation, test the water hourly and record results. Maintain this range continually and shock treat at the end of daily use.
Public spas	2.0	4.0–6.0	10.0	
Iodine, ppm				
	Levels not established	—	—	**NOTE:** Local health department officials should be consulted before use.
2. CHEMICAL VALUES				
pH	7.2	7.4–7.6	7.8	If pH is too low: • Rapid dissipation of disinfectant • Eye discomfort • Plaster and concrete etching • Corrosion of metals • Vinyl liner damage If pH is too high: • Low chlorine efficacy • Scale formation • Cloudy water

1. *Rules of Georgia Department of Human Resources Public Health, Chapter 290-5-57 Swimming Pools, Spas and Recreational Water Parks*
   These parameters are a sample, and are included for information purposes only.
   To prepare for the CMS Exam, don't use these parameters—use the ones in the *APSP Service Tech Manual, 4th Edition, v4.2, Unit 3: Water Quality.*

Parameter	Minimum	Ideal	Maximum	Comments
2. CHEMICAL VALUES				
Total Alkalinity (buffering), ppm as CaCo$_3$	60	80–100 for calcium hypochlorite lithium hypochlorite sodium hypochlorite 100–120 for sodium dichlor trichlor gas chlorine bromine compounds	180	If total alkalinity is too low: • pH bounce • Corrosion tendency If total alkalinity is too high: • Cloudy water • Increased scaling potential • pH tends to be too high
Total Dissolved Solids (TDS), ppm	300	1000–2000	3000	These values are offered as guidelines rather than absolute values to indicate concern for accumulation of impurities in the course of operation. Excessive high TDS may lead to hazy water, corrosion of fixtures, etc., and can be reduced by partial draining with addition of fresh water. High initial TDS may indicate poor water quality due to corrosive mineral salts, humus or organic matter. Consult local water authority. Increasing TDS indicates buildup of impurities to be controlled by partial drain/refill with fresh water.
Calcium Hardness, ppm as CaCo$_3$	150	200–400 to balance water	500–1000+	Operations of pools, spas and hot tubs at maximum hardness will depend on alkalinity (buffering) requirements of the sanitizer used. Maximum alkalinity and lower pH must be used with maximum hardness (over 500 ppm)
Heavy metals, ppm	None	None	copper 1.0 silver 0.1	If heavy metals, such as copper, iron, manganese, or silver are present: • Staining may occur • Water may discolor • Chlorine dissipates rapidly • Filter may plug • May indicate pH too low, corrosion, etc.
3. BIOLOGICAL VALUES				
Algae		None		If algae are observed: • Shock treat pool. (See Remedial Practices, Shock Treatment) • Supplement with brushing and vacuuming. • User approved algicide according to label directions. (See Remedial Practices below.)
Bacteria	None	None		If bacteria count exceeds maximum allowed: • Superchlorinate and follow proper maintenance procedures • Maintain proper disinfectant residual.
4. STABILIZER (if used)				
Cyanuric acid, ppm	10	30–50	100	If stabilizer is too low: • Chlorine residual rapidly destroyed by sunlight If stabilizer is too high: • May exceed local health department regulation • May reduce chlorine efficacy **NOTE:** Stabilizer is not needed in indoor or brominated pools and spas.

Parameter	Minimum	Ideal	Maximum	Comments
5. REMEDIAL PRACTICES				
Superchlorination frequency	Pool– monthly	Pool– every other week	Pool– weekly when the temperature is over 85 °F	**NOTE:** Some high use pools may need superchlorination 3 times a week or more as a preventative measure or when combined chlorine is over 0.2 ppm.
Superchlorination to establish break point, dosage in ppm	10 × combined chlorine level			When combined chlorine is over 0.2 ppm, superchlorinate by adding 10 times the combined chlorine ppm (eg. If combined chlorine is 0.3 ppm, superchlorinate by adding 3 ppm chlorine) Applied at the end of daily usage, hold this level for 1–4 hours to clarify the water, remove ammonia (combined chlorine), and kill any algae present. Can also be applied when no bathers are present and as required to maintain clear water and the required halogen residual.
Shock Treatment, dosage in ppm	10	—	—	Non-chlorine oxidizers are not considered biocidal, but may reduce organic contaminants.
Clarifying/ Floccing frequency	—	When needed	—	Use all clarifiers following manufacturer's directions.
Algicides				Follow manufacturer's directions. Use EPA-registered products.
Water Replacement				Water in spas that have high bather use may require partial or complete replacement of water periodically to dilute dissolved solids, to maintain water clarity and to do necessary routine maintenance.
Foam				Foam may harbor persistent microorganisms. If foaming is not adequately controlled, consider daily shock treatment, water replacement or an appropriate anti-foam agent. Follow manufacturer's directions.
6. TEMPERATURE				
Pool	78 °F	78–82 °F	88 °F[2]	If temperature is too low: • Bather discomfort
Therapy pool	—	—	96 °F[2]	• Increased chance of hypothermia If temperature is too high:
Spa	—	—	104 °F	• Health hazard • Bather discomfort • Excessive fuel requirement • Increased evaporation • Increased scaling potential • Increased use of disinfectants • Increased potential for corrosion
7. WATER CLARITY				
Water turbidity	Must be able to see main drain covers, or a standard black and white disc laying on the bottom of the deepest portion of the pool			If water is turbid: • Disinfectant level may be low • Filtration system may not be working • Improper chemical balance • Bottom should be clearly visible at the deepest part of the pool or spa. • Consult remedial practices

2. Maryland Chemical Operational Parameters. Source: State of Maryland, Department of Health and Mental Hygiene

Parameter	Minimum	Ideal	Maximum	Comments
8. OXIDIZERS				
Ozone, low output generators Contact concentration, mg/L when ozone is injected and not removed prior to entry into pool.	–	–	0.1	Serves as oxidizer of water contaminants. Indoor installations should have adequate ventilation.
Levels above the pool or spa	0	0	0.05	
9. OXIDIZER REDUCTION POTENTIAL (ORP)				
ORP	650 MV	–	–	When chlorine or bromine is used as the primary disinfectant, ORP can be used as a supplemental measurement of proper sanitizer activity. The use of ORP testing does not eliminate or supersede the need for testing the sanitizer level with standard test kits and ORP reading may be affected by a number of factors including: (1) pH, (2) probe film and (3) cyanuric acid. Follow manufacturer's recommendations.

Testing and correcting the water

- Test the water, following test kit instructions.
- Do a water balance calculation (p. 3-29).
- Determine what problems you want to correct, and by how much.
- Treat the problem (add the chemicals).
- Retest the water to confirm that the problem has been corrected.

Once you have tested the water and analyzed the results, you may not need to make any corrections. However if the water is not balanced, or if the sanitizer level is low, etc., you will need to make one or more adjustments. Determine what things you need to adjust, and by how much.

Re-test the water after 6–8 hours, to be sure that you have made the changes you wanted.

▶ NOTE: If you plan to add large quantities of chemicals to the pool in order to achieve water balance, do it in small amounts over several days, to avoid localized scaling.

Add chemicals in this order:

1. If changing the total alkalinity (TA), change this first.*
2. If changing the calcium hardness (CH), do this next.
3. If changing the pH, change this next.
4. Adjust sanitizer, cyanuric acid, other chemicals— no special order required.
* Freshly plastered pools only: Adjust calcium hardness first, then total alkalinity, then pH, and then add any other chemicals needed.

Always:

- Use water additives and treatment chemicals according to the label instructions. Not all chemicals are added in the same way!
- When you add chemicals directly into the pool or spa, *no one is allowed in the water* until the chemicals are completely dissolved and diffused throughout the pool or spa.
- Test the chemical levels to make sure they are swim-safe, before allowing people back in the pool or spa.

Courtesy of The Association of Pool & Spa Professionals

C3
Chemical Safety Summary

Oxidizers

The precautions for handling all oxidizers are similar. However, it is up to you to familiarize yourself with the requirements for each.

Name of Oxidizer
calcium hypochlorite
lithium hypochlorite
sodium hypochlorite
trichlor
sodium dichlor
1-bromo-3-chloro-5, 5-dimethylhydantoin
potassium peroxymonosulfate

Protective Equipment
- Eye goggles
- Hands—gloves (rubber, neoprene, or PVC)
- Body—Coveralls and impervious boots (rubber)
- Lungs—Provide ventilation where dust is likely. Wear NIOSH/MSA approved chlorine gas/dust mask if dust is excessive.

Handling Precautions
- Do not take internally
- Avoid contact with eyes, skin or clothing.
- Upon contact with skin or eyes, rinse with water.
- Avoid breathing dust.
- Store all containers in a cool, dry place.
- Do not store containers in direct sunlight.
- Do not store near combustible materials.
- Do not mix oxidizers.
- Use clean, dry utensils when handling oxidizers.
- Keep all oxidizer containers off wet floors.

Conditions & Material to Avoid
- Excessive heat. Oxidizers will decompose, releasing toxic gasses and heat.
- Solvents.
- Acids.
- Other pool chemicals such as acids, algicides, clarifiers, sequestering agents, surface cleaners, etc.
- Organic materials.
- Do not mix oxidizers.
- Do not mix oxidizers with anything but water. Always add chemicals to plenty of water. Never the reverse.

Acids

Acids are highly corrosive and must be handled with extreme care.

Names of Acids
muriatic acid (hydrochloric acid, dilute)
sodium bisulfate

Protective Equipment
- Eye goggles or full face shield when splashing may occur.
- Hands—gloves (rubber, neoprene, or PVC)
- Body—Coveralls and impervious boots (rubber)
- Lungs—Wear NIOSH/MSA approved chlorine gas/dust respirator for sodium bisulfate.

Handling Precautions
- Do not take internally
- Avoid contact with eyes, skin, or clothing.
- Upon contact with skin or eyes, rinse with water.
- Avoid breathing vapors (muriatic acid) and dust (sodium bisulfate).
- Store all containers in a cool, dry place.
- Always add acid to plenty of cool water. Never the reverse.

Conditions & Materials to Avoid
- Avoid contact with strong alkalies such as caustic soda, sodium carbonate, etc.
- Avoid contact with all oxidizers.
- Do not store in wet or moist conditions.
- Do not store in direct sunlight.

Balance Chemicals

Although acids are balance chemicals, they have been treated separately. The chemicals in this section are all basic (high pH) and increase pH, TA, and calcium hardness.

Names of Balance Chemicals
sodium bicarbonate
sodium sesquicarbonate
sodium carbonate
sodium hydroxide
calcium chloride-dihydrate

Protective Equipment
- Eye goggles.
- Hand—gloves (rubber, neoprene, or PVC)
- Body—impervious boots (rubber)
- Lungs—Wear NIOSH/MSA approved gas/dust mask or respirator where dust, mist, or spray may occur.

Handling Precautions
- Do not take internally
- Avoid contact with eyes, skin, or clothing.
- Avoid breathing dust, spray, or mist.
- Store all containers in a cool, dry place.

Courtesy of The Association of Pool & Spa Professionals

- Always keep containers closed.
- Caution: Considerable heat is generated when sodium hydroxide or calcium chloride dihydrate is dissolved in water. Use extreme care. Use luke warm water. Never add to cold or hot water.

Condition & Materials to Avoid
- Avoid contact with acids.
- Avoid contact with small water volumes.
- Avoid contact with organics and oxidizers.
- Do not store near acids.

C4
Quick Fix Formulas

To Fix	Chemical	Added to	Result
To raise total alkalinity	15 lbs of sodium bicarbonate	Add to 100,000 gallons of pool water	Raises total alkalinity 10 ppm
To raise calcium hardness	11 lbs of calcium chloride	Add to 100,000 gallons of pool water	Raises calcium hardness 10 ppm
To raise chlorine residual or 1 US gallon of sodium	1 lb of chlorine gas or $1\,^1/_2$ of calcium hypochlorite or pool water hypochlorite	Add to 120,000 gallons (1,000,000 lbs) of	Raises calcium residual 1.0 ppm
To lower chlorine residual	1 lb of sodium thiosulphate	Add to 100,000 gallons of pool water	Lowers chlorine residual 1.0 ppm

C5
Chlorine-Base Sanitizing Agents

Chlorine-based Sanitizing Agents
The most common forms of chlorine sanitizers used in pools and spas are:

Chemical Name	Common Name	% Available Chlorine	pH	Physical Form	Stabilized
Calcium hypochlorite	Cal Hypo	47%, 65% and 78%	~11	granular and tablets	no
Sodium hypochlorite	Liquid chlorine, or bleach	10–15%	~13	liquid	no
Lithium hypochlorite		35%	10.7	powder	no
Chlorine generators		Variable; commonly ~1% for brine type		salt—produces sodium hypochlorite solution	no
Sodium dichloro-s-triazinetrione	Dichlor	56% and 63%	6.5	granular	yes
Trichoro-s-triazinetrione	Trichlor	85% and 90%	3.0	granular and tablets	yes
Elemental chlorine	chlorine gas	100%	0–1	gas in cylinder	no

©The Association of Pool & Spa Professionals

C6
Use of Elemental Chlorine

General

Chlorine is one of the chemical elements. The gas has a characteristic odor and greenish yellow color and is about two and one-half (2 1/2) times as heavy as air. Chlorine is shipped in Department of Transportation specification steel containers; standard sizes contain either 100 or 150 pounds of chlorine. In the cylinder the chlorine has both a liquid and a gas phase. All cylinders are equipped with the Chlorine Institute standard chlorine cylinder valve.

Chlorine is a "hazardous material" subject to Department of Transportation requirements. When used for pool disinfection, chlorine is considered a pesticide and as such is subject to pertinent regulations of the U.S. Environmental Protection Agency.

Users of chlorine must be trained as to the proper procedures for handling chlorine and as to appropriate emergency procedures. Detailed information is available from chlorine suppliers and the Chlorine Institute, 2001 L Street, N.W., Washington, D.C. 20036.

Equipment and Installation

1. Chlorination equipment should be located so that equipment failure or malfunction will have minimum effect on evacuation of pool patrons in an emergency.
2. Elemental chlorine feeders (chlorinators) should be activated by a booster pump using recirculated water supplied via the recirculation system. The booster pump should be interlocked to the filter pump to prevent feeding of chlorine when the recirculation pump is not running.
3. The chlorinator, cylinders of chlorine and associated equipment should be housed in a reasonable gas-tight and corrosion-resisting housing having a floor area adequate for the purpose. Cylinders should always be stored in an upright position and properly secured.
4. All enclosures should be located at or above ground level. The enclosure should be provided with: ducts from the bottom of the enclosure to the atmosphere in an unrestricted area, a motor-driven exhaust fan capable of producing at least one air change per minute, and louvers of good design near the top of the enclosure for admitting fresh air. Warning signs should be posted on the doors. It is recommended that the doors to the chlorine room should open away from the pool.
5. Electrical switches for the control of artificial lighting and ventilation should be on the outside of the enclosure adjacent to the door.
6. Contents of a chlorine cylinder can be determined only by weight; therefore, facilities should include a scale suitable for weighing the cylinders. Changing cylinder(s) should be accomplished only after weighing proves contents of cylinder to be exhausted. Care must be taken to prevent water suck-back into the cylinder when empty by closing the cylinder valve.
7. Connections from the cylinders to the system depend on the type of chlorinator to be used and should comply with the chlorinator manufacturer's recommendation.
8. It is recommended that an automatic chlorine leak detector and alarm be installed in the chlorinator room.
9. Respirators approved by the National Institute for Occupational Safety and Health (NIOSH) should be provided for protection against chlorine. It is recommended that at least one approved self-contained breathing apparatus be provided. Respiratory equipment should be mounted outside the chlorine enclosure. Occupational Safety and Health Administration (OSHA) regulations require training and maintenance programs for respirators.
10. Containers may be stored indoors or outdoors. Full and empty cylinders should be segregated and appropriately tagged. Storage conditions should: (a) minimize external corrosion, (b) be clean and free of trash, (c) not be near an elevator or ventilation system, (d) be away from elevated temperatures or heat sources.

For additional information, contact The Chlorine Institute, Inc., 2001 L Street, NW, Washington, D.C. 20036, (202) 775-2790, and request a copy of the "Chlorine Manual" and the wall chart entitled "Handling Chlorine Cylinders & Ton Containers."

Continued

Operational Procedures

1. A specific person should be made responsible for chlorination operations and should be trained in the performance of routine operations including emergency procedures and leak control procedures.

2. Chlorine cylinders must be handled with care. Valve protection caps and valve outlet caps should be in place at all times except when the cylinder is connected for use. Cylinders must not be dropped and should be protected from falling objects. Cylinders should be used on a first-in, first-out basis. New, approved washers should be used each time a cylinder is connected.

3. It is recommended that a safety wall chart be posted in or near the chlorine enclosure and a second chart in the pool office near the telephone. Such charts are available from many suppliers and from the Chlorine Institute, 2001 L Street, N.W., Washington, D.C. 20036. The telephone number of the chlorine supplier should be shown on this chart.

4. Although chlorine suppliers make every effort to furnish chlorine in properly-conditioned cylinders, chlorine gas leaks may still occur. Pool personnel should be informed about leak control procedures and consideration should be given to providing a Chlorine Institute Emergency Kit A.

5. Chlorine suppliers are equipped with a Chlorine Institute Emergency Kit A, which contains devices for capping leaks at cylinder valves and some leaks which occur in the cylinder wall. Further information on these kits and training slides demonstrating their use are available from the Chlorine Institute.

6. As soon as a container is empty, the valve should be closed and the lines disconnected. The outlet cap should be applied promptly and the valve protection hood attached. The open end of the disconnected line should be plugged or capped promptly to keep atmospheric moisture out of the system.

7. To find a chlorine gas leak, use a plastic bottle containing 26° BE Ammonia capable of releasing only vapors when squeezed. A white cloud will result if there is any chlorine leakage. Never use water on a chlorine leak.

C7

30 ppm Shock Table for Algae Removal

Available chlorine (%)*	Volume of water						
	250 gals / 946 L	400 gals / 1,514 L	1,000 gals / 3,785 L	5,000 gals / 18,927 L	20,000 gals / 75.708 L	50,000 gals / 189.271 L	100,000 gals / 378.541 L
5	2.36 cups / 558 mL'	1.89 pts' / 893 mL'	2.36 qts' / 2.23 L'	2.95 gals / 11.20 L'	11.8 gals / 44.70 L'	29.5 gals' / 112 L	59.0 gals' / 223 L'
10	1.18 cups' / 279 mL'	.94 pts / 447 mL'	1.18 qts' / 1.12 L'	1.48 gals' / 5.58 L'	5.90 gals' / 22.30 L'	14.8 gals' / 55.80 L'	29.5 gals / 112 L'
12	.98 cups' / 234 mL*	.78 pts / 372 mL'	.98 qts / 932 mL'	1.23 gals' / 4.65 L'	4.92 gals' / 18.60 L'	12.3 gals* / 46.50 L'	24.6 gals' / 93.10 L'
35	2.86 oz / 81.1 g	4.58 oz / 130 g	11.4 oz / 324 g	3.57 lbs / 1.62 kg	14.3 lbs / 6.50 kg	35.7 lbs / 16.20 kg	71.5 lbs / 32.40 kg
60	1.67 oz / 47.3 g	2.67 oz / 76.0 g	6.67 oz / 190 g	2.08 lbs / 950 g	8.34 lbs / 3.79 kg	20.8 lbs / 94.70 kg	41.7 lbs / 19.00 kg
65	1.54 oz / 43.7 g	2.46 oz / 69.9 g	6.16 oz / 175 g	1.92 lbs / 875 g	7.70 lbs / 3.49 L	19.2 lbs / 8.74 kg	38.5 lbs / 17.50 kg
90	1.11 oz / 31.6 g	1.80 oz / 50.5 g	4.45 oz / 126 g	1.39 lbs / 635 g	5.56 lbs / 2.52 kg	1.3.9 lbs / 6.35 kg	27.8 lbs / 12.60 kg
100	1.00 oz / 28.4 g	1.60 oz / 45.5 g	4.00 oz / 114 g	1.25 lbs / 569 g	5.00 lbs / 2.28 kg	12.5 lbs / 5.70 kg	25.0 lbs / 11.40 kg

' For correct chlorine product to add refer to "How to use the Treatment Tables."

C8
Spa Disinfectants

	Chlorine	Bromine	Ozone
Most common form(s) for spa application:	Trichlor tablets dichlor (granular)	Organic bromine (BCDMH tablets) 1- and 2- step bromine salts (granular)	Gas; generated on site
Active disinfectant:	hypochlorous acid, hypochlorite ion	hypobromous acid, hypobromite ion, bromamines,	Ozone's "free radicals"
Proper ppm level:	1.0-3.0 residential 2.0-4.0 commercial	2.0-4.0 residential 4.0-6.0 commercial	—
Most effective e pH:	7.2-7.6	7.2-8.2	7.2-8.2
Lasting residual:	YES	YES	NO
Easy to measure:	YES	YES	YES
Requires other disinfectant:	NO	NO	YES
Requires shocking:	YES	YES	NO
Creates odors:	SOMETIMES	SOMETIMES	SOMETIMES
Irritates eyes/skin:	SOMETIMES	NOT USUAL	NOT USUAL
Affects balance:	YES	YES	NOT USUAL
Methods of adding:	Tablets, feeder or floater Dichlor, hand-fed	Tablets, briquettes, feeder or floater Bromide/oxidants, hand-fed	Ozone generator on, pump on

From *Basic pool and spa technology*, ed 2, 1992, The Institute.

Appendix D
Safety Guidelines

D1
Child Safety Alternatives for Pools

Product	Purpose	Type, Price
1. Self-closing/ self-latching devices for doors and windows.	To keep all doors and windows leading to the pool area securely closed, limiting access by unsupervised children.	Hinge pin replacement ($8-10) Swing arm ($15-30)
2. Door exit alarm	To warn parent or guardian when a child opens the door. Placed on/near door.	Door announcer/chime ($35-50); Home Security System
3. Fencing	To isolate swimming pool by way of 4-ft. enclosure. To temporarily isolate swimming pool, when children are visiting.	Chain-link ($1.80/ft.) Picket ($3-4.60/ft.) Ornamental (variable) Portable ($8/ft.)
4. Fence gate closer and latch	To close and latch fence gates securely, making pool inaccessible to a child.	Self-latching ($25-35) Adjust. height (N/A)
5. Fence gate alarm	To sound alarm when gate is open.	N/A
6. Infrared detectors	To sound alarm when area around pool perimeter is entered. Wireless detection.	Light-beam ($300-400) Body energy ($200)
7. Safety covers	To cover the pool with a complete and impenetrable barrier blocking access to water.	Manual closing ($800-2,300); Automatic closing
8. Pool alarms	To sound an alarm when something accidentally or without authorization enters the water. Placed in the pool.	Surface water (wave motion; $140); Pressure Waves (acoustic; $350)
9. Child alarms	To sound an alarm when the child exceeds a certain distance or becomes submerged in water. Clipped on the child.	Electronic monitoring system ($300); Clip-on transmitter ($250-$300)

Courtesy of The Association of Pool & Spa Professionals
From NSPI: *Basic pool and spa technology*, ed 2, 1992, The Institute.

D2
Pool Chemical Safety

Read the label

Clean-up and disposal—customer checklist

1. Never clean spills with bare hands.
2. Flush a spill with large amounts of water.
3. Do not vacuum a spill.
4. Never use a fire extinguisher on smoking chemicals.
5. Call the fire department immediately for large spills, fire, or disposal assistance.

Transport/storage of pool chemicals—customer checklist

1. Separate your chemicals in cardboard or plastic boxes. Ask your dealer for boxes if you did not bring them.
2. Avoid sudden swerves and stops when driving.
3. Clean spills immediately and properly.
4. Remove chemicals from your car immediately. Don't allow them to sit in the heat of your trunk.
5. Store your chemicals in a locked, dry, cool, well-ventilated shed used only for pool supplies.
6. Separate chemicals with cardboard or plastic in storage.

It's Good Business

Safety priorities checklist—for pool/spa store owner

1. Safety is YOUR responsibility. Make safe handling and storage or chemicals a priority. Know what to do in an emergency.
2. Either you or someone you've appointed should train all new employees in pool chemical safety.
3. Post the phone number of your fire department and rescue squad by your phone. Make sure your employees know where the numbers are posted.
4. Work with your local fire officials. Let them know your layout and what products you have in your store and warehouse.

Chemical delivery and storage—store checklist

1. Don't order more than you can safely store or sell in a season.
2. Refuse damage goods. Report damage to the supplier for instructions on disposal.
3. Store in a cool, dry, well-ventilated area.
4. Keep the warehouse clean at all times.
5. No smoking in the storage area.
6. Separate incompatible chemicals.
7. Stack at recommended heights.
8. Rotate stock.
9. Label hazardous areas with the proper NFPA 704 placards.

Transportation

Proper vehicle loading checklist—business deliveries and service

1. Keep your vehicle clean.
2. Separate incompatible chemicals.
3. Don't carry damaged containers.
4. Put heavy equipment on the rear floor.
5. Anchor your load securely.
6. Carry protective equipment for spills.
7. Post a placard for hazardous loads that exceed limits.
8. If your vehicle weighs more than 10,000 pounds or if your load is placardable, whatever your weight, you also must have a daily vehicle inspection report, your medical cards, and a list of all the regulated material in your load.

- ☐ Read the label and instructions.
- ☐ Use compatible chemicals.
- ☐ Do not inhale fumes.
- ☐ Do not over-stock
- ☐ Drive carefully.
- ☐ Never combine chemicals.
- ☐ Don't leave in car.
- ☐ Store in proper shed.
- ☐ Separate chemicals in storage.
- ☐ No smoking.
- ☐ Mix chemicals at poolside.

- ☐ Wear gloves and goggles.
- ☐ Use separate scoops.
- ☐ Handle with care.
- ☐ Separate chemicals during transport.
- ☐ Add chemicals to water.
- ☐ Mix only exact amounts.
- ☐ Keep away from children.
- ☐ Keep dry and off the floor.
- ☐ Flush with water.
- ☐ Do not vacuum.
- ☐ Clean spills properly.

Emergency Numbers

Fire_______________________________________

Police_____________________________________

Ambulance_________________________________

Physician__________________________________

Poison Center______________________________

Pool Service Company_______________________

Chemical Safety Summary

OXIDIZERS

The precautions for handling all oxidizers are similar. However, it is up to you to familiarize yourself with the requirements for each.

Name of Oxidizer	Protective Equipment	Handling Precautions	Conditions and Materials to Avoid
Calcium hypochlorite Lithium hypochlorite Sodium hypochlorite Trichlor Sodium dichlor Gas chlorine Bromine Potassium peroxymonosulfate Hydrogen peroxide	Eyes: Goggles or face shield Hands: Gloves (rubber, neoprene, or PVC) Body: Coveralls and impervious boots (rubber) Lungs: Provide ventilation where dust is likely. Wear NIOSH/MSA approved chlorine gas/dust mask if dust is excessive.	Do not take internally. Avoid contact with eyes, skin, or clothing. Upon contact with skin or eyes, rinse with water. Avoid breathing dust. Store all containers in a cool, dry place. Do not store containers in direct sunlight. Do not store near combustible materials. Do not mix oxidizers. Use clean, dry utensils when handling oxidizers. Keep all oxidizer containers off wet floors. See also *Chlorine Gas Safety*, p. 3-59	Excessive heat. Oxidizers will decompose, releasing toxic gases and heat. Solvents Acids Other chemicals such as algicides, clarifiers, sequestering agents, surface cleaners, etc. Organic materials **Do not mix oxidizers.** **Do not mix oxidizers with anything but water.** Always add chemicals to plenty of water, *never* the reverse.

ACIDS

Acids are highly corrosive and must be handled with extreme care.

Name of Acid	Protective Equipment	Handling Precautions	Conditions and Materials to Avoid
Muriatic acid (hydrochloric acid) Sulfuric acid Sodium bisulfate Cyanuric acid	Eyes and Face: Eye goggles or full-face shield when splashing may occur Hands: Gloves (rubber, neoprene, or PVC) Body: Coveralls and impervious boots (rubber) Lungs: Wear NIOSH/MSA approved respirator or dust mask designed for sodium bisulfate.	Do not take internally. Avoid contact with eyes, skin, or clothing. Upon contact with skin or eyes, rinse with water. Avoid breathing vapors (muriatic & sulfuric acid) and dust (sodium bisulfate). Store all containers in a cool, dry place. Always add acid to plenty of cool water, *never* the reverse.	Avoid contact with strong alkalies such as caustic soda, sodium carbonate, etc. **Avoid contact with all oxidizers.** Do not store in wet or moist conditions. Do not store in direct sunlight.

BALANCE CHEMICALS

Although acids are balance chemicals, they have been treated separately. The chemicals in this section are all basic (high pH) (except calcium chloride, which is neutral or slightly basic) and increase pH and total alkalinity (TA). Calcium chloride also raises calcium level.

Name of Balance Chemical	Protective Equipment	Handling Precautions	Conditions and Materials to Avoid
Sodium bicarbonate Sodium sesquicarbonate Sodium carbonate Sodium hydroxide Calcium chloride-dihydrate	Eyes: Eye goggles. Hands: Gloves (rubber, neoprene, or PVC) Body: Impervious boots (rubber) Lungs: Wear NIOSH/MSA approved gas/dust mask or respirator where dust, mist, or spray may occur.	Do not take internally. Avoid contact with eyes, skin, or clothing. Avoid breathing dust, spray, or mist. Store all containers in a cool, dry place. Close containers immediately after use. **Caution:** Considerable heat is generated when sodium hydroxide or calcium chloride dihydrate is dissolved in water. Use extreme care. Use *lukewarm* water. *Never* add to hot water.	Avoid contact with acids. Avoid contact with small water volumes. Avoid contact with organics and oxidizers. Do not store near acids.

Courtesy of The Association of Pool & Spa Professionals, 2012

Glossary

acid A chemical compound that provides hydrogen ions to lower the pH of water. Acids give readings of 6.9 or less on the pH scale. Muriatic acid is a common liquid swimming pool acid. Sodium bisulfate is a common dry swimming pool acid.

acid demand A measurement of acid needed to reduce pH or alkalinity. Usually used with the pH test.

activated carbon Used in the swimming pool industry to remove excess oxidizers, colors, and odors from the water. Usually comes in granular form.

ADA The American Disabilities Act (public law 101-336, passed 1990) gives civil rights protection to approximately 43 million citizens with disabilities similar to those rights provided to individuals on the basis of race, sex, national origin, and religion. It guarantees equal opportunity for individuals with disabilities in employment, public accommodations, transportation, state and local government services, and telecommunications. The law strictly prohibits discrimination in public places against individuals with disabilities.

algae The simplest form of plant life, microscopic and containing chlorophyll, that thrives on sunlight. There are many varieties that enter pools most often by wind or rain. Unsightly and slippery. Easier to prevent than kill. Green, black, and mustard algae are most common in aquatic facilities. There are more than 21,000 known species of algae.

algaecide A specialty chemical that aids in killing, controlling and preventing algae. Many varieties of algaecides are available; some cause foaming. Quaternary ammonia compounds (Quats) are popular algaecides.

algaecidal Being capable of **killing** algae.

algaestat A chemical that inhibits algae growth but is not very effective in killing algae that already exist.

alkaline The property of a compound that allows it to neutralize an acid; in pool water a reading of 7.1 or higher on the pH scale indicates alkaline water. Chemicals added to pool water to raise the pH and offset acidity are known as **alkalies**.

alkalinity The alkaline condition or the pH buffering capacity of water. Determined by the amount of bicarbonate, carbonate, and hydroxide present.

alum A filter aid that when added to a pool's filtration system crates a gelatinous floc on top of the filter bed which helps to precipitate solids out of solutions. The pH must be carefully controlled when alum is used. **Alumi-num sulfate** is a common flocculant. Alum is most often used with older, conventional sand and gravel filter systems.

ammonia A hydrogen/nitrogen compound that combines with swimming pool chlorine (FC) to produce chloramines (CC) that have obnoxious odors and cause eye burn.

ammonia hydroxide Used for detecting gas chlorine leaks, this ammonia and water alkaline mixture produces a white cloud in the presence of chlorine.

ammonia nitrogen Found on human bodies in the form of sweat, urine, or other waste. Combines with chlorine and bromine to produce chloramines and bromamines, which in turn produce odors and eye burn. Soap showers prior to entering the swimming pool can significantly reduce chloramine production.

ANSI American National Standard Institute develops a variety of standards. **ANSI** in cooperation with **NSPI** publish swimming pool and spa standards.

anthracite (anthrafilt) A filter aid composed of hard coal that can be added to the top of sand filters to help remove chemicals, odors, and tastes.

ARC The American Red Cross. National Headquarters are in Washington D.C. The ARC offers a variety of comprehensive courses in water safety, CPR, and first aid.

automatic feeders Electronically controlled pool equipment that monitor and adjust pool chemicals, particularly pH and chlorine levels.

available chlorine Active, unused chlorine that is available to oxidize organic materials and kill bacteria in pool water. This term is used to rating chlorine-containing products as to their total oxidizing power.

backwash A term used to describe one way of cleaning filter media. **Backwashing** calls for the reversing of the flow of water in a filtration system so that dirt trapped in the filter bed is pushed out to waste. Although all filters can be cleaned, not all filters can be backwashed.

backwash cycle The time required to backwash the filter media and elements completely.

backwash rate The flow rate required for effective cleaning of the filter media. Backwash rates are measured in gallons per minute (gpm) per square foot of filter area. The manufacturer's recommendations must be followed for proper backwashing rates.

bacteria One-celled organisms that can either be pathogenic (disease-producing) or nonpathogenic. A **bacteri-**

cide is a chemical that kills bacteria.

Baquacil A nonchlorine polymer used as a swimming pool sanitizer and algaestat.

barrier A fence, safety cover, wall, or a combination thereof that completely surrounds or covers the swimming pool and obstructs access to the swimming pool.

bather load The number of swimmers in a pool at a given time. Many state codes determine maximum **bather loads** that should not be exceeded. **Swimmer load** is perhaps the more appropriate term; the term **bather** is a remnant from the days when pools were referred to as **baths**.

balanced water Water that is neutral, that is neither corrosive (aggressive) nor basic (scale forming). Balanced water possesses the correct combination of minerals and pH levels.

base or basic A chemical that neutralizes acids, often through hydroxyl ions.

beginners area Those swimming pool areas with a water depth of three feet or less.

body coat Diatomaceous earth that builds up on filter elements during the filter cycle. If DE is added to the body coat on a regular basis it is often referred to as a body feed or slurry feed.

breakpoint The process of adding sufficient free available chlorine (FC) or other nonchlorine oxidants to convert chloramines and ammonia-nitrogen compounds to inert nitrogen gas. All chlorine added after break point is free and uncombined. **Breakpoint chlorination** is necessary to rid a pool of odors and eye burn caused by chloramines.

bridging When the body coat of Diatomaceous Earth filters becomes so thick that the DE coat on adjacent elements touch each other. At this point, filtering is impaired and DE must be removed from the elements.

broadcast A method of introducing granular or powdered chemicals to a pool by spreading them widely over the surface.

brominator A device designed to deliver bromine disinfectant to a swimming pool or spa at a controlled rate.

bromine A swimming pool disinfectant used to kill bacteria and algae. Bromine is often used in hot water spas and hot tubs.

bromamines Produced when free available bromine combines with ammonia and nitrogen wastes brought into the pool by swimmers. Unlike chloramines, bromamines continue to be effective disinfectants.

buffer A combination of weak acids and weak bases and their salts that help to resist changes in pH. Sodium bicarbonate is an example of a popular buffer used in pool water.

calcification Precipitation of calcium carbonate in hard water. Blocks and clogs circulation parts and plumbing.

calcium chloride (CaCl$_2$) A soluble white salt used to raise the calcium hardness of pool or spa water.

calcium hardness The calcium content of the water usually expressed in ppm's. Calcium hardness accounts for approximately 70% of the total hardness. "Soft" water has low calcium hardness and may corrode pool equipment, whereas "hard" water has high levels of calcium hardness and may clog pipes and filters.

calcium hypochlorite A dry, inorganic chlorine that is available in granular form or tablets. It contains 65% active available chlorine. Calcium hypochlorite is flammable and must be handled with care.

cartridge filter A relatively new type of swimming pool filter that utilizes synthetic, porous cartridges to filter water. Cartridge filters are very effective but are often difficult to clean. These filters are used on smaller rather than larger pools. **Depth-type cartridges** rely on the penetration of particles into the medium for removal and provide adequate holding capacity of such particles. **Surface-type cartridges** rely on the retention of particles on the surface of the cartridge for removal.

chelating agents Chemical compounds used to keep metals and minerals in solution so they do not precipitate out in the pool water.

chemical feeder A mechanical device used to dispense pool chemicals into the water. There are many different types of chemical feeders including **diaphragm, piston, erosion, peristaltic, dry, and vacuum**.

chloramines Produced by free available chlorine combining with ammonia and nitrogenous wastes introduced into pools by swimmers. Renders chlorine less effective and creates odors and eye burn. Must be "shocked" from the pool with large doses of additional free available chlorine. Also known as **combined chlorine (CC)**.

chlorinator A chemical feeder used specifically for dispensing chlorine into pools. **Gas chlorine feeders** are most often referred to as "**chlorinators**."

chlorine A halogen that is the most popular swimming pool sanitizer and serves as both a disinfectant and oxidizer for swimming pool water. Chlorine is available in many forms, some of which are safe to handle than others. Chlorine kills both bacteria and algae and oxidizes organic debris.

chlorine demand The amount of chlorine required to disinfect and oxidize all undesirable matter in the pool including ammonia and nitrogenous wastes plus chloramines, bacteria, and algae.

chlorine generator Equipment that generates chlorine, hypochlorous acid, or hypochlorite on-site for disinfection and oxidation of water contaminants.

chlorine residual The amount of free available chlorine remaining after the chlorine demand has been satisfied.

clarity Refers to how clear or transparent water is. Water clarity is determined by how easily objects can be detected underwater at depth. **Water clarity** should not be confused with **water quality**, which refers to bacteria and other contaminants.

clarifier May also be referred to as a **coagulant** or **flocculant**. A chemical that coagulates and neutralizes suspended particles in water. There are two basic types: inorganic salts of aluminum or iron, and water soluble organic polyelectrolyte polymers.

colorimetric A chemical testing procedure by which various shades and hues of colors are compared to determine chemical levels present in pool water. Most chlorine and pH test are colorimetric tests.

coliform A type of bacteria found in the intestines of warm-blooded animals. When coliform is found in pool water, disease-producing bacteria may also be present. *E* and *B Coli* coliform tests are performed by health officers or certified labs and are generally accepted as a standard of water contamination.

combined chlorine (CC) Also known as chloramines. CC is produced when inadequate levels of **free chlorine (FC)** combine with ammonia and nitrogenous waste introduced into the pool by swimmers. **CC** is undesirable in the pool, causing both odors and eye burn, and is the leading pool problem in busy swimming pools.

comparator The device used to compare colors during a colorimetric chemical test. Water sample colors are held next to and compared with the comparator colors to determine the chemical level of the sample.

coping The cap on the pool or spa wall that provides a finishing edge around the pool or spa. It may also be used to secure a vinyl liner to the top of the pool wall. **Coping** can be made of many different materials.

copper A metal found in some water supplies and also used in many plumbing fixtures. Blue/green water may indicate that high levels of copper exist in the water supply or corrosive water is corroding pool pipes or heater elements.

copper sulfate Once considered a popular algaecide, copper sulfate is rarely used in swimming pools today.

corrosion The "melting" or "eating away" of metal parts in swimming pools. Caused by aggressive, acidic, or soft water. This deterioration can be easily prevented by keeping the pH above 7.2 and by maintaining balanced water according to the Saturation Index.

covers Something that covers, protects, or shelters a swimming pool, spa, or hot tub. There are many different types of pool covers providing a variety of functions. They include **hard top covers** for spas and hot tubs, **winter covers** that keep debris out, **solar covers** that increase water temperature through solar activity, **thermal covers** that insulate and prevent evaporation, and **safety covers** that reduce the risk of drowning of children under five years of age.

cyanuric acid (CYA) A chlorine "conditioner" or "stabilizer" that extends the life of chlorine in outdoor pools. Cyanuric Acid protects chlorine from the dissipating effects of sunlight. Cyanuric acid can be added directly to the pool or it can be purchased already combined with chlorine in tablets or sticks. **Dichlor** and **Trichlor** are commonly used **stabilized chlorines**. CYA levels must be a minimum of 25 ppm in order to extend the life of chlorine but **should not exceed 100 PPM** in pools. According to the Environmental Protection Agency (EPA), high levels of CYA may lead to liver or kidney damage. CYA should not be used indoors.

diaphragm pump A common chemical feeder for pools. This positive displacement pump feeds chemicals to the circulation system at a rate that is easily adjusted. Should be cleaned regularly. This pump is characterized by a diaphragm and check valves.

diatomaceous earth (DE) A fine white powder used as a filter media. **DE** is capable of outstanding filtration, screening out particles as small as one micron in size. DE is composed of fossilized marine life skeletons called diatoms. Because these diatoms are porous, excellent water clarity results when DE filters are used. **Diatomite** is another name for **diatomaceous earth (DE)**.

disinfection The process of destroying **bacteria** and **viruses** in order to **prevent disease transmission. Disinfectants** are chemicals used to destroy these contaminants.

diving Entering the water headfirst from a springboard or diving platform. Requires training and supervision. Not to be confused with entering headfirst into shallow water from decks, docks, starting platforms, or others.

diving board A recreational mechanism for entering a swimming pool, consisting of a semirigid board that derives its elasticity through the use of a fulcrum mounted below the board. A jump board is a recreational mechanism that has a coil spring, leaf spring, or comparable device located beneath the board, which is activated by the force exerted in jumping on the board.

diving platform, stationary These are diving devices that are constructed on-site. May include natural or artificial rocks, pedestals, or towers. May be used for recreation or competition, depending upon construction, design, and dimensions.

diving equipment, competitive Includes competitive diving boards, platforms, and related equipment. Fulcrum adjusting diving stands are needed to provide adjustments for competitive diving. Use of this equipment requires training and supervision. All competitive diving equipment must meet **NCAA, US DIVING, OR FINA** standards. **Not intended for aboveground/inground swimming pools.**

DPD (N,N-diethyl-p-phenylenediamine) The preferred swimming pool colorimetric indicator used in test kits to determine levels of chlorine, bromine, ozone, and some other oxidizers. The darker the shade of red produced by DPD, the more oxidizer present.

dry acid (sodium bisulfate) This granular chemical is safer and easier to use than muriatic acid for **lowering** both **pH** and **total alkalinity**.

effluent Exiting or out-flowing water from a pool, pump, or filter.

electrode A sensor used in automatic pool controllers that aids in reading and controlling chemical levels. Electrodes are usually placed inside the pool circulation lines. Silver and copper electrodes may also be used to ionize the water for disinfection and algae control.

electrolysis Electrical current running through water produced by electrically charged ions. Electrolysis can cause corrosion of metal parts in pools.

erosion feeder A simple, canister-type chemical feeder that allows a steady, regulated flow of water through the container. Chemical tablets are placed in the erosion feeder where the water current erodes and dissolves the chemical. The erosion rate can be controlled by adjusting the flow rate through the feeder.

equalizer A line that is sometimes added between the bottom of the skimmers and the pool wall to prevent air from being sucked into the filter when the water level is below the skimmer box inlet. When the water level does drop, the equalizer automatically draws water from the pool into the skimmer and back to the filter.

feet of head A measurement of pressure or resistance in a hydraulic system. Feet of head is equivalent to the height of a column of water that would create the some amount of resistance. (100 feet of head equals 43 pounds per square inch.)

filter aid Any chemical or other substance that is added to the water to increase the filters efficiency.

filter cartridge See cartridge filter

filter cycle The length of filtering time between backwashing or other filter cleaning procedures. Longer filter cycles or runs usually mean less work for the pool operators.

filter sand A type of filter media composed of silica, quartz, or similar particles. Filter sand comes in different grades. Manufacturer's recommendations must be followed regarding types, grades, and life of filter sand.

filter septum The individual filter membranes found in a DE and some other filtration systems. Can be made of fabric, wire, or similar material. DE clings to the septa in order to trap particles suspended.

filtration The process of removing particulate matter and oils from water as it passes through a porous medium. Many types of filtration are available for swimming pools. A filter usually refers to the mechanical device that traps and strains the suspended particles from the water. Numerous external and internal parts are required for the filter to function properly.

Fireman's switch A mechanism adapted to the time clock that will turn the heater off long enough for it to cool down before the time clock turns the pump off.

Five-Minute Scanning Strategy© Developed by Tom Griffiths, Ed.D., Penn State University. Defines sweeping and scanning separately and requires a significant bodily change and safety check every five minutes in an attempt to improve vigilance.

flocculant A chemical compound added to some sand filters that aids filtration by creating a foaming, gelatinous mass (called the **floc**) on top of the filter bed, which traps finer particles that might normally pass through the sand. Also referred to as **aggregation. Alum** is a common **flocculate**.

flowmeter A device located on a recirculation line that measures flow rate in gallons per minute or liters per minute.

flowrate The rate of flow through a swimming pool recirculation system, most often expressed in gallons per minute. The flowrate is used to determine pool turnovers.

free chlorine Uncombined, usable chlorine that is free to kill bacteria and algae and oxidize organic material. This is the most active and desirable form of chlorine. Free available chlorine is composed of hypochlorous acid (HOCL) and hypochlorite ion (OCL).

Freeboard The clear vertical distance between the top of the filter medium and the lowest outlet of the upper distribution system in a permanent medium filter.

galvanic corrosion The corrosion of metals that takes place when two or more different metals are submerged in an electrolyte.

grab rail Tubular rails used to enter or exit a pool or spa, usually made of stainless steel or chrome plated brass.

gunite A dry mixture of cement and sand, sprayed onto contoured and supported surfaces to build a pool or spa. Water is added to the dry mixture at the nozzle.

gutter The return outlet that surrounds the perimeter of the pool. The gutter is the overflow trough located at the water's edge of most larger pools. Gutters are typically more effective than skimmers.

halogen Fluorine, chlorine, bromine, iodine, and astatine, all of which are found is Group VIIA of the Periodic Table. Most of the halogens are excellent disinfectants.

hair and lint strainer Protects the pool pump by screening out hair, lint, bobbie pins, etc. The removable mesh basket must be cleaned daily.

hardness (hard water) Water that contains high levels of calcium and magnesium compounds and other minerals. Hard water produces scale, which in turn clogs pipes, filters, and heaters.

headfirst entry An entry used by an untrained, recreational "diver." Not to be confused with the sport of springboard diving.

hot tub A spa constructed of wood with sides and bottoms formed separately. The whole tub is shaped to join together by pressure from surrounding hoops, bands, or rods; as distinct from spa units formed of plastic, concrete, metal, or other materials.

hydrogen peroxide (H_2O_2) An oxidizing agent that is often used with alternative sanitizers like UV light. Cannot be used by itself and must be handled with extreme care.

hydrochloric acid (muriatic acid) An extremely strong acid used to lower pH as well as a cleaning agent for diving boards, decks, etc. Also produced when chlorine gas is added to water.

hydrotherapy jets A fitting that blends air and water creating a high velocity, turbulent stream of air-enriched water. Used in spas and hydrotherapy pools.

hydrotherapy spa A unit that may have a therapeutic use but which is not drained, cleaned, or refilled for each individual.

hypochlorite A pool chemical containing chlorine used for disinfection and oxidation. Often refers to calcium, sodium, or lithium hypochlorite.

hydrogen The lightest chemical element that is a component of water and a product of many chemical reactions. Can be used to measure acidity and pH.

hydrogen ion The positively charged nucleus of a hydrogen atom. Can be used to measure the acidity of a solution.

hydroxyl ion A negatively charged particle composed of one hydrogen and one oxygen atom.

hypochlorinator Delivers liquid chlorine to a pool at an adjustable rate.

hypochlorous acid (HOCL) Produced when any chlorine type reacts with water. **HOCL** is the active disinfectant or **free chlorine** used in the treatment of pools and spas. **HOCL** is an excellent sanitizer, oxidizer, and algaecide.

impeller The part (vanes) of a centrifugal pump that spin and move pool water through the circulation system.

indicator A chemical reagent used to produce a color change in a water sample. Phenol red and DPD are two common pool test indicators.

influent Water flowing into a pump, filter, pool, or other vessel.

iodide A chemical compound containing iodine that will be released when placed in pool water. Potassium and sodium iodide are both used for pool disinfection.

iodine A halogen that can be used for swimming pool disinfection but is not common. Although it is an excellent bactericide, iodine is not an effective algaecide.

iron When found in high concentrations in water supplies, may precipitate out in red, brown, or murky colors. Staining often begins when the iron content is higher than .3 ppm. Water with high iron levels must either be filtered out before it reaches the pool plant and/or sequestered with a specialty chemical if in the pool itself.

ionization An electrochemical process using electrodes to convert neutral or noncharged atoms, molecules, or compounds to electrically charged ions. Ionization is used as an alternative sanitizer in some pools to reduce their dependence on chemicals. Staining may accompany ionization.

lifeline A line running across the surface of the pool dividing shallow and deep ends. Prevents nonswimmers from sliding down the slope into deep water. Floats are normally attached. This safety device may present a hindrance to lap swimming.

lithium hypochlorite (LiOCL) A dry, granular chlorine that is extremely soluble. This chlorine type is often used as a **shocking** agent but is quite expensive.

logarithm A mathematical term used in the pool industry to determine the pH scale; the power to which 10 (in the case of pH) must be raised to the reciprocal of the hydrogen ion concentration of pool water.

lower distribution system (underdrain) Those devices used in the bottom of a permanent medium filter to collect the water during filtering and distribute the water during backwashing.

magnesium hardness The amount of magnesium found in a water supply or sample; magnesium hardness and calcium hardness equal total hardness.

make-up water (source water) Outside (fresh) water used to fill or add water to swimming pools.

manometer An instrument using a column of liquid, usually mercury, to indicate flow rate in gallons per minute.

micron A unit of measure equalling 1/1000 of a millimeter or 1/1,000,000 of a meter.

microorganism A microscopic, invisible plant or animal often found in water.

muriatic acid Also known as hydrochloric acid or hydrogen chloride, this strong acid is used primarily to reduce total alkalinity and for cleaning chores around the pool. Muriatic acid is extremely corrosive and must be stored and handled with care. A toxic gas is produced when sodium hypochlorite and muriatic acid come in contact with each other. **Sodium bisulfate (dry acid)** is a safer alternative to muriatic acid.

neutral 7.0 on the pH; neither acid nor basic.

nitrogen An odorless, colorless, tasteless gas found combined in all living tissues. Nitrogen enters the pool combined with body oil, perspiration, and cosmetics and combines with free chlorine to produce chloramines. Chloramines result in odors and eye irritation. Nitrogen compounds also promote algae growth.

NSF National Sanitation Foundation

NSPI National Spa and Pool Institute. The major trade organization in the swimming pool industry.

NSPF National Swimming Pool Foundation. An educational foundation promoting swimming pool research, education, and safety. Also trains Certified Pool Operators.

organic wastes Introduced to pools by swimming entering the water and the surrounding environment. Include perspiration, urine, saliva, body oil, cosmetics, suntan lotion, etc. Extremely difficult to filter from pool water. Chemical oxidation is usually required to rid a pool of organic waste.

organisms Animal or plant life like algae or bacteria that can grow in pool water.

ORP The oxidation reduction potential produced by strong oxidizing agents in a water solution. **ORP**, or **REDOX**, is a measure of the oxidation level measured in millivolts by an **ORP METER**.

OTO Orthotolidine (OTO) is a colorimetric indicator used to detect total available chlorine. Darker shades of yellow indicate higher levels of chlorine. Effectively measures total chlorine, but OTO testing does not differentiate between free chlorine from combined chlorine, which is why DPD testing is preferred.

overflow system Refers to removal or pool/spa surface water through the use of overflows, surface skimmers, and surface water collection systems of various design and construction.

oxidation The process of changing a compound or molecule from a lower to a higher positive oxidation state. For example, the carbon atom of organic swimmer waste is oxidized to carbon dioxide, which has a higher oxidation state. An **oxidizing agent** (like hypochlorous acid) encourages and promotes oxidation.

ozone (O_3) An artificially on-site produced gas in the swimming pool industry used to disinfect and oxidize pool water. Ozone is a bluish, pungent gas that is a triatomic form of oxygen (O_3). Because of its poor residual properties, ozone is most often used as a supplemental oxidizer.

pathogen A microorganism-causing disease.

pH A measure of the acidity, basicity, or neutrality of water. The pH scale runs from 0.0 to 14.0. A pH below 7.0 is considered acid; a pH is considered basic. **Phenol red** (phenolsulfonthalein) is the most common reagent used for the pH test (6.8 to 8.4). Mathematically, pH is defined as the negative logarithm of the hydrogen-ion concentration in water.

polymer An agent used to clump, collect, or flocculate suspended particles in water. Used as a filter aid.

pools A vessel constructed for the purpose of swimming. May be designed specifically for relaxation, recreation, therapy, or competition. NSPI further classifies pools as **aboveground, onground, in-ground, residential, and commercial/public, splasher, and wading pools**. Public/commercial pools are further classified into numerous categories.

potable Safe drinking water that is free of bacteria.

potassium peroxymonopersulfate One type of nonchlorine shocking agent used to oxidize chloramines and organic waste.

ppm Parts per million. A measurement used in swimming pool testing that indicates the amount of chemical by weight in relation to 1,000,000 parts of water. For example, there are a million pounds of water in a 120,000 gallon pool. Therefore a pound of gas chlorine in a 120,000 gallon pool equals one part per million.

precipitate An insoluble compound produced by a chemical reaction between compounds that are usually soluble. The process in which soluble, invisible compounds in water become insoluble; visible is called **precipitation**. Calcium carbonate and iron are two common pool precipitates.

precoat A thin layer or coating of DE placed on the filter septum to start a filter cycle.

pressure differential The difference, usually measured in PSI, between two gauges.

PSI Pounds per square inch. Used to describe pressure in filter tanks or indicate head pressure.

pump A mechanical device, usually powered by an electric motor that causes hydraulic flow and pressure for the purpose of filtration, heating, and circulation of pool and spa water. Typically, a **centrifugal pump** design is used for pools and spas.

pump curve Characteristics of a pump graphically displayed that is invaluable in selecting and testing pump performance. Considers pump power, resistance, and flow variables.

quaternary ammonium compound ("Quat") An organic compound of ammonia used as an algaestat and germicide in pool and spa water. May cause foaming. Concentrations of 3 to 5 ppm are usually recommended for quats.

racing start The method of entry used by a competitive swimmer from the pool deck or from a starting platform to begin a race. Not to be confused with the sport of springboard diving.

rate of flow (flow rate) The amount of water passing through a circulation system measured at a given point on the system. Usually measured in gallons per minute (gpm) on a flow meter. Rate of flow is important in producing good water quality and clarity.

reagent Used for chemical testing; may come in tablets, liquid, or powder.

recirculation system The "closed loop" system used in swimming pools to filter, heat, and chemically treat the water. Composed of numerous parts including pipes, pumps, and filters.

Recreational Water Illnesses (RWI's) A variety of water-borne illnesses that can be contracted by following the fecal-oral route and are becoming more common in aquatic facilities and as defined by the CDC.

residual The amount of disinfectant or other chemical remaining in the swimming pool water. Although chlorine and bromine have good residual properties, some other disinfectants do not.

return inlet The aperture or fitting through which treated water under positive pressure returns to a pool or spa.

RID factor Three factors adversely affecting the performance of lifeguards. Failure to **RECOGNIZE** victims, **INTRUSION** of unnecessary, non-lifeguarding tasks, and **DISTRACTION** from the task of protecting swimmers. Developed by Frank Pia.

ring buoy A common lifesaving device that is circular and buoyant. Normally has a long line attached and is meant to be thrown to a distressed swimmer.

sand filter A swimming pool filter using specially graded sand or sand and gravel as the filter media to trap dirt and filter the water.

saturation index An extremely important tool used to check water balance. If used regularly, can help to prevent corrosion and scale. The saturation index is a simple mathematical formula that measures the interrelation of temperature, calcium hardness, total alkalinity, and pH to determine if water is acidic, basic, or neutral.

scale A precipitate composed mostly of calcium carbonate found on pool surfaces and other parts like the heater and filter. Often caused by high pH, high mineral content, or extremely basic water.

sequestering agent A specialty chemical added to swimming pools to keep metals and minerals in solution in order to prevent staining, scaling, and cloudy water.

shelf life The length of time a material (like a pool chemical) can be stored yet still remain suitable for its intended use. Many pool chemicals deteriorate when stored improperly (left uncovered or stored in sunlight, humidity, or in elevated temperatures).

skimmer A swimming pool outlet that functions like a gutter but is much smaller in size. Allows water to continually return from the surface of the pool to the filter system for cleaning and treating. A **skimmer weir** is a one-way door or flap in the skimmer box that continually adjusts to varying water levels so that the skimming action is continuous.

shocking Producing high levels of chlorine or nonchlorine oxidizer to rid a pool of all chloramines and other organic wastes. Often refers to **superchlorination** or **breakpoint**.

slip resistant A surface that has been treated or constructed is such a way as to significantly reduce the chance of the user slipping. The slip-resistant material must not cause an abrasion hazard.

slurry feed A liquid (water and DE mixed) body feed for DE filters fed to the filtration system by means of a slurry feeder. A slurry feed adds media to the filter elements or septa, thereby extending the filter cycle or "run."

soda ash (Na_2CO_3) A white powder (sodium carbonate) used to raise pH and total alkalinity in most swimming pools.

sodium bicarbonate ($NaHCO_3$) A strong, basic solution (pH 13) used to raise pH in some pools.

sodium hypochlorite (NaOCL, liquid chlorine) A popular swimming pool disinfectant that is 10% to 12% available chlorine with a pH of 13 and is lost in sunlight.

sodium thiosulfate A chlorine neutralizer that has many applications. It may be added directly to the pool to lower high chlorine levels resulting from superchlorination. Often sodium thiosulfate is added to cells for chemical tests like pH and total alkalinity to prevent faulty reading.

soft water Water that has low (less than 100 PPM) or insignificant levels of dissolved calcium and magnesium content.

spa A hydrotherapy unit of irregular or geometrical shell design. Typically contains water heated between 99° and 104° F. A public spa is operated by a owner, licensee, or concessionaire regardless of whether a fee is charged for use. Residential spas are basically used in the home. NSPI further classifies spas.

stabilizer Cyanuric acid (CYA) added to pool water or chlorine to protect outdoor pools and spas from the dissipating effects of the UV rays from the sun. The process of adding cyanuric acid to "save" or "stretch" chlorine is called **stabilization.** CYA levels should be at least 25 ppm to save chlorine but must not exceed 100 ppm.

sterilization The complete killing of all microorganisms by either heat or chemical disinfection.

superchlorination (shock treatment) Introducing extremely high levels of chlorine or some other "nonchlorine" shocking agent to destroy chloramines. This is also referred to as breakpoint and normally requires 10 times the chloramine count in free chlorine. Superchlorination may also be used to kill algae. At busy pools, superchlorination or "shocking" should be performed regularly.

surface skimming action Includes perimeter type overflows, surface skimmers, and surface water collection systems of various designs and construction.

swimmer load The total number of swimmers in the pool at a given time or period of time.

tamperproof Tamperproof equipment means that tools are required to alter or remove parts.

test kit A device used to monitor specific chemical residual or demands in pool or spa water.

titration A chemical testing procedure by which an indicator is added to a given test sample followed by the addition of a titrating solution that brings about a color change (endpoint). The number of titrating drops added to the sample to produce a color change is used to calculate the amount of chemical in solution. Calcium hardness and total alkalinity tests are often titration tests.

total alkalinity (TA) The total amount of carbonates, bicarbonates, and hydroxides in pool water. Total alkalinity buffers and controls pH. Low TA results in pH bounce, making it difficult to stabilize pH levels. High TA makes it difficult to change pH levels. Total alkalinity levels may be maintained between 80 ppm and 150 ppm, but the TA level must be compatible with the chemical disinfectant used and the pool shell.

total chlorine (TC) Total available chlorine is the sum of free-available (good) chlorine (FC) and combined available (bad) chlorine (CC).

total dissolved solids (TDS) A measure of the total amount of dissolved matter in water, including calcium, magnesium, carbonates, bicarbonates, metallic compounds, and others.

turbidity Cloudiness or lack of clearness (visibility) in water. Usually results from suspended particles in the water. Can be caused by a variety of reasons including low disinfectant levels, inadequate filtration, high chloramine levels, DE in the pool, unbalanced water, etc. When pool water becomes so turbid that the bottom is not easily recognized, the pool should be closed immediately.

turnover rate The number of times a quantity of water equal to the pool volume passes through the filtration system in 24 hours. Larger pools often have a six-hour (four turns) turnover or eight-hour (three turns) turnover, whereas smaller pools like spas may have a 30-minute turnover.

trichlor (trichlor-s-triazinetrione) A stabilized or organic chlorine that contains three available chlorine atoms. Trichlor has an available chlorine content of 89% and has a pH of 2.9, which is very acidic.

underdrain The plumbing at the bottom of most sand filters tanks that collects the filtered swimming pool water and returns it to the pool. The underdrains also distribute backwash water up through the filter bed for cleaning during the backwash cycle.

underwater light A lighting fixture located in the wall of some swimming pools below the surface of the water. A "wet niche" light is found immersed totally in pool water, whereas a "dry niche" light is housed in the pool wall behind a waterproof window. The advantage of the dry niche light is that it can be repaired or replaced out of the water.

upper distribution system Those devices designed to distribute the water entering a permanent medium filter in a manner so as to prevent movement or migration of the filter medium. This system shall also properly collect water during filter backwashing unless other means are provided.

vacuum filter Any pool filter where the pump follows the filter (effluent side) and "pulls" the water through the filter. Conversely, a pressure filter is preceded by pump (influent side) that "pushes" water through the filter. Pressure systems usually have hair and lint strainers, whereas most vacuum systems do not.

velocity The rate of water movement in feet per second.

vinyl liner That plastic membrane constructed of vinyl or vinyl compounds that acts as a container for pool water.

voids Spaces of gaps within a filter media.

weir The device included with a through-the-wall skimmer that controls the amount of surface water (flow) drawn into the skimmer and filtration system.

winterizing The procedure of preparing pools and spas for freezing weather. Includes chemical treatment of the standing water, plus physical and chemical treatment of the standing water, plus physical and chemical protection of the pool or spa and its equipment against freezing.

zeolites A filter and water chemistry supplement that is derived from volcanic ash. Is most often used as a sand filter supplement and is best known for absorbing ammonia.

** Glossaries from both the National Swimming Pool Institute (NSPI) and the National Swimming Pool Foundation (NSPF) were consulted for the Glossary found in this text.*

About the Authors

Dr. Tom Griffiths is the president and founder of Aquatic Safety Research Group, LLC. Recognized as an international leader in water safety, he has spent 38 years teaching, coaching, and managing aquatics at three major universities. Griffiths has produced videos, textbooks, articles, and presentations in various areas of aquatics focusing his efforts on safety. He has also conducted hundreds of aquatic facility and beach inspections across the nation and abroad and teaches full-day Aquatic Risk Management seminars. Perhaps his most significant contributions are the Five-Minute Scanning Strategy©, Griff's Guard Stations©, Disappearing Dummies, his research on Shallow Water Blackout, and the National Note & Float program. He has been an aquatic safety expert for more than 40 years and shares his knowledge, expertise, and experience worldwide.

Rachel Griffiths, MA, is the Communication Director for Aquatic Safety Research Group, LLC, conducting water safety research to help prevent drowning and providing education about water safety to the public. Rachel is also the president of Note and Float Life Jacket Fund, which donates life jackets to aquatics facilities to implement the Note & Float™ program. She is an excellent public speaker who presents cutting-edge water safety research. She has a bachelor's degree from the University of Maryland in communication and a master of arts degree from San Diego State University in communication. She publishes water safety articles, teaches aquatic risk management seminars, and has conducted and written reports for myriad aquatic facility audits throughout the country.

Contributing Authors

John Caden spent most of his career in the healthcare industry. He founded RehaMed International in 1996, which became the leading worldwide provider of swimming pool lifts. The company was acquired by SR Smith in 2009, and John served as the Accessibility Specialist for the company until his retirement in April 2013. John is a founding member of the APSP Commercial Council and served as a member of the board of directors for three years representing the council. John represents the APSP on the committee that is revising the ICC Standard A117.1 for Accessible Buildings and Facilities. John is an acknowledged authority on issues related to accessibility of pools and spas and is frequently asked to present on this topic.

Shawn P. DeRosa, JD, EMT is the Director of Aquatics and Safety Officer for Intercollegiate Athletics at The Pennsylvania State University. Shawn is a cum laude graduate of Suffolk University Law School. Shawn served as the Aquatics Program Coordinator for the Massachusetts State Park system, where he was responsible for policy and programmatic development for 66 aquatic facilities. Prior to joining Penn State, Shawn worked as the Northeast Regional Director for the National Recreation and Park Association and was a member of the adjunct faculty of Salem State College's Department of Sport and Movement Science, where he taught courses within the Sports Management and Leisure Services curricula. Owner of DeRosa Aquatic Consulting, Shawn provides education and training programs to pool operators in the United States and abroad. Shawn has been retained as an expert witness in a variety of aquatic cases, including drowning and spinal injury cases at both pools and beaches.

Gareth Hedges is Associate General Counsel for The Redwoods Group, a social enterprise that provides insurance and risk management services to YMCAs, Jewish Community Centers (JCCs) and nonprofit resident camps across the nation. The company's mission—whose motto is to Serve Others®—is to protect and improve the quality of life in the communities it serves.

Geoffrey Peckham, CEO of Clarion Safety Systems, has more than two decades of experience in actively advancing safety communications. He has led and continues to lead both the U.S. and international efforts to harmonize standards in the area of safety signs, labels, and markings; this includes contributing to the leadership and direction of ANSI, ISO, OSHA, and NFPA safety codes. Peckham serves as chair of the ANSI Z535 Committee for Safety Signs and Colors and chair of the U.S. TAG to ISO/TC 145 – Graphical Symbols. He has also been selected as a member of the U.S. TAG to ISO/PC 283, an ISO committee writing a new Occupational Health and Safety Management Systems standard that will, when finished, define global best practices for workplace safety.

Kevin Post earned his BS in computer science from the University of North Texas (UNT). He has spent most of his life around swimming pools, starting as a competitive swimmer at the age of 7 into his first jobs as a swim instructor and lifeguard. Working through college as a pool manger, he realized there was no escaping his passion for aquatics. After graduating, Kevin took the position of Aquatics Director at UNT's new Student Recreation Center. He later joined the Counsilman-Hunsaker team to share is knowledge and passion across the United States. He is a Certified Pool Operator Instructor through the National Swimming Pool Foundation and is a certified technical writer through the University of North Texas.

Dan Simons is a professor in the Department of Psychology and the Beckman Institute for Advanced Science and Technology at the University of Illinois. His research explores the limits of our own minds and the reasons why we often are unaware of our limits. His first book, *The Invisible Gorilla*, was co-authored by Christopher Chabris and was first published in 2010 (by Crown). It became a *NY Times* bestseller and has been translated into more than a dozen languages worldwide. He is also the founder and president of Viscog Productions, a company that produces and distributes DVD presentation tools that help teachers and speakers illustrate the limits of visual perception and attention.

Also Contributing to the Third Edition

American Swimming Pool and Spa Association
Association of Pool & Spa Professionals
Councilman-Hunsaker
Engineered Treatment Systems (ETS)
Eric Knight
Emperor Aquatics
Neptune-Benson
Pentair Aquatic Systems
Paddock Evacuator
Poseidon Technologies
Richard C. Scott
Ryan Smedema Safety Turtle
S. R. Smith
Swim SEAL
Taylor Technologies
Tom Schaeffer, Engineered Treatment Systems
Water Technology, Inc.
World Waterpark Association

Acknowledgments to Contributors to the First and Second Editions

Michael Beach
Annie Clement
PJ Heath
John McGovern
Charles M. Neuman ("Chuck")
Kerry Hoffman Richards
Richard C. Scott
Greg Wittstock

Index

American Swimming Pool and Spa Association

1108 Little River Dr.
Elizabeth City, NC 27909
Training Pool Operators Since 1997
1-877-766-5724 / 1-877-(Poolschool)

Classes are available in classroom, online, and blended formats

ALL COURSE PARTICIPANTS RECEIVE A COPY OF THE COMPLETE SWIMMING POOL REFERENCE by Dr. Tom Griffiths and Rachel Griffiths

Classes available include: National Licensed Aquatic Facility Technician
Basic Licensed Aquatic Facility Technician
Pennsylvania Aquatic Facility Technician

The **National Licensed Aquatic Facility Technician** course is designed to provide the knowledge necessary to safely and efficiently manage and operate swimming pools and spas. The National Licensed Aquatic Facility Technician course fulfills the mandated requirement that operators of public and commercial pools be trained through a nationally recognized course. The course is available in classroom, online, and blended formats. (Minimum 16 hours)

The **Basic Licensed Aquatic Facility Technician** course is designed to provide the knowledge necessary to safely and efficiently manage and operate swimming pools and spas. It is approved by many states that require operators of public and commercial pools be trained through a nationally recognized course. The course is available in classroom and online formats. (Minimum 8 hours)

The **Pennsylvania Aquatic Facility Technician** course meets the state of Pennsylvania requirement for 6 Core and 4 Category 24 Swimming Pool CEU's for Pesticide Applicators. This course is available in both classroom and online formats. (Minimum 8 hours)

www.swimmingpooloperator.com

WATERPARKS
INDOOR WATERPARKS
RESORTS
WATER PLAYGROUNDS
COMPETITION
MUNICIPAL
THERAPY & WELLNESS
UNIVERSITIES

PROGRAMMING
MASTER PLANNING
CONCEPTUAL DESIGN
DETAILED DESIGN
WATERPARK HVAC
WATER TREATMENT SYSTEMS

www.wtiworld.com

100 Park Avenue
P.O. Box 614
Beaver Dam, WI 53916

Ph. 1.920.887.7375
Fx. 1.920.887.7999

Wisconsin • Texas • Virginia • Arizona • U.A.E.

WORLD LEADERS IN AQUATIC PLANNING, DESIGN AND ENGINEERING

Get Connected

AQUATICS INTERNATIONAL magazine delivers award-winning editorial to commercial and recreational pool industry professionals.

AI Extra the premier newsletter for need-to-know aquatic news, offering an immediacy few can match.

Waterparks + Resorts a monthly newsletter featuring the latest news, trends, personalities and products.

ProView newsletter featuring ideas and insights from leading industry experts

AI Connect offers a dynamic, extensive social media network for aquatic pros. Here, more than 2,000 members talk shop, share insights, post content and more.

To Advertise, Contact: Gary Carr (323) 801-4922 | gcarr@hanleywood.com
To Subscribe: (888) 269-8410 | aqi@omeda.com

hanley wood

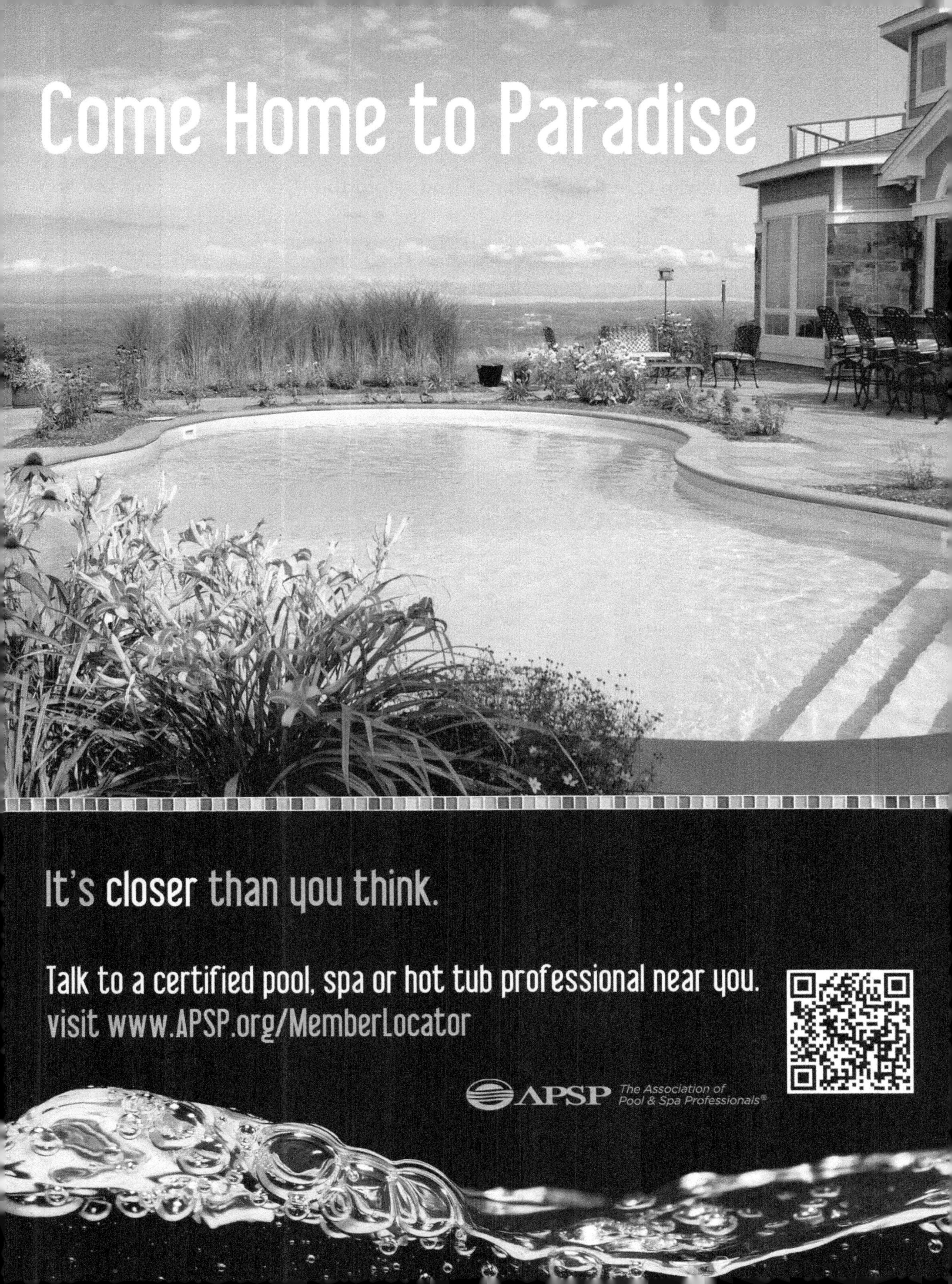

Come Home to Paradise

It's closer than you think.

Talk to a certified pool, spa or hot tub professional near you.
visit www.APSP.org/MemberLocator

Aquatic Risk Management

Tom Griffiths, Ed.D.
Rachel Griffiths, M.A.

Become "Armed" with Effective, Practical, and Affordable Risk Management Solutions

A fast-paced class using videos, PowerPoints and lively discussion.

Learn to minimize risks that could lead to catastrophic injuries.

Gain an understanding of the applicable standard of care.

Topics Include:

- 5 Minute Scanning Strategy
- Lifeguard Blindness: Physical, Perceptual, Internal noise
- Effective Signage
- Real Aquatic Court Cases
- Seven Deadly Sins
- Shallow Water Blackout
- Suction Entrapment

Aquatic Safety Audits

Objective, Thorough Walk through of your Facility

Identify strengths and weaknesses of your operation

Evaluate safety conditions and practices

Help reduce liability, reduce risk

Improve overall operations and safety - reduce expenses, increase income

Contact:
RachelGriffiths@AquaticSafetyGroup.com

www.AquaticSafetyGroup.com

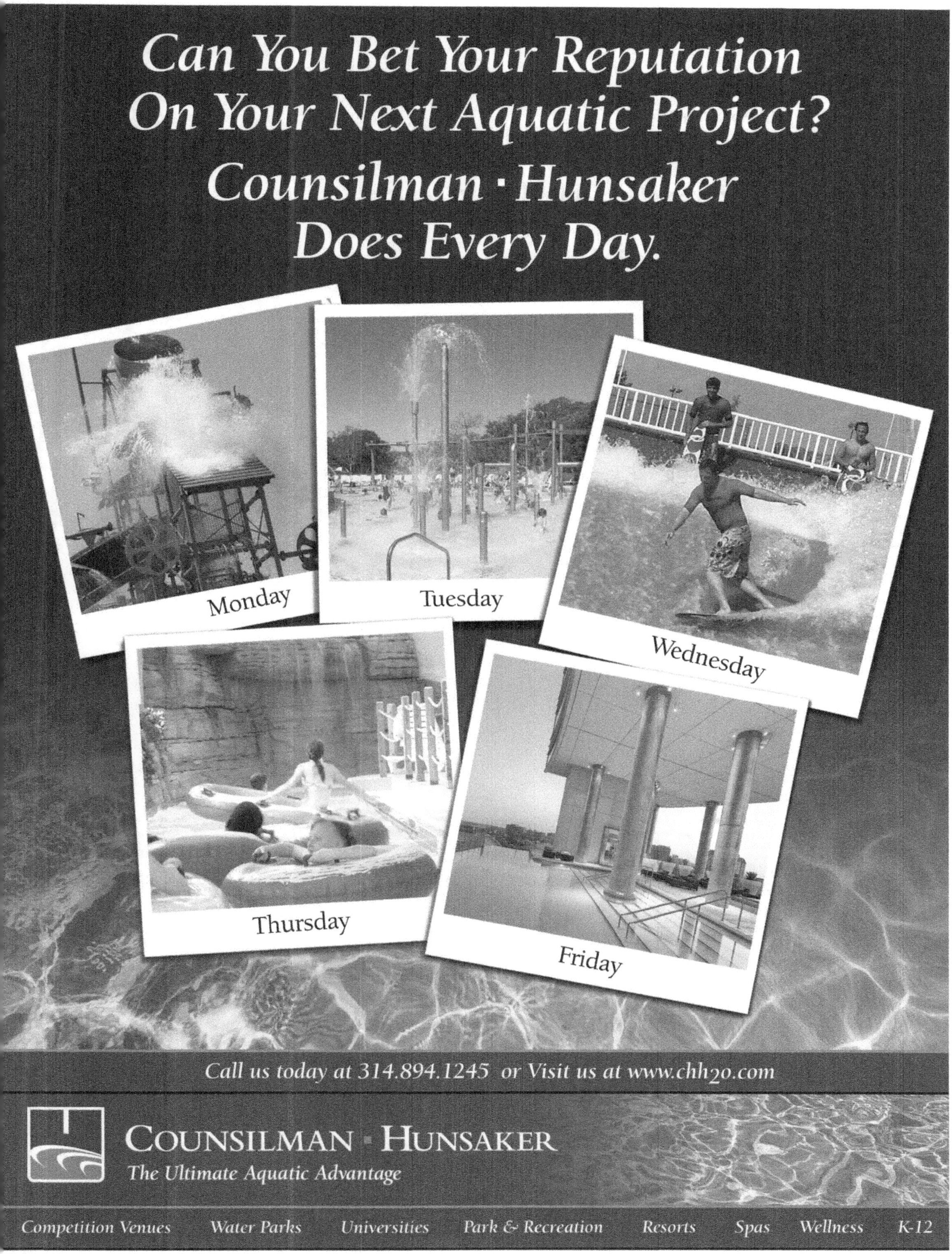

Can You Bet Your Reputation
On Your Next Aquatic Project?
Counsilman · Hunsaker
Does Every Day.
Monday
Tuesday
Wednesday
Thursday
Friday
Call us today at 314.894.1245 or Visit us at www.chh2o.com
COUNSILMAN · HUNSAKER
The Ultimate Aquatic Advantage
Competition Venues
Water Parks
Universities
Park & Recreation
Resorts
Spas
Wellness
K-12

Clarion®

Reducing Risk, Protecting People

Safety starts with sight.

Clarion's Pool Safety Sign System:

- Developed by leading experts in safety standards, signage and aquatics
- Designed with clear graphical symbols to draw attention to core safety messages
- The **ONLY** sign system on the market tested by viewers and proven to be quickly recognized and easily understood
- Complies with the latest standards to help fulfill your legal "duty to warn"

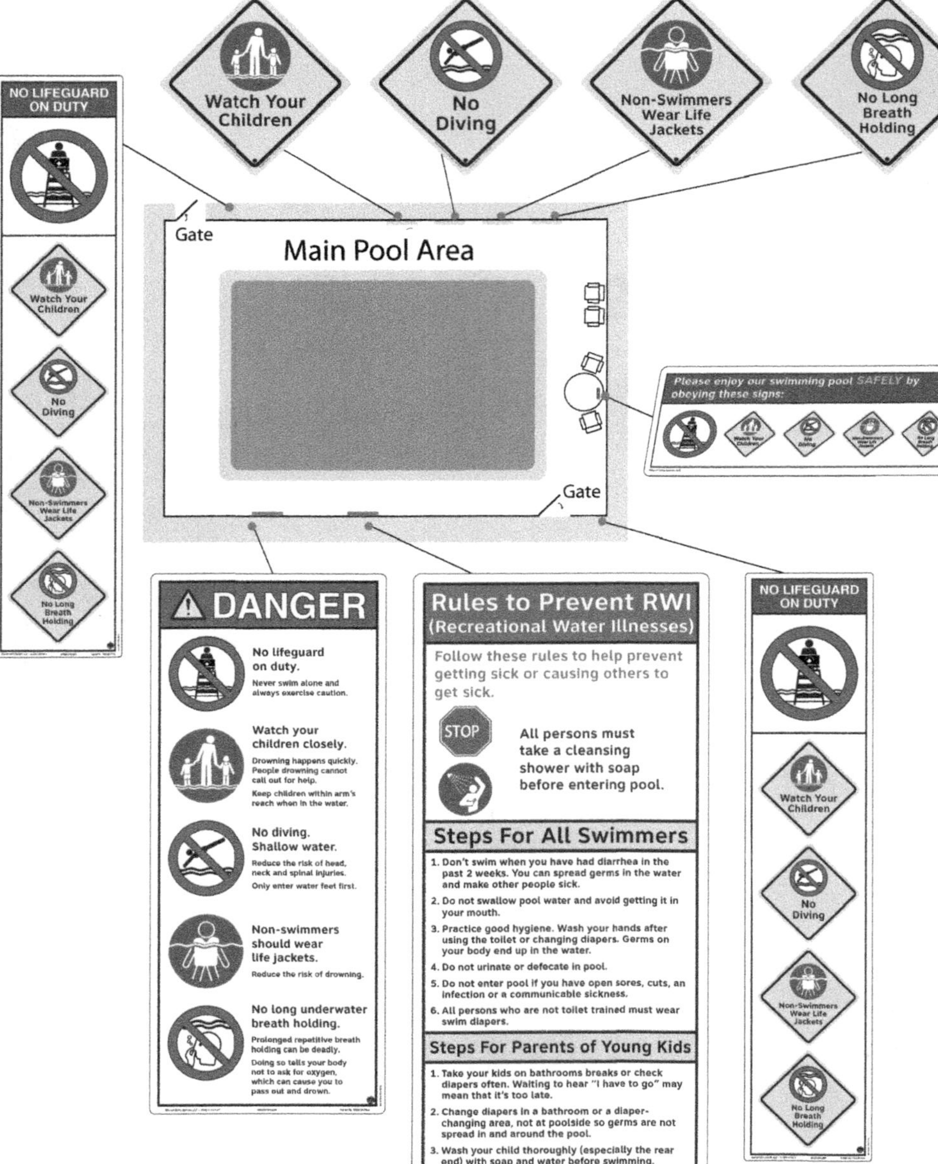

Build a Clarion Pool Safety Sign System to protect your pool with three simple steps:

1 Indoor or Outdoor?
Select indoor or outdoor signs.
- Indoor for non-glare textured material
- Outdoor for weather-durable material

2 Pick Your Signs' Size and Messages
Select 3 or 4 core warning message symbols and the right size of sign to fit your pool.

3 Effective Placement
Reinforce core safety messages with signage at pool entrances, perimeters, and lounge areas in order to fully inform.

(800) 748-0241

www.clarionsafety.com

sales@clarionsafety.com

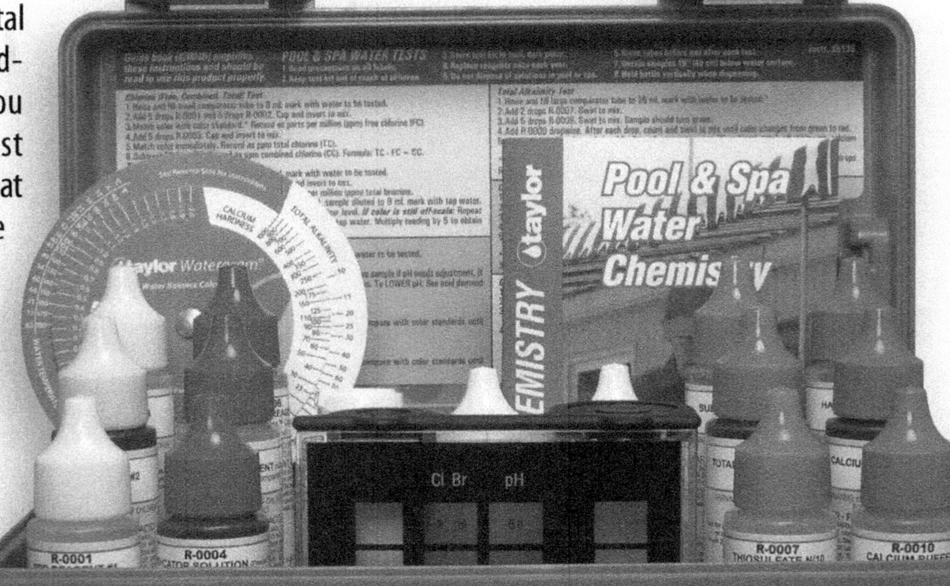

THE TRADITION OF EXCELLENCE
CONTINUES

From the manufacturer of Taylor liquid test kits and *sure*TRACK® test strips comes the **TTi™ 2000 Colorimeter,** a microprocessor-controlled, direct-readout instrument which completely eliminates the subjectivity of visual color comparisons. The TTi 2000 takes the reading for you, showing the test result in the large liquid crystal display window. No second-guessing color matches! You already know you can trust Taylor chemistries. Now get that same reliable performance from your handheld meter.

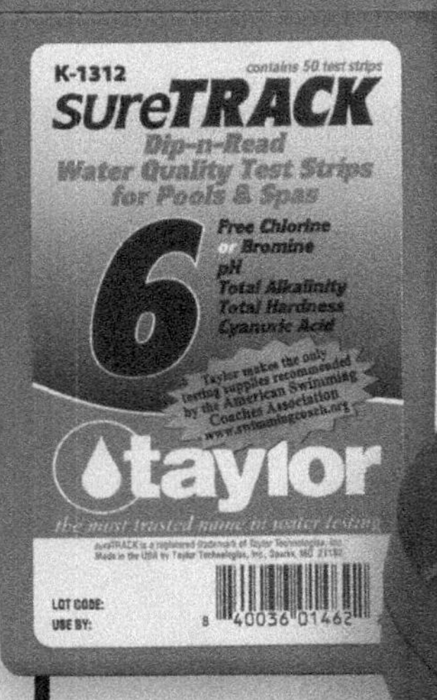

Taylor Technologies, Inc.
Made in the USA
800-TEST KIT (837-8548)
www.taylortechnologies.com
Watch our video demos

PARAGON®
DECK
EQUIPMENT

GRIFF'S GUARDING SOLUTIONS

Griff's Guard Stations are designed to provide maximum viewing and increased lifeguard effectiveness, supporting Tom Griffith's Five Minute Scanning Strategy. Dual access assures that swimmers are covered during shift changes. Our new stations are versatile, easy to move and assemble quickly.

GRIFF'S VISION GUARD STATION™
- Patent Pending Design
- Minimum Footprint Maximum Impact
- Lighter, Less Costly, and Ships Flat
- 3 Heights Available

ALL TERRAIN GRIFF'S GUARD STATION™
- Most Versatile Guard Chair Ever
- Super Portable – Tip and Roll With Ease Over Any Terrain
- Front and Back Guard Access

The Pool Management Group

Providing genuinely safe, smooth pool operations with minimized risk is complex. Together, The Pool Management Group and its 16 partner companies deliver outstanding levels of safety, efficiency, and customer satisfaction to our clients nationwide. Visit us online to learn more about The Pool Management Group, our partner companies, and our unique suite of comprehensive services.

www.poolmanagementgroup.com

Poseidon

EVERY YEAR HUNDREDS OF PEOPLE
DROWN OR NEARLY-DROWN
IN LIFEGUARD PROTECTED POOLS.

Lifeguards can not do it alone.

POSEIDON CAN HELP.

Watching every swimmer at every moment is impossible.
Poseidon detects a swimmer in trouble.

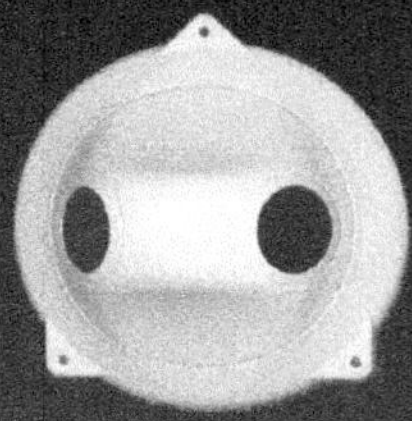

www.Poseidonsaveslives.com

© 2013 Poseidon Technologies, Inc

SafetyTurtle
Water Safety System

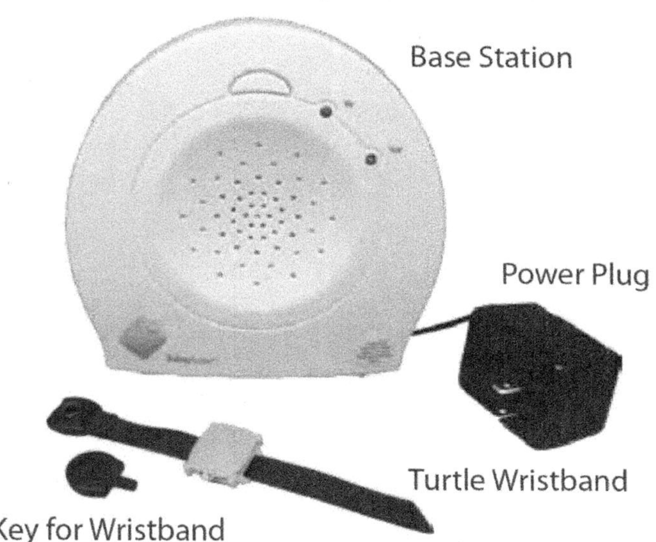

Base Station

Power Plug

Turtle Wristband

Key for Wristband

- Easy setup/ requires no installation
- Wristband triggers 115 dB alarm when immersed in water
- Protect your children, pets, or even adults
- Go mobile add optional battery pack and car charger
- A necessary "layer of protection"
- Get Peace of Mind Today

SafetyTurtle.com
877.467.6627

 RJE Technologies, Inc. 15375 Barranca Pkwy., Ste. B107, Irvine, CA 92618

everybody IN THE POOL

Whether you need serious equipment for a competitive swim environment or serious fun for a backyard pool, **S.R.Smith is your source for pool deck equipment.** In fact, we've been helping people get into pools for more than 80 years.

srsmith.com | poollifts.com | 800.824.4387 | info@srsmith.com

Member benefits may change, but our commitment to you never will.

Join the World Waterpark Association as a park or supplier member. You can tap into a **thriving community of water leisure professionals** and enjoy a great mix of **educational and innovative resources** built for you by the WWA and its members.

**Join today by calling +1-913-599-0300
Or join online at Waterparks.org**

SAGAMORE PUBLISHING | SAGAMORE JOURNALS

RELATED BOOKS AND JOURNALS